HUM
RIGHTS
WATCH
WORLD
REPORT
1998

Featured in World Report 1998

■ Featured in World Report 1998

HUMAN RIGHTS WATCH WORLD REPORT 1998

Events of 1997

New York • Washington • London • Brussels

Copyright © December 1997 by Human Rights Watch.
All rights reserved.
Printed in the United States of America.

ISBN 1-56432-176-2
ISSN 1054-948X

Human Rights Watch
485 Fifth Avenue
New York, NY 10017-6104
Tel: (212) 972-8400
Fax: (212) 972-0905
E-mail: hrwnyc@hrw.org

Human Rights Watch
1522 K Street, NW, #910
Washington, DC 20005-1202
Tel: (202) 371-6592
Fax: (202) 371-0124
E-mail: hrwdc@hrw.org

Human Rights Watch
33 Islington High Street
N1 9LH London
United Kingdom
Tel: (44171) 713-1995
Fax: (44171) 713-1800
E-mail: hrwatchuk@gn.apc.org

Human Rights Watch
15 Rue Van Campenhout
1000 Brussels, Belgium
Tel: (322) 732-2009
Fax: (322) 732-0471
E-mail: hrwatcheu@gn.apc.org

Website Address: http://www.hrw.org
Listserv address: To subscribe to the list, send an e-mail message to
majordomo@igc.apc.org with "subscribe hrw-news" in the body of the
message (leave the subject line blank).

HUMAN RIGHTS WATCH

Human Rights Watch conducts regular, systematic investigations of human rights abuses in some seventy countries around the world. Our reputation for timely, reliable disclosures has made us an essential source of information for those concerned with human rights. We address the human rights practices of governments of all political stripes, of all geopolitical alignments, and of all ethnic and religious persuasions. Human Rights Watch defends freedom of thought and expression, due process and equal protection of the law, and a vigorous civil society; we document and denounce murders, disappearances, torture, arbitrary imprisonment, discrimination, and other abuses of internationally recognized human rights. Our goal is to hold governments accountable if they transgress the rights of their people.

Human Rights Watch began in 1978 with the founding of its Helsinki division. Today, it includes five divisions covering Africa, the Americas, Asia, the Middle East, as well as the signatories of the Helsinki accords. It also includes three collaborative projects on arms transfers, children's rights, and women's rights. It maintains offices in New York, Washington, Los Angeles, London, Brussels, Moscow, Dushanbe, Rio de Janeiro, and Hong Kong. Human Rights Watch is an independent, nongovernmental organization, supported by contributions from private individuals and foundations worldwide. It accepts no government funds, directly or indirectly.

The staff includes Kenneth Roth, executive director; Susan Osnos, associate director; Michele Alexander, development director; Cynthia Brown, program director; Barbara Guglielmo, finance and administration director; Patrick Minges, publications director; Jeri Laber, special advisor; Lotte Leicht, Brussels office director; Susan Osnos, communications director; Jemera Rone, counsel; Wilder Tayler, general counsel; and Joanna Weschler, United Nations representative.

The regional directors of Human Rights Watch are Peter Takirambudde, Africa; José Miguel Vivanco, Americas; Sidney Jones, Asia; Holly Cartner, Helsinki; and Hanny Megally, Middle East. The project directors are Joost R. Hiltermann, Arms Project; Lois Whitman, Children's Rights Project; and Dorothy Q. Thomas, Women's Rights Project.

The members of the board of directors are Robert L. Bernstein, chair; Adrian W. DeWind, vice chair; Lisa Anderson, William Carmichael, Dorothy Cullman, Gina Despres, Irene Diamond, Fiona Druckenmiller, Edith Everett, Jonathan Fanton, James C. Goodale, Jack Greenberg, Vartan Gregorian, Alice H. Henkin, Stephen L. Kass, Marina Pinto Kaufman, Bruce Klatsky, Harold Hongju Koh, Alexander MacGregor, Josh Mailman, Samuel K. Murumba, Andrew Nathan, Jane Olson, Peter Osnos, Kathleen Peratis, Bruce Rabb, Sigrid Rausing, Anita Roddick, Orville Schell, Sid Sheinberg, Gary G. Sick, Malcolm Smith, Domna Stanton, Maureen White, and Maya Wiley.

ACKNOWLEDGMENTS

A compilation of this magnitude requires contribution from a large number of people, including most of the Human Rights Watch staff. The contributors were:

Fred Abrahams, Marcia Allina, Suliman Baldo, Jennifer Bailey, Rebecca Bell, Clary Bencomo, Doug Black, Peter Bouckaert, Sebastian Brett, Cynthia Brown, Widney Brown, Samya Burney, Bruni Burres, Scott Campbell, Holly Cartner, Jim Cavallaro, Jana Chrzova, Allyson Collins, Sara Colm, Sarah Cooke, Andrew Cooper, Georgina Copty, Erika Dailey, Sarah DeCosse, Rachel Denber, Alison DesForges, Richard Dicker, Helen Duffy, Hetty Eisenberg, Ra'id Faraj, Jamie Fellner, Janet Fleischman, Arvind Ganesan, Eric Goldstein, Stephen Goose, Patricia Gossman, Jeannine Guthrie, Julia Hall, Malcolm Hawkes, Steven Hernández, Sinsi Hernández-Cancio, Elahé Hicks, Trish Hiddleston, Joost Hiltermann, Megan Himan, Ernst Jan Hogendoorn, LaShawn Jefferson, Mike Jendrzejczyk, Mark Johnson, Sidney Jones, Tom Kellogg, Jane Kim, Robin Kirk, Jeri Laber, Gia Lee, Zunetta Liddell, Jeffery Locke, Diederik Lohman, Andre Lommen, Timothy Longman, Ivan Lupis, Bronwen Manby, Anne Manuel, Zachary Margulis-Ohnuma, Joanne Mariner, Maxine Marcus, Kerry McArthur, Michael McClintock, Hanny Megally, Evelyn Miah, Rita Mwiyeretsi-Motlanta, Sahr Muhammed Ally, Robin Munro, Smita Narula, Olga Nousias, Binaifer Nowrojee, Olajumoke Osode, Jagdish Parikh, Diane Paul, Christopher Panico, Ariana Pearlroth, Robby Peckerar, Alexander Petrov, Christina Portillo, Regan Ralph, Jemera Rone, Kenneth Roth, Awali Samara, Nejla Sammakia, Joseph Saunders, Emily Shaw, Virginia N. Sherry, Milbert Shin, Linda Shipley, Joel Solomon, Mickey Spiegel, Joseph Stork, Marie Struthers, Peter Takirambudde, Dorothy Thomas, Yodon Thonden, Alex Vines, José Miguel Vivanco, Ben Ward, Lois Whitman, and Juliet Wilson.

Cynthia Brown, Jeri Laber, and Michael McClintock edited the report, with editing and production assistance by Patrick Minges and Sahr Muhammed Ally. Various sections were reviewed by, Lotte Leicht and Joanna Weschler. Patrick Minges, Sahr Muhammed Ally, and Susan Osnos proofread the report.

CONTENTS

HUMAN RIGHTS WATCH/HELSINKI

HUMAN RIGHTS WATCH/MIDDLE EAST

HUMAN RIGHTS WATCH

POSTSCRIPT

INTRODUCTION

International human rights standards are built on the principle of universality, the fundamental premise that they apply equally to all nations without exception. Because every government has its own particular reasons for violating human rights—whether to silence an awkward critic or grant its military a bit more latitude in battle—exceptions to the principle of universality threaten the entire system for the defense of human rights.

The universality of human rights came under sustained attack in 1997. As in previous years, governments seeking to justify their authoritarian conduct found it convenient to challenge universality, usually in circumstances in which their repression precluded rebuttal by the people in whose name they claimed to speak. In the past year, a parallel and insidious challenge was also particularly pronounced—an unwillingness on the part of several major powers to uphold human rights in their dealings with key abusive countries, and an increasing reluctance to subject their own conduct to international human rights standards.

As this report describes, the major powers showed a marked tendency to ignore human rights when they proved inconvenient to economic or strategic interests—an affliction common to both Europe and the United States. China was the largest beneficiary of this selective commitment to human rights, but a new challenge from central Africa also met a disappointingly weak response. In addition, the U.S. government displayed the arrogance of a great power in obstructing the strengthening of international human rights standards and institutions. Its actions reflected a cynical view of human rights as standards to be embraced only if they codify what the U.S. government already does, not if they enshrine what the American people ought to achieve. The prospects for peace in Bosnia and an effective international system of justice were also jeopardized by the refusal of the North Atlantic Treaty Organization (NATO) to follow a British lead and arrest indicted war criminal suspects—a short-sighted abdication of responsibility due in large part to the Pentagon's overriding preoccupation with avoiding all possible risks to its troops.

Fortunately, as the most powerful governments wavered in their defense of human rights, a new set of actors, both governmental and nongovernmental, came to the fore. In negotiations to ban anti-personnel landmines and establish an International Criminal Court, alliances emerged of small and medium-sized states from both the North and the South. Many of the Southern governments, having experienced and overcome repression, brought an important voice of appreciation for human rights. With their success in circumventing the U.S. government's opposition to a landmines ban, these new coalitions could assume important leadership roles by insisting on the principle of universality and a strong defense of human rights when the commitment of the major powers is lacking.

What follows is Human Rights Watch's review of human rights practices in sixty-five countries. This report is released in advance of Human Rights Day, December 10, 1997, which launches celebrations of the 50th anniversary of the Universal Declaration of Human Rights the following year. The report covers events from December 1996 through November 1997. Most chapters examine significant human rights developments in a particular country; the response of global actors, such as the United States, the European Union, Japan, the United Nations, and various regional organizations; and restrictions on human rights monitoring. Other chapters address thematic issues. This introduction describes certain patterns and trends that Human Rights Watch has discerned in the course of its work over the past year.

This volume is Human Rights Watch's eighth World Report on global human rights practices. It does not include a chapter on every country where we work, nor does it discuss every issue of importance. The failure to include a country or issue often reflects no more than staffing and funding limitations, and should not be taken as commentary on the significance of the related human rights concerns. Other factors affecting the focus of our work in 1997 and hence the content of this volume include the severity of abuses, our access to information about them, our ability to influence abusive practices, and our desire to balance our work across various political and regional divides and to address certain thematic concerns.

Beyond the Major Powers: A New Global Partnership

The awarding of the 1997 Nobel Peace Prize to the International Campaign to Ban Landmines signaled a new era in which nongovernmental organizations (NGOs), working closely with sympathetic governments from the developed and developing world, can set the international human rights agenda despite resistance from some major powers. Inspired by the victory in the battle over antipersonnel landmines, a similar coalition is now seeking to establish a strong and independent International Criminal Court to bring the most culpable human rights criminals to justice. Other NGO efforts of note include attempts to hold multinational corporations to human rights standards, to continue integrating women's rights into the human rights agenda, and to secure the arrest of indicted war criminal suspects in Bosnia.

This important role for NGOs reflects their essential function in modern society. Isolated individuals rarely have the capacity to devise solutions to today's complex problems and secure their implementation. Only by banding together, by merging their expertise, voice, and influence, can individuals hope meaningfully to address today's challenges. Governments and increasingly corporations exert a powerful influence on society, but governments are often hostage to powerful special interests, while corporations are driven above all by the quest for financial profit. Frequently, neither serves as an effective conduit for the concerns of ordinary citizens. As the past year showed, NGOs can help to fill that void.

Landmines

The campaign against anti-personnel landmines illustrates this NGO role. Less than a decade ago, a handful of NGOs working in war-torn countries began to comprehend the terrible humanitarian cost of landmines. In such countries as Cambodia, Angola, Somalia, and Bosnia, it was apparent that scores of ordinary civilians fell victim to these indiscriminate weapons, often far from war zones or long after conflict had ended. By reporting on the scope and severity of the problem—landmines are estimated to kill or maim some 26,000 civilians each year—a small group of NGOs brought the issue to international attention. With time, the International Campaign to Ban Landmines grew from its six founding members, including Human Rights Watch, to a vibrant coalition of over 1,000 NGOs in more than sixty countries.

The NGOs actively solicited and gained some major governmental allies, as when France agreed to call for an international conference to review international law regulating landmines, or when a U.S. senator, Patrick Leahy, sponsored legislation suspending the use and export of landmines. But what was notable about the landmines campaign was the central role played by governments that were not major powers. Spanning North-South lines, these included Austria, Belgium, Canada, Mexico, Mozambique, Norway, and South Africa. NGOs encouraged these governments to pursue a ban despite the resistance of some major powers. NGOs also brought expertise to the drafting of a ban treaty and mobilized a global network of allied organizations to build public pressure for a ban. The importance of the NGO campaign was recognized during the final treaty negotiations in Oslo, when the International Campaign was given official observer status, with access to all deliberations and the right to make interventions—a first for NGOs in an arms control or humanitarian law treaty negotiation.

Also instrumental to the success of the landmines effort was the decision to proceed toward a treaty outside the straitjacket of the recent United Nations preference for "consensus," in which every government is given a veto. Rather than insisting that all governments embrace the new treaty from the start, the plan was to establish a strong international norm and then pull in reluctant governments through moral pressure. Since governmental obstruction could no longer take place during the arcane, back-room maneuvering of U.N. negotiations, the public could readily see whether governments joined the ban or not. Public pressure thus proved to be a powerful factor.

As this report is released in early December 1997, more than one hundred governments are expected to assemble in Ottawa to sign a treaty unconditionally banning the use, production, stockpiling, and transfer of anti-personnel landmines—the first time that states have outlawed an entire weapons system that has been in widespread use. The moral force created by this alliance between NGOs and governments has succeeded in attracting even some of the reluctant major powers—the United Kingdom, France, and Japan—but not yet such governments as the United States, China, Russia, India, or Pakistan. Efforts will now turn toward persuading the holdouts to join the rest of the world.

An International Criminal Court

The power of this partnership between NGOs and small and mid-sized governments was also evident in the progress made toward a permanent International Criminal Court (ICC). The ICC would be a genuinely international court, with its own judges, prosecutors and investigators, which would be available to try those responsible for genocide, war crimes or crimes against humanity when national judicial systems fail to do so. It would add the threat of criminal prosecution to the human rights movement's traditional tools of stigmatizing abusive governments and denying them certain forms of aid. Just a few years ago, the ICC was only a dream. Today, it appears on the verge of becoming a reality, as plans are being set for the treaty establishing the court to be finalized in Rome in July 1998. Most strikingly, this feat has been accomplished despite the resistance of the permanent five members of the U.N. Security Council. Again, NGOs played a central role in this progress.

A strong and independent court could be a powerful supplement to the Security Council, since it promises to deter the gross abusers of human rights who lie behind most of today's threats to international peace. Unfortunately, allowing narrow self-interest to take precedence over the duty entrusted them to uphold international security, the permanent Security Council members seemed to see the ICC only as a threat to their power and sovereignty. Led by the United States, with backing from France and, at times, the United Kingdom, these governments formally endorsed an ICC while trying to weaken it and subordinate it to their Security Council prerogatives. They proposed that a broad range of prosecutions be approved in advance by the Security Council, that the ICC prosecutor be denied the right to initiate prosecutions on his or her own, that the number of crimes that the ICC is allowed to address without the consent of interested governments be limited, and that the ICC lend extraordinary deference to national judicial proceedings.

A group of human rights organizations from the United States, Europe and the developing world, again including Human Rights Watch, has sought to block this short-sighted effort. A caucus of women's rights advocates and organizations also played an important role in highlighting the need to incorporate crimes of sexual and gender violence as an integral part of an ICC. Bringing expertise about the legal and political issues to be resolved, these organizations have helped to build a broad coalition of some forty states from the developed and developing world to transform what might have become a North-South controversy into one that pits most of the world against the permanent Security Council members and a collection of implacable opponents of human rights institutions. Thus, a broad range of voices from the South, including Argentina, Egypt, Ghana, Malawi, South Africa, and South Korea, have joined traditionally supportive states from the North. Because many of these Southern governments have completed transitions from authoritarian to democratic government, they speak with special authority about the importance of having an institution of justice that would remain above pressures for impunity from local forces.

The coalition of NGOs and these "like-minded" states still faces major obstacles in securing an independent and effective ICC. As described more fully below, a big challenge facing the governmental friends of an ICC is abandoning an approach that links the success of the ICC to early ratification by the United States—linkage that will only force the ICC to the level of one of its least enthusiastic supporters. It is time to leave the United States behind until the day that it transcends the great power arrogance toward international human rights institutions that currently prevails in Washington. The new partnership between NGOs and small and mid-sized governments offers hope that this will occur.

Multinational Corporations

The collective power of NGOs is also seen in the growing movement to hold multinational corporations accountable for their human rights practices. The growth of the global economy means that multinational corporations today wield considerable influence on human rights. As economically influential actors, they can help bolster a repressive regime or steer it toward greater observance of human rights. As the operators of major business enterprises, they can set an example of indifference to or respect for these rights.

Governments have shown little interest in the issue of corporate responsibility for human rights, for fear of jeopardizing trade and investment opportunities. The trade agreements negotiated by governments have so far either ignored labor rights standards, as in the case of the World Trade Organization (WTO), or relegated them to weak side agreements, as NAFTA did. For example, the Clinton administration in 1997 unsuccessfully sought "fast-track authority" to negotiate trade agreements, but without any commitment to securing labor rights protection as an integral part of such agreements. In December 1996, the administration tried to introduce labor rights into WTO discussions, but it lacked credibility because it had not ratified the core conventions of the International Labour Organisation. While establishing a White House task force of business and labor leaders in the apparel industry and asking them to negotiate voluntary standards, the administration refused to press for legislated human rights standards or even to articulate its own preferred standards.

Yet today, multinational corporations in growing numbers are adopting codes of conduct that incorporate human rights standards. Some corporations are genuinely concerned about human rights and seek voluntarily to improve their practices. Many, however, are responding to public pressure built by NGOs in the developed and developing world, including Human Rights Watch, together with labor unions and the press. In the place of official legal regimes, NGOs are monitoring corporate practices, denouncing misconduct, and arousing public outrage over corporate abuses. To avoid tarnishing their public images, these corporations have taken preemptive steps by adopting human rights standards to guide their operations. Increasingly, the debate is not about whether corporations should respect human rights standards, but about which standards they have a duty to uphold and how best to monitor whether they are doing so.

While there are many NGOs reflecting a variety of interests, one overriding NGO concern is ensuring that competition among businesses is not waged through repression. Wages or factory costs can be kept low by denying workers the opportunity to speak out and organize around issues of salary and working conditions. But governments should not be encouraging competition through the suppression of the rights of workers.

Much remains to be accomplished before multinational corporations will reliably act to enhance respect for human rights. The codes adopted by many corporations remain disturbingly vague. Most do not address such difficult issues as working in countries where independent trade unions are barred, as in China, Vietnam, or Indonesia, or where operations depend for their security on police, military or paramilitary forces that have a history of abuse, as in mining or oil or gas-producing areas in Burma, Colombia, Nigeria or Indonesia. Only the rare code enables independent monitoring of a company's compliance—a step that is essential to the credibility of company vows to respect rights standards.

Yet, NGO pressure helped to achieve results in 1997. To cite three examples in which Human Rights Watch took the lead, General Motors agreed to stop testing women job applicants for pregnancy (previously the company had refused to hire pregnant job seekers); Phillips-Van Heusen became the first operator of a maquiladora (export-processing plant) in Guatemala to negotiate with a labor union, and then reached a collective bargaining agreement; eighteen U.S. manufacturers of anti-personnel landmine components pledged to cease their involvement in landmine production; numerous companies pulled out of Burma; and even oil companies like Royal Dutch/Shell and British Petroleum voiced a still-to-be-tested interest in complying with human rights standards.

Ultimately, corporate respect for human rights cannot depend on NGO monitoring alone. The collective resources of NGOs are too small for them to be the exclusive avenue of enforcement. Government action will be needed, at both the national and international levels, to obligate corporations to respect human rights standards. But, today, while governments are unwilling to insist that corporations not profit from repression, a vibrant and burgeoning NGO movement is leading this campaign.

Lost Luster for the "Asian Concept of Human Rights"

For several years, a number of Asian governments have attacked the universality of human rights by trumpeting a supposed "Asian concept of human rights." Asian officials, particularly in China, Burma, Singapore, Malaysia, and Indonesia, have long insisted that Asian people prefer order to freedom, and that this order is the best means to secure economic growth. These claims have always

been suspect, since they were usually made by those in power. The economic and environmental crises that plagued Southeast Asia in 1997 undermined their credibility all the more. The lack of free debate about important public issues and the practice of closed official decision-making produced unaccountable governments whose policies exacerbated these crises. It became clear that freedoms of expression and association, far from the impediments to order that Asian leaders decry, were essential to producing responsive governments that would safeguard the basic well-being of Asian people.

Malaysian Prime Minister Mahathir bin Mohamad provided the best illustration of the emptiness of the economic justification for repression. In July, he proposed a review of the Universal Declaration of Human Rights, as if the freedoms of expression and association that it guaranteed were inapplicable to Asia. By the end of the year, taking advantage of the diminished risk of contradiction that comes from the absence of free public debate, he deepened his country's economic crisis by attempting to deflect blame for it to foreign currency speculators.

A similar lack of accountability in Indonesia lay behind its economic crisis as well as the environmental crisis originating in Indonesian forest fires that produced a thick, unhealthy haze over much of Southeast Asia from September to November. Corruption and nepotism drove the economic crisis, while sweetheart land deals and irresponsible land-clearing methods created the environmental crisis. Each was the direct result of a government that was not answerable to its people.

The importance of civil and political rights to the physical well being of people was also demonstrated in North Korea, where a devastating famine threatened millions with starvation. Severe restrictions on public debate within the country led to disastrous economic policies, precluded a clear understanding of the extent of the problem, and undermined effective international and national responses.

A New Challenge to Human Rights in Central Africa

As the Asian threat to the universality of human rights lost credibility, a parallel challenge emerged in Central Africa and attracted surprising sympathy in the West. Unlike the Asian variant, which was stated in cultural terms, the African challenge sought to justify deviations from human rights standards in political terms, as temporarily necessary to rebuild nations recently liberated from highly repressive regimes. Ugandan President Yoweri Museveni, the leading intellectual author of this theory of "nonparty democracy," argued that in these times a "movement" is adequate to meet the needs of the people. Under the slogan of "African solutions to African problems," supporters of this concept offered what was essentially a recycled version of the one-party state, except that they advocated capitalism instead of socialism as the economic base of the state. Like its Asian counterpart, the "movement system" was used in 1997 to justify tight control on speech, assembly, association, and democratic institutions. This thin cover for repression found adherents among the new generation of leaders in Eritrea, Ethiopia, Rwanda, and the Democratic Republic of the Congo (DRC), who have been dubbed the "soldier princes."

Within the DRC, government forces aided by soldiers from Rwanda, Uganda and Angola killed thousands of civilians, most of them Rwandan refugees, as they fought the war that deposed Mobutu Sese Seko and installed Laurent Kabila as president. Inside Rwanda, the government army murdered thousands of noncombatants in the course of an indiscriminate campaign against a brutal insurgency, which itself took many civilian lives. Leaders of the DRC and Rwanda did not challenge the validity of international humanitarian law prohibiting such slaughter. Instead, they tried to hide or minimize the extent of the killings by impeding independent investigation of the crimes. At the same time, they argued—as in the case of violations of civil and political rights—that the killings were justified by the context of overthrowing a tyrant in the DRC and combatting forces responsible for the genocide of 1994 and now waging war again in Rwanda.

Policymakers in Europe and North America showed moral myopia towards violations of civil and political rights and even the massive slaughter of civilians. Well aware of the complexity of the central African crises, they hesitated to discourage the initiative shown by the "soldier princes," whose decisive action would, they hoped, contribute to stability in the region. They believed that the dynamic, media-savvy, militarily competent leaders represented a potential for moving beyond the tragedies of the past—a solution that could pull along a considerable part of the continent. They also seemed eager to minimize discussion of abuses in order to move on to talks about exploiting the vast mineral wealth of the DRC.

The U.S. government was particularly conspicuous in its tolerance of grave human rights violations. It provided strong political support and some military training to Rwanda before and during the time when its troops were waging war in the DRC and hunting down civilians in the rainforest. U.S. officials in Rwanda and Washington covered up the Rwandan presence in the DRC and obfuscated the number of civilians at risk in the region, hence delaying and eventually contributing to the halt of an international force designed to protect them. The U.S. government also consistently put the best face on the conduct of Rwandan government troops and officials within Rwanda, refraining from firm and prompt condemnation of abuses. U.S. embassy officials in Kigali even suggested that independent critics should not publicize these abuses.

With the exception of the European humanitarian aid commissioner, Emma Bonino, and Belgian Minister of Cooperation Reginald Moreels, most European leaders kept quiet about atrocities committed in the DRC. A delegation of the European Commission initially recommended resuming structural aid in light of the "positive political environment" that it found on a visit to the DRC.

Ultimately, both the U.S. and European governments declared that the DRC must cooperate with a U.N. investigation into the massacres in order to receive assistance. They thus tacitly recognized that, as in the case of Mobutu's Zaire, aid to the DRC government would be squandered, or even underwrite repression, unless the government was made accountable under a regime of respect for human rights and the rule of law. But the international community's efforts to demand accountability were weakened by its own past record of inaction in the face of the Rwandan genocide and Mobutu's many years of repression. U.S. insistence that donors meet for a preliminary consideration of aid to the DRC in September, before the U.N. investigation had begun, suggested that it was not firmly committed to insisting on justice. For much of the year, local leaders played skillfully on the international community's past mistakes to justify obstructing the investigation into the massive civilian slaughter. As this report went to press in mid-November, the DRC government had vowed to allow the U.N. investigation to go forward, although it remained unclear whether this vow would be respected.

International inaction at the time of the slaughter suggested that future massive killings would also provoke no interference from abroad, a particularly dangerous proposition given the current insurgency in Rwanda, the ongoing civil war in Burundi, and the renewed combat in eastern DRC. The tardy and uncertain demands for justice in the DRC also threatened to undermine the international effort to secure justice for the Rwandan genocide, which could now be viewed as a matter of convenience rather than principle. Failure to insist on justice for the victors in the DRC while prosecuting the genocidal losers of the Rwandan conflict risked sending the message that it was not violations of international law that were being punished but rather such violations in defeat.

The government of Ethiopian President Meles Zenawi also benefited from this deferential attitude on the part of the international community. Despite government restrictions imposed on opposition political parties, critical press reporting, and independent associations, both the E.U. and the U.S. increased aid to the country without using this financial leverage to secure improvements in the government's human rights performance. The augmented U.S. aid included increased military assistance in the name of fighting Sudanese terrorism.

International acquiescence in the abuses of these new leaders is particularly disappointing because it came just when much of southern Africa was showing great promise on human rights. The fostering of strong human rights cultures by the governments of South Africa, Botswana, Malawi, and Namibia showed how wrong it is to condemn the rest of the continent to lesser expectations.

The international community did manage to exert useful pressure to curb abuses on two older-style leaders, in Kenya and Zambia, and to maintain pressure for democratization in Nigeria.

The Danger of Indulging Great Power Arrogance on Human Rights

In addition to the challenges to the universality of human rights emanating from Asia and Africa, a growing threat emerged in 1997 in the unwillingness of the U.S. government to subject itself to international human rights law. This arrogance was most apparent in U.S. efforts to block the strengthening of human rights standards and institutions, but it also could be seen in the U.S. government's unwillingness to permit the application of existing international standards at home. Within the U.S. government, the Pentagon has been the principal opponent of full participation in the international human rights system. But ultimate responsibility lies with President Clinton for refusing to override its parochial objections.

There are many reasons that the United States might be expected to embrace international human rights law. With its strong constitutional rights tradition, the United States should be particularly comfortable with a rights-based international legal regime.

And as a global economic and military power, the United States would seem to have an interest in curtailing the threats to commerce, public welfare, and international peace that serious abuses of human rights often portend. Instead, the U.S. government's attitude toward international human rights law remained one of deep distrust.

A Narrow Embrace of Human Rights

In the case of the handful of treaties it has ratified so far, such as the International Covenant on Civil and Political Rights (ICCPR) or the International Convention on the Elimination of All Forms of Racial Discrimination (CERD), it carefully entered reservations, declarations, and understandings in any area that it perceived expanded on existing U.S. law. This stingy form of ratification reflected a view that international human rights law was to be embraced only if it codified current U.S. practice, not if it required any improvement. Apparently to guard against any evolution in the strength of international protection, the U.S. government ratified these treaties in a way that denied U.S. citizens the right to insist on compliance before either U.S. courts or international institutions. The result was that ratification became an empty gesture for external consumption rather than an act that strengthened rights protections for Americans.

The U.S. government's one report on its compliance with the ICCPR reflected the same attitude. It reviewed the rights enshrined in U.S. constitutional law without any effort to examine whether that law ensured that Americans enjoyed the rights guaranteed them by international standards in practice. This is hardly an academic point, since, as Human Rights Watch reports have shown, U.S. practice falls short of international standards in such areas as police abuse, the treatment of prisoners, abuse by the Border Patrol, the treatment of asylum seekers, and the application of the death penalty. As this report goes to press, the U.S. government is also more than two years late in issuing its required reports under CERD and the Convention Against Torture and Other

Cruel, Inhuman or Degrading Treatment or Punishment.

In addition, the U.S. government has so far refused to ratify several core human rights treaties. One egregious example is the Convention on the Rights of the Child, which has been ratified by 191 governments—representing every country of the world except for Somalia, which has no recognized government, and the United States. The U.S. government has also not ratified the Convention on the Elimination of All Forms of Discrimination Against Women; the International Covenant on Economic, Social and Cultural Rights; the Additional Protocols of 1977 to the Geneva Conventions of 1949 (which prohibit such forms of warfare as the indiscriminate bombing of civilians); the American Convention on Human Rights, and several key labor rights conventions of the International Labour Organisation. When, in September and October 1997, the U.N. special rapporteur on extrajudicial, summary, or arbitrary executions visited the United States to look into the arbitrariness with which the United States applies the death penalty and police officer's use of lethal force, Washington gave him the cold shoulder by relegating him to low-level officials.

Blocking New Human Rights Standards and Institutions

In the past year, the U.S. government has actively obstructed the emergence of human rights standards designed to strengthen international law and institutions, as shown in the U.S. position on landmines, child soldiers, and the International Criminal Court. On landmines, President Clinton endorsed their "eventual" abolition but, meanwhile, sought to insert various loopholes and exceptions into the unconditional ban offered by the Canadian government and now embraced by more than one hundred countries. The Clinton administration's principal argument was that it needed landmines to defend South Korea, but since many governments have similar reasons for wanting to retain a landmines option, the U.S. position threatened to undermine a ban by riddling it with exceptions. The

Pentagon also sought to exempt permanently from an anti-personnel landmines ban certain types of self-destructing "smart" mines—those that come in mixed systems with anti-tank mines—even though other governments during the treaty negotiations rejected U.S. efforts to redefine these anti-personnel mines as mere "submunitions." The Pentagon would undoubtedly incur some cost and risk in genuinely stopping its use of landmines, but so will many of the one hundred other governments that will be signing the treaty in Ottawa in the interest of building a norm that could help save thousands of innocent landmine victims each year.

The U.S. government also stands virtually alone in opposing a ban on the use of children under the age of eighteen as soldiers. Stopping the use of child soldiers by governments and armed opposition groups in such countries as Liberia, Sudan, Uganda, Burundi, and Sri Lanka—an estimated quarter of a million children are under arms worldwide—would end a practice that leaves the children physically at risk, emotionally traumatized, and a danger to anyone they encounter. Such a ban would be attached as an optional protocol to the Convention on the Rights of the Child. The U.S. government has opposed codifying this ban even though, as noted, it is one of only two countries not to have ratified the underlying treaty, and it would be entirely optional whether signatories to the principal treaty would also endorse the protocol. The only apparent reason for the Clinton administration's obstruction is that the Pentagon finds it somewhat easier to reach its enlistment goals if it entices seventeen-year-olds to sign up for military service. Although only about one percent of the U.S. military is composed of such underage recruits, the Pentagon refuses to give up this recruitment practice in the interest of building a strong international norm against the use of child soldiers.

On the International Criminal Court, as noted, the U.S. government insisted on various restrictions that would weaken the court's independence and effectiveness. The goal seemed to be avoiding even the remotest possibility that an American soldier, pilot, or political leader might end up in the dock of the ICC. But that insistence on an effective U.S. exception—one that the other four permanent members of the Security Council were quick to demand for themselves—risked the universality on which any international system of justice must be built.

This attitude was best seen in the U.S. position on the requirement that the Security Council consent to any prosecution stemming from a situation that the council is confronting under its authority to address threats to peace under Chapter VII of the U.N. Charter. Washington's stated fear was that prosecution of those behind genocide, war crimes, or crimes against humanity might jeopardize efforts to establish peace. But by suggesting that prosecutions might be a mere bargaining chip, to be sacrificed in the course of peace negotiations, this position would only embolden those committing atrocities, by offering a way to avoid prosecution when it comes time to talk peace. That would only accentuate the threat to peace that these abusive individuals present.

That self-protection might have been the dominant American motive could be seen in the U.S. response to a compromise suggested by Singapore. Under this compromise, if prosecutions would clearly threaten peace efforts, the Security Council could halt or delay them, but only by a majority vote of the whole council. But the United States insisted on Security Council permission before prosecutions go forward, meaning that, by virtue of its veto, the U.S. government could single-handedly block any prosecution.

Even if the U.S. were to succeed in weakening a future ICC through such restrictions, there is little chance that the administration would submit the ICC treaty to the current U.S. Senate, with its marked disdain for international human rights institutions, let alone that the Senate would consent to ratification. Yet the administration persists in weakening an historic institution simply because, at some unknown date in the future, the Senate might find an enfeebled court palatable.

It is time for the international community to stop indulging this obstructionist behavior. The landmines negotiations may promise a new approach. By sidestepping the U.N.'s recent preference for "consensus" in negotiations for new human rights standards, the proponents of the landmines treaty, led by Canada, insisted that the United States either accept an unconditional ban or face the ensuing opprobrium. A similar approach should be taken in other negotiations. Negotiators for a ban on child soldiers should insist that the United States ratify the Convention on the Rights of the Child as a condition for taking a position on the minimum age for soldiers. Negotiators for an International Criminal Court should refuse to allow the United States to weaken this institution on the distant hope that the U.S. Senate might someday embrace it.

If the U.S. government persists in its current attitude toward international human rights law, the international community should simply leave the United States behind. Just as it took the United States forty years to ratify the Genocide Convention and twenty-five years to ratify the International Covenant on Civil and Political Rights, so it may be some time before the United States is willing to adopt new human rights standards or embrace a strong and independent ICC. In the case of the ICC, it is better to accept that the United States will not be a founding member of the court than to allow the U.S. government to undermine such an important institution in the hope that it can be made acceptable to the U.S. Senate at this moment in its history. While U.S. financial and political backing for the ICC will still be necessary—to help fund prosecutions and apprehend indicted suspects—such support is likely to be easier to secure when the pursuit of a particular brutal tyrant is at stake than in the abstract. As for the rest of the world, its support—also essential—is more likely for a court that is truly universal than for one that enables a handful of major powers to exempt themselves and their allies from prosecution.

Weak Pressure on China

China continued to pose a major dilemma for the international community: how to exert human rights pressure on a repressive country that is also a key trading partner, potentially the world's largest market, a growing military power, and a permanent member of the U.N. Security Council? China showed no hesitation in responding to one country's human rights criticism by excluding its nationals from lucrative business contracts, or in buying key votes at the U.N. from small countries with promises of assistance. Asian allies, worried about China's military build-up, warned against too strident a human rights posture, fearing that it would only exacerbate a siege mentality among some of China's leaders. Policymakers in Washington worried about how irritants in the U.S.-China relationship, of which human rights was one, might affect China's willingness to play a constructive role in resolving tensions on the Korean peninsula or stopping weapons proliferation.

The question of striking the right balance between economics, security, and human rights was a real issue, but some countries seemed more concerned about striking deals. Nowhere was this more evident than at the annual meeting of the U.N. Commission on Human Rights in Geneva, one of the few multilateral fora left for raising human rights concerns in China. France, Germany, Spain, and Italy capitulated to China's commercial seduction by trading the usual European Union sponsorship of a U.N. resolution critical of China's human rights practices for the prospect of more Chinese purchases of their jointly produced Airbus planes. Nor did these governments respond forcefully in defense of their fellow E.U. members when China retaliated economically against Denmark and the Netherlands for sponsoring the resolution and speaking in favor of it. For similar commercial motives, Japan, Canada, and Australia abandoned their traditional sponsorship of the U.N. resolution in return for a toothless bilateral human rights "dialogue"; indeed, Japan gave China $867 million in aid in 1996, more than to any government other than Indonesia. The developing world displayed no greater commitment to human rights as it succumbed to Chinese threats, bribes, and blandishments.

With China's shuttered civil society, pervasive torture, extensive religious repression, and thousands of political prisoners, there are few more deserving candidates for condemnation by the U.N. Human Rights Commission. Yet China's success in fending off condemnation year after year is itself an affront to the universality of human rights and an effective proclamation that powerful countries are exempt from human rights scrutiny.

Although the U.S. government did sponsor the U.N. resolution on China, it waffled so long, and lobbied its allies for support so ineffectively, that the result seemed more a cosmetic gesture than a genuine effort to censure China. Indeed, because the U.S. government agreed to sponsor the resolution only after Vice President Al Gore visited Beijing in March and secured U.S.$685 million worth of contracts for the Boeing Corporation—at a time when Human Rights Commission deliberations were already in full swing—the U.S. contention that its allies should risk their own commercial ambitions rang hollow. The United States and the European Union desperately sought a few Chinese concessions on human rights to justify abandoning the U.N. effort, but even the concessions under discussion did not justify withdrawing the condemnation effort and the rare form of multilateral leverage that it provided. It is only to be hoped that the United States and European governments heed the European Parliament's resolution of October 1997 calling for early and joint sponsorship of a China resolution in 1998.

The international community was no more effective in deploying the other sources of leverage at its disposal. One of the potentially most useful, and least costly, forms of leverage was summitry. Summits took place with the leaders of France, Sweden, Russia, and Japan, but for Chinese President Jiang Zemin, the most important of these meetings was the long-sought summit in Washington, a visit that would for all practical purposes

end China's post-Tiananmen stigma and help consolidate his position at home. But the Clinton administration largely squandered this opportunity to secure human rights concessions before the summit.

The only concession offered by Beijing in advance of the summit (which had previously been promised to France as a condition of its not sponsoring the China resolution at the U.N. Human Rights Commission) was China's decision to sign the International Covenant on Economic, Social and Cultural Rights (ICESCR), though not the International Covenant on Civil and Political Rights. The significance of that step must be judged in light of Beijing's persistent and pervasive use of torture despite its earlier ratification of the Convention Against Torture. Indeed, although the ICESCR upholds the right to form independent labor unions, China indicated no willingness to uphold this right, and Washington did nothing to press American businesses to insist on it.

At the summit, President Clinton took the important step of engaging in a candid, public exchange with President Jiang about human rights. Shortly after the summit, China released Wei Jingsheng from prison for exile in the United States. The release was unexpected and welcome, but such periodic, isolated releases have little impact on the overall human rights situation in China. Because China's repressive laws remain in place, there is nothing to prevent the Chinese government from using other prisoners as hostages in the next round of international negotiations or, indeed, from making new arrests.

In the past, China has responded to pressure when its human rights practices were clearly linked to something of concern to Beijing. There are plenty of possibilities for such linkage today—everything from China's admittance to international institutions like the World Trade Organization to the date for President Clinton's return visit to Beijing. World Bank loans are also a possibility—$2.8 billion were extended in fiscal year 1997, more than to any other government—if the administration were able to secure support, at least to hold up loans, from other major donors. But the administration's refusal to link China's human rights performance to anything that mattered to Beijing made it easy for Chinese leaders to ignore U.S. concerns.

Over the past year, the Clinton administration seemed to spend more time and effort fending off critics of its China policy than it did pressing China to respect human rights. Administration officials, including Secretary of State Madeleine Albright, obfuscated the policy choices facing the administration by repeatedly presenting U.S. policy toward China in terms of a false dichotomy between "isolation" and "engagement." This simplistic argument diverts the public from asking how, while engaging China on a variety of topics, the U.S. government could effectively put pressure on Beijing to respect human rights. Another favorite ploy of the administration was to argue that the U.S.-China relationship is too important to be held "hostage" to human rights concerns—a truism that, again, deliberately avoids the questions about how pressure could be exerted for human rights within the larger relationship. When the administration confronted China on copyright piracy, missile sales, market access, or Taiwan, no one suggested that this pressure would "isolate" China or hold the relationship "hostage" to a single issue.

The administration also tried to steer the human rights conversation toward promoting the rule of law. This approach, the administration contended, was the best of all possible options: pressure would be unnecessary, since it was hoped that the Chinese government could be convinced that its economic development required greater legal regularity, and the introduction of the rule of law over time might be good for human rights. Building the rule of law is certainly important, but it is a long-term project which does nothing to redress the suffering of today's victims of torture and political imprisonment. Moreover, as demonstrated by Singapore's form of judicial repression of dissent, building the rule of law in the commercial realm does not necessarily ensure an independent judiciary and the rule of law in the political realm. Most important, the rule of law secures human rights only if the law itself respects those rights. So long as Chinese law continues to regard any criticism of the Chinese government as a threat to state security, so long as Chinese law permits the detention of any independent labor activist or religious leader, improvements in the rule of law will only secure more efficient repression. And China has demonstrated no inclination to change its law without the tough pressure that the administration studiously avoided exerting.

The international community should stop settling for tokenism and insist that Beijing take structural steps that will make a difference for significant numbers: granting humanitarian organizations access to prisons, opening all of China and Tibet to scrutiny by independent journalists and human rights monitors, or releasing the many nonviolent offenders among the 2,000 prisoners serving time for "counterrevolution," a crime which no longer exists (China having substituted new "state security" crimes with expanded scope). But none of these changes is likely to occur without the sustained international pressure that was so lacking in 1997.

Europe: More Direct Policy Linkage with Human Rights

While Europe failed as miserably as the United States in putting pressure on China, it demonstrated a somewhat greater willingness elsewhere to link aid and trade benefits to the recipient's respect for human rights. Although such linkages are built into U.S. law, they are routinely ignored in Washington. Indeed, many of the largest recipients of U.S. aid—Israel, Egypt, Turkey, Colombia, Armenia—faced little or no pressure from Washington in 1997 to improve their human rights records.

The European Union pursues a different approach, by concluding legally binding agreements with recipients of aid and trade benefits that are explicitly conditioned on human rights performance. The test of these agreements will be in their implementation, and E.U. adherence to them has been inconsistent. But in 1997, they gave rise to some promising interventions.

European insistence on the principle of linkage was best illustrated in the case of Mexico. The Mexican government sought to weaken the standard clause conditioning its trade and cooperation agreement with the European Union on its respect for human rights. Although at first the European Commission agreed, protest led the Council of Ministers to insist on the standard clause, and Mexico relented. New agreements with human rights clauses were also in the process of ratification for Israel and Tunisia. Similarly, the European Parliament continued to block payment on human rights grounds of some $470 million in adjustment fees under its 1995 customs union agreement with Turkey. The European Commission cut off Burma's low-tariff access to the E.U. market under the Generalized System of Preferences (GSP) because of its use of forced labor—the first time that this human rights clause in the European GSP program had been invoked. And the E.U. adopted a "common position" toward Cuba, conditioning full economic cooperation on specified human rights improvements.

On the question of membership, the European Union identified specific human rights concerns that stood as obstacles to the eventual admission of Bulgaria, the Czech Republic, Hungary, Romania, and Slovakia. It also suspended its "critical dialogue" with the Iranian government in April, and temporarily withdrew most E.U. ambassadors, following a verdict in a German court holding the "Iranian political leadership" responsible for the murder of the leader of a Kurdish armed opposition group and three companions in Berlin in 1992. British Foreign Secretary Robin Cook, speaking for Britain in its capacity as E.U. chair at the time of the April 1998 Asia-Europe meeting (ASEM), announced that Burma would not be invited to the meeting, despite its admission to the Association of Southeast Asian Nations (ASEAN), because of its human rights record.

The Council of Europe—an institution whose raison d'être is the promotion of human rights—also had an inconsistent record. In 1996, it admitted Russia and Croatia de-spite serious human rights problems, and neither made improvements in 1997 to justify this experiment in "constructive engagement." Only where there was less at stake did the Council of Europe take a more principled stand on human rights: it suspended Belarus's special guest status in January 1997 because of President Aleksandr Lukashenka's toughening repression, and continued to bar admission of the Caucasus countries on human rights grounds.

There were some significant blemishes on Europe's record in promoting human rights. Despite the increasingly authoritarian rule of Albanian President Sali Berisha, the European Commission had provided his government with some $560 million since 1990—more per capita than anywhere else in Eastern Europe—while the United States had supplied $236 million in the same period. The rationale for this uncritical support was Berisha's willingness to open Albanian ports and airstrips to Western troops operating in Bosnia. But by propping up Berisha's increasingly authoritarian government, the international community helped to fuel the violent political upheavals in Albania in 1997 that left 2,000 dead. France granted visas to several members of the Nigerian government in violation of E.U. sanctions. France also remained Algeria's largest donor, despite the Algerian government's refusal to permit independent investigation of the large-scale slaughter of civilians in the villages surrounding Algiers or to intervene against the attackers. And France gave generously to Tunisia, despite its broad crackdown on human rights activists and the political opposition under the guise of fighting Islamist militants.

Bosnia and Rwanda: The International Criminal Tribunals

Significant progress was made in 1997 toward securing justice before international tribunals for those behind the genocides in Rwanda and the former Yugoslavia. But this experiment with international justice remained at risk because President Bill Clinton, British Prime Minister Tony Blair, and French President Jacques Chirac refused to order their troops in the NATO-led, 30,000-strong force in Bosnia (the Stabilization Force, SFOR) to arrest the Bosnian Serb political and military leaders at the time of the genocide, Radovan Karadzic and Ratko Mladic.

The International Criminal Tribunal for Rwanda made the most progress in the past year. With Kenya's arrest and surrender of seven allegedly leading participants in the genocide, the Rwandan Tribunal had twenty-three of thirty-five indicted defendants in custody, including the apparent mastermind of the genocide, Col. Theoneste Bagasora. Chief Prosecutor Louise Arbour replaced the deputy prosecutor for Rwanda with an apparently far more engaged, energetic, and effective individual, Bernard Muna, and she took steps to address the administrative, staffing, and morale problems that affected the tribunal. In an important development and precedent, the tribunal filed its first indictment for rape and sexual abuse committed during the genocide. The tribunal also appointed a gender advisor in the witness protection unit as a first step toward addressing the specific needs of female victims and witnesses.

The International Criminal Tribunal for the Former Yugoslavia also advanced in 1997. It concluded its first trial, of Dusan Tadic, and secured his conviction on numerous counts; he was sentenced to twenty years in prison. It also accepted a guilty plea of Drazen Erdemovic and sentenced him to ten years in prison.

In addition, the Yugoslavia tribunal made some important progress in securing the custody of indicted defendants. In June, a lightly armed U.N. force in Croatia arrested one indicted Serb suspect. In July, British troops arrested a secretly indicted Bosnian Serb suspect in Prijedor and killed another in a firefight. In October, Croatia, facing tough diplomatic and economic pressure from the United States, the European Union and the World Bank, arranged the "voluntary" surrender of ten ethnic Croat suspects, including the highest-ranking Bosnian Croat facing charges. As of mid-November, of the seventy-eight known to have been indicted by

the Yugoslavia tribunal, twenty were in custody awaiting trial, six were known or believed to be dead, and fifty-two were at large. All of the suspects in territory controlled by the Bosnian Federation and a majority of the suspects in Croatia and Croatian-controlled parts of Bosnia were thus in custody. Those still at large were primarily in Serbia or Serb-controlled parts of Bosnia.

While economic pressure succeeded in securing the cooperation of the Croatian government in surrendering suspects, there was no evidence that such pressure alone would result in the surrender of the remaining ethnic Serb defendants. It thus appeared likely that these indicted suspects, particularly Karadzic and Mladic, would find their way to the Hague only if they were arrested by the NATO-led international force in Bosnia.

The British arrest effort in July punctured two of the most overworked excuses for NATO's refusal to make these arrests. First, despite NATO's worst-case predictions, there was no serious retaliation against NATO troops or other international workers; as in the past, those tempted to attack international workers were scared off by warnings of severe consequences at the hands of the formidably armed NATO troops. Second, despite NATO's repeated protests that it had not "encountered" any of the suspects—its current mandate requires an "encounter" as a condition for making an arrest—it became clear that NATO could easily arrange such "encounters" if it chose.

After July, however, various NATO governments offered one excuse after another for deferring further arrests. They argued that arrests might upset Russia (when its acquiescence in NATO expansion was needed), disrupt the Bosnian municipal elections of September, spark Serb nationalism during the Bosnian Serb parliamentary elections of November, or disrupt the fragile peace. Above all, the U.S. military leadership remained determined to avoid subjecting its troops to the risk of apprehending indicted suspects, regardless of the stakes involved. Although, as noted, a functioning justice system would help to deter tyrants who today pose some of the greatest risks to international security, the Clinton administration refused to make this case to the American people, apparently terrified of the political costs of suggesting that casualties might be incurred in the course of making arrests.

It was also disappointing that Britain, France, and their European allies—which had already incurred casualties in the interest of establishing peace in Bosnia—were so deferential to Washington's excessive fear of casualties when it came to building the justice system necessary to keep that peace. Britain overcame this undue deference to American sensibilities once, but seemed unwilling to act again without Washington's participation. And France showed no willingness at all to proceed with arrests.

As Human Rights Watch showed in a series of reports on particular municipalities in Bosnia, the failure to apprehend these accused killers was the single biggest obstacle to ethnic reintegration and a secure peace in the country. The men who presided over ethnic slaughter during the war continued, through their control of local police forces and paramilitary networks, to use violence and intimidation to silence dissent and prevent ethnic minorities from returning home. Peace is unlikely to survive the ultimate withdrawal of NATO troops while these accused murderers remain at large.

NATO did take steps to weaken Karadzic by seizing his radio transmitters and disarming some of his police force. It also overtly backed his political rival, Bosnian Serb President Biljana Plavsic. The hope seemed to be that NATO might succeed in shifting the balance of power in Republika Srpska away from Karadzic and perhaps even encourage others to force his surrender. But Plavsic, also a confirmed Serb nationalist and past supporter of "ethnic cleansing," refused to cooperate with the Yugoslavia tribunal, despite her professed support for the Dayton peace accord. And NATO's overt involvement in Bosnian Serb politics, rather than in the principled support of international justice, risked promoting the same kind of popular outrage that its immersion in local politics did in Somalia in 1993.

NATO's paralysis in Bosnia also dimmed hopes for the emergence of a meaningful international system of justice. A future international criminal court could contribute to deterring atrocities only if their authors face a reasonable likelihood of apprehension, trial, and punishment. So long as war criminals and genocidal killers can dismiss indictments as bluster—an empty accusation that the major powers have no intention of backing—the ICC will be condemned to serve as a paper tiger, and the international community risks squandering this first opportunity in fifty years to fulfill the promise of the Nuremburg and Tokyo tribunals.

New Hope and Persistent Challenges for Human Rights at the United Nations

The election of Kofi Annan as U.N. secretary-general and his appointment of Mary Robinson as U.N. high commissioner for human rights gave a tremendous boost to those who look to the United Nations to fulfill the obligations under its charter to protect human rights. Yet significant challenges still face the U.N., particularly its lead refugee agency and its central human rights body.

The Secretary-General

In sharp contrast to his predecessor, the new secretary-general, Kofi Annan, spoke frequently, forcefully, and thoughtfully about human rights. In his first press conference, in February, he stressed the importance of human rights to the four main areas of U.N. activity: peace and security, humanitarian affairs, economic and social affairs, and development. The high commissioner for human rights was invited to be represented on all thematic management teams and to take part herself in the secretary-general's new cabinet-style senior management group.

The secretary-general also frequently emphasized that many of the world's ills, particularly problems of security, cannot be solved without addressing human rights. "Human rights are part of human security" is a phrase he coined and repeatedly used, including in a speech in Shanghai. As a series of massacres took place in the villages surrounding Algiers while the Algerian government did little to stop the carnage and blocked independent investigation into its origins, the secretary-general spoke out forcefully and stressed the "urgent" need for international involvement to end the slaughter. Challenging the Algerian government's view that the killing was a strictly internal affair, the secretary-general said, "As the killing goes on...it is extremely difficult for all of us to pretend that it is not happening, that we do not know about it, and that we should leave the Algerian population to their lot." He also stepped in decisively to remove, or, in one case, to transfer, a number of the U.N. officials whose corruption, incompetence, or obstruction had hindered the work of the International Criminal Tribunal for Rwanda.

From a human rights perspective, the biggest disappointment of the secretary-general's first year in office was his inconsistent support for fundamental principles of human rights investigation in his dealings with the government of the Democratic Republic of the Congo. Worst was his capitulation to the demand of the DRC government that Roberto Garretón, the U.N. special rapporteur for the country, be removed as head of the U.N.'s investigation into the massacre of tens of thousands of Rwandan refugees as they fled across northern Congo. Garretón had issued a report in April calling attention to the massacres as they were underway—precisely the kind of preventive effort that the U.N. should applaud. But with the active support of the U.S. government, the U.N. rewarded him for his effort by removing him from the U.N. investigative team. This capitulation emboldened the DRC government to insist on further concessions, which U.S. Ambassador to the U.N. Bill Richardson traveled to Kinshasa to grant, including restrictions on the timing of the U.N. investigation, limits on the investigators' access to certain Congolese witnesses, a prohibition on recommendations of prosecution by the investigators, and the right of the DRC government to examine and comment on the inves-

tigators' report before it is released to the public.

The breach of the principle that abusive governments do not get to choose their investigators came back to haunt the U.N. In July, Burundi apparently followed the DRC's lead and asked, unsuccessfully, to remove its highly capable special rapporteur, Paulo Sérgio Pinheiro. And in October and November, Iraq demanded the removal of the American members of the U.N. team investigating Baghdad's production of weapons of mass destruction. While the U.S. government threatened war with Iraq over this incident, it never reaffirmed the general principle that Washington helped to undermine.

The new secretary-general also faces challenges in living up to his commitment to integrate human rights into all U.N. activities. The marginal role given human rights monitoring in such U.N. operations as UNOMIL in Liberia was a good example. UNOMIL regularly subordinated human rights to political concerns, and U.N. human rights monitors made no effort to monitor the behavior of abusive international troops from the regional ECOMOG force. The normally respected U.N. mission in Guatemala, MINUGUA, also tarnished its reputation in 1997 by, in the supposed interest of peace talks, suppressing evidence that the army had forcibly "disappeared" a rebel captive. The secretary-general will need to stress that strong and consistent human rights reporting is essential to any effort to build peace.

Also of concern is whether the secretary-general will deliver on his promise to increase work on women's rights throughout the U.N. He has made little if any progress, and his reform plan made scant reference to the issue.

The High Commissioner for Human Rights

Mary Robinson, the new high commissioner for human rights, was a welcome replacement for her predecessor, whose low-key approach and penchant for quiet diplomacy squandered the principal tool available to the high commissioner: the ability to use the moral authority of the office to shame governments into ending abusive practices. As the former president of Ireland, Mary Robinson skillfully used a ceremonial office to make high-profile statements on a range of important human rights issues. The challenge facing her now as high commissioner is to deploy the enormous potential of her office as a powerful and public voice for the oppressed worldwide.

The U.N. Commission on Human Rights

A major difficulty facing the U.N. Commission on Human Rights is the determination of a group of abusive governments and some of their regional allies—including China, Cuba, Egypt, Indonesia, Iran, Malaysia, Nigeria, Pakistan, Philippines, and Sri Lanka—to cripple the U.N.'s human rights machinery. A principal focus of this attack was the U.N. Working Group on Arbitrary Detention, which these governments pressured to defer to the judgments of domestic courts, limit the application of the International Covenant on Civil and Political Rights, and "give views rather than take decisions" about cases of unjust detention. In a related move, these countries convinced the commission for the first time to censor the report of one of its independent rapporteurs. And in a series of resolutions that were tabled but deferred for action until March and April 1998, these countries sought to prohibit rapporteurs and working groups from speaking with the press during their investigative missions (the moment of maximum press interest) and similarly to "rationalize" the work of the commission's investigative and reporting bodies.

Much of the reason for this attack on the U.N.'s most effective human rights institutions is the commission's indifference to the human rights record of its membership. Commission members include not only countries that routinely flout basic human rights standards, such as China, Belarus, and Rwanda, but even countries that refuse to permit U.N. special rapporteurs to conduct on-site investigations, such as Cuba and, until recently,

Sudan. It is time to end the charade that permits abusive governments to join the U.N.'s highest human rights body for the principal purpose of shielding their human rights conduct from criticism and enfeebling the U.N.'s capacity to defend human rights.

The major good news at the commission was the willingness of many African governments to break with regional alliances on the vote regarding the appointment of a special rapporteur for Nigeria. South Africa and Uganda voted for the resolution, while the other African governments on the commission abstained.

The U.N. High Commissioner for Refugees

The recent global tendency to downplay the protection of refugees in the interest of providing humanitarian relief exploded in disaster in 1997 in what became the Democratic Republic of the Congo. For over two years, the U.N. High Commissioner for Refugees (UNHCR) had been forced to tolerate a situation in which the camps it operated in Zaire housed not only legitimate refugees but also killers from Rwanda's genocide of 1994. When Rwandan troops took advantage of an uprising in eastern Zaire to attack the refugee camps where guerrillas had set up base, 600,000 refugees were returned home to Rwanda. Many returned voluntarily, but a significant number were sent back against their will to face severe repression by Rwandan authorities—a blatant violation of the principle of *nonrefoulement* which is at the core of UNHCR's mandate. Within weeks, another 470,000 Rwandan refugees were forcibly returned from Tanzania, also largely with UNHCR acquiescence.

Much of the responsibility for this state of affairs fell to the major powers, which refused countless pleas from UNHCR and NGOs to provide a military force to separate victims from oppressors in the camps run by UNHCR. Instead, these governments pursued a simplistic humanitarianism in which they preferred to pump upwards of $1 million a day into the camps—a total of $2.5 billion—rather than take the political and military risks necessary to separate combatants from genuine refugees. The failure to end this combustible mix fueled a new armed conflict and, through the parallel massacres that it triggered, the apparent slaughter of tens of thousands of refugees as they fled across Zaire/DRC. Even when large-scale massacres of refugees were underway, a number of governments, led by the United States and Canada, began planning for a military force to protect the Rwandans, but they finally decided not to intervene, in part because they refused to accept UNHCR's information about the number of people at risk. According to UNHCR, 213,000 refugees remain unaccounted for.

Some blame for this tragedy must also be shared by Sadako Ogata, the high commissioner, who might have rallied greater international support had she been more outspoken about the problem of refugees camps controlled by *genocidaires* rather than at first denying that the problem existed. Similarly, UNHCR in recent years has tended to disfavor its traditional strategy of protecting refugees in exile, in favor of promoting the return of refugees to their country of origin, even in circumstances in which their safety cannot be ensured. Again, the international community's unwillingness to pay for the long-term protection of refugees in exile is a major factor in this shift. But UNHCR made this shift easier by tacitly endorsing the premature or involuntary return of refugees in several cases.

For example, when Rwandan troops overran the camps and forced the refugees to return to Rwanda, UNHCR legitimized the expulsion by announcing that conditions in Rwanda were "safe," hardly an accurate depiction of a country where government and insurgent forces were engaged in indiscriminate attacks on civilians. Similarly, until very late in the process, UNHCR facilitated rather than protested the forced return of Rwandan refugees in Tanzania. UNHCR also observed but did not protest the apparently involuntary return of some Burmese refugees in Thailand, and it gave Burmese refugees in Bangladesh a deceptively rosy picture of the conditions they would encounter if they returned home.

UNHCR also gave insufficient attention to protecting women refugees from sexual violence. The problem was vividly illustrated by a study of Burundian refugees in Tanzania which showed that 25 percent had been sexually assaulted while in UNHCR-run camps.

By year's end, UNHCR seemed to be rethinking its downgrading of protection. Rather than sanction the continuing forcible return of Rwandan refugees near Kisangani in the DRC, it publicly announced that it could not guarantee the safety of those being returned, and thus distanced the agency from this unlawful action. When Gabon summarily returned a small group of refugees to Rwanda, UNHCR sent a high-profile mission to Kigali to inquire into their safety. UNHCR also urged European governments to refrain from the "hasty deportation of rejected Algerian asylum seekers in the midst of an upsurge of violence in Algeria." In addition, UNHCR initiated a useful dialogue with human rights groups about protection issues.

Restoring protection to the central role that it traditionally occupied at UNHCR is clearly the greatest challenge facing the agency. Whether it succeeds in fulfilling its core protective responsibilities will depend not only on its success in gaining support from the major governmental powers but also on its candor in reversing the disturbing downgrading of protection that has infected UNHCR operations in recent years.

Closing Doors to Refugees

As noted, UNHCR's protection shortcomings reflect a growing determination among powerful governments to shed their responsibility for refugees. With the Cold War ideological incentives for admitting refugees long gone, the West increasingly shut its doors to those facing persecution. Illustrative was a U.S. law implemented in April that authorized the use of summary procedures to evaluate the claims of asylum seekers who arrive in the United States without proper travel documents, as a large percentage of those fleeing persecution do. Frequently tired after a lengthy journey, confused, unable to speak English, and without the assistance of counsel, asylum seekers face immediate return home unless they can convince a low-level immigration agent, operating without public scrutiny, that they should be given an opportunity to demonstrate a credible fear of persecution. UNHCR and others have criticized this procedure because of the likelihood that it will deliver refugees back to their persecutors.

The U.S. government also continued its heavy reliance on the detention of those asylum seekers whose claims survive this cursory review. Detention frequently occurred not because an asylum seeker was shown to pose a risk of flight if his or her claim were denied, but for the apparent purpose of deterring asylum seekers from arriving on U.S. shores.

Meanwhile, the European Union adopted rules that enabled its member states to reject asylum claims if the applicant had previously passed through a "safe third country." The E.U. aggressively pursued agreements with countries to the east and south to accept the return of asylum seekers, often without adequate guarantees that their claims would be heard and fairly assessed. This practice led to the prospect of refoulement through a chain of deportations to supposedly "safe third countries." Similarly, many E.U. governments agreed not to consider requests for asylum from residents of other E.U. states—a blanket prohibition that again violates the refoulement prohibition. In addition, the E.U. adopted a narrow view of the persecution that gives rise to asylum by excluding persecution by rebel groups, even when local governments lack the means or will to provide protection, and it favored temporary protective status in lieu of the more complete and durable rights to be accorded under the Refugee Convention. Germany and Switzerland began to demand that refugees return to Bosnia even though violence and intimidation prevented the vast majority from returning to their homes in areas where they would now be an ethnic minority.

Among other countries that turned their backs on refugees, Russia routinely beat, extorted, and expelled refugees, especially from the countries of the former Soviet Union, and Thailand forcibly returned 20,000 refugees to Burma and denied entry to thousands more.

National Efforts to Establish Accountability

At the national level, progress was made toward holding abusive officials accountable under the law in several countries, particularly in Latin America.

* In Peru, a military court convicted the head of the Army Intelligence Service (SIE), Carlos Sánchez Noriega, and three of his subordinates, and sentenced them to eight years in prison, for the torture of a fellow SIE agent. The agent was suspected of having leaked information regarding secret army intelligence plans to blow up a television station and intimidate well known journalists and human rights defenders.

* In Guatemala, the so-called Law of National Reconciliation, which was enacted in December 1996 and allows judges to grant amnesty for crimes other than "disappearance" and torture that occurred in the context of the country's lengthy armed conflict, did not lead to the amnesty of human rights offenders that many had feared. Guatemalan judges rejected amnesty applications in all cases involving human rights abuse, and no member of the military was granted amnesty. Guerrillas received amnesty only for crimes of subversion but not for violent abuses such as murder.

* In Colombia, the Constitutional Court ruled that cases involving extrajudicial executions, torture, forced disappearances, and rape by the security forces must be tried in civilian, not military, courts. The army had used military courts to avoid accountability for its atrocities. However, no pending cases had yet been transferred to the civilian courts.

In three African countries, justice proceeded painfully slowly. Ethiopia's trial of seventy-two top-ranking officials of the former military government of the Derg was still pending, while another 2,246 facing "genocide" charges had been in custody for three to five years without trial. In Rwanda, trials began of some genocide suspects, and a handful of convictions were handed down, but 120,000 suspects remained in prison, crammed into facilities meant to accommodate a mere fraction of their number. Rwanda's rudimentary justice system, which was in the process of being rebuilt after having been destroyed during the genocide, gave most prisoners little prospect of trial. In Burundi, the trial of soldiers accused of having assassinated President Melchior Ndadaye in 1993 was adjourned in the first half of 1997, but trials of civilians accused of killings following the assassination continued. Six of those convicted were executed by hanging in July.

In Asia, the Japanese government rejected the recommendation of the U.N. special rapporteur on violence against women that it provide individual compensation to 200,000 women forced into sexual slavery by the Japanese army during World War II; instead, it established a voluntary fund. Pol Pot's imprisonment by Khmer Rouge troops in Cambodia raised momentary hopes that he would be surrendered for trial before an international tribunal for his role in the deaths of some two million people during Khmer Rouge rule from 1975 to 1979. However, the Khmer Rouge opted instead for a show trial that had nothing to do with the atrocities of the 1970s, and a coup by Second Prime Minister Hun Sen against his royalist coalition partner effectively ended the international momentum to bring Pol Pot to trial.

The United States had a mixed record in 1997 of allowing scrutiny of its own role in human rights abuse. On the positive side, the Central Intelligence Agency (CIA) released documents confirming that in the 1980s it had known about the interrogation and torture of civilians by a military death squad in Honduras and that its agents had visited at least one clandestine prisoner, all while the U.S. government was defending Honduras's human rights record. The CIA also declassified 1,400 pages of documents about its involvement in a coup that overthrew the elected government of Guatemalan President Jacobo Arbenz in 1954. The documents revealed the agency's encouragement of political assassination and murder.

By contrast, the Clinton administration continued to protect Emmanuel "Toto" Constant from deportation to Haiti. Constant, who under Haiti's 1991-94 military dictatorship was on the CIA payroll as the head of the paramilitary organization known as FRAPH, was wanted in Haiti for his role in FRAPH's extensive acts of political violence. The U.S. embassy in Port-au-Prince also continued to refuse to return to the Haitian government approximately 160,000 pages of documents and other material seized in 1994 from FRAPH and the Haitian military. While these documents could be invaluable to Haitian prosecutors, the Clinton administration continued to insist on redacting the names of all Americans—an apparent effort to avoid embarrassing revelations about the involvement of U.S. intelligence agents.

An Expanding Set of Actors Promoting Human Rights

Once, only a handful of Western governments played an active role in promoting human rights across national boundaries. Today, similar efforts by numerous regional groupings and coalitions have come to the fore. Although many of these new actors were no more consistent than Western governments in their human rights advocacy, they demonstrated that concern with human rights across national boundaries is a vigorous reality in the South.

In Latin America, the Organization of American States (OAS) in September 1996 amended its charter to allow the hemisphere's governments to ostracize any government that comes to power by a coup d'etat. The OAS governments stressed that it is in each country's interest to promote constitutional, democratic governments. At the Iberoamerican Summit in November 1996, the governments of Latin America, together with Spain and Portugal, issued the Viña del Mar Declaration, which proclaimed their support for democracy, human rights and fundamental liberties. Even Cuban President Fidel Castro signed the declaration, although the Cuban government promptly sentenced one dissident to eighteen months in prison for challenging the government to comply with it. Following a campaign led by Human Rights Watch, OAS governments also voted in 1997 to reject a nominee with an unsavory human rights past who had been nominated by Guatemala to serve on the respected Inter-American Commission on Human Rights. The candidate, Francisco Villagrán Kramer, had been Guatemala's vice president for three years under a highly abusive dictatorship and then formed a political alliance with another former dictator with a comparably ruthless record.

In Asia, the Association of Southeast Asian Nations (ASEAN) postponed Cambodia's admission after the coup in July led by Hun Sen. However, ASEAN simultaneously admitted Burma, despite its worse record of suppressing political dissent.

In Africa, the Southern Africa Development Community (SADC) played an assertive and notably positive role in pressing for a strong and independent International Criminal Court. South African President Nelson Mandela also made a speech before SADC in which he stressed that respect for each member state's sovereignty and non-interference in each other's national interest could not blunt the SADC governments' common concern for democracy and human rights. However, SADC admitted the Democratic Republic of the Congo despite the massacres of refugees that occurred there. And South Africa itself had a mixed record in promoting human rights abroad: it refused to sell weapons to Turkey because of its human rights abuses, but sold the Rwandan government military equipment despite its continuing atrocities, and gave police equipment to the DRC despite the massacres there. President Mandela also gave vocal support to the DRC's Laurent Kabila and a high-profile embrace to Libya's autocratic leader, Mu'ammar al-Qadhafi.

The Organization of African Unity (OAU) actively promoted the landmines ban, but also rallied behind the Kabila government in the DRC despite its complicity in mass killings. The OAU's African Commission on Human and Peoples' Rights continued to be a disappointment: it sent commissioners to Sudan, Mauritania, Senegal, and Nigeria, but they allowed themselves to be manipulated by governments, often failed to meet with opposition or human rights groups, and did not issue a public report.

At least through the first ten months of 1997, governments of eastern and central Africa maintained sanctions against Burundi which had been imposed following the July 1996 coup. The governments of the Economic Community of West African States (ECOWAS), using regional troops known as ECOMOG, intervened against a coup in Sierra Leone. Despite a history of abusive conduct, ECOMOG also played a generally positive role in Liberia in 1997 following the appointment of a new commander.

The Commonwealth maintained its suspension of Nigeria on human rights grounds. A new group of Francophone nations, organized in November, agreed to make respect for democracy and human rights a main value.

Progress and Retrenchment Around Elections

Elections advanced human rights in several countries in 1997, and at times the international community played a useful role in promoting free and fair elections. Other times, however, the international community showed itself still to be excessively preoccupied with elections as a surrogate for respect for human rights.

In Mexico and Iran, elections represented a major step forward. Mexico's congressional and municipal elections in July, reflecting reforms instituted by President Ernesto Zedillo, were the first in which opposition parties could compete on a level playing field with the long-governing Institutional Revolutionary Party (PRI). For the first time, the PRI lost its majority in the lower house of congress and the mayoralty in Mexico City, the country's second most important post. In Iran, although competition in the presidential elections in May was highly restricted—the Council of Guardians, an appointed body responsible for upholding Islamic principles in government policy, rejected all but four of 238 candidates—Mohammad Khatami, who had been opposed by the ruling clerical establishment, emerged the victor with a campaign that vowed to guarantee the rights of citizens and to institutionalize the rule of law.

By contrast, in Indonesia, the ruling Golkar party won parliamentary elections in May in what it called a "festival of democracy" after allowing only two opposition parties, one of which had been forced to remove its leader. Both the E.U. and the U.S. criticized the electoral process. In Croatia, President Franjo Tudjman was re-elected president in balloting that the Organization for Security and Cooperation in Europe described as seriously flawed because of slanted coverage by the state media and an eleventh-hour assault by a Croatian army captain on the leading opposition candidate, which forced him to spend the days leading up to the election in the hospital. In Slovakia, the government first delayed an opposition-proposed referendum on the direct election of the president and then subverted it through the apparently deliberate misprinting of referendum ballots. In Colombia, guerrilla attacks on candidates in local elections led 900 candidates to withdraw.

In Nigeria, Gen. Sani Abacha, who took power in a 1993 coup, continued cynically to implement his seemingly endless program of "transition" to democratic rule. Local elections held in March were neither free nor fair, as various official bodies screened candidates and excluded those with connections to pro-democracy, human rights, or opposition groups. On the national level, two of five officially registered political parties declared General Abacha their preferred candidate for president; possible alternative candidates for the three other parties withdrew after intimidation or arrest.

In Cambodia, Second Prime Minister Hun Sen overthrew the elected government and then promised "free and fair" elections for May 1998. The United States, while cutting some aid, refused to call this coup a coup because under U.S. law a total suspension of aid would have been required. Japan resumed aid a mere month after the coup and refused to criticize the appointment of a new prime minister to replace the elected prime minister who had been overthrown, although Japan did refuse to give any new assistance until after the 1998 elections.

The international community played a positive role in pushing for free and fair elections in Zambia and Kenya. In Zambia, donor governments put strong pressure on Lusaka when it prevented the principal opposition candidate from running for president and imposed other restrictions on the exercise of civil and political rights leading up to November 1996 elections. That pressure was maintained when, following the elections, the Zambian government blocked attempts by the main opposition party to hold a peaceful rally and harassed NGOs that had been involved in election monitoring and had found the election not free and fair. In Kenya, pressure from donor governments in response to Nairobi's manipulation of voter registration and restrictions on the formation of opposition political parties yielded significant electoral reforms.

In the Balkans, some policymakers showed that they still gave too much credence to elections as a surrogate for the resolution of more fundamental human rights problems. In the Federal Republic of Yugoslavia (FRY), the international community put effective pressure on then-Serbian President Slobodan Miloševi to reverse his annulment of opposition victories in November 1996 local elections, but when he relented, the European Union, in April 1997, granted the FRY preferential trade status despite ongoing serious abuses against ethnic minorities and Belgrade's continuing refusal to surrender indicted war criminal suspects on its territory. The U.S. government adopted a more principled stand by maintaining restrictions on Belgrade's access to nonhumanitarian aid, loans, and trade benefits. In Bosnia, the international community, determined to show progress in the stalled Dayton peace process, pushed for municipal elections in September despite severe restrictions on physical movement and access to the media by opposition parties and candidates.

Religious Persecution

Persecution of minority or disfavored religions remained a serious problem in many parts of the world. The issue gained prominence in the United States as evangelical Christians raised their voice against the persecution of fellow Christians in various parts of the world, although the global problem of religious persecution extended well beyond any particular religious group. Legislation pending in the U.S. Congress would sanction other governments for the most extreme forms of persecution, such as murder, torture, and prolonged detention, but left unaddressed some of the most common forms of religious oppression faced by believers.

In China, "unofficial" religious congregations were subjected to a widening government campaign aimed at forcing them to register with state-sanctioned religious bodies or face dissolution. Those affected included all Buddhists, Protestants, Muslims, Catholics, and Daoists. The Chinese government also denies legitimacy to popular religion, the belief structure of the vast majority of Chinese citizens, labeling its practices "feudal superstition." Members of the Catholic "underground" churches and of unregistered Christian "house churches" faced harassment and detention. In February, in Tongxiang, Zhejiang province, a select Communist Party-led team mounted a five-month campaign to curb the influence of religious figures who refused to submit to state control. The campaign featured strengthened daily supervision of religious activities, a stepped-up registration campaign, and "strict surveillance of underground bishops and priests and 'self-styled' missionaries who cannot yet be punished according to the law." In Xinjiang province, the government targeted "underground" Muslim religious activities, banning the construction or renovation of 133 mosques, arresting forty-four "core participants in ille-

gal religious activities" in the Yili region, and breaking up more than one hundred classes "illegally" teaching the Koran. In Tibet, Buddhist monks and nuns were forced into reeducation programs in which they were supposed to denounce the Dalai Lama and acknowledge the legitimacy of the Chinese government's selection of the new Panchen Lama. In response to a national directive, Chinese officials in many provinces ordered "excessive" Buddhist temples destroyed or converted to other uses.

In Burma, the persecution of the Rohingya Muslim minority continued in Arakan (Rakhine) state, causing new outflows of refugees to Bangladesh. Apparently acting at government instigation, Buddhists monks also attacked Muslims in the central Burmese city of Mandalay in March. Government-tolerated rioters attacked mosques and Muslim-owned shops, and soldiers ordered some Muslims to convert to Buddhism or leave the country.

The Sudanese government continued to wage a highly abusive war against residents of the southern part of the country—a conflict with religious, ethnic, and regional dimensions. The government also condoned kidnapping and enslavement of southerners and denied permits for church-building in Khartoum. In Pakistan, sectarian violence between Sunni and Shi'a Muslim groups left 200 dead, while so-called blasphemy laws and related laws regulating religion were used to harass, intimidate and punish religious minorities, particularly Christians and Ahmadis. In Saudi Arabia, the Sunni government prohibited all non-Muslim religious manifestations. Shi'a Muslim citizens of Saudi Arabia faced widespread official discrimination, including the banning of books on Shi'ism and tight restrictions on the private construction of Shi'a mosques or community centers.

The Iranian government continued to tolerate or encourage violent religious zealots known as Partisans of the Party of God (Ansar-e Hezbollah) to assault and intimidate writers and intellectuals, disrupt gatherings of those critical of government policies, and carry out raids on the offices of independent magazines and newspapers. Baha'is and evangelical Christians faced widespread persecution, including death sentences against two Baha'is accused of spying for Israel and, since 1994, the unexplained murder of three Christian leaders. An official council of clerics and jurists vetted candidates for public office for their "piety," and the constitution restricted the presidency to a male Shi'a Muslim, excluding not only all women but also the 20 percent of the population that is Sunni Muslim or belongs to other religious minorities.

In Egypt, the state's discriminatory treatment of the Christian minority remained unaddressed, including the requirement that congregations secure presidential permission prior to constructing or repairing churches. Coptic Christians in southern Egypt continued to be targeted by armed Islamist militants; in February, eight young Copts were massacred inside a church, and in March, gunmen entered a village and methodically killed thirteen residents, nine of them Copts. Armed opposition groups also invoked religion to kill civilians in Algeria and Israel.

In Russia, "traditional" religions tried to protect their privileged position from the influx of "new" religious groups through a new law revoking almost all rights of religious groups that had been in Russia for fewer than fifteen years. Macedonia proposed a similar law. In Bulgaria, non-Orthodox Christian groups, including Jehovah's Witnesses and World of Life, were refused official recognition and, along with Mormons, were the subject of public attacks and official discrimination. The chief prosecutor also warned that certain Protestant churches would face revocation of their legal recognition if they continued to evangelize. In Greece, the constitution gave only the Greek Orthodox church official status and prohibited proselytism.

In Uzbekistan, the Muslim community faced official curbs on the use of loudspeakers for the call to prayer, steps to prevent female students from wearing Islamic headscarves in schools and colleges, and the closure of Islamic teaching establishments. A Baptist teacher was also charged with conducting illegal church services (facing a possible three years in prison) and his congregation prevented from holding further meetings. To stop proselytizing by predominately Protestant groups, the Uzbekistan authorities confiscated 25,000 copies of the New Testament in Uzbek translation.

In Indonesia, the trial in October of a well-known Catholic priest and social activist in Jakarta on charges of harboring student radicals accused of subversion was widely interpreted as a government effort to brand opposition leaders in heavily Muslim Indonesia as non-Muslim. The Iraqi government interfered with Shi'a religious observance at shrines in Karbala by blocking the annual pilgrimage to the tomb of Imam Husayn.

In Turkey, the military forced the ouster of the Islamic-led coalition government of Prime Minister Necmettin Erbakan and were threatening to outlaw his Welfare Party. The Erbakan government's stated offense, as alleged in the indictment to close the party, was attempting to allow a greater role for Islam in public life, such as allowing female civil servants to wear headscarves and, in the case of some party leaders, calling for the adoption of Islamic law (sharia).

In Cuba, the government sentenced one leader of an independent Christian organization to four years in prison, in part, it appeared, for his unsuccessful attempts to obtain legal status for his organization.

Attacks on Human Rights Monitors

Because the revelation of a government's human rights crimes can be deeply stigmatizing, some governments went to great lengths to silence the messenger, including murder. In apparent retaliation for their work, fifteen human rights monitors in 1997 were killed, forcibly "disappeared," or died in suspicious circumstances. This was more than double the toll for 1996, with all but one of the victims in Colombia or Rwanda. Many other human rights monitors faced detention and harassment.

Killings in Colombia

Colombian human rights activists suffered a wave of murders, with eight killed or "disappeared" in 1997, making the country one of the most dangerous places for human rights monitoring. On May 19, Mario Calderón, an employee of the Center for Research and Popular Education (Centro de Investigación y Educación Popular, CINEP); Elsa Alvarado, his wife and a former CINEP employee; and Carlos Alvarado, Elsa's father, were killed by masked gunmen in their Bogotá apartment, apparently in retaliation for their human rights work.

Nazareno de Jesús Rivera, a member of the Segovia Human Rights Committee, was murdered on March 9. The same day, colleague Jaime Ortiz Londoño was forcibly "disappeared." On March 12, the Army's Fourteenth Brigade displayed Rivera's body to the press, falsely claimed that he was "a guerrilla killed in action," and showed reporters Ortiz's identity documents. On March 23, a former member of the same group, Margarita Guzmán, was killed in her office, apparently for her work investigating Rivera's death and Ortiz's "disappearance."

Víctor Julio Garzón, the secretary general of an agrarian association and a well-known human rights defender, was killed by unidentified gunmen in his Bogotá office on March 7. Garzón was a member of the Meta Civic Committee for Human Rights, which had been all but extinguished after its members were systematically killed. Although international outrage followed the 1996 murder of Josué Giraldo, president of the Meta Civic Committee for Human Rights, no arrests were made in his case, which remained in preliminary investigation along with most other investigations into past killings of Colombian human rights monitors.

A government worker who was investigating links between the security forces and paramilitary groups, former Yondó, Antioquia, ombudsman Gustavo Núñez, was pulled from a public bus by paramilitaries near Barrancabermeja and killed on August 8.

Killings in Rwanda

In early February, five staff members of the U.N. Human Rights Field Office for Rwanda (UNHRFOR) were murdered in southwestern Rwanda by assailants who ambushed their vehicle. Three of the five were Rwandan, Jean-Bosco Munyaneza, Aimable Nsensiyumvu, and Agripin Ngabo; one was Cambodian, Sastra Chim Chan; and one was British, Graham Turnbull. Rwandan authorities attributed the attack to a band of insurgents, several of whom they said they had killed in an encounter soon after.

In late January, a former judge and human rights activist, Innocent Murengezi, "disappeared" just after leaving court in Kigali. He had been one of only three Rwandan lawyers willing to defend persons accused of genocide.

Killing in Ethiopia

The acting president of Ethiopia's Teachers' Association (ETA), Assefa Maru, was shot and killed by the police in early May. He was also a member of the executive committee of the independent Ethiopian Human Rights Council. Maru was shot in the street on the way to his office. Witnesses claimed that at least four police teams took part in the assassination.

Violence and Threats to Safety

Human rights defenders in Colombia were also the targets of threats and surveillance by members of the security forces. Wilson Patiño, a human rights activist from Remedios, Antioquia, was forced to leave the area after armed men came to his home on March 20, apparently to kill him. On May 24, Neftalí Vanegas Perea, a human rights defender in Ocaña, Norte de Santander, narrowly escaped an assassination attempt by armed men believed to be working in league with the security forces. The offices of the Association of Family Members of the Detained and Disappeared (Asociación de Familiares de Detenidos y Desaparecidos, ASFADDES) were the target of a June 24 bombing that destroyed the group's archives. Later, organization members in Medellín and Riosucio,

Chocó, received several threats, including that of a telephone caller who claimed that "the bomb was only a warning, so it would be better if you left the office." Two branch offices were later closed for fear of attacks, and the group's president and her family were forced to leave the country for their safety.

Other human rights workers in Colombia reported receiving threats related to their work. After a series of massacres in the Middle Magdalena region, five human rights workers associated with the Regional Corporation for the Defense of Human Rights (Corporación Regional para la Defensa de los Derechos Humanos, CREDHOS) were informed that their names appeared on death lists being circulated by paramilitary groups. In September, members of the Association for the Promotion of Social Alternatives (Asociación para la Promoción Social Alternativa, MINGA) said that suspicious men were watching their offices and were following the MINGA and ASFADDES members working there.

Human rights advocate Francisco Soberón, head of Peru's Pro-Human Rights Association (Asociación Pro-Derechos Humanos, APRODEH), faced repeated anonymous death threats, apparently in retaliation for APRODEH's defense of a respected judge facing arbitrary legal proceedings and a police whistle-blower facing persecution.

In Bolivia, on January 25, National Police agents arrested Waldo Albarracín, president of the Permanent Assembly of Human Rights (Asamblea Permanente de Derechos Humanos, APDH), and reportedly tortured him for more than three hours. The police agents reportedly beat Albarracín all over his body, including his genitalia, and subjected him to death threats and near-asphyxiation. Albarracín was later hospitalized with serious wounds.

In the eastern town of Kindu, Democratic Republic of Congo, the military commander ordered the closure of the premises of the rights group Haki Za Binadamu, after he received a letter in which the group denounced the unlawful detention of suspects in criminal

and civil cases in a military camp. Two of Haki's workers were detained and tortured; one was left hospitalized and in a coma.

After suffering enormous losses during the genocide, the five Rwandan human rights associations attempted to resume work but activists who criticized the authorities or urged the presumption of innocence for those accused of genocide were harassed and threatened.

A pattern of state-tolerated intimidation of civil liberties lawyers and other political activists continued in Andhra Pradesh, India, where the state government was engaged in a longstanding conflict with armed Maoist groups collectively known as Naxalites. In April and May a group calling itself the "Green Tigers"—a reportedly fictitious name used by a police counterinsurgency unit—claimed responsibility for assaults on two senior members of the Andhra Pradesh Civil Liberties Committee (APCLC) and a protest singer, and threatened to attack four other prominent civil liberties activists.

In September, a police official entered the offices of the South Asia Human Rights Documentation Centre (SAHRC) in New Delhi and questioned the director, Ravi Nair, about the group's activities. When Nair requested that the official provide proper identification, he left. Nair later received a call from the deputy commissioner of police who threatened to arrest him and give him "special treatment" if he did not cooperate.

In October, R. N. Kumar, an activist from the Committee for Initiative and Action in Punjab, received anonymous death threats over the telephone. Kumar had been instrumental in bringing about investigations into the "disappearances" of more than 980 people in Punjab between 1984 and 1994. Also in October, Babloo Singh Loitongbam of the Committee on Human Rights in Manipur was interrogated by police in Imphal, Manipur, after he criticized India's human rights record before the U.N. Human Rights Committee in July.

In Pakistan, human rights activists continued to receive more threats from religious groups than from government agents. Asma

Jahangir, a prominent human rights lawyer and chairperson for the Human Rights Commission of Pakistan, continued to receive threats from religious organizations opposed to the Lahore High Court's decision in the Saima Waheed case, which upheld the validity of this twenty-two-year-old Pakistani woman's marriage in the face of a challenge from her father.

Several members of the Belarusian Helsinki Committee (BHC) were arrested during demonstrations in March, April, and June. One of them was acquitted in court while the others received warnings, fines, or sentences of administrative detention. Police beat up two monitors of the organization during demonstrations on March 14 and April 2. The BHC came under renewed attack on October 20, when three men who identified themselves as "young Belarusian patriots" assaulted and threatened twenty-one-year-old Nadezhda Zhukova, a trial and demonstration observer, as she left the Leninsky District Court.

Arrests, Detentions and Mistreatment

In late 1996 and 1997, local authorities in the Russian provinces arrested at least four human rights activists and brought charges against them for such things as libel, contempt of court, making death or other threats, and having sexual intercourse with a minor. All activists had provided free legal advice to people in their regions and acted as public defenders at court hearings.

In Kyrgyzstan, the Yntymak Society, an organization that advances the housing concerns of migrant workers in Bishkek, came under attack by the government following peaceful demonstrations outside a government building. On July 7, twelve demonstrators, including human rights activist Tursunbek Akhunov, were arrested by police while picketing the building.

On March 14, a three-judge panel found the Turkish translator and publisher of a 1995 Human Rights Watch report on arms transfers to and human rights violations in Turkey, Erturul Kürkçü and Ayenur Zarakol, guilty of the charge of defamation. The court gave Kürkçü a ten-month prison sentence, suspended for two years, and fined Zarakol 1.5 million Turkish Lira, about $7.50.

In May, Dr. Tufan Kose was found guilty of "negligence in denouncing a crime" and Mustafa Cinkilic, a lawyer, was acquitted of "disobeying the orders of authorities." The case against both men, representatives of the Human Rights Foundation of Turkey, Adana branch, stemmed from their refusal to provide authorities with the names and records of 167 victims of torture who sought treatment in Adana.

In Indonesia, on March 22, the police and military broke up the national meeting of Indonesia's largest human rights organization, the Indonesian Legal Aid Foundation (Yayasan Lembaga Bantuan Hukum Indonesia, YLBHI) at the Graha Asri Hotel in Bandung, West Java, on the grounds that YLBHI had not applied for an official permit to hold the meeting. Two local organizers, Wirawan and Hemasari, as well as the hotel manager, were taken to the local police station in Cidadap (Kapolsek) and later transferred to the regional police office (Kapolwiltabes) in Bandung, where they were interrogated.

Khemaïs Ksila, a vice president of the Tunisian Human Rights League, was arrested on September 29, the day he launched a well-publicized hunger strike to dramatize the price he himself had paid for his human rights work: dismissal from his public-sector job, a ban on his travel abroad, and police surveillance. He was accused of "disseminating false news" and inciting others to disturb the public order, and was still in detention as of early November.

In Algeria, the office of lawyer Mohamed Tahri, whose clients included relatives of "disappeared" persons, suffered a suspicious burglary during the weekend of June 12-13, in which the only items missing were personal documents and correspondence with clients. The break-in occurred only days after Tahri was featured speaking about human rights in *Le Monde* (Paris) and on French television. On October 20, Tahri was arrested and held for seven hours after demonstrating in Algiers with about fifty women seeking information on missing relatives.

Rachid Mesli, an Algiers lawyer who had been openly helpful to Amnesty International (AI) during and since its 1996 mission to Algeria, was sentenced after an unfair trial to three years in prison, on charges of "encouraging" and "providing apologetics" for "terrorism." During his initial interrogation and trial, the judge questioned Mesli about his contacts with AI.

On July 27, Israel renewed for six months the administrative detention of Sha'wan Jabarin, fieldwork coordinator at Al-Haq, the Palestinian human rights organization. He had been held off and on for a total of nearly five years since 1989, all of that time without charge or trial.

On October 26, Palestinian security forces arrested Khaled Amayreh, a journalist and human rights activist, after he published a report on the torture of Hamas detainees in a Palestinian Authority center near Hebron. Amayreh said later that he was held for almost two days and verbally abused by Jibril Rajoub, head of the Preventive Security Service in the West Bank. He was released without charge.

Odilia Collazo Valdés, president of Cuba's Human Rights Party (Partido Pro Derechos Humanos, PPDH), suffered repeated arrests during 1997, as did other PPDH members, including Maité Moya Gómez and Jorge Luis Rodríguez. On October 23, a Cuban court in Santa Clara convicted eleven members of the PPDH of "association to commit criminal acts" and "disobedience," with sentences ranging from one year of house arrest (one woman) to one-and-one-half years in prison or work camp (for nine). René Gómez Manzano, an attorney with the Agromontista Current (Corriente Agromontista), a legal defense group, and leader of the Internal Dissidents' Working Group, remained in detention in mid-November.

In Syria, five activivsts from the Committee for the Defense of Freedom and Human Rights continued to serve prison sentences of up to ten years. Roberto Monte, a human rights activist who worked in the state

of Rio Grande do Norte, Brazil, was sued for defamation for accusations he made against a high-ranking police official.

Seven human rights activists in the Dominican Republic complained of police harassment in October and November, apparently linked to a national strike. In early November, Danilo de la Cruz, a member of the Dominican Committee for Human Rights (Comité Dominicano de Derechos Humanos, CDDH) who police had fired on in 1996, was detained and held incommunicado for over one week. During that time, police repeatedly interrogated him about the activities of CDDH and tortured him by beating him, handcuffing him to a metal tube, and refusing to provide him with sufficient food or water.

In China, Liu Nianchun, a principal sponsor of the League for the Protection of the Rights of the Working People; Zhou Guoqiang, a labor rights activist and lawyer; and Gao Feng, a religious dissident, had their sentences extended (288 days for Zhou and 216 for the others) for failure to reform. All three were serving labor reeducation sentences in Shuanghe Labor Camp in Heilongjiang province, although by October Luu had been transferred to an unknown location. When Liu protested and began a hunger strike on May 22, he was thrown into a small dark punishment cell, denied sufficient water, and tortured with electric shocks. He was extremely ill with a blocked intestine, swollen lymph nodes, and mouth ulcers, and had lost over forty pounds, but prison authorities ignored his requests for medical treatment

Also in China, it became known in January 1997 that five dissidents from Guiyang had received lengthy sentences. A verdict dated May 27, 1996 listed sentences for Chen Xi, Liao Shuangyuan, Huang Yanming, Lu Yongxiang, and Zeng Ning ranging from two to ten years' imprisonment for "organizing and leading a counterrevolutionary group," participating in such a group, and engaging in counterrevolutionary propaganda and incitement. Seven others, Xu Guoping, Wang Jun, Hu Kangwei, Chen Zongqing, Yi Hua, Tao Yuping, and Wang Quanzheng, have been

detained since 1995 in the same case and are
not known to have been tried. In May 1995,
Chen Xi initiated an "Open Letter to the
Communist Party Central Committee" which
advocated democratic reform, respect for
human rights, and release of political prisoners. Liao signed the petition, while Huang and
Lu distributed it.

HUMAN
RIGHTS
WATCH
WORLD
REPORT
1998

HUMAN RIGHTS WATCH

AFRICA

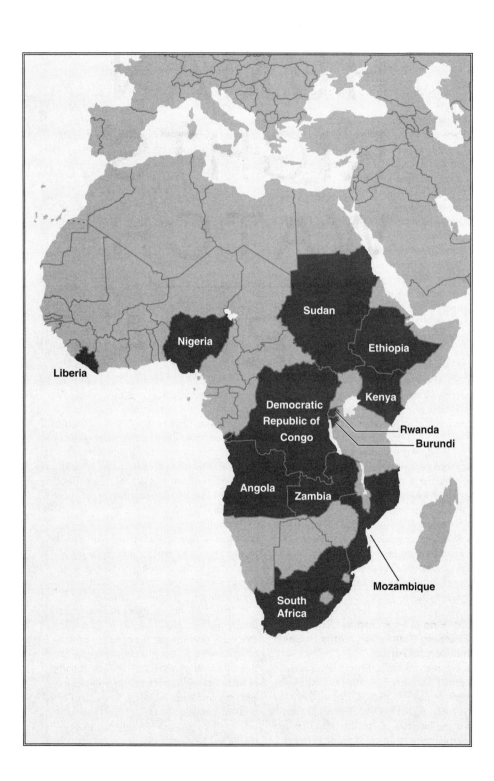

HUMAN RIGHTS WATCH/AFRICA OVERVIEW

Human Rights Developments

African Solutions to African Problems

The year 1997 saw a major political realignment of the African continent, with the sudden collapse of the dictatorship of Mobutu Sese Seko in Zaire before the troops of the Alliance of Democratic Forces for the Liberation of Congo-Zaire (ADFL), led by Laurent Kabila. The installation of Kabila as head of state of the renamed Democratic Republic of Congo (DRC) brought to international attention a political trend underway since the late 1980s. Kabila joined President Museveni of Uganda and the rulers of Rwanda, Ethiopia and Eritrea as the newest representative of a "new generation" of African leaders. Kabila's conquest, with its dependence on assistance from neighboring states, also demonstrated that some African rulers were shedding old rules regarding the inviolability of territorial integrity and "non-interference" in the internal affairs of other states.

While in many cases the new rulers had replaced governments distinguished primarily by the extreme repression they had inflicted on their own populations—in Rwanda a government guilty of genocide—the slogan of "African solutions to African problems" seemed designed also to disguise a rejection of the interdependence of human rights in some domains, and a refusal to permit autonomous monitoring of those rights in others.

Old Wine in New Bottles: The Emerging Political Systems in East and Central Africa

In Uganda, Ethiopia, Eritrea, Rwanda, the parts of southern Sudan controlled by the rebel Sudan Peoples' Liberation Army (SPLA), and in the DRC, leaders claimed that the interests of stability required and justified the restriction of political rights.

In this view, most African states were not ready for multiparty democracy and would become so only after the development of a thriving economy and an established middle class. The political systems the new leaders advocated were characterized by restrictive legal structures that undercut core democratic values of freedom of association and speech. Opposition parties, civil society, and the media were permitted to exist, but only to the extent that they agreed not to challenge the party in power. Despite claims to the contrary, the ideology appeared to be a reinstatement of one-party rule, with the one difference that countries such as Democratic Republic of Congo, Ethiopia, Rwanda and Uganda, not only tolerated but actively encouraged private enterprise.

In Uganda during 1997 Museveni's National Resistance Movement (NRM), in power since 1986, continued to implement its "no-party" political system, and placed increasingly severe restrictions on the activities of political parties. The 1995 constitution had already restricted the functioning of political parties by prohibiting a wide range of political activities. A bill that was under consideration as of this writing, the Political Party Bill of 1997, would further regulate the activities of political parties.

The Ethiopian government did not tolerate party politics, cracked down on critical reporting in the media, and aggressively sought to subdue labor and professional associations and other emerging civil society organizations.

In Eritrea, the governing People's Front for Democracy and Justice (PFDJ) was the sole party operating in the country. Eritrean officials were on record dampening expectations of an early introduction of a multiparty system. Severe restrictions on civil society and core freedoms including freedom of expression persisted in 1997.

In Rwanda, increasingly tight control by the military made clear how far the government had moved from the apparently civilian coalition established after the victory of the Rwandan Patriotic Army (RPA). The RPA clearly dominated the new Rwandan government, prevented public activities by opposition political parties, and discouraged the development of civil society.

In the DRC, once installed in Kinshasa, the new government did not encourage much hope of a departure from the practices of its predecessor. It disbanded peaceful marches and imposed stifling restrictions on the broadcast media.

Kenya, Burundi, Sudan and possibly Tanzania, were the only holdouts against the general pattern of the emerging system in east and central Africa. Yet the government of Daniel arap Moi in Kenya, despite a formal commitment to a multiparty system, displayed almost as much intolerance of political opposition as the "new" leaders in neighboring countries. The Kenyan government met the clamor for greater political freedom with police repression.

The military government of Burundi continued to curb political activity in 1997. Although the National Assembly and political parties were tolerated and recommenced their activities in late 1996, they functioned under severe impediments.

Sudan's National Islamic Front (NIF) used the power and structures of the state to consolidate its hegemony. The government continued its enforcement of severe restrictions on fundamental rights.

Forced Migration and Abuses of Civilians in Armed Conflict

One of the most overt manifestations of the new distribution of power in central Africa, and of the willingness of African leaders to step in to "solve" African problems, was the forced return of Rwandan refugees from Zaire, Tanzania, and Burundi beginning in late 1996. These vast population movements created a humanitarian and security crisis of mammoth proportions on the continent, already host to the largest number of refugees and displaced persons in the world.

During the campaign to overthrow the Mobutu government, the ADFL attacked refugee camps established in eastern Zaire. Some of those driven out of the camps were participants in the 1994 genocide in Rwanda; others were innocent, victims of developments beyond their control. The ADFL forces, often led by Rwandans, hunted down those in flight, killing many thousands of civilians as well as armed elements and preventing humanitarian agencies from delivering the food, water and medicine needed to keep the remainder alive. Mobutu's Zairian Armed Forces (Forces Armées Zairoises, FAZ), Rwandan *interahamwe* militia, and mercenaries also committed gross violations of international humanitarian law. Following the installation of Kabila's government, ADFL forces continued to use excessive force against civilians, in an attempt to put down rebellions in the eastern part of the country.

The events in Zaire had been preceded by less brutal but no less serious violations of international refugee law in other countries hosting Rwandan refugees. In late 1996, the Tanzanian government had given an ultimatum for approximately 600,000 Rwandans to leave by December 31, 1996. The Tanzanian authorities used teargas and batons to push refugees over the border. A similar forced repatriation of approximately 80,000 Rwandan refugees had taken place from Burundi in October and November 1996.

In Rwanda, meanwhile, government soldiers and rebel forces engaged in large-scale massacres of civilians and other abuses. In Burundi, both government forces and various guerrilla movements massacred civilians identified by their ethnicity in efforts to establish control over different regions. The government forced hundreds of thousands of civilians into regroupment camps where they were abused by soldiers and often suffered from lack of food and medicine.

The refugee crisis facing Africa was not limited to the Great Lakes region. Violence in the coastal provinces of Kenya displaced an estimated 100,000. Some four million displaced persons in Sudan, the largest such population in the world, continued to suffer from the government's efforts to hamper or seriously delay assistance from the large U.N. relief operation. Three major rebel forces, the Lord's Resistance Army (LRA), the Allied Democratic Forces (ADF), the West Nile Bank Front (WNBF), and its offshoot the Ugandan National Rescue Front II (UNRF II) that challenged the Uganda People's Defense Forces (UPDF), the government army, were all responsible for serious abuses of human rights. The LRA, in particular, regularly abducted children. An estimated 240,000 civilians were displaced by the fighting between the LRA and government troops. The Uganda government encouraged civilians to leave their homesteads and move into "protected camps" in close proximity to military bases but where conditions were poor. In western Uganda, a similar humanitarian crisis was developing because of the fighting between the Allied Democratic Forces (ADF) and the UPDF.

In the Republic of Congo (Brazzaville), previously a relatively stable contrast to Zaire/Congo-Kinshasa, presidential elections scheduled for July were postponed as the country sank into a full-scale civil war between the forces of President Pascal Lissouba and those fighting on behalf of ex-President Denis Sassou-Nguesso. Sassou-Nguesso's fighters captured the capital, Brazzaville, on October 16, with Angolan government assistance. An estimated 3,000 civilians were killed by the fighting and thousands more fled the capital; approximately 33,000 of them crossing the Congo river to Kinshasa.

In Sierra Leone, a civilian government elected in 1996 was overthrown on May 25, 1997 by soldiers in alliance with the Rebel United Front (RUF), a brutal rebel force that had waged a six-year war against successive governments. Hundreds of civilians were killed in indiscriminate shelling and almost 40,000 refugees fled to neighboring Liberia or Guinea, leaving behind those who would face soaring food prices and starvation. Meanwhile, despite the end of the Liberian civil war, almost 500,000 Liberian refugees re-

mained in neighboring countries. During 1997 there were also increased clashes between Senegalese government army troops and the Movement of the Democratic Forces of Casamance (MFDC), a rebel group advocating independence for the Casamance region of southern Senegal. Hundreds of civilians lost their lives in this conflict.

Once again, the dismal plight of Angola's people, precariously caught between war and peace, blighted the southern African region's hopes for progress. Some 300,000 Angolan refugees remained in neighboring countries, although several thousand returned to Angola independently. An estimated million or more people displaced people inside Angola were also unable or unwilling to return to their homes because of insecurity.

Weapons flows continued to both the Angolan government and the Union for the Total Independence of Angola (UNITA) despite the peace accord. In the Great Lakes region too, as in Sudan, proliferation of weapons encouraged human rights abuses.

Progress and Setbacks in Democratization

Despite the dispiriting news from the countries that captured the headlines during 1997, many African countries continued to make progress, however hesitant, toward the establishment or consolidation of democratic governments. A score of countries were headed by leaders that had been chosen in elections judged by international observers to have been free and fair. Nevertheless it was evident that much improvement was still needed.

In West Africa, flawed—some would say rigged—elections, inadequate electoral preparations, boycotts, and widespread election-related violence were the hallmarks of presidential, parliamentary, and municipal elections in Cameroon, Gabon, and Togo during the year.

In Cameroon, in the run up to both presidential and parliamentary elections, repeated affirmations by President Paul Biya of commitment to "democracy building" were belied by his government's conduct. In the absence of an independent electoral commission to oversee the process, the government harassed opposition party members, intimidated voters, restricted movement in the opposition stronghold of John Fru Ndi's Social Democratic Front, banned opposition campaigning in one district, and engaged in questionable voter-registration and ballot-counting practices which disenfranchised many and provided multiple registration to others. At the same time, the government engaged in a campaign against the independent press, harassing and arresting journalists for criticizing government officials, policies and practices, and shutting down newspapers at will, sometimes seizing editions at newsstands. Cameroon's three main parties boycotted the presidential polls.

In neighboring Gabon, political tension escalated amidst disorganization and mismanagement during the run up to staggered parliamentary polls held in December 1996 and January and February 1997. Allegations of electoral fraud dominated the process. Similarly, in Togo, controversy related to electoral fraud and blatant political manipulation dominated the news headlines relating to elections.

Legislative elections in Burkina Faso, however, were comparatively free of allegations of mismanagement and fraud, even though the ruling CDP—headed by President Blaise Campaore—took over 90 percent of the seats. The government reexamined two bills which had already been approved, concerning the structure of the national electoral commission and the electoral code, due to demands from the political opposition and civil society.

In Mali too, though April elections for the National Assembly were marred by poor organization and widespread confusion at polling stations, several factors helped redeem Mali's tarnished democratic credentials. First, the elections were supervised by an independent electoral commission composed of ten government representatives, ten members of civil society, seven members of the opposition and seven from the ruling party. Second, the results were annulled by a Constitutional Court that found the irregularities to be technical, rather than manipulative, in nature. The government respected the Constitutional Court decision, and fresh elections were held (which were easily won by the ruling party). Additionally, Mali boasted a free press.

The demand for an independent electoral body was a focus of political controversy during the year in Senegal. Finally, President Diouf agreed to the creation of a National Electoral Observatory. While the Observatory would include opposition representatives, it would, however, have a purely supervisory mandate. Elections would continue to be organized by the Ministry of Interior.

For Liberia, 1997 was the year its brutal seven-year war ended, through an election on July 19 that swept former faction leader Charles Taylor and his party into power with 75 percent of the vote. International observers judged the poll to be free and fair. Following his victory, President Taylor stated that he would head a government that respected human rights. Liberian and international observers were encouraged but skeptical of this claim, given Taylor's reputation as a warlord.

Nigeria remained the most significant country not at war to fail to join the trend to democratization of the continent. Gen. Sani Abacha continued to implement a "transition program" supposedly to lead to free and fair elections, but blatant manipulation of the process deprived it of all credibility. The rule of law edged closer to collapse, as the government ignored court orders and arbitrarily detained opposition members, human rights activists and journalists.

Southern Africa: Hope for the Future

Many of the most positive developments on the continent during 1997 came from Southern Africa, as the region benefited from South Africa's continuing transformation to a democratic state and its generally positive engagement with its neighbors. In South

Africa itself, so much had changed that it was easy to forget how recently South Africa had ceased to be under the yoke of apartheid. Despite clouds on the horizon—notably the threat of violent crime and repressive response, but also the failure of the government to deliver on many of its pre-election promises—the progress was impressive. As regards its external policy, however, South Africa seemed to vacillate between real support for human rights principles—as in its leading position within the international movement to ban landmines—and short-sighted "realism" based only on building geopolitical alliances—as in its decision to resume arms supplies to Rwanda, despite good evidence of abuses committed against its own citizens by the Rwandan government.

The change of government in South Africa influenced developments in its closest neighbors, as political landscapes continued to adjust to new regional geopolitical realities. Throughout 1997, Swaziland remained in the throes of a constitutional crisis, as one of the world's last remaining absolute monarchies fiercely resisted domestic and international pressure—including pressure from the South Africa government and labor movement—for a transition towards a constitutional monarchy. Lesotho, too, theoretically a constitutional monarchy with a multiparty system for some years, was gripped by a constitutional crisis for much of 1997. On the whole, the omens were good that neither country could resist the subregional trend to genuine democratization and accountable government much longer.

In Botswana, long one of the most politically and economically stable African countries, a tradition of democratic government strengthened during 1997, as the opposition to the ruling party became more lively and coherent. Following a referendum, the country amended its constitution to lower the voting age, to create an independent electoral commission that would have multiparty representation, and to limit future presidents to two terms of office. In Namibia, by contrast, rumors persisted of plans to amend

the country's constitution to allow President Sam Nujoma to run for the presidency for a third term on the grounds that he was still a "young man."

In Malawi and Mozambique, both countries with terrible legacies to overcome, 1997 saw continuing progress in the consolidation of democracy. Despite three decades of repressive rule by former president Kamuzu Banda, hardly good training for consensus and coalition building, the government of President Bakili Muluzi in Malawi made steady progress, even without a parliamentary majority. And in Mozambique, human rights practices continued to improve, although political and legal institutions remained fragile and the economy one of the poorest in the world.

It was a turbulent year in politics in Zimbabwe. Although President Robert Mugabe and his Zimbabwe African National Union won elections easily, his government faced popular protest at a level not seen before. Impoverished veterans of the liberation war, outraged that apparently healthy cabinet ministers were drawing generous disability pensions, demonstrated in Harare. Other civil society groups maintained vigorous criticism of the government. Zimbabwe's Supreme Court demonstrated its independence by striking down legislation that gave the ruling party sole access to large sums of state money. In response to criticism from human rights groups, the government proposed new legislation to replace the draconian Law and Order (Maintenance) Act. However, the new bill would retain several of the restrictive aspects of the latter. Restrictions on fundamental rights remained in practice in place, and in many respects Zimbabwe remained a one-party state.

The performance of Zambia, once regarded as one of the brightest hopes for democratization in Africa, was the most disappointing in the region. Discredited and facing near bankruptcy, the Chiluba government made superficial improvements regarding its human rights record during 1997, with a view to addressing this obstacle to aid flows being resumed.

Accountability

The events of the year once again demonstrated the importance of ensuring that those responsible for past abuses of human rights be made accountable, if a transition program is to be successful. In this context, the South African Truth and Reconciliation Commission continued to attract international attention as one of the most original and positive efforts in Africa and in the world to ensure accountability during a transition process.

In Liberia, however, international efforts to negotiate peace dispensed with accountability in an effort to find a political solution; the peace accord that ultimately led to the installation of the Taylor government granted a "general amnesty to all persons and parties involved in the Liberian civil conflict in the course of actual engagements."

Where trials of former rulers did take place, often after total victory in war—or even total victory in elections—they were often stalled by lack of court resources or lack of evidence. In Ethiopia, the trial of the seventy-two top-ranking officials of the former military government of the Derg were still pending by the last quarter of 1997. Malawi's Supreme Court in July dismissed an appeal by the government against the acquittal of former dictator Kamuzu Banda on murder charges, finding that the government's appeal was "a hopeless case."

In Rwanda, military and administrative officials responded to the massive return of Rwandans from abroad by arresting many accused of genocide. They made these arrests often without legal authority. Against the negative backdrop of increasing violence by both the government and the insurgents, the beginning of trials for genocide offered one sign of hope, even though the first trials failed to meet international standards in several respects.

Under a new team of administrators and prosecutor, the International Criminal Tribunal on Rwanda (ICTR), began to show signs of recovery from previous professional and administrative maladies.

It seemed self-evident that a year following the endorsement by the Organization of African Unity (OAU) summit of a "plan of action to end impunity in Africa," African leaders should support, facilitate and encourage the investigations of the large-scale slaughter of civilians in Congo. However, representatives of African states, meeting in Kinshasa at the invitation of OAU Chairman and Zimbabwean President Robert Mugabe, expressed their support for Kabila in the face of accusations of mass killings. They denounced with "dismay the persistent unsubstantiated disinformation campaign against the Democratic Republic of Congo" and "condemned this campaign of vilification and the unjustified pressures being exerted on the Democratic Republic of the Congo." Rwanda, Uganda, and Angola were joined in their uncritical support for the new government by South African President Nelson Mandela, who referred to Kabila as "an outstanding figure, a dynamic leader" and appeared ready to accept Kabila's assurances that allegations of massacres were false.

In Zimbabwe, a report compiled by the Catholic Commission on Justice and Peace alleged that 3,000 innocent people had been murdered and many more made victims of gross atrocities when the government suppressed a 1980s rebellion in the Matabeleland region. Mugabe claimed that the reports about such abuses were only meant to cause trouble, and justified the actions of the army as having been committed during a time of war. In Namibia, the ruling South West African Peoples' Organization (SWAPO) still failed to provide a complete account of detainees who went missing during the period before independence.

Regional and subregional organizations

A notable feature of 1997 was the apparent invigoration of regional bodies in Africa including the Southern Africa Development Community (SADC), which discussed a strengthening of its institutions; and the Economic Community of West African States

(ECOWAS), which intervened in Sierra Leone just as its Cease-fire Monitoring Group (ECOMOG) was winding down its operation in Liberia. An inter-African peacemaking-cum-peacekeeping force, the Mission de Suivi des Accords de Bangui (MISAB), with troops drawn from Mali, Senegal, Chad, and Gabon, was tasked to monitor the January 25 Bangui peace agreement in Central African Republic. Commanded by a Malian general and ex-President Amadou Toumani Touré of Mali, MASIB forcibly disarmed ex-mutineers and their civilian allies in support of President Ange-Félix Patassé. MISAB's mandate was extended to cover scheduled 1998 elections. Nevertheless, actions taken by these bodies responded to geopolitical considerations in which human rights considerations appeared largely absent.

SADC, the strongest subregional mechanism in Africa, benefited from the leadership of South Africa. In a September speech at the annual SADC summit, held in Blantyre, Malawi, President Nelson Mandela of South Africa implored his colleagues to think seriously about their commitment to democracy and human rights if the organization was to retain its credibility. Mandela strenuously argued that SADC's basic principles of respect for each member state's sovereignty and of non-interference in each other's national interest could not blunt its common concern for democracy and human rights. Mandela went on: "The right of citizens to participate unhindered in political activities in the country of their birthright is a non-negotiable basic principle to which we all subscribe. We, collectively, cannot remain silent when political or civil movements are harassed and suppressed through harsh state action." He then posed what he termed difficult questions that had nonetheless to be addressed by SADC. These included: "Can we continue to give comfort to member states whose actions go so diametrically against the values and principles we hold so dear and for which we struggled for so long and so hard?"

Yet despite the robust principled fervor in Mandela's speech, the same SADC summit went on to admit the Democratic Republic of Congo to membership despite the international outcry over the large-scale massacres of civilians and Congo's blockage of international efforts to investigate them.

Within ECOWAS, Nigeria overshadowed its smaller and less powerful neighbors; yet the ECOWAS states also showed themselves for perhaps the first time prepared to resist Nigeria's adventurism. When Nigeria asked for retrospective endorsement for its armed intervention in Sierra Leone, ECOWAS states mandated it only to maintain a blockade designed to drive out the coup leaders, and not to engage in further offensive military action. While ECOWAS condemned the military coup in Sierra Leone, with Nigeria the chair of the body, there was no possibility of similar condemnation of the military regime in Nigeria itself, still less of a call for sanctions.

The Right to Monitor

The rapid growth of indigenous human rights organizations continued, although the democratic space that was available for domestic and international groups to monitor respect for human rights in Africa varied widely. A few governments, including South Africa, Botswana, Malawi, Mauritius and Mali, showed a genuine commitment to pluralism and in these countries civil society flourished. In other countries, such as Mozambique, while civil society was still comparatively weak, private monitoring groups expanded their scope significantly. Elsewhere, for example in Kenya or Zambia, sophisticated local monitoring groups resisted government attempts to close down their activities. In certain historically closed societies, such as Mauritania, human rights groups made progress in carving out space for themselves even though serious government restrictions on such activity remained in place. But in several countries including, Burundi, Cameroon, Democratic Republic of Congo, Nigeria and Rwanda, governments refused to permit autonomous monitoring.

National Human Rights Commissions

Almost as striking as the growth in nongovernmental organizations in Africa has been the trend to establish national human rights commissions, government-funded but nominally independent. Countries where national commissions functioned during 1997 included Uganda, Kenya, Ghana, Cameroon, Nigeria, Malawi, Zambia, and South Africa. Emerging from electoral success in July, President Charles Taylor joined this trend by announcing plans for the creation of a commission on human rights, though as of this writing, its terms of reference were still being drafted. In Rwanda, as well, the national assembly was working on legislation to establish a human rights commission.

The challenge that faced these national commissions was whether their actions would help to improve government respect for human rights in practice and bring relief to victims of abuse. Human rights commissions were generally timid and shied away from thorough investigations. Often mandates were tightly limited and jurisdictions narrow. Commissioners were often closely associated with the appointing authorities.

Questions affecting their significance included the following: Would the commissions possess real investigatory power? Could the commissions institute real and serious investigations? Would the commissions go beyond perfunctory investigations and pursue agendas that encompass issues of national importance? Did the commissions have the requisite budget and infrastructure? Did the commissions have the independence required to investigate the government's actions and make public their findings? Ultimately, the real test of the national human rights commissions in Africa would be in their actions.

South Africa's Human Rights Commission, showed the greatest signs of taking an active part in criticizing the government and actively pressing human rights concerns. In October it issued its first subpoena against a government department.

The activities of Ghana's Commission on Human Rights and Administrative Justice also generated wide publicity and demonstrated how such bodies, even when initially apparently created by a government in the belief that they would take no action, can nevertheless develop lives of their own.

But less independent commissions in Zambia, Kenya and Nigeria boded ill for their possibilities of robust defense of human rights in the future.

The Role of the International Community

Human rights crises in Africa loomed large on the international landscape during 1997. Though even in the most difficult situations the means to act, were available, the conviction needed to take firm action to protect human rights was often lacking. Responses to Africa's problems continued to be fire brigade and bandaging operations that at most, only achieved short term and often cosmetic improvements. Many responses caused, or had potential for causing, more harm than good.

Perhaps of most concern was the forgiving attitude to violations committed by the new brand of leadership that championed the mantra "African solutions to African problems." These leaders were for the most part young, dynamic, educated, articulate, and extremely media savvy. The curious blend of idealism and ruthlessness, principle and pragmatism fascinated Western policy makers and the media. The erosion of human rights standards was adroitly explained away by the leadership as being the necessary cost of getting these countries on track after many years of political mismanagement. Further, in select cases, their geostrategic alliances, especially with Washington, rendered them significantly immune to international pressure. The ability of some of these governments to show economic success made them particularly attractive and acceptable to the major Western donors.

The international community was quick to overlook or excuse repressive tendencies by these "soldier princes" on the grounds that, compared to the past, they had brought improvements such as greater political stability, economic prosperity, and democratization. This comparative approach to human rights set a disturbing pattern which allowed for some African states to be held to a different, and lesser, set of human rights standards.

The international role with regard to over a million Rwandans that fled to the DRC in 1994 typified the international failure of leadership. The international community preferred to pay the high cost of upkeep for the camps, U.S.$ 1 million a day at one point, to the costs—financial, military and political—of separating genuine refugees from the military and others who had no right to this status.

When the ADFL attacked the camps, the international community once more addressed simply the humanitarian issues of facilitating repatriation and delivery of aid. Having decided against armed intervention, the international community was reduced to repeatedly deploring the ADFL attacks against refugees and obstruction of humanitarian assistance. In the face of reports of large-scale atrocities, they engaged in public protestations and private diplomacy, all which seemed equally ineffective. Even after the United Nations special rapporteur on Zaire, Roberto Garretón, presented evidence that massacres had occurred in his April 2, 1997 report to the United Nations Commission on Human Rights, the U.N. made no intervention that might have averted subsequent slaughter. All along it seemed that the international community acted as if focus and firmness in demanding justice was an obstacle to stability and prosperity for the region, rather than its precondition.

Moreover, by sitting mute on the sidelines, the international community became an unwilling accessory to a radical erosion of one of the great humanitarian postulates which had come to be a major plank in international relations since World War II: the right to *non-refoulement*, that nobody should be coerced to return to a homeland

where he or she had reason to fear abuse. By remaining silent and by participating in the forced return of Rwandan refugees from what was then Zaire and Tanzania, the international community had shamefully abandoned its responsibility to protect refugees.

United Nations
The turbulent events in the Great Lakes region forced the U.N.'s structures to focus on conflict resolution and management. In September 1997, the U.N. Security Council held a ministerial meeting to consider the need for concerted international efforts to promote peace and security in Africa. The council asked the secretary-general to produce a report by February 1998 containing concrete recommendations regarding the sources of conflict in Africa, ways to prevent and address these conflicts, and how to lay the foundation for durable peace and economic growth.

For his part, U.N. Secretary-General Kofi Annan stated that he believed Africa was entering a "new wave of progress," based on peace, democracy, human rights, and sustainable development—the "pillars of good governance." He noted a "new consensus that the primary responsibility for the solution of Africa's problems rests with Africans themselves."

The U.N. High Commissioner for Refugees (UNHCR) appeared unable, and in some cases unwilling, to fully address the complexities of the refugee crises that unfolded in the Great Lakes region. The waning support by African governments and the international community for protection of refugee rights, the unchecked militarization within and attacks on refugee camps, threats to UNHCR staff, and increased weapons flows further obstructed the ability of UNHCR to provide safety and assistance to refugees.

UNHCR initially remained silent in the face of the forced repatriation of Rwandan refugees in late 1996, but became more vocal toward the end of 1997 as criticism mounted against the agency for its retreat from protection. Only after the bulk of Rwandan refugees remaining in Zaire/Congo had been slaughtered or subjected to extreme hardship did UNHCR begin to protest more strongly. For instance, in September, UNHCR strongly protested the forced repatriation of some 800 Rwandan and Burundian refugees (some 550 of whom were women and children) from Kisangani in the DRC who to Rwandan by the Kabila government.

The silence of UNHCR this year was made worse by the realization that the Rwandan refugee crisis might have been mitigated had greater efforts been taken by UNHCR, with the assistance of the international community, to exclude human rights violators and military elements from the refugee population at the outset. Following the clearing of the camps in the DRC, UNHCR initiated this kind of exclusion in the Central African Republic, Gabon and Malawi. For the Rwandan refugees, it was a case of too little, too late, but these were nonetheless commendable initiatives that should be strengthened for the future.

U.N. assistance and protection for the internally displaced remained disjointed and unfocused. Due to the lack of a U.N. agency with an exclusive mandate to the deal with the internally displaced, U.N. programs continued to be run on an ad hoc basis with varying degrees of success. Recognizing this limitation, the U.N. administrative reforms unveiled by the secretary-general in July, specifically stated that the U.N. needed to improve its programs for the internally displaced. The United Nations Development Program (UNDP) played a larger role in reintegration programs for the internally displaced, although its programs continued to dodge the protection and human rights needs of the displaced. Although efforts to address this fundamental omission were underway at UNDP, they remained at the initial stages of policy formulation.

In Rwanda, the U.N. human rights field office restricted its representatives to the capital and other secure regions after five of its employees were killed in an ambush. Only in mid-year did it resume vigorous reporting on military massacres of civilians and the killing of detainees by the authorities. By skillful negotiation, Rwanda succeeded in replacing a U.N. special rapporteur with a far less powerful special envoy. Moreover, immediately after the U.N. human rights field office published reports on military massacres of civilians and other abuses, the Rwandan government intensified its campaign to end the operation of the field office. Burundi excluded altogether the special rapporteur named to monitor its compliance with human rights standards.

Despite a major lobbying effort by the Nigerian government, however, the 1997 session of the U.N. Commission on Human Rights resolved to appoint a special rapporteur on Nigeria. In a notable departure from the African solidarity that characterized much voting at the U.N., South Africa and Uganda voted for the resolution, while the other African countries on the commission abstained.

The U.N. was weak on rights issues in Angola. Although it maintained a Human Rights Unit there, with monitors deployed in most provinces, it achieved little, except holding a series of high profile workshops on rights and submitting reports for U.N. Special Representative Maitre Alioune Blondin Beye's submissions to the Security Council. Beye's insistence that robustly exposing rights abuses would undermine the peace process contributed to making the U.N.'s human rights efforts impotent.

The Commonwealth

The Commonwealth undertook some initiatives in the human rights field, with most activity related to human rights focused on Africa. A Commonwealth Ministerial Action Group (CMAG), held a number of meetings during the year to review developments in the Gambia, Nigeria, and Sierra Leone, the countries most blatantly in violation of the Harare Commonwealth Declaration of 1991, which commits member states to respect human rights and democracy. At the end of October, the Commonwealth Heads of Government Meeting (CHOGM) decided to maintain Nigeria's suspension from the organization. Nigeria was warned that it faced expulsion if it failed to bring in a democratic system by October 1998. Additionally, the same meeting decided that pending the restoration of the elected government, the Armed Forces Revolutionary Council regime in Sierra Leone would remain suspended from the Commonwealth.

Aid and Human Rights: The European Union and World Bank

The approach of the European Commission and the World Bank, both major donors to Africa, was narrow and focused on economic considerations at the expense of human rights. Under Article 5 of the Lomé Convention, governing access by African Caribbean and Pacific (ACP) countries to European Union (E.U.) markets, respect for human rights and democratic principles was an "essential element" for those states to receive development aid from the European Union through the European Commission.

Under the leadership of James Wolfensohn, the World Bank sought during 1997 to improve its record in fighting African poverty and to assure its status as the flagship of the international development agencies. But questions still abounded whether the World Bank was not wittingly or unwittingly propping up undemocratic regimes in Africa. Mr Wolfensohn claimed that under his leadership the Bank had begun to reach out to human rights groups. The Bank's 1997 World Development Report, laid special emphasis on the need for upgrading the effectiveness of the state as a prerequisite for economic development and improved social welfare. But apart from highlighting the need for investment-friendly legal systems, the Bank in its report appeared to have deliberately factored democracy and human rights out of its formula for resolving Africa's crisis of governance.

The narrow, economics-based approach was demonstrated in the decision of the European Commission and World Bank to concentrate most of their economic assistance efforts on three countries in Africa:

Mozambique, Ethiopia, and the Ivory Coast. All three countries were certainly in need of such assistance, but an equivalent focus was not placed on support for initiatives to improve respect for human rights either in those countries or elsewhere. Moreover, at the July 11-12 Consultative group meeting on Zambia, the Bank had strenuously but ultimately unsuccessfully sought, in the face of objections of bilateral donors, to downplay the issue of good governance.

France

In what promised to be a significant shift, France's new socialist government announced plans to revise its policy toward Africa, apparently based on a less interventionist approach to the politics of France's former colonies in Africa. The ongoing reconsideration of French policy could lead Paris eventually to revise its defense and military assistance agreements with a number of these former African colonies. Nevertheless, enduring neo-colonial pacts between France and her ex-colonies continued in 1997 to imply strong political, economic and potentially military support, despite their records of human rights abuses. Yet French policy toward Africa was increasingly determined by economic interests, including the interests of large French oil companies such as Elf-Aquitaine.

These changes implied a desire to distance France from the record of backing human rights abusers like the late Mobutu of Zaire, and Habyarimana of Rwanda. Apart from the considerations of cost, the retreat was due to a generational change, with the younger French leaders intent on "normalizing" relations with Africa. Africa meant less and less to the French electorate, even if the politicians had wished to preserve the neo-colonial relationships. The new government seemed inclined to go further and faster to reduce the permanent French military presence in the region, a force of 80,000, from seven to five bases: in Senegal, Gabon, Chad, Ivory Coast, and Djibouti. Bases in Cameroon and the Central African Republic would close. The French government also downgraded its "cooperation" department (to the level of a junior ministry), as well as the post of minister for "francophonie"—or French cultural promotion.

During the 1990s, Angola, Kenya, Nigeria, South Africa, and Uganda, none of which were francophone countries, emerged as major destinations of French exports. The civil war in Congo-Brazzaville suggested a new, more oblique, but no less self-interested involvement especially in potentially lucrative markets. In his fight to wrest power from ex-President Lissouba, Sassou Nguesso was reportedly supported by France in a bid to defend the interests of French oil giant Elf-Aquitaine in Congo-Brazzaville. The overall impact of France's policy review could be significant on the poorer and less lucrative francophone countries, as aid and investment flows declined. A withdrawal of aid and other commitments might spell increasing instability in French "clients" in the short-term. In the absence of automatic political, diplomatic and military protection, former clients would at the same time become less immune to domestic and international pressure to democratize and respect the rule of law and human rights.

United States

In financial year 1997, U.S. aid to Africa was somewhat reduced from the previous year, at just under U.S. $700 million. The focus of U.S. assistance began to change, with the bulk of U.S. assistance being channeled to countries deemed to be democratizing and achieving a better economic performance.

Two major U.S. initiatives for Africa were under development during 1997. Just before the June G7 Denver summit, the U.S. announced plans to promote a series of trade measures with Africa intended to encourage free-market reforms of the continent's most promising economies. The new trade initiative, which was prompted by a draft legislation, African Growth and Opportunity Act, would support sustainable economic development by increasing trade between the U.S. and Africa, rewarding economic reform and promoting good governance. While the draft

legislation included specific human rights language about which countries would be eligible for the program, the administration had not set forth any specific human rights criteria, focusing instead on issues of governance.

Meanwhile, between July and September, U.S. Special Forces trained a battalion of troops in each of Uganda, Malawi, and Senegal to form part of the African Crisis Response Initiative (ACRI), an all-African military peacekeeping force suggested by the U.S.

The primary purpose of the ACRI was said to be to have African units ready for quick deployment to crisis zones, compatibly equipped and capable of working together. It was hoped such a force would stabilize conflict zones so humanitarian aid could be provided to civilians. Such deployments might require the use of force. Among the issues that remained to be resolved were: how the force would be equipped, what the command and control structure would be, how decisions on deployment should be made, and how the force would be linked to regional organizations such as the OAU and SADC. In October 1997, Department of State Special Coordinator for the ACRI Marshall MacCallie stated that ACRI training included "basic soldier skills, peacekeeping procedures, logistics management, human rights observance, and techniques of working with refugees, humanitarian organizations, and civilian authorities."

In what appeared to be a competing initiative, in mid-October, French Foreign Minister Hubert Verdine visited Addis Ababa, Ethiopia, home of the OAU, where he held meetings with OAU Secretary-General Salim Ahmed Salim, and pledged U.S. $30 million in 1998 to help train and equip an African peacekeeping force.

In its bilateral relations with individual African states, the U.S. government adopted a selective approach, critical of the human rights practices of some states while remaining silent on major restrictions on core freedoms in others. For example, during 1997 the U.S. adopted a notably firm and public stand on human rights in Kenya. Ambassador Arlene Render took a strong stand on the Chiluba government in Zambia, calling for change and the implementation of democratic values.

In Nigeria, outgoing U.S. ambassador Walter Carrington was perhaps the most outspoken of the diplomatic representatives resident in Lagos. This earned him both a farewell party given by human rights organizations, and the attention of the security forces in breaking up that party. The U.S. administration indicated that it was undertaking a review of Nigeria policy, but failed to adopt a strong line—even when British elections produced a government much more prepared to cooperate in international efforts to isolate the military government.

The United States adopted a different approach in its dealings with such countries as Uganda and Ethiopia. It turned a blind eye on restrictions on political rights while building special relationships with Uganda and Ethiopia with reference to the geostrategic issues of the Great Lakes area and the Horn. The U.S. continued to be supportive and upbeat about Museveni's economic reforms and rewarded Uganda generously for its cooperation with the IMF and the World Bank.

Throughout most of the year, the U.S. continued firm support for the government of Rwanda, despite the evident abuses by its military both at home and in the DRC. Embarrassed by publicity about U.S. military assistance to Rwanda, initially described as soft and humane and later revealed to include combat training, the U.S. in fact bore far greater responsibility for continuing political support for Kigali—support which helped shield its government from criticism. However, after initial weakness in the face of Kabila's objections to U.N. investigatory commission, the U.S. eventually said that it was insisting that it be permitted to carry out its mission in the DRC.

The Work of Human Rights Watch

Throughout 1997, Human Rights Watch pressed African governments and the international community to meet their responsibilities regarding the promotion and protection of human rights in Africa. Against a background of a mixture of grim news and hopeful developments, the work of Human Rights Watch incorporated a key strategic consideration: a balance between tragedy and crisis on the one hand, and recognition and encouragement of positive developments and stemming the negative on the other. While our brief continued to cover all of Africa south of the Sahara , we made a core group of countries priorities for more intensive research and advocacy: Angola, Burundi, DRC, Eritrea, Ethiopia, Liberia, Mozambique, Nigeria, Rwanda, South Africa, Sudan, Zaire, Zambia, and Zimbabwe. We monitored major human rights abuses, including the treatment of refugee and internally displaced populations from Burundi, DRC, Kenya, Liberia, and Rwanda ; the impact of landmines in southern Africa ; abuses perpetrated by foreign soldiers in internal conflicts in the DRC; the progress of transitions to democracy in the DRC, Liberia and Nigeria; as well as ongoing human rights violations in a wide range of countries.

Human Rights Watch fielded investigative missions to Burundi, the DRC, Ethiopia, Liberia, Nigeria, South Africa, Sudan, and Zambia and maintained an office in Rwanda for part of the year to closely monitor the crisis in the Great Lakes region. Human Rights Watch also collaborated with the Human Rights Watch Arms, Children's Rights and Women's Rights Projects in their missions to Ethiopia Eritria,, Kenya, Uganda, and southern Africa. In conjunction with the Arms Project, Human Rights Watch produced a comprehensive report on the impact of landmines in southern Africa as part of a largely successful campaign to ban antipersonnel landmines around the world. In August collaborative work with the Women's Rights Project brought about a follow-up report on domestic violence in South Africa.

Joint work with the Children's Rights Project led to two investigative missions to Kenya and Uganda that generated two major reports and related advocacy activities on street children in Kenya and the abduction of children in northern Uganda.

Concerned that the international community was retreating from protection of refugees and internally displaced persons, Human Rights Watch devoted substantial resources to the monitoring of the situations of refugees and internally displaced persons, particularly in Burundi, the DRC, Kenya, Liberia, and Rwanda. We published a report that chronicled the violence perpetrated against civilians in eastern Zaire, a significant percentage of whom were refugees from Rwanda. In June, we published a seminal report on the failure of the United Nations Development Programme (UNDP) to adequately protect internally displaced persons, using UNDP's program in Kenya as a case study, and offered recommendations for improvement. While the United Nations struggled to get its own investigation in the DRC underway, we uncovered evidence confirming reports of large-scale massacres. In a major report released in October, we documented civilian killings perpetrated by all sides during Zaire's civil war through testimonies and photographs, offering our evidence to the United Nations Investigative Team. Thousands of those slaughtered were Rwandan refugees previously resident in camps in eastern DRC. A report was also completed on the situation of Liberian refugees.

In regular briefings, reports and other documentation provided to African states and donors, both bilateral and multilateral, we strongly advocated the denial of economic assistance to abusive governments as a tool for promoting reform. In a report released in July, we strongly urged the World Bank Consultative Group Meeting on Zambia to keep international aid to Zambia conditioned on respect for human rights. We increased attention to the European Union (E.U.), Commonwealth and the African Commission on Human and Peoples'

Rights (ACHPR) and local NGOs in sub-Saharan Africa. Through reports, letters and meetings we sought to influence the policies of the E.U. (including its member states) and the Commonwealth Heads of Government Meeting (CHOGM), especially on Nigeria. At the October CHOGM biennial summit we released a major updating report on the deeply flawed transition program in Nigeria. We established a greater presence at the ACHPR through regular attendance at its meetings and written submissions to the commissioners that detailed our concerns on key human rights issues in Africa. Human Rights Watch remained involved in several networking efforts by human rights NGOs including the network associated with the ACHPR. We made the building of a more interactive and continuous relationship with African human rights activists a priority in our research and advocacy programs.

Human Rights Watch sought to encourage the international community, as well as national judiciaries, to hold human rights abusers accountable. In Rwanda, staff of a project of Human Rights Watch and the International Federation of Human Rights Leagues (FIDH) assisted in organizing and training a team of Rwandan observers to monitor national trials of persons accused of genocide. The observers began publishing reports on the conduct of the trials. A group of human rights organizations prepared an amicus curaie brief for the International Criminal Tribunal for Rwanda (ICTR) to urge that charges of rape be included in some of the indictments of persons accused of genocide. The brief, based largely on research by Human Rights Watch and FIDH , resulted in the amendment of the indictment in the first case tried by the ICTR. A Human Rights Watch researcher served as expert witness in trials at the ICTR and also gave testimony twice before a Belgian Senate Commission investigating the role of Belgium in the Rwandan genocide.

Recognizing the pivotal role of South Africa's Truth and Reconciliation Commission (TRC) in the quest for the institutionalization of accountability in the region, Human Rights Watch also deepened its monitoring of the TRC . We expanded the pre-existing constructive dialogue with the TRC and remained a key source of comparative expertise and information relevant to matters in which the TRC was actively engaged.

For a listing of relevant reports and missions, see page 459 at the end of this report. Partial listings also follow each country chapter.

ANGOLA

Human Rights Developments

Angola remained in an open-ended transition from a single-party state in a state of war to multiparty democracy. The government, dominated by the Movement for the Popular Liberation of Angola (MPLA), and the armed opposition Union for the Total Independence of Angola (UNITA) restricted freedom of movement, arbitrarily abducted or detained civilians and intimidated journalists. Both sides violated cease-fire agreements: indiscriminate attacks on civilians were a persistent feature of military operations.

Serious violations of the cease-fire by both UNITA and the government increased in 1997. In the early part of the year, the majority of reported cease-fire violations were attacks by soldiers on civilians designed either to control the movement of food aid in contested areas or to stop people from moving into areas controlled by the other side. Other cease-fire violations were committed by the government's military moving up to frontlines. In March flash points were the northern provinces of Lunda Norte, Lunda Sul, Uíge and Zaïre. There were also some clashes in Huíla and Benguela provinces. The Angolan Armed Forces (FAA) had been increasing troop concentrations on the periphery of the UNITA heartland since February and in May increased incursions into disputed territory in Huila and in the Lundas. By September the mili-tary situation was characterized by persistent tensions affecting almost the entire country, but particularly the provinces of Lunda Norte, Lunda Sul and Malange. The main fighting was in June. In a fortnight's fighting, the army captured an estimated 10 to 15 percent of UNITA's diamond-producing areas in an operation that expanded government control over a corridor from Dundo to Luena. Most of the fighting was confined to the Lunda provinces but attacks were also made on UNITA positions in Bié, and later in Soyo (Zaïre province) and Huíla. The fighting diminished in mid-June but did not cease until the end of the month. From July the Angolan presidency called for a suspension of military activity inside Angola, meanwhile lobbying hard internationally for U.N. sanctions against UNITA and providing military equipment and 1,000 troops in support of military leader Denis Sassou-Nguesso's successful efforts in overthrowing democratically elected President Pascal Lissouba in Congo (Brazzaville) in October. Lissouba had aligned himself with UNITA.

Between June and September there were many new reports of troop mobilization, the movement of military equipment, and forced conscription. The U.N. verified several attacks by UNITA on government positions, including in Lunda Norte province as well as attacks by government forces on villages in Huíla province. The most serious attacks were by UNITA in Lunda Norte at Posto de Fronteira Nordeste on July 2, where UNITA forces razed to the ground a village of approximately 150 inhabitants. At Posto Fronteira Muaquesse on July 24, UNITA forces attacked a northern village burning houses and killing several civilians. UNITA also reenlisted demobilized UNITA troops for deployment at strategic locations controlled by UNITA, such as Dambi near Uíge and Vinte Cinco near Huambo.

The quartering and reintegration process was slow and interrupted by the renewed fighting. Although the operation only started in earnest in February 1996, by the time the ceremony was held to swear in the new joint army on July 10, UNITA had quartered 70,660 troops in its fifteen camps for demobilized fighters. Of these, 22,686 reportedly deserted after having been registered at the camps. UNITA provided the army with 10,899 of the troops quartered, including senior officers, far short of the 26,300 UNITA personnel expected to be incorporated into the national armed forces. By August a total of 21,175 UNITA soldiers had been officially demobilized and had left the quartering areas. Under the Lusaka Protocols UNITA was also obliged to quarter 62,500 soldiers for demobilization. A high proportion of those quartered were also found not to have been regular UNITA troops however, and U.N. figures show that 7,600 were under the age of eighteen.

In July, after repeated delays, UNITA provided the U.N. with details of the security guard maintained by UNITA chief Jonas Savimbi and UNITA's so-called "mining police," citing the total strength of these forces as 2,963. In September, following U.N. pressure, UNITA submitted a new figure which acknowledged troops of 6,052. However, the minister of defense asserted that UNITA had still some 35,000 armed personnel under its control.

The government had confined to barracks 5,450 rapid reaction police in thirteen locations. However, between June and August the government deployed 424 rapid reaction police in Lunda Sul and Lunda Norte provinces without informing the U.N. and declared its intention to terminate its agreement to confine the rapid reaction police to barracks nationwide. U.N. and observer pressure on the government stopped the government from redeploying its rapid reaction police, but paramilitary training of other police units—such as how to use machine—guns was observed by the U.N. indicating that the government might be attempting to prepare civilian police for tasks not compatible with their normal job description.

The new Government of Unity and National Reconciliation (GURN) was inaugurated on April 11 and included the MPLA, UNITA and the Democratic Party of Angola (PDA). The leader of UNITA, Jonas Savimbi was not present at the ceremony, although confidence-building by U.N. negotiators had made the incorporation of senior UNITA figures into the Luanda-based government possible. The government was to have taken office in January, but this deadline was not met. Critical issues were the quality and quantity of housing for UNITA officials and the size of their personal security force. A second deadline was set for the end of February; this deadline failed with the status of Jonas Savimbi as the central issue. The MPLA had offered Savimbi the post of one of two vice-presidents in February 1996, but Savimbi had turned this down. This issue remained a key negotiating point, with UNITA looking for the post to have direct military authority. The U.N. in December 1996 sought to separate the issue of Savimbi's status from the formation of a government of national unity.

The U.N. Security Council gained additional time to pressure UNITA when the deadline shifted to March. The U.N. team was anxious to make the GURN effective prior to its scheduled departure in August. UNITA joined the GURN in April, in the face of continuing pressure and the changing situation in Zaire.

The handover of territory under UNITA control to the government of Angola was also slow. In May UNITA cited "technical reasons" for a delayed handover of fifteen municipalities in Benguela province. Following U.N. and troika (Russia, Portugal and U.S.) pressure on UNITA, the U.N. announced that the expansion of state administration in the area would recommence on May 26. After pressure from the U.N. following the killing of a Brazilian peacekeeper near the town of Vila Nova by suspected UNITA supporters, UNITA handed over Vila Nova to a high-level government delegation on May 28. A few days later in the Quibala district of Cuanza Sul, UNITA supporters protesting at the handing over of the territory assaulted and injured Isaias Samakuva, head of the UNITA delegation to the Joint Commission and N'zau Puna, a

UNITA defector who is now a vice-minister of the interior. By late October 108 localities out of 337 had been handed over by UNITA to government control.

The civil war in neighboring Zaire was a significant factor in the power struggle in Angola. UNITA had been supporting President Mobutu Sese Seko, who in turn provided supply lines for arms and a marketing route for diamonds. In February and March the Angolan government sent two battalions of Katangese Angolans (originally from Shaba province in Zaire) to help Laurent Kabila, the leader of the rebel forces in (then) Zaire. In June Kinshasa fell to the rebel forces and Zaire became the Democratic Republic of Congo (DRC). The immediate impact on Angola was that UNITA lost its supply lines through Congo and the ability to hide troops over the border became severely limited.

Up to 15,000 Hutu refugees also entered northern Angola from DRC in April and May. Many of these refugees entered UNITA zones and access to them by humanitarian agencies was obstructed. There were reports that UNITA used some of these refugees as porters and also conscripted young men into its military. In June the Angolan army claimed its troops had arrested twenty-four armed Rwandans.

UNITA continued to resist compliance with the agreement to hand over all of its weapons, in particular its heavy weapons and sophisticated ground-to-air missiles. The U.N. claimed that 30 to 40 percent of those weapons handed to it were in poor condition or unserviceable and that the ammunition was in poor condition and averaged just eleven rounds per rifle. By late-1997 UNITA had provided to the U.N. some 33,867 personal arms and 5,120 crew-served weapons systems but there were many reports of ongoing caching of weapons across the country and the opening of caches for the distribution of arms when hostilities broke out.

Weapon flows continued to the government despite the peace accord. Although arms shipments significantly declined in 1996 and in the first half of 1997, they increased in the second part of the year. In late 1996 the government sent fighter aircraft to Israel for reconditioning and in early 1997 the government purchased new helicopter-gunships from Russia. New shipments of weapons in August and September were delivered in Luanda port, unloaded from Polish and Danish registered ships. The government also put in an order with Russia for some twenty Su-24s fighter-bomber aircraft and there were reports of a U.S. $230 million arms deal with France. A U.S. firm also attempted to sell six reconditioned C-130 Hercules aircraft for around $72 million. From an official budget of $2.6 billion, the government claimed it would spend over $302 million on arms. The true figure for planned expenditure was unknown. The hiding of significant arms payments from the budget, including paying off older loans, defied the transparency required by the International Monetary Fund to secure an agreement leading to much needed debt rescheduling under the Paris Club.

UNITA continued for much of 1997 its U.N. sanction-busting operations, bringing in new weapons and supplies over land and on secret flights from Congo-Kinshasa and Congo-Brazzaville to airstrips in the diamond-rich Lunda provinces. UNITA appeared to have obtained much of its weaponry from private sources, rather than foreign governments, although there was some evidence that DRC provided arms in early 1997 prior to the fall of the Mobutu government. UNITA also exported weapons and provided support for Mobutu until May, when it focused all its efforts on using DRC to bring in supplies before the fall of Kinshasa to Kabila's forces. From August UNITA's supplies came mainly on private aircraft from Pointe Noire and Maya Maya international airport in Congo-Brazzaville although some flights originated from South Africa, Zambia and possibly Mozambique. Three senior officials at Zambia's Ndola Airport were suspended in September following investigations that found they permitted unauthorized landings for the aviation division of Metex international, a South African company. It appears that Metex conducted commercial activities, including the airlifting of fuel from Ndola airport to UNITA in Angola, in violation of a 1993 U.N. embargo on UNITA. Pilots told Human Rights Watch that runways and airstrips in UNITA areas were recently lengthened and improved, such as at Andulo (Bié) and Luzamba (Lunda Norte). Bulgarian weapons featured prominently in these transfers. The U.N. reported that between July 1 and 30 it had recorded over 120 flights landing at UNITA-controlled airstrips scattered throughout the central and eastern parts of the country. The U.N. was not permitted to inspect what was being delivered.

Both parties, but particularly UNITA, imposed restrictions on U.N. verification activities. The government also failed at times to provide information on movements of troops and military equipment and on occasions U.N. military observers were stopped from conducting inspections. Armed UNITA personnel detained a U.N. investigation team and their helicopter for over twenty-four hours at Calibuitchi on July 11 and 12 and a U.N. team's attempt to verify allegations that UNITA was storing weapons in eight containers at Chingongo on July 12 was also stopped. A World Food Program helicopter was also arbitrarily seized by armed UNITA soldiers in June in Moxico province.

Some 40,000 people remained trapped against their will by UNITA in its former headquarters, Jamba, in the south, where conditions were very bad. Although UNITA claimed it had invited the international community to evacuate them, in effect UNITA refused to allow civilians to move out of UNITA zones. There was increasing evidence during the year that UNITA was also using Jamba for military training and that illegal flights carrying weapons and other supplies were landing there. The Namibian authorities exacerbated the situation by keeping its border near Jamba closed, fearful that an open border would permit a mass exodus of Jamba residents onto Namibian soil.

Planting of new mines in UNITA-controlled areas was also reported. One such incident was along the Saurimo-Cacolo road on July 4, resulting in three people killed and the injury of many others when a civilian vehicle struck an anti-tank mine. Demining experts that visited the scene concluded the mine was newly placed. Other incidents were confirmed by the U.N. in Malange, Lunda Norte and Lunda Sul. The government was also responsible for laying new mines in Cabinda.

The availability of weapons contributed to a significant rise in armed crime and banditry. Banditry in Benguela and Lunda Sul provinces was particularly bad. The government was expected under the Lusaka Protocols to disarm the civilians it armed in 1992, when up to a million AK-47s were issued in Luanda alone. The numbers handed over to police by mid-year were disappointing: 102 crew-served weapons, 2,642 firearms of various types and 21,100 rounds of ammunition. In August the government announced its suspension of disarmament of the civilian population pending the completion of the normalization of state administration. It insisted that the civilian population in both government and UNITA-controlled areas be disarmed simultaneously.

The circulation of people and goods continued to be restricted by the maintenance of illegal checkpoints and the escalation of acts of banditry in various areas of the country. By September, with deteriorating confidence in the peace process, old checkpoints had been reactivated and new ones were set up in both government and UNITA areas.

As a result of delays in implementing the peace process, some 300,000 refugees in neighboring countries were not repatriated, although several thousand returned to Angola independently. An estimated million or more displaced people inside Angola were also unable or unwilling to return to their homes because of insecurity.

In Luanda politically and economically motivated violence by state security forces and common criminal violence were often indistinguishable. A large number of violent crimes, including robbery, vehicle hijackings, assault, kidnaping, rape and murder were committed by members of the military and police both in and out of uniform. The government's Rapid Intervention Police "Ninjas" were also reported in 1997 to have summarily executed people caught in the act of committing crimes. There have also been gun battles between police and military or with bandit groups in the suburbs resulting in significant numbers of civilian casualties.

There are also a growing number of small armed separatist groups operating in northern Angola. Front for the Liberation of the Cabinda Enclave (FLEC) separatist groups have for several decades operated in the oil-rich Cabinda enclave. The government restarted negotiations in 1995 with the armed factions but in 1997 these negotiations broke down and there was an increase of military activity including incidents of new landmine warfare and indiscriminate shelling of villages. Dom Paulino Madeca, the Catholic bishop of Cabinda, in March accused government troops of massacring civilians in the Mayombe forest. Kidnaping for ransom also occurred in Cabinda. In February a Malaysian national died after being kidnaped by the FLEC-Armed Forces of Cabinda (FAC) faction.

The state press remained tightly controlled and the few independent media outlets chose carefully what they published. Several journalists were killed in suspicious circumstances. António Casimiro, Cabinda correspondent of *Televisâo Popular de Angola* was murdered at his home on October 30, 1996. Dom Paulino Madeca, the bishop of Cabinda, said the killers were police officers led by a civilian; the authorities blamed Cabindan separatists. Two inquiries were opened into the killing, but their findings have not been published. During the swearing in of the GURN in April, President José Eduardo dos Santos called for "greater transparency and freedom" in the media. In practice this has not happened. The government continued to refuse to allow the U.N. to open a short-wave radio station, despite many Security Council resolutions requesting it to do so. The governor of Huíla province, Kundy Paihama also prevented the sale of the private newspapers *Agora, Folha 8,* and *Comercio Actualidade* because they published stories critical of the government. The independent local radio station in Lubango, Rádio 2000, was also prevented by the authorities in April from retransmitting Voice of America programs.

The transformation of UNITA's radio VORGAN into a nonpartisan private station (called Rádio Despertar) made little progress despite being a requirement of the Lusaka Protocols and a notification in writing by UNITA to the government in September that would fulfill its obligations. Despite repeated promises by UNITA officials, the radio station continued to broadcast propaganda hostile to the government and inflammatory public announcements against the peace accords. Some of the broadcasts targeted U.N. and other international staff working in Angola for their alleged partisanship in favor of the government.

In 1993 the Council of Ministers decided to transfer control of the judicial system and prisons system from the Interior Ministry to the Justice Ministry. However, this transfer has not yet happened. The court system is comprised of a Supreme Court with municipal courts under it. The president appoints Supreme Court judges for set terms, with no requirement that they be confirmed by the National Assembly. By July 1997 twelve of the sixteen seats of the Supreme Court remained vacant.

The constitution also guarantees freedom of association and assembly, but in practice the government controls both tightly. Union leader Miguel Filho of SINPROF, the teacher's union, was in early 1997 held at gunpoint by armed men and robbed of all papers and possessions in what union officials claimed was an official move to suppress a series of strikes and demonstrations he was organizing.

The Right to Monitor

Local human rights monitoring was not encouraged by the government. Some churches engaged in civic education and conflict resolution work were involved in discreet human rights education, despite government hostility, equating human rights activity as involvement in "politics." A number of church groups appealed to the government and to UNITA to speed up the implementation of the Lusaka accords and called on church leaders to be nonpartisan.

The Angolan nongovernmental organization (NGO) Action for Rural Development and the Environment (ADRA) linked up with the Association of European Parliamentarians for Action on [Southern] Africa (AWEPA) to organize workshops on civic education and increase knowledge of the provisions of the Lusaka Protocols. With the support of Amnesty International, the Angolan Human Rights Association, also distributed information about human rights. Development Workshop, an independent Angolan NGO, also worked with fisherman and market women in Luanda to improve their knowledge of basic political rights. On November 28, 1996 the Angolan Campaign to Ban Landmines (CABM) was launched. It was increasingly active in campaigning against landmines and collected 60,000 signatures in a petition calling for a total ban. The CABM also organized exhibitions in Kuito, Malange and Lubango and was active in lobbying National Assembly members. The Angolan government supported the Ottawa process for a total ban of antipersonnel landmines.

The Role of the International Community

United Nations

In a climate of international frustration over peacekeeping, there was strong pressure, particularly from the U.S., not to allow the operation of the 7,000 strong United Nations Angola Verification Mission (UNAVEM III) to drag on indefinitely. Largely for this reason, UNAVEM III's mandate was renewed for only short periods in 1997.

It had been originally planned that UNAVEM III would complete its mission in February 1997. However, due to slippage in the Lusaka Protocols' timetable, the plan changed to a phased withdrawal. Four of the six infantry battalions, together with additional support units and some military headquarters personnel were repatriated by June. The remainder were to have left by August but this was postponed because of the deteriorating security situation. The end of June saw the expiry of the mandate of UNAVEM III. It was replaced by the United Nations Observer Mission to Angola (MONUA). MONUA was comprised of 1,500 "rapid reaction troops" deployed in six companies to assist 345 Civilian Police (CIVPOL) and just eighty-five military observers. The Security Council ruled in October that the drawdown of MONUA's military units was to be completed by the end of November and that MONUA's mandate was extended to January 30, 1998.

In August the Security Council threatened a further package of sanctions against UNITA unless it fulfilled outstanding obligations under the Lusaka Protocols by the end of September. The sanctions included freezing UNITA bank accounts, blocking foreign travel of its officials and closing of its offices abroad. But on September 29, the Security Council agreed unanimously to postpone for a month implementation of the sanctions until October 30. Because UNITA failed to make further progress on its Lusaka Protocols obligations during October, the Security Council adopted unanimously Resolution 1135 on October 29, which imposed the new sanctions package on UNITA from 00.01 EST on October 30.

The Human Rights Unit of UNAVEM held a small number of regional seminars on human rights education in government and UNITA-controlled zones. It did not, however, conduct much investigative work into ongoing human rights abuses, and published just one report in mid-December. The unit failed to win the confidence of local groups. Six cases of human rights violations were submitted in July by MONUA to the ad hoc group on human rights at the Joint Commission. Between June and August police observers investigated twenty cases of alleged human rights abuses and MONUA staff visited prisons in the Luanda area. The staff of the Human Rights Unit declined in July with the departure of six human rights monitors funded by the European Union (E.U.).

European Union
On January 13, the European Commission granted a humanitarian aid package of ECU 14 million to Angola which would be administered by the European Community Humanitarian Aid Office (ECHO). The humanitarian aid projects would actually be conducted by the International Committee of the Red Cross (ICRC), United Nations agencies, and various NGOs. ECHO's two priorities in Angola were medical aid and feeding programs.

On February 3, the European Union stated that it was very pleased with the progress toward the Lusaka Protocols in Angola, particularly with the induction of UNITA officers into the Angolan Army. However, the E.U. was concerned with the delays in establishing a Government of Unity and National Reconciliation. The E.U. also praised the governments of Portugal, the United States of America, and the Russian Federation for their efforts in the peace process in Angola.

On August 13, the European Union criticized UNITA's failure to comply with the demilitarization demands highlighted in Security Council Resolution 1118, and requested UNITA compliance with the terms of the Lusaka Protocols as well as information on the status and whereabouts of its military forces.

United States
The U.S. remained one of the most influential forces in the Angolan peace process and dominated the export market and investment sector. In 1996 the U.S. bought more than half of Angola's exports (mostly oil), worth some U.S.$5 billion. The U.S. also led investments, with private capital expected to exceed $4.3 billion in 1997. Chevron alone will account for up to roughly $3 billion of investments up to the millennium.

In 1997 the U.S. provided $150 million in emergency funding for post-war reconstruction, in addition to being one of the main contributors to the U.N. force there. In August two Republican members of the Senate Foreign Relations Committee, Chairman Jesse Helms of North Carolina and John Ashcroft of Missouri, strongly objected to the proposed sale of six U.S. manufactured C-130 aircraft to Angola. A U.S. firm, Military Professional Resources Inc. (MPRI), assisted in the training of the new unified army.

A central focus of U.S. policy in Angola remained the implementation of the Lusaka Protocols and the avoidance of a return to conflict. Early in the year a series of demarches were presented to the Angolan government over its involvement in the DRC crisis and again in October over intersection in Congo-Brazzaville. UNITA also received a number of demarches about its foot-dragging and noncompliance with the conditions of the Lusaka Protocols.

U.S. embassy officials in Angola maintained irregular contact with nongovernmental organizations working on human rights issues, which was reflected in the Angola section of the *Country Reports on Human Rights Practices in 1996*. The report presented an accurate description of human rights conditions in the country. Human Rights Watch/Africa was unaware, however, of any public statements from the embassy condemning human rights violations when they occurred during 1997.

BURUNDI

Human Rights Developments
The opposing sides in the four-year-old civil war in Burundi raped, tortured, and killed thousands of civilians and looted and destroyed civilian property in 1997. The Tutsi-dominated armed forces used extensive violence against the majority Hutu population in order to crush support for Hutu rebel groups. Shortly after Buyoya returned to

power in a July 1996 coup, the military government began a program of forced resettlement of hundreds of thousands of Hutu civilians in areas of rebel activity. In the policy known as regroupment, officials ordered civilians to assemble at designated sites, generally around military posts.

After gathering those who complied with the orders in camps, the military conducted "cleanup" operations, going systematically through the countryside, looting and burning homes, and hunting down anyone who resisted being regrouped. The armed forces killed thousands of unarmed civilians, many of them women, children, and elderly, for refusing to be regrouped and drove survivors into the camps. The camps themselves represented a clear violation of the right to freedom of movement and, despite government claims that the camps were created "to protect the civilian population," amounted to concentration camps.

Inside the camps, the Hutu population continued to face persecution. The military summarily executed hundreds of people they suspected of supporting rebel groups and arrested, tortured, and killed many others who violated camp rules, such as curfews. The camps were seriously overcrowded, without water and other facilities and the creation of the camps seriously disrupted agricultural production, leading to chronic malnutrition and illness. Within the camps, rape by soldiers and forced labor for camp residents was common. Although the province of Kayanza began dismantling its regroupment camps in late August, camps remained in Bubanza, Bujumbura-Rural, Cibitoke, Karuzi, and Muramvya, and new camps were created in the southern provinces of Bururi and Makamba.

The armed forces frequently retaliated against Hutu rebel activity by attacking Hutu civilians. Among the worst army attacks on civilians was a December 12, 1996 attack in Kayanza in which 114 people were killed; repeated attacks in Giheta commune of Gitega in late 1996 and early 1997 in which hundreds of civilians were killed; and a May 14 attack on Mugendo parish near Magara,

Bujumbura-Rural in which soldiers killed forty-two people during a religious service. Attacks on refugees returning from the Democratic Republic of Congo (DRC) and Tanzania in early 1997 killed several hundred. The military also carried out numerous attacks targeting specific individuals who were summarily executed or "disappeared." Areas most affected by such attacks included Isare, Kanyosha, Kabezi, and Muhuta communes of Bujumbura-Rural; Rutegama, Bukeye, and Bugarama in Muramvya; and Burambi, Buyengero, and Rumonge in Bururi. Most of those killed or taken and presumed dead were business people, teachers, catechists, or other community leaders, whom the armed forces feared could organize resistance among the population, or young men, whom the armed forces feared might someday join the rebel groups. In some cases, soldiers raped women before killing them.

Hutu rebel groups also targeted civilians. The largest of the groups, the Forces for the Defense of Democracy (FDD), faced a major setback with the closure of their bases in DRC in late 1996, and was further weakened by the regroupment policy which cut them off from popular support. The FDD launched a major offensive in southern Burundi in March. The FDD was able to occupy the area around Magara in Bujumbura-Rural and around Nyanza-Lac in Makamba and to expand the territory under its control in Burundi.

The most widespread human rights abuse by the FDD and other rebel groups was looting from the civilian population, but the rebels also killed a number of unarmed civilians, both Hutu and Tutsi, in indiscriminate attacks. The FDD killed more than one hundred people in an April 17 attack at Kayogoro in Makamba, and on April 30 FDD combatants killed forty people at a Catholic school at Buta, Bururi, in an attack that gained international condemnation because nearly all of those killed were children. The FDD ambushed a number of civilian vehicles on the main Lake Tanganyika road and several other roads in the country. In July and August, fighting in Bubanza and

Cibitoke between the FDD and a rival rebel group, the Party for the Liberation of the Hutu People (PALIPEHUTU), left several hundred Hutu dead and drove thousands to flee the area.

The warring parties began a massive arms buildup, and resorted increasingly to the use of landmines. An increasing number of injuries and deaths in mine explosions were reported during the year.

The armed forces nearly doubled in size, from 25,000 to 40,000, in less than two years. The military conscripted secondary school and university students (including women), members of youth gangs, and children reportedly as young as ten. Virtually all recruits have been Tutsi, further exacerbating the lack of ethnic balance in the armed forces. To facilitate the expansion, training was reduced from one year to three months.

Following the FDD advance in the south, the armed forces distributed arms to Tutsi civilians and began military training for Tutsi men in Bujumbura and elsewhere, substantially expanding a civilian defense program begun in 1996. Civilian militia have been involved in a number of violent attacks in Burundi in recent years, and the expansion of civilian militia appeared to give government sanction to such activities. Nevertheless, the Tutsi militia were involved in fewer violent incidents in 1997 than in the recent past.

The Buyoya regime engaged in preliminary talks with FDD representatives in Rome, a development that was announced publicly in May. Although some Tutsi factions objected to holding discussions with a group they accused of genocide, Buyoya expressed a commitment to finding a peaceful settlement to the conflict. Negotiations to be moderated by former Tanzanian president Nyerere were scheduled for August 25, but the government and the largely Tutsi UPRONA party withdrew at the last moment. Buyoya subsequently stated that he would participate in future talks.

Political activity continued to be restricted in 1997. The National Assembly and political parties operated under critical constraints. Hutu politicians faced continued harassment. In February, agents of the Center for National Documentation arrested and tortured FRODEBU executive secretary Domitien Ndayizeye. In a March raid, agents confiscated FRODEBU computers and documents, and arrested and tortured Augustin Nzojibwani, FRODEBU secretary general, in an attempt to extract the password to the computers. On August 2, Paul Sirabahenda became the twenty-third FRODEBU member of parliament to be assassinated since 1993.

Conflict increased among Tutsi political factions. Former president Bagaza remained under house arrest for much of the year, and other Tutsi politicians who had publicly challenged Buyoya, such as leaders of the youth group SOJEDEM and Charles Mukasi, an UPRONA leader, were brought in for questioning or placed under house arrest at various times during the year. Following the revelation that the government was secretly engaging the FDD in talks, Bagaza's party, the Party for National Recovery (PARENA), as well as a disgruntled faction within Buyoya's party, UPRONA, organized demonstrations in the streets of Bujumbura. A series of mine blasts in Bujumbura in May and June were also attributed to these factions. A rift between Buyoya and other UPRONA leaders gradually expanded during the year.

The judicial system continued to be a major concern. The number of people detained in national prisons increased from 6,100 in December 1996 to more than 9,000 in August 1997, the majority held without charge. Prosecutions for participation in the 1993 ethnic massacres began, largely of Hutus accused of participating in attacks on Tutsi. On July 31, six people were executed for participating in the 1993 massacres after a brief show trial without legal representation. Fourteen more people were condemned to death in August. Both trials were travesties of due process intended solely to make a political point. At the same time, a case against military officers accused of involvement in the assassination of President

Ndadaye in October 1993 made little progress. To date, the numerous assassinations of Hutu politicians remain uninvestigated.

A number of provinces adopted a reconstruction program in 1997, using community councils to arrange repayment for the destroyed property of victims of ethnic violence. While many people, including Hutu politicians, supported the principle of compensation for damages, in practice the program was used by Tutsi to profit from Hutu and to pursue personal grudges with little consideration for justice. Those who were accused of having pillaged and were unable to pay the damages assigned faced imprisonment. In Karuzi, where the Hutu residents of regroupment camps are being required to pay Tutsi even though their own homes had also been destroyed and all of their property stolen or destroyed.

The Right to Monitor

Local human rights groups remained constrained in their operations. The drop in militia violence reduced one of the main dangers to human rights work. However, it appears that the decline in harassment of human rights groups reflects their reduced activity. Many people were surprised when the most credible group, ITEKA, signed on to a letter calling for an end to the sanctions against Burundi.

The Burundian Association for the Defense of the Rights of Prisoners began a program of monitoring the treatment of the growing prison population. The group had difficulty receiving authorization to enter prisons and speak with prisoners, but the appointment of a more moderate justice minister in May may resolve this issue.

The United Nations Human Rights Center in Bujumbura expanded from five to twelve monitors in 1997, but they found their operations severely constrained. The government, given an opportunity prior to publication to respond to the center's monthly reports, regularly delayed its response and sought to prevent the publication of the reports. The liaison committee provided for by the authorization agreement with the government was only formed in January, and most of the government representatives on the committee did not participate. In January, a campaign against the center began in the media and elsewhere, and vandalization of center cars and other harassment soon followed. Security concerns also limited the ability of the center to conduct research in parts of the country with extensive human rights problems.

The Role of the International Community

United Nations

U.N. agencies worked to alleviate serious problems of health and nutrition brought about by regroupment, a military policy in violation of the rules of war, while seeking to avoid lending support to the government. Meeting humanitarian needs without seeming to condone the policy at the roots of the problem proved challenging, and some agencies such as UNICEF and Food and Agriculture Organization of the United Nations (FAO) suggested that the humanitarian concerns should override political concerns. Nevertheless, in a discussion of the situation in Burundi on May 30, the Security Council expressed "deep concern" about the regroupment policy and called upon the government "to allow the people to return to their homes without any hindrance."

The United Nations also assumed a role in supporting negotiations, though the primary role in this has been taken by the neighboring states through the Organization of African Unity (OAU). A number of high level delegations visited Burundi in 1997 to monitor the human rights and humanitarian situations. In February and November, the special human rights rapporteur for Burundi, Paulo Sergio Pinheiro, issued strongly worded reports condemning abuses in Burundi. In July, the U.N. rejected the request by the government of Burundi that Pinheiro be replaced . Pinheiro later deplored the July 31 execution of six persons which he had sought to prevent because the persons were condemned to death without the benefit of legal counsel.

In a July 15 statement, the U.N. secretary-general firmly turned down a request by the Burundi government for the formation of an international tribunal on ethnic violence in Burundi, believing that the government of Burundi was not interested in a truly independent tribunal but would instead seek to politicize its operations.

United States
The United States vocally opposed the creation of the regroupment camps. The U.S., a major funder of the World Food Programme (WFP) and other programs in Burundi, refused to allow American money to be used in building infrastructure in the camps, for fear this would encourage the camps to become permanent. The U.S. supported efforts to encourage negotiations between the warring parties in Burundi. Several high level delegations visited the region to lend support to the talks.

European Union
As the war in the former Zaire set off a new refugee crisis in late 1996, the European Parliament responded with a report prepared by British member Richard Howitt, which sought to create a swift European Union (E.U.) reaction by simplifying the cumbersome bureaucratic structure for approving refugee aid. The Parliament approved the report on November 12.

The European Parliament on December 12 strongly condemned continued fighting in the African Great Lakes Region, but divisions within the E.U. prevented the deployment of a multi-national peacekeeping force. In a March meeting, delegations from the European Parliament and the African, Caribbean, and Pacific Countries approved a compromise resolution on the crisis in the Great Lakes Region condemning the presence of troops and foreign mercenaries in Zaire and inviting all governments involved in the conflict to withdraw their troops and abstain from further interference.

The European Commission on March 26 set aside 100 million ECU over four years to help relieve the debts of poor African, Caribbean, and Pacific countries. The money was earmarked for eleven countries, including Burundi, to ensure that development programs would not be hindered by excessive debt burdens.

On May 7, the European Union condemned the continued violence in Burundi and in particular the massacres and atrocities committed against the civilian population. The European Union condemned the execution in July of six prisoners after unfair trials on charges of genocide.

A May 20 declaration welcomed President Buyoya's announcement of negotiations taking place in Rome with the National Council for the Defense of Democracy (CNDD) and called on the government to disband the regroupment camps at the earliest opportunity. In August, the European Union expressed its full support for the opening of multiparty negotiations at Arusha in Tanzania. It urged the parties in Burundi to refrain from setting preconditions which might create obstacles to negotiation and urged them to "support the peace process which should be conducted in a climate of trust and calm."

OAU and Regional Collaboration
The regional heads of state have taken a leading role in supporting a peaceful settlement to the civil war and a return to civilian rule. The sanctions imposed against Burundi immediately after the July 1996 coup were modified in April 1997 to allow the import of humanitarian goods, but at a meeting in August, regional leaders reiterated their commitment to maintaining sanctions. Presidents Moi of Kenya and Kabila of the DRC, who had announced in July their intentions to ignore the sanctions, appear to have been convinced at the August meeting to respect the sanctions.

Former Tanzanian President Nyerere continued to play a leading role in organizing talks between the government and rebel groups, despite some complaints from the government that he was biased in favor of the rebel movements.

The transfer of power in the former Zaire substantially improved Burundi's relations with that country. Buyoya developed cordial relations with Kabila, with the two leaders exchanging a number of diplomatic visits. Meanwhile, relations with Tanzania deteriorated. The Buyoya regime accused the Tanzanian government of waging a campaign against Burundi by allowing the FDD to establish bases in the country and by pushing for a maintenance of sanctions. In September, Tanzania accused Burundi of mining their mutual border and of making incursions into Tanzanian territory.

Relevant Human Rights Watch reports:

Stoking the Fires: Military Assistance and Arms Trafficking in Burundi, 12/97
The War Against the Civilian Population in Burundi, 12/97

THE DEMOCRATIC REPUBLIC OF CONGO (Formerly Zaire)

Human Rights Developments

The rebel Alliance of Democratic Forces for the Liberation of Congo (ADFL) ousted President Mobutu of the then Zaire and seized power in mid-May after a seven-month campaign. The Mobutu government's moves to strip the ethnic Tutsi Banyamulenge of their citizenship and drive them from the country sparked the rebellion, which was later joined by other groups. Even before the war erupted, however, the country was on the verge of disintegration. The failed transition to democracy and Mobutu's rule through kleptocracy had left the country with a col-

lapsed economy, an unruly military, a president whose term in office had long since expired, and an unelected parliament.

An intricate regional crisis added to the potency of Congo's internal political and ethnic conflict. An estimated one million refugees from neighboring Rwanda had settled in eastern Congo, and among them were thousands of armed exiles from the former Rwandan Armed Forces (ex-FAR) and its militia the *Interahamwe*. The refugees were mainly Hutu who had fled to Congo fearing retribution for the 1994 genocide during which more than 500,000 minority Tutsis and moderate Hutus were killed. The killing frenzy only stopped after rebels of the Tutsi-dominated Rwanda Patriotic Army (RPA) toppled the Rwandan government which had orchestrated the genocide. Mobutu's government helped the remnants of the ex-FAR to rearm, and persistently refused to cooperate with the International Criminal Tribunal for Rwanda in apprehending and extraditing persons indicted for genocide.

Rwanda's government seized on the Banyamulenge uprising as an opportunity to disband the refugee border camps and destroy the ex-FAR and Interahamwe. RPA troops took part in the rebel offensive, and the ADFL also received military and diplomatic support from the governments of Uganda, and Angola, among other regional powers.

While the fighting forced an estimated 600,000 refugees back into Rwanda, hundreds of thousands of others fled further west into Congo, among them tens of thousands of armed elements. The United Nation's High Commissioner for Refugees (UNHCR) estimated that 213,000 refugees remained unaccounted for as of the last quarter of 1997. Human Rights Watch investigations and others have gathered evidence indicating that fleeing refugees were pursued relentlessly, falling victim to human rights abuses committed by all parties to the conflict. The deserting and demoralized soldiers of the former Zairian army (FAZ) looted supplies and raped scores of civilians in their flight, including Congolese as well as refugees, and destroyed schools, churches, and clinics. Likewise, armed elements from the ex-FAR and its militia used force and random killings to prevent other refugees from repatriating to Rwanda and tended to use unarmed refugees as human shields in their flight, leading to many deaths of civilians in cross fire. The ADFL troops, and their Rwandan RPA backers, in turn, engaged in extensive and systematic massacres of refugees, many of whom were hunted down on the run and at temporary encampments. The killers often forced the local population to clean up massacre sites. An exacerbation of local ethnic tensions and violence caused civil war to return to North and South Kivu in 1997, as remnants of the ex-FAR allied themselves with local rebel groups, attacking government forces and local Tutsi populations.

On May 17, 1997, the day Kinshasa fell to its troops, the ADFL issued a declaration by which it suspended the transitional constitution, disbanded the transitional parliament and government, and appointed its own chairman, Laurent Désiré Kabila, as president of the republic. A constitutional decree proclaimed by the new president on May 28 empowered him to legislate by decrees, head the government, and appoint and dismiss ministers and judges. Despite this latter provision, the decree acknowledged the independence of the judiciary. Congo's continued obligations under human rights and humanitarian treaties to which it was party were expressly acknowledged. Upon taking office, President Kabila promised a transitional agenda that would lead to legislative and presidential elections in two years. The first step in that process was taken when in mid-October he issued a decree establishing a commission to draft the new constitution.

As a political movement, the ADFL undertakes in its statutes to be open to the affiliation of other political parties, organizations of civil society, as well as individuals, who would adhere to its "ideological base." This is defined in the statutes as the ADFL's belief that all power emanates from the people and is founded on inalienable human rights. In practice, political parties were asked to dissolve themselves into the alliance in order to be part of the government, and members of existing opposition parties were appointed to government positions in their individual capacities.

The government had yet to integrate ADFL soldiers from different regions, ethnic backgrounds, or from neighboring countries under a unified command structure, and frequent frictions and confrontations continued to occur between military units of different backgrounds. The problem of deteriorating discipline, particularly after the failure of the government in securing the timely payment of salaries to the military, contributed in turn to growing insecurity as soldiers attempted to extort money from civilians, or indulged in armed banditry

Incidents in which indiscriminate gunfire took a high toll abounded all over Congo, including the killing, on the night of July 6 to 7, 1997, of fifteen persons in Kinshasa by a patrol of unruly ADFL soldiers. A confrontation on the night of August 21-22 in the Ceta military camp, between soldiers distinguished by the Kinshasa press as "Tutsi" and "Congolese," left at least three soldiers dead. On August 30, soldiers fired in the air to control a large crowd of teenagers in the municipal swimming pool of N'Sele, Kinshasa. In the resulting panic, at least twenty-four young men and women died.

As it took over, the ADFL arrested and confiscated the property of prominent dignitaries of the Mobutu era, in many cases without due process of law. There were about fifty detainees of this category in Kinshasa by August 1997. Six of whom were interviewed by Human Rights Watch in an August meeting in a Kinshasa detention center.

In Lubumbashi, there were eighty-nine detainees, about twenty of whom were prominent politicians, in the cells attached to the headquarters of the new political police, the National Intelligence Agency (ANR), when a local rights group visited it on July 31,

1997. Many were detained for months following denunciations arising from civil and criminal disputes without appearing before a court. Conditions were harsh: prisoners slept on the cemented floors, looked poorly nourished, and sanitation was lacking. Political prisoners who spoke to Human Rights Watch, including a former governor, a former mayor of Lubumbashi, and the former chairman of Mobutu's party, said they were not informed of the reasons for their detention, and alleged that prisoners held in connection to their suspected roles in civil and criminal cases were routinely beaten.

The ADFL banned political activities throughout the country. In Kinshasa, government troops periodically attacked the headquarters of political parties with popular followings, dispersed their peaceful marches with gunfire, and abducted, detained, and tortured their militants. Soon after Kabila's inauguration, government troops dispersed demonstrations by supporters of the Union for Democracy and Social Progress (UDPS) protesting the exclusion of the UDPS, and its leader Etienne Tshisekedi, from the transitional government. Shortly after Tshisekedi's participation as principal speaker in a political rally at Kinshasa University, troops descended on his residence late on June 26, and arrested him and his wife and held them overnight. Authorities also arrested and badly tortured a student, Richard Mpiana Kalenga, who they suspected was an organizer of the rally.

On July 25, a group of soldiers opened fire on demonstrators returning from a peaceful march that the Unified Lumumbist Party (PALU) organized to press for more political participation. One PALU militant was killed, and many were injured. In the afternoon of the same day, soldiers raided the headquarters of PALU, which is also the residence of Antoine Gizenga, a veteran politician and PALU president. They beat party militants with iron bars, belts, and gun butts before taking them into custody. They locked the elderly Gizenga and his wife in a bathroom, and then went on a rampage, looting the family's personal possessions

and ransacking the property of the party.

The bustling private press of Kinshasa maintained a critical tone vis-a-vis the new government that reflected an independence it had successfully fought for under Mobutu. While initially tolerating this, authorities cracked down on coverage of "sensitive" information such as security issues or corruption in government ranks. Polydor Mubunga, editor of the *Le Phare*, was placed under house arrest in mid-September after publishing an article claiming that Kabila was recruiting his own presidential guard. Ali Kalonga, director of the official Congolese Press Agency, was detained for weeks in August 1998 after he authorized a story about the suspension and house arrest of the finance minister following allegations of corruption. The government also took measures which, if fully implemented, would threaten the very existence of the private media. In late May, one of the first decisions of the new information minister was to ban advertising through privately-owned radio and television stations. On August 18, the national police issued an order banning the sale of newspapers on the main streets of Kinshasa. The private press considered this as a "declaration of war" as its distribution was entirely dependent on street vendors.

The Right to Monitor

Groups who stepped in to denounce abuses by agents of the new government quickly became the target of punitive measures. In Kinshasa, at least three rights activists were detained for short periods in separate incidents in retaliation for a joint campaign by rights groups for detained Mobutists and other political prisoners to be charged or released. In the eastern town of Kindu, the military commander ordered the closure of the premises of the rights group Haki Za Binadamu, after he received a letter in which it denounced the unlawful detention of suspects in criminal and civil cases in the military camp. Two of Haki's workers were detained and tortured: as a result of which one fell into a coma and was hospitalized. In response to the outcry that followed, the authorities in the province accused them of involvement in a "plot"—to provide false information to the U.N. team investigating the massacres of refugees that occurred in the vicinity of the town during the war.

The Role of the International Community

United Nations

By the time the refugee camps of eastern Congo were dismantled by the ADFL attacks in October 1996, the international community had channeled an estimated U.S. $2.5 billion into relief for the Rwandan refugees in the region. This effort was seriously undermined by the failure of the U.N. and world powers to enforce the separation of armed exiles, suspected of crimes against humanity, from bona fide refugees.

With the rebellion in eastern Congo rapidly developing into a generalized civil war, the U.N. Security Council endorsed on February 18, 1997, a five-point plan prepared by Mohammed Sahnoun, the joint U.N. and Organization of African Unity (OAU) special envoy for the Great Lakes region, which called for an immediate end to the fighting; the withdrawal of all foreign forces, including mercenaries; reaffirmation of the territorial integrity of all states in the region; protection and security for all refugees, and the convening of an international conference to resolve conflicts in the region. Sahnoun's diplomatic efforts to mediate a peaceful settlement for the war on the basis of this plan were hampered by the ADFL's outright military success.

On March 6, 1997 the U.N. high commissioner for human rights asked the special rapporteur for Zaire (now Congo), to investigate allegations of refugee massacres in ADFL-held areas. Following a short field mission, the rapporteur, Roberto Garretón of Chile, on April 2 issued a short report, identifying more than forty possible massacre sites and calling for further investigations through the mechanisms of the Human Rights Commission. The commission resolved in mid-April that the special rapporteur, jointly with the special rapporteur on extrajudicial, summary or arbitrary executions, and a member of the Working Group on Disappearances, carry out a mission to investigate the allegations of massacres and other issues related to the situation in that country since September 1996.

The ADFL, however, adamantly refused to allow the team to enter territories under its control to conduct its probe and said it rejected the team's leader, Roberto Garretón, apparently because of his earlier report. The U.N.'s subsequent agreement to this condition led Human Rights Watch, together with other human rights organizations, to write, on June 13, to the U.N. secretary-general pointing out the dangers involved in allowing countries under investigation to choose their own investigators. In subsequent discussions with the Congolese government, the U.N. failed to persuade it to accept the team mandated by the commission. To overcome the delays created by the government's veto on the team's leader, the Security Council agreed to the secretary-general's proposal, on July, 8, to create an investigative team under his own authority. The team thus formed arrived in Kinshasa on August 24 to a hostile reception.

When the U.N. team attempted to launch the investigation in the western city of Mbandaka, the government blocked it and said the investigation could only focus on the east. An impasse followed, leading the U.N. to recall the three main investigators to New York "for consultations." In late October, U.S. ambassador to the U.N. Bill Richardson and President Kabila reached an agreement in Kinshasa that was expected to clear the way for the probe to begin in early November. Kabila agreed to drop territorial limitation on the coverage of the probe, and the U.N. agreed that the team would not recommend any punitive measures or interfere in Congo's internal affairs.

The Congo continued to host a U.N. human rights field office. Agreed to in August 1996 under the previous government, the office was originally proposed by special rapporteur Garretón to assist him in collecting information and maintaining contact with the government. The primary mandate of the office was to monitor human rights abuses, though some technical cooperation activities were envisaged. With only one professional from the U.N. Human Rights Center assigned to Kinshasa, the office was understaffed and underresourced at a time when its presence could have played a vital role in the promotion and protection of human rights in the country.

Organization of African Unity

South Africa's initiative, in February 1997, to host indirect talks between representatives of the ADFL and an advisor of President Mobutu ultimately led to direct talks between Kabila and Mobutu in May. The thrust of South Africa's diplomatic drive was to get Mobutu to relinquish power in exchange for a commitment from the ADFL to form a broad-based transitional authority. Battlefield advances, however, allowed the ADFL to prevail without concessions.

The ouster of Mobutu created an atmosphere of euphoria in much of the region, which peaked at the 33rd session of the OAU summit, held in early June in Harare, during which leaders welcomed Kabila and the ADFL's triumph. This in turn led to strong expressions of support for Kabila when he came under increasing international pressure to cooperate with the U.N. probe and to commit himself to early democratic elections. On May 27, President Mandela and Uganda's Yoweri Museveni accused Western governments of "demonizing" Kabila and defended his orders to prohibit political activities. Museveni reminded journalists that he had taken similar action against political parties in his own country and said he believed that African societies, which he characterized as preindustrial, were "not ready" for multiparty democracy.

European Union

The European Union (E.U.) suspended economic assistance to Mobutu's government in 1992, citing Article 5 of the Lome Convention IV (1989) which makes respect for human rights and democratic principles an "essential element" of the convention. The European Commission however disbursed an exceptional humanitarian aid package of U.S.$309.81 million between 1992 and 1996 for rehabilitation and infrastructure programs, mainly through nongovernmental organizations (NGOs) and civil organizations of the health sector. The E.U. also earmarked an additional $35 million for electoral assistance and set up an European Electoral Unit for that purpose, although most of these funds were not disbursed due to the Mobutu government's decision to postpone the elections.

The E.U. issued a declaration on May 23, on the transfer of power in Congo, in which it stipulated what it expected from the new authorities, namely: that they respect the electoral calender announced by Kabila, and commit themselves to democracy and the respect of human rights. The E.U. also urged the new government to protect refugees and allow humanitarian access to them, and to allow the U.N. probe to go ahead as a matter of urgency.

The signals from the E.U. and some of its member states, however, were mixed. The humanitarian aid commissioner, Emma Bonino, kept the pressure on the new government by publicly denouncing its denial of humanitarian access to refugees, and by repeatedly and publicly pressing for a neutral investigation of reports of refugee massacres. But in a statement made on May 28, E.U. Development Commissioner Joao de deus Pinheiro said that Kabila was right in setting law and order and stabilization as his first priority, agreeing on this with President Mandela. Belgium, for its part, indicated its willingness to resume its development aid to Congo, following a visit by Belgian Secretary of State for Development Cooperation Reginald Moreels in early August. The *troika* of European Union foreign ministers also visited Kinshasa in early August. The delegation was headed by current E.U. President Jacques Poos, Dutch Foreign Minister Hans Van Mierlo, British Deputy Foreign Minister Tony Lloyd, and a representative of the European Commission. It welcomed the end of the dictatorial rule of Mobutu and the arrival of a new government that had expressed its intention to found its policy on the principles of democracy, respect of human rights, and the rule of law. On the question of refugees, the ministerial troika welcomed the government's acceptance of the U.N. investigative mission and raised the question of access by humanitarian organizations to refugees and the security of their personnel. The delegation said it would recommend, in its report to the E.U. Council of Ministers, the gradual resumption of structural aid to the new government in light of the prevailing "positive political environment."

In response to the restriction of the U.N.'s delegation to the capital, Kinshasa, for nearly four weeks, the E.U.'s Presidency had sent a letter to Congo's foreign minister asking an immediate lifting of the obstacles blocking the team. Should this fact-finding mission not succeed, it said, in a press release, "the new prospects of cooperation between the European Union and the Democratic Republic of Congo would be jeopardized."

The Luxembourg Presidency spoke to the European Parliament on September 24, declaring that there was no rift in the E.U. about cooperation with Congo, only that cooperation would henceforth be conditional on respect for human rights. Kabila quickly reacted describing the E.U. position as a plot "hatched by Western powers" acting under the cover of humanitarian agencies.

United States

The U.S. suspended its economic assistance to Congo in 1991 under statutory provisions prohibiting foreign aid to countries in default on their loans to the U.S. government. This followed decades of unconditional U.S. support for Mobutu, its longtime Cold War ally, during which the U.S. continued to pour in millions of dollars and to facilitate World Bank and International Monetary Fund support while Mobutu and his cronies openly siphoned these funds into their own pockets.

Suspicions were rife in Congo at the outbreak of the war that the United States was backing the rebels, leading to a wave of anti-American feelings in late 1996. These suspicions were in part rooted in the knowledge of the considerable political, economic, and military support that the U.S. extended to Rwanda, which in turn had provided decisive military assistance to the ADFL's campaign. In congressional hearings in December 1996, Vincent Kern, Deputy Assistant Secretary of Defense, downplayed U.S. military assistance to Rwanda, describing it as the "softer, kinder, gentler" side of military training, and said it didn't include instruction for combat situations and basic military training. However, under further NGO, press, and congressional scrutiny, the Department of Defense issued a report on August 19, 1997 which detailed one program of basic military training, including combat skills, of some Rwandan troops partially conducted by the U.S. Army Special Forces.

In a July 1997 interview, Rwanda's strongman and minister of defense, Paul Kagame, said he informed the State Department officials in August 1996 that Rwanda was ready to dismantle the camps if the international community failed to remove them from the border area, and, according to him, the U.S. "took decisions to let it happen."

Following the attack on the camps, and the return of hundreds of thousands of refugees to Rwanda, the U.S. embassy in Kigali agreed with the Rwandan government's estimates that only "tens of thousands" of refugees remained behind, instead of estimates of 200,000 to 450,000 made by humanitarian agencies operating on the ground. By the time a general agreement was reached on the higher estimate, a plan for a multinational force to assist the refugees and facilitate their repatriation was abandoned.

The U.S. subsequently criticized the ADFL for the large-scale abuses alleged in areas under its control, and in statements in January 1997, the U.S. ambassador to Congo agreed with the Mobutu government's charge that the country was being "attacked" by

Rwanda and Uganda, contradicting assertions from the U.S. embassy in Kigali that "there was no proof" of Rwandan military presence in Congo. Unwilling to hold Rwanda accountable for its alleged share of responsibility in these killings, the U.S., however, stepped up its pressure on the ADFL as of March and April, when the U.S. demanded guarantees from the ADFL of access to the refugees by aid workers and insisted on access for human rights investigators.

In the meantime, the administration obtained the agreement of Congress to a limited assistance of $10 million, to be allocated mainly in grants to UNICEF's immunization program, NGO assistance, and to the reform of the legal system. In late September, spokesman Jamie Rubin of the U.S. State Department warned President Kabila that the U.S. government's relations with Kinshasa "will be determined to some significant extent by his willingness to allow the U.N. human rights team to do its job."

Relevant Human Rights Watch reports:
What Kabila is Hiding: Civilian Killings and Impunity in Congo, 10/97
Zaire: Transition, War, and Human Rights, 4/97
Zaire: "Attacked on all Sides": Civilians and Civil War, 4/97

ETHIOPIA

Human Rights Developments
The government of the Federal Democratic Republic of Ethiopia (FDRE), established in August 1995 after elections boycotted by opposition groups, continued to build the federal state structures provided for by the 1994 constitution. These centered on ethnically-based regions having legislative, executive, and judicial powers within their geographical areas. The governing Ethiopian People's Revolutionary Democratic Front (EPRDF), and its founding and core constituent, the Tigrean People's Liberation Front (TPLF), continued to exert strict control over this process.

Ignoring constitutional rights, the government of Prime Minster Meles Zenawi did not tolerate pluralist party politics, cracked down on critical media reporting, and aggressively sought to coopt labor and professional associations, and other civil society structures. It actively promoted the policy of ethnic federalism, while successfully dominating the emerging ethnically-based political system by favoring regional parties affiliated to the EPRDF and clamping down on opposition groups in the conduct of regional and national elections from 1992 to 1995.

The Oromo Liberation Front (OLF) and the Ogaden National Liberation Front (ONLF), broke with the transitional government in 1992 and 1994 respectively and later launched armed insurgencies against the government. Recently formed radical Islamist groups, including the Islamic Front for the Liberation of Oromia, and Al Ithad Al-Islami (Islamic Unity), which operated in the Somali Region, fought sporadically with the government.

The government continued to arbitrarily detain hundreds of civilians in remote regions where separatist dissident groups operated. After raids on three border towns in Somalia in August 1996 and December 1996/January 1997, the government claimed it had destroyed Al Ithad Al-Islami's bases. The fundamentalist group continued, however, to claim responsibility for a campaign of bombings of hotels and restaurants, among other civilian targets, in the capital and other cities. The government arrested dozens of ethnic Somalis on suspicion of membership in Al Ithad. In early November, the government accused prominent members of the Oromo community of involvement in bombings in the capital and elsewhere and of OLF membership. As of this writing, at least fifteen remained in detention without charge in the police Central Investigation Bureau. Those detained for their suspected sympathy for rebel groups were usually held in unofficial detention centers, such as the premises of peasant associations, or army camps. Torture and ill-treatment, at the hands of members of rural militias attached to the governing coalition and other security forces, were common. Political killings by state agents were also reported, mostly in areas remote from the capital. The absence of effective judicial oversight and the restriction of the work of most rights monitoring groups to the capital has meant most of those suffering abuse have had no recourse to legal remedy or to public denunciation.

The government kept the officials of regional parties and local governments on a short leash, through a system of quarterly assessments by subordinates, known as *Gimgamas*, whereby soldiers evaluated their commanders in a process the TPLF believed to have improved the military performance of the Front. Following a series of appraisals in the ranks of the Oromo People's Democratic Organization (OPDO), Kuma Demeska, the chief administrator of Oromiya Region, declared in April that the OPDO had purged its ranks of 250 executive district officials and detained eighty others. In mid-August, the regional council of Gambella Region "endorsed" a proposal, presumably by the regional party, to detain the top four officials in the deposed state's government. The government often accused the purged officials of corruption or of manifesting "narrow nationalism," a reference to their suspected sympathy for dissident groups.

The government's attempts to silence the boisterous Addis Ababa private press continued, but detentions were shorter than in the past. Six journalists were serving prison sentences handed down under the press law for articles they had published. Fourteen other journalists faced similar charges. High levels of bail were set relative to journalists' incomes, an economic punishment that was effective in inducing the media to exercise self-censorship rather than face further arrests.

The government also sought to extend the application of the press law to international correspondents resident in or visiting the country, whose coverage had largely escaped censorship in the past. The Ministry of Information sent guidelines to foreign correspondents in early June, requiring resident correspondents to obtain annually renewable work permits and to respect the "laws of the country, its culture, and its traditions." In late June, Alice Martin, correspondent of the British Broadcasting Corporation (BBC), was forced to leave Ethiopia after the immigration authorities refused to renew her residency permit three days after she assumed the presidency of the association of foreign correspondents.

Activists loyal to the government succeeded in April 1997 in taking control of the Confederation of Ethiopian Trade Unions (CETU). What the new leaders termed "normalization" followed a protracted confrontation with its elected leadership that started in October 1994. At the time, CETU's chairman publicly criticized the negative impact of the government's structural adjustment program on public sector workers, the majority of unionized workers in the country. Destabilizing tactics were used against two of nine federations which remained loyal to the previous leadership. The Federation of Commerce, Technical, and Printing Industries, a group of EPRDF loyalists called in the police on November 4, 1996 to support its claim to lead the federation and to eject the previous team from the union's premises. The last federation to remain loyal to the previously-elected CETU leadership was the Banking and Insurance Trade Unions' Federation. Its largest and most influential union, that of the Commercial Bank of Ethiopia, became the target of pressure such as the freezing of its bank account in April 1997 and the disruption of its meetings. These measures appeared to have ended when its leadership agreed to join the new CETU after its "normalization," and did so in August.

In early May, police shot and killed Assefa Maru, the acting president of Ethiopian's Teachers' Association (ETA), which continued to oppose ethnic federalism and its implications in the field of education. The police statement claimed that the union official, who was also an executive committee member of the independent Ethiopian Human Rights Council, resisted when police caught him "making preparations to destroy economic establishments, and assassinate individuals holding public office" with other accomplices. Human Rights Watch interviews with eyewitnesses and relatives of the accused who are now in custody, as well as photographic evidence, indicated that Assefa Maru was shot in the street on the way to his office. According to the testimonies, at least four police teams took part in the assassination-style killing.

Fearing for his safety, the general secretary of the ETA went into voluntary exile after this incident. The ETA's president, Taye Wolde Semayat, started his second year in prison in May, pending the conclusion of his trial on charges of leading an anti-government armed group. The remaining four members of ETA's executive committee also experienced government harassment. Abate Angore, who headed the members' affairs department, was arrested in March 1996 and spent two months in detention for protesting a police raid on ETA premises. On September 21, 1996, he was again arbitrarily detained in the Southern Region when regional authorities found ETA literature with him. He was released in mid-March 1997. ETA reports that as of mid-year at least seventy teachers were held in Arbe Minch because regional authorities suspected them of loyalty to the ETA.

Despite legal provisions requiring only that authorities be notified prior to political meetings and demonstrations, the government restricted freedom of assembly by a de facto permit system, routinely dispersing "illegal" events. In order to obtain an early release, demonstrators detained during protests in Addis Ababa in March and May had to submit written petitions admitting illegal actions and promising not to participate in demonstrations in the future.

The trial of the seventy-two top-ranking officials of the Derg is still pending. It opened in December 1994 with forty-seven defendants before the court and the rest tried in absentia. In February, the special prosecutor stated that his office had brought charges, mainly for the crime of genocide, against a total of 5,198 persons, 2,246 of whom had been in detention by that time for up to five years, while the remaining 2,952 were charged in absentia. In March, three new trials of Derg-era defendants opened before the Federal High Court in Addis Ababa. The new trials immediately ran into delays similar to the ones that marked the first Derg trial. On the other hand, defendants who were to stand trial before regional high courts were still waiting for their trials to start as of this writing. A serious crisis in the Ethiopian judiciary had left federal courts with a backlog of some 70,000 "ordinary cases."

The judiciary remains in deep crisis. The government purged dozens of qualified judges, mainly on political grounds, following the 1991 political change. In addition, the restructuring of the judiciary into federal and regional court systems led to further delays, which were aggravated by the lack of resources and trained personnel. The credibility of the new police force, which the government said would be established under civilian control and made accountable before the law, suffered a serious setback as a result of the reported role of the police in the killing in May 1997 of Assefa Maru. Efforts to establish a human rights commission and ombudsman under the auspices of the Council of Peoples' Representatives have yet to produce tangible results.

The Right to Monitor

The government continued to deny the human rights monitoring Ethiopian Human Rights Council legal status, while refusing to respond to its reports and petitions on behalf of individual victims of alleged abuses, claiming that it was a "political" organization. The organization's bank account was frozen in 1995, although its work from its Addis Ababa office has been tolerated. In December 1996, a group of activists founded a Human Rights League, which, by early November 1997, was also denied status as a legal entity: six board members of the league were among the Oromo leaders detained in November. Two of them, the elederly Hussein Abdi and Beyene Belissa, were reportedly ill-treated in police custody. The Ogaden Human Rights Committee, established in 1995, continued to operate clandestinely following the closure of its office, in Gode, Somali Region, after a night raid in June 1996. It published its reports outside the country. The Oromo Ex-Prisoners For Human Rights group was also forced into hiding but continued to monitor the human rights situation in Oromiya regional state and to publish its reports outside the country.

The International Committee of the Red Cross (ICRC) reported that since the beginning of the year its delegates have been able to conduct visits to an increasing number of detention centers and prisons, to assess detention conditions, and to extend limited assistance to detainees. The ICRC also publicly reported that representations it made to authorities on detention conditions had in various cases led to improvements. For 1996, the ICRC reported that it had visited 6,117 persons held in 129 places of detention in connection with the change of regime in 1991, or for reasons linked to national security, and registered 3,537 new detainees. Human Rights Watch visited Ethiopia in July and August 1997 and met with officials and human rights workers.

The Role of the International Community

The European Union and the World Bank Consultative Group

In December 1996 Ethiopia hosted the meeting of its World Bank-sponsored Consultative Group, the first such meeting held in Africa. Fifteen bilateral and twelve multilateral donors participated, together with a government team headed by Prime Minister Meles Zenawi. Donor delegates applauded Ethiopia's achievements in macroeconomic and structural adjustment programs and urged the government to improve its partnership with civil society through increased dialogue and consultations with groups affected by the economic policies. At the end of the meeting, they pledged over US$2.5 billion in new commitments for the fiscal years 1996/97 through 1998/99.

Reflecting the prevailing inclinations in donor circles, the European commissioner for development and external relations with African, Caribbean, and Pacific countries, Professor Joao de Deus Pinheiro, indicated on February 4, 1997, that the E.U. had increased its grants to Ethiopia, Kenya and Uganda by between 10 and 45 percent. Asked whether E.U. aid was tied to human rights improvements, Pinheiro said one had to be pragmatic in making funding decisions: "You cannot isolate human rights from the basic rights of the citizen to food, shelter, opportunities . . . all these things are important in assessing the progress of a country." According to the ambassador of a major bilateral donor country, high-ranking Ethiopian officials often articulated similar arguments when foreign diplomats raised specific human rights concerns and called for government investigations of reported abuses.

On February 25, 1997, delegations from the World Bank and the European Commission, met to discuss issues concerning a collaborative effort in Africa. The European Commission and World Bank teams agreed to concentrate their efforts on poverty alleviation and private sector development in three countries: Mozambique, Ethiopia, and the Ivory Coast. The E.U.'s development commissioner stressed that growth, the development of human resources, and the reduction of poverty must go hand in hand with respect for human rights, democratic principles, and the rule of law. Despite this, the E.U. and the donor community at large had yet to bring meaningful pressure to encourage Ethiopia to comply with human rights and other good governance benchmarks.

September 18, 1997, the European Parliament passed a resolution condemning human rights violations by Ethiopian security forces, seeking the release of all prisoners of conscience and respect for freedom of the press. The killing of Assefa Maru reportedly jolted the government of the United Kingdom into freezing the renewal of an aid package earmarked for the modernization and training of the police force. When the U.K. later offered a revised version of the agreement, incorporating human rights values in the training and reference to judicial oversight, the Ethiopian side reportedly rejected the training. Diplomatic tensions developed between the two countries when the U.K. pressed in vain for the government to open an independent investigation of the incident. The E.U. and other donors supported preparations sponsored by the Council of Peoples' Representatives to convene an international conference in December 1997 for consultations on the creation of a human rights commission and the office of a human rights ombudsman.

United States

Ethiopia ranked second among recipients of U.S. bilateral economic assistance in Africa in Fiscal Year 1997, with approximately $104.6 million in U.S. aid. Private U.S. trade and investment activities also grew significantly, with some 120 U.S. investors starting operations in the country. Assistance reflected the increasing reliance of the U.S. on Ethiopia as the linchpin of its strategy for the containment of the spread of militant political Islam in the region and the stabilization of Somalia.

The U.S. renewed bilateral military assistance to Ethiopia after the fall of the Derg, providing training in demining, basic soldiering skills, and in the area of military justice. In November 1996, the U.S. announced that it was supplying Ethiopia, Uganda, and Eritrea with military hardware totaling $20 million in a program intended to "contain" Sudan. In late September 1997, a U.S. official stated that the government was going to increase the levels of its military aid to these "front line states," while engaging the government of Sudan in an aggressive dialogue meant to press it into abandoning its support of Islamist groups in the region. Ethiopia was also among the first five countries chosen for U.S. training for peacekeeping within the U.S. initiative known as the African Crisis Response Initiative.

Officials of the Clinton administration rarely used these close economic and strategic ties to press Ethiopia for concrete human rights improvements. The U.S. ambassador to Ethiopia frequently voiced supportive statements on its positive achievements, while remaining largely silent on rights abuses; in contrast, the Department of State's annual country reports on Ethiopia provided fairly accurate descriptions of the state of human rights there. The statement by the then Secretary of State Warren Christopher during his October 1996 visit, in which he called on the Ethiopian government to respect the freedom of the private press and abide by other human rights standards, was a rare and welcome exception to this pattern.

KENYA

Human Rights Developments

Levels of violence steadily rose throughout the year as the early 1998 deadline for elections drew closer. The crisis was precipitated by the government's refusal to enact previously promised reforms to allow genuine political liberalization. National and international pressure increased on President Moi to take steps to address the lack of accountability and corruption that have characterized his nineteen-year rule. President Moi responded with a characteristic combination of recalcitrance and heavy-handed brutality, all the while making promises to bring about change that it failed to be implemented.

Throughout the year, measures to restrict the activities of the political opposition and to undermine a national voter registration process continued. By year's end, the government's actions left grave doubts as to whether a free and fair multiparty election in Kenya was possible. Opposition supporters continued to complain of disruption of their meetings by police or local authorities, as well as the denial of permits to hold meetings by police or local authorities. The National Electoral Commission remained a presidentially-appointed body and was blatantly used by the government to its advantage. By rejecting all but new national identity cards as a basis to receive voter registration cards and denying the new cards to many, the procedure was manipulated to disenfranchise an estimated one million eligible voters. The government continued to ignore or deny registration applications from over a dozen political parties, including Safina, a party formed by top members of the Kenyan opposition in 1995 and heavily attacked by President Moi at the time. The block on registration exacerbated political struggles between factions in the opposition parties since no new parties could be formed. The government continued to curb free speech by not relinquishing its monopoly on the broadcast media, severely restricting the ability of the political opposition to disseminate information, while using the media to promote the ruling party.

By mid-year, a pro-democracy alliance made up of the political opposition, religious, and human rights groups, had organized to call for the repeal of laws (some dating back to the colonial period) that allowed Moi to manipulate the political system to his advantage. Among those that violated international standards included the Preservation of Public Security Act, that allowed indefinite detention without trial and restrictions on freedom of movement; the Public Order Act, that restricted freedom of association; the Defamation Act and Penal Code provisions on sedition, that restricted the right to freedom of expression; and the Societies Act, that restricted registration of associations, including political parties and trade unions.

Peaceful rallies and strikes called by the pro-democracy alliance, the National Convention Executive Council (NCEC), were met with force and in one case resulted in violent protest action. The police brutally dispersed rallies on May 31, July 7, August 8, and October 10. Ultimately, thirteen pro-democracy protesters were killed by police

using teargas, bullets and batons and some 500 people were arrested. During the course of the dispersals, protesters were shot at point-blank range. Police even stormed the Anglican Cathedral where a prayer meeting was underway, tear-gassing and clubbing parishioners. During the August 8 rally, two police were beaten to death by protesters.

Following international and national pressure, President Moi ordered police to stop breaking up the non-violent political protests and promised limited reforms. In the face of the political pressure, the government ordered the attorney-general to issue draft bills to repeal some of the repressive laws and announced the creation of a parliamentary commission to review the constitution and to reevaluate laws used to stifle debate. However, these efforts did not translate into meaningful changes. For instance, the proposed Peaceful Assemblies Bill that was to replace the Public Order Act continued to retain restrictive provisions such as the wide discretionary rights of local government officials to close down meetings. The government also remained firm on its refusal to have any constitutional reform prior to the elections on the grounds that time was short. Opposition leaders said that the proposed reforms did not go far enough and pointed out that constitutional reform had been promised by the government after the last 1992 election. Nonetheless, the pro-democracy alliance suspended its campaign of civil disobedience in August to allow a group of clergymen to mediate. In July, the government announced that it would introduce further legal reforms and set up a commission to look into constitutional reforms.

Kenya's universities continued to be targeted by police in 1997, and a climate of fear and intimidation gripped the universities after four students were killed at three different campuses. On December 17, 1996, Festus Okong'o Etaba, a first-year student at Egerton University, was shot and killed by police during a student demonstration seeking a partial refund of fees. The following day, police shot and killed Kenneth Makokha Mutabi and Eric Kamundi, who were among a group of students at Kenyatta University who had gathered peacefully to mourn the death of Mr. Etaba and to protest the use of lethal force by police against unarmed students. On February 23, Solomon Muruli, a Nairobi University student leader, was killed after a suspicious early morning explosion and fire in his dormitory room. The university was briefly closed by the government in February following a student protest over Muruli's death. The university was again a target of a police raid during the pro-democracy rallies: After breaking up one of them, police raided the university and attacked students at the architecture faculty while they were sitting their exams. The students were beaten and shot and a professor was left unconscious with broken bones. By October, the government had yet to hold anyone responsible for any of these incidents. The deaths of the students were only the most visible and dramatic consequences of a deep crisis at Kenya's universities.

In August, a series of ethnically-driven attacks in the Coast Province killed some forty people and displaced over 120,000. The attacks, by armed gangs from coastal ethnic groups, razed businesses and homes belonging to people from inland tribes. Leaflets were distributed in some areas in which certain groups were attacked which stated "The time has come for us original inhabitants of the coast to claim what is rightly ours. We must remove these invaders from our land." Several people were killed by machetes. The warnings and the attacks were strikingly similar to the "ethnic" violence which had taken place prior to the 1992 elections in the Rift Valley, and targeted some of the same ethnic groups. In those attacks, substantial evidence showed that the Moi government had been behind the attacks against ethnic groups perceived to support the political opposition. Since the violence followed shortly after voter registration ended, some Kenyan human rights activists surmised that the attacks at the coast had been instigated by the government, after voter registration data had indicated that it would lose the coast province. The govern-

ment maintained that the violence was the work of local criminals taking advantage of the volatile political climate. Some 300 arrests were made by the police, including several ruling party members, and strong statements condemning the violence were made by the government. However, by October it was still unclear who was behind the violence, although the gangs had reportedly been organized and trained some months prior to the attacks.

The government continued to consolidate the political gains of the state-sponsored "ethnic" violence of the early 1990s. At that time, some 300,000 people from ethnic groups perceived to support the opposition were driven from their land in large-scale attacks. The government instigated the violence after it was forced to concede to demands for a multiparty system, in order to punish and disenfranchise ethnic groups associated with the opposition, while rewarding its supporters with illegally obtained land. This land, located largely in Rift Valley Province, is in an area which boasts the largest number of parliamentary seats and some of the most fertile land in the country. Throughout the year, local government officials continued to countenance fraudulent land transfers and land sales under duress in Rift Valley Province further entrenching the gains.

Street children in Kenya continued to be the subject of harassment and abuse by Kenyan police. They were subject to frequent arrests and group roundups simply because they were homeless. Although government officials asserted that the children were rounded up with the intention of helping the children, the manner in which the children were treated, both by police and in the institutions where they were housed, belied this. Children were routinely beaten by police and held in station lockups, with adults, for days and even weeks before they were charged and remanded to detention centers for long periods of time pending adjudication of their cases. The complex and outdated legal provisions and enforcement mechanists resulted in the criminalization and mistreatment of street children.

The government continued to use the judiciary for political ends. No progress was made during 1997 by the legal task forces formed by the attorney general in 1993 to amend or repeal repressive legislation. The trial of prominent opposition figure Koigi wa Wamwere and two others on charges of armed robbery continued on appeal, although by January, the government had released them all on bail. The lower court trial which resulted in a prison sentence in 1995 was criticized by local and international human rights and bar organizations for not conforming to international standards.

In July, the Kenyan government cooperated with the International Criminal Tribunal on Rwanda and arrested eighty Rwandan genocide suspects, pending formal application for their extradition. Seven of the arrested Rwandans were indicted by the tribunal on charges of genocide and were handed over by the Kenyan authorities to the tribunal in Arusha, Tanzania. The arrests were significant since those arrested were among the most prominent of the alleged perpetrators that had sought asylum in Kenya, and President Moi had previously stated that he would not cooperate with the tribunal. Unfortunately, the arrests of the seven Rwandans was followed by a sweep of arrests against foreigners in Kenya, including a number of duly recognized refugees. Some were held without charge for short periods in order to extort money.

The Right to Monitor

A wide array of local human rights organizations were engaged in monitoring human rights in Kenya, among others the Catholic Justice and Peace Commission, Center for Governance and Democracy, Concerned Citizens for Constitutional Change, International Commission of Jurists (Kenya), the International Federation of Women Lawyers (FIDA-Kenya), the Kenya Anti-Rape Organization, the Kenya Human Rights Commission (KHRC), the Legal Advice Center, Public Law Institute, and Release Political Prisoners (RPP). The national Council of

Churches of Kenya (NCCK) and the Catholic Church were also outspoken on human rights issues.

In particular, the National Convention Executive Council (NCEC), a pro-democracy alliance, made up of a coalition of religious, human rights and political groups, came under strong government attack in 1997. The demonstrations and rallies organized by the NCEC were forcibly dispersed and the NCEC was heavily criticized by the government for calling for democratic reforms. Two Kenyan television editors were suspended from their jobs from July to October after screening footage of police brutality at the Anglican Cathedral. Two nongovernmental organizations that work with street children reported that their staff members were harassed by Nairobi police for their attempts to help street children (these organizations requested anonymity). One staff member was arrested along with street children during a street sweep.

The government-sponsored Human Rights Committee, formed in May 1996, was virtually silent in the face of human rights abuses in 1997, giving credence to the widespread belief that this body was created merely to offset international criticism of Kenya's record.

The Role of the International Community

Prior to the 1992 elections, Kenya's main donors played a key role in pushing the government to concede to domestic demands for a multiparty system. Since then, donor pressure waned significantly despite continuing human rights abuses in Kenya, and aid was steadily resumed on the basis of economic reforms. In 1997, donors took a more unified public stand around human rights, although they stopped short of placing human rights conditions on donor aid. In a series of joint statements, several donor countries criticized the deteriorating human rights situation in Kenya.

In February, the U.S. and Japan issued a joint statement condemning police brutality against opposition party members. In

April, the U.S., the European Union and Japan condemned inflammatory racist remarks made by senior opposition party members against members of the Kenyan Asian community. The same month, the U.K., U.S., Japan and twelve European embassies issued a joint statement condemning the harassment of opposition leaders and called on the government to "allow political leaders, candidates and all citizens freedom of speech and assembly, which are essential to free and fair elections." In May, twenty-two embassies, including those of all of Kenya's main aid donors, presented a joint position to the Kenyan government that outlined areas of concern including access to the ballot, access to the electorate, access to information, and freedom of assembly. In June, another joint statement was issued that called on the Kenyan government to protect its citizens from violence and to uphold their rights of freedom of expression, assembly and association. In July, in response to the police attacks on peaceful demonstrators, the same alliance condemned the police brutality and called on President Moi to have an "open and frank" dialogue with the opposition.

A Consultative Group meeting of all Kenya's donors scheduled for July 11 to discuss new aid commitments was postponed by the government. By October, no new date had been set. In response to the mounting international criticism, President Moi attacked "foreigners" for telling Kenyans what to do and called on the international pressure to end, stating "they should understand that the country and its people have been pushed far enough."

In July, the International Monetary Fund suspended its Enhanced Structural Adjustment Facility, a U.S. $220 million loan agreement, that had been signed in 1995, because the government had not taken sufficient steps to combat corruption. This was followed by similar action on the part of the World Bank that suspended a $71.6 million Structural Adjustment credit to Kenya pending action on economic reform. Although human rights abuses did not prompt the decisions of the international financial institutions, the suspensions coincided with international censure over the government's brutal crackdown on pro-democracy advocates, and contributed to the mounting pressure for Moi to take steps to reform.

European Union

Following the police brutality against the pro-democracy alliance rallies, the European Parliament adopted a resolution on May 15 urging the European Council and the European Commission to look into the situation. The European Parliament also requested that the government of Kenya find out who was responsible for these attacks and bring them to justice. On July 15, 1997, responding to a question floored by Graham Watson, British MEP, concerning the upcoming elections in Kenya, Commissioner Joao de Deus Pinheiro replied by saying that if the elections were not handled fairly, the European Union might consider cutting aid.

The European Parliament adopted a resolution on July 17 that condemned human rights violations in Kenya. The resolution requested that the Kenyan government stop all forms of repression and violations of the freedom of expression as well as ensuring that the upcoming elections would be held in a fair manner. Commissioner Sir Leon Brittan stated that the European Union (E.U.) was deeply concerned with the worsening situation in Kenya. He also stated that the European Commission was currently discussing these concerns with the Kenyan government with the assistance of the Donor's Democratic Development Group.

Following police brutality at the August 8 pro-democracy rally, the E.U. issued a declaration condemning the violence. The E.U. requested that the groups responsible for the recent outbreaks of violence cease their actions and settle their differences in a peaceful fashion. On September 19, 1997, the European Parliament adopted a resolution stating that it "strongly condemn[s] all incidents of political violence organized by state security forces." This resolution also requested E.U. support to make sure that the forthcoming elections will be conducted in a fair manner. The European Parliament also requested the E.U. to monitor the human rights situation and to provide aid to the refugees in the Mombasa region. This resolution came in the wake of the ethnically-based violence in the Coast Province that left tens of thousands homeless.

United States

The U.S. adopted a notably more firm and public stand on human rights in 1997. This change could be credited largely to the appointment of Ambassador Prudence Bushnell in October 1996, and the importance newly accorded to human rights in both bilateral and multilateral settings. The year was marked by public statements condemning human rights violations. In February, the U.S. Embassy issued a statement deploring the death of student activist Muruli. In July, the U.S. ambassador observed that the preconditions for free and fair elections were not yet in place" and that the government's actions "limit the choice of the people and do not reflect great progress in efforts to strengthen democracy." The State Department also publicly deplored the police brutality and in a strongly-worded statement noted that "[t]he real source of political violence in Kenya is not just the government's unacceptable "strong-arm" tactics, but its failure to take the essential, concrete steps to create a free and fair electoral climate." In August, Ambassador Bushnell stated unequivocally that "the U.S. will not be a silent witness to human rights abuses. We will condemn the use of excessive force. We call on the government and opposition alike to respect the rights guaranteed to Kenyans under their constitution and international conventions."

In July, the Africa Subcommittee of the House International Affairs Committee held hearings on "U.S. Policy Toward Kenya." In August, a bipartisan group of U.S. senators sent a letter to President Moi calling for the government to end the violence and to initiate constitutional review. In 1997, U.S. aid to Kenya totaled U.S. $34 million, including humanitarian aid. Approximately two-thirds of this aid was allocated to program assistance, which was directly almost entirely to nongovernmental organizations.

Relevant Human Rights Watch reports:

Failing the Internally Displaced: The UNDP Displaced Persons Program in Kenya, 6/97
Police Abuse and Detention of Street Children in Kenya, 6/97

LIBERIA

Human Rights Developments

On July 19, 1997, Liberia's seven-year civil war was finally ended through an election that swept former faction leader Charles Taylor and his party, the National Patriotic Party (NPP), into power with 75 percent of the vote. Thousands of Liberians were killed during the war. Almost half the population remained displaced, and the country's infrastructure was virtually destroyed. Despite the presence of regional peacekeepers since 1990, joined by a United Nations (U.N.) military observer mission in October 1993, fighting resumed numerous times in the course of the war, and the number of factions proliferated over the years. All the factions were responsible for terrorizing the local populations in order to loot and to discourage support for rival factions. The widespread atrocities against civilians included extrajudicial executions; torture, including rape; forced labor; and extortion. The factions consisted predominantly of bands of armed fighters, many as young as ten years of age, with no formal military training.

Ultimately, over a dozen peace accords and almost twenty cease-fire agreements were signed during the countless negotiations for peace. The repeated breakdown of the peace process could be attributed to a number of factors including: the creation and support of anti-Taylor factions by the former government army and the regional peacekeeping force; the internal factionalization of existing armed groups on ethnic lines; economic incentives for these groups to continue the war; the regional peacekeepers' lack of adequate leadership, training, and financing; and the failure of the U.N. military observer mission to address the problems in the regional peacekeeping force, the Economic Community of West African States Cease fire Monitoring Group (ECOMOG).

The timetable for disarmament, demobilization, and elections that brought the conflict to an end was agreed to by the factions in August 1996, under the auspices of the Economic Community of West African States (ECOWAS), following an April 1996 killing and looting spree by the factions in Monrovia. According to the peace accord, ECOMOG was to deploy to create a series of safe havens throughout the country beginning on November 7, 1996; disarmament and demobilization of combatants, and repatriation of refugees was to proceed from November 22 through January 21, 1997; and elections were scheduled for May 30, 1997.

Although this timetable was delayed somewhat and not all the objectives were achieved—particularly the return of refugees and the demobilization of combatants—disarmament began on November 22, 1996, and was concluded after a seven-day extension on February 7, 1997. Some 21,315 combatants, including 4,360 children and 250 women, were disarmed out of an estimated total of 33,000. The fighters demobilized ranged from six-year olds to people in their seventies.

The U.N. estimated that some 15,000 to 20,000 children had directly participated in violent acts, were forced to kill or maim, were exposed to fighting, and were themselves brutally victimized. Some fought with factions as a means of survival. The physical and psychological status of these children varied from place to place, but they all shared trauma, uncertainty about their future, insecurity, and above all, a desire to go back to school or to learn some trade. Unfortunately, the demobilization programs for former fighters did not adequately address the needs of child soldiers.

Although not all weapons were turned in and the command structures within the factions remained intact for the most part, the collection of some 10,000 weapons and 1.24 pieces of ammunition resulted in a notable demilitarization of the society. During the last weeks of the voluntary disarmament period, there was a dramatic increase in the numbers of weapons collected, although the factions continued to hoard weapons. Discoveries of hidden weapons continued well after the end of voluntary disarmament, and some 3,750 weapons and 152,500 pieces of ammunition were uncovered shortly before the election through cordon and search operations by ECOMOG.

Due to the short timetable for the implementation of the peace process, little more than confiscation of weapons occurred before the election. Combatants were not systematically given psychological counseling, training or other vocational opportunities, or even transported and integrated into their home communities. The lack of time also led to insufficient resources and planning for long-term demobilization programs. The growing number of armed robberies in the Monrovia area may signal that some of these former fighters were turning to criminal activity.

Following disarmament, preparations for the election proceeded with international oversight, and despite some delays, the election was successfully held on July 19, 1997. The election was certified by the U.N. and ECOWAS, and judged credible by hundreds of international and national observers. Although there were some reports of overzealous West African peacekeepers "helping" voters choose, the casting of the ballots appeared to be generally free of fraud, as did the count.

However, the larger context in which the election was held placed limitations on how free and fair the election could be. The timetable leading up to the election was extremely tight, and a number of the prerequisites agreed to in the peace accord, such as the return of the refugees and the demobilization of soldiers, were not completed prior to the election. As a result, hundreds of thousands of Liberian refugees outside the country were not eligible to vote in the election. Due to the lack of demographic information, the rainy season, and the logistical difficulties of functioning in a war-torn place, the polling stations did not always correspond to population density. The lack of identification papers, a common problem after seven years of chaos, allowed for some minors under the age of eighteen to register. The short time available for civic education was inadequate in light of the high illiteracy rate.

Campaigning resources for the candidates were markedly disparate. Charles Taylor, having controlled and looted the bulk of the country's revenues from logging, diamond and iron ore mines for most of the war, was able to use these vast resources to campaign more effectively—using a helicopter to reach distant areas, monopolizing the broadcast media with looted equipment, transporting voters (including refugees from neighboring countries) to polling sites, and handing out money, rice and tee shirts to voters. Ellen Johnson-Sirleaf, who came in second with 9.6 percent of the vote, had cashed in her pension from her previous U.N. job to raise campaign funds.

Most importantly, the implicit threat that Charles Taylor would resume the fighting if he lost was high on the minds of Liberian voters. Many categorized their vote as "a vote for peace." Others expressed a genuine support for Taylor saying that "he said he would destroy this country and he did. Now he is saying that he will rebuild it and he will."

Of the thirteen parties that contended the election, three were headed by former warring faction leaders. Charles Taylor and his party, the National Patriotic Party (NPP), won 75.3 percent of the vote, followed by Ellen Johnson-Sirleaf and her Unity Party (UP) with 9.6 percent of the vote, and the All Liberian Coalition Party (ALCOP) led by former faction leader Al-Haji Kromah that won 4.0 percent. The other ten candidates

and their parties shared the remaining 11.1 percent. Due to the system of proportional representation used in this election, legislative seats were won by parties on the basis of the percentage of the presidential vote (with a minimum threshold to qualify for a legislative seat). As a result, Charles Taylor's party, the NPP, won 75 percent of the seats in the bicameral legislature.

On August 2, 1997, Charles Taylor was sworn into office. In his victory and inauguration speeches, President Taylor declared his intention to head a government that respected human rights, stating his commitment to an independent judiciary, human rights, respect for the rule of law, and the equal protection of the law, and announcing the creation of a Commission on Human Rights and a Commission on Reconciliation. More significantly, the first set of government appointees did not draw from those in Taylor's faction who were most notorious for committing egregious human rights violations. These announcements served to dispel somewhat the fears harbored by some in Liberia's human rights community—based on the Taylor faction's past record of egregious abuses and conscription of child soldiers.

Close to one million Liberians, mostly rural women and children, remained displaced within and outside the country in 1997. According to the U.N. High Commissioner for Refugees, a mid-year count indicated approximately 500,000 refugees, mostly from Lofa and Nimba counties in northern Liberia, in neighboring African countries: 210,000 in Ivory Coast; 210,000 in Guinea; 13,600 in Sierra Leone; 17,000 in Ghana; and 6,000 in Nigeria. Accurate figures for the internally displaced were not available, but estimates put the numbers of internally displaced in the Monrovia area at between 250,000 to 500,000. Provision of assistance and protection remained a problem, particularly for Liberian refugees in Guinea.

The Right to Monitor

A number of human rights groups functioned relatively freely in Monrovia in 1997, including the Catholic Church's Peace and Justice Commission, the Center for Law and Human Rights Education, the Liberian Human Rights Chapter, the Association of Human Rights Promoters, Liberia Watch for Human Rights, National Human Rights Monitor (NAHRIM), Movement for the Defense of Human Rights (MODHAR), Human Rights Monitor, Liberia Civil and Human Rights Association (LCHRA), Liberia Democracy Watch, Civil Rights Association of Liberian Lawyers (CALL), Fore-runners of Children's Universal Development (FOCUS), Center for Democratic Empowerment, and the Association of Female Lawyers in Liberia (AFELL).

The election of Taylor led to apprehension on the part of some in the human rights community that their activities would be restricted; this had not materialized in the first months of the new government. In the September draft bill for the creation of the governmental Commission for Human Rights, the bill listed a select list of nongovernmental groups from which its commissioners would be drawn from: The National Human Rights Center of Liberia (a coalition group), the National Bar Association, the Liberian Council of Churches, the National Moslem Council and the Press Union of Liberia. While these groups were desirable choices, the exclusion of other nongovernmental organizations which had been outspoken on abuses committed during the civil war by the Taylor faction was questionable.

The Role of the International Community

UNOMIL

In 1993, the U.N. Security Council created the U.N. Observer Mission (UNOMIL) to help supervise and monitor the peace accords in conjunction with ECOMOG. UNOMIL's mandate was to report on ceasefire violations and violations of humanitarian law. In late 1995, UNOMIL was also entrusted with the mandate to "investigate and report to the Secretary-General on violations of human rights..."

Although UNOMIL's initial human rights efforts were minimal throughout, the human rights component of the mission eventually grew from one person to three. The effectiveness of the three human rights officers in Liberia was limited by a lack of resources, the insecurity in the country, the marginalization of the human rights unit within UNOMIL, and the willingness of the international community to dispense with human rights concerns in the search for political solutions. The investigative findings of the human rights team were often not acted upon either by UNOMIL or by the U.N. Secretariat.

Moreover, UNOMIL never actively took on the task of providing international scrutiny of the misconduct of ECOMOG troops—a role that only UNOMIL could have played given the circumstances. Reports of human rights violations by ECOMOG troops were ignored by the U.N. even when brought to the attention of UNOMIL and the U.N. Secretariat by its own human rights unit.

Following the election, UNOMIL was deemed to have fulfilled its mandate and most of the staff departed. Nine UNOMIL military observers remained until the end of September to assist in sorting and classifying the 10,000 weapons and 1.24 million pieces of ammunition that were taken during the demobilization process.

The U.N. sought agreement with President Taylor for a small U.N. political office to be created, following the withdrawal of UNOMIL, to serve as a focal point for post-conflict peace-building activities of the United Nations in Liberia and have overall authority for coordination of the U.N. system in the country. The proposed role for this U.N. office, which was still under negotiation in late October, was to provide advisory assistance to the government in defining post-conflict priorities, the mobilization of international funds for Liberia, and to coordinate and liaise between the government and the international community.

ECOMOG

Since the beginning of the fighting in Liberia, the West African peacekeeping force ECOMOG has consistently played a role— as a ground breaking example of regional initiatives at times and a troublesome contributor to the violence and lawlessness at others. The poor conduct of ECOMOG during the April 1996 fighting contributed to the decision to assign a new Nigerian field commander, Maj. Gen. Victor Malu, and to rotate out many of the troops. The introduction of qualified leadership as well as regular payment of salaries to the ECOMOG troops improved the levels of professionalism and public confidence in the West African peacekeeping force in 1997. From the end of 1996 until the election, ECOMOG played a critical role in ending the civil war by supervising the disarmament and electoral processes.

Following the election, ECOMOG's mandate was extended until January 1998 to allow ECOMOG to "help consolidate and strengthen security in the country, and to assist with the restructuring and training of the Armed Forces of Liberia, as well as the police and security services." Due to ECOMOG's history in Liberia, this was an area of major concern. Although Maj. Gen. Malu's appointment as the force commander led to a much higher level of professionalism, reports of abuse by ECOMOG troops continued in 1997. ECOMOG's actions in cordon and search operations during the demobilization process raised concerns over the serious human rights violations that were reported. ECOMOG engaged in arrests and detention without due process and beatings and torture of those in their custody; in at least two cases men died in custody. Both were seized on suspicion of hoarding weapons.

European Union

The European Union (E.U.), through the European Commission's Aid Coordination Office in Liberia, continued to provide the country with assistance in the fragile transition period. The E.U. focused not only on immediate assistance needs, such as clean water, but also on the process of post-war reconstruction, including support for retraining of ex-combatants, the transportation of returning refugees, and the electoral process.

The European Commission program plans following the election focused on assistance to civil society and education, with significant E.U. funding available because the allocated funds for Liberia had accumulated unspent during the seven year war. E.U. representatives in Monrovia stated that respect for human rights was to be an important factor in their decision-making process to provide aid. However, the benchmarks to condition aid to human rights needed to be further articulated.

United States

The U.S. remained a significant contributor to Liberia, providing close to U.S. $100 million in assistance in 1997, including approximately $30 million to ECOMOG, $30 to 50 million in humanitarian assistance, and $9 million for elections. Having assisted with the training of 500 police by the International Criminal Investigation Training Assistance Program (ICITAP) for the July 19 elections, the U.S. committed to continue assistance to the rebuilding of the Liberian National Police and the judiciary, through ICITAP. However, in September, the U.S. suspended its police training program following the appointment of NPFL-stalwart Joe Tate, who was notorious for his lack of respect for the rule of law as police commissioner under the previous Transitional Government.

Through its Agency for International Development (USAID), the U.S. developed a plan to participate in Liberia's redevelopment conditioned on a number of factors, including good governance and human rights. According to the State Department, human rights indicators were considered in the decision-making process to provide aid to the Taylor government. As with the E.U., the benchmarks to condition continued aid to human rights needed to be further articulated.

Relevant Human Rights Watch report:
Emerging from the Destruction: Human Rights Challenges Facing the New Liberian Government, 11/97

MOZAMBIQUE

Human Rights Developments

Human rights practices continued to improve in many parts of the country. However, human rights concerns remained, including restrictions on the rights to freedoms of expression and movement by the former armed opposition, Mozambique National Resistance (RENAMO), heavy-handed policing, and appalling prison conditions.

Over 146 police were expelled from the police force in the capital, Maputo, alone in 1997, many for serious breaches of the police disciplinary code, such as drunkenness on duty and prolonged abandonment of their posts. A small number were accused of violence against civilians, extortion and contraband trading, including trade in light weapons. Police brutality more commonly went unpunished. For example Azarias Estevâo Piquei was badly beaten up by police in Maputo's suburb of George Dimitrov by three police from the police's fifteenth precinct when he refused to pay a bribe; Manuel Mateus suffered serious head injuries from police from the same police station on the same day. To date no prosecution of the police involved has taken place.

Police treatment of suspects in the capital appeared to have improved following President Chissano's dismissal in November 1996 of Interior Minister Manuel António and his deputy Edmundo Alberto and the appointment of the new minister, Almerino Manhenje. The change followed repeated scandals, and intense pressure on the president from the media, civil society, and foreign donors to dismiss António. Remarks by António in January 1996 that the deaths by starvation of prisoners in Interior Ministry cells were "their own fault" caused a particu-

lar outcry. One of the first actions by the new interior minister was on December 4 to attend a training course for 750 police officers at which he issued a blistering attack on corruption and abuse of power in the police force. Manhenje singled out several police precincts in Maputo for criticism, including the thirteenth and fifteenth. A fact-finding visit by Human Rights Watch in March, to seven police stations in Maputo, found that assault, the treatment of suspects, and the conditions in which remand prisoners were held had improved.

On January 30 Maputo City Court sentenced four policeman to seven year jail terms on charges of manslaughter for their part in torturing a suspect to death in June 1996. The victim, Frenque Tchembene, had been accused of stealing a Toyota Hilux. Police from Maputo's seventh precinct detained him on June 2, 1996, and at the station tried to beat him into revealing the whereabouts of the vehicle. Tchembene's wife, Mauharawa Hamido, witnessed this and was beaten herself. The intervention of the Mozambican Human Rights League (LDH) resulted in the police sending Tchembene to hospital, but he died there of injuries sustained while in police custody.

From late December, newly trained policemen were seen patrolling parts of Maputo particularly prone to crime, areas a few months earlier consciously avoided by the police. Police behavior remained a serious concern outside Maputo and was the source of the majority of complaints Human Rights Watch/Africa received from Mozambique in 1997. Arbitrary detention, torture and extortion were common allegations.

In May RENAMO engaged in a series of angry demonstrations around the country, protesting at alleged "misgovernment" and the cost of living. In Beira demonstrations on May 5 and 12 ended with riot police using tear gas and arresting thirty-one RENAMO protesters for illegally demonstrating without a permit. On May 15 in Chimoio police dispersed a crowd of fifty people before a march had begun. Six people were injured, two of them seriously. Two people were arrested.

Prison conditions remained a source of grave concern. Abuse in prison was largely due to overcrowding and lack of food and medical attention, but prisoners regularly reported police beatings, rape, and demands of money in exchange for freedom or food. Chimoio's provincial prison, "Cabeça do Velho," the scene of appalling conditions and deaths in 1995 and 1996, attracted public attention again in 1997 for its poor conditions. Following the appointment of a new interior minister in November, the conditions of the ministry's jails improved, although they still suffered from shortages of food, poor hygiene, and over-crowding. The Ministry of Justice began an initiative in its jails in Sofala, central Zambézia, and Manica provinces whereby prisoners were given their own plots of land to cultivate food crops and in Quelimane prisoners were contracted out as laborers to local businesses.

In January the LDH found that despite its formal agreement with the Ministry of Interior on prison access police demanded bribes to allow one of its lawyers to visit detainees in Beira's police cells. The LDH entered a cell with an official capacity of nineteen people, in which sixty-seven prisoners were held. Hygiene was poor. Those prisoners with relatives looking after their needs had plastic bags in which to defecate and bottles in which to urinate; others used the floor. Sofala Provincial Attorney Nazarinho Mourinho visited several prisons in Beira run by the Interior Ministry in December 1996 and concluded that they did not meet the minimum conditions for accommodating human beings. Mourinho also discovered many children under the age of sixteen in the cells, although under Mozambican law the civil responsibility for crimes committed by minors falls on their parents or guardians and international standards do not permit minors to be held with adults.

RENAMO continued to rule some areas it controlled at the end of the war five years ago, and to exclude government officials from conducting their duties, although the extent of its control declined significantly from 1996. In Maringue, RENAMO's headquarters during the war, the ruling Front for the Liberation of Mozambique (FRELIMO), first secretary, Albertino Sandeangane, reported in February that RENAMO had threatened to attack him and his staff, to destroy his office, and to burn his party's flag. In Inhaminga, in the central province of Sofala, armed and uniformed men belonging to RENAMO's "presidential guard" interfered with police work and intimidated local residents. The district police commander, Alves Joâo, accused RENAMO supporters of forcing him to release suspects even before investigations were underway by threatening to beat him and his men up. Chazuco Jojo, the newly nominated administrator of Inhaminga claimed in July that members of this armed RENAMO force continued to restrict movement in the area, while subjecting residents they suspected of having FRELIMO sympathies in Cheringoma municipality to beatings. In the municipalities of Muembe and Mavago in Niassa province, RENAMO reportedly prevented people from leaving, sometimes by force.

RENAMO alleged that its officials have been harassed by local government officials and FRELIMO members in some areas. In Inhangoma locality at a political rally the local administrator reportedly pointed a pistol at the head of the local chief, a RENAMO member, and forced him to repeat insults about RENAMO. There were also reports that civil servants in Tete who were members or supporters of RENAMO were systematically harassed because of their political affiliation.

Accountability for human rights abuses during the 1977 to 1992 civil war continued to be discussed in the media, but both FRELIMO, RENAMO and many church and traditional religion groups continued to advocate impunity, arguing that this made possible healing and reconciliation at the local level through healing ceremonies and other rituals.

Landmines in Mozambique have claimed some 10,000 victims: more than 1,000 people have been injured by mines since the October 1992 peace accord. Landmines constitute one of the most immediate obstacles to postwar redevelopment, and hinder delivery of relief aid, resettlement, and agricultural and commercial reconstruction. Human Rights Watch believes that the frequently cited U.N. estimate of two million mines in Mozambique is too high, with the real total in the tens or hundreds of thousands. But the number of mines was not the measure of the problem. Mozambique clearly has a problem that threatens civilians daily and is curtailing economic reconstruction. A limited number of mines have continued to be planted since the peace accord, by both government and RENAMO forces, in some cases simply to wage local vendettas. Bandit groups, criminals and poachers have also used mines.

President Chissano announced in October 1995 that Mozambique was prepared to head an international campaign against antipersonnel mines, but little concrete action was taken for the next year and one-half as the Mozambican military wanted to retain the option of using landmines. However, as Maputo's hosting in February of the 4th International NGO Conference on Landmines approached, the greatly increased attention to the issue domestically, regionally and internationally spurred a policy decision. On February 26, Mozambique's foreign minister addressed the four-day conference and announced an immediate ban on the use, production, import and export of antipersonnel mines. Destruction of Mozambique's stockpile was not addressed.

Throughout 1997 there were localized incidents of banditry, especially along the Zimbabwean border in the Sussundenga, Mossurize and Barue municipalities. The government announced that between November 1995 and November 1996 its police discovered fifty arms caches, collecting more than 1,000 guns and hundreds of mines and grenades. They also reported that in the same period they "neutralized" 214 bands of robbers and recovered 105 cows and 337 cars. Press reports of the discovery of new arms caches appear weekly. Destroying the arms caches left over from the war became a priority issue for meetings between President Chissano and RENAMO leader Afonso Dhlakama. Both men were concerned about the dangers of bands of men outside their control carrying landmines. In December 1996 they agreed to set up a working group, with members appointed by the government and RENAMO to deal with the dismantling of arms caches. Clandestine shipments of weapons were also reported to have transited Mozambique in November 1996 through Nacala port to an unknown destination. The Institute for Security Studies in Pretoria witnessed weapons being unloaded there, stored, and then transferred onto South African-registered light aircraft. This arms and contraband pipeline was run by Portuguese businessmen resident in South Africa and appeared to have had links with senior officials in Mozambique. Although the government publicly denied such a trade occurred, Human Rights Watch was told privately by officials that an official investigation is underway.

The Right to Monitor

The Mozambican Human Rights League (LDH) was instrumental in bringing a criminal complaint against six police involved in the torture and manslaughter of Frenque Tchembene which resulted in a seven year prison sentence for the six in January. The LDH also played an important role in campaigning for the removal of Interior Minister Manuel António in November 1996. The LDH's work remained mainly Maputo-focused but it attempted to expand its scope to other provinces during the year.

In conjunction with the Commonwealth Non-governmental Office for South Africa and Mozambique, the LDH held a conference in Maputo in April on the role of parliamentarians in the promotion and defense of human rights.

The Association for the Defence of Human Rights (ADDH) visited some prisons in Maputo in 1997 and wrote several letters to the press. The Order of Lawyers of Mozambique (OLM) lobbied for higher standards for the legal profession and a redefinition of the national standards for accreditation as an attorney. In September UNESCO held an international conference in Maputo on the Culture of Peace and Good Governance. The conference attracted widespread media interest especially over the rights of the child and the fate of child combatants.

The Mozambican Campaign to Ban Landmines (CMCM) also obtained a high media profile before and after the Maputo-held 4th International NGO Conference to Ban Landmines in February and presented to President Chissano its petition of over 100,000 signatures in support of a total ban. During the Oslo summit in September, to prepare the Ottawa treaty, the CMCM mobilized 500 people to demonstrate outside the U.S. embassy in Maputo to lobby against the U.S. position for exclusion and exemption clauses to be added to the Ottawa draft treaty.

The Role of the International Community

European Union, United Nations and the World Bank

The World Bank's Consultative Group on Mozambique (the Paris Club) confirmed pledges worth more than U.S.$ 560 million in new loans to the government in July. Although donors raised concerns about the growth of corruption and drug trafficking in Mozambique they remained generally supportive of the post-election government. Crime and police behavior was a major donor pre-occupation. The Swiss government had threatened to cut aid unless the government made serious efforts to cut crime. On November 12, 1996, following the firing of Interior Minister António, the Swiss embassy in Maputo announced that it would not go ahead with aid cuts. The German, Netherlands and Spanish governments pledged over $10 million for a police training program, coordinated by the United Nations Development Program (UNDP), although

by late 1997 this program was not operational.

On February 25, delegations from the World Bank and the European Commission met to discuss issues concerning a collaborative effort in Africa. The European Commission team, headed by the European Commissioner for Development and External relations with Africa, the Caribbean and the Pacific (ACP) countries, Professor João de Deus Pinheiro, and the World Bank team, headed by the World Bank regional vice-president for Africa, Mr. Jean-Louis Sarbib, agreed to concentrate their efforts on poverty alleviation and private sector development in three countries: Mozambique, Ethiopia, and in Ivory Coast. They also decided that their upcoming meetings should be held in the three African countries mentioned above to encourage more participation on their part.

United States

Bilateral U.S.-Mozambican relations improved generally. The new U.S. ambassador designate to Maputo, Dean Curran was sworn in on November 7, sixteen months after he was first nominated following the departure of Dennis Jett, but this had little to do with bilateral relations. The departure of Dennis Jett as U.S. ambassador to Mozambique in July 1996 ended the U.S. embassy policy of boosting RENAMO's image, aimed at trying to improve their confidence in the peace process. The *State Department's Country Reports on Human Rights Practices for 1996* was more balanced.

Total U.S. aid to Mozambique in 1997 was estimated at U.S.$ 51 million making it one of the main international donors. The U.S. also renewed Title 3DO480 food aid worth U.S. $ 4 million after several years suspension because of a diversion scandal (Eritrea, Ethiopia and Haiti were the other recipients of this total package of U.S. $30 million in food aid in 1997).

U.S. administration visits to Mozambique were kept at deputy assistant secretary level and included a visit from the department of the treasury during the year.

The Clinton administration demonstrated its continued interest in Mozambique in April by arranging a drop-by meeting by Secretary of State Madeleine Albright with President Chissano in Washington during a meeting he had with the deputy-assistant secretary for African Affairs.

NIGERIA

Human Rights Developments

Arbitrary detentions, torture, summary executions, censorship and, perhaps most fundamentally, denial of the right of the Nigerian people to choose their own government continued under Gen. Sani Abacha's military government. A program of transition to civilian rule announced on October 1, 1995, and due to culminate in a transfer of power to an elected federal government on October 1, 1998, remained in place, but state governorship and assembly elections were postponed by several months. Local government elections held in March were neither free nor fair. Two of the five officially registered political parties declared that General Abacha was their preferred candidate for president; possible alternative candidates for the other three withdrew following intimidation or arrest, and a public campaign for Abacha to succeed himself was sponsored by a number of nominally independent groups. A draft constitution prepared in 1995 in a process under military control, to come into effect with the end of the transition program, was still not published, leaving Nigerians in the dark as to the future form of the government for which they were supposed to be voting. Chief Moshood K.O. Abiola, the presumed winner of the June 12, 1993 elections, annulled by the military, remained in prison for his third year.

Opposition activists were harassed, jailed, or driven into exile—or threatened with indefinite detention or summary execution should they return from abroad. In March, exiled Nobel Prize winner and outspoken critic of the government Wole Soyinka was charged with treason, together with fifteen others, of whom twelve were held in detention inside Nigeria. A series of bomb blasts apparently directed at members of the military government was cited as the basis for the charges. Soyinka and the others, including Chief Anthony Enahoro, leader of the National Democratic Coalition (NADECO) formed from the remnants of Abiola's banned Social Democratic Party, denied involvement, and the government offered no evidence that any of them were involved. Cases involving treason, a capital offense, are tried before a military tribunal, without right of appeal. Bail was denied for those held in the country, who remained in detention as of this writing. Chief Olabiyi Durojaiye, a NADECO leader arrested in December 1996, was detained without charge, despite court orders for his release. Those convicted in 1995 of involvement in an alleged coup plot, including four journalists and pro-democracy campaigners such as Beko Ransome-Kuti, also remained incarcerated. Ransome-Kuti was refused permission to attend the funeral of his brother, Fela Kuti, the great Nigerian musician and thorn in the side of successive military regimes, who died on August 2.

Decrees suspending constitutional protections of citizens' rights, allowing detention without trial and criminalizing criticism of the government or its policies, remained in force The courts remained barred from inquiring into the legality of detentions without trial or examining government actions.

Chief Gani Fawehinmi, human rights lawyer and leader of the National Conscience Party, Femi Aborisade, his deputy, and human rights lawyer Femi Falana, all detained without charge in January and February 1996, were released in November 1996. A number of activists were held for shorter periods during 1997, including Tunji Abayomi, director of Human Rights Africa, who was held for three days during August.

Although one of the strongest in Africa, the independent press remained under threat. In January, Minister of Information Walter Ofonogoro announced the government's intention to set up a press court that would try journalists who "report untruths" and to enforce Decree No. 43 of 1993 requiring newspapers to apply annually for publishing licenses. This threat was repeated at intervals throughout the year, encouraging self-censorship. The government was particularly sensitive to events relating to NADECO or detained presidential candidate Moshood Abiola: for example, armed policemen prevented an anticipated press conference to mark Abiola's August 24 birthday, and on August 30, guests were turned back by police from the planned launch of a book, *Abiola, Democracy and the Rule of Law*, by journalist Richard Akinola.

Individual journalists faced harassment of various kinds, ranging from a requirement to complete forms indicating the purpose of their travel if they left the country, to intimidation and arrest. Ladi Olorunyomi, journalist and wife of exiled journalist Dapo Olorunyomi, was detained for six weeks from March 20. In February 1997, Moshood Ademola Fayemiwo, the publisher of the defunct *Razor* magazine, was detained by Nigerian agents in the Benin Republic and moved to Lagos, where he was still held as of this writing. Godwin Agboroko, editor of the *Week* magazine, was detained from December 1996 to May 7, 1997; George Onah, journalist with the *Vanguard*, was released on May 14 after a year in detention. Many other journalists were detained for shorter periods and often beaten. In July, the editor of the Owerri-based newspaper the *Horn*, Oni Egbunine, was arrested by soldiers and beaten into a coma. In the same month, Edetean Ojo of the *Guardian* daily newspaper was prevented from traveling to a conference in Kenya. The broadcast media remained under virtual government monopoly, although some opposition radio stations broadcast on short wave from outside the country.

Meetings and rallies organized by human rights or pro-democracy groups were routinely disrupted by members of the security services. Rallies to mark the anniversary of the June 12, 1993 elections were banned, and those that went ahead anyway were disrupted by the large security force contingents deployed for the occasion. In September 1997, a farewell party arranged by human rights groups for the outgoing U.S. ambassador, Walter Carrington, was broken up by security police. Union activities continued to be restricted, in particular in the oil sector and on university campuses. Frank Ovie Kokori, secretary-general of NUPENG, the National Union of Petroleum and Natural Gas Workers, held since August 1994, and Milton Dabibi, secretary-general of PENGASSAN, the Petroleum and Natural Gas Senior Staff Association of Nigeria, held since January 1996, remained incarcerated. NUPENG and PENGASSAN continued to be controlled by government-appointed sole administrators, as did the umbrella organization, the Nigerian Labour Congress, to which all unions are compulsorily affiliated. Labour leaders involved in a strike by civil servants in Kaduna were detained in June. The Academic Staff Union of Universities (ASUU) remained banned. In April, a new decree banned the Nigerian Labour Congress and its member unions from affiliating with the International Labour Organization. Shiite leader Sheikh El Zak-Zaky, detained in September 1996, was charged in July 1997 with publication of materials capable of undermining the security of the nation. He was not produced in court and remained in prison.

March local government elections were marked by numerous irregularities. Those eligible to vote were coerced into registering by threats of reprisals—such as exclusion of children from school—in case of refusal to participate. Candidates were screened by the National Electoral Commission of Nigeria (NECON), by the State Security Service, and by the National Drug Law Enforcement Agency. In this process, any candidate with connections to pro-democracy, human rights or opposition groups was excluded. Tribunals sitting to decide winners in constituencies where election results were contested often ruled in favor of the candidate paying the largest bribe, rather than on the merits of the case. Some local government chairs were forced to stand down "on security grounds" after their election had been confirmed. A new decree was promulgated allowing the head of state to remove the chairs of local government councils at will. In a number of cases, decisions by NECON, supposedly an independent body, regarding the election process were directly overruled by the military.

Nigerian citizens not actively involved in politics also faced a consistent pattern of human rights violations. The security forces carried out summary executions and torture, while prison conditions remained life threatening. Different state governments operated special task forces with names like "Operation Sweep" or "Operation Storm" that were supposedly aimed at cracking down on criminal activity. These task forces were amongst the most abusive units of the Nigerian security forces. Many of those arrested by these units were convicted of "armed robbery" before special tribunals which did not respect international standards; those found guilty were executed by firing squad without the right to appeal. Tens and possibly hundreds were arbitrarily executed in this way.

In Ogoniland, home of the Movement for the Survival of the Ogoni People (MOSOP), of which Ken Saro-Wiwa was leader before his execution in November 1995, severe repression continued during 1997. Nineteen Ogonis remained in prison facing charges of murder before a special tribunal in connection with the same events as those for which Saro-Wiwa and eight others were killed. A previously unknown twentieth defendant in the case, detained at a different location for two years, joined those held in Port Harcourt prison. There was no progress in their case, and their health steadily deteriorated. A number of others suspected of sympathy for MOSOP were extrajudicially executed in Ogoniland; others were detained without trial.

Elsewhere in the oil-producing areas of the Niger Delta, police and soldiers responded to any threat of protest against oil company activity with arbitrary arrests, beatings and sometimes killings. From March to May, serious ethnic violence erupted in the oil town of Warri, Delta State, over the relocation of a new local government headquarters by the military administrator of the state. In the course of the crisis a number of Shell flow stations were occupied by youths, and Shell personnel were held hostage for several days. Hundreds of youths were detained for several weeks in connection with the violence; an unknown number were killed by security forces suppressing the disturbances. The decision of the military administrator of Osun State to relocate another local government headquarters also led to violence in Ile Ife in August 1997 in which tens of residents died. In other states, government decisions led to similar but less serious clashes.

The Right to Monitor

Nigeria's numerous and sophisticated human rights groups continued their monitoring, advocacy and education activities throughout the year, despite routine harassment by the authorities. Officers of the State Security Service (SSS) regularly visited the offices of human rights organizations to intimidate staff, destroy property and confiscate publications; human rights activists were detained on a number of occasions; others were prevented from traveling abroad to attend international gatherings at which Nigeria was to be discussed. The government-appointed National Human Rights Commission, created in 1996, held or attended a number of noncontroversial meetings, but failed to make any serious criticism of ongoing human rights violations.

The Role of the
International Community

The Commonwealth

The Commonwealth Ministerial Action Group (CMAG) appointed by the Commonwealth Heads of Government Meeting (CHOGM) in November 1995 met several times during 1997. In July, CMAG held hearings on the situation in Nigeria, to which

Nigerian human rights and opposition groups were invited to make submissions, as were international groups including Human Rights Watch. CHOGM, a biannual gathering that met at the end of October 1997, considered Nigeria's suspension from the Commonwealth, imposed in 1995, and the continuing mandate of CMAG. As expected, CHOGM decided to continue the suspension but not to expel Nigeria. The mandate of CMAG was also extended.

United Nations

The U.N. Commission on Human Rights adopted a resolution in April 1996 in which it requested two thematic special rapporteurs (on the independence of judges and lawyers and on extrajudicial, summary or arbitrary executions) to submit a report at the next session of the commission in 1997. Extended negotiations with the Nigerian government for the special rapporteurs to undertake a mission to Nigeria finally collapsed shortly before the 1997 session, due to the Nigerian government's failure to agree to their standard terms of reference, and the special rapporteurs eventually published a report on the basis of information supplied by other organizations. The hard-hitting report concluded that, among other things, "the rule of law is on the verge of collapse, if it has not already collapsed" and that Nigeria was in violation of a number of its international obligations. The report made a series of recommendations, including for the appointment of a country-specific rapporteur on Nigeria by the commission. On April 7, the commission adopted a resolution expressing its deep concern at continuing human rights violations in Nigeria and inviting the chair of the commission to appoint a special rapporteur on Nigeria. Soli Sorabjee, former attorney general of India, was appointed to the position in October 1997.

European Union and its Member States

Sanctions imposed by the European Union (E.U.) following the November 1995 executions of Ken Saro-Wiwa and eight other human rights activists, renewable on a six-monthly basis, remained in force during 1997, but no moves were made to strengthen these measures. A number of resolutions and measures on Nigeria were adopted by E.U. structures during the year, including by the European Parliament and the General Affairs Council.

In March, E.U. Council President Mr. Pronk expressed the view that relations between the E.U. and Nigeria had worsened on a political level. At the same time, the Netherlands, holding the presidency of the E.U., invited Nigeria to attend a meeting in Maastricht of the ACP-E.U. Joint Assembly, bringing together parliamentarians from the E.U. and the African-Caribbean-Pacific (ACP) countries. The European Parliament objected to the invitation, protesting that the invitation broke E.U. sanctions on Nigeria. The Dutch foreign ministry said that the visa restrictions only applied to "Nigerian authorities traveling to Europe for private reasons." The Joint Assembly adopted a resolution condemning the human rights situation in Nigeria and calling on the European Council to impose an oil embargo on Nigeria and to freeze the financial assets held in the E.U. by members of the Nigerian Government. The assembly also reaffirmed the need for a total ban of arms exports to the country and for E.U. Member States not to grant visas to members of the Nigerian Government. The Joint Assembly did, however, approve humanitarian aid to be sent to the most vulnerable groups and those worst affected by sanctions.

Following May elections in the United Kingdom, the new Labour government immediately began to take a much stronger line on Nigeria than the Conservatives had done. Foreign Secretary Robin Cook stated that human rights would dominate British policy concerning Nigeria and that strict sanctions should be imposed on Nigeria. On June 25, 1997, he lashed out against Nigeria saying that, "Nothing has happened in Nigeria to justify lifting the suspension." A new French government, however, resisted attempts to isolate Nigeria, and granted visas to a number of members of the Nigerian government, apparently in violation of E.U. sanctions.

Organization of African Unity and its Member States

African countries were in general reluctant to condemn Nigeria's human rights record in strong terms. Nevertheless, the intransigent position of Nigeria towards the U.N. special rapporteurs did lead to sufficient irritation in the African group at the U.N. Commission on Human Rights for South Africa and Uganda to vote for the resolution appointing a special rapporteur on Nigeria and most of the other African members to abstain. African countries also supported the ACP-E.U. Joint Assembly resolution calling for an oil embargo on Nigeria.

South Africa took a somewhat stronger line toward Nigeria during 1997 but continued to give contradictory signals. After South Africa made some comments supportive of respect for human rights in Nigeria and backed the appointment of a U.N. special rapporteur the Nigerian minister of information, Pfonagora, responded by referring to South Africa as "a white country with a black head," accusing unnamed western countries of "driving a wedge" between South Africa and Nigeria in order to weaken the continent. Yet, though President Mandela called the statement "unfortunate and ill-informed," he emphasized the "brotherly cooperation" with Nigeria over regional mediation efforts in the former Zaire. Ofonagoro later claimed to have been misquoted by the press. In September, Nigerian Foreign Minister Tom Ikimi met with Mandela and delivered a private letter from Gen. Abacha; South African Deputy President Thabo Mbeki was due to visit Nigeria before the end of the year.

Following a military coup in Sierra Leone in May led by army officer John Koroma, in which the elected government of Ahmed Tejan Kabbah was overthrown and Koroma was installed as president, Nigeria led an effort by the Economic Community of West African States (ECOWAS) Monitoring Group (ECOMOG) to reinstate the previous government. The intervention led—as apparently had been intended—to statements of support from the secretary-general of the Organization of African Unity (OAU), Salim Ahmed Salim, as well as many individual African (and western) states and Commonwealth Secretary-General Emeka Anyaoku. However, Nigeria's favored military solution was rejected in August by a meeting of ECOWAS heads of state, at which Ghana, Guinea and Côte d'Ivoire opposed Nigeria and successfully argued for the imposition of sanctions on Sierra Leone instead. Several hundred civilians were killed in the Sierra Leonean capital, Freetown, some of them in indiscriminate shelling by Nigerian forces.

The African Commission on Human and Peoples' Rights, an organ of the OAU, sent a fact-finding mission to Nigeria in March 1997. The mission took place at the time that the U.N. special rapporteurs were (unsuccessfully) negotiating their own entry to Nigeria, and the commission did not itself insist on similar terms of reference. The mission agenda was organized by the Nigerian government, and its members were criticized by Nigerian human rights organizations for failing to allocate sufficient time to meet with human rights and pro-democracy groups to obtain information about human rights abuses. The delegates did not visit any of the political detainees held by the Nigerian government other than the "Ogoni 20," who were not individually interviewed in private. The mission did not submit a written report to the April 1997 session of the commission, though one was expected at the following session in November.

United States

The section on Nigeria in the Department of State's *Country Reports on Human Rights Practices for 1996* was thorough and accurate, existing measures to press Nigeria to respect human rights remained in place, and the U.S. issued strong statements condemning military rule and human rights violations. No further concrete measures to put pressure on the Nigerian government were adopted or proposed. At various points during the year, the Clinton administration indicated that it was reviewing its Nigeria policy. No conclusion was announced to this review and it was stated that the government's commitment to human rights and democracy in Nigeria remained firm; nevertheless, there were some worrisome indications that the U.S. government might be prepared to make concessions in these areas in return for access to the Nigerian government to discuss "technical" issues relating to drug trafficking and civil aviation. For the fourth time, Nigeria was denied counter-narcotics certification under Section 481 of the Foreign Assistance Act (FAA), thus requiring the U.S. to vote against Nigeria in six multilateral development banks, including the International Bank for Reconstruction and Development and the African Development Bank and to refuse all FAA and Arms Control Export Act assistance to Nigeria. Direct flights to Nigeria remained banned due to safety concerns.

A draft "Nigeria Democracy Act" first introduced in November 1995 was reintroduced in Congress in June 1997 by Representative Donald Payne, proposing further sanctions, including a ban on air links and on new investment in the energy sector and a freeze on assets of members of the Nigerian government held in the U.S. In September, the House Committee on International Relations held hearings on U.S. policy toward Nigeria. The U.S. remained by far the largest importer of Nigerian oil, taking about 40 to 50 percent of its output, and any international steps taken towards an oil embargo therefore depended on U.S. action and cooperation.

A number of U.S. cities adopted resolutions preventing purchase from suppliers with businesses in Nigeria (affecting in particular U.S. oil companies Mobil and Chevron), and in June a conference of mayors meeting in San Francisco adopted a resolution welcoming such measures in support of democracy in Nigeria. Independent missions to Nigeria by ex-president Jimmy Carter and especially by the American Baptist Convention were criticized by Nigerian human

rights groups for taking at face value the government's stated intentions to restore Nigeria to democratic government. A thirty-eight member monitoring team sponsored by U.S. groups observed the March local government elections but failed to denounce any of the multiple defects of the transition process. The Nigerian government continued to launder its image in the U.S. with a high profile lobbying campaign.

Relevant Human Rights Watch report:
Transition or Travesty? Nigeria's Endless Process to Return to Civilian Rule, 10/97

RWANDA

Human Rights Developments

In late 1996, the Rwandan government sent its soldiers across the border into eastern Democratic Republic of Congo (DRC) to empty camps that sheltered more than one million Rwandans. In the months that followed, Rwandan troops and their Congolese allies chased down camp residents who fled west across DRC, killing thousands of noncombatants as well as the soldiers and militia accompanying them. During 1997 the government of Rwanda launched other military operations within its own frontiers that killed thousands more unarmed civilians as it tried to put down a growing insurgency.

As in prior years, Rwandan authorities professed adherence to international human rights standards and claimed that civilian killings were the unintended consequence of operations justified by the needs of self-defense. They failed, however, to act effectively to punish violators or to halt abuses.

The insurgents, based largely in Rwanda after the camps were closed, also killed civilians by the hundreds as well as attacking government soldiers. With no publicly acknowledged political leadership, they escaped sanction by the international community, whose one effort to halt their violence—an arms embargo imposed in 1994—

was poorly enforced.

Some 6,000 civilians were killed in the first nine months of 1997, the majority by the Rwandan Patriotic Army (RPA), the rest by insurgents or by assailants whose affiliation was unclear. This death toll represents nearly a four-fold increase over the previous year, when the U.N. Human Rights Field Operation in Rwanda (UNHRFOR) reported 1,575 persons killed in similar circumstances.

In late 1996, over a million Rwandans lived in exile in DRC after having fled the victory of the Rwandan Patriotic Front and the establishment of the current government in 1994. Although most people in the camps were noncombatants, tens of thousands of others were soldiers, militia, and civilian authorities responsible for the genocide of at last half a million Tutsi in Rwanda. Nourished by the international community and shielded by the massive civilian population which they manipulated for their own interests, the leaders of the former government and Rwandan Armed Forces (Forces Armées Rwandaises, FAR) used the camps to regroup, rearm and launch incursions into Rwanda. The international community preferred to pay the high cost of upkeep for the camps, one million dollars a day at one point, to the costs—financial, military and political—of separating genuine refugees from military and others who had no right to this status. Human rights and other humanitarian agencies called repeatedly for the removal of soldiers from the camps and the Rwandan government made clear that it would act if the international community did not. As the ex-FAR continued their incursions and preparations for full-scale invasion, Rwanda profited from the cover of an uprising by the Alliance of Democratic Forces for the Liberation of the Congo (ADFL) to join a campaign which both ousted long-term dictator Mobutu Sese Seko and smashed the camps. (*See* Democratic Republic of the Congo.)

Some 600,000 Rwandans then returned home, many of them glad to be free of the control of the former authorities. Others came back to Rwanda against their will, victims of a forcible repatriation forbidden by interna-

tional refugee law. Still others fled west and northwest, some of them forced to accompany the retreating ex-FAR and militia. For the next six months, ADFL forces, often led by Rwandans, hunted down those in flight, killing civilians as well as armed elements and preventing humanitarian agencies from delivering the food, water and medicine needed to keep them alive. By July 1997, the United Nations High Commissioner for Refugees (UNHCR) had located some 286,000 Rwandans in DRC and adjacent countries and had assisted some 234,000 of these persons to return to Rwanda. An additional 213,000 remained missing, many of them presumably dead either from military attack or hunger and disease.

Several weeks after the massive return from DRC, more than 470,000 Rwandans came back from exile in Tanzania. The return of smaller numbers from Burundi during 1996 brought the total of returnees to more than 1,300,000.

The government of Rwanda had always urged those abroad to come home, preferring to contain its adversaries within the country rather than fight them across borders. Authorities ensured a generally orderly and prompt dispersal of returnees to their home communes, at first postponing arrests of persons who could be accused of genocide and keeping local populations calm. In the course of the year, however, more than two hundred returnees were killed, including some fifty ex-FAR officers and their families. In most of these case, no assailants were apprehended. Local authorities in Mukingo commune, Ruhengeri prefecture, reported that some 500 returnees who were being held for questioning were taken away by truck during the middle of the night of April 29 by government soldiers and have not been seen since. In addition, two ex-FAR officers returned from abroad were said to have committed suicide while imprisoned at a brigade lockup in Rubavu commune.

Beginning in January, insurgents attacked genocide survivors and other Tutsi who had returned to Rwanda after the 1994 Rwandan Patriotic Front (RPF) victory. In raids on taxis and schools in February, March and April, assailants targeted only Tutsi and spared Hutu, indicating an intent to continue the 1994 genocide and to eliminate witnesses who could testify about the earlier slaughter. In August, insurgents killed seventeen genocide survivors and 131 Congolese refugees, most of them ethnic Tutsi, who were housed in a camp in northwestern Rwanda. In a mid-October attack on a similar camp in Mutura commune, insurgents killed at least thirty-seven persons and wounded many more. At the end of October some 2,000 survivors of the genocide and other Tutsi sought shelter in the town of Ruhengeri, leaving homes in rural areas where they feared attacks by rebels.

The insurgents, who gathered in larger groups as the year progressed, attacked more important targets, such as government installations, and fought more substantial skirmishes against the army beginning in May, primarily in the northwestern part of the country. Although authorities asserted repeatedly that the insurgents had been beaten, the rebels were able to lay siege to the important town of Gisenyi for seven hours in early October. The government soldiers had to bring reinforcements and artillery from Ruhengeri in order to defeat some 1,000 insurgents who also shot mortars into the town. Insurgents and government soldiers clashed again in Ndusu, Gatonde, and Nyarutovu communes in Ruhengeri later in October. Most military action was concentrated in the northwest, but armed men, apparently insurgents, carried out several attacks in the northeast, including one in Buyoya in early September where they killed a local official, his wife, six children and two guards, in the western prefecture of Kibuye, and in the central prefectures of Gitarama and Gikongoro.

The government responded to attacks with an excessive and indiscriminate use of force, by October killing an estimated 3,500 unarmed civilians in the course of military operations. These operations generally followed attacks on government soldiers, Tutsi civilians, and local government officials or the reported presence of insurgents in a community. Soldiers and government officials also killed hundreds of civilians in circumstances other than military operations. In August, soldiers reportedly executed some 150 detainees at the communal jails in Kanama and Rubavu in northwestern Rwanda. In the southern prefecture of Butare, two soldiers killed eleven detainees in Muyira commune in January and an RPA guard killed another eleven at Maraba commune in May. A prison guard in the commune of Rutongo killed eight detainees in early August. On January 24, at a public meeting in Karengera commune, Cyangugu prefecture, soldiers carried out the extrajudicial execution of two persons suspected of murder, repeating violations from the previous month when four persons were shot dead by soldiers in the presence of civilian authorities in Satinsyi commune, Gisenyi prefecture, and Mubuga commune, Gikongoro prefecture.

Soldiers and administrative officials have confined hundreds of civilians in military camps or facilities under military control after having arrested them in cordon-and-search operations in areas of conflict and in urban centers like the capital. U.N. human rights monitors and representatives of the International Committee of the Red Cross (ICRC) were ordinarily denied access to such facilities, making it impossible to know how many persons were held or the conditions of detention.

After two particularly egregious cases of military abuses, the killing of at least 137 civilians in Kigombe commune in early March and the slaughter of hundreds at Mahoko market in Gisenyi prefecture in August, authorities reportedly opened investigations and arrested the local commanding officers—in each case a major—and other soldiers. Some 1,300 soldiers faced charges in the military justice system, but more than half of these were ex-FAR accused of genocide or crimes against the current government. Military courts tried 114 cases, but only two involving human rights abuses attracted public notice. In December 1996, Col. Fred Ibingira, the commander of government troops who massacred some 2,000 displaced persons at the Kibeho camp in April 1995, was tried and acquitted of charges of murder and the use of arms without orders. He was found guilty of failing "to prevent criminal acts through immediate action" and was sentenced to eighteen months imprisonment, a period which he was said to have already spent in pre-trial custody, and to a fine of about U.S. $30. Lieutenant Colonel Murokore, Ibingira's immediate subordinate, was also charged in 1995, but by 1997 he was freed, apparently without trial, and the military prosecutor's office said that it expected no further prosecutions related to the Kibeho killings. (Both Ibingira and Murokore reportedly fought in the DRC operation.) In a judgment in September remarkably like that of the Ibingira case, a military court acquitted several soldiers of serious charges related to the killing of 110 civilians at Kanama in September 1995 and found them guilty of failing to come to the assistance of people in danger. They were sentenced to twenty-eight months in prison, of which they were said already to have served twenty-four, and were fined about $30. In both trials, the prosecutors presented weak cases, tapping very little of the abundant evidence available. In the second case, they had taken most of the testimony in the weeks immediately preceding the trial, although the events had taken place nearly two years before.

Gen. Paul Kagame, the effective head of government, repeatedly stressed the importance of political over military solutions to problems, but the government experienced growing difficulty in finding political solutions. Illustrative of this development was the apparently forced resignation of Col. Alexis Kanyarengwe from the post of minister of the interior following his public protests against killings by government soldiers in March in his home region of Ruhengeri. Prior to the killings, Kanyarengwe had helped assure support of the government in Ruhengeri. The government removed the prefect of Ruhengeri, apparently because he too had spoken out against military excesses,

and replaced him with Boniface Rucagu, whom authorities had previously accused of having led the genocide. Arrested several times but never brought to trial, Rucagu was apparently thought to be the only person who might bring order to the northwestern prefecture. Members of the National Assembly, particularly survivors of the genocide, protested the choice bitterly, but to no avail.

Among the civilians slain by October 1997 were 108 administrative and nineteen judicial officials. Insurgents were reportedly responsible for most of these crimes as they sought to punish supporters of the government. In a few cases, army or other state officials were accused of the killings. Whatever the source or sources of the violence, it discouraged moderates from accepting official duties.

A journalist critical of the government, Appolos Hakizimana, was assassinated in April. His associate, Amiel Nkuliza, also critical of the government, was threatened with death immediately thereafter and was arrested two weeks later on charges of having incited ethnic hatred.

In a number of cases, unidentified assailants killed Rwandan employees of international agencies, such as UNICEF, UNHCR, and the World Food Program. Government soldiers in January shot at two employees of the nongovernmental organization (NGO) Concern, killing one of them. Many other employees of humanitarian agencies have been threatened. In other cases, the assailants murdered eight foreign residents by mid-year. On January 18, armed men, some of them in military uniform, attacked three buildings in the town of Ruhengeri that were occupied by foreign staff of Save the Children, Medecins sans Frontieres, and Doctors of the World. Driven away from two of the buildings, assailants gained entry to the third, where they murdered three Spanish medical workers and seriously injured an American, who later was obliged to have his injured leg amputated. The government soldiers in the immediate vicinity failed to intervene but later arrested the guard of the premises who had witnessed the whole attack; an RPA soldier shot him the next day, supposedly because he was trying to escape custody. In another case, insurgents killed a Belgian nun when they attacked the school she directed in Satinsyi commune, Gisenyi prefecture, on April 28 and were reportedly also responsible for murdering a Chinese engineer in Kivumu commune, Kibuye prefecture on June 24. A teacher, reportedly once an RPA soldier, shot and killed a Canadian priest during a mass in Kinigi commune, Ruhengeri prefecture on February 2. The attacks on foreign nationals, including attacks on human rights monitors described below, caused many NGOs to withdraw their staff from insecure areas in the west and northwest. This reduced the number of outside witnesses and diminished the amount of information available about incidents of violence.

Against the backdrop of increasing violence by both the government and the insurgents, the beginning of trials for genocide offered one sign of hope. With considerable foreign assistance in the training of personnel, the judicial system was operating with 910 judges, far more than the number in service before the genocide. By mid-year, courts had handed down judgments in 142 cases, in which sixty-one persons were found guilty and condemned to death, eight were acquitted, and the rest found guilty and sentenced to varying prison terms up to life in prison. As of October, five of those sentenced to death had appealed and seen their appeals rejected, but none of the condemned had been executed. Following the procedure set by a 1996 law on the genocide, twenty-five persons pleaded guilty and made detailed confessions in order to be eligible for a lighter penalty. In September, the first decision was handed down concerning one of some 2,000 minors facing charges of genocide. The accused, found guilty of crimes committed when he was fourteen years old, was given a reduced sentence of three years because he had confessed.

The first trials failed to meet international standards in several respects, most importantly because the accused had no legal representation. The government of Rwanda acknowledged the right of the accused to a defense, but declared itself unable to pay for legal assistance. A small NGO, Avocats sans Frontières, arranged for attorneys from other African and European countries to represent some defendants, but lacked resources to meet the overwhelming demand. In addition, their staff did not provide assistance in insecure areas. During the year, the conduct of trials in a number of courts improved: prosecutors called witnesses to court more often, instead of merely presenting a written summary of their testimony; the accused was given more time to review the charges; and judges more often granted reasonable requests for adjournments. These improvements, while significant, did not take place in all courts, nor did they alleviate the persistent problem of threats against defense witnesses, lawyers, and judges.

In August forty-four lawyers were sworn in to the newly established bar, but almost all of them refused to defend persons accused of genocide. One of the three Rwandan lawyers who agreed to do so, Innocent Murengezi, "disappeared" when he left a court building at the end of January. Although the minister of justice and U.N. human rights monitors made efforts to trace him, he had not been located eight months later and was presumed dead.

With the massive return of Rwandans from abroad, military and administrative officials once more began making arrests without legal authority to do so and without following legal procedure, thus reviving practices that had diminished last year with the improved functioning of the judicial system. They also began once more holding detainees in irregular places of detention in various sectors of the communes. Near the end of 1997, an estimated 40 percent of those detained in prisons and 80 percent of those detained in other facilities had no files establishing charges against them. This made it appear impossible for authorities to comply with provisions of a 1996 law setting the end of 1997 as the deadline for having appropriate warrants drawn and preliminary appearances before judges for all those arrested on or before September 8, 1996. By October, more than 120,000 persons were held in inhumane conditions, crammed into prisons and communal jails meant to house a fraction of that number. In the early part of the year, prisoners in several central prisons received no or very little food for up to ten days, supposedly because of lack of firewood for cooking. Due to insecurity in some regions, representatives of the ICRC were unable to visit an estimated 30 percent of jails in communes and police brigades.

The reintegration of the returnees has exacerbated social and economic problems chronic to the heavily overpopulated, agricultural country. Those who fled Rwanda in 1994 have returned to find their homes, fields, businesses and jobs in the hands of others, many of them persons who followed the RPF back to Rwanda from their own years of exile. The government has guaranteed the property rights of those who fled in 1994, but has implemented the promise in relatively few cases. The Ministry of Defense has confiscated properties of some of those accused but not yet tried on charges of genocide and has decreed that tenants occupying those properties must work out rental agreements with its officials. In April, the government announced that returnees who wanted to seek employment or to attend school would first have to pass through a one-month program of re-education. Those already employed were told to leave their jobs until they had undergone this process and employers were warned not to hire any returnees who had not completed re-education. By August several re-education camps had begun operating, but they could accomodate only a very small number of those who must complete the program before beginning work or study.

The Right to Monitor

The five Rwandan human rights associations suffered enormous losses during the genocide. In attempting to resume work, activists who have criticized the authorities or urged the presumption of innocence for those accused of genocide were harassed and threatened. Virtually all Rwandans—including lawyers and judicial personnel—ordinarily refer to those accused of genocide as the "presumed guilty." In February 1997, Alphonse-Marie Nkubito, the founder of the first Rwandan human rights organization, the Rwandan Association for the Defense of Human Rights (Association rwandaise pour la defense des droits de l'homme, ARDHO), died suddenly. Authorities failed to investigate allegations that he had been murdered, leaving suspicions and fear among his colleagues and others. Soon after Nkubito's death, Abbe Andre Sibomana, president of the Rwandan Association for the Defense of Human Rights and Public Liberties (Association rwandaise pour la défense des droits de la personne et des libertés publiques, ADL) and Rosalie Mukarukaka, secretary general of ADL, were detained and interrogated by the police. Emmanuel Hitimana, a researcher for ARDHO was also detained for seven days in a communal jail and was warned to stop doing human rights work. Murengezi, who "disappeared" in January, was also a human rights activist.

Rwandan human rights researchers who tried to investigate the killing of detainees at the Maraba communal jail in May (see above) were not permitted to view the bodies or to interview the wounded and other detainees. Military authorities excluded Rwandan activists seeking to investigate RPA abuses from areas of the northwest, declaring the communities to be areas of military operations.

Under these pressures, three of the five human rights groups gave up rigorous monitoring of government abuses and have devoted themselves to less dangerous tasks, like human rights education.

In early February, five staff members of the United Nations Human Rights Field Office for Rwanda (UNHRFOR) were murdered in southwestern Rwanda by assailants who ambushed their vehicle. Three of the five were Rwandan, one was British, and one was Cambodian. Rwandan authorities attributed the attack to a band of insurgents, several of whom they said they had killed in an encounter soon after. Several weeks before, two Rwandan and two foreign UNHRFOR staff members were beaten and robbed and their vehicle burned, apparently by insurgents. Following the February killings, all staff were recalled to the capital for the rest of the month. When the U.N. field team resumed operations, staff could not regularly monitor the areas of greatest insecurity, the very regions where they were most needed.

The Role of the International Community

As in 1996, the international community continued to offer political, economic and military support to Rwanda. Governments were generally ready to overlook or to excuse Rwandan abuses as a cost of rebuilding a nation shattered by genocide or to accept without challenge official denials of responsibility when the identity of the perpetrators was unknown. International actors rarely criticized abuses, whether victims were Rwandans or even citizens of their own nations. Condemnation of the murder of the U.N. human rights monitors was so muted as to dishearten their colleagues. Foreign diplomats in Kigali accepted the show of justice in the Ibingira court martial without comment, fearing that too much attention to the case would be "counterproductive," according to one European diplomat.

South Africa, which had interrupted arms sales to the previous government, resumed selling weapons to Rwanda, apparently unconvinced by human rights groups, canvassed by the National Conventional Arms Control Committee, that had argued against this. The African National Congress (ANC) issued a statement concerning the weapons sales commending the Rwandan government for its "positive role in bringing about peace in the region as a whole and their country in particular." The South African endorsement was only one indication of the widespread support enjoyed by the Rwandan governement among African leaders ready to overlook its human rights abuses in light of its political and military successes.

United Nations

According to the Rwandan government, the U.N. lost the moral authority to condemn human rights abuses in Rwanda when it failed to intervene in the genocide in 1994. Exploiting this premise and the justification that current killings resulted from a need to defend against insurgents, Rwanda persuaded the U.N. Commission on Human Rights to end the mandate of the special rapporteur on Rwanda, replacing him with a "special representative" who lacked the authority to report on alleged abuses and was limited to advising on how to improve the human rights situation.

Using similar arguments, Rwanda began a campaign to end monitoring by UNHRFOR. Reports by the field operation, regularly submitted to Rwandan authorities before publication, rarely criticized the government firmly. Like the local organizations, UNHRFOR devoted considerable resources to less risky human rights activities, like promoting human rights and assisting in development of the judiciary. When UNHRFOR did produce two exceptionally strong reports in late July, the government stepped up its efforts to have the monitoring operation ended. Diplomats in Kigali, reflecting the policy of their governments, provided little political support to UNHRFOR.

The International Criminal Tribunal for Rwanda (ICTR), established by the U.N. Security Council in 1994 to prosecute those responsible for the genocide and other violations of international humanitarian law, improved its performance markedly in 1997 after the replacement in February of the registrar and deputy prosecutor. Under the new leadership, tribunal staff in general functioned more efficiently and the prosecutor began grouping several accused persons for a single trial, a strategy which promised to expedite the process. The opening of a second courtroom made it possible to try two cases simultaneously, an important step since the ICTR already had twenty-one indicted persons in custody. In October, the first three trials were nearing conclusion and the prosecution hoped for judges to begin their deliberations by the end of the year.

The tribunal, now adequately funded by the international community, still suffered severe shortages of qualified personnel, a lack exacerbated by the end of a long-standing practice that allowed member states to second personnel to U.N. agencies. At mid-year, more than half the posts of investigator were vacant.

In 1997, Cameroon joined the list of states (Belgium, Kenya, Switzerland, Zambia) that had assisted the tribunal in arresting suspects, delivering four accused persons to the ICTR, including Col. Theoneste Bagosora, one of the top leaders during the genocide. Kenya also helped the ICTR once again, this time with the arrest of the former prime minister of Rwanda and seven other suspects, who were subsequently handed over to the custody of the tribunal. One accused person is imprisoned in the U.S., awaiting transfer to the ICTR.

European Union

The European Union, particularly satisfied to have most of the refugees back home, provided a fresh infusion of emergency funds, some thirty-five million ECU to assist in their resettlement. In terms of development assistance, the E.U. continued to contribute particularly to the judicial and police systems, giving some four and a half million ECU. Italy provided some U.S.$10 million for the re-education camps and France joined the ranks of international donors to the current government for the first time with some $2.5 million worth of assistance in education and health. Austria cancelled a Rwandan debt of $17 million. As reports increased of killings of civilians by RPA soldiers, critics of continued unconditional assistance to the Rwandan government became more vociferous in Belgium, the Netherlands, and Ireland, but their efforts had produced no restrictions in aid by October. Similarly, an E.U. discussion of an arms embargo on the entire Great Lakes ended with no action.

United States

The U.S. emerged this year as the most important foreign supporter of the Rwandan government, a role symbolized by U.S. military assistance. In itself a relatively small program, the military training attracted much attention because of human rights violations by RPA soldiers both in Rwanda and in DRC. At a congressional hearing in December 1996, Assistant Secretary of Defense Vincent Kern asserted that the U.S. provided the "softer, kinder, gentler" kind of military training, with emphasis on human rights issues, civil-military relations, and leadership training. In August, after further congressional prodding, the Department of Defense reported having provided one course that taught combat skills as marksmanship in the months just before the DRC operation. U.S. embassy staff in Kigali were reluctant to acknowledge abuses by government forces, although they maintained that they raised such issues privately with Rwandan authorities. In one UNHRFOR briefing about RPA killings of civilians, the U.S. ambassador challenged the report so vigorously that "he looked like the Rwandan government lawyer," according to one observer present at the meeting. After the RPA arrested soldiers for the 1997 killings in Kanama, the U.S. ambassador publicly commended military authorities for "hold[ing] the army accountable," but he said nothing about the judgment that same day that acquitted soldiers charged with murdering 110 civilians at Kanama in 1995. (*See* above.)

Like E.U. nations, the U.S. provided substantial assistance, some $28 million, for refugee resettlement and more than one million dollars for rebuilding courts and training communal and national police.

As reports increased of abuses by government soldiers, Washington policymakers debated what course to follow in Rwanda but by late in the year, there had been no apparent change in policy.

SOUTH AFRICA

Human Rights Developments

The African National Congress (ANC) continued to dominate South Africa's government of national unity (GNU) as it reached the middle of its first term of office. Members of the Inkatha Freedom Party (IFP) were included in the cabinet, but the National Party, which had resigned from the GNU in 1996, remained in opposition. In August, the resignation by former president F. W. de Klerk as leader of the National Party reflected the disarray of the former party of apartheid, as the political landscape continued to adjust to the new realities of universal suffrage. A number of new milestones in South Africa's transformation were passed, most importantly the coming into force, on February 4, following certification by the Constitutional Court, of the constitution drafted during the period since the elections of April 1994. The constitution, which replaced an "interim" constitution adopted in December 1993 and in force since April 1994, included a bill of rights guaranteeing to all in South Africa the range of civil, political, economic, social and cultural rights.

The Truth and Reconciliation Commission (TRC) continued its hearings and investigations during the year. The commission was set up in December 1995 with a mandate to establish a record of gross violations of human rights from 1960 to 1994 and to grant amnesty to perpetrators of crimes committed with a political motive who fulfilled certain conditions, including full disclosure of their acts. It was due to finish its public hearings in December 1997, except for those related to amnesty applications, and to submit a report in July 1998. By the end of August 1997, almost 7,000 individuals had applied to the commission for amnesty (the great majority of them prisoners convicted of crimes with little apparent political motive), of which 1,700 had been dealt with and about seventy-five applications granted. Those indemnified against prosecution or civil liability included former ANC members as well as former security police. The main political parties faced cross-examination on their submissions to the TRC, leading the National Party to "withdraw its cooperation" from the commission following hearings in May at which former president de Klerk received sharp criticism for his failure to acknowledge National Party abuses. The National Party also launched a court challenge to the commission calling for the dismissal of its vice-chair and an order that it carry out its work without bias, though this case was later settled on the basis of an apology. The Inkatha Freedom Party maintained its opposition to TRC proceedings, alleging a "witch-hunt" against its members. A number of individual Inkatha and security force members also refused to cooperate with the commission, which launched court action to compel their appearance. No senior members of the National Party or Inkatha Freedom Party applied for amnesty, despite increasing evidence of their involvement in systematic efforts to promote political violence and assassinate members of the liberation movements. The commission held special hearings during the year related to the role of health professionals, the media, business, and the legal system in human rights violations. Other commissions of inquiry investigated other aspects of the past, including the activities of the former homeland governments and the "Shell House massacre," a 1994 march past ANC headquarters in Johannesburg at which a number of Inkatha supporters were shot dead by ANC security guards.

As investigations continued into the violations of the past, efforts to reform the institutions responsible continued. In April 1997, an Independent Complaints Directorate (ICD) assumed responsibility for the investigation (or supervision of internal investigations) of all complaints against the police. Legislation to amend section 49 of the Criminal Procedure Act, allowing police to shoot fleeing suspects, was approved by cabinet. A three-year moratorium on recruiting new police officers was lifted in May, and 1,200 posts were advertised (for which there were over 600,000 applications); these officers were to undergo training under a new curriculum including a substantial human rights content. Nevertheless, allegations of police involvement in torture, extra-judicial executions, and organized crime continued throughout 1997. In July, the ICD announced that it had recorded 191 cases of deaths in custody or as a result of police action during the first three months of its existence (fifty-six of these were custodial deaths), suggesting a total of close to 800 deaths in one year. Even though the legislation establishing the ICD obliged police to report all such deaths, the ICD suspected that not all cases were being reported to it; yet the numbers significantly increased from those reported in previous years (226 deaths were reported in 1995).

In December 1996, the Department of Justice announced an ambitious legislative program for 1997. Laws introduced to parliament or passed during the year included an act to remove corporal punishment and the death penalty from the statute book; an act to provide for the establishment of a national prosecuting authority and a national director of public prosecutions; and an act to establish an office for witness protection within the Department of Justice. The provision of legal aid to indigent individuals accused of criminal offenses increased greatly, as defendants began to exercise their constitutional right to demand legal representation at state expense "if substantial injustice would otherwise result." In April, a Johannesburg High Court ruled that a convict who had not been informed of his right to a lawyer should be released, after serving fifteen months of a ten-year sentence.

Such reform efforts were blighted by continuing high rates of violent crime, especially organized political violence. KwaZulu-Natal remained the worst-affected province, although the declining trend of violence since 1994 continued. The situation in the long-troubled Midlands area of the province was particularly worrisome, with an upsurge in violence following the expulsion from the ANC of Richmond leader Sfiso Nkabinde in

April, amid (longstanding) allegations that he had been a police informer and was involved in hit squad activities. Although a police special investigation unit arrested Nkabinde and seventeen others in September and charged them with a number of murders, violence continued. Violence flared up intermittently elsewhere in KwaZulu-Natal, and the thousands of people displaced by over a decade of conflict in the province remained largely unable to return home. Groups monitoring the violence alleged continuing police complicity in organized political violence, as well as the involvement of individuals trained in paramilitary skills as part of the Inkatha Freedom Party under the previous government. ANC and IFP discussions of a local peace plan continued, without conclusion, including controversial proposals for amnesty to be granted to "warlords" on a more generous basis than under the legislation establishing the Truth and Reconciliation Commission.

Organized violence also persisted in other parts of South Africa, including the Qumbu and Tsolo areas of the Eastern Cape (where over a hundred people were killed during the year), and in Bushbuckridge, where a dispute continued as to whether the community should be part of the Northern Province or Mpumalanga. A political resolution to the Bushbuckridge crisis appeared to have been reached with a July agreement for joint administration, although protests continued. Troops were deployed in the Eastern Cape to carry out peacekeeping duties, amid allegations that the perpetrators of violence enjoyed immunity or even support from the police. In August, a special court began to hear cases related to the Eastern Cape violence, though human rights organizations feared its lack of an independent investigative capacity would seriously reduce its effectiveness.

In November 1996, the Regulation of Gatherings Act, drafted by a panel of local and international experts in 1993, was implemented, providing for management of public demonstrations by the police and local authorities and placing an obligation on organizers of a march to notify the authorities within seven days of the planned event. The carrying of "dangerous weapons" at public gatherings was banned throughout the country in October 1996. Despite these measures, public demonstrations continued to lead on occasion to violence and sometimes deaths. In February, demonstrations in townships south of Johannesburg by the South West Joint Civics Organisation (SOWEJOCA) led to three deaths, blamed by a commission of enquiry on SOWEJOCA, though police were also criticized for lack of proper crowd control. In March 1997, a march by the IFP to commemorate the "Shell House Massacre," itself resulted in three people dying of gunshot wounds in incidents connected to the demonstration. The activities of an apparent vigilante group calling itself People Against Gangsterism and Drugs (PAGAD), formed in 1996 in the impoverished Cape Flats townships, led in some areas to violent conflict with drug gangs which police appeared powerless to check.

Prisons remained seriously overcrowded and plagued by gang violence between prisoners. Assaults on prisoners by prison staff also remained common. In February, prisoners at Helderstroom prison in the Western Cape were beaten by a correctional services "rapid reaction unit" called in to quell disturbances in the prison. In May, hundreds of prisoners were allegedly beaten by the same unit at Pollsmoor prison in Cape Town, following a search for illegal weapons. Police investigations led to charges being brought against a number of staff. In March, the commissioner for correctional services stated that the use of disused mineshafts was being considered for some prisoners, whom he described as animals. This suggestion was endorsed by the minister for correctional services, but was apparently dropped after an outcry from human rights organizations. In April, the minister for correctional services announced plans for the building of seven new prisons, two of them "super-maximum security" facilities. More positively, the first secure care facilities for children who had committed serious

crimes were opened during 1997 with the aim of ensuring that children would not in the future be held with adults in prisons and that children would have access to educational and rehabilitative programs. Many children nonetheless remained in adult prisons.

During 1997, a number of initiatives were taken to improve the government's response to issues of violence against women, with a range of measures unveiled on August 9, Women's Day in South Africa. The Department of Welfare announced plans to distribute "crisis kits" for rape victims at police stations, including disposable underwear, toiletries, and the telephone numbers of counselors. The Department of Justice, which ran a campaign against violence against women from November 1996 to March 1997, developed new guidelines for all government departments involved in the handling of sexual violence against women and children. The police service began to establish special units across the country to handle cases of family violence, child abuse and sexual offenses. For most women, however, the response of the police and justice system remained inadequate if not abusive in its own right. On February 1, abortion during the first trimester became generally legal in South Africa for the first time. The Gender Commission established by the constitution was appointed and began to function during 1997, although it had yet to make its mark with substantial achievements. Following the 1996 publication of a discussion paper on the law relating to obtaining restraining orders in cases of domestic violence, the South African Law Commission published draft legislation which incorporated many of the recommendations of women's organizations, although some concerns remained.

Public concern at a perceived "flood" of undocumented immigration to South Africa, and accompanying xenophobia, led to a number of violent attacks on foreigners engaged, for example, in informal street trading. The police response to such attacks was often inadequate. Furthermore, allegations of police brutality against foreigners (as against South Africans) continued, and at least one asylum applicant died immediately after being released from police custody, apparently as a result of assault by policemen. A government-appointed committee held hearings and published a draft Green Paper on migration policy which advocated a more rights-based approach than was currently in force.

During the course of the year South Africa—and in particular President Nelson Mandela—became increasingly involved in mediation efforts to resolve some of the conflicts on the African continent. Most high profile and possibly least well-conceived were South Africa's hosting of talks between the representatives of President Mobutu Sese Seko of Zaire and Laurent Kabila, leader of the rebel forces that ultimately took over the government. Other mediation efforts focused on Angola, Sudan and Lesotho. South Africa was quick to recognize Kabila's new government and announced the donation of R.1.5 million (U.S.$350,000) worth of police equipment to his government. Mandela appeared to discount reports of the involvement of Kabila's forces in massacres of civilians in eastern Zaire. South Africa supported the decision of the U.N. Commission on Human Rights to appoint a special rapporteur on Nigeria, while at the same time apparently attempting to rebuild friendly relations with the Nigerian government. In June, the chair of South Africa's national Human Rights Commission, Barney Pityana, was elected to membership of the African Commission on Human and Peoples' Rights by the Organization of African Unity summit in Harare.

South Africa made strenuous efforts to market its weapons overseas during 1997, striking significant deals with Malaysia and the Gulf States. South Africa nevertheless continued its policy of allowing a greater degree of transparency and democratic control over arms sales than many other countries. The government insisted, however, that it would not reveal the names of purchaser countries if they did not want their identities known; and it tried, unsuccess-

fully, to keep knowledge of a major deal with Saudi Arabia from the public. Controversially, sales of military equipment to Rwanda, suspended in November 1996 due to concerns at conflict in the region, resumed in July following reported assurances that such materiel would not be used outside the country; continued gross human rights violations in Rwanda did not apparently affect the decision. Allegations were also made during the year that South African-made weapons were being used by both sides in the civil war in Sudan. Although the government denied that any official sales had been made, it was alleged that arms supplied to Uganda were being transferred to Sudanese rebel forces without protest from South Africa. More positively, South Africa took a lead within Africa and internationally in calling for the banning of anti-personnel mines and in May began destroying its own stockpile during a meeting of African heads of state in South Africa to discuss the issue. South Africa refused to sell weapons to Turkey, due to concerns about its human rights record. Legislation was introduced to parliament regulating the provision of military assistance by South African individuals or companies in other countries, aimed at the activities of such groups as the security outfit Executive Outcomes.

The Right to Monitor

There were no restrictions on the right to monitor human rights in South Africa during 1997. In July, state arms manufacturer Denel (Pty) Ltd., brought criminal charges under apartheid-era legislation against the *Sunday Independent* and other newspapers for disclosing details of a large arms deal to an unnamed country and sought injunctions to prevent the *Sunday Independent* and the weekly *Mail and Guardian* from publishing the name of the country (later revealed to be Saudi Arabia). Temporary injunctions were later lifted by the High Court, and Denel announced it was withdrawing criminal charges. Independent statutory bodies mandated to monitor government activity—including the Human Rights Commission, charged with promoting respect for human rights and investigating violations, and the Public Protector, with a brief to investigate misconduct in public administration—published a number of reports. The cabinet approved an Open Democracy Bill, designed among other things to increase public access to government information.

The Role of the International Community

Multilateral and bilateral relations with South Africa focused largely on promotion of trade and macroeconomic policy; however, significant assistance was also committed to development and human rights projects and U.N. structures began to monitor South Africa's new commitments under international treaties.

United Nations

At the invitation of the South African government, following its ratification in 1996 of the U.N. Convention on the Elimination of All Forms of Discrimination Against Women, the U.N. special rapporteur on violence against women, its causes, and consequences, Radhika Coomaraswamy, visited South Africa in October 1996. In February 1997, a report on South Africa was published resulting from this mission. The special rapporteur concluded that "without a complete overhauling of the criminal justice apparatus, the retraining of its members and the creation of a more representative service, violence in general, and violence against women in particular, will never be contained." The report noted that government measures to address questions of violence against women had been in place for a short time and that therefore their effectiveness could not yet be measured.

European Union

The "European Programme for Reconstruction and Development in South Africa," through which European Union (E.U.) aid to South Africa was channelled, placed priority on human rights, health, education, rural and urban development, strengthening local communities and protecting the environment. In February 1997, the European Union pledged R.40 million (U.S.$8.5 million) to nongovernmental projects in South Africa, including R.9 million (U.S.$2 million) to the Institute for Democracy in South Africa (IDASA) to promote peace and democratization efforts in KwaZulu-Natal. In April 1997, members of the South African government and the European Commission met in Pretoria to hold their first annual consultations on the European Programme, including preparation of a Multi-Annual Indicative Programme which would provide resources of ECU 375 million (U.S.$420 million) to South Africa. The aid was to fund social services, democratization, and private sector aid.

A number of European countries also gave aid on a bilateral basis, including Swedish assistance to the Truth and Reconciliation Commission to enable it to complete its work on time and continued U.K. assistance in efforts to reform the police service.

United States and Canada

A bilateral U.S.-South Africa commission headed by Vice-President Al Gore and Deputy President Thabo Mbeki met during the year to promote trade and investment between the U.S. and South Africa. While the U.S. government announced that it would progressively reduce its aid grant to South Africa as the focus of bilateral relations shifted increasingly to trade, U.S. Agency for International Development continued to support both governmental and nongovernmental bodies involved in improving access to justice, based on a pledge of U.S.$600 million committed in 1994 to be spent over three years. In October, the U.S. government pledged a further R.220 million (U.S.$50 million) to be spent on education, justice, and health care. The Canadian government also continued support for programs aimed at reforming the criminal justice system.

Relevant Human Rights Watch reports:
Violence Against Women and the Medico-Legal System, 8/97
Still Killing: Landmines in Southern Africa, 5/97

SUDAN

Human Rights Developments

Sudan, once promoted as the bridge between the Arab and African worlds, was distinguished by human rights abuses arising from the government's determination to create an Arab Islamic state, including discrimination against Sudanese non-Arabs and non-Muslims. Non-Arabs made up 60 percent of the 26.7 million population and non-Muslims about 40 percent.

Government forces committed gross abuses of international humanitarian law in the fourteenth year of the civil war against the rebel Sudan People's Liberation Movement/Army (SPLM/A), fighting in the south and the central Nuba Mountains. The war widened as a new eastern front was opened by the National Democratic Alliance, a broad coalition including northern Muslims as well as southerners and marginalized peoples in the SPLA, other armed opposition groups, and traditional political parties.

The government defended itself against massive international criticism and tried to garner international support, by claiming to be the victim of a Western Christian conspiracy to destroy an Islamic state. But the ruling National Islamic Front (NIF) represented a politicized form of Islam and repressed even Muslim leaders and sects that challenged its hegemony. In April, police even dispersed a simple protest by the Khatmiyyah (one of Sudan's largest Muslim sects) of the government's postponement of the commemoration of their religious leader's death.

Political parties remained banned and expression restricted, except in debate by NIF members: in the press, some NIF members advocated a return to a multiparty state. In another slight opening, the government permitted a faction of the Democratic Unionist Party to establish offices and allowed its leader to engage in public debate, without having the status of a political party. The editor of Alwan, a nongovernment daily, did not have such latitude, however, and went on trial in September because of an article reporting on fighting in the south.

Sudan contains nineteen major ethnic groups (with almost 600 subgroups), speaking more than 115 tribal languages. Arabic is the official language. The government's strategy in the war zones (where African non-Arab populations predominate) was to turn African peoples against one another. It fomented hatred against the Dinka, the most numerous southern, African people; the majority of the SPLA leadership is Dinka. The government consolidated its military relations with former SPLA factions including Riak Machar's rebel force (the second largest rebel force in Sudan and the one with the allegiance of most Nuer, cousins of the Dinka). It moved Machar's troops into Juba to fortify it against SPLA attack, thus positioning troops for a war of southerner versus southerner—part of its divide and rule strategy.

In March 1997, the SPLA retook the government garrison towns of Yei and Kajo Keiji in Eastern Equatoria. The government, withdrawing from these areas, left landmines which injured many civilians, while at an international conference it took the important step of indicating its willingness to ratify an international treaty banning the manufacture and use of antipersonnel landmines.

The government reacted sharply to the opening of the eastern front (which appeared to threaten any oil pipeline that might be built to Port Sudan and possibly the water supply for the capital), the SPLA's advances in the south, and the December 1996 flight into exile of former prime minister and head of the Umma Party Sadiq al Mahdi. It stepped up forced recruitment, arbitrary arrests, and trials in military tribunals. It signed a "peace accord" with former rebel groups (with whom it had already been at peace for years). The oil resources of Sudan lie largely in Machar's Nuer territory, where an international consortium including Malaysian and Chinese investors led by Canadian-chartered Arakis Oil Company is drilling. The peace accord, not negotiated with or signed by the SPLA, the main rebel force, would permit a referendum among southerners (but not Nubas, Beja or other marginalized peoples) on the issue of self-determination in an undetermined period of time.

The government suspended all university classes but those of a women's college in late 1996 and ordered college students to "volunteer" for the Popular Defense Forces (PDF), the government's politicized Islamist militia, and to go to the southern front. Graduating high school seniors were required to go to PDF camps for a two-month PDF training course before they could receive their certificate of graduation (necessary for university attendance and employment).

In June some 65,000 unmarried males not in school were conscripted into the army for twelve to eighteen months. Many tried to dodge conscription, and the army began to round up young men at public events and checkpoints. The government, however, showed no interest in its soldiers and militia once captured by the SPLA; it even refused to permit an exchange of letters with their families.

A group of military officers and civilians was detained in Port Sudan and tried in 1997, continuing a trend of trying all political suspects—where they were tried at all—in secret military courts where fair trial protections were absent. Two were jailed and five officers received lesser penalties, with acquittals of five others. Another military court, convened in August 1996, completed the trial of another group of alleged coup plotters in mid-1997. The convicted coup leader ultimately received a fifteen-year prison sentence; nine defendants were acquitted and the remaining defendants received sentences ranging up to five years.

As is by now customary, the government released political prisoners during Al Eid religious holidays. The government continued to detain lesser-known persons suspected of subversion after that date, however, with dozens remaining in prison without charges or trial. Alleged members of the banned Sudan Communist Party continued to be singled out for long-term arbitrary detention. Several hundred women inmates of Omdurman Women's prison were released on grounds of overcrowding. Arrests of women peddlers continued, however, and the number of female inmates rose again.

Pressures brought on women to conform to a vague "Islamic woman" code continued. In late 1996 the Khartoum State government tried to impose sex segregation in public buses.

Sudan has the largest population of internally displaced in the world—some four million, largely the product of the prolonged war. Many lost homes, assets such as cattle and crops, and family members, and were forced to move.

The government remained intent on pushing internally displaced persons in the capital, disproportionately southerners and Nubas, back to their home areas, treating them as second class citizens and violating their right to freedom of movement. It suppressed their community organizations and self-help efforts by arbitrarily arresting community leaders, destroying homes without notice or compensation, and uprooting families to desert areas remote from water and jobs. It banned all but Islamic relief organizations from working outside these "official" displaced persons camps.

Those relocated to these camps generally had no right of tenure even there and were constantly threatened with removal to even more remote areas. In 1997, the government bowed somewhat to international pressure and issued some tenure permits in a minority of cases. Its basic policy remained unchanged.

Churches, schools and community centers built by the displaced in Khartoum's shanty towns also were razed by government bulldozers, with the pretext of "urban renewal." The government denied any religious discrimination but admittedly refused to grant any permits to build churches in Khartoum for the last twenty-five years, while routinely issuing permits for the construction of new mosques.

The government destroyed one church in the Omdurman slums during Easter week, in the face of parishioners' protests.

Humanitarian and even commercial access to the SPLA-controlled areas of the Nuba Mountains remained barred by government fiat, causing hundreds of thousands of civilians extreme hardship. This stringent blockade deliberately created a situation of desperate poverty, while in government areas international relief was conditionally provided to lure people from the SPLA. Those who resist were subjected to government bombing, looting (particularly of foodstuffs), and raids forcibly relocating Nuba from SPLA zones, destroying their communities, churches and mosques, and placing them into misnamed "peace camps" under tight government control, where the African cultures of the Nuba were subjected to destruction by forced separation of families, sexual abuse, and forced Arabization and Islamization.

In the south, the government also denied humanitarian access to areas of assessed civilian need for military strategic reasons without regard to human deprivation. According to the U.N. secretary-general's special envoy for humanitarian affairs for Sudan, the government ban on the use of C-130 aircraft, the only one capable of airdropping food in remote regions, from September 1995 to July 1996 caused more than 500,000 people in Bahr El Ghazal and 200,000 in other areas to suffer from serious hunger and related problems; the C-130 was banned again from late March 1997 to mid-June 1997 with similar effect. The government further significantly delayed barge convoys carrying food along the Nile corridor. Nevertheless the government complained that the U.N. was not responding to calls for relief when some 8,300 civilians fled into government-controlled Juba after the fall of Yei and Kajo Keiji.

In northern Bahr El Ghazal, frequently placed off limits to the U.N. by the government, civilian villages were subjected to military raids by government troops, in which the raiders took cattle, grain, and women and children as slaves or war booty. The government denied allegations of slavery as the evidence continued to surface of these continued slave-taking raids. The raiders enjoyed complete immunity from investigation or prosecution for this universally-outlawed practice. A long-awaited government report to the U.N. on slavery did not contribute to the analysis or solution of the problem.

The government denied accountability for former rebel forces whom it supplied and quartered. In a bizarre incident at the end of 1996, Cmdr. Kerubino Kuanyin Bol (a former SPLA commander supplied and paid by the government) took an International Committee of the Red Cross (ICRC) plane, crew, and five patients hostage, absurdly demanding millions of dollars in ransom. After protracted negotiations, the plane and crew were released in exchange for relief food and trucks, leading other relief agencies to fear becoming extortion targets. The five patients, SPLA former combatants, were never released, and the government maintained that they had joined the Sudan army, refusing to permit the ICRC to visit them. The ICRC refused to return to Sudan until the five were accounted for.

The government's conspicuous lack of captured SPLA combatant prisoners, during the fourteen-year course of the war, led to the conclusion that there was a government policy, forbidden in international law, of executing captured SPLA combatants. The only exception (which tended to prove the rule) was the government's acknowledged capture and detention of Eritrean and Ugandan prisoners (combatants) captured inside southern Sudan; their presence served to support the government's allegations that troops from neighboring Ethiopia, Eritrea and Uganda were fighting inside Sudan alongside the SPLA. As in prior years, these three governments claimed in turn that the Sudanese government was sponsoring, quartering and supplying rebel groups attacking them.

The SPLA released the Ugandans it captured in Yei, claiming that half the 3,000 killed and captured there were from the West Nile Bank Front, a Ugandan rebel group allegedly sponsored by the Sudan government and based in Sudan. The SPLA acknowledged holding about 1,600 captured in clashes with government forces, some 300 of whom had been held since 1985, inside Sudan. The ICRC was permitted to visit but conducted no activities inside Sudan after its December 1996 problems with the government.

The Sudan government's sponsorship of the Ugandan Lord's Resistance Army (LRA), a rebel group with an appalling human rights record of abducting, killing, torturing, and sexually abusing Ugandan children, was visible when it permitted relatives of some kidnaped children to visit an LRA camp inside Sudan. In a report on the LRA, Human Rights Watch called on the Sudan government to use its influence to release the children and to cease military and other aid to the LRA until the LRA's abuses stop.

LRA activity in northern Uganda also affected the Sudanese internally displaced. In one of many incidents, relief trucks carrying food to southern Sudan were ambushed in June by the LRA in Uganda, killing eight.

Government aerial bombardment by high-flying Antonov planes increased as towns fell to the SPLA; Yei was bombed four times in the weeks after the SPLA captured it. The government's bombs fell on towns behind the frontline, such as Maridi, killing one and injuring thirteen while destroying eighteen civilian homes there in March; in June another twelve bombs killed one woman and injured eight. Labone, where an estimated 32,500 internally displaced lived on the Ugandan border, was bombed by the government in July with fourteen civilian casualties, and again in October with additional casualties. Government helicopter gunships attacked civilians in the Nuba Moun-

tains and around Juba. In September the government even dropped cluster bombs on a prisoner of war camp in Yei which held government soldiers and militia, killing three.

When former U.S. president Jimmy Carter's advance team was in Yei to prepare for Carter's meeting with SPLA leader John Garang to discuss the peace accords, the government bombed that town. As a result the meeting did not take place.

The SPLA remained largely unaccountable to the civilian population it governs, although efforts have been made, by the U.N. and others, to assist the SPLA's civilian administration in the south. Institutions are not yet firm, there is no clear avenue for redress, and the style of governance appears to depend largely on the personality of the local commander. After the SPLA took Yei, for example, its soldiers committed a series of gross abuses against civilians, including murder, looting, and rape. This pattern was followed in several other captured towns. The lawlessness in Yei persisted until a new commander was brought in. He restored order by imposing military discipline, including use of a firing squad. In the Nuba Mountains, the SPLA was more respectful of the civilian population, in part because of political leadership of the Nuba commander and the emphasis on Nuba solidarity; this was accomplished without any U.N. assistance.

In too many cases, justice is never done and impunity rules, as in the case of Paul Anade Othow, who was in the SPLA, then in Riak Machar's faction of the SPLA, and then went to work with the government. The SPLA recaptured Pochalla (an Anuak area and Anade's place of origin) in 1996, and detained Anade, but then he "disappeared." Efforts by the family and Human Rights Watch to receive an answer from the SPLA on his whereabouts have come to naught, as have inquiries on other "disappearance" cases.

The SPLA continued forced recruitment of underage boys, including those in schools, even in the Nuba Mountains. Civilians protested the taking of their sons. Since

1996 the SPLA permitted UNICEF to engage in family reunification in its territory, including a group of 306 in late 1996. Many children so reunited were originally separated from their families by the SPLA for recruitment purposes.

Six missionaries who complained to the SPLA about forced recruitment of schoolchildren as young as twelve, and their teachers, in Mapourdit were detained in August 1996 and the priest beaten by a local SPLA military intelligence officer. They were not released until the church publicly protested, making international headlines. An investigation was ordered by the SPLA commander-in-chief. The officer responsible was said to have been detained. One year had elapsed, however, with no report and no hearing.

Looting and diversion of food continued to be a problem in several SPLA zones. Action Against Hunger, a French nongovernmental agency, claimed that it was expelled by the SPLA because it was about to investigate why a high rate of malnutrition existed in Labone despite adequate supplies of relief food for the civilian population. It was suspected that the SPLA deliberately kept some children in a thin and sickly state to justify continued high levels of relief food the SPLA could divert. The SPLA took thousands of Sudan army and militia prisoner in Yei, Rumbek and other garrison towns it captured, but was unable to provide adequate food or medical care to the prisoners.

The Right to Monitor

No nongovernmental human rights groups functioned openly inside government-controlled areas of Sudan. The Sudan Human Rights Organization (SHRO), whose members went into exile after the 1989 coup, has many branches outside Sudan but none inside; a government-organized group by the same name functions inside Sudan but is not known ever to have criticized the government.

Prior to the coup, the bar association had played an active role in defending legal rights, only to be banned and later permitted to reopen under NIF control. Individual lawyers defended those tried for politically-related crimes and some managed to have themselves named as "friends" of the conspiracy defendants in military tribunals, where their role was sharply circumscribed.

Women advocating the abolition of female genital mutilation were permitted to work on this health issue by the government, which supports the abolition of this practice.

In the Nuba Mountains, a nongovernmental human rights organization with support from abroad was created in 1995; its eleven monitors collected substantial information on government abuses, but their mandate did not include investigating SPLA abuses. Elsewhere in SPLA-controlled zones, however, no local human rights organization of any type existed; those persons most likely to form such an organization were too afraid for the physical safety of the monitors to do so. A brief Human Rights Watch visit to Yei was welcomed, however, and access to prisoners of war permitted.

The Role of the International Community

United Nations

Despite worldwide condemnation of the dire human rights situation in Sudan, efforts in the U.N. Commission on Human Rights to establish a program of U.N. human rights monitors or officers for Sudan, while approved on paper, remained stalled by the commission and the Sudan government resistance. Potential donors, including the United States and European Union countries, failed to seize the initiative to break the impasse.

Numerous U.N. human rights and other bodies condemned abuses in Sudan. They all noted persistent and serious human rights problems. Sudan remained under mild Security Council sanctions for its failure to extradite three alleged participants in the assassination attempt on Egyptian President Hosni Mubarak in Ethiopia in 1995.

The government's campaign against the U.N. special rapporteur on human rights,

Gaspar Biro, continued. It bowed to pressure at the U.N. Commission on Human Rights to permit the rapporteur to visit Sudan in August 1996, after a hiatus of several years. After his return in January 1997, however, he spent less than two days before the prosecutor general informed him that the government could no longer be responsible for his safety due to the anger of "the masses" at military developments on the eastern front. The special rapporteur had no choice but to leave. Remarkably, the U.N. Resident Representative openly criticized the rapporteur's decision, and reportedly later instructed U.N. staff not to meet with him. The special rapporteur made a return visit to Khartoum in September 1997.

UNICEF, the lead agency in the southern sector of Operation Lifeline Sudan (OLS), a program to assist the war-affected inside Sudan, has had a human rights dimension in its program since 1994. The OLS entered into "humanitarian ground rules" with the main rebel groups whereby they committed themselves (bilaterally) to respect international humanitarian law, children's rights, and U.N. and nongovernmental organizations' operations. This effort substantially increased SPLM/A and civilian awareness of and familiarity with human rights and humanitarian law concepts, roles and duties in the south, leading to an improved human rights climate.

Organization of African Unity

The African Commission on Human and People's Rights sent a delegation to Sudan in December 1996 to investigate human rights. This was the first human rights mission ever undertaken by the commission.

European Union

The ACP-European Union Joint Assembly in March deplored the violations of human rights in Sudan and condemned the government's obstruction of humanitarian aid to the Nuba Mountains. The European Parliament resolved in May to maintain sanctions, including an arms embargo, on Sudan on account of human rights violations and other problems. It voiced deep concern over the proliferation of war zones in the area and abuses of human rights, for which all warring parties were held responsible. Suspension of development aid was continued until there was an improvement in human rights. Humanitarian aid continued.

United States

The U.S. sent a State Department human rights official to present U.S. concerns about human rights to the Sudan government and, separately, to the SPLA. The U.S. Embassy in Khartoum remained functioning at a low level, with no U.S. citizen diplomatic personnel residing in Sudan as a sign of security concerns and diplomatic displeasure.

The U.S. announced in late 1996 that it would provide U.S. $20 million in surplus military equipment to Eritrea, Ethiopia and Uganda, for defensive purposes (referring to the government of Sudan's purported support for rebel forces from each of those countries). It also sent fifty elite U.S. Army Special Forces troops to Uganda to train Ugandan military forces for participation in African peacekeeping, arousing the suspicions of the Sudan government that the U.S. would train the SPLA and the Ugandans to fight in Sudan; the U.S. and Uganda denied this.

Multiple U.S. sanctions, required by U.S. law on account of the military coup that overthrew an elected government and the State Department's finding that Sudan supported terrorism, remained in force on Sudan. Humanitarian aid continued.

U.S. Treasury Department regulations created a loophole in the anti-terrorism sanctions in August 1996 permitting U.S. businesses to invest in Sudan. The loophole did not come to public attention until an article in The Washington Post in April 1997, after which bills were introduced in the U.S. Congress to close the loophole. In early November, the loophole was closed by executive order.

Legislation was proposed in the U.S. Congress in mid-1997 that would require the imposition of stiff sanctions on countries engaging in religious persecution. The government of Sudan was singled out by name in this draft legislation for engaging in religious persecution.

ZAMBIA

Human Rights Developments

On November 18, 1996 presidential and parliamentary elections were held in Zambia, five years after the first multiparty elections in November 1991. President Frederick Chiluba and his Movement for Multiparty Democracy (MMD) were returned to power with the majority of the contested seats in what was in reality a hollow defeat of an opposition that had chosen to boycott the electoral process. The opposition's candidate, former president Kenneth Kaunda had been barred from running on the grounds that his parents were not born in Zambia. Numerous human rights violations before the vote—centered on the MMD's manipulation of the constitutional reform process—had seriously undermined the electoral process by tilting it strongly in favor of the MMD. International ambivalence over rights conditions in the run-up to the election had resulted in a decision by the major donors to maintain an aid freeze that specifically targeted balance of payments support. Discredited and facing near bankruptcy, the Chiluba government made some largely superficial attempts over 1997 to improve its human rights record, in hope of restoring aid flows.

On October 28, 1997, President Chiluba announced that he had crushed a military coup against his government and that those "that rise by the sword will fall by the sword." He spoke several hours after state radio had reported that the president had been overthrown and coup leader "Captain Solo" had taken over. Military units loyal to the government had quickly surrounded the radio station: after some sporadic gunfire, one rebel was killed and Captain Stephen Lungu, alias "Capt. Solo" and fifteen other alleged coup plotters were arrested. President Chiluba declared a state of emergency on October 29.

Zambia Information Service Acting Deputy Director Mundia Nalishebo was suspended with five other state media journalists on November 25, 1996 after allegations were made that they had collaborated with an election monitoring group that had found the elections neither free nor fair. Since November 18, 1996, four journalists from the independent press have been imprisoned for their writing and had criminal charges brought against them; six journalists from the state-run television service were suspended and then dismissed.

The most-publicized case was the jailing of the *Post*'s Masautso Phiri, detained on February 11 for contempt of court after writing that "there was a rumor doing the rounds in Lusaka" that judges were accepting bribes to rule in President Chiluba's favor in the presidential petition. Judges whom Phiri had previously criticized heard his case and sentenced him to three month's imprisonment, with no right of appeal. He was the first Zambian journalist jailed for contempt.

Most ominously, the government introduced a draft Media Council Bill, which, by forcing journalists to register with the state, would have stripped those unregistered of the right to work and punished the unauthorized practice of journalism with jail terms and fines. After considerable controversy and international outcry, the state suspended consideration of the bill in April.

At his inauguration speech on November 21, President Chiluba warned nongovernmental organizations (NGOs) that they should not "instruct" the authorities, and in the following days, the government threatened to pass legislation to restrict their operations if they continued to act in an "anti-patriotic" manner. Following the announcement by the Committee for a Clean Campaign (CCC) that the elections had not been free and fair, the situation deteriorated. On November 24 and 25, police raided the Lusaka offices of the Zambia Independent Monitoring Team (ZIMT), the Committee for a Clean Campaign (CCC), and the offices of the Inter-Africa Network for Human Rights and Development (AFRONET), seizing files, documents, bank books and statements, computer diskettes and pamphlets. Many of these still have not been returned, and charges of receiving financial and material assistance from foreign governments and organizations were brought against these organizations.

The Foundation for Democratic Process (FODEP), which also concluded that the elections were not free and fair, was similarly targeted by the government. FODEP's tax exempt status was suddenly revoked and on December 19, 1996, it received a tax demand for outstanding tax arrears for K27 million (approximately U.S.$21,000): shortly afterwards, tax authorities confiscated all of the funds in FODEP's bank account.

The opposition was also harassed in the post election period. The main opposition party, the United National Independence Party (UNIP), was prevented from holding a peaceful rally in Ndola in February by police. Relatives of senior UNIP officials have also been subject to harassment: Vida Ngoma, the eighty-year-old aunt of Betty Kaunda, former president Kaunda's wife, was detained and kept in a cell for two days—with a man's corpse—after police searched her house without a warrant.

On August 23 UNIP leader Kaunda and Opposition Alliance chairman Roger Chongwe were shot and wounded by police as they were leaving a political rally in Kabwe. Bullets grazed the head of former president Kaunda, and struck Roger Chongwe in the cheek and neck. Several other people were also injured by police, who arrested twenty-one people and destroyed the podium at the rally site. The Zambian authorities also enforced a twenty-four-hour news blackout on the state-run Zambia National Broadcasting Corporation. Police arrested and assaulted Masautso Phiri of the *Post*, who took pictures at the rally of the police exerting excessive force on the public. A public enquiry into the shooting is underway.

An opposition petition challenging the fairness of the elections and President Chiluba's constitutional right to the presidency before the Supreme Court was a focus of Zambian political life, as the opposition produced evidence it claimed showed President Chiluba to be of Zairian parentage. Some of the witnesses brought to testify in this case were harassed, with death threats being reported by some witnesses. One witness, Theresa Mulenga Kalo, was arrested and held for several days by police after she testified and three others reportedly went into hiding.

A permanent Human Rights Commission was established by the government in March 1997, with a mandate to hear individual claims of human rights abuse and the maladministration of justice. The hasty process by which the government appointed its members, most of whom lacked robust human rights credentials, drew broad domestic criticism. The commission also lacked permanent premises, phone lines, and resources. The promotion of the commission's creation internationally, with a view to improving Zambia's image, also contrasted with its public profile in Zambia. Officials of the government printing office in Lusaka told Human Rights Watch that the documents concerning the commission were available "only to diplomats," after initially denying they had ever been printed. These documents were, however, widely distributed to international donors; indeed there is reason to believe that the creation of the commission was rushed so that it would be in place prior to the April 25 preliminary meeting of the Consultative Group of donors, in London.

While the Chiluba government adopted the language of support for human rights, it took several steps backward in human rights observance. On January 24, eight condemned prisoners at Mukobeko Maximum Prison were secretly executed on the same day that President Chiluba pardoned 600 inmates. Neither the names of the eight or their alleged crimes were officially released. But Human Rights Watch confirmed that they were executed on January 24, obtained the names and prison identification numbers of the eight, and identified the courts where they were sentenced and the crimes for which they were convicted. All of the executed had spent many years on death row—between ten and fifteen years in some cases. Notably, all of the condemned prisoners were sentenced to death during the Second Republic, years before the MMD government came to power in 1991. It is unclear why President Chiluba ordered their execution in January and whether any of the prisoners had any outstanding rights of appeal. As of April 1, there were 127 prisoners on death row, one of whom was a woman.

The Right to Monitor
The NGOs that conducted independent monitoring of the November 1996 elections were subjected to intensified harassment in the first few months of 1997. In particular, the umbrella coalition of the Committee for a Clean Campaign (CCC), the Zambia Independent Monitoring Team (ZIMT), the Foundation for Democratic Progress (FODEP), and the Inter-Africa Network for Human Rights and Development (AFRONET) took the brunt of state intolerance for expressing the view that the elections were not free or fair.

The government continued to be critical of the national origins of NGOs and foreign support for them. After receiving the credentials of the new ambassadors of Sweden, China and South Africa in late December 1996, President Chiluba accused several NGOs of serving foreign interests and warned that "non-indigenous" NGOs were potential sites of "mercenary" operations. He charged that Zambia had no indigenous NGOs. At the opening of parliament on January 17, President Chiluba said that local election monitors who questioned the legitimacy of the November poll were "unpatriotic" and that the government intended to introduce new legislation to control such "wilful" behavior. He said he planned new laws "which would make election monitoring teams and all NGOs accountable to both their members and to society."

International human rights monitoring groups experienced no government obstruction, although senior government officials were reluctant to discuss human rights issues with them. The Paris-based media watchdog Reporters Sans Frontières visited Zambia in May and published a report on the state of the media, urging the government to scrap the media council bill.

The Role of the International Community
The international community's efforts seeking improved human rights and good governance practice in Zambia have been exemplary. The resolve to offer renewed balance of payments support in return for positive actions by the Zambian government had results in the run-up and aftermath of the July 10-11 Consultative Group meeting in Paris.

Aid of up to U.S. $1 billion a year was central to the economic reform program of President Chiluba. As the country's largest source of foreign exchange, aid accounted for some 70 percent of gross domestic product. A decline in the production of copper, which in previous years accounted for more than 95 percent of export earnings (a fall only partially compensated by a rise in world prices), has created a growing dependency on aid. In 1992, at the height of donor goodwill, Zambia received $1.2 billion in non-emergency aid, three times the average in Africa, as well as $400 million in emergency aid. In 1996 the aid pledged was just $800 million, down a third from the 1992 figure. The World Bank had $120 million in aid allocated for 1997 in comparison to the 1996 figure of $140-150 million.

The difference between the 1992 and the 1996 figures was the result of Zambia's increasing aid needs being met with tougher conditions set by the international donor community. At the heart of the debate on the role of aid in economic reconstruction were issues of good governance, accountability and democratic practice.

Two Consultative Group meetings, scheduled for December 1996 and March

1997, were deferred, presumably with the purpose of putting further pressure on the Zambian government to reform. On April 25, at the Zambian government's request, a pre-Consultative Group meeting with the donors was held in London. The Zambian government presented itself as having made considerable progress on governance and economic reform. On the basis of that meeting, the donors agreed to convene the next Consultative Group meeting in Paris on July 10-11. During the Paris meeting human rights issues were raised over both days, although the World Bank had attempted to limit discussion of governance issues to a pre-meeting on July 9. The meeting concluded that a further meeting was needed in December 1997 prior to full-balance of payments resumption by members. The resumption of balance of payments would be conditional on unspecified governance and economic targets being met.

European Union, Norway and Japan

In a statement on November 20, 1996 the European Union (E.U.), said it was "pleased" that the November 18 elections were peaceful and orderly, but expressed concern at the discontent of some parties with the process. The E.U. urged the new Zambian government to avoid confrontations with political parties and also to stress political and economic reform.

On December 9, 1996 the German embassy announced that it had cut part of its bilateral aid to Zambia in protest against the political impasse. Other E.U. countries, notably the Netherlands and Sweden, also raised their concerns about human rights standards with the government. Britain and Finland voiced their rights concerns in private. Norway, a non-E.U. member, also played an important role: its ambassador, Jon Lomay, in May declared that Norway was still concerned about the implementation of good governance and would continue to monitor the situation closely. The Japanese government's Lusaka mission also continued to emphasize the need for good governance. The Republic of Ireland's diplomatic mission in Lusaka, which has shown little enthusiasm about public criticism of human rights practices during 1996, spoke out strongly in April about the media council bill.

United States

Ambassador Arlene Render took a strong critical stand toward the Chiluba government, calling for change and the implementation of democratic values in society when she presented her credentials in early 1997. She urged the Chiluba administration to embrace civil society as an essential engine and balancing force for change and transformation. Zambian Minister Without Portfolio Michael Sata accused the United States government of hostility toward the Zambian government and of taking a hard-line stance, despite the country being considered a yardstick for democracy in Africa. But U.S. Ambassador Render and a visiting State Department deputy director for Southern Africa said that Washington would be unrelenting in its demand for good governance in Lusaka, which the U.S. saw as inseparable with economic performance.

Relevant Human Rights Watch reports:

Reality Amidst Contradictions: Human Rights Since the 1996 Elections, 7/97
Elections and Human Rights in the Third Republic, 12/96

HUMAN
RIGHTS
WATCH

AMERICAS

HUMAN RIGHTS WATCH/AMERICAS OVERVIEW

On September 25, in a ceremony at the Organization of American States (OAS) headquarters in Washington, D.C., the OAS amended its charter to allow the hemisphere's governments to ostracize from the group any government coming to power by coup. This welcome step underlined the growing consensus in the region that maintaining constitutional, democratic governments is in each nation's best interests. And indeed, with scant exceptions, the region comprising Latin America and the Caribbean stood out as one of the few parts of the world where elected civilian government seemed firmly ensconced.

The history of the area makes clear that elected governments have offered the greatest possibility for enjoyment of human rights; in the past, the rupture of constitutional order in every case brought serious and systematic human rights violations. In this sense, the 1997 congressional and municipal elections in Mexico, the first in which opposition parties could compete with the long-governing Party of the Institutionalized Revolution (Partido de la Revolución Institucionalizada, PRI) on a level playing field, marked a significant step forward for democracy in the region. Cuba—where an unelected government completed thirty-eight years in power—remained the exception to the trend toward greater political space.

But while elected government may be a precondition for human rights to be respected, the region's dismal record shows that it is by no means sufficient. Massive and serious human rights violations plagued the region in 1997, regardless of the regular alternation in power of elected governments. Indeed, the lack of respect for human rights in countries as diverse as Colombia, Peru, Venezuela, Brazil, Argentina, and the Dominican Republic showed that elections are only the first step toward genuine democracy. Massacres, extrajudicial executions, disappearances, torture and other forms of police brutality, along with inhumane prison conditions stubbornly continued.

Many of the region's elected governments accepted legitimate criticism of their abusive human rights practices, abandoning the defensive reactions of the past. Many realized they stood only to benefit from opening communication with human rights monitors. The exceptions remained the governments of Fidel Castro in Cuba, which continued to deny international human rights groups access to the island while harassing and prosecuting those attempting to monitor rights domestically; the government of Alberto Fujimori in Peru, which denounced human rights groups' motives even as it adopted some of their recommendations; and the Ernesto Zedillo government in Mexico, which admitted to shortcomings in police behavior but expelled international human rights monitors and categorically rejected their findings. Indeed, the only governments in the region which continued to violate human rights as part of central government policy were Cuba and Peru.

Even governments that accepted international criticism failed to make human rights protection a priority by designing programs and dedicating resources to the eradication of torture, police brutality, arbitrary detention, and other widespread abuses, as well as the impunity with which these acts were committed.

Human Rights Developments

In Colombia, thirty-five massacres claimed the lives of 272 individuals in the first eight months of the year, and some 450 more died in individual political assassinations during the same period. The bulk of the carnage was attributable to paramilitary groups, usually working with military acquiescence and in some cases with military support; according to the Colombian Commission of Jurists (CCJ), a respected human rights organization, 76 percent of the human rights violations recorded in 1997 were the work of paramilitaries, 17 percent were the work of guerrillas, and 7 percent were the work of state agents. In Peru, torture remained a common practice employed by police against both accused terrorists and common criminal suspects, and even against a member of the army intelligence service accused of leaking information to the press. In Mexico, political violence in rural areas—in some cases with official involvement or acquiescence—remained acute, and the justice system showed a marked tendency to be lenient with the government's supporters and severe with its opponents. In Brazil, amateur videotapes capturing random police brutality shocked a nation seemingly inured to the fate of criminal suspects. In Venezuela, security forces resorted to systematic abuses, including torture, extrajudicial executions, and the disproportionate use of lethal force in their efforts to control crime in urban areas.

President Fujimori's government in Peru demonstrated its lack of respect for the rule of law by a dizzying series of maneuvers including the sacking of three of the seven members of the Constitutional Court after they ruled against a third presidential term for Fujimori. The judges' removal effectively put the court out of business for settling constitutional conflicts.

Prison conditions in many parts of the region were so bad as to constitute serious human rights violations, and a majority of those held had not been convicted of any crime; indeed, some detainees were held for years in preventive detention, in violation of the presumption of innocence. Some 90 percent of Honduran, Paraguayan, and Uruguayan inmates were unsentenced, while in the Dominican Republic, Panama, Haiti, El Salvador, Peru, and Venezuela, the proportion of unsentenced inmates ranged from 65 to 85 percent. In the Dominican Republic, we found one prisoner who had been held for ten years without trial.

Meanwhile, in a serious setback to international human rights protection mechanisms, Jamaica announced in late October that it would become the first country in the world to withdraw from the Optional Protocol to the International Covenant on Civil and Political Rights. North Korea renounced the covenant itself in August. The Jamaican move, which will have the effect of preventing individuals whose rights may have been violated by the Jamaican government from appealing to the United Nations Human Rights Committee, was apparently intended to deny death row inmates an opportunity for U.N. review.

While the overall picture in 1997 was of continued serious violations, several positive developments occurred. The signing of a final peace agreement in Guatemala, bringing an end to three decades of armed conflict, contributed to a continuing decline in the number of human rights violations linked to counterinsurgency operations. Peru's government in October suspended the use of "faceless courts" to try terrorist suspects. Those courts had presented numerous and profound due process violations. Persons accused of the aggravated form of terrorism, in Peru termed "treason," will continue to be tried by military courts, although the judges will no longer remain anonymous. The amendment of Brazil's criminal code to codify torture as a crime marked a step forward in an effort to eradicate that practice. And in Colombia, President Ernesto Samper introduced two pieces of important legislation: one, would ensure that gross violations of human rights be prosecuted in civilian, rather than military, courts, and a second would make forced disappearance a crime. In Venezuela, the Supreme Court on October 14 knocked down as unconstitutional a 1956 vagrancy law which allowed administrative detention for up to five years of possible delinquents without proof of individual wrongdoing.

Perhaps the most ominous development in 1997 was the persecution in several countries of some of the region's most outstanding reporters and news media. Thin-skinned officials in Panama, Argentina, and Peru lashed out at their critics among the press, demonstrating an intolerance for criticism more characteristic of authoritarian regimes than democratic governments. In Cuba, harassment of the small independent press corps continued unabated.

In Argentina, in January, news photographer José Luis Cabezas was handcuffed, beaten, shot dead and set on fire, in a chilling reminder of the dangers of investigating police corruption. At this writing, three provincial police officers have been detained in connection with the case. On September 11, the only Argentine Navy officer to have voluntarily confessed to serious human rights abuses during the military dictatorships from 1976 to 1983 was abducted by armed men with police credentials. During the two hours he was held, former Capt. Adolfo Scilingo was beaten and threatened, and the initials of journalists to whom he had told his story were carved in his face. His captors threatened to kill Scilingo as well as those journalists: Mariano Grondona, Magdalena Ruiz Guiñazú, and Horacio Verbitsky. President Carlos Menem's reaction to this gangland-style incident, in which he suggested that Scilingo was not to be believed, followed unfortunate comments he had made shortly before the attack, in which Menem appeared to suggest that the limits of press freedoms could be determined by violence.

The government of Ernesto Pérez Balladares in Panama took steps to suppress freedom of expression by setting in motion a deportation order against Peruvian journalist Gustavo Gorriti, associate editor of the daily *La Prensa*. Gorriti's articles covering corruption in official circles irked those in power, who sought to oust the award-winning reporter based on specious legal grounds. Gorriti's investigative unit had written about drug money flowing into President Pérez Balladares's campaign and alleged irregularities in the accumulation of television networks by the president's cousin. However, in a significant victory for press freedom, the government reversed itself in October, allowing *La Prensa* to retain Gorriti in a senior position in Panama and vowing to seek derogation of legislation limiting the role of foreign nationals in the media.

In Peru, the government launched a campaign against the Israeli-born majority shareholder in Lima's Channel 2 television, Baruch Ivcher Bronstein. Channel 2 was the first to broadcast an interview with Leonor La Rosa, an army intelligence agent severely tortured by her employers on suspicion of having leaked information about planned persecution of the press. An escalating campaign of harassment against Ivcher culminated in the July 13 revocation of his Peruvian nationality, followed by takeover of the television station by the pro-government minority shareholders. Other journalists faced serious harassment, including Blanca Rosales, managing editor of the daily *La República*, who was abducted, beaten, and threatened by unidentified armed men before being released.

Cuban authorities continued to intimidate journalists. Among those arrested were Héctor Peraza Linares, codirector of the Habana Press news agency, and Raúl Rivero, the head of Cuba Press. On February 26, a group of government supporters gathered outside the homes of Cuba Press journalists Tania Quintero and Ana Luisa Baeza, throwing objects and shouting. Joaquín Torres Alvarez, the director of Habana Press, was beaten in May by several assailants whom he later identified as members of the State Security forces and representatives of his neighborhood's communist party office.

In Mexico, gunmen murdered Jesús Bueno León of the Guerrero state weekly *7 Días;* Bueno had written that he believed state officials planned to kill him in retaliation for his reporting. After covering police excesses in Mexico City in September, four reporters were abducted and tortured by unidentified assailants.

In December 1996, a new series of television regulations went into effect in Colombia, including limitations on the broadcasting of violent images which could, if enforced, seriously restrict news coverage, among other things, the measures restricted airing statements from guerrilla or other criminal organizations. Although the regulations have not produced attempts at censorship as of this writing, their implementation granted the government tremendous leeway to limit television coverage. Colombian cameraman Ricardo Velez fled the country in September after receiving serious threats on his life related to a suit for damages he filed against the army. Soldiers had beaten Velez while he filmed repression of a protest march in 1996.

In June, the Inter-American Commission on Human Rights published a report finding that the government of Chile had violated the right to freedom of expression by banning the sale of a book written by Francisco Martorell in 1993. The book, *Diplomatic Impunity*, concerned the circumstances leading up to the departure of the former ambassador of Argentina in Chile, Oscar Spinosa Melo. The commission called on the government of Chile to lift the ban on the book.

Meanwhile, when President Rafael Caldera of Venezuela recommended that a November 1997 Iberoamerican summit in Caracas suggest measures to protect the "right to truthful information," this concept—suggesting governmental control over press content—provoking well-deserved approbrium from press watchdog groups.

The Right to Monitor

Human rights monitors continued to face threats, harassment, and physical violence in several countries in the region, and in many cases governments failed to take measures to investigate, prosecute, and punish those responsible. In a dangerous continent, Colombia remained the killing field for human rights defenders. Mario Calderón and Elsa Alvarado of the Center for Research and Popular Education (Centro de Investigación y Educación Popular, CINEP) were killed by masked gunmen in their Bogotá apartment, apparently in retaliation for their human rights work. Alvarado's father was also killed and her mother seriously wounded in the same incident. On September 28, authorities arrested five people who may have taken part in the killing. Among the other human rights monitors killed by unidenti-

fied gunmen in Colombia in apparent retaliation for their work were Nazareno de Jesús Rivera of the Segovia Human Rights Committee, Margarita Guzmán a former colleague who pressed for an investigation, and Víctor Julio Garzón, a member of the all-but-extinguished Meta Civic Committee for Human Rights. A third member of the Segovia Human Rights Committee, Jaime Ortiz Londoño, was forcibly disappeared. Several other monitors have been forced to leave the country because of death threats. On October 26, the guerrilla group known as the National Liberation Army (Ejército de Liberación Nacional, ELN) kidnapped two election observers from the Organization of American States in an effort to frustrate municipal elections. The guerrillas freed the observers after more than a week.

In Cuba, where monitoring the human rights policies of the government runs afoul of numerous provisions of the penal code restricting free expression and association, those who attempted to defend human rights faced harassment and prosecution. On July 15, authorities detained human rights lawyer René Gómez Manzano along with three other prominent dissidents. At this writing, the four leaders remain in prison facing possible trial for enemy propaganda.

Human rights advocate Francisco Soberón, head of Peru's Pro-Human Rights Association (Asociación Pro-Derechos Humanos, APRODEH), faced repeated anonymous death threats apparently in retaliation for APRODEH's defense of a respected judge facing arbitrary legal proceedings and a police whistle-blower facing persecution.

In Bolivia, National Police agents arrested Waldo Albarracín, president of the Permanent Assembly of Human Rights (Asamblea Permanente de Derechos Humanos, APDH) on January 25 and allegedly tortured him for over three hours. The police agents reportedly beat Albarracín all over his body, including his genitalia, subjected him to death threats and near-asphyxiation. Albarracín was later hospitalized with serious wounds.

Church-related human rights groups in Mexico continued to come under attack. Padre Camilo Daniel, founder of Chihuahua's Commission of Solidarity and Defense of Human Rights (Comisión de Solidaridad y Defensa de los Derechos Humanos, COSYDDHAC), and his secretary were threatened with death in January. On February 15, armed men ambushed a group of investigators from the Fray Bartolomé de las Casas Human Rights Center in the Chiapas town of Sabanilla, wounding José Montero in the arm. Also in Chiapas, assailants tried unsuccessfully to burn the offices of the Coordinating Group of Nongovernmental Organizations for Peace (Coordinadora de Organismos No Gubernamentales por la Paz, CONPAZ).

In Venezuela, members of the Human Rights Office of the Vicariate of Puerto Ayacucho, state of Amazonas, came under attack for their work on behalf of the Amazonian Indians. Following inflammatory criticism of the office by local politicians and members of the regional government, two vehicles belonging to the office were damaged by acid.

In November, Human Rights Watch honored Carlos Rodríguez Mejía, a distinguished human rights attorney from the Bogotá-based Colombian Commission of Jurists (Comisión Colombiana de Juristas, CCJ), in our annual celebration of human rights monitors from around the world. Rodríguez is a founding member of the CCJ, one of Colombia's most effective human rights groups. It was largely through Rodríguez's efforts that the U.N. agreed to set up a special office of its High Commissioner for Human Rights in Bogotá to press the government to protect human rights.

The Role of the International Community

United Nations

The presence of the United Nations human rights mission in Guatemala, known as MINUGUA, continued to contribute to reduced levels of politically motivated human rights violations. Nonetheless, the mission's prestige suffered a blow with the delay in publication of its investigation into the forced disappearance of a guerrilla captured by the army in October 1996. To its credit, MINUGUA continued to press the case despite stonewalling by the government.

The U.N. High Commissioner for Human Rights opened a field office in Colombia, a long-awaited move that held the promise of reducing violations. In April, the U.N. Human Rights Committee in New York lamented that "gross and massive human rights violations continue to occur in Colombia." It expressed its "deep concern" over evidence that paramilitary groups "receive support from members of the military" and that "impunity continues to be a widespread phenomenon." Torture in Mexico also received well-deserved scrutiny from the U.N. In its conclusions reached in April, the Committee Against Torture praised legal reforms but strongly faulted the systematic practice of torture in the country. In August, Nigel Rodley, the U.N. special rapporteur on torture, visited Mexico to document the nature and extent of violations.

United States

The State Department's annual *Country Reports on Human Rights Practices* provided an accurate and detailed description of the human rights problems and practices in the region. In a departure from past practice, the Clinton administration in 1997 also took steps to raise human rights issues to a more prominent position in its agenda with the region, on some occasions issuing public statements in countries where it had previously been silent. In Colombia, the U.S. embassy publicly expressed its concern over military authorities' verbal attacks on civilian investigators who linked Gen. Farouk Yanine to the Puerto Araujo massacre, the first time it had spoken publicly on a human rights case. And despite strong pressure from members of Congress eager to fund Colombian anti-narcotics campaigns regardless of human rights violations by the army, the Clinton administration held up aid to the military until August, when the Colombian armed forces agreed to human rights conditions. At this writing, it is unclear how the conditions will be implemented and to what extent the U.S., in making aid determinations, will rely exclusively on the Colombian defense ministry's evaluation of its own troops' human rights record.

In Peru, U.S. officials issued strong statements on the sacking of three members of the Constitutional Court and on the revocation of Ivcher's citizenship. Meanwhile, private pressure from the administration contributed significantly to convincing the government of Panama to reverse its plan to deport investigative journalist Gustavo Gorriti. In particular, the influence exerted by First Lady Hillary Rodham Clinton during her visit to Panama in October appeared to have had an important impact. In Mexico, Secretary of State Madeleine Albright met with local human rights organizations, a significant symbolic action given the hostility these groups face from the authorities.

Efforts to make public the U.S. role in past human rights violations in the region inched forward, as the Central Intelligence Agency (CIA) completed, but did not make public, an internal study of its ties to a military death squad in Honduras. CIA documents released in August confirmed that the agency knew about the interrogation and torture of civilians by that unit in the 1980s and that agents visited at least one of its clandestine prisoners. Documents declassified in 1997 about U.S. involvement in the coup that overthrew the elected government of Jacobo Arbenz in Guatemala in 1954 provided a chilling inside look at the methods used and promoted by the agency, including targeted political assassination and mass murder.

Meanwhile the Clinton administration acted to protect from deportation Emmanuel "Toto" Constant, wanted in Haiti for massive and serious human rights violations committed by a paramilitary group he headed during the military dictatorship. Constant received CIA payments in Haiti while directing the Front for the Advancement and Progress of Haiti (Front pour l'Avancement et Progrés d'Haïti, FRAPH). Moreover, the U.S. embassy in Port-au-Prince refused to return to the Haitian government the approximately 160,000 pages of documents and other materials seized from FRAPH and Haitian military headquarters in 1994, documents that could assist prosecutors' efforts to punish human rights violators.

While discussions of free trade issues dominated his tour of Latin capitals in October, President Clinton made important statements on behalf of freedom of expression in Argentina, where attacks on journalists ascended in 1997 with apparent government tolerance. During the president's trip to Mexico and Central America in May, Clinton failed to mention human rights.

European Union

In December 1996, the European Union Council of Ministers adopted a new, stronger policy toward Cuba, making full economic cooperation conditional on human rights improvements. Unfortunately, European investors in Cuba, as well as Canadians and others, failed to adopt effective strategies to ensure respect for labor rights in their Cuban workplaces, where government-dominated projects denied basic rights of free association and speech.

An effort by Mexico to negotiate a trade and political cooperation agreement with the European Union without the E.U.'s standard human rights clause was defeated when the Zedillo government, in July, agreed to the insertion of the full human rights clause.

In July, the European Parliament issued a strong resolution calling on the Fujimori government to reinstate the magistrates of the Constitutional Court who had been dismissed by the Congress; to guarantee freedom of expression; and to abolish the practice of torture.

Some European embassies and diplomats took high-profile roles in attempting to lessen political violence and the suffering it caused in Colombia. In April, Netherlands Amb. Gysbert Bos made a three-day visit to the Middle Magdalena region, in part to draw attention to a rise in paramilitary activity and displacement. The E.U. continued to pressure Colombia to improve its human rights record, and announced in September its full support for a negotiated settlement to political conflict.

The Work of
Human Rights Watch

In 1997, we published book-length reports in English and Spanish on rural violence in Mexico, prison conditions in Venezuela, and violations of children's rights in Guatemala. Our report on police brutality in Brazil was published in English and Portuguese. Human Rights Watch released each report in the respective nation's capital, followed up with a week discussing our conclusions and recommendations with senior government officials, European Union and U.S. ambassadors, human rights organizations, and the press. As part of this and other in-country advocacy trips, the division's executive director met in 1997 with the presidents of Brazil, Colombia, and Venezuela to urge attention to human rights violations.

Several issues we have pressed jointly with other human rights organizations for years produced results in 1997: In Peru, the government suspended the use of civilian faceless courts used to try terrorist suspects; in Brazil, legislation was passed to codify torture; and in Colombia legislation was introduced to try human rights cases in ordinary, rather than military courts. Cases that we have litigated before the Inter-American Commission on Human Rights and the Inter-American Court of Human Rights together with the Center for Justice and International Law (CEJIL) and local partners bore results as well: the court found that the government of Peru had violated the American Convention on Human Rights in the detention, torture, rape, and prosecution before faceless military and civilian courts of María Elena Loayza Tamayo and ordered her release, a move the government complied with shortly thereafter; and the commission mediated a friendly settlement in the case of the extrajudicial execution of a human rights activist and wounding of a second in Colotenango, Guatemala, in 1993. The settlement required the government to prosecute and punish those responsible and provide reparations to the community for numerous abuses suffered at the hands of military-sponsored civil patrols. Also in Peru, the government released Luis Cantoral Benavides, whose case we had taken to the Inter-American Court of Human Rights. Our legal representation of author Francisco Martorell at the Inter-American Commission also brought a victory when the commission in June released its final report on the case, finding Chile had violated his right to freedom of expression by banning the sale of his book. In July 1997, the United States National Administrative Office (U.S. NAO, the body charged with hearing cases of alleged violations by Canada or Mexico of the North American Agreement on Labor Cooperation, commonly referred to as the labor rights side agreement of the North American Free Trade Agreement, NAFTA) accepted for review a petition filed by Human Rights Watch and the National Association of Democratic Lawyers (Asociación Nacional de Abogados Democráticos), which charged the Mexican government with failure to enforce its domestic labor code or set up effective mechanisms to adjudicate labor disputes. The U.S. NAO was expected to issue its findings by the end of November 1997.

In June, a campaign we organized involving press, regional governments, and human rights organizations from several countries succeeded in defeating a candidate promoted by Guatemala to join the Inter-American Commission on Human Rights. The candidate's career of political alliances with military dictators made him unsuitable for the post. We also protested violations of freedom of expression across the continent and pressed the Clinton administration to raise the issue during the president's October trip to Latin America.

For a listing of relevant reports and missions, see page 459 at the end of this report. Partial listings also follow each country chapter.

BRAZIL

Human Rights Developments

Several well-publicized incidents of police brutality and corruption constituted the principal human rights developments in 1997 in Brazil. Despite encouraging good faith efforts by many authorities, including at the federal executive level, human rights violations continued to be severe and varied.

On March 31, Brazil's widely viewed television news program *Jornal Nacional* broadcast an amateur video showing military police extorting, beating, torturing, and humiliating persons randomly stopped at a roadblock in Diadema, a working class suburb of São Paulo. In one scene, the police without provocation shot and killed an unarmed passenger in a car after a random stop. The explicit images, which were filmed on at least two separate occasions, sent shock waves throughout Brazil and the world. The videos confirmed what human rights groups had been reporting about the frequently violent and unprofessional nature of military police in São Paulo. Subsequent journalistic investigations revealed that dozens of complaints about these kinds of violence and corruption had been lodged with police authorities in Diadema in the months preceding the March televised incident, without results.

A week later, on April 7, the same national news program exhibited another amateur video, this time depicting extortion, severe beatings, and humiliations inflicted by the Rio de Janeiro military police in Cidade de Deus, a poor community on the city's outskirts. The Cidade de Deus video shifted the focus of debate to the national nature of the problem, as well as to programs of the Rio State Secretariat of Public Security that promoted and paid bonuses to police officers involved in acts of bravery. In the days following the video's airing, reports surfaced demonstrating that three of the six policemen involved were receiving monthly pay bonuses for bravery. In the midst of this debate, Human Rights Watch noted, in a detailed report released at this time that, in practice, "bravery" bonuses were awarded to police officers that had killed criminal suspects, regardless of the circumstances. Human Rights Watch's research showed that in a one-year period, from May 1995 to April 1996, at least 179 police officers were promoted in Rio de Janeiro in connection with incidents that claimed the lives of seventy-two civilians and six police officers. The victims' autopsy reports showed that in some of these cases, they were the victims of summary executions, rather than shootouts, as the reports authorizing bravery rewards contended.

Throughout 1997, Rio de Janeiro authorities continued to promote and pay bonuses to police involved in acts of bravery. In April, the Bar Association of Rio de Janeiro, citing the Human Rights Watch report, filed an unsuccessful challenge to the constitutionality of the bravery measures in state court. Following reports in September in Rio dailies to the effect that fourteen ranking military police officers indicted for their involvement in a gambling racket had received pay raises and promotions for bravery, State Representative Carlos Minc introduced legislation into the Rio State Legislative Assembly seeking to limit the bonuses and promotions to police not facing indictment for serious crimes. In October, the Superior Institute of Religious Studies (Instituto Superior de Estudos Relgiosos, ISER) a leading nongovernmental organization (NGO), released a report demonstrating that the Rio police had killed at least 942 civilians in the period from January 1, 1993 through July 31, 1996. The ISER study included analysis of the autopsy reports demonstrating that at least forty of these 942 civilians had been shot at point-blank range. Figures regarding the high incidence of bullets to victims' heads and chests and the percentage of shots from behind suggested that the number of summary executions may well have been substantially higher. The study also demonstrated that the number of persons killed by the police in the city of Rio rose from sixteen per month prior to May

1995, when the current public security secretary, Gen. Nilton Cerqueira, assumed control of Rio police forces, to thirty-two per month afterwards. In this same period, the Rio police killed 3.4 times as many civilians as they wounded.

Despite attention focused on the São Paulo military police due to the Diadema incident, official figures showed that in 1997 military police killings of civilians in the state continued to decline. In the first eight months of 1997, military police in the São Paulo metropolitan area killed eighty-six civilians while on duty and fifty-one more while off duty. In those same eight months, the military police suffered eight fatalities on duty and twenty-four off-duty deaths. In 1996, the number of civilians killed by military police in São Paulo, both on and off duty had fallen to 183, the lowest full-year total in a decade. Twenty-seven police (twenty-one while off duty) were killed during this same period. By contrast, four years earlier, in 1992, the military police killed 1,190 civilians in São Paulo while suffering fifty-five fatalities. These reductions were widely believed to be related to the creation and continued operation of the Office of the Ombudsman for the Police, as well as a state program (Programa de Acompanhamento de Policiais Envolvidos em Ocorrências de Alto Risco-PROAR) that required police officers to be removed from street duty, at least temporarily, when involved in fatal shootings. In December 1995, the State Secretariat of Public Security had extended the PROAR program to include police officers involved in killings while off duty.

Nonetheless, throughout 1997, São Paulo police violated basic human rights. On May 20, military police stormed the Fazenda da Juta housing complex, which had been occupied by squatters for several months. When the squatters resisted eviction by throwing rocks and sticks, the police, not specially trained for such operations and without adequate equipment such as shields and helmets, fired at the squatters, killing three. One of the victims was killed by a single bullet to the back of the head, suggest-ing a summary execution. Another squatter was killed by bullets to the chest, which a police officer contended he fired in self-defense after being knocked to the ground. The coroner's report, however, indicated the victim had been shot twice through the chest in a straight line, casting doubt on the police officer's version of events.

In September, the involvement of two São Paulo military police officers in the kidnapping and murder of an eight-year-old boy prompted the State Secretary of Public Security to fire the commander of the State Military Police. During the same week, in Brasília, military police officers orchestrated the kidnapping of the young daughter of a federal congressman, who was released after a rescue operation. These two incidents once again prompted intense debate on the issue of police violence and corruption.

In April and May, shortly after the images in Diadema and Cidade de Deus aired on television, a special state parliamentary inquiry in Minas Gerais state gathered evidence of the widespread practice of torture in police precincts in Belo Horizonte. Members of the state parliamentary inquiry commission appeared in one infamous precinct with a video camera and filmed a room that detainees had described as a torture center. The video corroborated the statements given to the parliamentary commission both in terms of the location of the torture center and its characteristics: the room included rivets to hang a "parrot's perch," a bar on which prisoners are extended during torture sessions, and a water faucet and two exposed wires, presumably used for electric shock torture. Despite this and other evidence, Minas Gerais Gov. Eduardo Azeredo denied that the police in Minas Gerais practiced torture and refused to order a full investigation.

Two months later, the Minas Gerais military police organized a massive strike. Demanding higher wages—military police in Minas Gerais received a starting wage of roughly U.S.$400 per month—the police organized a strike that paralyzed the state for two weeks in June. By the end of the month, the governor ceded to the striking police officers' demands, authorizing a 50 percent base salary hike. The Minas Gerais dispute touched off similar protests or wage demands in more than a dozen other Brazilian states in July and August.

Prompted by this police unrest as well as increasing popular and media attention to the severe problem of police corruption and violence, a national working group led by newly appointed National Secretary for Human Rights José Gregori studied needed changes to improve public security throughout Brazil. In September, as a result of the work of these groups, President Fernando Henrique Cardoso proposed a series of legislative and constitutional modifications in police structure, including an amendment to eliminate military courts entirely, to authorize the states to unify the civil and military police should they so choose, and to protect witnesses to incidents of police abuse. If implemented, these measures could significantly reduce the incidence of gross human rights violations committed by state agents. However, it was unclear whether these reforms would be given priority by Brazil's Congress, whose record for enacting human rights measures continued to be poor in 1997. At this writing, the legislative package is still pending in Congress. So, too, are dozens of other important proposals included in the National Human Rights Plan, released on May 13, 1996. Since then, the Brazilian Congress managed to approve only a handful of measures. Apart from a law criminalizing torture passed in the wake of the Diadema incident, the only other public security reform passed by Congress since the plan's release was Law 9.437, which criminalized illegal weapons possessions, signed into law on February 20.

Prison conditions throughout Brazil continued to violate international standards in 1997. The primary violations involved official violence directed against detainees or complicity in prisoner-against-prisoner violence; overcrowding; unsanitary conditions; and lack of access to recreation, education and other benefits. Substandard conditions were exacerbated in police precincts' detention centers, where prisoners were held for months and even years. In São Paulo, nearly 30,000 detainees were held in precincts, which according to the most generous official estimates, had capacity for fewer than 16,000. The São Paulo daily *Folha de S. Paulo* reported eighty rebellions in precincts and eleven more in penitentiaries in the state in the first six months of 1997, up from seventy-one rebellions in precincts and eight in penitentiaries in all of 1996. By early October the number of revolts in penitentiaries rose to fifteen. In September, São Paulo authorities announced the signing of contracts to build seven prisons with a total capacity for 5,544 detainees. If completed on schedule, along with the planned construction of fourteen more prisons, these centers of detention would provide space for an additional 17,520 prisoners by the end of 1998.

To their credit, São Paulo authorities rarely used deadly force to control prison and precinct rebellions. This was not always the case, however, in all of Brazil in 1997. On July 29, military police entered the Róger penitentiary in João Pessoa, Paraíba, to end a prison riot in which a group of prisoners had seized the warden, three guards, and two fellow prisoners as hostages. Subsequent medical examinations demonstrated that seven of the eight prisoners killed had been severely beaten and likely tortured and then summarily executed, a conclusion that the state governor himself accepted. Two months later, military police responded to another rebellion in the same facility killing one detainee. Investigations by the João Pessoa municipal human rights commission showed that the prisoners were armed with sticks and that the police response was, at a minimum, disproportionate. In October, two more prisoners were killed during an escape attempt.

The problem of prison and precinct overcrowding was exacerbated in 1997 by the existence of prisoners held in these detention facilities beyond the terms of their sentences. In September, ad hoc investigatory commissions composed of members of the State Bar Association, the State Attorney General's Office and representatives of the State Legislative Assembly documented irregularities observed during surprise visits in the state of São Paulo. For example, the ad hoc commissions found several detainees held beyond the terms of their sentences, scores of others eligible for parole or early or day release programs, as well as one case of a detainee held for more than two years based on a provision which allows thirty-day renewable detention periods.

In 1997, rural conflicts continued to seize headlines as the Movement of Landless Rural Workers (Movimento dos Trabalhadores Rurais Sem Terra, MST) intensified its efforts to force the government to take land reform measures. In numerous incidents throughout 1997, land occupations by the MST and other groups of landless resulted in armed conflicts. According to the Pastoral Land Commission (Comissão Pastoral da Terra, CPT), through mid-October 1997 twenty-five civilians had been killed in these land conflicts. While in 1996, the military police were responsible for most of those killed in land conflicts (including nineteen squatters in a single incident in El Dorado do Carajás on April 17, 1996), in 1997, according to the CPT, hired gunmen killed a much greater proportion of the victims in land disputes.

Figures for 1996 and partial figures for 1997 demonstrated an increase in both the number of land disputes and the violence practiced in their resolution. In 1996, forty-six individuals were killed in land conflicts, an increase from the thirty-nine deaths in conflicts registered in 1995. The CPT also registered a significant rise in the number of conflicts in 1996 (653) compared to 1995 (440), as well as the number of persons involved, which rose from 318,458 in 1995 to 481,490 in 1997. Although figures for 1997 were not available, the CPT reported that throughout the year, this trend of escalating land conflict and increasingly violent resolution continued in 1997.

A positive development in the campaign against rural violence and impunity was the June 27-29 jury trial and conviction in Imperatriz, Maranhão state, of three landowners for ordering the 1986 targeted assassination of Father Josimo Moraes Tavares, regional director of the Pastoral Land Commission. Landowners Guiomar Teodoro da Silva, Adailson Gomes Vieira and Geraldo Paulo Vieira, arrested in 1994 and held in pre-trial detention since then, were sentenced to fourteen, eighteen and nineteen years' imprisonment, respectively. The conviction of the crime's intellectual authors in this case was exceptional: according to the CPT, of 976 land-related killings and 891 cases of attempted homicide registered from 1985 through the beginning of 1997, only fifty-six cases had gone to trial. In only fourteen of the trials, those who ordered the killings were prosecuted, with seven cases resulting in convictions.

In an unfortunate use of the criminal justice system against land reform activists, a trial court in Pedro Canário, in the eastern state of Espírito Santo, convicted landless leader José Rainha on June 10 for the 1989 murders of landowner José Machado Neto and military police officer Sérgio Narciso. Despite overwhelming evidence that José Rainha was hundreds of miles away when the killings occurred, the jury convicted, and the presiding judge sentenced him to twenty-six-and-a-half years in prison, on the grounds that he organized the land occupation and helped the peasants leave after the murder. Witnesses on Rainha's behalf included a military police colonel from Ceará, the former agriculture secretary for Ceará (now a federal congressman), and other elected officials from Ceará, all of whom testified that Rainha was in Ceará and not Espírito Santo during the time of the land conflict. The trial was tainted by other irregularities, including the presence of several persons on the jury with ties to one of the victims. At this writing, no date has been set for Rainha's second trial, guaranteed to him under Brazilian law.

Forced labor, the practice whereby laborers are recruited with false promises of high wages and then maintained against their will in work camps, continued to occur in 1997, although at rates believed lower than prior years. The CPT's figures for 1996 showed a significant decline in the number of victims involved in forced labor compared with 1995. While the number of cases of forced labor fell only slightly from twenty-one to nineteen, the number of victims plummeted from 26,047 to 2,487. This dramatic decrease was widely believed to be the result of joint programs of civil society, principally the CPT and rural labor unions, and the federal government's Ministry of Labor, particularly in the state of Mato Grosso do Sul. In that state, in which thousands had been held captive in coal pits in prior years, efforts to eliminate forced labor proved successful. In Minas Gerais, the work of a parliamentary commission of investigation helped reduce the number of victims of forced labor from 10,040 in 1995 to 790 in 1996.

In September, federal authorities announced plans to expropriate lands used for forced labor. The minister of land affairs announced that those workers who had been forced into debt bondage at the Flor da Mata estate in São Félix do Xingu, southern Pará state in the Amazon region, would be settled on the estate and that the government would follow this new policy with other areas in which forced labor is practiced. Legal experts, however, argued that such expropriation was beyond the authority of the federal government and required the enactment of legislation specifically authorizing such expropriations. At this writing, legislation that would empower the federal government to expropriate land used for forced labor operations is pending in Congress.

After convictions in April and November 1996 in the first two trials of military police officers involved in the July 1993 murder of eight sleeping children and adolescents in the Candelária plaza in downtown Rio, prosecution efforts suffered serious setbacks in late 1996 and 1997. First, in December 1996, two police officers and one civilian were acquitted after the prosecution failed to press the case against the defendants despite strong evidence, including witness statements, attesting to the involvement of two of the men. Then, in April 1997, former police officer Nelson Cunha, who had been convicted in November 1996 and sentenced to 261 years in prison, was acquitted of all homicide charges by a second jury. This, despite Cunha's confession that he was in the car with the killers and that he personally shot and injured survivor and key witness Wagner dos Santos in the head. Cunha, who admitted pointing the gun at the youth's head, claimed the gun went off accidentally as the car was moving. Cunha continued to serve a separate sentence of eighteen years for attempted murder based on his initial conviction.

For other high-profile massacres, impunity continued to be the rule. More than five years after the 1992 massacre at Carandiru prison, where 111 prisoners were killed, no one was brought to trial, although the case had been transferred from the military to the ordinary courts. The prosecution of police responsible for the August 1993 massacre of twenty-one residents of the Vigário Geral favela in Rio de Janeiro inched forward in 1997. In April, a jury in Rio convicted former military police officer Paulo Alvarenga, the first of more than fifty defendants to be tried, to more than 400 years in prison, of which he will have to serve thirty.

In the early morning hours of April 20, 1997, four young men and one teenager doused Pataxó Indian Galdino Jesus dos Santos, asleep on a bench in Brasília, with gasoline and then set him afire, producing severe burns which caused his death at a local hospital a few hours later. Dos Santos was attending a conference on indigenous rights in celebration of the National Indian Day. He returned to the hostel where he was staying shortly after closing and was forced to sleep outside. Subsequent investigations established that the boys had seen dos Santos asleep, proceeded to a gas station, and then returned to set him afire. Despite this and other evidence, Judge Sandra De Santis Mello reduced charges against the defendants from murder to assault and battery followed by death, accepting their position that they lacked any intent to kill or seriously harm dos Santos. Both the initial incident and the subsequent judicial decision touched off protests and calls for greater governmental efforts to protect the rights of indigenous peoples. At this writing, the defendants still face prosecution.

One encouraging trend during 1997 was the increased cooperation between governmental authorities and civil society in the area of human rights. In the northeastern state of Pernambuco, the state government continued to finance a witness protection program run by an NGO. In 1997, the Ministry of Justice took steps in conjunction with local governmental authorities to transplant this program to five other states. In June, the federal government created the National Secretariat for Human Rights within the Ministry of Justice, which worked closely with NGOs to develop programs jointly and to press for the implementation of measures included in the National Human Rights Plan. In São Paulo, the Ombudsman's Office for Police continued its energetic oversight of police abuse that contributed to significant reductions in police violence against civilians. The Human Rights Commission of the Federal Chamber of Deputies continued to denounce human rights violations throughout Brazil, holding numerous hearings in several locations to expose local abuses and provide fora for local activists and also pressed the Chamber and the Senate to pass sorely needed human rights legislation. In Rio Grande do Sul, the State Legislative Assembly's Human Rights Commission published its third annual "Blue Report," the most thorough catalogue of human rights violations in the state. Across the country, state legislative assemblies either formed human rights commissions or strengthened those that already existed; this same phenomenon occurred at the municipal level as well. Through these measures, government agents strengthened their relationships with their nongovernmental counterparts while

assuming responsibility for vital oversight of citizens' rights.

The Brazilian government participated in the Oslo negotiations to draft the landmines treaty. The Ministry of Foreign Affairs expressed its intent to attend the December conference in Ottawa and to sign the landmines treaty at that time. In March, Brazil took an initial step toward recognizing the illegitimacy of the occupation of East Timor by sending its first official delegation to the former Portuguese colony since the 1975 Indonesian invasion. Brazil also received a September visit by Nobel Laureate José Ramos Horta. During his previous visit to Brazil in November 1996, Ramos Horta was received by President Cardoso.

The Right to Monitor

The Brazilian government imposed no formal obstacles to human rights monitoring, and Brazil continued to maintain an active civil society including human rights organizations, religious groups, civic associations, and unions. In addition, in 1997 a number of state legislatures and city councils formed human rights commissions which played an increasingly important role, alongside those governmental commissions that already existed, in this watchdog capacity. In May, the São Paulo state legislature established an Ombudsman for the Police, a position previously created by gubernatorial decree. In September, the state legislature in Minas Gerais created an ombudsman's office based on the São Paulo model.

Unfortunately, this trend was not universal. In many parts of Brazil, authorities continued to be antagonistic towards human rights monitors. Human rights activists in the northeastern state of Rio Grande do Norte faced both death threats and law suits for their courageous efforts to rid the police of violent officers. The death threats rarely triggered serious investigations on the part of the appropriate authorities. A list of ten activists who promote investigations of corrupt and violent police in Rio Grande do Norte began to circulate at the end of 1996. The first person on that list, attorney Gilson

Nogueira, was murdered on October 20, 1996, and in May 1997, despite significant evidence of police involvement in his killing, federal prosecutors ended their investigation into the matter with no indictments.

Throughout 1997, Rio de Janeiro authorities responded to legitimate criticism of police violence by attacking the sources. This aggressiveness applied to Human Rights Watch, after our report on police brutality, as well as to local and national critics.

The Role of the International Community

European Union

The European Union (E.U.) financed numerous NGOs dedicated to the defense of human rights in Brazil in 1997. Member states of the European Union encouraged Brazil to comply with international human rights norms through regular meetings with federal officials both in Brazil and on official government trips to Europe. At year's end, several governments expressed interest in providing instructors and financing a program directed by the International Committee of the Red Cross (ICRC), to train Brazilian police in methods that respect fundamental human rights. This ICRC training program would build on two courses which it led in 1997 for representatives of the military police forces of each of Brazil's twenty-six states and federal district. National Human Rights Secretary José Gregori sought financial support from E.U. governments for police training in human rights during several visits to Europe in 1997. At this writing, however, plans for such financing have not been completed.

United States

In 1997, the U.S. gave relatively little direct assistance to Brazil. For Fiscal Year 1998 the U.S. administration requested U.S. $225,000 for training through the International Military Education and Training Program (IMET) and U.S. $1 million in antinarcotics assistance, as well as U.S.$600,000 targeted to police forces in Brazil. The U.S.

government finalized plans to open an Federal Bureau of Investigation office in Brasília to combat drug trafficking during fiscal year 1998, although according to the U.S. embassy, no clear timetable for its operation has been established at this writing.

During the year, the U.S. government sponsored numerous visits for human rights activists, judges, and prosecutors to the United States through the administration of justice and United States Information Services programs, as well as visits to Brazil by experts on alternative sentencing and the federalization of human rights crimes, both issues contemplated by the Brazilian National Human Rights Program. The State Department's chapter on Brazil in its *Country Reports on Human Rights Practices for 1996* accurately portrayed the varied human rights problems that Brazil faces, as well as the advances and setbacks provoked by governmental policies.

In October, President Bill Clinton visited Brasília, São Paulo and Rio de Janeiro. In Brasília, Clinton met with his counterpart Fernando Henrique Cardoso, as well as the presidents of the Chamber of Deputies and the Senate. Unfortunately, President Clinton failed to address the issue of human rights publicly during the trip.

Relevant Human Rights Watch report:

Police Brutality in Urban Brazil, 4/97

COLOMBIA

Human Rights Developments

Even as the administration of President Ernesto Samper took limited steps to curb violence and address impunity, the human rights situation in Colombia deteriorated. Political violence was particularly intense in areas contested by guerrillas and by paramilitaries operating with the acquiescence and in some cases the support of the army. All parties routinely attacked perceived enemies within the civilian population, meaning that noncombatants—among them farmers, elected officials, teachers, banana workers, merchants, and children—remained Colombia's most frequent victims of political violence. Thousands of Colombians fled violence to join the rapidly growing ranks of the forcibly displaced. Meanwhile, poor conditions in Colombia's jails led to a series of protests, several of which became violent and resulted in casualties among guards and prisoners.

Although exact figures remained difficult to confirm and many cases went unreported or uninvestigated, it was clear that political violence increased, especially as October 1997 municipal elections neared. According to our records, there were at least thirty-five massacres in the first eight months of 1997—twenty-seven committed by presumed paramilitaries and eight committed by presumed members of the Revolutionary Armed Forces of Colombia (Fuerzas Armadas Revolucionarias de Colombia, FARC), the country's largest guerrilla group. In all, these massacres claimed 272 lives. More than 450 Colombians also died in targeted assassinations, with the largest identified group being peasants.

Human Rights Watch recorded a reduction in the number of cases attributed to the security forces, either acting alone or with paramilitary groups, while guerrilla violations increased. In the past, the army openly backed paramilitaries. Human rights organizations in Colombia called on the government to take concerted action against paramilitaries to demonstrate that they were not supported or tolerated by the armed forces. It was significant, therefore, that even as the police and military incorporated human rights into their public statements and held meetings with human rights groups, words did not translate into consistent action against paramilitaries, who operated freely in heavily militarized areas and significantly expanded their operations. The state's failure to arrest paramilitary leaders or pursue their units constituted tacit approval for their violations and meant that paramilitaries waged an unhindered campaign of terror throughout most of the country.

According to the Colombian Commission of Jurists (CCJ), a respected human rights organization, 76 percent of the violations recorded were the work of paramilitaries, 17 percent were the work of guerrillas, and 7 percent were the work of state agents. Human Rights Watch recorded twenty-four cases of extrajudicial executions and eight forced disappearances attributable to the army during the first six months of 1997. On January 10, for example, 18th Brigade soldiers apparently executed three youths detained in a Saravena, Arauca, slum, beating and shooting them in front of witnesses. In addition, in regions like the Middle Magdalena and southern Cesar department, army units patrolled openly with groups of armed civilians, killing and threatening supposed guerrilla supporters.

When abuses were investigated, the military continued to use its tribunals to cover them up, most notably in the case involving Gen. (ret.) Farouk Yanine Díaz, charged with ordering the 1987 massacre of nineteen men near Puerto Araujo, Santander. On June 23, then-army commander Gen. Manuel Bonett, appointed the investigative judge on the case, announced he would close further investigation of Yanine's involvement. He did so despite solid evidence implicating Yanine. The case had been prepared by the Attorney General's Human Rights Unit, which continued to do credible investigations. Similar evidence collected by the Human Rights Unit had served to convict the civilian paramilitaries accused of carrying out the Puerto Araujo massacre.

In a welcome decision, the Constitutional Court ruled in August that unresolved cases involving extrajudicial executions, torture, forced disappearances, and rape by the security forces must be tried in civilian court, not military tribunals. Writing for the majority, magistrate Eduardo Cifuentes Muñoz held that human rights crimes "have absolutely no connection to the role of State agents according to the constitution. [A]ny order to commit such a crime merits no obedience whatsoever."

However, as of this writing, no pending cases, including that of General Yanine, have been transferred to civilian courts for trial. In an effort to ignore the ruling, military tribunals continued to hear cases involving serious human rights violations, including the December 1991 massacre by police and local paramilitaries of twenty Páez Indians, among them five children, near Caloto, Cauca. On September 23, a military tribunal declared that the massacre constituted an act of service meant to "help (the victims) coexist peacefully" and released the anti-narcotics police captain found to have planned and helped carry out the killings. Although the Samper administration presented a bill to congress that would reform the military penal code to reflect the Constitutional Court decision, as of this writing it was unclear what its fate will be.

Overall, the paramilitary group known as the Peasant Self-Defense Group of Córdoba and Urabá (Autodefensas Campesinas de Córdoba and Urabá, ACCU) amassed the worst record, committing at least twenty-two of the massacres reported in the first eight months of 1997. In July, over one hundred ACCU members arrived in Mapiripán, Meta, by air, then killed and beheaded at least seven men in the local slaughterhouse. Part of the group's much-publicized plan to form a national alliance of paramilitary groups and reach areas formerly considered guerrilla strongholds, the Mapiripán attack lasted for five days without any reaction by police or military forces based in the area, despite pleas from the local judge. Residents told journalists that as many as thirty more people may have been killed, beheaded, and thrown into the Guaviare river. Most of the residents fled after the attack. In a press interview published after the massacre, ACCU leader Carlos Castaño vowed that in the future, there would be "many more cases like Mapiripán."

Elsewhere, the ACCU expanded its influence, moving south from the Caribbean coast into the departments of Bolívar, Magdalena, Santander, Sucre, and Cesar, with massacres, killings, death threats, and forced displacement marking its advance. Since October 1996, the ACCU has repeatedly entered Panama, where it has killed and threatened local villagers it accuses of providing guerrillas with food and medicine.

Despite the announcement of a U.S. $1 million reward for information leading to the capture of ACCU leader Castaño, nothing was done to capture him or his forces. After highly decorated army Col. Carlos Velásquez reported in 1996 that his superiors at Urabá's 17th Brigade had failed to pursue the ACCU, rather than investigate his information fully, the military cashiered him. Near San José de Apartadó, for instance, a combined force of paramilitaries and army soldiers reportedly executed José Macario David Góez, a mentally retarded man, on March 27. Afterward, soldiers apparently dressed David's body in a military uniform and presented him to the press as a guerrilla killed in combat.

Other paramilitaries also operated in Colombia virtually unimpeded by the authorities, among them the Northeast Self-Defense Group (Grupo de Autodefensa del Nordeste, GAN) around Segovia and Remedios in Antioquia. Since the 1980s, when paramilitaries allied with the army's Bomboná Battalion carried out a series of massacres, this region has been tormented with political killings. After the killings of three human rights workers in March (*see* The Right to Monitor, below), authorities convened a "security meeting" to discuss ways to prevent further attacks. Nevertheless, on August 2, the GAN reportedly took seven people from their homes in Remedios, including former mayor and Patriotic Union member Carlos Rojo Uribe, then executed five of them on the road to Segovia. Rojo and teacher Luis Alberto Munera, also a member of the Segovia Human Rights Committee, were taken to Segovia, where they were shot. In September, some alleged GAN members were arrested.

During the year, several peace initiatives were begun, but, as was obvious from behavior of the parties to the conflict, there was no real commitment to negotiating an end to the fighting. As October 26 elections neared, elected officials and candidates throughout Colombia came under increasing attack. Both the National Liberation Army (Ejército de Liberación Nacional, ELN) and FARC vowed to stop elections in a dozen departments. The ACCU and its allies in the United Self-Defense Groups of Colombia (Autodefensas Unidas de Colombia, AUC) coalition announced in May that they would prevent pro-guerrilla "proselytizing" in areas of conflict, which candidates considered a threat against those who failed to embrace their views.

Within a month after aspirants had to submit their names to the National Electoral Registry, authorities reported that over 900 had cancelled their candidacies due to threats. While similar elections in 1994 were suspended in nine municipalities, as of mid-September, there were fifteen municipalities without mayoral candidates. In the words of one candidate who withdrew, "to be a candidate for mayor or even town council in many rural areas. . .is to search out a death foretold."

In the first eight months of 1997, government authorities reported that ten mayors had been murdered, representing towns in eight departments. In addition, thirty-six town council members were killed. Even candidates' family members were the frequent targets of death threats and kidnaping. Colombia remained the world's leader in reported kidnappings, close to half of which were carried out by rebels. According to government authorities, between November 1996 and August 1997, forty-one mayors were kidnaped.

Both paramilitaries and guerrillas also threatened journalists. Among them was Alfredo Molano, who reported that in August he received a paramilitary threat suggesting that he was a "subversive encysted" in the government because of his work for the government's High Commissioner for Peace. In turn, the FARC announced in June that it would consider journalists who wrote what they considered "apology for militarism" legitimate military targets.

Far from protecting threatened mayors, the security forces appeared largely powerless or unwilling to pursue their attackers. To the contrary, mayors themselves became the targets of army investigations for supposed ties to guerrillas. An army intelligence report leaked to the newsweekly *Semana* in May alleged that 650 municipal governments— more than half of those in Colombia—had either direct ties with guerrillas or collaborated with them. Dozens of mayors protested, saying the information was tantamount "to putting a gravestone over our heads." The mayor of Sogamoso, Boyacá, a Catholic priest, filed formal charges against the government for defamation, and the army later disavowed its report.

Instead of moving aggressively to protect the civilian population and ensure its neutral status, the government promoted Rural Watch Cooperatives Cooperativas de Vigilancia y Seguridad Rural, CONVIVIR), made up of civilians authorized to gather intelligence for the security forces, join maneuvers, and use weapons banned for private ownership, including machine guns, mortars, grenades, and assault rifles. Although CONVIVIRs receive a government license, the identities of their members remain anonymous even to local authorities.

In 1997, we received credible reports that CONVIVIRs in the Middle Magdalena and southern Cesar regions were led by known paramilitaries and had threatened and killed Colombians deemed sympathetic to guerrillas or who refused to join. On February 3, a CONVIVIR patrolling with the army's Fourteenth Brigade near the village of San Francisco, in Santander, apparently executed Norberto Galeano, Reynaldo Ríos, and a seventy-year-old man, then dismembered their bodies. Two months earlier, the same group had been linked to the massacre of at least seven people in the nearby villages of La Congoja and Puerto Nuevo, prompting the mass displacement of over 700 villagers.

Along with the CCJ, fourteen human rights groups filed a suit with the Constitutional Court calling for Decree 356, which regulates CONVIVIR, to be declared unconstitutional. In its brief, the CCJ argued that through CONVIVIR, the Samper administration was arming civilians in violation of the constitution. Given Colombia's tragic history of paramilitary violence, executive director Gustavo Gallón noted in an August 26 hearing before the court, a decree that "permits the organization and development of paramilitary groups. . .is contrary to the essence of the State's rule of law."

Dozens of government officials, mayors, and religious leaders also objected to CONVIVIR, among them Attorney General Alfonso Gómez Méndez, who argued that CONVIVIR involved civilians in the armed conflict, thus excluding them from the humanitarian protections granted by Protocol II Additional to the Geneva Conventions. "With the organization of CONVIVIR," Gómez noted, "the Colombian state once again has fallen into the error of promoting the creation of 'armed individuals,' who intensify problems of illegal repression and war without quarter."

In August, even President Samper admitted that some CONVIVIRs "have transgressed their legal boundaries to assume combat roles." Subsequently, the government announced that it would suspend the creation of new CONVIVIRs.

Guerrillas also committed serious abuses during 1997, among them massacres. On March 9, presumed members of the FARC's 34th Front opened fire on an ice cream parlor in Currulao, Antioquia, killing nine people, including parlor owner Danilo Valencia Naranjo.

The FARC was believed to have sent the April book bomb that killed Pedro Agudelo, the seventeen-year-old son of Hope, Peace and Liberty party (Esperanza, Paz y Libertad) leader Mario Agudelo.

The FARC made a practice of attacking civilian targets, putting the lives of noncombatants at serious risk. In January, guerrillas apparently activated a bomb in front of a Medellín skyscraper, killing four passersby and wounding forty-one others.

In September, one of Colombia's largest hydroelectric plants was the target, causing the government to recommend that families begin limiting their use of electricity.

The ELN also committed serious violations, among them targeted killings. According to press reports and information gathered by human rights groups, the ELN was responsible for at least forty-nine political killings in the first nine months of 1997. Among the victims were farmers, mayors, an employee of the attorney general's office, and children. In addition, the ELN apparently killed several security force agents *hors de combat*, among them three soldiers captured and executed on August 3 near El Playón, Santander.

The ELN stepped up its use of car bombs, registering dozens of attacks in the first six months of 1997. In an attack on March 17, a car bomb in Cúcuta, Norte de Santander, apparently detonated by the "Resistencia Yariguíes" Front of the ELN, killed eighteen-month-old Martha Liliana Riveros and left several others wounded.

Kidnapping remained a common tactic of paramilitaries and guerrillas, who routinely took family members of combatants as hostages. Since 1996, the ACCU kidnapped over a dozen family members of guerrillas, seven of whom were released on March 26 under the auspices of the International Committee of the Red Cross (ICRC).

Several political kidnappings led to deaths. On May 5, the FARC announced that Congressman Rodrigo Turbay Cote, kidnapped in 1995, had died while being transported along the Caguán river in his native department of Caquetá, apparently after falling from a canoe. In retaliation, paramilitaries who had kidnapped two family members of an ELN commander announced that they were executed in May.

Three Americans kidnapped by the FARC in 1993 remained missing as of this writing—Richard Tenenhoff, David Mankins, and Mark Rich. The FARC was also implicated in the execution-style slaying of two kidnap victims, Austrian Johan Kehrer and German Alexander Scheurer, in the Chocó jungle in March.

The forced displacement of civilians continued to be part of the strategy of war used by all sides, particularly paramilitaries. In March, the Consultancy on Human Rights and Displacement (Consultoría para los Derechos Humanos y el Desplazamiento, CODHES), nongovernmental organization (NGO), estimated that between 1985 and 1996, 920,000 people had been displaced by violence, an average of one in every forty Colombians. According to the United Nations Children's Fund (UNICEF) in Colombia, 72 percent of the displaced were children.

The year was marked by forced displacements on a massive scale not seen previously. In March, more than 13,000 people, most from black minority communities, fled their homes along the Riosucio river in the northwest department of Chocó after paramilitaries took control in December 1996 and the army carried out indiscriminate air attacks two months later. After a difficult journey through the jungle during which several people reportedly died, the army blocked the passage of peasants fleeting to the town of Mutatá. The refugees were prohibited from making the journey. There were credible reports that a soldier fired on a group of the displaced attempting to reach Mutatá in April and seriously injured two people, including a girl. A court later found the government, specifically the army, responsible for causing the forced displacement, and ordered authorities to ensure the families' safe return to their homes.

Nevertheless, as of this writing, thousands of displaced from Riosucio continue to live in crowded camps at Pavarandó Grande, without sufficient food, water, or health care. Paramilitaries threatened to enter the camp to kill displaced, and reportedly assassinated several people in nearby towns.

The Samper administration responded to mass displacement by creating the post of "presidential counselor for the "displaced" in April, adopting a revised national plan on displacement in May, and promulgating Law 387 in July, which dealt specifically with assistance, protection, and prevention is-

sues. Advocates criticized the government for promoting the return of the displaced to their homes without guaranteeing their safety, highlighting mandatory registration requirements and lack of funds as serious flaws in the new law. The United Nations High Commissioner for Refugees (UNHCR) opened an office in June by invitation of the Colombian government, but no formal agreement about the scope of the agency's activities had been reached at the time of this writing.

Doubts about the government's ability to effectively address the problem of forced displacement were deepened by the case of 280 families violently evicted by paramilitaries from the Bellacruz Ranch in the department of Cesar in February 1996. With twenty-six of at least twenty-eight arrest warrants against the implicated paramilitaries still outstanding, the families were unable to return, and most were resettled on unirrigated land that allowed only a precarious existence. In May, the Constitutional Court issued an injunction protecting the rights of the Bellacruz peasants after the governor of Cundinamarca refused to allow the families, whom she accused of being subversives, to resettle in her jurisdiction.

In April, some 300 Colombians were forcibly repatriated from Panama to Bahía Cupica, Chocó, after the UNHCR was denied access to interview them in Panama. Safe conditions for their return did not exist, and the repatriated families were evacuated from Bahía Cupica on an emergency basis in September after paramilitaries circulated a list of twelve people they intended to kill or kidnap.

In Colombia's jails, prisoners cited severe overcrowding, lack of medical care, and isolation as the reasons behind a series of coordinated protests that began in January and continued through June. A census by the National Penitentiary Institute, responsible for administering Colombia's prisons, showed that although Colombia has the capacity to house 30,000 prisoners, as of April 1997, it reported holding 42,000 inmates, half of whom were still awaiting trial for common crimes and rebellion. In the

Valledupar prison, in Cesar, armed inmates and imprisoned members of the ELN killed four prison guards and took sixteen other people hostage, including a fourteen-year-old girl, in April before agreeing to surrender to authorities and releasing the hostages unharmed.

Given the serious problems of internal displacement, hostage-taking, and violence, the ICRC took an increasingly important role in Colombia, boosting its in-country staff to forty-three people and maintaining nine offices. The organization brokered prisoner exchanges, visited prisoners and hostages, aided the wounded and displaced, and assisted threatened Colombians to flee the country. According to ICRC estimates, their office assisted in the release of forty hostages between August 1996 and March 1997. The ICRC also gave presentations on international humanitarian law to ACCU members and guerrillas.

The Right to Monitor

Human rights defenders continued to be the targets of attack and threats. On May 19, Mario Calderón, an employee of the Center for Research and Popular Education (Centro de Investigación y Educación Popular, CINEP), Elsa Alvarado, his wife and a former CINEP employee, and Carlos Alvarado, Elsa's father, were killed by masked gunmen in their Bogotá apartment, apparently in retaliation for their human rights work. Although Alvarado's mother was seriously wounded, the couple's eighteen-month-old son was unharmed. On September 28, authorities in Medellín arrested five people who may have taken part in the killing.

In Segovia, Antioquia, GAN continued to work in close coordination with the army's Bomboná Battalion, an alliance considered complicit in the March 9 murder of Nazareno de Jesús Rivera, a Segovia Human Rights Committee member. The same day, colleague Jaime Ortiz Londoño was forcibly disappeared. On March 12, the Army's Fourteenth Brigade falsely displayed Rivera's body to the press as "a guerrilla killed in action" and showed reporters Ortiz's identity documents. On March 23, a former member of the same group, Margarita Guzmán, was killed in her office, apparently for her work for the authorities investigating Rivera's death and Ortiz's "disappearance."

Also on March 7, Víctor Julio Garzón, the secretary-general of an agrarian association and a well-known human rights defender, was killed by unidentified gunmen in his Bogotá office. Garzón was a member of the Meta Civic Committee for Human Rights, all but extinguished after its members have been systematically killed. Although international outrage followed the 1996 murder of Josué Giraldo, president of the Meta Civic Committee for Human Rights, at this writing, no arrests have been made in his case, which remained in preliminary investigation along with most other investigations into past killings of human rights monitors.

Community leaders who spoke out about human rights continued to be targets. On October 6, FARC members, apparently angered by the decision of San José de Apartadó residents not to supply food, abducted and killed Luis Hernando Goes, Luis Fernando Aguirre, and Ramiro Correa. The three were members of a civic group working to make the town neutral territory in the battle among guerrillas, paramilitaries, and the army. Another civic leader, Francisco Tabarquino, had been killed by paramilitaries on May 17.

Government workers who investigated cases involving links between the security forces and paramilitaries were also killed or forced to leave the country for their safety. Among them, former Yondó, Antioquia, ombudsman Gustavo Núñez was pulled from a public bus by paramilitaries near Barrancabermeja and killed on August 8.

Other human rights defenders were the targets of threats and surveillance by members of the security forces. Wilson Patiño, a human rights activist from Remedios, Antioquia, was forced to leave the area after armed men came to his home on March 20, apparently to kill him. On May 24, Neftalí Vanegas Perea, a human rights defender in Ocaña, Norte de Santander, narrowly escaped an assassination attempt by armed men believed to be working in league with the security forces.

The offices of the Association of Family Members of the Detained and Disappeared (Asociación de Familiares de Detenidos y Desaparecidos, ASFADDES) were the target of a June 24 bombing that destroyed the group's archives. Subsequently, organization members in Medellín and Riosucio, Chocó, received several threats, including that of a telephone caller who claimed that "the bomb was only a warning, so it would be better if you left the office." Two branch offices were later closed for fear of attacks, and the group's president and her family were forced to leave the country for their safety.

Other human rights workers reported receiving threats related to their work. After a series of massacres in the Middle Magdalena region, five human rights workers associated with the Regional Corporation for the Defense of Human Rights (Corporación Regional para la Defensa de los Derechos Humanos, CREDHOS) were informed that their names appeared on death lists being circulated by paramilitaries. In September, members of the Association for the Promotion of Social Alternatives (Asociación para la Promoción Social Alternativa, MINGA) said that suspicious men were watching their offices and were following the MINGA and ASFADDES members working there.

In response to the killings of human rights defenders, thirty-six human rights groups, unions, religious groups, and indigenous groups petitioned the government in May and again in June for investigations into attacks, the punishment of those responsible, an end to the military's verbal attacks on their work, and guarantees of protection. A key demand was for an aggressive and immediate law enforcement effort to identify, track down, and arrest members of paramilitary groups and their security force patrons, an effort, the groups noted, that should be given equal status with punishing drug traffickers and guerrillas.

In a partial acknowledgment of the seriousness of the situation, President Samper issued a directive honoring the work of human rights defenders and explicitly barring government officials, including the army, from making statements that "falsely accuse or belittle the right to a defense, due process and the honor [of human rights defenders]" on July 16. Subsequently, groups met with the government, and on September 9, Colombia's Human Rights Day, President Samper announced the creation of a Human Rights Council to coordinate actions among the government's multiple human rights offices.

The Role of the International Community

United Nations
April 7 marked the official opening of the Bogotá office of the U.N. High Commissioner for Human Rights, led by Amb. Almudena Mazarrasa and staffed by five experts and a deputy director. At this writing, it is too early to judge the effectiveness of the office, but at least one of the objectives in establishing it was achieved: the office pressed the government on issues of concern to the commission, including reforms to the military penal code and CONVIVIR. Experts traveled throughout the country and held regular meetings with government officials, representatives of human rights groups, and Colombians wishing to deliver complaints.

Nevertheless, the Human Rights Committee continued to lament Colombia's failure to implement its repeated recommendations, and noted that "gross and massive human rights violations continue to occur in Colombia." The Committee expressed its "deep concern" over evidence that paramilitary groups "receive support from members of the military" and that "impunity continues to be a widespread phenomenon."

European Union
Some European embassies and diplomats took high-profile roles in attempting to lessen

political violence and the suffering it caused. In April, Netherlands Amb. Gysbert Bos made a three-day visit to the Middle Magdalena region, in part to draw attention to a rise in paramilitary activity and displacement. The visit was seen as especially important given that the Netherlands occupied the presidency of the EU.

For its part, the EU continued to pressure Colombia to improve its human rights record, and announced in September its full support for a negotiated settlement to political conflict.

The European Community Humanitarian Office (ECHO) donated U.S. $5 million dollars in emergency aid to international NGOs to assist the thousands of people forcibly displaced earlier in the year in Urabá.

Organization of American States

The Organization of American States agreed to send a team to Colombia to monitor municipal elections in areas where guerrillas and paramilitaries had threatened candidates. Two monitors, a Guatemalan and a Chilean, were kidnapped by the ELN and held for more than a week before being released. For its part, the Inter-American Human Rights Commission continued to hear Colombian cases and took part in several efforts to resolve cases through so-called "friendly negotiation" between victims and the government. However, in several high-profile cases, including the 1990 Trujillo massacre and the 1994 Villatina massacre, this effort had not, at this writing, borne tangible fruit.

In October, two Colombian human rights groups formally presented to the commission the case involving Navy Intelligence Network No. 7 and its involvement in the killings of at least sixty-eight people from 1991 to 1993 in and around Barrancabermeja, Santander. The case was detailed in *Colombia's Killer Networks: The Military-Paramilitary Partnership and the United States*, published by Human Rights Watch in November 1996.

United States

The United States pursued a contradictory policy in Colombia. On the one hand, the Clinton administration for the first time made human rights an important part of U.S.-Colombia relations. In 1997, the State Department issued its most detailed and critical human rights report ever, concluding that "the [Colombian] armed forces committed numerous, serious human rights abuses." In addition, the report noted, "the Samper administration has not taken action to curb increased abuses committed by paramilitary groups, verging on a policy of tacit acquiescence."

This report was followed by an April letter from Secretary of State Madeline Albright to Sen. Patrick Leahy, co-sponsor of a 1996 amendment that placed human rights conditions on some antinarcotics aid. In the letter, Secretary Albright announced that the spirit of the amendment would be applied to all anti-narcotics aid, including monies suspended after Colombia was "decertified" a second time in a row for failing to meet U.S. goals in fighting drugs. In an unusual move, the U.S. embassy publicly expressed its concern over the tone used by military authorities to attack civilian investigators who linked General Yanine to the Puerto Araujo massacre, the first time it had spoken publicly on a human rights case.

For its principled stand, the administration was harshly criticized by some Republicans in the U.S. Congress, who argued that human rights concerns hampered the drug war. Led by the International Relations Committee and its chair, Rep. Benjamin Gilman, Republicans attempted to remove the Leahy amendment from the 1998 Foreign Operations bill, an initiative that failed.

Although the Clinton administration acknowledged that Colombia's human rights situation continued to be serious, it also pushed hard for aid to the military to fight drugs, arguing that funds would be channeled to units without bad records. After months of tense negotiations, the Colombian and U.S. governments signed an end-use monitoring agreement on August 1, freeing

$70 million of the $100 million slated to reach Colombia in 1997, much of it for the army and navy. Among the items sent were communications equipment, night vision scopes, and parts for helicopters and river patrol boats. Police continued to receive aid throughout the year, including munitions and weapons. However, the agreement on military aid left monitoring to the Colombian Defense Ministry, not U.S. officials, who were severely limited in their ability to verify any reports.

CUBA

Human Rights Developments

Cuba voiced muffled support for human rights and representative democracy in the past year, as it moved toward greater economic engagement with Europe, Canada, Asia, and Latin America. But the government revealed an intransigent reliance on political oppression to crush internal opposition through its repressive measures against dissidents, failure to amnesty political prisoners, continuing blockage of human rights monitoring, creation of new laws restricting human rights, and refusal to dismantle oppressive legal structures.

In one of Cuba's strongest statements favoring human rights, President Fidel Castro Ruz signed the Viña del Mar Declaration, endorsing support for democracy and respect for human rights, fundamental liberties, and the principles consecrated in the United Nations Charter, at the Sixth Iberoamerican Summit of leaders in Chile in November 1996. On January 9, 1997, however, Cuba flaunted its disdain for the agreement by arresting Héctor Palacios Ruiz, the president of the Democratic Solidarity Party (Partido Solidaridad Democrática, PSD), charging him with contempt for the authority of President Castro and seizing his copies of the Viña del Mar Declaration. Palacios Ruiz, whom the Cuban government sentenced to eighteen months' imprisonment on September 4, had challenged the

government's willingness to comply with the declaration in an interview with a German journalist.

Palacios Ruiz's trial, and Cuba's refusal to amnesty political prisoners, highlighted the government's reliance on its prison system as the backbone of its repressive tactics. Once again, in the past year the government failed to reform a penal code that criminalized the exercise of fundamental rights under provisions such as "enemy propaganda," "contempt for authority," "illicit association," "dangerousness," and "illegal exit." Cuban courts routinely denied basic due process guarantees, including sufficient and timely access to lawyers, the right to present witnesses and evidence for the defense, and open courtrooms free of intimidation.

Among the dissidents prosecuted in the last year was Enrique García Morejón, a member of the Christian Liberation Movement (Movimiento Cristiano de Liberación, MCL), sentenced in February 1997 to four years in prison for enemy propaganda. The court alleged that he had distributed flyers saying "Down with Fidel," but reportedly the charge arose from his collecting signatures for the MCL's unsuccessful attempt to obtain legal status. In May 1997, Cuban authorities sentenced Ana María Agramonte Crespo, a member of the Nationalist Action Movement (Movimiento de Acción Nacionalista), to eighteen months for contempt for authority and resistance to authority. A Cuban court condemned Ricardo De Armas Hernández, a member of the PSD in Matanzas, to nine months for dangerousness in May. Confined in the harsh Agüica prison, De Armas reportedly suffered beatings by prisoners held for common crimes in August. In August 1997, a court convicted Luis Mario Pared Estrada,, a leader of the Thirtieth of November Party "Frank Pais" (Partido 30 de Noviembre "Frank Pais"), of dangerousness and sentenced him to one year. In September, a Havana court convicted his colleague, Maritza Lugo Fernández of bribery, for allegedly trying to pay a prison guard to bring a prisoner a tape recorder.

A Cuban court also convicted Néstor Rodríguez Lobaina, the president of Youth for Democracy (Jóvenes por la Democracia), of contempt for authority and resisting arrest on April 10, 1997, sentencing him to eighteen months. In September, several prison guards beat him after he began a hunger strike to protest prison conditions. On June 17, 1997, a court sentenced Radames García de la Vega, a vice-president of Youth for Democracy, to eighteen months for contempt for authority. In late July, the government convicted Heriberto Leyva Rodríguez, a vice-president of the same group, of contempt for authority of the Santiago court, reportedly based on his testimony at Garciá de la Vega's appeal hearing earlier that month.

The dissidents convicted of political crimes in 1997 joined over 800 additional political prisoners in Cuba's extensive prison system. Prison conditions remained poor for all inmates, and dissidents suffered particularly abusive treatment. Political prisoners often suffered dramatic weight loss due to meager food rations; serious, and sometimes life-threatening, health problems due to insufficient medical attention; and, in some cases, abuses at the hands of guards or common criminals, with whom they routinely were mixed. Prison authorities forced some imprisoned dissidents to spend periods in isolation cells, restricted their visits, or transferred them far from family members. The punitive and intimidatory measures against political prisoners that caused severe pain and suffering violated Cuba's obligations under the Convention against Torture and Other Cruel, Inhuman or Degrading Treatment or Punishment, which it ratified in 1995. Once again, in the past year the government forbade access to its prisons by international human rights monitors and humanitarian groups, including the International Committee of the Red Cross (ICRC).

Guards at the Kilo 8 prison, which is known for its extremely harsh conditions, persisted in their abusive treatment of Jesús Chamber Rodríguez. He suffered deteriorating health due to confinement in punishment cells, insufficient medical attention, poor nutrition, and denial of access to sunlight for weeks at a time. Chamber Rodríguez began serving a ten-year sentence for enemy propaganda in 1992, but Cuban authorities sentenced him to four more years in 1996 for contempt of authority, apparently based on his criticizing prison conditions and shouting "down with Fidel." Jorge Luis García Pérez, known as Antúnez, who began serving seventeen years for enemy propaganda, sabotage, and "evasion" in 1990, also received harsh treatment from prison authorities. Prison guards responded to Antúnez's hunger strikes, in protest of prison conditions, by denying him family visits and medicine. In September, guards at the Guantanamo prison beat Antúnez after he criticized the government.

Cuban failures to provide medical care left many political prisoners in critical condition. Omar Del Pozo Marrero, a doctor who received a fifteen-year sentence in 1992 and was held at the Combinado del Este prison, suffered severe hypertension and malnutrition in 1997, due to insufficient medical care, bars on his access to sunlight for several week periods, and restrictions on family visits. Prison authorities at Kilo 8 did not provide Eduardo Gómez Sánchez, who was sentenced in 1994 to twenty years for illegal exit and rebellion, with appropriate treatment for a liver ailment that turned his skin yellow and caused vomiting, diarrhea, and weight loss.

Cuba's efforts to stifle criticism reached inside prison walls as well, where prisoners protesting inhumane treatment faced retaliatory measures, including beatings, isolation, and criminal prosecution. On January 21, 1997, a Cuban court convicted Víctor Reinaldo Infante Estrada, whom a Cuban military court sentenced to thirteen years in prison in 1992, to one additional year for contempt of authority. The court based Infante Estrada's second sentence on his denouncing abuses at the Agüica prison, where he was held. In May, when he demanded improved medical treatment, the prison authorities punished him again, by confining him to an isolation cell for over one month.

Security forces harassed and arbitrarily detained scores of nonviolent activists in the past year. Government repression touched broad sectors of civil society, including academics, human rights activists, labor organizers, religious leaders, youth groups, and unofficial political parties. Cuban authorities notified many dissidents that they were at risk of criminal prosecutions if they did not abandon their "counter-revolutionary" activities or leave the country. Activists fled Cuba in response to these warnings, including Miguel Angel Aldana, a leader of the Martiana Civic Association (Asociación Cívica Martiana), who left for the United States in April 1997, after Cuban authorities threatened him with a four-year sentence for dangerousness. Cuba employed diverse methods to control dissident groups: conducting unauthorized searches; firing employees; seizing fax machines and photocopiers; making unsupported allegations of links between activists and terrorists (specifically regarding the eleven bombs that targeted Cuban tourist destinations between April and September); and, denying dissident groups any legal recognition. The government also heightened harassment of homosexuals, raiding several nightclubs known to have gay clientele and allegedly beating and detaining dozens of patrons.

Official intent to silence dissenting voices was glaringly manifest in the July 15, 1997 detentions of four prominent, nonviolent leaders of the Internal Dissidents' Working Group (Grupo de Trabajo de la Disidencia Interna, GTDI): professor Félix Antonio Bonne Carcasses, economists Marta Beatriz Roque Cabello and Vladimiro Roca Antúnez, and attorney René Gómez Manzano. On May 5, the group held a well-attended press conference encouraging a boycott of elections planned for late 1997. In June, the GTDI issued a statement titled *The Motherland Belongs to All* (*La Patria es de Todos*), which challenged Cuba's exclusive recognition of one political party. Cuban authorities categorized the dissidents' peaceful protests as "counter-revolutionary crimes." At this writing, the four leaders remain in prison facing possible trial for enemy propaganda and revealing state secrets, reportedly about the Cuban electoral system.

Cuba continued to exercise strict control over labor rights during 1997, refusing to allow the formation of any independent unions. The Foreign Investment Law required all investors to hire employees through the government-controlled employment agency, which apparently selected some workers based on political viewpoints. Independent labor activists faced government harassment. State security agents interrogated Manuel Antonio Brito López, the secretary general for the Union of Independent Workers (Unión de Trabajadores Independientes), in Havana on July 12, advising him to restrict his movement until August 6, the final day of the International World Festival of Youth and Students.

In preparation for the October 1997 Fifth Communist Party Congress, in late May the government released a position paper titled *The Party of Unity, Democracy, and Human Rights that We Defend*, which praised Cuba's allegedly spotless human rights record. Yet, the document called upon the "truly free" press to "guarantee the continuity of socialist, patriotic, and anti-imperialist ideas and values, and the Revolution itself...." Meanwhile, the government manifested its disdain for genuine press freedoms throughout the year. In July, Cuban authorities sentenced Lorenzo Paez Núñez, a journalist with the Habana Press agency in Pinar del Río, to eighteen months for contempt and defamation of the police, based on his having reported alleged police abuses.

Cuban authorities relied heavily on both short-and long-term detentions to intimidate journalists. Authorities detained Héctor Peraza Linares, the co-director of Habana Press, in Pinar del Río on June 23, only releasing him in September. Raúl Rivero, the head of Cuba Press, was arrested on July 28 and August 12. Cuban authorities freed Cuba Press journalist Efrén Martínez Pulgarón in mid-September, without charges, following his August 13 detention. Cuba employed other dissuasive tactics as well. On February 26, the authorities harassed Tania Quintero and her colleague Ana Luisa Baeza, of Cuba Press, with "repudiation meetings" (*mítines de repudio*) in which groups of up to sixty government sympathizers gathered outside the women's homes, throwing objects and shouting criticisms. Following a February 21 arrest, Joaquín Torres Alvarez, the director of Habana Press, was beaten in May by several assailants whom he later identified as members of the State Security forces and representatives of his neighborhood's Communist Party office.

The government permitted a small number of permanent international news bureaus to operate in Cuba, including, as of March 19, the U.S.-based Cable News Network (CNN). While the U.S. government approved licenses for nine additional media to open Cuba bureaus, the Cuban government did not allow these companies to do so. In February 1997, new regulations granted Cuban authorities the right to reprimand or withdraw credentials from foreign reporters who had failed to demonstrate "objectivity," accurately represent the facts, or comply with journalistic ethics.

Additional Cuban legal initiatives further narrowed the exercise of free expression, association, and movement. In December 1996, Cuba passed the Law Reaffirming Cuban Dignity and Sovereignty (Ley de Reafirmación de la Dignidad y Soberanía Cubanas, also known as the Gag Law). A response to the Helms-Burton law, which tightened the U.S. embargo, the law created broad restrictions on free expression, criminalizing even the appearance of support for U.S. policies. Cuban authorities then insisted on public manifestations of support for the law. In early 1997, the government circulated a pro-law petition, the Declaration of the Mambises of the Twentieth Century (Declaración de los Mambises del Siglo XX, the "mambises" fought for Cuban independence), to mass organizations, schools, universities, and workplaces. On April 7, Cuban authorities briefly detained Fidel Emilio Abel Tamayo, the father of one of several schoolchildren who had refused to sign the declaration in March.

In April, Cuba extended its control over citizens' movements with the passage of Decree 217, which directed all but "legal" residents to leave Havana. President Castro praised the initiative's potential for minimizing "indiscipline." By late April, the official Cuban press announced that the government had returned more than 1,600 "illegal residents" of Havana to their home provinces "using persuasive methods." Cuba also retained its prohibition on unapproved emigration and continued to prosecute for "illegal exit." In October 1996, Cuban authorities sentenced Abel Denis Ambroise Sanville to fourteen months for illegal exit.

Cuba attempted to weaken United Nations human rights mechanisms. As it had in 1996, Cuba pushed for a narrower mandate for the U.N. Working Group on Arbitrary Detentions, which previously had censured Cuba. At the Human Rights Commission's fifty-third session in Geneva in March and April 1997, Cuba successfully lobbied to restrict the Working Group's scope. Cuba also co-sponsored a resolution urging member states not to employ coercive economic or political measures against countries in response to negative human rights practices.

The Right to Monitor

The government barred international human rights groups' access to the country, as well as access by the ICRC and the U.N. Special Rapporteur. In September 1997 Human Rights Watch requested permission to conduct independent investigation in Cuba, having been denied access since 1995. In October, the request was denied.

Odilia Collazo Valdés, the president of the Pro Human Rights Party (Partido Pro Derechos Humanos, PPDH), suffered repeated arrests during 1997, as did other PPDH members, including Maité Moya Gómez and Jorge Luis Rodríguez. On October 23, a Cuban court in Santa Clara convicted eleven members of the PPDH of "association to commit criminal acts" (asociacion para delinquir) and "disobedience," with sentences ranging from one year of house arrest (María Felicia Mata Machada) to one and one-half year in prison or at a prison work camp (José Antonio Alvarado Almeida, Ileana Peñalver Duque, Roxana Alina Carpio Mata, Lilian Meneses Martínez, Arélis Fleites Méndez, Marlis Velázquez Aparicio, Iván Lema Romero, Danilo Santos Méndez, Vicente García Ramos, and José Manuel Yera Meneses). The trial occurred after the activists held a hunger strike to protest the government's detention of another PPDH member, Daula Carpio Mata. The judge reportedly allowed the defense attorney less than ten minutes to present testimony from all of the defendants. On October 29, the court sentenced Carpio Mata to sixteen months internment in a work camp for assault, following her outspoken criticisms of an earlier trial.

René Gómez Manzano, an attorney with the Agromontista Current (Corriente Agromontista), a legal defense group, and leader of the Internal Dissidents' Working Group, remains in detention at this writing. After repeated prior denials, Cuba granted Elizardo Sánchez Santacruz, the leader of the Cuban Commission for Human Rights and National Reconciliation (Comisión Cubana para los Derechos Humanos y la Reconciliación Nacional) permission for international travel in early 1997 and did allow him to return to Cuba. On May 30, the Cuban government detained Sánchez's colleague, Moisés Rodríguez Quezada, for seventy-two hours, warning him to abandon his work or leave Cuba.

The Role of the
International Community

United Nations
In November 1996, the General Assembly again voted to condemn the U.S. embargo against Cuba. In April 1997, the fifty-third session of the U.N. Human Rights Commission again censured Cuban human rights practices. As in prior years, Cuba dismissed the resolution as slanderous. Cuba's efforts,

described above, to weaken U.N. human rights mechanisms met with some success. The government refused to allow the Special Rapporteur on Cuba, Swedish diplomat Carl-Johan Groth, to conduct in-country research, but he nonetheless provided excellent coverage of Cuban human rights developments.

Organization of American States
In March, the Inter-American Commission on Human Rights issued a detailed report on Cuba's lack of compliance with the American Convention on Human Rights. Acknowledging that the Cuban government was excluded from the inter-American system in 1962, the commission nonetheless stressed that the Cuban state retained its obligations to uphold international human rights standards for its population.

European Union
On December 2, 1996, the European Union (E.U.) Council of Ministers adopted a new, stronger policy toward Cuba, known as the "common position," to "encourage a process of transition to pluralist democracy and respect for human rights and fundamental freedoms...." The policy made full economic cooperation conditional on human rights improvements, including penal code reform, the release of political prisoners, an end to harassment of dissidents, the ratification of international human rights conventions, and respect for the freedoms of speech and association. When its review of political and economic developments in Cuba revealed no notable progress, on June 26, the E.U. renewed the common position for an additional six months. Unfortunately, European investors in Cuba, as well as Canadians and others, failed to adopt effective strategies to ensure respect for labor rights in their Cuban workplaces, where government-dominated projects denied basic rights of free association and speech.

Canada
Canada's role as a leading foreign investor in Cuba provided it with important leverage for pressuring Cuba to make genuine human

rights reforms during 1997. Yet, Canada's most significant human rights initiative, the January 1997 joint declaration between the Canadian and Cuban foreign ministries, included no concrete agenda for improvements in Cuban human rights practices. Relying on the principle of "effective influence," the accord, which also addressed foreign investment, taxation, banking, and other issues, provided that Cuba and Canada would cooperate on human rights issues by holding seminars, training judges, and "exchang[ing] experiences" relevant to Cuba's intent to support a citizen's complaint commission. Unfortunately, the Cuban government, which detained several dissidents during the negotiations, showed little sign of taking the accord seriously. A Cuban Foreign Ministry spokesman stated that "it is a blatant exaggeration to say that the inclusion of the issues of human rights in a broad and diverse joint declaration with Canada implies the existence of problems in this regard on the island." At this writing, the joint accord has resulted in informal bilateral talks on human rights in Havana early in the year, closed seminars on children's and women's rights in May and June, and preparatory meetings regarding legal reforms and a Cuban citizen complaint commission.

United States

In the past year, the U.S. government could not point to human rights gains in Cuba arising from its anachronistic thirty-year policy of isolation. President Clinton acknowledged that the policy had failed in April, when he noted that the embargo had not created "an appreciable change in the Cuban regime...." The embargo, which was solidified in 1996 with the passage of the Cuban Liberty and Democratic Solidarity Act (also known as the Helms-Burton law), continued to restrict the rights to free expression and association and the freedom to travel between the U.S. and Cuba, thus violating Article 19 of the International Covenant on Civil and Political Rights, a treaty ratified by the United States. The government's granting of ten licenses per-

mitting U.S. media outlets to operate in Cuba was a positive step, but still reflected tight government control over communication between the two countries.

DOMINICAN REPUBLIC

Human Rights Developments

The Dominican government committed serious human rights abuses during President Leonel Fernández Reyna's first year in power. Police and members of the military used excessive force against criminal suspects, prisoners, and individuals participating in peaceful public demonstrations, and routinely violated due process rights. Dominican prisoners, particularly minors, suffered in deplorable conditions, and some 85 percent of detainees were held without trial, many for long periods.

On February 23, police reacting to a disturbance in the Azua prison reportedly killed three unarmed boys in cold blood. Two police lieutenants, one named Méndez and another known as "Gomera," reportedly lined up the seventeen-year-old boys, Roberto Rafael Corporán, José Ignacio Payano Núñez, and José Paredes Gutiérrez, against an interior wall of the prison and fired repeatedly at them with shotguns, killing them while other inmates pleaded for the three youths' lives. The government opened an investigation, initially concluding that the three boys had been killed while trying to escape the prison, but have not released final results of its inquiry at this writing.

On November 18, 1996, at least one-hundred heavily-armed Dominican police entered a squatters' settlement known as "El Café," on the outskirts of Santo Domingo, to evict approximately 600 families. The police fired weapons and tear gas, wounding at least ten residents. One police officer reportedly fired at Alfredo D'Oleo Encarnación, who was unarmed and standing on his patio, killing him. The government has not concluded its investigation of the El Café incident at this writing.

Dominican security forces using excessive force killed over thirty other individuals in the past year. The police and military involved in shootings frequently invoked the defense that they had been fired upon before shooting, but witnesses often contradicted their accounts. Among these cases, on March 7, army Sgt. Roberto Reyes Familia was riding his motorcycle in Santo Domingo when a vehicle side-swiped him. Reyes Familia fired at the vehicle, killing Antonio Santos Caraballo. On September 26, police invoked self-defense in the deaths of two suspected criminals in the Capotillo region of Santo Domingo, but onlookers allegedly saw police shoot the suspects after they had laid down their weapons. In May, police conducting a drug raid in Capotillo allegedly saw José Ramírez swallow a package of crack cocaine. As the police beat him with their weapons, Ramírez began to foam at the mouth and lost consciousness. The police left Ramírez at the scene. He died three hours later, as neighbors were transporting him to a hospital. While the immediate cause of Ramírez's death remained uncertain, police used excessive force in beating him and were negligent in failing to provide him with medical assistance.

Police reportedly tortured several detainees in the past year. On January 27, police arrested Ramón Vizcaino and his wife Rosie Cuevas in Vicente Noble and transported them to the national police headquarters in Santo Domingo. On three occasions over two days, officers in the robbery department beat Vizcaino, using a baseball bat and grabbing his testicles, while insisting that he admit to assisting with an escape plan for the Monte Plata prison. The police then held him for over one month, without providing him with medical treatment for injuries from the beatings, including a hernia. Police also reportedly tortured several suspects by hanging them by handcuffs or thumb screws for extended periods and denying them food, water, and access to toilets.

Dominican police routinely ignored due process protections, such as providing access to lawyers and observing the forty-eight-hour limit on holding detainees in police lock-ups. They also arbitrarily detained criminal suspects' family members as hostages, to entice the suspects to turn themselves in. Police detained Ramona Pozo, the seventy-year-old mother of Ramón Pozo, for three days in July, until her son surrendered to police in Haina.

Dominican authorities used excessive force at several public demonstrations. On April 24, a peaceful demonstration marking the 1965 U.S. invasion of the Dominican Republic was disrupted by shots fired from a Navy minibus. Sailors shot Joseliu Perdomo through the back of the leg and wounded several other demonstrators. Police opened fire on the nonviolent crowd at a Santo Domingo rally against rising telephone rates in June, leaving Araceli Pensón and Virtudes Alvarez with injuries from shotgun blasts and wounding several others.

Late in the year, police committed serious human rights violations in response to nationwide protests of persistent power outages. On October 22, police reportedly arrested Damian Edis Paredes, who was demonstrating in Santo Domingo, severely beat him and then executed him with several shots, including one in his mouth. The same day, police apparently employed excessive force when they fired numerous tear gas canisters into a demonstration, leading to the death by asphyxiation of thirteen-year-old Marlene Vargas Santana, who was in her nearby home. Hundreds of Dominican activists were arbitrarily detained in apparent government efforts to get protest organizers off the streets prior to a planned November national strike.

A backlog of criminal cases left the prisons extremely overcrowded: during 1997, 85 percent of the Dominican prison population of approximately 12,000 prisoners had never been tried. Prisoners routinely struggled to find sufficient nutrition and a place to sleep, lived in filthy, dangerous conditions, and received insufficient medical care. The police and military authorities charged with running the country's prisons received no specialized training. The difficult conditions led to several prison riots. On June 5, detainees at the Mao prison rioted in protest of poor conditions and corruption, including the reported selling of infirmary cells to healthy prisoners for up to 3,000 pesos (U.S. $231). After a few days of negotiations, police stormed the prison, injuring dozens of detainees. Police wounded sixteen-year-old Jorge Santiago Contreras, who was confined to an isolation cell and unarmed, with a shotgun blast. Another youth, seventeen-year-old Edward Moíses Sí Peña, was shot in the back.

Stunning travesties of justice resulted from the judicial system's weaknesses, prevalent corruption, and transfers of detainees far from their homes, which prohibited most prisoners from genuine access to lawyers and the courts. Scores of detainees spent months and years in Dominican prisons without being tried or found guilty of any crime. Prisoners who had been confined to Dominican prisons for exceptionally long periods without trial included: Zenóm Ramírez Ogando, who was detained in 1987 but never sentenced (his trial for homicide remained in the investigation phase); Rafael Sosa Félix, who was detained without trial since April 1991; Marino de la Rosa Beltrén, who was detained in 1991 without charge; and Valentín Almonte y Almonte, who was arrested in March 1994 but whose case file had been lost. Condemned prisoners faced additional impediments. Although a court ordered liberty for Rafael Orlando Caminero Guerrero on April 26, 1991, when he completed his ninety-day sentence in La Victoria for painting a stolen car, authorities had failed to free him as of August 1997. Ramón de la Rosa Peguero was condemned to six months in La Victoria and a 1,500 peso ($115) fine in March 1995. He completed his time in September 1995 and paid his fine but, at this writing, still awaits a judicial order freeing him.

Dominican authorities failed to provide minors, the prison system's most vulnerable population, with appropriate care. In violation of the United Nations Convention on the Rights of the Child, a treaty ratified by the Dominican Republic, the government confined hundreds of minors, both convicts and those in preventive detention, in adult prisons, and neglected to provide them with sufficient protection, education, or rehabilitation. The government's purported evaluation center for minors, Casa Albergue, was the site of serious abuses, including a November 1996 incident that left Juan Pablo Medina and Ricardo Torres dead when police refused to release the boys from their cells despite a mattress fire in the area. In May 1997, police at the center were angered by an argument with seventeen-year-old Carlos de la Cruz Severino. Six officers beat him with baseball bats, including blows to his genitals and neck. The abuses of detained minors highlighted the government's complete failure, since 1994, to enforce a new minors code.

The Law Against Intrafamiliar Violence, which was enacted into law in February, resulted in a handful of convictions late in the year. The law increased sanctions for domestic violence and improved procedural protections for victims of family violence.

Haitians continued to suffer discriminatory treatment by the Dominican government. More than 21,000 Haitians were expelled in 1997. The Dominican military carried out a particularly intense campaign in February and March, during which soldiers in some cases failed to respect the Haitians' due process rights, beat detainees, and would not allow detainees to notify family members of their expulsion. Dominican authorities also deported several Dominicans, after disregarding documents demonstrating their citizenship. On September 23, Dominican soldiers arrested Manuel Antonio Estéban Fermín, a Dominican citizen, in Santo Domingo and expelled him to Malpasse, Haiti. An Air Force captain leading the operation reportedly destroyed Estéban Fermín's national identity document and expelled him because of the dark color of his skin. In dozens of cases, government officials denied the constitutional citizenship rights due to children born of Haitian parents in the Dominican Republic. In March, Telma Reyes, a civil official in Sabana Grande de Boya, justified her denial of citizenship to ten children of Haitian descent by saying that she had received an order to do so from migration authorities. She further explained that she thought that granting the children citizenship would threaten the motherland's purity. At this writing, the Dominican government still has not submitted its report to the U.N. Committee on the Elimination of Racial Discrimination, which was due in March, and the committee considered the report "excessively overdue." The Dominican government, which is obligated to submit reports to the committee every two years, last satisfied this requirement in 1990.

Impunity for human rights violations persisted in the past year. While the Dominican police fired more than one-hundred officers for crimes and human rights abuses in August and September 1997, in an effort to purge the institution, Dominican courts brought few human rights violators to trial. The 1994 "disappearance" case of university professor Dr. Narciso González Medina remained open, but the government failed to clarify responsibility for the case and did not detain a single suspect. At this writing, the case is pending before the Inter-American Commission on Human Rights. On a positive note, the government denied a petition to try Gen. (ret.) Salvador Lluberas Montás, also known as "Chinino," in military, rather than civilian, court for the 1975 murder of journalist Orlando Martínez.

A transparent selection process for Supreme Court judges culminated in August, with the swearing-in of a new court amidst hopes that it would set a new, professional tone for the decrepit legal system. But this positive step was countered by the president's September firing of Guillermo Moreno, the well-respected attorney general for Santo Domingo, who had taken a firm stance against human rights violators.

The Right to Monitor

Under the government of President Fernández, Dominican human rights activists worked with greater freedom than they had under the previous administration, when police intimidation and anonymous telephone threats were the norm. However, several human rights activists complained of close police surveillance in October and November, prior to a planned national strike. In early November, Danilo de la Cruz, a member of the Dominican Committee for Human Rights (Comité Dominicano de Derechos Humanos, CDDH) who police had fired on in 1996, reported that police officers were following him. Virgilio Almánzar, the president of the CDDH, also was under police surveillance. His five and nine-year-old sons were followed to school by two police officers on November 3, 1997. While the government provided some access to its prisons and detention centers for minors, that access was, on occasion, unduly restricted. The Dominican government cooperated fully with the visit of representatives of the Inter-American Commission on Human Rights.

The Role of the Organization of American States

A delegation from the Inter-American Commission on Human Rights (IACHR) of the Organization of American States conducted a four-day human rights investigation in the Dominican Republic in June. The IACHR delegation explored broad human rights concerns and concluded its mission with the issuance of a detailed press release that pointed to human rights deficiencies and proposed concrete steps for improvement. The commission members have not concluded the final report of their visit at this writing.

Following an October hearing, the "disappearance" case of Narciso González remained before the IACHR at year's end.

GUATEMALA

Human Rights Developments

Emerging from more than three decades of internal warfare, Guatemala in 1997 faced soaring criminal violence, an incomplete police reform, continued impunity for human rights violations as well as common crimes and profound uncertainty over the post-conflict role of the military. The signing of a final peace accord in December 1996, capped a steady decline in recent years in the most egregious politically motivated human rights violations. Most notable was the decline in "disappearances," which since the late 1960s had become a regular practice of the Guatemalan military. Security forces carried out one case of forced disappearance in late 1996, which did not come to light until 1997. The Mission of the United Nations in Guatemala (Misión de las Naciones Unidas en Guatemala, MINUGUA) was investigating two additional cases at this writing. Other abuses did not diminish as evidently. MINUGUA confirmed nineteen extrajudicial executions in the first six months of 1997—compared with twenty-two confirmed cases in the previous semester— as well as several cases of ill-treatment, arbitrary detention, and excessive use of force, mostly by the police. Whereas in the past the victims tended to be those perceived by the security forces as ideological opponents—such as journalists, human rights advocates, trade unionists, or peasant organizers—the victims of recent abuses were predominantly poor suspects in cases of common crime.

Although political repression sharply declined, Guatemala remained awash in violence as common crime soared, including car thefts and kidnappings carried out by rings in which members of the security forces were reportedly involved. Efforts by the government in 1996 to prosecute officials and other organized-crime figures languished in 1997, reflecting the overall weakness of the judiciary and law-enforcement bodies and the government's failure to get its witness protection program off the ground. Indeed, while the continued presence of MINUGUA and the end of the conflict kept politically motivated human rights abuse at an all-time low, citizens had no recourse against lawlessness, an insecurity that prompted dozens of cases of lynchings.

A clandestine military unit's forced disappearance of guerrilla Juan José Cabrera, alias "Mincho," showed that the powerful Presidential General Staff (Estado Mayor Presidencial, EMP) continued to conduct secret and violent operations outside the law. The stubborn insistence of government officials in covering up the guerrilla's "disappearance" and apparent slaying reflected the army's longstanding refusal to accord captured combatants fundamental human rights. The guerrilla leadership also showed an alarming willingness to suppress information on the case, to the extent that the commander of Mincho's rebel force, the Revolutionary Organization of the People in Arms (Organización Revolucionaria del Pueblo en Armas, ORPA) was quoted in the press as denying his militancy in the guerrilla group.

The EMP's secret unit known as the Anti-Kidnapping Command (Comando Anti-Secuestros) reportedly captured Mincho, along with Augusto Rafael Baldizón Núñez, alias Commander "Isaías," on October 19, 1996, after the guerrillas had abducted an elderly wealthy woman. The woman's abduction, and her subsequent release in exchange for Commander Isaías, broke down the peace talks and deeply embarrassed both sides. In this context, the "disappearance" of Mincho was kept quiet by both government and guerrillas, and only confirmed by MINUGUA seven months later, after the international and domestic press loudly criticized the observer mission's silence. On May 20, MINUGUA issued a statement holding the EMP responsible for slaying Mincho "at the moment of his capture," without further describing the circumstances of the death. At this writing, Mincho's body has not been found. Noting its secret role in other anti-kidnapping operations, MINUGUA criticized the EMP for "broadly exceeding its duties and following procedures contrary to the law and the rule of law, to the detriment of an effective policy of citizen security."

The government of Alvaro Arzú reacted defensively to MINUGUA's report, denying that a second guerrilla was captured or killed along with Isaías. Moreover, a public statement by the president's public relations secretary denied that the EMP had been involved in any anti-kidnapping actions and flatly rejected the U.N. mission's request to interview those security force members involved in the operation in which Mincho allegedly perished. The government's open refusal to facilitate MINUGUA's inquiry in the case marked a rare break with this and the previous government's policy of public support for the U.N. mission. While that support may have often masked behind-the-scenes obstinacy, the government's defiant reaction on the Mincho case marked a low point in cooperation with the mission since its establishment.

The EMP—officially charged with providing security for the president—has for decades been implicated in domestic spying and political assassination. Its covert branch has gone through many incarnations and was until recently known as the "Archivos." Although then-President Ramiro de León Carpio announced the dissolution of the Archivos shortly after taking office in 1993, then-EMP head Gen. Otto Pérez Molina told Human Rights Watch a year later that only its operational arm had been suppressed, while intelligence activities continued. The EMP's Anti-Kidnapping Command is widely perceived to be the reincarnation of the operational unit. In 1997, the Anti-Kidnapping Command was reportedly involved in several cases of torture or ill-treatment of kidnapping suspects before turning them over to the National Police. Under the peace agreement, the government had promised to suppress all "clandestine security machinery" and to put domestic intelligence-gathering in civilian hands. The EMP's Anti-Kidnapping Command violated that commitment.

Military influence over the police—facilitated by a constitutional provision granting the military a role in internal security—has long obstructed effective investigations of human rights violations and contributed to the creation of an abusive police culture. Efforts spawned by the peace accords to create a new, professional, and purely civilian police force were undercut by several developments, including a delay in the promised passage of a constitutional reform limiting the military's role to external defense. In February, the congress passed a new police law, which fell short of the detailed commitments contained in the peace accords regarding police academy training for the new force. Moreover, the government failed to set up an adequate screening mechanism to avoid reintegrating into the new force agents who had been implicated in human rights violations in the past. As a result, more than a dozen police with records of serious human rights violations were admitted into the academy for training. Many members of the now-disbanded Mobile Military Police were surreptitiously admitted to the academy as well, after the briefest of stints at the Treasury Police allowed them to pass as members of that civilian institution, according to MINUGUA.

Impunity for human rights violations persisted, with some exceptions. A conviction was won in the November 1994 murder at the hands of police of university student Mario Alioto López Sánchez. On July 31, a trial judge sentenced Carlos Venancio Escobar Fernández, formerly the deputy director of the National Police Fifth Precinct, to a thirty-year prison term for the slaying. In addition, then-Interior Minister Danilo Parinello Blanco, Vice Minister Mario Mérida González, and National Police Director Salvador Figueroa were each sentenced to ten years for issuing orders that led to the killing, a judgment subsequently overturned on appeal.

Despite this milestone, impunity for human rights violations remained the most common outcome of judicial proceedings, as the shocking exoneration on May 19 of former military commissioner Cándido Noriega Estrada demonstrated. Noriega's acquittal on charges of thirty-five murders, forty-four kidnappings, eight rapes, and dozens of other crimes followed proceedings in which the mostly indigenous prosecution witnesses suffered intimidation, threats, and sorely deficient translation from their native Quiché into Spanish. The murders occurred on three occasions in 1982, in which Noriega and another military commissioner, Juan Alesio Sanmayor, reportedly led groups of soldiers through the community of Toluché, in the department of El Quiché, identifying villagers as guerrillas for extrajudicial execution by the military.

Noriega's actions were typical of the early 1980s, in which civilian auxiliaries to the army, both military commissioners and civil patrollers, joined together with soldiers in widespread slaughter of perceived guerrilla supporters. Several initiatives were underway in 1997 to uncover and reliably document the abuses that characterized the conflict. Nongovernmental organizations, including the Human Rights Office of the Archbishop of Guatemala, launched massive fact-finding programs. And in July the Historical Clarification Commission established under the peace accords formally began an official study on the subject. Although the commission's mandate bars it from identifying the individual perpetrators of abuse or providing evidence for prosecutions, the naming of respected Guatemalan and international figures to lead the effort raised hopes that its contribution could be significant in bringing to light and to official acknowledgment the immense suffering inflicted on the civilian population during the armed conflict, largely at the hands of the forces designated by law for citizens' protection.

These initiatives also began to expose previously unreported laws-of-war violations by the guerrillas. In August, the Archbishop of Guatemala's forensic team began an exhumation of victims of a 1982 guerrilla massacre that reportedly claimed as many as 180 civilians—including women and children—in Chacalte, El Quiché department.

Indeed, Guatemala's highlands were littered with hundreds of clandestine cemeteries from the period, and although many have been exhumed in the 1990s, few prosecutions have resulted. The main obstacles to successful prosecutions included the routine intimidation of prosecutors, judges, witnesses, and relatives of victims, as well as negligence and corruption on the part of the authorities. Nonetheless, in 1997, several military officers were charged in connection with the December 1992 massacre of 162 people—among them sixty-seven children under age twelve—in a hamlet known as "Las Dos Erres" in the department of Petén.

The so-called Law of National Reconciliation passed in December 1996 raised the possibility that judges could grant amnesty for crimes deemed to have occurred in the context of counterinsurgency. While the law specifically prohibited the granting of amnesty for crimes of "disappearance" or torture, the absence of a precise prohibition of amnesty for extrajudicial executions left room for frightened judges to exonerate suspects in such cases. As of this writing, judges had denied every request for amnesty made by defendants in human rights cases; indeed, no member of the military had been granted amnesty. Guerrillas received amnesty for crimes of subversion, but not for violent abuses such as murder.

Initiatives the government announced in 1996 to combat impunity met with mixed results. A witness protection program created by law in 1996 lacked resources and had a negligible impact on the very real practice of intimidating witnesses and judicial officials. A special crimes task force established in 1996 to handle new cases in which security forces were implicated, or in which judicial or police authorities, human rights monitors or international observers became victims, had some successes in solving common crimes under its mandate.

Meanwhile, progress was suspended on the transfer to civilian courts of hundreds of cases of common crimes committed by members of the armed forces, incidents that had come under military court jurisdiction. Landmark legislation in 1996 mandated the shift in jurisdiction, but, at this writing, Guatemala's Constitutional Court had yet to rule on a legal challenge to the law.

In January, a ten-year conviction was handed down against former military commissioner Carlos Morales Sosa for the April 1993 murder of street youth Henry Yubani Alvarez Benítez; this conviction followed two other encouraging sentences in late 1996 for murders by police and private security guards of street children. Impunity remained intact, however, for eleven murders of street children that occurred in 1996; some of these cases appeared to represent a kind of "social cleansing" and at least one was carried out by a member of the security forces.

Children's rights suffered a setback when the government delayed implementation of a new Minors' Code scheduled to take effect in September. As of this writing, the Congress had postponed implementation of the code until at least March 1998. The code represented a vast improvement over current legislation, extending important procedural protections to children accused of crimes, including the right to a lawyer at the government's expense. It forbade placing children in protective custody in juvenile detention centers or imprisonment for status offenses, such as running away or being homeless. Research by Human Rights Watch documented ongoing abuses against street children and those held in juvenile detention in Guatemala, including arbitrary detention of street children, sometimes merely for being homeless; due process violations during adjudication hearings; and the practice of holding children deemed to need the state's protection together with juvenile offenders. The investigation also found children vulnerable to serious mistreatment from staff members and other detainees, sometimes with staff acquiescence.

During 1997, for the first time, a maquiladora union negotiated a contract with a company in the export processing sector. In November 1996, the Labor Ministry failed to determine whether or not the union had mustered sufficient strength to compel the company to bargain under Guatemalan law. Nonetheless, after the conflict between the union and the Phillips-Van Heusen company attracted international attention, the union's sufficient base of support was established, a pattern of anti-union activity was uncovered, and the company voluntarily entered into negotiations with the union, producing the unprecedented contract.

The Right to Monitor

Human rights monitors, especially those pressing for justice in cases of human rights violations, continued to face death threats, surveillance, and intimidation by unidentified assailants, incidents that the government failed to investigate. In the first months of 1997, individuals affiliated with the Association for the Advancement of Social Sciences in Guatemala (Asociación para el Avance de las Ciencias Sociales en Guatemala, AVANCSO) faced threats and harassment, apparently in relation to the prosecution underway of the alleged intellectual authors of the 1990 extrajudicial execution of AVANCSO co-founder Myrna Mack.

An attempt by the Arzú government to promote the election of an unqualified candidate to the Inter-American Commission on Human Rights of the Organization of American States (OAS) was defeated in June by a The candidate, Francisco Villagrán Kramer, spent nearly three years in office as vice-president under the regime of Gen. Romeo Lucas García (1978-1992), during which government death squads eliminated an entire generation of political and grassroots leaders, and later formed a political alliance with former military dictator Efraín Ríos Montt, whose regime replaced death squad operations with the widespread slaughter of peasants by the army. Human rights organizations deemed Villagran Kramer unsuited for leadership in the hemisphere's most important organization for the protection and promotion of human rights.

The Role of the International Community

United Nations

The role of the United Nations in moderating the difficult peace process that culminated in the December 1996 agreement, combined with the presence since late 1994 of more than one hundred human rights observers, has been pivotal in reducing politically motivated human rights abuses. Other branches of the world body also played critical roles, such as the independent experts named by the U.N. Commission on Human Rights since 1990, who consistently highlighted the structural factors contributing to human rights abuse in Guatemala. A significant number of the recommendations contained in the reports of Independent Expert Christian Tomuschat and his successor, Mónica Pinto, have been met over the last few years, such as the dissolution of the civil patrols and military commissioners, both civilian groups deputized by the army with great license to commit abuses. Some of the recommendations, such as the creation of an intelligence service fitting for a democratic society, have been fulfilled in name only. Nonetheless, the Human Rights Commission did not renew Pinto's mandate when it met in Geneva in March and April, instead offering the government "advisory services" on human rights and committing the secretary-general to submit a report on human rights by the end of 1997. Although the human rights situation has undeniably improved, the lack of full compliance with the recommendations of the independent experts ought to have been grounds for extension of the expert's mandate. In August, the U.N. Sub-Commission on the Prevention of Discrimination and the Protection of Minorities, in an effort to avoid duplication of work carried out by other U.N agencies, officially ended fifteen years of examination of the human rights situation in Guatemala as well. This reduction of international mechanisms closely watching the human rights situation left great responsibility in the hands of MINUGUA by year's end. MINUGUA's prestige suffered from its delay in taking a position on the "disappearance" of the guerrilla known as Mincho, provoking tensions in what had previously been exemplary relations between the mission and local human rights groups.

United States

No longer a supplier of overt military aid, the United States became a source of modest financial contributions to the peace process. Military aid that had been frozen since 1990 was converted into a fund to assist in the demobilization of combatants. The administration also pledged a U.S. $1 million contribution to the Historical Clarification Commission. In September, the commission formally requested the Clinton administration to declassify records concerning human rights abuses committed during the armed conflict. Guatemalan authorities in September requested documents pertaining to the trial underway of the alleged intellectual authors of the 1990 extrajudicial execution of Guatemalan anthropologist Myrna Mack. U.S. government archives, especially those of intelligence agencies that historically worked in tandem with Guatemala's military intelligence, most likely contain a wealth of information critical to the truth-seeking process underway in Guatemala. In addition to assisting investigations and prosecutions inside Guatemala, the release of U.S. documents is likely to expose important aspects of U.S. policy that contributed to human rights violations in Guatemala.

In May, the Clinton administration released 1,400 pages of Central Intelligence Agency (CIA) documents regarding its covert operations in Guatemala in the 1950s, including plans to assassinate leading officials of the leftist government of Jacobo Arbenz, who was overthrown by a CIA-sponsored military coup. Although only a fraction of the classified files the agency maintains on the coup, the documents released provided a chilling inside look at the methods used and promoted by the agency, including targeted political assassination and mass murder. These documents underscored the need for a thorough airing of the U.S. role in promoting human rights violations in Guatemala and elsewhere.

Documents released as a result of a lawsuit filed by Jennifer Harbury, the wife of disappeared Guatemalan guerrilla commander Efraín Bámaca Velásquez, show that U.S. agencies had information about her husband's fate within days of his March 12, 1992 capture and clandestine detention by the army. Yet this information was denied to Harbury, a U.S. citizen, for more than two years, during which time she engaged in three hunger strikes demanding information regarding Bámaca's fate.

Relevant Human Rights Watch reports:
Guatemala's Forgotten Children, 7/97
Corporations and Human Rights: Freedom of Association in a Maquila in Guatemala, 3/97

HAITI

Human Rights Developments
Haiti's struggle to establish a solidly democratic government in the past year was marred by political confusion. Elections in April were disputed, with tentative results announced only in August. Controversy surrounded the Provisional Electoral Council. Prime Minister Rosny Smarth resigned in June, and, at this writing, the government cannot agree on his successor. Noting Haiti's still tentative security situation, the United Nations extended the mandate of peacekeeping troops and civilian police advisors in the United Nations Transition Mission in Haiti (UNTMIH) for six months, until November 30, 1997.

Despite these upheavals, the public steadily clamored for justice, with demonstrations marking the anniversaries of political assassinations. But the government failed to dedicate needed resources to confront impunity. Only the Haitian National Police (HNP) revealed a willingness to discipline and fire human rights violators within its ranks. As Haitian courts imposed minimal criminal sanctions on abusive police officers or simply dismissed charges against them, HNP human rights violations persisted. Officers beat detainees, killed criminal suspects or others with an excessive use of force, and, albeit in fewer cases than in 1996, committed extrajudicial executions.

On November 4, 1996, HNP agents killed five men in the Delmas area of Port-au-Prince. HNP officers reportedly executed one of the men after having handcuffed him, while apparently killing two with excessive force and two in unclear circumstances. By July 1997, the HNP's inspector general's office (IG), an internal police disciplinary body, had fired seven officers for the incident, who later were tried and acquitted. The U.N./ Organization of American States International Civilian Mission in Haiti estimated that the police killed twenty criminal suspects with an excessive use of force from January to August 1997, and reportedly extrajudicially executed three individuals during that period, one of whom died after police beat him severely.

Haitian police frequently beat detainees, both in urban areas, where violent crime contributed to officer frustration and violence, and in the provinces. Seven police beat Chena Pierre Martial, a congressman from Trou-du-Nord, in August, after he reportedly evoked one officer's jealousy at a local dance. The IG later fired the seven agents. In September, police in Cayes arrested Yvon Chéry, the director of a local news station, beating him and detaining him overnight, reportedly because they were angry that Chéry had argued with police about an alleged traffic violation the day before. Police routinely held detainees in lockups beyond the forty-eight-hour maximum period prescribed by law.

Police abused their authority by engaging in violent criminal activity, including murder and drug trafficking. On May 20, HNP agent Antoine Bien Aimée killed his cousin, Eddy Bien Aimée, and wounded another cousin, Luckner Bien Aimée, allegedly over a petty dispute. In late July, several officers from Jéremie, in the department of Grande Anse, were arrested for armed robbery in the Delmas area of Port-au-Prince. The HNP Grande Anse departmental commander, Fritz Jean, who had provided the vehicle used in the robbery, violated police procedures by ordering three of the arrested officers, his apparent co-conspirators, released. At this writing, Jean retains his position and neither he nor any HNP agent has faced trial for the incident. On October 2, off-duty HNP agent Jude Merzy fired into a crowd leaving a soccer match in Grand Goâve, killing one man and wounding several others.

The IG disciplined dozens of officers for human rights and other abuses and sent over thirty cases to the Haitian courts in 1997. By September, the IG had fired over 160 officers for serious violations of police regulations, such as crimes or human rights abuses. The IG's work earned it the ire of fellow police, and inspectors took extra security precautions in the face of frequent threats of violence, some of which were made directly by police charged with abuses, urging them to cease their investigations or withdraw criminal complaints. However, the Haitian courts did not keep pace with the IG's progress; most police abuse criminal cases referred to the courts by the IG, ranging from simple assault to homicide, did not go to trial or were marred by irregularities.

Weaknesses in the judicial system and an apparent lack of governmental will precluded prosecutions for human rights violations that occurred under Haiti's military dictatorships as well. The justice ministry's November 1996 creation of the National Penal Unit (Unité Pénale Nationale, UPENA), to assist with human rights prosecutions, ended in failure by February 1997, when the unfunded unit collapsed. The government set aside no funds for victim reparations for the deaths of family members or serious injuries resulting from military violence. The Special Investigations Unit, a team formed in late 1995 with international support and charged with investigating politically motivated crimes, made few advances. The Haitian government did little to challenge the United States government's refusal to return thousands of incriminating documents it had seized from the Haitian military and the paramilitary group, the Front for the Advancement and Progress of Haiti (Front pour l'Avancement et Progrés d'Haïti, FRAPH) in FRAPH was responsible for human rights atrocities under the military government that ruled Haiti from 1991 to 1994 and reportedly was founded with Central Intelligence Agncy assistance. The International Lawyers' Bureau, a special prosecution team supported by the justice ministry and focusing on two cases, stood out for having made progress toward successful human rights trials.

The lawyers' bureau continued preparation for trials of those accused of the December 1993 massacre of at least thirty residents of Cité Soleil and the 1994 massacre of at least fifteen individuals in Raboteau, near Gonaïves, both of which were committed by Haitian soldiers and FRAPH members. Over twenty defendants, including military officials, were in detention for the Raboteau case, although one escaped in March. The U.S. government impeded progress on the Raboteau and Cité Soleil cases by failing to produce documents detailing its own investigations of each case. U.S. authorities, including Amb. William Swing, conducted these inquiries shortly after each incident had occurred. In June, the U.S. State Department denied Haiti's request for expedited delivery of the Cité Soleil materials and in October, the U.S. rejected Haiti's March request for expedited delivery of the Raboteau materials.

Several of the human rights cases that did go to trial were marred by apparent corruption or prosecutorial incompetence. In late July, Adrien Saint Julien, the former military commander in Marchand Dessalines, a community near St. Marc, was tried for the murders of Loukens Pierre and Antoine Pauleus in 1992. At trial, the prosecutor failed to present critical evidence and the judge permitted jury members to speak to the defense attorney. One juror abandoned the trial before its completion, potentially skewing the outcome of the trial. Nevertheless, the judge permitted jury deliberation and Saint Julien was acquitted. Despite the existence of other criminal complaints against Saint Julien, authorities released him shortly after the trial. On September 15, former soldier Thélusmé Jean-Gilles was acquitted in Jacmel for the October 1993 murder of Marie Délène Nicolas, a local supporter of then-ousted President Jean-Bertrand Aristide, after the prosecution neglected to present essential elements of the case. On September 19, in Jacmel, a former section chief (*chef de section*, a military auxiliary in a small town), Baguidy Calixdé, who was accused of the 1994 killing of a reputed Aristide supporter, Pachino Dord, in Leogane, was brought to trial despite the observance of a national day of mourning for victims of a ferry disaster. Court officials failed to notify the witnesses and the victim's family that the trial was going forward. Amid allegations that the defendant's family had bribed the judge, the judge allowed the trial to proceed. Since no witnesses were available to testify, the prosecutor asked that charges be dropped. The court complied and released Calixdé.

As public confidence in the police and the judicial system crumbled, vigilante violence continued in Haiti, with a handful of deaths each month of suspected criminals at the hands of angry mobs. In mid-September, residents of the rural community of Sevrin in the south-west killed Louinor Jean-Louis and his wife, Vesta Jeune, with machete blows, after accusing them of engaging in sorcery that contributed to an infant's death.

Judicial failures to respect due process and to try old cases resulted in over 80 percent of Haiti's prison population being held in preventive detention, often for excessive periods. As of August 1997, several women at the Fort National prison and men at the National Penitentiary had been held without trial for over two years, while over two dozen boys had spent over sixteen months at Fort National without trial. In mid-August, Haitian courts ordered several supporters of the Mobilization for National Development (Mobilisatión pour le Développement National, MDN) released for insufficient evidence. They had been detained in 1996 for allegedly threatening state security. A handful of prisoners remained in detention on charges of failing to pay debts, in violation of the International Covenant on Civil and Political Rights, a treaty ratified by Haiti.

The National Penitentiary Administration (Administration Pénitentiaire Nationale, APENA) improved prison conditions somewhat, providing cleaner facilities and better nutrition for prisoners. However, general conditions in Haiti's overcrowded prisons remained dismal. A few complaints surfaced of beatings by APENA guards, but these were not addressed due to the absence of clear procedures for disciplining APENA staff. Overcrowding prevented the necessary segregation of prisoners according to age and legal status. Of greatest concern, the concentration of over seventy male minors, both convicts and preventive detainees, in two cells at Fort National contributed to multiple rapes of younger, weaker prisoners by older or stronger fellow inmates. Prison authorities admitted that they lacked other holding facilities that would allow them to isolate victims from their attackers. In provincial prisons, few minors were held with adults.

On October 6, three off-duty APENA guards reportedly gunned down Louis Emilio Passe, a congressional deputy from Dame Marie. He died several days later. At this writing, one APENA guard is under arrest, while two remain at large.

The Right to Monitor

Haiti did not impede independent human rights monitoring in 1997. The Office of Citizen Protection (Office de la Protection du Citoyen, a human rights ombudsman) received start-up funds early in the year, but at this writing, the government has not allocated it operating funds. The Inter-American Commission on Human Rights briefly visited Haiti in August to investigate the shooting of one of its members, former Haitian

Justice Minister Jean-Joseph Exumé. The commissioner apparently was the victim of a carjacking.

The Role of the International Community

United Nations and the Organization of American States

The U.N. maintained a peacekeeping presence in Haiti in the past year, with UNTMIH's fifty military and 250 civilian police personnel. In light of planned withdrawals of U.N. forces, Canada pledged to maintain 700 troops in Haiti until the end of the year and the U.S. Support Group Mission of approximately 500 troops remains in Haiti at this writing. The reduced staff of the U.N./OAS International Civilian Mission, who briefly served as electoral monitors in April, planned to continue their low-profile human rights observation and training for local groups until year's end.

United States

The U.S. government refused again to return to the Haitian government the approximately 160,000 pages of documents and other materials seized from FRAPH and Haitian military headquarters in 1994. The U.S. continued to insist that the documents only would be returned after U.S. citizens' names had been excised, apparently for the illegitimate purpose of covering up U.S. complicity in political murder and other abuses, particularly the role of U.S. intelligence assets with the military government and FRAPH. Ambassador Swing stated that his government already had removed information identifying U.S. citizens from 113 pages of the materials. The refusal to return Haitian property to Haitian prosecutors, in conjunction with the U.S. government's failure to provide details of its own investigations of the Cité Soleil and Raboteau massacres, obstructed justice for Haitian human rights victims.

In August, the State Department acted to prevent the deportation of FRAPH leader Emmanuel Constant, who had received regular CIA payments while directing the paramilitary organization. Arguing that Constant's return to Haiti might cause instability and burden the judicial system, the State Department allowed him to remain in New York with a work permit. This kept Constant beyond the reach of Haitian prosecutors, despite high-ranking Haitian officials' assurances that he could receive a fair trial.

Its refusal to cooperate with Haiti's struggle against impunity seriously damaged U.S. credibility. More positively, the U.S.-backed Legal Assistance Program provided representation to Haitian prisoners, reportedly resulting in 3,000 releases.

In June, the Senate passed the DeWine amendment, which would deny U.S. visas to those who had been "credibly alleged" to have committed or ordered political killings in Haiti. If passed into law, the bill, which remains in conference at this writing, would require the State Department to report each year to Congress on compliance with the provision.

Relevant Human Rights Watch report:

Human Rights Record of The Haitian National Police, 1/97

MEXICO

Human Rights Developments

Although the Mexican government continued to pay rhetorical attention to human rights, serious violations and impunity remained the norm during 1997. Authorities failed to address human rights violations stemming from acute rural tensions, the army's confrontation with leftist guerrillas, and a much-needed but ill-designed campaign to fight organized and common crime. In case after case, Mexican officials refused to engage in constructive dialogue with Mexican and international human rights organizations, preferring to obfuscate or ignore human rights issues rather than offer workable solutions to well-documented problems. At the heart of many abuses lay Mexico's police and justice systems, which often functioned at the expense of, rather than in support of, human rights.

Despite the serious human rights violations that took place during the year, the country made important strides in expanding political rights. On July 6, Mexicans voted in mid-term elections, casting ballots in a poll historic in both procedure and outcome. The elections represented an important consolidation of the right of Mexicans to exercise their political freedoms. Mexican and international observers agreed that procedural irregularities were minimal, in contrast to previous elections. Electoral reforms instituted over recent years permitted much freer balloting; for the first time ever, for instance, the Federal Electoral Institute (Instituto Federal Electoral, IFE) operated independently from the government, and IFE officials administered the elections fairly in most parts of the country. Contrary to the trend in the rest of Mexico, however, serious irregularities did take place in Chiapas. There, according to Civic Alliance Chiapas (Alianza Cívica Chiapas, ACC), a local branch of the national good-governance group, more than 150 voting booths were burned or robbed. Supporters of the leftist Zapatista Army of National Liberation (Ejército Zapatista de Liberación Nacional, EZLN), which launched an armed uprising in January 1994, and partisans of the ruling Institutional Revolutionary Party (Partido Revolucionario Institucional, PRI), who organized into armed groups in northern Chiapas, carried out the attacks.

The outcome of the vote sent a shock wave through Mexican politics, as the PRI lost control of the Chamber of Deputies, Mexico's lower house of congress, for the first time since the party was formed seven decades ago. The elections also resulted in opposition leaders assuming pivotal positions that had always before been occupied by members of the PRI, such as speaker of the Chamber of Deputies and mayor of Mexico City.

Though historic, the vote offered little hope of immediate improvements in the human rights situation, an outcome that would require the new congress to act as a counterbalance to the arbitrary actions of the traditionally authoritarian executive branch of government. Congress could, for instance, press state governors to end impunity for human rights violations, hold authorities accountable for abuses documented by the government's National Human Rights Commission (Comisión Nacional de Derechos Humanos, CNDH), and require the executive to take meaningful action to end human rights violations and ensure that violators faced justice. At this writing, it is too soon to know if congress would assume such a role.

In addition to the advance constituted by the elections, Mexico deserved credit for the important role it played as one of eight countries leading a diplomatic effort to draft a convention banning anti-personnel landmines. Begun in October 1996, the negotiations, which eventually came to include eighty-nine countries, resulted in September in the signing of a convention on the total prohibition of anti-personnel landmines.

On the domestic front, however, Mexican officials took much less seriously numerous and serious human rights problems that needed urgent attention. In rural Mexico, violence continued unabated. In April, Human Rights Watch issued findings covering Chiapas, Sinaloa, Guerrero, and Oaxaca states. A common feature of much rural violence was the misuse of the structures of government—prosecutors' offices, the police, and courts—to harass real or perceived opponents of the ruling party, reinforcing victims' assumption that the justice system could not effectively and impartially mediate community conflicts stemming from political differences, economic rivalries, or religious discord. In Chiapas, for example, Human Rights Watch reported that while many of the assassinations, abductions, threats, and expulsions in rural Mexico were carried out by private individuals, government agents often facilitated such abusive acts, failed to prosecute the perpetrators, or appeared to use the judicial system to achieve partisan goals. Moreover, in many cases, officials participated directly in abuses.

Those problems remained serious throughout the year. In northern Chiapas, community conflict continued to lead to expulsions and murder. For instance, Juan López Jiménez, a leader of the pro-PRI armed group called Peace and Justice, was assassinated on June 15 in Sabanilla municipality. In what appeared to be a reprisal, four members of the opposition Party of the Democratic Revolution (Partido de la Revolución Democrática, PRD) were killed on June 22 and 23.

As this incident made clear, violence in the region was not one-sided. A pattern emerged, however, in which prosecutors and police frequently turned a blind eye toward abuses committed by government supporters but fiercely prosecuted alleged acts of violence committed by real or perceived government opponents. In a positive move, starting in May Chiapas state officials released at least twelve people who had been wrongly jailed in such circumstances. The detainees had gone on hunger strike in November 1996 to force government review of their cases. At this writing, others claiming to be wrongly detained are still in jail.

Serious human rights violations also continued to take place in the context of the government's fight against the leftist Popular Revolutionary Army (Ejército Popular Revolucionario, EPR), which first appeared in June 1996. In Guerrero state, Mexican human rights groups documented a series of abuses committed by the army and police in their zeal to combat the guerrillas. A July 1997 report by the Miguel Agustín Pro Juárez Human Rights Center (Centro de Derechos Humanos "Miguel Agustín Pro Juárez," PRODH) found a pattern of army abuses consisting of "illegal searches, arbitrary detentions, physical torture, detentions beyond legally allowed limits, death threats, incommunicado detention in military barracks, and psychological torture that include simulated executions." Detainees were typically blindfolded, held incommunicado for periods of between several hours and several days, tortured, and interrogated about the EPR, then released or turned over to the public prosecutor's office. For instance, unidentified men took Magencio Abad Zeferino Domínguez, from Olinalá municipality, from his home on December 27, 1996, and questioned him about the EPR. According to a report prepared by the Tlachinollán Human Rights Center of the Mountain (Centro de Derechos Humanos de la Montaña Tlachinollán), Zeferino was kept blindfolded during his entire detention and suffered torture consisting of near-drowning and electric shocks. His abductors moved him to several locations. In one of the detention centers where Zeferino was held, he encountered Luis Gonzaga Lara, another man from Olinalá municipality who had been abducted on December 27 and questioned about the EPR. The unidentified men who interrogated Gonzaga told him, "See, why didn't you want to say who had painted the letters?"—a reference to an incident a week earlier in which soldiers arbitrarily detained him and questioned him about a political slogan painted on the wall of his house. It appeared, therefore, that the December 27 abductions of Gonzaga and Zeferino were carried out by security forces. Eventually, both men were released.

Such abuses also took place in Oaxaca state, another region where the EPR was active. In Loxichas, Mexican human rights groups tallied scores of arbitrary detentions, temporary "disappearances," and incidents of torture carried out in operations coordinated by the police and military. The crackdown began in August 1996, following an EPR attack in the region that was part of a coordinated assault by the guerrilla group in several states, and continues as of this writing. On August 4, for instance, Oaxaca state police detained and blindfolded Juanario Crispín Almaráz Silva, from San Agustín Loxicha. According to the Fray Francisco Vitoria Human Rights Center (Centro de Derechos Humanos "Fray Francisco Vitoria"), he was beaten severely and interrogated about the EPR, then transported to a

Mexico City prison. The following day, he was released without charge. Celerino Jiménez Almaráz had not been so lucky. Police wounded him after breaking into his home in San Mateo Río Hondo on April 24. According to his wife, Jiménez tried to flee, even though he had been wounded in the leg. His body was found two days later; police said he died in an armed confrontation.

Government officials also engaged in serious abuses under the guise of promoting the government's fight against illegal drugs. In May officials did so after someone stole half a ton of cocaine from the San Luis Río Colorado, Sonora state, Office of the Federal Attorney General (Procuraduría General de la República, PGR). The drug had been confiscated from traffickers. Agents of the special anti-drug unit of the police detained Alberto Gómez García, one of the robbery suspects, on May 27, held him incommunicado, and moved him from location to location in Mexico, torturing him by methods including near-suffocation and electric shocks. On June 3, federal prosecutors announced that they had been holding Gómez under a type of arrest known as "*arraigo*," in which the detainee is not held in jail but cannot move from a designated area. Eventually, on June 22, Gómez's family was permitted to see him while he was held under arraigo in Mexico City's Hotel Edison. The PGR informed Human Rights Watch in September that the torture allegations and complaints of procedural irregularities were being investigated by the PGR's Internal Criminal Investigations Unit (Visitaduría General) and Internal Administrative Investigations Unit (Contraloría Interna).

Mexican human rights groups have also documented a growing problem of "disappearances" in northern Mexico, apparently related to drug trafficking. PRODH chronicled at least sixteen between June 1996 and August 1997 in Sinaloa state. In many cases it was not clear if the victims were detained by police or soldiers, or, if such officials were responsible, if the authorities were working with the goal of fighting drug trafficking in general or were in the employ

of a drug trafficker looking to weaken a rival gang. Rómulo Rico Urrea, for instance, remains missing since September 1996. A report by the *New York Times* in March described evidence of links between the abductors and Gen. Jesús Gutiérrez Rebollo, who was named in December 1996 to head Mexico's anti-drug efforts, then removed and jailed on allegations that he was in the employ of drug traffickers. In October, the same newspaper reported that more than fifty people have been reported "disappeared" in Chihuahua, most of them after being detained by police.

Torture in Mexico remained a serious problem in the cases of suspected guerrillas and in detentions related to common crime. In its third periodic report submitted to the United Nations Committee Against Torture (CAT), the Mexican government provided an excessively formal description of the torture problem in Mexico, focusing on legal reforms and provisions designed to combat torture while ignoring the inefficacy of these measures. In its conclusions reached in April, the CAT noted the positive nature of some of the legal reforms and education initiatives undertaken by the government but strongly faulted the "profound dichotomy" between legal and administrative structures and the continuing systematic practice of torture in the country. Mexican human rights groups prepared detailed documentation on torture in anticipation of the August visit of Nigel Rodley, the U.N. special rapporteur on torture. Rodley's visit to Mexico was his first to Mexico in his U.N. post and followed years of requests to the Mexican government for permission to make the trip.

During 1997, public security continued to demand attention from Mexican policy makers, as common and organized crime grew in magnitude. President Ernesto Zedillo noted in his state-of-the-union address in September that "public insecurity in the streets is the most serious concern facing Mexicans." He lamented, too, that much of that insecurity came from the fact that Mexicans continue "fearing both those who commit crime and those who should fight it, because frequently [those who should be fighting crime] cover it up or tolerate illegal acts." Nowhere were public security concerns—and human rights violations stemming from police operations —more clear than in Mexico City, where techniques developed to combat crime hinged upon the violation of civil liberties, including freedom of movement and due process. Police cordoned off streets or entire neighborhoods, detained all present, and only later released detainees not deemed suspicious. The abuses stemming from this anti-crime strategy reached tragic proportions on September 8, when, after responding to a reported robbery in the Buenos Aires district, a police officer was killed in an apparent shoot-out with the suspects. Three people reported by witnesses to have been detained by police were found murdered the next day. Three other people detained by men in plain clothes and missing since September 8, were found dead on September 30. In October, police arrested at least two dozen police officers, one of whom was accused of aggravated homicide. After the incident, authorities dissolved the "Jaguars" Special Dissuasive Group (Grupo Especial Disuasivo "Jaguares"), the Mexico City police force from whose ranks came the officer accused of aggravated homicide. At this writing it was not clear how far up the chain of command the investigation would reach.

As police took ever-stronger actions to fight crime, journalists covering crime increasingly faced harassment, physical attacks, and even death. Gunmen killed at least two journalists during the year, Jesús Bueno León of the Guerrero state weekly *7 Días* and Benjamín Flores Guerrero, with the Sonora state daily *La Prensa*. Prior to his murder, Bueno had written that he believed state officials planned to kill him in retaliation for his reporting. In the Flores Guerrero case, state authorities arrested two men they accused of carrying out the assassination at the behest of a man believed to be a drug trafficker.

Other physical attacks against journalists also took place during the year. In separate incidents in September, for instance, unidentified assailants kidnapped two reporters with the daily *Reforma*. On September 5, after interviewing family members of PGR agents accused of drug trafficking, Daniel Lizárraga was driven around in a taxi by men who interrogated him about the interviews and threatened him to stop covering the subject. Before releasing Lizárraga, the assailants stole materials related to the story, including his interview notes. Just days before, on August 25, assailants kidnaped, beat, and threatened *Reforma* reporter David Vicenteño, who was covering the "disappearance" of a Mexico City police agent. Then, on September 13, men dressed in civilian clothing kidnaped René Solorio, a reporter with the *Hechos* news program on TV Azteca. The assailants tortured the journalist by placing a plastic bag over his head and threatening to execute him. They warned him and his boss, anchor Javier Alatorre, to drop stories critical of police operations in Mexico City. The station had recently broadcast a news story with footage showing armed robbers talking with police officers after committing robberies. The following day, *Hechos* reporter Ernesto Madrid suffered a similar attack. On September 17, a reporter from the daily *El Universal* who had covered the same story broadcast on "Hechos" was beaten.

Mexican journalists and foreign correspondents in the country also continued to face the harassment of criminal libel suits, which, according to the New York-based Committee to Protect Journalists (CPJ), carried with them the threat of a maximum of eleven months in prison. Among those facing defamation charges were Ninfa Deandar, editor of Tamaulipas state daily *El Mañana de Nuevo Laredo*, who has suffered death threats, and Sam Dillon and Craig Pyes of the *New York Times*. Other journalists were threatened with court action if they did not submit to prosecutors' questioning regarding information published in their newspapers.

In the area of labor rights, Mexicans continued to suffer violations stemming from lax government enforcement of labor standards and legal structures that impeded the organization of independent unions. For instance, Human Rights Watch documented the government's failure to enforce anti-discrimination law in export-processing factories known as maquiladoras and pro-government bias within federal labor tribunals. In 1996 and 1997, Human Rights Watch filed complaints about these problems before the United States National Administrative Office (U.S. NAO) (see The Role of the International Community). The U.S. NAO was created by the North American Agreement on Labor Cooperation (NAALC), commonly referred to as the labor rights side agreement of the North American Free Trade Agreement (NAFTA), to handle such matters. Union activists also faced threats, physical attacks, and reprisals for union organizing.

An important appeals-court decision in June offered hope that certain longstanding legal restrictions on union freedoms in Mexico would be eliminated. Based on a challenge made by the Single Union of Workers of the Fishing Ministry (Sindicato Unico de Trabajadores de la Secretaría de Pesca, SUTSP)—the union on whose behalf Human Rights Watch filed one of the U.S. NAO cases mentioned above—a court ruled unconstitutional provisions of a federal labor law that prohibited more than one union from organizing in any single government entity, such as a ministry. While the decision constituted an important success for freedom of association advocates, it was not clear what impact the decision would have, since federal labor law did not define the rights of second, minority unions in the federal workplace and the June legal decision did nothing to fill the legal void. Until Mexican law specified the rights of second unions—including their ability to receive union dues and have time off for official union activities—the formation of more than one union in federal workplaces would prove meaningless. Indeed, though the court decision gave SUTSP the right to exist along with a pro-government union within the

Ministry of the Environment, Natural Resources and Fishing (Secretaría del Medio Ambiente, Recursos Naturales y Pesca, SEMARNAP), SUTSP was not able to work as a union. At this writing, SUTSP is working through the courts to have its rights defined.

The Right to Monitor
The Mexican government continued to react vehemently against international human rights pressure, dismissing well-documented human rights reports and even expelling foreign human rights monitors. As in past years, Mexican human rights groups faced serious threats and attacks during 1997.

Church-related human rights groups continued to come under attack throughout Mexico. In Mexico City, a series of death threats received by members and collaborators of PRODH tapered off by the end of the 1996, but armed men appeared outside the group's Mexico City offices in May after the group gave assistance to foreigners threatened with expulsion. After keeping watch on the offices for a week, the men disappeared. Following a series of death threats against PRODH in 1996, some of which were delivered in writing and by hand to the group's Mexico City address, authorities installed a closed-circuit video camera outside PRODH's offices and instructed police to patrol the area near the building where the group worked. Judicial investigations into the threats, however, led nowhere, as authorities failed to follow up leads provided by PRODH.

Chihuahua's Commission of Solidarity and Defense of Human Rights (Comisión de Solidaridad y Defensa de los Derechos Humanos, COSYDDHAC) came under renewed threat in January, when the organization's secretary and founder were told to leave or they would be killed. COSYDDHAC had received similar threats during 1996. On February 15, following increasing pressure against members of the Fray Bartolomé de las Casas Human Rights Center (Centro de Derechos Humanos "Fray Bartolomé de las Casas"), a group of investigators from the center were attacked in Sabanilla, ambushed as they tried to leave the municipal center. Though they had traveled to the troubled municipality to gather information, they decided to leave after finding police unwilling to help them; as they left the community, armed men stopped them on the road and opened fire when the group tried to reverse its vehicles. José Montero from the center was wounded in the arm.

Also in Chiapas, the Coordinating Group of Nongovernmental Organizations for Peace (Coordinadora de Organismos No Gubernamentales por la Paz, CONPAZ) came under renewed attack. On October 7 and November 4, 1996, and February 9, 1997, unidentified assailants tried unsuccessfully to burn the group's offices. On November 7, 1997, a CONPAZ member group, Chiltak, received anonymous death threats naming several people who would be killed. Then, on May 7, the group's director, Gerardo González, received death threats by telephone.

The government showed disdain for international human rights reporting by rejecting information and reports by international human rights organizations, including Human Rights Watch and Amnesty International. The day that Human Rights Watch published its report on rural violence, for instance, the Foreign Ministry issued a statement asserting that the government was concerned about human rights protection but accusing Human Rights Watch of "Trying with its partial and unobjective report to distort the real human rights situation in Chiapas, Guerrero, Oaxaca, and Sinaloa." The statement, typical of the government's hollow human rights rhetoric, dismissed the report as dealing with "presumed violations that have been resolved or are in the process of being resolved."

When Human Rights Watch challenged the accusations, the Foreign Ministry pointed out three cases that it considered resolved or in process of being concluded. In the report on rural violence, Human Rights Watch had noted the arrest of the aggressors in two of the cases indicated by the government. Of dozens of other cases detailed in the report, however, the Foreign Ministry failed to indicate any one in which a government official had been prosecuted for having committed a human rights violation.

The government's unwillingness to engage in serious dialogue on human rights issues was reiterated in September, when high-level government officials refused to meet with a delegation headed by Amnesty International Secretary General Pierre Sané. Following this incident and a similarly embarrassing confrontation with French human rights organizations, the government announced the creation of the Inter-Ministerial Commission on Mexico's International Human Rights Obligations. At this writing, the commission has yet to begin its work of coordinating actions designed to ensure that Mexico lives up to these obligations.

Mexican authorities, however, did more to limit human rights monitoring than just issue vacuous press releases and close the door to dialogue. In April, the government expelled Vilma Núñez and Benjamín Cuéllar from the Paris-based International Federation of Human Rights (Federation Internationale des Ligues des Droits de l'Homme, FIDH) and Georgeanne Potter of the Boston-based Unitarian Universalist Service Committee. Authorities later apologized to Potter and told her she would be permitted back into the country. Also in April, officials pressed twelve European peace activists to leave the country because they participated in a protest march in Chiapas. The Mexican Foreign Ministry also sought to limit the access of human rights groups to the Inter-American Commission on Human Rights. Under the guise of improving the commission's procedures, Mexico pushed for changes that would have eviscerated the commission. Under the Mexican proposals, the offices of government ombudsmen— rather than nongovernmental organizations— would be the principal conduit for cases to come before the commission, the commission's reports would be confidential, and, according to the legal advisor to Mexico's Foreign Ministry, those who presented cases to the commission would not be permitted to be from "a third country or international organization far from the historical and cultural reality of Mexico." The government's proposals were not adopted.

The Role of the International Community

European Union

Mexico and the European Union (E.U.) agreed in October 1996 to begin formal talks on a trade, political, and cooperation agreement. In June, Mexico and the European Commission, which negotiates the terms of agreements with non-member states, reached agreement on an interim accord, but the pact was rejected by the E.U.'s Council of Ministers on the grounds that the interim agreement did not include the EU's standard human rights clause. Mexico had succeeded in stripping from the clause reference to its internal human rights policies. In July, Mexico agreed to the insertion of the full human rights clause.

Though ultimately unsuccessful at weakening the European Union's human rights clause, in July Mexico did manage to block U.S. $340,000 in E.U. aid for the Mexican Academy of Human Rights (Academia Mexicana de Derechos Humanos, AMDH) for monitoring elections in Mexico City. The government of Mexico argued that the Europeans had no standing to give money to a nongovernmental group without the government's consent and argued that the Europeans should not interfere with internal electoral proceedings. In April, a ruling party legislative initiative in the Chamber of Deputies would have made it illegal for Mexican election monitors to finance their work with foreign money. Faced with widespread criticism, the proposal was finally withdrawn.

United States

Continuing a trend begun several years ago, the United States increased its public support for Mexican human rights organizations, an important and positive contribution to the local human rights community. Secretary of State Madeleine Albright met with representatives of Mexican human rights groups during a visit to Mexico in May, and the U.S. Embassy in Mexico City maintained close contact with such groups. In another positive move, the U.S. government sent an unprecedented State Department mission to Mexico to focus exclusively on human rights issues. Headed by Deputy Assistant Secretary of State Steven Coffey, the mission resulted from the Mexican government's objection to the State Department's annual human rights report, released in February. The hard-hitting State Department report covered the main problems in Mexico well, finding, "Major abuses included extrajudicial killings, torture, illegal arrests, arbitrary detention, poor prison conditions, illegal searches, violence against women, discrimination against women and indigenous persons, some limits on worker rights, and extensive child labor in agriculture and in the informal economy."

Although the human rights report left no doubt about Mexico's rights problems, and the State Department showed vigor in supporting the Mexican human rights community, this did not mean that the U.S. government was willing to press Mexico for human rights improvements. In this critical area, U.S. policy toward Mexico appeared consistent with prior years: tense bilateral issues involving trade and the economy, drugs, and immigration elbowed aside human rights concerns.

The U.S. Labor Department continued to examine two labor rights cases submitted under the NAALC. On January 27, the department's U.S. NAO issued a report on a case involving SUTSP, which had been submitted in June 1996 by Human Rights Watch, the International Labor Rights Fund (ILRF), and Mexico's National Association of Democratic Lawyers (Asociación Nacional de Abogados Democráticos, ANAD). The petition showed that SUTSP had been unable to exercise its right to freedom of association since early 1995 and that no Mexican government agency effectively enforced freedom of association laws. Even when SUTSP received legal recognition of its union status, officials in SEMARNAP—the environment ministry, where SUTSP was organized—refused to recognize the union. The problem remains as of this writing.

The petitioners in the SUTSP case also argued that certain portions of Mexico's federal labor law violated freedom of association standards, and thereby the NAALC, by establishing that only one union could exist in any federal government agency, such as a ministry, and that Mexico's Federal Conciliation and Arbitration Tribunal (Tribunal Federal de Conciliación y Arbitraje, TFCA) was not impartial, as required by the NAALC. Petitioners urged the U.S. NAO to review Mexican compliance with its labor law in light of both domestic and international standards.

In its January 1997 report, the U.S. NAO requested that the U.S. Labor Department analyze jointly with its Mexican counterpart the issue of how Mexican labor standards related to international labor standards, but did not request that action be taken on any issue directly related to the SUTSP case. Through a mechanism termed "ministerial consultations," the two countries decided to hold a conference called Seminar on International Treaties and Constitutional Systems of the United States, Mexico, and Canada. The long and detail-oriented information-gathering process undertaken by the U.S. NAO in the SUTSP case, including December 1996 public hearings, proved an important method of shining public light on serious Mexican labor rights problems. At this writing, however, it has not resulted in any specific actions designed to solve those problems. In fact, the January U.S. NAO report failed to include in its analysis much of the well-documented information presented by the petitioners. For instance, the U.S. NAO cited SUTSP appeals court victories to conclude that no freedom of association violation had taken place, arguing that courts had restored freedom of association rights to the union. However, the U.S. NAO did not factor into its decision evidence that, despite the court victories, the union members were never able to exercise their rights, since no government official allowed them to do so. Similarly, the U.S. NAO found no labor tribunal bias in the SUTSP case but did not directly address the petitioners' complaints. For instance, to determine that no bias existed in the tribunal, the U.S. NAO pointed to SUTSP victories when it appealed labor tribunal decisions, even though the ability to appeal a decision shed no light on the workings of the tribunal whose decision was appealed. Further, the U.S. NAO found that, given its structure, the tribunal would appear to be biased in some cases that came before it, but, even given this finding, decided that no further action needed to be taken on the bias issue, even though the NAALC required labor tribunals to be completely free of bias.

In the second case processed by the U.S. NAO during 1997, Human Rights Watch, ILRF, and ANAD accused the Mexican government of failing to enforce anti-discrimination laws by permitting mandatory, hiring-related pregnancy testing of female job applicants in maquiladoras. The complaint also alleged that victims of this discrimination did not have effective access to labor tribunals to resolve the issue. Submitted in May, the NAO decided to accept the case for review and began a months-long process of gathering information on the issues raised. The Mexican government responded to the case by asserting that pregnancy testing violated neither Mexican nor international law. At this writing, the U.S. NAO is still gathering information on the issues raised by petitioners. In October, the U.S. NAO announced that it would hold public hearings on the case on November 19.

A third case was briefly reviewed by the U.S. NAO but later withdrawn by the petitioners.

Relevant Human Rights Watch report:
State Responsibility for Rural Violence in Mexico, 4/97

PERU

Human Rights Developments

During 1997 a series of attacks on the autonomy of bodies established to protect constitutional rights, on the independence of the judiciary, and on freedom of the press revealed the authoritarian style of the government of President Alberto Fujimori with increasing clarity. In May, the pro-Fujimori majority in Congress crippled the recently elected Constitutional Court by dismissing three of its members, an action which prompted the court's president to resign in protest. The congressional action was in response to the court's issuing of a ruling challenging Fujimori's constitutional right to stand for election for a third consecutive term. The government arbitrarily deprived an Israeli-born media owner of his Peruvian nationality and expropriated his shares in his television station after he broadcast an interview with an army intelligence agent who had been detained and tortured by her superior officers. Peru's shadowy National Intelligence Service (Servicio Nacional de Inteligencia, SIN), whose de facto head Vladimiro Montesinos is a close adviser of the president, was widely suspected of ordering a series of violent attacks on journalists and prominent politicians, as well as widespread surveillance and illegal phone tapping of public personalities such as government ministers and a former presidential candidate. Evidence emerged that members of the La Colina army death squad, whose members were released from prison under an amnesty law passed in June 1995, were still regular visitors at army headquarters in Lima.

Peru's anti-terrorist police continued to engage in torture, and grave abuses were attributed to soldiers stationed in zones where armed anti-government groups operated. No advances were made in passing badly needed legislation to prevent and punish torture, although several bills had been before Congress since March 1996. Conditions in special prisons reserved for those accused or convicted of terrorist crimes continued to violate international norms. Hundreds of innocent prisoners who had fallen foul of the so-called "faceless" anti-terrorist courts, which violated rights to a defense and a fair trial, remained in prison. By November 1, President Fujimori had released 227 innocent prisoners convicted or under trial by these courts after the special Ad-hoc Commission appointed in 1996 to review such cases recommended their pardon. Finally responding to intense criticism of the courts by domestic and international human rights organizations, the government did not renew their mandate when it expired in mid-October; henceforward those accused of terrorism would be tried by ordinary judges. Those accused of the more serious crime of treason would continue to be tried by military courts, but the identity of the judges would cease to be secret.

Armed opposition groups, the Shining Path (Sendero Luminoso) and the Túpac Amaru Revolutionary Movement (Movimiento Revolucionario Túpac Amaru, MRTA), continued to violate international humanitarian law, although the scale of abuses by both organizations declined with the level of armed activity. The MRTA's spectacular seizure on December 17, 1996, of hundreds of hostages at the residence of the Japanese Ambassador in Lima flagrantly violated the prohibition on hostage-taking contained in the Geneva Conventions. After releasing hundreds of the hostages, the MRTA continued to hold seventy-two—among them government ministers, judges, and diplomats—for more than four months, until the army and police stormed the residence, securing their release on April 22, 1997.

Two members of the security forces and a Supreme Court judge, Carlos Giusti Acuña, died during the rescue. Soldiers and police killed all fourteen guerrillas found in the building. The government refused to investigate the circumstances of the hostage-takers' deaths to determine whether they were produced by a legitimate use of force or whether some may have been killed after their surrender or capture.

No significant new activity by the MRTA was reported during the year. Activity by the Shining Path appeared to decrease during the hostage crisis, but the organization remained active, particularly in Lima and in remote parts of the departments of San Martín, Ucayali, Cusco, Ayacucho, and Huánuco. There was no sign of any change in its tactics, which continued to violate basic principles of international humanitarian law. According to Peruvian human rights groups, between January and August the organization selectively killed eighty-seven people, of whom sixty-nine were civilians. On May 15, the seventeenth anniversary of the beginning of its armed campaign, the Shining Path exploded a car bomb outside a police station in the working-class area of Ate Vitarte, in Lima, wounding several people.

For the first time in many years, Peruvian human rights organizations had not recorded any cases of extrajudicial execution or "disappearance" by the armed forces or the police by the end of October. Government forces, however, continued to resort to torture when interrogating guerrilla suspects. One month before the end of the hostage crisis, the 31st Division of the Peruvian Army detained more than forty peasants in Alto Yurinaki and other remote villages of the province of Chanchamayo, Junín department, where they believed an MRTA guerrilla column had originated. The arrests followed the television screening of a newsclip which showed youths wearing MRTA bandanas training in a jungle camp in the area. An army communiqué accused the peasants, identified in the press by their names, mugshots, and supposed aliases, of belonging to an MRTA column which had planned to attack the Villa Rica army counterinsurgency base with the help of conscripts who had infiltrated the base. Between February 24 and March 12 the supposed infiltrators, who had themselves been detained and tortured, accompanied soldiers round the area identifying villagers, who were then arrested, tortured, and forced to identify others.

During the Alto Yurinaki operation, seventeen-year-old Emerson Wistrecher Cánepa was detained at about 4:00 p.m on March 9. He was beaten, hung by the feet, kicked in the stomach and plunged head first into a tank full of water laced with detergent. This treatment went on for several days, while soldiers forced him to accompany them to look for a supposed weapons cache. The weapons allegedly found were previously buried by the army in a hole in the ground, according to local residents. On March 21 a Channel 15 television interview showed Wistrecher after his release, still with ugly wounds on his wrists caused by the electric cables used to tie them. The footage also showed the back room of a small grocery store where the soldiers had tortured Wistrecher, complete with a car battery used for giving electric shocks and a receptacle still containing water and detergent. The antiterrorist police released most of the detainees after finding no evidence to charge them, despite the advance publicity given by the army to their presumed guilt. In a television interview on March 30, President Fujimori promised to investigate the allegations of torture, but to our knowledge, the Ministry of Defense did not carry out any investigation, nor were those responsible for the torture detained or charged.

Army intelligence agents also tortured one of their own subordinates whom they had arrested on suspicion of leaking information to the media about secret army plans to intimidate members of the opposition press. On April 6, "Contrapunto," a Channel 2 television program, featured a shocking interview with thirty-six-year-old Leonor La Rosa Bustamante, which had been secretly filmed at her bedside in Lima's military hospital. The camera showed severe burns and scarring on the fingernails of her right hand, and she could walk only with assistance. La Rosa, herself an active agent of the Army Intelligence Service (Servicio de Inteligencia del Ejército, SIE, a department of the SIN), said that the SIE held her for five days in January in the basement of the General Command (Comandancia General) of the Peruvian Army, known as the "Little Pentagon" (Pentagonito), and SIE agents beat her and tortured her with electricity. La Rosa was admitted to the Military Hospital with head injuries. On her discharge she was given fifteen days convalescence leave. When she returned to work on February 11, her superior officers again arrested her and took her back to the basement, where they interrogated her under torture for a further week. On February 19, after hemorrhaging as a result of the beatings, she was re-admitted to the military hospital, where she suffered respiratory failure. She told Channel 2 reporters and congressmen who visited her bedside that her interrogators suspected her of leaking information to the press on secret army intelligence plans to blow up a television station and intimidate well-known journalists and human rights defenders, including television personality César Hildebrandt and lawyer Heriberto Benítez.

On May 9 a military court convicted the head of the SIE, Carlos Sánchez Noriega, and three of his subordinates for the torture of La Rosa, and sentenced them to eight years imprisonment. The proceedings were conducted according to summary military procedures and held in secret, making it impossible for outsiders to assess the evidence or whether higher officials may have ordered or acquiesced in the torture. In August the Supreme Court resolved in favor of the military a dispute over jurisdiction with the civilian court that was also investigating the case, and which had issued an order for an inspection of the SIE's detention facilities. The ruling preempted the inspection and the possibility of public access to the investigation.

The link between the targets of the SIE's intimidation campaign appeared to be their role in denouncing army human rights abuses. Benítez, a prominent human rights lawyer, represented former Gen. Rodolfo Robles Espinoza, who was forced into early retirement when he publicly revealed the involvement of an army death squad, known as the Colina Group, in extrajudicial execu-tions and "disappearances" in 1992. The members of the death squad were jailed for human rights crimes but released under a government amnesty promulgated in June 1995. Since his return from exile in Argentina, Robles had received repeated anonymous threats. On November 26, 1996 army intelligence agents beat and abducted him in retaliation for his denouncing the Colina Group's role in a bomb attack the previous October against the Puno transmitter of Global Television, which had been critical of the government. The army released Robles in early December after domestic and international protest forced the government to approve an amnesty for him. However, harassment of Robles and his family continued. On March 26, 1997, four unidentified assailants tried to abduct Robles's son, Jaime Robles Montoya, who was driving his father's car at the time. Leonor La Rosa testified that she had seen members of the Colina Group frequenting army headquarters, providing more evidence that the main beneficiaries of the 1995 amnesty were still on active service.

Included in Channel 2's feature on Leonor La Rosa was an investigation into the "disappearance" of Mariella Lucy Barreto Riofano, also a SIE agent and a friend of La Rosa. The program revealed that a dismembered corpse found in plastic bags on a roadside north of Lima on March 23 belonged to Barreto, and that she had been the mistress of Capt. Martín Santiago Rivas, former head of the Colina Group. The newspaper La República had reported in February that Barreto was also under investigation by the SIE in relation to leaked information about intelligence activities. At this writing those responsible for her murder remain at large.

Other attacks against journalists and opposition politicians were also attributed by human rights groups to the SIN, although the government insisted they were the work of ordinary criminals. On March 19 in Lima, unidentified gunmen kidnapped and beat three occupants of a jeep owned by Javier Diez Canseco, a congressman of the United Left (Izquierda Unida), who is known in

Peru for his campaigning on human rights issues and the object of death threats and attacks in the past. In the vehicle, apart from the driver, were Patricia Valdez, an Argentine human rights advocate, and Diez Canseco's bodyguard, who was shot in the leg. The three were beaten and threatened and eventually dropped off; the car was found later a burned-out wreck by the roadside. On April 1, four heavily armed men abducted Blanca Rosales, general editor of *La República* shortly after midnight close to the paper's offices in central Lima while she was driving home with a colleague, Juan de la Puente. The men beat and threatened Rosales but, like the occupants of Diez Canseco's jeep, later allowed her to escape. *La República*, a left-of-center opposition newspaper, has campaigned for years against the SIN and the Colina Group. In June, César Hildebrandt, presenter of the television program *En Persona,* demanded that the Interior Ministry guarantee his family's safety after the program aired revelations by La Rosa about a plan in December 1996 by the SIE to kill him; he also received a telephone call threatening the safety of his son. Within days after the revelations became public, an *En Persona* film crew was attacked by three armed men of military appearance who broke into a house where they were about to film an interview. A week later, three armed men assaulted and beat up journalist Luis Angeles Laynes, political editor of the popular newspaper *Ojo,* in a Lima street; *Ojo* staffers had earlier received threatening phone calls.

While these attacks remained anonymous and the government disclaimed responsibility, it openly denounced other journalists and media proprietors who published unwelcome disclosures, and opened selective prosecutions against them for alleged tax debts. The main target was Baruch Ivcher Bronstein, an Israeli-born magnate and majority shareholder in Channel 2 television, the station which aired the explosive La Rosa interview. In the days following that broadcast, helicopters circled over the station, and police investigators arrived there to gather information about alleged import

tax evasion. Captain Julio Salas, a police officer placed in charge of the customs investigation, later stated that a superior had told him the investigation was ordered by the SIN. When the intended harassment received adverse publicity, the government halted the investigation and publicly denied it had ever begun. Salas, who refused to comply with instructions to deny his role in the investigation, was threatened and intimidated by his superiors, and on two occasions, unknown assailants attacked his wife in the street. On May 23, the army issued a communiqué denouncing Ivcher, who had taken refuge in Miami, for allegedly trying to damage the armed forces' prestige. This was followed by a warrant for his arrest by the military justice authorities. The government then introduced an unexpected change in the immigration rules, warning naturalized Peruvians that they risked losing their citizenship if they engaged in treasonous behavior. On July 13 it revoked Ivcher's Peruvian nationality, citing alleged irregularities in his application for citizenship, which had been granted thirteen years before and never previously questioned. This action violated Peru's constitution (Article 2:21), which holds that no one may be stripped of his or her nationality, as well as international treaties ratified by Peru.

Minutes before the decree appeared in the official gazette, Ivcher's television station, Channel 2, broadcast the results of an investigation which purported to show that the SIN had tapped the phones of at least 197 businessmen, politicians, and public personalities, including Foreign Minister Francisco Tudela, as well as former United Nations secretary-general and opposition presidential candidate, Javier Pérez de Cuellar. President Fujimori, Prime Minister Alberto Pandolfi, and the head of the SIN, Julio Salazar Monroe, all strenuously denied the report. They claimed that private individuals were responsible and could easily obtain the necessary eavesdropping equipment. Communications experts, however, indicated that the sale of electronic eavesdropping equipment was restricted to government agencies, while a television investigation revealed that the government of Peru had updated its electronic surveillance equipment in 1994.

By various legal means Fujimori's party, Change 90-New Majority (Cambio 90-Nueva Mayoría, C90-NM) tried to weaken the critical function of autonomous constitutional bodies set up to safeguard individual rights and the rule of law. In May, C90-NM's parliamentary majority dismissed three members of the Constitutional Court after impeaching them for publishing a ruling that a law passed by Fujimori to enable him to stand for a second re-election in the year 2000 was inapplicable. Article 112 of the constitution does not permit a second re-election, but the impugned law had interpreted the article as excluding terms of office prior to the promulgation of the constitution in 1993. The impeachers argued that the court had no quorum for the ruling, but four of the seven judges on the court disagreed. The firings caused protests across the nation and provoked strong objections from the judiciary, the attorney general, the Office of the People's Defender (Defensor del Pueblo), and the Catholic Church, as well as concern by the Inter-American Commission on Human Rights. Prior to her dismissal, one of the judges, Delia Revoredo, found herself under investigation by a Callao court for the import of a car in a case which had long been closed, and she alleged that her home had been under surveillance.

Measures purported to reform the judiciary, which was drastically purged after Fujimori's coup in 1992, came under severe questioning from politicians, the public, and the judges themselves, as it became increasingly clear the goal was to tighten executive control over the court system. A poll conducted in August revealed that less than one in five members of the Lima population had any confidence in the judiciary, and judges themselves complained of insecurity after a wave of firings by the Executive Commission of the Judiciary, whose head, former navy Capt. José Dellepiane, was appointed in 1996 by the government to overhaul the courts. Five years after Fujimori's drastic

intervention of the judiciary, 80 percent of Peru's judges still had only provisional status, and their lack of tenure made them notoriously vulnerable to pressure from the executive branch. The director of the Academy of the National Magistrates' Council (Consejo Nacional de la Magistratura, CNM), which is responsible for training judges, estimated that it would take three or four years for the CNM to fill all the vacant posts with permanent appointees. Meanwhile, the commissions set up in 1996 to coordinate the restructuring of the courts and the Public Ministry were criticized for inefficiency as well as being headed by loyal government appointees. Members of Congress from the government as well as the opposition made new proposals in August to restructure the reform process, including a controversial proposal to reduce the training requirements of new judges to speed up new appointments. As a result of Fujimori's intervention, the courts' traditional inefficiency has been compounded by a growing subservience to the executive branch.

In a disturbing development which illustrated the above problems, conflicts between civilian courts and military tribunals over the applicability of constitutional guarantees such as writs of habeas corpus were resolved in favor of the military by the Supreme Court. When Attorney General Miguel Aljovín Swayne ordered legal action against the Superior Council of Military Justice (Consejo Superior de Justicia Militar, CSJM) for failing to comply with three separate habeas corpus writs issued by the Chamber of Public Law of the Lima appeals court, the CSJM's president threatened to open impeachment proceedings against Aljovín. Then the CSJM presented a disciplinary complaint against the Lima appeals court judges who had granted the habeas corpus. In June, a Supreme Court panel summarily relieved Judges Sergio Salas Villalobos, Elizabeth Roxana MacRae Thays, and Juan Cancio Castillo Velásquez of their duties on the appeals court. One of the cases it had been due to hear was an appeal for constitutional protection (*amparo*) by Baruch Ivcher against the decision depriving him of his Peruvian nationality.

The Supreme Court also dismissed the attorney general's accusation against the CSJM, arguing that the military justice authorities could disregard any habeas corpus which was "illegal." Instead, it ordered the three appellate judges prosecuted for breach of public duty (*prevaricato*). The panel which ruled on the case was composed of temporary judges without tenure, and who were therefore vulnerable to pressure from the military and the executive. On September 4, the Executive Commission of the Public Ministry decided not to order the prosecution of the three judges.

In July, then-Minister of the Interior Carlos Saucedo issued a shocking order that Judge Elba Greta Minaya Calle, of the 37th Penal Court of Lima, be prosecuted for terrorism and other crimes for granting a habeas corpus writ against the National Police. Due to a public outcry, the terrorism accusation was dropped, but disciplinary proceedings against Judge Minaya—widely respected for her independence and integrity—remain open at this writing.

Congress renewed the mandate of the adhoc commission established in 1996 to review cases of prisoners unjustly accused or sentenced for terrorism until February, 1988. By November President Fujimori had released 227 innocent prisoners on the recommendation of the commission, but hundreds more remained in jail. As of this writing, the government has refused to renew access of the International Committee of the Red Cross (ICRC) to maximum-security prisons, which it suspended during the hostage crisis. Visits by the ICRC, which does not publish its findings but communicates them privately to the government, have proven effective in reducing the incidence of ill-treatment, including torture and forcible disappearance, of detainees. The continued denial of ICRC access underlined the government's disregard for the rights of detainees accused of terrorism and treason. Prison conditions for high-security prisoners continued to be extremely harsh. In April and August, 161 high-security prisoners jailed for terrorist offenses were transferred to a new prison at Challapalco, located at more than 14,000 feet in the Peruvian Andes, where temperatures drop to twenty degrees below zero centigrade (four degrees below zero Fahrenheit). These conditions constituted a serious risk to health, and the remoteness of the site meant that the prisoners were virtually cut off from the outside world, violating international norms.

In June the government introduced new prison regulations for prisoners accused or convicted of "terrorist" crimes, which may ameliorate some of the worst features of the prison regime. Prisoners were to be allowed weekly, instead of monthly, visits from the families, and their children would be allowed to visit them every week, instead of every three months. Prison privileges were to be earned by good conduct, but new prisoners, regardless of the nature of their offense, still had to spend a year under the harshest regime, locked up in their cells and allowed out for only one hour a day.

The Right to Monitor

The Pro-Human Rights Association (Asociacion Pro-Derechos Humanos, APRODEH), which played a prominent role in bringing human rights violations to public attention, suffered harassment, including persistent surveillance and anonymous death threats. The threats coincided with APRODEH'S assistance to the beleaguered judges and police captain Julio Salas. On August 14, APRODEH staff received five threatening phone calls asking about Judge Minaya, insulting them and threatening to make them "disappear". Later that afternoon a black Volkswagen followed Minaya's car when she visited APRODEH'S Lima office. When APRODEH staff questioned the driver, he confirmed that he was following the judge. On September 4, a man turned up at the office claiming to bring a message in an envelope from Judge Minaya. The letter was an anonymous warning to APRODEH'S director, Francisco Soberón, not to meddle in the case of police Cap. Julio Salas and accusing both Salas and Soberón of accepting a bribe of $30,000 from Baruch Ivcher. "Stop meddling in what does not concern you, you have been warned, son of a bitch," the letter said. The same person left another letter in the home of María Jesús García Sánchez, Salas's companion, accusing Salas of treachery and threatening to kill him "like a dog." On the following day, Soberón, María Jesús García, Salas's lawyer Dr. Miro Toledo, and Sofía Macher, executive secretary of Peru's respected nongovernmental human rights umbrella group, the National Coordinator of Human Rights (Coordinadora Nacional de Derechos Humanos, CNDH) held a press conference to denounce the threats. Two hours later, each of them received a threatening phone call from a women who announced that she personally would kill María Jesús García. The latter received three messages on her beeper from a person impersonating Soberón summoning her to an urgent meeting.

The Role of the International Community

United States

The United States ambassador in Lima, Dennis Jett, assumed a higher profile on human rights and civil liberties in 1997 than has been embassy practice in previous years, a gratifying step away from the policy of quiet diplomacy we have criticized in the past. Jett's timely interventions may have helped avoid a deteriorating human rights situation becoming much worse. On at least six occasions Jett spoke out on human rights issues, including torture, freedom of the press, due process in anti-terrorist trials, and judicial independence. On April 9, for example, Jett told reporters who questioned him on the La Rosa case that a prompt investigation of the torture could improve Peru's international image. One month later, military justice officials announced that four officers had received eight-year sentences by military courts, an unprecedentedly swift response. The ambassador described the dismissal of the three Constitutional Court judges as "defi-

nitely a step backwards in the process of consolidation of Peruvian democracy." On the Ivcher case, State Department spokesperson Nicholas Burns accused the government of depriving Ivcher of his Peruvian nationality for political reasons and pointed out that "this action raises fundamental questions about freedom of the press and of expression."

Though these interventions were poorly received by the Peruvian government, they set an important tone for Peru's relations with the United States, reminding Peruvian authorities that the U.S. would not be silent on human rights in exchange for cooperation in other spheres, such as economic policy and anti-narcotics efforts.

However, the United States' role in Peru was marred by a continuing ambiguity concerning its relationship with Vladimiro Montesinos, de facto head of the SIN. Montesinos, who is reported to have worked for the Central Intelligence Agency, is widely seen in Peru as enjoying Washington's support, a notion that the United States did nothing to dispel. Moreover, Washington reportedly maintains a covert assistance program with the SIN to combat drug trafficking. This apparent liaison with a unit deeply involved in anti-democratic activities undermines the impact of public statements made by Jett and the State Department.

European Union

The European Parliament issued a strong resolution on July 22 calling on the Fujimori government to reinstate the magistrates of the Constitutional Court who had been dismissed by the Congress; to guarantee freedom of expression; and to abolish the practice of torture.

VENEZUELA

Human Rights Developments

As in previous years, human rights violations in 1997 were closely linked to the battle against crime in Venezuela's cities. Facing the difficult challenge of policing the poor and increasingly crime-ridden neighborhoods that surround Caracas and other Venezuelan cities, security forces resorted to systematic abuses, including torture, extrajudicial executions, and the disproportionate use of lethal force. Time-honored methods used to cover up illegal killings, together with an antiquated legal system that obstructed prompt and impartial investigations, ensured that the perpetrators of these abuses tended to go unpunished. Despite efforts by government authorities to improve prison conditions, convicted prisoners and those awaiting trial continued to be held in circumstances that violated international standards.

The pace of police abuses showed no sign of letting up from the prior year, as Venezuelan police forces, including the Technical Judicial Police (Policía Técnica Judicial, PTJ), continued to commit serious human rights violations, including summary executions. In some cases, police executed individuals thought to be dangerous criminals, or sought revenge for the killing of police agents. In other instances, police shot suspects fleeing arrest or the scene of a crime. In still other cases, police committed abuses unrelated to their police work, such as during fights or to settle personal grudges. According to the Network in Support of Justice and Peace (Red de Apoyo por la Justicia y la Paz, Red de Apoyo), police committed at least ninety extrajudicial executions between January and August, a figure that was comparable to the prior year's tally.

In investigating arbitrary killings by the police, Human Rights Watch found that many killings appeared to have been planned beforehand and that the police appeared to follow standard procedures designed to avoid accountability. Officers often wore hoods to protect identification, shepherded onlookers away from the scene beforehand, and fired guns into the air after the killing to simulate a firefight. To cover up abuses, they sometimes removed the corpse before crime-scene investigators arrived, on the pretext of taking the victim to a hospital, planted weapons or drugs on the victim, or removed his or her clothing and personal identification. Officers also intimidated relatives or witnesses to dissuade them from denouncing what they had seen. In several cases, post-mortem medical examinations performed by the Medical Legal Institute, a national forensic agency that is subordinate to the PTJ, failed to disclose information on the number and location of gunshot wounds.

In a typical execution, PTJ officers killed José Gregorio Rondón on July 4 in his home in the Catia neighborhood of Caracas. The police arrived at 5:00 a.m., forced their way into the house, and overpowered Rondón, who was in bed on the first floor. His sister, Ana Rosa, saw him lying on the floor with a policeman's foot pressed to his head, before the police locked her and her mother into a downstairs room, from where they heard shots fired. After releasing the two women, police told Ana Rosa that Rondón had been shot because he had tried to resist arrest. They removed the body and took it to the morgue. The police arrested Rondón's sister and took her to PTJ headquarters in Carabobo Park, where they threatened her with torture and imprisonment if she did not sign a statement incriminating her brother.

Systematic police abuses were also reported from other states, such as Anzoátegui, on Venezuela's Caribbean coast. At 6:30 p.m. on August 1, agents belonging to the Metropolitan Police (Policía Metropolitana, PM) detained Aníbal José Vargas, an eighteen-year-old soccer enthusiast, while he was training for a local team in a poor neighborhood in the city of Barcelona. According to local residents, the police confused him with a criminal, and despite the fact that Vargas showed them identification, one officer ordered another to shoot Vargas; the youth was shot at close range with an explosive bullet, dying almost instantly. The policeman responsible fired additional shots to simulate a gunfight. A police report issued to the press said that the victim had died in an exchange of gunfire.

Although police authorities said that officers accused of committing killings had been detained or suspended pending judicial examinations, such investigations faced almost insuperable obstacles. A legal procedure unique to Venezuela allows cases against police to be sidetracked for long periods of time. Known as an averiguación de nudo hecho—a requirement that public officials undergo a preliminary investigation before an official criminal investigation can take place—these proceedings are intended to be completed within ten days but often languish for months or years. Their effect was to shield those responsible from prosecution, since criminal charges cannot be filed until the preliminary investigation is completed. Meanwhile, the officer can remain in service. Frequently, the police agency accused in abuse cases failed to respond to repeated orders from the courts for the information needed for the case to pass to trial. Moreover, until the official has been arrested and formal charges have been filed, court investigations remain secret. After several years of waiting for a result, relatives of victims of police killings told Human Rights Watch that they still had no access to the court's findings.

In addition to summary executions, torture continued to be used by police routinely in criminal investigations. According to a report issued in December 1996 by United Nations Special Rapporteur on Torture Nigel S. Rodley, security forces "resort frequently to the use of torture as a method of obtaining information or as a punishment, especially among low-income sectors of the population, in a society characterized by high levels of crime." After publication of the special rapporteur's report, the number of reported torture cases has significantly increased. During the first eight months of 1997, the Red de Apoyo documented 767 reports of torture or ill-treatment, an increase of more than 300 over the comparable figure for 1996. The police forces most frequently cited by the special rapporteur were the PM, which operates under the jurisdiction of the governor of Caracas; the PTJ, responsible to the minister of justice; the Directorate of Services of Intelligence and Prevention (Dirección de los Servicios de Inteligencia y Prevención, DISIP), which is subordinate to the interior minister; and the various state police forces, which are responsible to state governors.

Luis Evelio Quintero, a driver for a food company, reported that he was unjustly detained and tortured by PTJ agents to get him to confess to a robbery he did not commit. On February 4, Quintero's truck was hijacked, and he and another man in the truck were dumped on a highway east of Caracas, after which they reported the crime to the PTJ in nearby Guarenas. On February 28, another truck from the same company was robbed. The owner went to the PTJ to denounce the theft, and the PTJ subsequently arrested both Quintero and his driving partner, took them to the PTJ station in El Llanito, Miranda state, and held them in detention for eight days, the maximum permitted by the law. During this time, they were taken in the evenings to a deserted house some thirty minutes from the police station. They beat Quintero and applied electric shocks all over his body. After handcuffing his wrists behind his body, on several occasions they hoisted him in the air and let him hang for thirty minutes. As a result of the hanging, Quintero's left hand was paralyzed.

José Francisco Palencia Ruiz, a nineteen-year-old former volunteer fireman who worked at a forestry station, was detained on July 8 by members of the Baruta municipal police and tortured to get him to confess to robbing a safe deposit box in the station. Palencia was handcuffed and hung by the cuffs from a beam, while he was beaten and kicked in the stomach. A plastic bag was put over his head several times while the police tried to force him to confess. At one point his torturers beat him repeatedly to get him to confess to having stolen a larger amount of money.

The PTJ could hold suspects for eight days before placing them at the disposal of a judge, an excessively long period that provided ample opportunity for mistreatment. In any case, the time period was often ignored. Human Rights Watch is not aware of a single torturer who has been punished, despite ample documentation on torture cases prepared by Venezuelan and international human rights groups. Among the many factors contributing to impunity was the subordination of the Medical Legal Institute to the PTJ, one of the police agencies most frequently implicated in torture. In addition, cursory and slipshod examinations and the fact that autopsies are secret make evidence of torture difficult to prove. Another factor was the "nudo hecho" procedure; often, the procedure was delayed so long that the crime became subject to a statute of limitations before the preliminary investigation was completed and charges could be filed.

Overcrowded, understaffed, physically deteriorated, plagued by official corruption and abuse, and rife with weapons, guns, and gangs, Venezuela's prisons languished in a seemingly permanent state of crisis. Although the Ministry of Justice, charged with administering the country's prison system, took some steps toward reform, the prisons' overall structural problems were not noticeably eased. The January closure of the violent and overcrowded Retén de Catia prison, although it eliminated a notorious symbol of the country's prison woes, exacerbated overcrowding at the remaining penal facilities in Caracas. Nationally, with over 25,000 inmates crammed into thirty-two penal institutions, the prison population continued to far exceed the available capacity.

Most notable among the prisons' chronic problems was their extreme violence, which remained at the highest levels in the region. According to newspaper accounts, eighty-two prisoners were killed during the first eight months of the year—a number that, while shockingly high, represented a substantial decline from previous years. One of the most violent prisons was Tocuyito, in Valencia, where at least twenty-nine prisoners were killed—many by gunshots—between January and September. In Tocuyito and other prisons, such killings were almost entirely the product of inmate-on-inmate violence. Heavily armed, and supervised by a small number of untrained, underpaid guards, the prisoners themselves

effectively controlled the prisons, as even the minister of justice publicly acknowledged.

The year was punctuated by exceptionally brutal outbursts of prison violence. On August 28, a surprise attack of one group against its rivals at El Dorado prison, a remote jungle facility in southeastern Venezuela, resulted in twenty-nine dead and numerous injured. Even prior to the violence, the deplorable conditions of the "Casa Amarilla," the area of the prison where the murders took place, had led the Public Ministry to call for its closure.

The prisons' severe overcrowding and unhygienic conditions, combined with their appalling lack of medical care, encouraged the emergence and spread of disease. Tuberculosis was the most common illness, according to the Public Ministry, which in August reported 1,011 confirmed cases in the prisons. In May, cholera broke out in Sabaneta prison, a densely populated, decaying facility in western Venezuela: eighty-five prisoners reportedly fell ill, while almost 600 others required treatment. Cases of cholera were also reported in La Planta prison in July and in El Rodeo II in September. In a promising effort to stem the spread of disease, the government of Miranda state instituted a pilot project of sending large medical teams into local prisons for short-term sweeps, conducting tests, providing vaccinations, and distributing much-needed medical supplies.

In the wake of the El Dorado prison massacre, the new minister of justice, who was appointed in March, promised that in less than a year the prison crisis would be brought under control, and described an array of measures meant to accomplish this goal, including the development of a new corps of prison guards who would be better paid and better trained. Given the lackluster history of Venezuelan prison reform efforts, however, such claims must be judged on the strength of their results rather than on the encouraging scope of their ambition. The Ministry of Justice did, in June, conduct a detailed census of the prison population, a first step toward classifying prisoners to separate pre-trial detainees from convicted offenders, and first-time petty criminals from dangerous recidivists. It also established a new prison ombudsman's office, a post with greater independence than provided previous such monitors.

Over two-thirds of the Venezuelan prison population was made up of pre-trial detainees and others at some stage in the criminal justice process—people who might be incarcerated for several years before being acquitted of the charges against them— indicating that a durable solution to Venezuela's prison crisis required action from other government authorities as well. In particular, the country's criminal justice system was in need of radical reform, an effort implicating the legislature and the judiciary, among others.

Minister of Justice Hilarión Cardozo acknowledged the gravity of the situation in the country's prisons and agreed to proposals on prison reform made by the Forum for Life, a consortium of nongovernmental organizations. However, the government agreed to implement only a few of the forum's overall recommendations.

Local human rights groups reported indiscriminate arrests, torture, and arbitrary killings in Apure state, along Venezuela's border with Colombia, where constitutional guarantees continued to be suspended due to incursions by Colombian guerrilla groups. On February 6, for example, National Guard (GN) troops shot dead Juan José Rodríguez Bastidas, a teacher, and Jesús Castellanos Vasco, a three-year-old Colombian boy, when they were traveling by boat down the Arauca river. The shooting occurred an hour after an armed cross-river clash between the GN and Colombian guerrillas. As the boat went past a GN river control post, the police opened fire, claiming afterward that they had been responding to shots fired from the Colombian bank. However, according to witnesses, no shots from the Colombian side preceded the GN attack, and the police gave no warning prior to opening fire. Four other passengers in the boat were wounded. On the same day, GN troops shot dead Ignacio José Briceño, a twenty-eight-year-old cattleman, when he failed to heed an order to halt at a GN mobile control post in El Molino.

Having attracted considerable criticism in 1996 for human rights violations, the Venezuelan government took some steps in 1997 to put human rights on its policy agenda. In contrast to prior years, the government publicly recognized that human rights violations took place in the country. President Caldera officially dubbed 1997 the "Year of Human Rights" and announced the formation of a National Commission of Human Rights (Comisión Nacional de Derechos Humanos, CNDH), composed of key cabinet ministers and the governor of Caracas. He instructed the commission to formulate a "national agenda" on human rights. Unlike national human rights commissions or ombudsmen in other Latin American countries, however, the Venezuelan CNDH was not given powers to investigate or make recommendations on individual cases of human rights violations. Its role was limited to coordinating information between ministries on human rights issues, responding to intergovernmental human rights bodies, and acting as a liaison with domestic monitoring groups. By October, the CNDH still lacked a secretariat, staff and budget, and had met only on five occasions. In a positive development, the Supreme Court declared unconstitutional a 1956 law, called the Law of Vagrants and Undesirables, that allowed authorities to detain people administratively for up to five years. Frequently, the law had been used to detain unemployed people or others deemed undesirable.

One of the first meetings of the CNDH was held to discuss an official reply to the U.S. State Department's *Country Reports on Human Rights Practices for 1996*. The twenty-three-page Venezuelan government response, released on February 4, accused the United States of supplanting the supervisory competence of the human rights bodies of the United Nations and the Organization of American States, and implied that the State Department report was flawed because it presented facts out of context and ignored the instability of Venezuela's recent past.

In another international arena, Venezuela's response to a treaty banning landmines was troubling. Of eighty-nine countries that took part in negotiations to draft a convention on a comprehensive ban on the weapons, Venezuela was one of four that indicated that it was unlikely to sign the treaty, which was approved in September.

The Right to Monitor

Members of the Human Rights Office of the Vicariate of Puerto Ayacucho, state of Amazonas, came under attack for their work on behalf of the Amazonian Indians. During the last week of May, local politicians and some members of the regional government, who were trying to frustrate the drafting of a law to protect Indians' land rights, launched a series of attacks against the Vicariate in the press and on the radio, accusing its members of promoting divisions and violence between Indians and white settlers. On May 27, a vehicle belonging to Luis Jesús Bello, the general coordinator of the Human Rights Office, and another that belonged to a Salesian nun were damaged when acid was thrown on them.

On June 7, an unidentified person in the street insulted and threatened an engineer working for the office. On June 9, the Superior Court of Puerto Ayacucho ruled that a lawsuit filed by the Public Ministry of Amazonas State against the Human Rights Office for "usurpation of functions" was unwarranted and ordered that it be dropped.

The government sought to improve its relations with the country's large network of nongovernmental human rights organizations. During 1996 and in earlier years, government officials had often tried to discredit and stigmatize the local groups. During 1997, however, the organizations were invited to participate in meetings with government officials to contribute to a list of needed human rights reform measures. The first of these meetings took place on July 4, when the Forum for Life met ministers and lower-ranking officials and presented a detailed list of recommendations, and the Forum for Life welcomed the meeting as a first positive sign.

The Role of the United States

The Venezuela section of the State Department's *Country Reports on Human Rights Practices for 1996* painted an accurate picture of the serious human rights situation in Venezuela. The U.S. Embassy chose not to intervene in the debate caused by the publication of the CNDH's response to the State Department human rights report. Human Rights Watch learned of no public pronouncements made by the United States on human rights issues.

Relevant Human Rights Watch report:

Punishment Before Trial: Prison Conditions in Venezuela, 3/97

HUMAN RIGHTS WATCH

ASIA

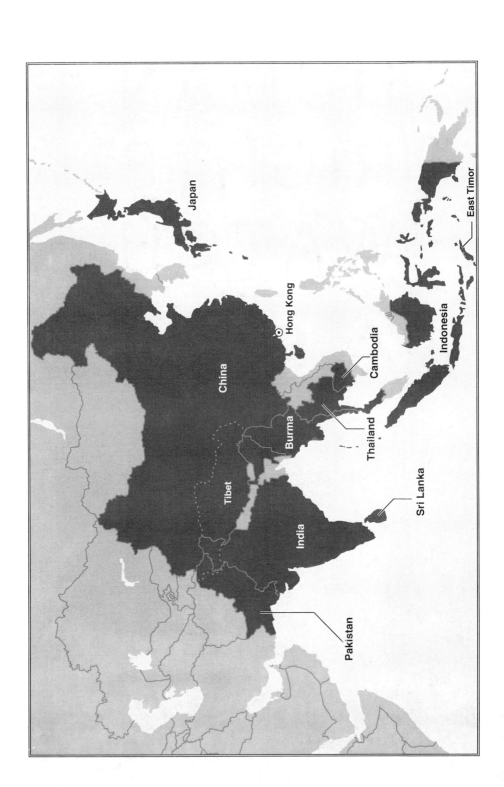

Contrary to expectation, the reversion of Hong Kong to China did not have the most impact on human rights in Asia during the year. The famine in North Korea, the currency crisis in Southeast Asia, and the forest fires in Indonesia unexpectedly vied for that honor. All served to weaken the shibboleths about human rights and economic development in Asia, highlighting the issue of government accountability. The fires, the economic crisis, and the coup in Cambodia also raised questions about the staying power of "Asian solidarity" that has been such a block to regional human rights initiatives in the past.

War, work, and religion were three other themes running through human rights developments in the region during the year. Ongoing internal armed conflicts in Afghanistan, Sri Lanka, East Timor, India's northeast, Kashmir, and the border areas of Burma continued to produce serious abuses by both government and opposition forces and a growing population of refugees and internally displaced people. Labor rights remained a top priority of activists in the region, with bonded labor an ongoing issue across South Asia, forced or compulsory labor a continuing problem in Burma, Tibet and Vietnam, and restrictions on the right to organize source of deep concern in Indonesia and China. International campaigns also highlighted abuse of workers in Asian-invested plants producing international name-brand footwear. The political use of religion by Asian governments caused human rights violations in Pakistan, China, Indonesia, Burma, and Vietnam, while arbitrary detention and torture continued to be a problem across the region.

Human Rights Developments

On the surface, the problems in North Korea and Southeast Asia could not have been more different. The secretive Stalinist government in Pyongyang, clinging to a home-grown ideology of self-sufficiency, seemed to be frozen politically, socially, and economically in the 1950s. In contrast, the urban elite of the capitalist, foreign investment-friendly societies of Thailand, Malaysia, Singapore, and Indonesia seemed in some ways to have already crossed the bridge to the twenty-first century. It was the governments of these "miracle economies" of Southeast Asia, together with China, that produced the spurious "Asian values" claim, arguing that the welfare of the community through economic development had to take precedence over protection of individual rights, and that Asians valued efficiency over democracy. Many western analysts bought the argument, often adding that a strong, centralized leadership not beholden to particular constituencies and capable of taking unpopular decisions at critical times was responsible for the soaring rates of economic growth.

But when the Asian bubble burst in July, with the collapse of the Thai currency and dangerous smog spread over Southeast Asia, the comparison to North Korea did not seem so farfetched. North Korea's catastrophe was only a more extreme version of a central problem besetting Southeast Asia: lack of government accountability. It seemed to underscore the accuracy of philosopher Amartya Sen's contention that famines— as opposed to crop failures— only take place in countries with tight restrictions on freedom of expression.

The absence of checks on executive power also contributed to Southeast Asia's woes. One lasting image for the year may well be the larger-than-life videoscreens of Malaysian Prime Minister Mahathir and financier George Soros trading accusations at the World Bank meeting in Hong Kong in September over who was responsible for Southeast Asia's economic crisis. Mahathir blamed Soros and western speculators in general, going so far as to suggest that Soros was out to punish the Association of Southeast Asian Nations (ASEAN) for admitting Burma as a member in July. Soros countered that the crisis in the region might have been averted by a freer press and less corruption.

Certainly Malaysia, Singapore, and Indonesia continued to punish those who released damaging information about the government or who portrayed government leaders in a negative light. Singapore continued to rely on criminal defamation suits, with two opposition politicians, Jayaretnam and Tang Liang Hong, the particular objects of its wrath. Meanwhile, in Thailand Prime Minister Chavalit established a "News Analysis Center" under the Ministry of the Interior, ostensibly to ensure accurate reporting at a time when the government was blaming negative press articles for some of the country's economic problems.

Lack of government accountability and corruption are also believed to have been factors in the forest fires that raged through Sumatra and Kalimantan, Indonesia, in the latter half of the year. One cause of the fires was a prolonged drought, but another was the Indonesian government's granting of timber concessions to Soeharto family cronies and the clearing of land for palm oil plantations, both over the opposition of local peoples and both resulting in the destruction of wide swathes of rainforest. The argument that controls on freedom of expression and association lessened the possibility of finding correctives to bad development policies had fallen on deaf ears as long as the negative impact of those policies stayed within national boundaries. By late 1997, with the smog causing serious health hazards in at least three countries besides Indonesia, the argument was beginning to carry more weight.

One result of the problems in East and Southeast Asia was that Indian democracy gained new respect. Singaporean officials, in particular, had been fond of pointing out that if India and the Philippines were examples of Asian democracy, they wanted none of it. Open political processes, in their view, produced chaos and perpetuated poverty. China, with all its human rights problems, was doing more to improve the standard of living of its people than India. That view began to change during the year. More realistic assessments of long-term growth in the region laid stress on the importance of the rule of law, independence of the judiciary, political accountability, and the need for building up popular consensus to sustain economic reform programs, and the same analysts bewitched by the "Asian values" argument of the mid-1990s were beginning to see India as perhaps a better investment prospect than China.

The currency and forest fire crises in Southeast Asia, combined with the coup in Cambodia, also brought into question the notion of "Asian solidarity" in a way that had implications for human rights. While frictions among South Asian countries had long been public and bitter, the governments of East and Southeast Asia had tended to observe a code of silence with respect to each other's practices. Not only did they traditionally refrain from any public criticism of their neighbors, but they even allowed the more repressive countries of the region to set the lowest common denominator for human rights. Thus, in November 1996, the youth wing of the ruling party UMNO, backed by Malaysian police, broke up a conference on East Timor and deported the largely Asian participants, so as not to cause offense to Indonesia. In August 1997, apparently for the same reason, the Singaporean government requested the Foreign Correspondents' Association to cancel a planned lecture by Indonesian opposition politician, Megawati Soekarnoputri. No government official would publicly criticize Burma or China for its human rights practices, arguing the case instead for quiet persuasion. The code of silence was adopted partly as a reaction to western pressure on human rights—a statement on May 25 by U.S. State Department spokesman Nicholas Burns saying Burma should not be admitted to ASEAN was widely believed to be the act that convinced the last holdouts in ASEAN to drop their objections—and partly for self-protection of the individual member governments. It meant, among other things, that it was ludicrous to even think of a regional governmental Asian human rights charter, court, or commission because there was such a reluctance to interfere in what were perceived as the domestic affairs of one's neighbors. Indeed, according to the *Economist* magazine in July, ASEAN "has given the impression of being a club without even minimal standards of political behavior." ASEAN's call in July, at Prime Minister Mahathir's instigation, for a review of the Universal Declaration of Human Rights, did nothing to dispel that impression.

But cracks in the facade of unity were showing. The most important factor was the Cambodian coup of July 5-6, carried out by Hun Sen just before Cambodia was to be formally admitted as a member of ASEAN. Singapore was one of the first countries to speak out against the violence, and ASEAN as a whole held an emergency meeting within days of the coup and decided to put Cambodian membership in the regional body on hold. As ASEAN mounted a mediation effort led by Indonesian Foreign Minister Ali Alatas, Malaysian Deputy Prime Minister Anwar Ibrahim coined the phrase "constructive intervention,, as opposed to "constructive engagement," to describe the body's newfound role.

Then, as the Asian currency crisis deepened, Malaysians wondered publicly whether if they had voiced concerns about Thailand's problems earlier, some of the spillover effects of the problem might have been avoided. In October, a Singaporean paper, *The Sunday Times*, made similar comments about the forest fires. It said that while information about Indonesia as the source of the smog problem had been apparent as early as May 1997, Singapore's Environment Ministry requested the press not to publish the information because of "regional sensitivities," according to an October 12 Reuter dispatch. The paper acknowledged that keeping the information from the public in Singapore and elsewhere also meant that there were no demands on Indonesia from affected governments to take action to address the problem. "If only everyone concerned who had been monitoring the situation closely had spoken out about it early, clearly and loudly enough, the region may not have suffered the unmitigated environmental, public health and economic disaster that followed," Reuter reported the paper as saying. If governments of the region became well aware of the transnational impact of poor economic and environmental policy, it remained to be seen whether they would be willing to break the code of silence on their neighbors' human rights practices.

In other areas, long-festering problems remained much the same, with armed conflict remaining a major source of human rights violations. In Kashmir, elections in 1996 did little to reduce the incidence of rape and extrajudicial executions on the part of the Indian armed forces and groups working with them during 1997. In Afghanistan, summary trials and executions by Taliban forces got less attention than the group's efforts to ban women and girls from education and employment outside the home. In East Timor, attacks by guerrillas on army posts just before and after the May 29 elections sparked widespread arbitrary detention of young East Timorese men, often accompanied by torture, on the part of the Indonesian military; the guerrillas were also responsible for executions of civilians suspected of having links to Indonesian military intelligence.

Labor issues continued to be high on the agenda of local human rights groups. In China, new studies by researcher Anita Chan showed a system of bonded labor in some of the footwear manufacturing plants that have grown up in the country's booming coastal provinces, whereby migrant workers, recruited from inland provinces, are required to pay their employers a deposit for a temporary work permit which is then deducted from wages. She also documented widespread physical abuse of workers, including the use of electric batons by private security guards with links to the Chinese police. Chinese labor activists were among those who received particularly harsh administrative sentences during the year, and Chinese independent union organizer Han Dongfang, now resident in Hong Kong, remained banned from entering the mainland. In Burma, ongoing forced labor prompted the European Union to halt tariff benefits for Burmese agricultural exports. In Vietnam, reports of abuses of Vietnamese workers by Korean and Taiwanese managers in footwear factories were coupled with the Vietnamese government's announcement in May that families would be required to donate labor to the construction of the most massive infrastructure project in Vietnam's history, the construction of a north-south road running the length of the country. Bonded labor problems in South Asia, particularly India, Pakistan, and Nepal received new attention from the World Bank and other development agencies, with renewed emphasis on projects to eliminate bonded child labor in selected industries such as sericulture (silk production). In Indonesia, much of the labor activism was focused on a draft labor law that continued restrictions on freedom of association as well as on the issue of working conditions in Asian-owned plants in Java producing shoes for the Nike company. Independent labor union leader Mochtar Pakpahan moved back and forth between a hospital bed and his trial on subversion charges in a Jakarta court, as members of his union contined to face harassment, including brief detentions, during the year.

Finally, political manipulation of religion and communalism was another theme prevalent in Asia during the year. In Pakistan, in a gesture to religious conservatives, the government made permanent the *qisas* or retributive penalties mandating that punishments for certain crimes be equal to the harm caused. Persecution of the Rohingya Muslim minority continued in Burma's Arakan (Rakhine) state, causing a new outflow of refugees to Bangladesh, and attacks by Buddhist monks on Muslims in the central Burmese city of Mandalay in March were widely believed to have been instigated by the government as a way of increasing popular support. In Indonesia, it remained unclear whether government agents were involved in a series of outbreaks of communal violence prior to the May 29 elections, but the October trial of a well-known Catholic priest and social activist in Jakarta, on charges of harboring student radicals accused of subversion, was widely interpreted as a government effort to brand opposition leaders in heavily Muslim Indonesia as non-Muslim. In China, the government increased its control of organized religious activities, claiming that religion was being used by foreign powers to subvert and destabilize the country. The stepped-up control affected Protestants and Catholics, Muslims in Xinjiang and Tibetan Buddhists.

The Right to Monitor

Independent human rights organizations did not exist in Afghanistan, Bhutan, Burma, Brunei, China, North Korea, Singapore, or Vietnam. Where they were allowed to function, they remained vulnerable to various forms of intimidation, with individual activists facing threats, arrests, and sometimes death for their advocacy of rights and social justice. India continued to be one of the most dangerous places for human rights activists to work. Most of the attacks occurred in areas of conflict where human rights monitors were accused of sympathizing with armed opposition groups. Activists working with low caste or other marginalized groups in more remote rural areas were also targeted. Nevertheless, when rights organizations in the region acted in concert to advocate for common goals or to come to the assistance of beleaguered colleagues, they displayed remarkable strength. Governments, corporations and international financial institutions like the World Bank were forced to acknowledge their importance and include them (albeit sometimes grudgingly) in decision-making.

Regional networks expanded during the year, with nongovernmental organizations (NGOs) from India, Bangladesh, Nepal, Pakistan and Sri Lanka joining colleagues from East and Southeast Asia for strategizing on common concerns, including the impact of economic globalization and protection of labor and migrant rights in the context of the Asian-Pacific Economic Cooperation (APEC) organization. They (unsuccessfully) worked to prevent Burma from joining ASEAN and combatted national security legislation that infringed on civil rights. The Internet also played an increasingly important role in day-to-day communications among distant groups, allowing rapid responses to arrests of colleagues, threats to organizations, and other breaking news. Government attempts to control the Internet had little noticeable impact on the widening electronic network, in part because the governments most determined to put controls in place, such as China, Vietnam and Singapore, were also those where independent organizations were weakest.

In December 1996, more than one hundred activists from some twenty countries attended the Asia Pacific NGO Human Rights Congress in New Delhi, India. The meeting sought to enhance coordination among Asian rights groups to pressure governments, increase nongovernmental consultation in policy making, and counter attacks on the universality of human rights by Asian governments. The congress was an initiative of the Asia-Pacific Human Rights NGO Facilitating Team, a body of Asian NGOs that was formed in 1994 following the Vienna World Conference on Human Rights.

In January and February, nongovernmental activists throughout the region joined in celebration when Malaysia's attorney general dropped charges against participants in the banned Second Asia-Pacific Conference on East Timor (APCET II), which had been forcibly dispersed in Kuala Lumpur in late 1996. The attorney general also agreed to prosecute four members of a pro-government group who participated in the violent dispersal.

The case filed in 1995 by the Malaysian government against human rights activist Irene Fernandez continued to be a priority for NGO colleagues worldwide. Fernandez, director of Tenaganita (Womens' Force), was charged with publishing "false informa-tion" for her reporting on abuses of migrant workers in Malaysian immigration detention facilities. The case focused international attention on the growing phenomenon of migrant workers in Asia and the need for human rights protections.

Throughout the year, Asian activists concerned with the plight of migrant workers launched campaigns on behalf of endangered or stranded workers. The Asia-Pacific Mission for Migrant Filipinos in Hong Kong released a global appeal in August regarding stranded Filipino migrants in Saudi Arabia. The human rights organization SUARAM , based in Malaysia, circulated an appeal on behalf of Bangladeshi migrant workers who had been detained in Malaysia after they protested labor rights violations by a Japanese factory owner.

In June, pressure on the World Bank by well-coordinated networks of Indian and international NGOs concerned about the use of child labor and bonded child labor in World Bank-funded projects led the bank to convene meetings with Indian NGOs to determine means by which it might address child labor issues. The Bank agreed to canvas existing projects to determine if they employed children and to ensure that social assessment work on child labor be carried out for projects in preparation that posed a serious risk of employing child labor. The overall response of NGO participants in these meetings was cautious but positive. They stressed the need for the bank to emphasize prevention through quality primary education as well as the need for law enforcement.

National human rights commissions in the region (India, the Philippines, Indonesia, Australia, and Sri Lanka among them) continued to meet and forge links with each other, holding out the possibility that some kind of more formalized network might emerge.

The Role of the International Community

The lure of the market in the region, or concerns about its health following the currency collapse in Southeast Asia, overrode human rights concerns for most of the international community. This was particularly true with respect to China. No government successfully resolved the dilemma of how to exert pressure to improve human rights practices on this important trading partner and emerging superpower with a key voice on regional security, proliferation and other concerns. Integrating China into the global system of human rights norms and accountability remained a vague objective without a concrete strategy. The Group of Eight (G8), meeting in Denver in July, which might have hammered out such a strategy, focused only on Hong Kong. Most governments opted to drop political or economic pressure on human rights altogether and to substitute "dialogue" and support for long-term, uncontroversial rule of law programs.

Another source of potential leverage, limits on arms transfers to abusive governments, was virtually ignored, with the exception of an international campaign to ban arms to Indonesia because of human rights violations in East Timor. Foreign Minister Robin Cook, responding to pressure in the U.K., announced in September that he would apply the new British guidelines on an "ethical" foreign policy and ban £1 million worth of arms sales to Indonesia, for reinforced Land Rovers that the government called armored personnel carriers and sniper rifles. The U.S. Congress also formalized and extended an existing ban on some arms transfers to Indonesia.

United Nations

The U.N. continued to have a visible presence in Asia, with a special rapporteur on Burma (who was nevertheless denied access to the country); a special representative on Cambodia and an active field office in Phnom Penh of the U.N. Centre for Human Rights; and a special representative of U.N. Secretary-General Kofi Annan to work on East Timor. Officials from the U.N. Department of Political Affairs continued to be active in trying to help resolve conflicts in the region.

Several visits by the "thematic mechanisms" of the U.N. Commission on Human Rights took place during the year. The special rapporteur on religious intolerance visited India in December 1996, but the special rapporteur on torture, who had requested a visit, was not invited. The special rapporteur on summary and arbitrary executions visited Sri Lanka, and the Working Group on Arbitrary Detention went to China in October. The U.N. Human Rights Commission kept pending a decision on whether or not to take up human rights problems in Thailand (related to its treatment of Burmese refugees) under a confidential review procedure known as "1503."

Some progress was made in ratifying international human rights treaties or complying with treaty obligations. In January, Thailand's ratification of the International Covenant on Civil and Political Rights entered into force. In March, Pakistan reestablished dialogue with the U.N. Committee on the Elimination of Racial Discrimination after a ten-year lapse. In October, Sri Lanka became the first South Asian country to accede to the Optional Protocol to the International Covenant on Civil and Political Rights. China signed (but not necessarily ratify or accede to) the International Covenant on Economic, Social, and Cultural Rights before the end of the year.

Regional Bodies

The ninth summit in May of the South Asian Association for Regional Cooperation (SAARC) provided a forum for the prime ministers of India and Pakistan to meet and begin talks on Kashmir—the first meeting of its kind in eight years. While there was no immediate impact on the human rights situation in Kashmir, most observers believe that the human rights problems could not be resolved without addressing the underlying political conflict.

ASEAN's plans to admit Burma as a member, which it did in July, prompted the creation of the so-called Alternative ASEAN, a coalition established in October 1996 of more than fifty primarily Southeast Asian nongovernmental organizations to mobilize pressure within the region to address Burma's human rights record.

The Asia Pacific Economic Cooperation (APEC) forum steadfastly refused to examine human rights issues, although the Canadian government, as the 1997 host of APEC in Vancouver, provided some support for discussions about "civil society" in the various APEC working group meetings leading up to the Vancouver heads of state meeting. That meeting in late November was preceded by a "People's Summit" drawing hundreds of activists from throughout the region to discussions of labor rights and freedom of expression.

Donors and Investors

The annual consortium group (CG) meetings of international donors convened by the World Bank, and in some cases cosponsored by Japan, are a potentially useful venue for governments to raise human rights concerns, but the meetings on Cambodia, Indonesia and India had mixed results. The Cambodia donor meeting took place in Paris literally days before the July coup, but the strong message sent by several governments about corruption and the elections was largely eclipsed by events. The Indonesia CG in Tokyo was largely a missed opportunity to press Jakarta on key issues such as treatment of nongovernmental organizations and abuses related to the May elections, though some donors brought up these issues in private bilateral discussions. At the India CG in Paris, a number of governments urged action on child labor and bonded child labor issues—as they did at the previous year's CG in Tokyo—which clearly had an impact when combined with initiatives at the World Bank.

The Asian Development Bank (ADB), on the other hand, was slow to implement its "governance" policy adopted in August 1995, although it did sponsor a panel on governance and a seminar on work with nongovernmental organizations at its annual meeting in Fukuoka, Japan, from May 10 to 14. Nearly forty such organizations (including Human Rights Watch) from thirteen countries in the region were accredited to attend. The Burmese finance minister, Gen. Win

Tin, made an abortive effort to lobby the ADB to resume funding to SLORC suspended since 1988. The ADB continued an ongoing dialogue with the NGO Working Group, based in Manila, where the ADB is headquartered. By the end of the year, the ADB planned to issue an updated policy on nongovernmental organizations and one on gender and development.

Among private investors, governance issues took on greater relevance in many countries throughout the region. The flight of capital from Cambodia following the coup—including, most dramatically, from Southeast Asian countries—sent an unmistakable political signal to Hun Sen. Foreign investors, including major U.S. oil companies like Texaco, continued to pull out from Burma in response to both consumer pressure and a desire to distance themselves from the country's dismal human rights image. Equally significant were moves by companies to examine the impact of expanding trade and investment in the Asia-Pacific region, the need for open legal systems and accountable governments, and how to handle increasing demands in the region for worker rights.

The private sector became increasingly sensitized to consumer campaigns on Burma, East Timor, U.S. and foreign "sweatshops," and child labor issues. (Nike's effort to monitor its own code of conduct through a brief inspection trip to Vietnam, China and Indonesia by former U.S. Amb. Andrew Young is described in the section on Corporations and Human Rights.) Legislation in Massachusetts banning the state from purchasing goods and services from companies investing in Burma prompted a complaint from European countries to the World Trade Organization of discriminatory trading practices; muncipalities around the U.S., from Madison, Wisconsin to New York City, enacted similar Burma-related bans. Meanwhile, similar legislation was pending in Massachusetts at the end of the year with regard to Indonesia and East Timor.

The U.S.House of Representatives adopted legislation in the House in late September, requiring the U.S. Export-Import Bank to give preference in its export assistance programs in China to U.S. companies agreeing to a specific "code of conduct." (China receives about $1 billion a year in export credits from the Bank). Though the bill had not come to a Senate vote at this writing, its passage in the House indicated a growing consensus on the importance of the private sector's role in promoting human rights.

The Work of
Human Rights Watch

Many of the themes touched on above were covered by the Asia division of Human Rights Watch in reports and advocacy efforts. We responded immediately to the July coup in Cambodia, interviewing newly arrived refugees in Bangkok and using information from sources in Phnom Penh to put pressure on the international community to respond forcefully to summary executions and other human rights abuses committed by forces linked to Hun Sen. In addition to assisting opposition parliamentarians and others forced into temporary exile, we issued a report on the range of abuses that followed the coup. That report, cited in newspaper editorials in the U.S. and Europe, had as one of its key recommendations that the international community not press forward with support for elections scheduled for May 1998 until basic safeguards for human rights were in place.

We undertook two exploratory missions to investigate links between human rights violations and the famine in North Korea.

Concerns about the erosion of civil liberties in Hong Kong under the Special Administrative Region government provided an important focus of work in Brussels, Washington, and Hong Kong itself. Those concerns were outlined in a response we prepared in February to the British government's report on how the International Covenant on Civil and Political Rights was being implemented in Hong Kong. At that time, less than five months before the reversion to Chinese rule on July 1, several disturbing steps had already been announced by the Chinese government. We continued to monitor the independence of the courts and the press and analyze legislative developments, commenting publicly each time a key decision was taken. We helped arrange visits to the U.S. for human rights defenders in Hong Kong to ensure they could personally raise their own concerns with policymakers in Washington, and we co-sponsored a seminar on the rule of law in Hong Kong in Washington in March to ensure that those concerns were aired before a larger audience, including the private sector. In June, we issued a joint report with the Human Rights Monitor, a local human rights organization in Hong Kong, after undertaking the first-ever international assessment of prison conditions there. The report, which gave a reasonably clean bill of health to Hong Kong prisons, was intended both to establish a precedent for prison access after the reversion and to set benchmarks for assessing prison conditions under S.A.R. administration. Finally, in the months and weeks prior to the reversion, our Hong Kong office made a major effort to ensure that Chinese dissidents resident in Hong Kong were safely resettled in third countries prior to July 1.

The consequences of internal armed conflict and religious and communal persecution were central to our work on refugees, asylum seekers, and displaced people. In March, we issued a report on the status of the remaining Vietnamese boat-people in Hong Kong. In July and August, we issued reports on members of Burmese ethnic minorities who had fled to Thailand and Bangladesh respectively. Both reports were based on missions to the region and interviews with newly arrived refugees; one report was issued jointly with Refugees International. Incidents of involuntary repatriation prompted an ongoing dialogue with the United Nations High Commissioner for Refugees (UNHCR) about how best to protect the refugees involved, as well as protests and appeals, together with other nongovernmental organizations, to the Thai government to stop pushing Burmese refugees back over the border. The refugee exodus from Cambodia to Thailand following the Cambodia coup was also cause for concern. On Thailand, Cambodia, and Burma, Human Rights Watch worked in close cooperation with the Jesuit Refugee Service.

Human rights abuses associated with the conflict in East Timor produced a report in September, citing violations by both the Indonesian armed forces and related paramilitary groups and the East Timorese guerrillas. The report placed particular emphasis on the failure of the Indonesian government to address the problems of arbitrary detention and torture of those suspected of supporting the armed opposition. In Kashmir, our investigations into human rights abuses associated with the conflict there, including by Indian soldiers and former militants working with them, led to visa denials for our staff members and consultants.

A major report on religious repression in China appeared in October, as did a report on communal violence in West Kalimantan, one of Indonesia's most severe outbreaks of ethnic conflict in decades. The latter report was based on two missions to Kalimantan, one in January and one in July.

Much of our advocacy work during the year focused on labor rights. On Burma, we submitted information on forced labor to an International Labour Organisation commission of inquiry and presented testimony on the same subject at a hearing by the U.S. Labor Department on June 27. Our work on forced labor also contributed to key European Union decisions on withholding tariff benefits for Burma. As noted above, we pressed the issue of bonded labor in India with the World Bank and were in regular touch with our Indian counterparts to follow up on what steps the Indian government and international donor agencies were taking toward its eradication. In an effort to ensure that all those engaged domestically and in-

ternationally on the bonded labor issue in India had access to the same information, we prepared the first in a series of electronic newsletters on developments in the World Bank, the Indian Supreme Court, local government initiatives in India, and bilateral aid programs. On Indonesia, we continued to give labor rights abuses a high priority in Washington-based advocacy, particularly as a petition we submitted in 1995 to the U.S. Trade Representative's office calling for a resumption of the USTR's review of Indonesia's labor practices remained pending during the year.

Restrictions of rights on the grounds of national security remained a major area of concern. In April, we issued a report together with Human Rights in China focusing on China's New Criminal Code. The report documented the replacement of crimes of "counterrevolution," used to sentence most dissidents, with offenses against state security and provided the basis for an ongoing campaign during the year to get cases of convicted "counterrevolutionaries" reviewed with a view toward their release. We joined colleagues in Hong Kong in protesting new legislation there allowing the government to ban organizations and demonstrations on the grounds of national security and provided documentation on U.S. case law to help refute the S.A.R. government's contention that the new laws were no more restrictive than laws in the United States.

More generally, we continued to work for attention to the "traditional" human rights problems of political imprisonment and torture in China, Burma, and Indonesia. The steady diminution of international pressure on China to improve its human rights practices was the focus of a report released in March, just before the U.N. Human Rights Commission meeting, empasized Chinese diplomacy and Western hypocrisy. It was also the focus of numerous briefings, testimonies, newspaper commentaries, and other interventions by our Brussels and Washington offices.

We continued to work closely with our colleagues in the Human Rights Watch children's and women's rights projects. In January, we published a report on children's rights in Burma and took part in a hearing on Burma held in Geneva by the Committee on the Rights of the Child. Research on the trafficking of women in Asia continued, with a particular focus on Thai women trafficked to Japan. In July, we helped a small group interested in the trafficking of Indonesian girls to Malaysia find funding and establish themselves as a nongovernmental organization. A joint investigation with the Human Rights Watch Women's Rights Project, on the state's response to victims of sexual violence in Pakistan, began with a mission in November 1996 (*see* the WRP section).

We testified three times in the U.S. Congress during the year, on Indonesia, Hong Kong, and the general subject of democracy in Asia; we also submitted a written statement for a Senate hearing on Cambodia. Our Washington staff briefed members of Congress and their staff traveling to Asia, hosted Burma "roundtable" meetings with U.S. policymakers, nongovernmental organizations and members of the media; and met frequently with senior White House, State Department, and foreign embassy officials. We maintained regular contact with the World Bank, both at the staff and management level as well as with the U.S. executive director's office. In efforts to ensure good communication with the private sector on human rights issues in China, Hong Kong, Indonesia and Burma, we maintained a steady dialogue with relevant business and trade associations.

In the European Parliament, our Brussels office organized support for a resolution calling on the E.U. to back a China resolution at the U.N. Commission on Human Rights in April. In October, it helped mobilize support for a similar resolution for the commission's 1998 session. On Hong Kong, our Brussels and Washington offices worked in close coordination to secure expressions of support for the pro-democracy movement in its efforts to challenge actions by the S.A.R. government. Those efforts intensified prior to the visits by S.A.R. Chief Ex-

ecutive Tung Chee-hwa to the U.S. and Europe in September and October respectively.

The U.N. and its various agencies played an important part in our work during the year. In addition to the Burma and China advocacy described above, we appeared before the annual meeting of the U.N. Decolonization Committee to present material on human rights violations in East Timor and submitted to the Human Rights Committee a critique of the Indian government's report on its compliance with treaty obligations under the International Covenant on Civil and Political Rights.

Our advocacy work with Japan continued to be a key priority, with a staff mission in May and regular contacts with the Japanese embassy in Washington. These proved particularly useful during the Cambodian crisis. We also published commentaries on Asian human rights issues in the Japanese press.

As in the past, we worked closely with nongovernmental organizations in the region, sharing information, exchanging views on strategy (particularly with respect to labor issues), and cooperating in research. We continued an advocacy campaign with Indian rights groups on the issue of bonded child labor and took part in an ongoing campaign initiated by Asian organizations to promote the freedoms of association, assembly, and expression in the region. In defense of our embattled Asian colleagues, we wrote to the Indian government on behalf of threatened human rights activists in Kashmir and Andhra Pradesh. In March, our NGO liaison visited Malaysia to attend the trial of Irene Fernandez; later the same month, we helped lead sessions on using international law and on forging linkages among NGOs as part of a two-week Asian regional study session on human rights, sponsored by the Asian Forum for Human Rights and Development (Forum-Asia) and the Programme for the Promotion of Non-Violence in Thai Society at Chulalongkorn University. In November, we cosponsored a seminar called "Open Markets, Open Media" at the annual APEC summit; the seminar highlighted the the effect that the region's trade liberalization has had on freedom of the press.

For a listing of relevant reports and missions, see xxxx at the end of this report. Partial listings also follow each country chapter.

BURMA

Respect for human rights in Burma continued to deteriorate relentlessly in 1997. The opposition National League for Democracy (NLD) continued to be a target of government repression. NLD leaders were prevented from making any public speeches during the year, and over 300 members were detained in May when they attempted to hold a party congress. There were no meetings during the year of the government's constitutional forum, the National Convention, which last met in March 1996; the convention was one of the only fora where Rangoon-based politicians and members of Burma's various ethnic movements could meet. The government tightened restrictions on freedom of expression, refusing visas to foreign journalists, deporting others and handing down long prison terms to anyone who attempted to collect information or contact groups abroad. Persecution of Muslims increased. Armed conflict continued between government troops and ethnic opposition forces in a number of areas, accompanied by human rights abuses such as forced portering, summary executions, rape, and torture. The ruling State Law and Order Restoration Council (SLORC) continued to deny access to U.N. Special Representative to Burma Rajsoomer Lallah. Despite its human rights practices, however, Burma was admitted as a full member of the Association of Southeast Asian Nations (ASEAN) in July.

Human Rights Developments
In late January, the SLORC announced the sentencing of thirty-four people in connec-

tion with large-scale protests during the closing months of 1996. All were accused of being members of the defunct Communist Party of Burma and received a minimum of seven years' imprisonment. Eleven of those sentenced were NLD members. The end of 1996 had been marked by a series of student demonstrations, the first in five years, in Rangoon, Mandalay and other major cities. The demonstrations began in October as a protest over police beatings of three students from the Rangoon Institute of Technology and by early December had spread to the main Rangoon University campus where they grew to include 2,000 students and at least as many members of the public. Armed riot police and soldiers eventually stormed the crowd, arresting hundreds. On December 4, the government released a statement announcing that 609 people had been detained, of whom 487 were students and 122 were "agitators." The statement claimed that the students had all been released, but there was no information regarding the fate of those classified as agitators, nearly one hundred of whom were believed to remain in detention by the end of 1997.

During the December 1996 demonstrations the government had closed all educational institutions, from universities to primary schools, in Rangoon and in many other cities including Mandalay, Prome, Taunggyi, Moulmein and Sittwe, forcing the students to return to their homes. The dispersal of university students made it impossible to collect accurate information about arrests. The primary schools finally reopened seven months later, after the ASEAN meeting in July. As of November, most high schools, colleges and universities remained closed.

Military barricades set up in late 1996 on the road leading to the house of opposition leader Aung San Suu Kyi were maintained until May. After that, army checkpoints remained in place near the house, which was also the unofficial headquarters of the NLD, and at times of high tension the barricades themselves reappeared. For most of the year, Aung San Suu Kyi remained under virtual house arrest, having to ask for permission to leave her home in order to meet local and international media. Her phone line was frequently cut. Despite this, the NLD was allowed to hold three celebratory gatherings during the year in Daw Suu's home. On January 4, some 1,000 party members and guests marked the forty-ninth anniversary of Burma's independence. On February 12, the NLD held Union Day celebrations at the house, although a military barricade prevented at least half the guests from attending. In the days that followed, thirteen NLD members who had played a prominent role on the celebrations were reported to have been arrested, including Dr. Than Nyein, an NLD organizer and coincidentally the brother-in-law of the SLORC's top official, Secretary-1 Khin Nyunt. Than Nyein was later released, but his medical license was revoked. In April the NLD held New Year celebrations attended by some 600 supporters, all of whom had to register at the army checkpoint. The event raised funds for the families of NLD members in jail.

For the second year running, the NLD attempted to hold a party congress on the anniversary of the May 1990 election which it had won. Some 316 NLD members were prevented from attending the gathering, though few were actually detained. Those few were held in government guest houses for up to two weeks, while others were placed under temporary house arrest or otherwise warned not to go to Rangoon. Shortly thereafter, U Aye Win, Daw Suu's close adviser, was arrested. By November he remained without charge in unlawful detention in Insein jail in Rangoon and was in poor health, having spent long periods in the prison hospital after an operation in July.

On June 13, five NLD activists were arrested: U Ohn Myint an eighty-year-old party adviser; Khin Maung Win (known as Sonny), a photographer; Cho Aung Than, a cousin of Daw Suu; his sister Daw Khin Ma Than, and her husband U Myint Swe. U Ohn Myint was released after questioning, but on the same day trade unionists U Myo Aung Thant, U Khin Kyaw and his wife, all members of the exiled Free Trade Union of Burma

(FTUB), were also arrested at Rangoon airport on arrival from Thailand. In a press conference on June 27, Lt. Gen. Khin Nyunt accused the group of having collaborated with "overseas anti-government activists and advocates of destruction within the country" to bring in money for the NLD from overseas and to transmit information from Burma. He described them as puppets of the U.S. government. Myo Aung Thant and Khin Kyaw were also accused of smuggling in explosives in a rice cooker. On August 15 a court inside Insein prison sentenced Cho Aung Than, Daw Khin Ma Than, and U Myint Swe to ten years under the Unlawful Associations Act and the 1950 Emergency Provisions Act (EPA), section 5(e), which allows for seven years of imprisonment for anyone who "causes or intends to spread false news, knowing beforehand it is untrue." Myo Aung Thant was sentenced to life imprisonment for treason. The fates of Khin Maung Win and U Khin Kyaw were not known.

Other NLD members, elected members of parliament and supporters faced harassment and arrest from late 1996 through 1997. Over twenty NLD parliamentarians were forced to resign their seats. All had reportedly received threats that if they did not resign, members of their families would suffer reprisals ranging from arrest to permanent dismissal from public sector jobs. Seven members of parliament were arrested: U Hla Min, Saw Oo Reh, U Hla Myint, U Min Swe, U San Myint, U Tin Aung, U Saw Lwin, Dr. Hla Win, and Dr. Than Aung, bringing the number of elected parliamentarians in prison to thirty-three. At least fourteen NLD party organizers and activists, the majority from Irrawaddy division, were also arrested. Most were charged under the EPA; others were charged with criminal offenses, a tactic frequently used by the SLORC to discredit the opposition.

In July, in the only formal meeting during the year between the government and the opposition, Secretary-1 Khin Nyunt met with U Aung Shwe, NLD chairman. There were no other moves towards political reconciliation. On September 17, the NLD refused a further offer of talks because they did not include Aung San Suu Kyi.

On September 28, the NLD was permitted to hold a ceremony marking the ninth anniversary of the founding of the party. While the government gave express permission to allow 300 members to attend, some 700 were reported to have arrived at Daw Suu's house. All those attending had to give their personal details to military intelligence officers at the house, and some thirty NLD activists were denied permission to attend and were removed from the area.

Prison conditions remained poor and, in Myitkyina, Thayet, Myingyan and Tharrawaddy jails, reportedly deteriorated. U Tin Shwe, sixty-seven, a NLD central committee member, died on June 8 after nearly six years in Insein jail. The official report said he had died of heart disease in Rangoon General Hospital. During the year at least five political prisoners had to receive emergency medical treatment. Many of the most prominent political prisoners were transferred to jails far from their families, making visits difficult and the provision of extra food and medicines almost impossible.

On April 7, Cho Lay Oo, the daughter of Secretary-2 of the SLORC and Commander in Chief of the Army Lt. Gen. Tin Oo, was killed when she opened a parcel bomb sent to their home. It was the second bomb attack in four months; the first, on December 25, 1996, had killed five people and injured seventeen at the World Peace Pagoda in Rangoon, shortly before Lt. Gen. Tin Oo arrived to pay his respects. The SLORC blamed both attacks on armed opposition groups, the exiled All Burma Students Democratic Front (ABSDF) and the Karen Nation Union (KNU), and implicated the NLD as an "above-ground destructive element" with whom these groups were alleged to have contact. In May the government published an editorial in the official newspapers denying rumors that the bombs were a result of internal discord among military officers. By the end of the year, no arrests had been made in relation to either attack.

Muslims continued to be the target of discrimination throughout the country. On March 16, a group of monks in Mandalay provoked a confrontation at a mosque over the attempted rape of a Buddhist girl by a local Muslim, apparently in an attempt to whip up anti-Muslim sentiment. In the three days of riots that followed, four mosques and nearly 400 Muslim-owned shops and houses were destroyed. The violence spread to Rangoon, Sittwe, Moulmein and Prome, and in most areas eyewitnesses reported that security forces made no attempt to stop the rioters or to protect Muslims and their property. In Rangoon, seven mosques were attacked.

A disproportionately high number of Muslims joined ethnic Karen refugees fleeing Papun and Duplaya township during the year. Muslim refugees reported that soldiers had destroyed their mosques and schools and had ordered them to convert to Buddhism or leave the country. In Arakan state, refugees of the Rohingya Muslim minority returning from Bangladesh reported continued persecution by the Burmese military because of their race and religion. Some 270,000 Rohingyas had sought refuge in Bangladesh in 1991 and 1992. Of those who returned home, some 20,000 fled once again to Bangladesh in 1997.

By October, the number of internally displaced in Burma was estimated to be over 300,000. Forced relocations and a major military offensive against the KNU during the year drove some 150,000 people from their homes. Shan state, where over 100,000 people had been forced to leave their villages in 1996, was particularly hard-hit. The relocation program, aimed at cutting off support for ethnic rebels, was extended to new areas, and many of those displaced in 1996 were forced to move again to sites on the outskirts of government-controlled towns. The relocations were accompanied by killings, rape, and other forms of torture, and scores are believed to have died from malnutrition and related diseases due to poor conditions at the government-controlled sites. In other areas, relocated villagers were forced to work on road building projects. As many as 400 Shan villagers were reportedly killed by the Burmese army during May and June when they returned to collect food, or in reprisal attacks by the Burmese military after clashes with rebel soldiers. Others were killed by SLORC soldiers at the Thai border when they could not afford to bribe their way out of Burma.

Forced relocations also continued further south in Karenni state, where over one hundred villages had been removed during 1996. Conditions there remained dire, with the lack of sanitation, food and medical care leading to scores of deaths from malaria and other diseases. Villagers sent to the camps were forced to build fences around the periphery, turning the camps into virtual prisons. In July, eleven additional villages were forcibly relocated to Laikha district, bringing the total of displaced in Karenni state to over 25,000. Government efforts to block rice supplies coming into areas where rebels were active, combined with a sharp downturn in the Burmese economy and massive inflation, led to severe malnutrition in Shan, Karenni and Arakan states.

In Karen and Mon states and Tenasserim division, new fighting broke out in January after the failure of peace talks and the Karen National Union's continued support for Aung San Suu Kyi expressed in the Mae Tha Raw Hta statement of January 14, led to the major offensive against the KNU's last remaining strongholds. The offensive began on February 7, and by February 28 an estimated 80,000 Burmese troops had forced the KNU to abandon territory in these areas. Some 20,000 Karens fled to areas inside Burma or to Thailand in advance of the Burmese troops. In addition to displacement, Karen, Mon and Tavoyans living in these areas were subject to summary executions, arbitrary arrests, portering for the army and other forms of forced labor.

Even after fleeing to Thailand, Karenni and Karen refugees were not free from attack by Burmese government or government-backed groups. On January 3, a group of forty Burmese soldiers marched into a Karenni camp in Thailand's Mae Hong Son district and killed two people. Nine others were seriously injured. Four weeks later, members of the Democratic Karen Buddhist Army (DKBA), a militia group backed by the government, attacked three Karen refugee camps further south in Thailand's Mae Sot district. Three refugees were killed in the attacks, and 7,000 refugees were left without shelter as parts of camps were razed. On April 27, the DKBA attacked Ta Per Poo camp in Thailand's Umphang district.

The Right to Monitor

The press remained under tight government control. No indigenous human rights organizations were permitted to form, and no international human rights groups were permitted to visit during the year. On October 24, NLD organizer Kyow Din, who had been accused of passing on information to others that would cause "fear or alarm," died in a prison hospital. His death was attributed to natural causes, but his incarceration for his monitoring activites almost certainly contributed to his ill health. U.N. Special Rapporteur Rajsoomer Lallah was denied access to the country for the second straight year. Only NLD members were able to speak out against human rights abuses with some degree of freedom, but during the year it became increasingly difficult and dangerous for them and other Burmese to report on events in the country. Of the NLD members arrested during the year, many had appeared in international newspaper and television reports. Journalists themselves became the subject of attack, with photographer Myo Thant and his Japanese colleague, Shigefumi Takasuka, of the daily *Yomiuri Shimbun*, being badly beaten during the December 1996 demonstrations. Many other foreign journalists, especially those who had worked on Burma in the past, were denied visas during the year, and nine freelance journalists were deported.

Access to ethnic minority areas in particular remained very restricted. No U.N. agencies or international nongovernmental organizations were permitted to assist the displaced in the Shan, Karenni and Karen states, despite their requests to do so. Local church groups managed to provide some relief to the displaced, but did so without government permission.

In January, Burma's treatment of children came under scrutiny at the Committee on the Rights of the Child. The government sent a large delegation to Geneva in January to discuss with the committee its initial report on Burma's compliance with the Convention on the Rights of the Child. The leader of the delegation denied all allegations of human rights abuses against children. No nongovernmental organizations working in Burma, foreign or local, submitted reports to the committee for fear of government retaliation.

The Role of the International Community

The international community continued to be deeply divided between those countries advocating isolation of Burma and those calling for engagement. Limited economic sanctions imposed by the U.S. and Europe, and support within ASEAN for Burma's admission as a full member in the regional body, highlighted the difference in approach.

United Nations

Demands for an improvement in human rights and democratic accountability remained strong in the United Nations. The General Assembly in December 1996 and the U.N. Commission on Human Rights in March 1997 passed consensus resolutions calling on the SLORC to cooperate more with the U.N. system, particularly with the special rapporteur. In May, the U.N. secretary-general's representative, Alvaro de Soto, was permitted a four-day mission to Burma, where he met with the leaders of the NLD and other political parties as well as with Lt. Gen. Khin Nyunt. He was not able to meet ethnic minority representatives, however, nor with other members of the SLORC.

In June, the International Labour Organisation (ILO) initiated a commission of inquiry into allegations of forced labor in Burma. Such a step had only been taken against nine countries in the ILO's seventy-eight-year history and, depending on the results of the inquiry, could lead to Burma's expulsion from the ILO. The commission was expected to investigate for one year and to hear testimony from victims of forced labor. The ILO was planning to seek access to Burma to verify allegations.

European Union

The European Union (E.U.) continued to maintain a ban on provision of arms and military equipment to Burma, kept military attachés out of its embassies in Burma, and continued its suspension of non-humanitarian aid. In late 1996, it added provisions which banned entry visas for senior members of the SLORC, their families, and others in the Burmese security forces who formulate, implement or benefit from policies "which impede Burma's transition to democracy." It also called for suspension of high-level bilateral governmental visits between officials of the E.U. and Burma.

In early November 1996, the European Commission tried to send a mission to Burma to investigate forced labor, but the Burmese government denied the mission entry, saying that since there was no forced labor in Burma, there would be nothing to investigate. In December, the commission approved a decision to cut Burma's low tariff access to the European Union market through the Generalized System of Preferences (GSP) program because of forced labor and said the cut, which affected industrial exports, would remain in force until forced labor was abolished. It was the first time the human rights clause of the European GSP program had been invoked. On March 25, following action in the European Parliament, the Council of Ministers suspended Burma's GSP benefits for agricultural products as well. On July 28, in his address before the E.U./ASEAN Ministerial meeting, European Union Council President Jacques Poos announced that the E.U. had extended its common position on Burma that effectively prevented Burma from being included in the 1980 EC-ASEAN cooperation agreement.

In Britain, the newly elected Labour government, which had promised to put human rights at the heart of foreign policy, announced in June that it not only would continue the suspension of all government-sponsored trade tours to Burma but would actively discourage U.K. companies from investing there. In September, Foreign Minister Robin Cook also stated that despite having been accepted as a member of ASEAN, Burma would not be invited to attend the Asia-Europe meeting (ASEM) to take place in London in April 1998. In addition to these moves Western governments continued to give financial aid to Burmese refugees in camps in Thailand and Bangladesh, and European governments also gave aid to assist victims of severe flooding in Irrawaddy division in September.

United States and Canada

The U.S. also acted on human rights concerns. On October 2, 1996, the U.S. Senate passed the fiscal year 1998 Foreign Assistance Act, which included a provision giving the president authority to ban visas for all Burmese officials and to prohibit new investment by U.S. citizens or companies if the Burmese government physically harmed, rearrested or exiled Aung San Suu Kyi or committed large-scale repression against the political opposition. The visa restrictions were imposed the following day. Discussion continued on what constituted large-scale repression until April 22, when President Clinton announced his decision to impose the investment ban. As of October, however, the Treasury Department had yet to issue the implementing regulations.

Canada took similar action on August 7 when Foreign Minister Lloyd Axworthy announced the withdrawal of the General Preferential Tariff to Burma and a measure requiring all firms trading in Burma to apply for export permits. Axworthy also urged all Canadians to "refrain" from investing in Burma.

ASEAN

Western moves to pressure the SLORC for reform were offset by Burma's admission into ASEAN and by an increase in investment from ASEAN countries. In the run up to the ASEAN ministerial meeting in Kuala Lumpur in July, it was not clear whether Burma would be admitted, especially following the ASEAN decision to delay Cambodian membership. Regional nongovernmental organizations, members of parliament and other prominent groups, led by the Kim Dae Jung Foundation and the Alternative ASEAN network, protested Burma's imminent entry. But the sanctions enacted by the U.S. and E.U. prior to the meeting seemed only to harden ASEAN resolve to accept Burma as a full member and defy what was projected as an example of western imperialism. The Japanese government supported Burma's entry into ASEAN, while also warning that this should not provide "cover for oppression." Tokyo continued its ban on ODA (Official Development Assistance) to Rangoon and attempted to use the aid leverage as a carrot to promote improvements. (*See* Japan section for details.)

Relevant Human Rights Watch reports:

No Safety in Burma, No Sanctuary in Thailand, 7/97
Children's Rights and The Rule of Law, 1/97

CAMBODIA

Fundamental freedoms in Cambodia suffered a harsh reversal with the July coup d'état by Second Prime Minister Hun Sen of the Cambodian People's Party (CPP) against his coalition partner, First Prime Minister Prince Norodom Ranariddh of the Front Uni National pour un Cambodge Independent, Neutre, Pacifique, et Cooperatif (FUNCINPEC). Once touted as the United Nations' greatest peacekeeping success, the fractious and ill-fated coalition government installed after U.N.-supervised elections in

1993 disintegrated with the eruption of two days of heavy fighting in Phnom Penh and factional battles in the provinces. Before the coup, both factions of the coalition government had taken actions to undermine press freedom and freedom of association, and government officials at all levels enjoyed virtual immunity from prosecution for human rights violations. Afterwards, new problems arose with key members of FUNCINPEC and other parties fleeing to Bangkok, and thousands of refugees fleeing across the northern and western borders into Thailand. Many inside and outside Cambodia raised questions as to whether conditions for free and fair elections could be established by May 1998 when the first post-U.N. ballot was scheduled. The coup also served to stop the momentum that had been building internationally to find ways to bring Pol Pot and other Khmer Rouge leaders to justice for crimes against humanity.

Human Rights Developments

Relations between Ranariddh and Hun Sen had rapidly deteriorated since March 1996. Both factions had spent more than a year building up their own private armies, police forces, and bodyguard units. In February 1997, factional fighting erupted in Battambang province between FUNCINPEC and CPP forces, with human rights workers reporting as many as twenty soldiers killed during the armed clashes.

On March 30, a grenade attack on a peaceful rally in front of the National Assembly led by KNP President Sam Rainsy left at least sixteen dead and more than one hundred wounded. The two prime ministers continued to build up their personal arsenals and private armies, with Hun Sen's security forces numbering at least 1,500 and Ranariddh's approaching 1,000.

Tensions continued to escalate as the two factions competed to recruit defecting Khmer Rouge units, as well as to build new rival political alliances, which led to virtual paralysis of the fragile coalition. The beginning of the National Assembly's planned three-month session, slated originally for

April 21, was postponed after divisions broke out within FUNCINPEC, with a renegade faction led by Minister of State Ung Phan and Siem Reap Governor Toan Chay announcing their intention to oust Ranariddh. During the ensuing political stalemate, the National Assembly failed to convene for nearly six months, holding up passage of crucial legislation regulating the upcoming elections, nongovernmental organization (NGO) activity, political parties, and access to broadcasting frequencies.

When military authorities in late May seized a shipment of weapons and ammunition, addressed to Ranariddh and marked "spare parts," the first prime minister said he "did not have any choice" but to procure weapons in order to protect himself from CPP forces. On June 17, fighting broke out in the streets of Phnom Penh for several hours between Ranariddh's personal security unit and troops under CPP loyalist National Police Chief Hok Lundy, in which several people were killed.

The coup followed less than three weeks later. On July 5 and 6, sections of Phnom Penh were pounded by exploding mortars, tank blasts, and automatic weapon fire as forces loyal to Hun Sen seized the airport as well as the headquarters and military bases of FUNCINPEC. The national headquarters of the main opposition party, the Khmer Nation Party (KNP), was ransacked and looted, as were dozens of businesses, factories, and private homes. In Phnom Penh, at least sixty-five people died, and more than 200 were wounded in the two days of fighting.

The forcible ousting of Prince Ranariddh, whose party won a plurality of seats in the 1993 elections, was followed by an apparently systematic campaign of intimidation, torture, and summary executions of at least forty-one FUNCINPEC members by Hun Sen's forces. In addition, more than 500 FUNCINPEC soldiers were temporarily confined in detention centers—with at least thirty tortured in custody—while dozens of other FUNCINPEC officers disappeared and remain unaccounted for. Dozens of opposition members of parliament, political workers, labor union activists, and journalists fled to Thailand, where many regrouped as the Union of Cambodian Democrats. Others made accommodations with the CPP or escaped to FUNCINPEC zones in northwestern Cambodia. In a development that more than anything else symbolized the resumption of civil war, more than 40,000 Cambodians fled to the Thai border to escape factional fighting in northwestern Cambodia that began in July. By the end of the year, approximately 400 Cambodians had applied for asylum with the U.N. High Commissioner for Refugees (UNHCR) in Bangkok.

After the coup, Hun Sen moved to consolidate his power through action in the courts and the rump National Assembly. On August 6, despite the absence of twenty exiled parliamentarians, the National Assembly removed Ranariddh's parliamentary immunity from criminal prosecution and confirmed Hun Sen's choice for a new first prime minister, Foreign Minister Ung Huot, a member of FUNCINPEC. A warrant was subsequently issued for Ranariddh's arrest for allegedly buying and importing illegal weapons in May 1997.

The constitutionality of installing Ung Huot as a prime minister without removing Ranariddh was questionable on several grounds, including the fact that the National Assembly lacked a quorum for its Permanent Committee, which sets the body's agenda, and the National Assembly vice president, who is required to approve the appointment of new prime ministers, was in exile in Bangkok.

In September, the Phnom Penh Municipal Court issued two rulings with possible repercussions for exiled opposition leaders. On September 9, Cambodia's most prominent political prisoner, former KNP security chief Srun Vong Vannak, was sentenced to thirteen years in prison for conspiracy to murder Kov Samuth, deputy chief of the Criminal Department of the Interior Police, who was the brother-in-law of Hun Sen's wife. In violation of the penal code, Vannak was held for almost a month without access to a lawyer and forced to confess under duress by police, according to his defenders. The court's decision could set the stage for the filing of criminal charges against KNP President Sam Rainsy as a co-conspirator in a bid to bar him from running in the 1998 elections.

In another move to neutralize opposition parties, on September 17 the Municipal Court determined that the Son Sann faction of the Buddhist Liberal Democratic Party (BLDP), which sided with Ranariddh, could no longer use the BLDP party name or logo. Additional measures to block electoral participation by some exiled politicians are contained in a draft electoral law approved by the Council of Ministers and forwarded to the National Assembly in October. The law would require candidates to live in Cambodia for at least a year before the election and bar convicted criminals from running.

To further strengthen his hand, Hun Sen proposed a cabinet reshuffle in September to eliminate ministers loyal to Ranariddh and replace them with pro-CPP figures from FUNCINPEC and BLDP. However, the National Assembly rejected the slate of candidates proposed by Hun Sen in an initial vote conducted on September 16.

In an effort to get beyond international condemnation for atrocities committed during and after the coup and legitimize the new regime, Hun Sen began to focus his public statements on the 1998 elections. As early as July 13, he pledged that the media and human rights organizations could continue to operate. In a public relations gesture in August, he unveiled an "anti-crime" plan to depoliticize the military, root out corruption in the armed forces, and bring an end to kidnapping and extortion. The eight-point plan has largely been used to arrest offenders who are members of FUNCINPEC, now that they have no protection from political patrons.

A climate of fear throughout the country after the coup, along with the exodus of opposition leaders and journalists, seriously undermined prospects for free and fair elections slated for May 1998. Many in and outside Cambodia believed elections should take place only if the government ended its persecution of the opposition, brought human rights abusers to justice —particularly those responsible for executions during and after the coup—lifted restrictions on the press, ensured the safe return of exiled politicians, and established a neutral electoral administration.

The problem of impunity continued to plague Cambodia, with police, army, and government officials often shielded from conviction for criminal offenses or politically motivated crimes through Article 51 of the Civil Service Law, which forbids the prosecution of government employees without prior ministry approval. To date, no instance of political violence since the 1993 elections—aside from the murder of Hun Sen's wife's brother-in-law, which may not have been politically motivated—has resulted in a serious government investigation.

The lack of an independent judiciary also continued to pose a problem. A Supreme Council of Magistracy, mandated by Cambodia's constitution to appoint and discipline judges, was expected to meet for the first time in November, but a Constitutional Council that is to provide independent confirmation of legislative compliance with the constitution had yet to be established.

One of the most high-profile events of the year was the July 25 public denunciation of Khmer Rouge leader Pol Pot by other Khmer Rouge members, not for genocide or crimes against humanity committed during the 1970s but for the execution of Khmer Rouge Defense Minister Son Sen and an attempted purge of other Khmer Rouge leaders in June 1997. While the international press referred to the event as a trial, almost all the elements of a trial were absent. Many observers believe the eighty-minute proceeding, which sentenced Pol Pot to life imprisonment, was a maneuver designed to bestow legitimacy on the rebel faction in its new alliance with FUNCINPEC.

The status of fundamental freedoms of association, expression, and assembly—mandated by the Paris Peace Accords,

Cambodia's 1993 constitution, and its signing of international human rights treaties—suffered a huge setback in 1997. Hundreds of Cambodian NGOs, political parties, and labor unions that had sprung up since the U.N. peacekeeping mission were forced to close or operate much more cautiously in the climate of intimidation following the coup, avoiding direct confrontation with authorities. With so many important opposition leaders in exile, the remnants of the parties that remained in Cambodia largely acted as satellites of the CPP. Given the current political climate, it was unclear by year's end whether local rights organizations would be able to conduct more than symbolic election monitoring efforts in 1998, or whether the two main NGO coalitions that have formed—the Committee for Free and Fair Elections (COMFREL) and the Coalition for Free and Fair Elections (COFFEL)—would dissolve or become irrelevant.

An activist trade union movement sprang up in 1997, with the National Assembly passing a new labor law in January 1997 that gave workers the right to form and join independent trade unions, strike, and bargain collectively. The law was criticized on several grounds, including the lack of protections for civil servants, who constitute 85 to 90 percent of salaried workers in Cambodia. Since the enactment of the Labor Law, the government failed not only to implement it in a fair and neutral manner but actively interfered in workers' rights to organize and bargain collectively, favoring CPP-affiliated unions over independent unions or those linked to the KNP. Following the coup, trade union leaders received threats, and many went into hiding or left the country.

Press freedom was also dealt a blow in 1997. The CPP consolidated its hold over the electronic media during the coup, taking control over FUNCINPEC television and radio stations on July 7. Even before the coup, different political parties had complained about unequal access to the airwaves. In March 1997, Ranariddh threatened to call out tanks against the Ministry of Information, charging that government broadcasters gave preferential radio and television coverage to the CPP. The Ministry of Information repeatedly denied applications for broadcasting licenses by opposition parties such as the KNP or the Son Sann faction of the BLDP.

In May 1997, a CPP-affiliated television station in Sihanoukville was attacked by soldiers armed with rocket launchers, killing technician Pich Em and wounding several others. Three days later, the co-prime ministers instructed government radio and television stations not to broadcast political attacks between the prime ministers and their political parties, ostensibly in an effort to de-escalate violence incited by the diatribes aired in the media. The ban was not enforced, and CPP party propaganda continued to dominate the state media.

Print journalists remained largely free to publish what they wanted throughout the year, although that did not mean they operated in an environment conducive to freedom of expression. During 1997, at least three journalists or media workers were killed: two while covering the March 30 demonstration in front of the National Assembly and another in May during the armed attack at the government radio station in Sihanoukville. In addition, several editors and journalists received threats or were physically attacked, including the editor of the pro-FUNCINPEC newspaper *Kumnit Koan Khmer* (Thought of Khmer Children), who survived a beating and shooting attack in January by assailants in police uniforms. In February, following a pattern of increasingly vitriolic attacks on King Sihanouk in the press, several pro-CPP reporters were threatened or attacked, according to the League of Cambodian Journalists. In addition, sixteen journalists were injured in the March grenade attack at the National Assembly. In October, Thong Uy Pang, the editor of the pro-CPP newspaper, *Koh Santepheap,* survived a grenade attack on his home, which he attributed to high-ranking CPP officials he had accused of corruption. Since 1993, however, none of the perpetrators of violent attacks or murders of

journalists have been brought to justice.

As of July 1997, approximately fifty newspapers and magazines were publishing in Cambodia, representing a wide spectrum of political affiliations. In the week following the coup, all newspapers not affiliated with the CPP suspended publication, and several journalists went into hiding or fled the country. By August, in addition to the pro-government press, a number of non-CPP affiliated newspapers had resumed publication, sometimes carrying pieces highly critical of Hun Sen. The Ministry of Information reported in August that thirty-two newspapers were publishing again in Cambodia, including seven foreign-language publications.

In late August, the Ministry of Information ordered a private printing house to stop publishing the opposition newspaper *Moneakseka Khmer* (Khmer Conscience), ostensibly at the request of the paper's editor, who was in Thailand; the ministry said he had not authorized the paper to resume publication. In September, the Interior Ministry filed court charges and announced the thirty-day suspension of *Prayuth* (The Fight) newspaper under Article 12 of the Press Law for allegedly damaging "national security and political stability" by publishing inflated casualty figures from the military offensive in northwestern Cambodia. In October, the Ministry of Information cancelled a public affairs program on television produced by the Khmer Institute for Democracy (KID), a human rights organization, charging that KID Director Lao Mong Hay had attacked the government as undemocratic. Also in October the Ministry reprimanded the pro-government *Chakroval* (Universe) newspaper for publishing insulting stories about the King, suspended *Andarakhum* (Intervention) newspaper for twenty-five days for publishing a faked photograph implying government troops support for resistance leaders, and shut down the *Banteay Srei News* on the grounds that it lacked a license.

In the first half of the year Cambodians frequently exercised their right to freedom of assembly, albeit in circumstances that were often tense and confrontational. The KNP organized dozens of mass rallies, with hundreds and sometimes thousands of people demonstrating against garment factory owners, the state visit of Burmese leader Than Shwe, the lack of an independent judiciary, and illegal logging. In addition, farmers calling for flood relief or settlement of land disputes and merchants protesting marketplace rent hikes staged more spontaneous rallies in front of the National Assembly or the Royal Palace, and newly formed labor unions not affiliated with the KNP organized spirited marches, rallies, and demonstrations as well.

Most of the Sam Rainsy-led demonstrations were carried out under the constant threat of violence or provocation by extremely large numbers of police in attendance. In January, police used a water cannon in one instance, and electric shock batons in several other demonstrations, to disperse garment worker marches and rallies. Police forcibly dispersed another rally in January at the Tack Fat garment factory, beating up several protesters and shooting at the tires of Sam Rainsy's car as he attempted to leave the area.

The deadly March 30 grenade attack against an authorized demonstration led by Sam Rainsy was a clear violation of freedom of assembly. An FBI investigation into the grenade attack, conducted because an American was injured, reportedly implicated the bodyguard unit of Hun Sen, although the report itself has not been made public. After the March grenade attack, Ministry of Interior officials said that they would most likely reject all requests for public demonstrations on a case-by-case basis for the time being, although the ministry never issued a written policy to that effect. A significant exception was made to the ministry's unwritten policy on August 3, when Buddhist monks and nuns led more than 1,000 people on a march through the streets of Phnom Penh to call for peace and nonviolent conflict resolution.

Cambodia increasingly served as an illegal transshipment point in 1997 for the smuggling of illicit drugs, timber, and women and children for prostitution, with high-level dealers and mafia-like businessmen operating under the protection of well-placed political patrons. Cambodian business tycoon Teng Boonma, president of the Cambodian Chamber of Commerce, was blacklisted by the United States from obtaining a U.S. visa because of alleged involvement in narcotics trafficking. After the coup, Boonma admitted providing U.S. $1 million to Hun Sen to abate widespread looting by paying marauding soldiers to return to their barracks. Boonma also told the *Phnom Penh Post* that he had contributed $50,000 each to three parliamentarians—Ung Phan, Toan Chay, and Doung Khem—who shifted their allegiance from Ranariddh to Hun Sen in April 1997.

Cambodia's co-prime ministers and the armed forces presided over the illegal exploitation of the country's forests, resulting in severe social, ecological, and environmental consequences. Because of their connections to the prime ministers or high-ranking military officials, logging companies frequently carried out their activities with impunity. Protests by local people about illegal logging, as well as efforts by local officials to supervise or control logging in forested areas, frequently met serious intimidation, armed opposition, and even murder by soldiers or security forces attached to logging companies. In April 1997, a Siem Reap provincial forestry official was murdered by soldiers when he tried to stop logging trucks from passing a checkpoint. Illegal loggers also used landmines to block police, forestry officials, and local people from entering logging areas.

Journalists who covered illegal logging activities risked their personal safety, as reporters had been threatened or murdered in the past for investigating the issue. After the English-language *Cambodia Daily* newspaper published an article in March linking the giant Malaysian logging company, Samling/ SL International, to illegal logging, Samling filed a criminal defamation suit against the paper. The Cambodian courts said no criminal defamation was involved and reduced the case to civil status. As of November, no decision had been reached.

The Right to Monitor

In the wake of the March grenade attack and July coup, most of the indigenous human rights organizations scaled back high-profile activities such as monitoring and investigating human rights abuses out of fear of reprisals from the government. After the coup, a number of Cambodian human rights organizations began to consider the need to re-structure their activities out of concern for the safety of their staff and clients. Possible scenarios included dissolving the large human rights organizations and helping to form smaller local NGOs focusing on development work or less controversial issues such as children's rights. Another possibility under consideration by at least one group was to form a new human rights organization located in a neighboring country, monitoring the situation from there. Human rights education and training programs by Cambodian NGOs continued largely unfettered.

With most of the domestic opposition in hiding, exile, or practicing self-censorship, the United Nations Center for Human Rights (UNCHR) in Phnom Penh emerged as the only body that could effectively monitor and deter human rights violations without serious reprisals. In the face of human rights criticism about executions and torture during the coup, Hun Sen demanded an apology from the UNCHR and the replacement of its staff, accusing the UNCHR of falsely reporting executions and convincing dozens of members of the National Assembly to flee unnecessarily. He also announced plans to establish his own human rights committee to monitor abuses.

UNCHR staff encountered official resistance while attempting to carry out investigations after the coup, despite Hun Sen's appointment of a special advisor to maintain contact with the center. Initial UNCHR requests for access to some detention sites in July were denied, and in August an AK47 was fired over the heads of investigators at a grave site. In another instance, UNCHR investigators in the field heard radio traffic from government soldiers debating whether to kill them or not. The U.N.'s decision in September not to fill Cambodia's seat at the General Assembly heightened tensions further between Hun Sen and U.N. agencies in Phnom Penh. Balancing out Hun Sen's animosity towards UNCHR, on August 29 King Sihanouk cited staff from UNCHR and Amnesty International for exceptional service to the country.

Since the coup, international and regional human rights organizations such as Forum Asia, Human Rights Watch, and Amnesty International have sent fact-finding missions to Cambodia and/or Thailand, where many of the self-exiled parliamentarians were initially based.

The Role of
the International Community

Donors from the major industrialized countries and the World Bank poured aid into Cambodia until July, when virtually all international programs were placed under review. Member countries of the Association of Southeast Asian Nations (ASEAN), usually reluctant to criticize their neighbors, took a strong public stance against the coup by postponing admission of Cambodia into ASEAN. Several countries with embassies in Phnom Penh, the U.S. and Australia among them, were criticized for failing to offer meaningful support during and immediately after the coup to opposition members in danger.

United Nations

U.N. Special Representative for Human Rights in Cambodia Thomas Hammarberg made several visits to Cambodia in 1997. After a visit in March, he raised concerns about the poor functioning of the judicial system and the government's inaction on confidential UNCHR reports about violence against journalists and torture committed by the military. He also addressed the issue of impunity, referring in particular to "crimes against humanity" committed by the Khmer Rouge from 1975 through 1979 and calling for the establishment of a "truth commission" to conduct a full investigation into their activities. In July, Hammarberg was quick to denounce Hun Sen's military takeover as a "violent coup d'état...which has displaced the lawfully elected government of Cambodia." In September, Hammarberg met with Second Prime Minister Hun Sen to discuss a report prepared by UNCHR on more than forty cases of extrajudicial executions and torture. Hammarberg called for an impartial investigation into violence surrounding the coup and for the government to reveal the location of all detention centers, prisons, and cremation sites.

On September 19, the U.N. Credentials Committee decided not to fill Cambodia's seat at the fifty-second session of the General Assembly.

Europe

On November 7, 1996, the European Commission (EC) signed the first formal agreement with Phnom Penh designed to aid in Cambodia's reconstruction after more than twenty-five years of conflict. The agreement included assistance for refugees, education, rural development, human resources, environment, mine clearance, and human rights. A Joint Declaration annexed to the agreement stipulated that it could be suspended in the event of serious human rights violations.

In January, the EC approved a humanitarian aid package worth ECU 1.5 million to be distributed by the European Community Humanitarian Office (ECHO), which would enable nongovernmental organizations to carry out a six-month program focusing on heath and de-mining.

Following the March 30 grenade attack at a KNP rally, the European Parliament adopted a resolution in emergency debate, urging the EC to remind Cambodia of the importance of the human rights clause in the November cooperation agreement. The resolution welcomed the establishment of an independent committee of inquiry and insisted that Cambodian authorities identify those responsible for attacks on political

parties and bring them to justice.

At the same time, the Council of Ministers, the decision-making body of the E.U., prepared to formally sign the November agreement. The council's signature would mean that the agreement would then have to be ratified by the European Parliament and the Cambodian National Assembly. In mid-June, the European Parliament Committee on Development and Cooperation adopted a report recommending approval of the cooperation agreement, despite its rejection by the Committee on Foreign Affairs, Security, and Defense Policy because of continuing widespread corruption and deforestation in Cambodia. The development committee argued that the agreement's solid human rights clause might help consolidate democracy. The report was put before the plenary on October 1 and 2 and was returned to the development committee so that fundamental conditions on aid could be drafted in light of the July coup.

With close to two-thirds of Cambodia's national budget of U.S.$792 million derived from foreign aid, the potential leverage of international donors is considerable. At the Second Consultative Group (CG) meeting of donors in Paris, convened on July 1 and 2, 1997, international donors pledged U.S.$450 million to Cambodia. But the coup, three days after the CG meeting, led several countries to suspend financial and technical aid. The most unequivocal response came from Germany, which suspended all aid.

United States

The United States suspended all aid for thirty days following the coup, followed in August by suspension of all but humanitarian aid and aid given through nongovernmental groups, cutting its funding by two-thirds. The U.S. embassy in Phnom Penh was criticized, however, for refusing sanctuary and providing minimal assistance to Cambodians facing political persecution during and after the coup. The U.S. also avoided calling the CPP takeover a coup so as not to trigger sanctions that by law must be imposed when a democratically elected government is overthrown. In September, however, the United States played a crucial role in the U.N. Credentials Committee's decision to delay filling the Cambodia seat at the General Assembly.

The position of Cambodian asylum seekers in Bangkok was complicated by international bureaucratic obstructions. The U.S. embassy did not offer emergency visas to Cambodians who feared for their safety, telling them instead to request political asylum from the embassy in Bangkok. An August 2 statement by the State Department announced that the U.S. government would consider cases of Cambodian asylum seekers that the United Nations High Commissioner for Refugees (UNHCR) determined to be refugees in need of third-country resettlement, but because the Thai government refused to acknowledge anyone as a refugee, only allowing the designation "persons of concern to UNHCR," that avenue appeared to be blocked.

Asia
Following the coup, the Association of Southeast Asian Nations (ASEAN) made an unprecedented decision to postpone Cambodia's membership in the body, originally slated to take place in late July, and tried unsuccessfully to mediate the conflict. After an August 11 meeting of ASEAN foreign ministers, the grouping avoided taking a stand on the legitimacy of Ung Huot's appointment as first prime minister by announcing that it "recognized states not governments."

Australia suspended its military aid to Cambodia on July 15 but continued its general humanitarian aid program. Ambassador Tony Kevin was quoted in a leaked cable after the coup as calling Hun Sen a "democrat at heart" and was quietly supportive of Ung Huot, who holds dual Australian-Cambodian citizenship.

Japan, Cambodia's largest aid donor, while not officially suspending or terminating aid, halted its programs temporarily, following the lead of other donors and out of concern for the safety of its aid workers. But

on July 26, despite having previously stated four conditions for resuming aid—including assurances of "fundamental human rights and political freedom"—the Japanese Foreign Ministry announced resumption of aid to Cambodia. On October 16, Japanese Foreign Minister Keizo Obuchi reportedly told senior Cambodian officials that Ranariddh should be allowed to return to Cambodia to participate in the 1998 elections. China, on the other hand, gave its full support to Hun Sen.

As of August 4, the Thai embassy in Cambodia—under pressure from Hun Sen—stopped issuing visas for Cambodians to travel to Thailand.

World Bank
On September 23, the World Bank and the International Monetary Fund announced an indefinite suspension of their aid programs to Cambodia. The IMF stated that it was freezing Cambodia's U.S.$120 million, three-year loan because of concerns about corruption and logging. The World Bank, which has provided approximately U.S.$85 million to Cambodia since 1994, announced that it would not renew its funding support to Cambodia until the IMF resumed its programs.

Relevant Human Rights Watch reports:
Cambodia Aftermath of the Coup, 8/97
Deterioration of Human Rights in Cambodia, 12/96

CHINA AND TIBET

Despite China's ongoing violations of human rights, the international community with few exceptions continued to let itself be intimidated into silence by threats of commercial sanctions. It expressed more concern during the year over the prospect of the erosion of civil liberties in Hong Kong than over the virtual elimination of the dissident movement on the mainland. The release of Wei Jingsheng, China's best-known prisoner, in November, shortly after the U.S.-China summit, was a victory for international pressure, particularly for the Clinton administration and concerned individuals and organizations around the world who had worked on Wei's behalf. But, one man's release, however significant, changed little in terms of the overall human rights situation. Thousands of political prisoners remained behind bars, and prison conditions continued to be poor with consistent reports of torture and denial of medical care. "Unauthorized" religious congregations were subjected to a widening government campaign aimed at forcing them to register with state-sanctioned religious bodies or face dissolution. Suspected supporters of nationalist movements in Tibet, Xinjiang and Inner Mongolia were subjected to increasingly severe policies of surveillance, harassment and persecution. In Xinjiang, where the level of political violence was high, the crackdown extended well beyond those directly engaged in violent acts. Much-heralded legal reforms had little impact on those detained for peaceful expression of their beliefs. Assaults on freedom of expression, through print and electronic media, continued. In view of this pattern of abuse, the failure of some of China's key trading partners to make a credible effort to censure China at the U.N. Commission on Human Rights was particularly striking.

Human Rights Developments

Chinese authorities continued to hold dissidents and other activists in incommunicado detention before trial and then to sentence them harshly. The release of Wei Jingsheng was therefore not an indication of an increased tolerance for dissent. In December 1996, Ngawang Choephel, a thirty-five-year-old U.S.-based Tibetan ethnomusicologist, was sentenced to eighteen years in prison by a Lhasa court for alleged "espionage" in connection with research he had been carrying out in Tibet. Around the same time, Li

Hai, a former philosophy student from Beijing University who had been detained incommunicado since May 1995, was sentenced to nine years in prison on state secrets-related charges for compiling a list of names and other details of Beijing residents still in prison in connection with the 1989 prodemocracy movement. Also in December, Wang Ming, a longtime Sichuan-based activist and former editor of several unofficial journals from the 1978-81 Democracy Wall movement, was sentenced without trial to three years' "reeducation through labor" for writing and distributing a document titled "A Manifesto for Citizens' Freedom of Speech." Hu Kesi, an editor of the Hong Kong magazine *Pacific Economy* who had been secretly detained the previous March, received a similar administrative sentence in connection with unspecified alleged dissident activities in Shanghai. Chen Longde, a veteran dissident from Hangzhou also serving a three-year labor reeducation term, was sent back to his cell after receiving only cursory medical treatment for serious injuries sustained when he leapt from a three-story prison building to escape persistent torture.

In January, five prominent dissidents from Guiyang, detained since mid-1995 for advocating democratic reform, were tried and sentenced for alleged "subversive activities." Chen Xi, leader of the group and a lecturer at Guizhou Jinzhu University, received a ten-year prison term. The other men received sentences ranging from two to five years.

The defeat in April of an effort at the Geneva-based U.N. Human Rights Commission to censure China for human rights violations was soon followed by reports of serious ill-treatment of detained political dissidents. That month, Yao Zhenxian began a hunger strike at Dafeng Labor Reeducation Camp to protest the frequent beatings, deprivation of family visiting rights, and confiscation of correspondence that both he and his brother had endured since their joint detention in April 1996. His brother, Yao Zhenxiang, is a Shanghai dissident who had fled to France in 1994 and then returned to China in 1996 after receiving official reassurances for his safety.

In May, labor rights activist Liu Nianchun, serving a three-year labor reeducation term in Shuanghe Labor Reform Camp in the far northeast of the country, also staged a hunger strike in protest against the authorities' unlawful extension of his own prison term and those of two other Beijing dissidents, fellow labor rights activist Zhou Guoqiang and a Christian activist named Gao Feng. The sentence extensions (288 extra days for Zhou, and 216 days each for Liu and Gao) were ordered by the prison governor because the dissidents had continued to refuse to write confessions since the time of their initial sentencing hearings. As punishment for carrying out the hunger strike, Liu was subsequently subjected to beatings with electric shock batons, denied water for an extended period, and placed in solitary confinement. As of September, he was reported to be suffering from a blocked intestine, swollen lymph nodes and extensive mouth ulcers but had received no medical treatment. Similarly, Zhou Guoqiang, whose original three-year jail term was earlier extended by one year after he made a failed escape attempt, was said to be receiving no treatment for his prison-contracted tuberculosis.

Wang Guoqi, an independent labor activist serving an eleven-year sentence in Beijing, was denied all family visits during 1997 on the grounds that he had "failed to memorize the prison rules."

The medical condition of several other prominent Chinese political prisoners also deteriorated during the year. Gao Yu, a woman journalist serving a six-year sentence for allegedly "leaking state secrets" in articles written for the Hong Kong press, was denied release on medical bail despite suffering from a deteriorating heart condition, repeated loss of consciousness, and skin disease. (In May, when Gao was awarded the UNESCO World Press Freedom Prize, the Chinese government threatened to withdraw in protest.)

Wang Dan, the principal student leader of the 1989 prodemocracy movement serving an eleven-year sentence for continuing to speak out against the government's human rights record, was reported to be suffering from an enlarged prostate gland, a stomach disorder, and persistent headaches and dizziness. Despite repeated requests from his family and several governments, Chinese authorities as of October were still refusing to release him on medical parole.

In June, a Shenzhen court finally announced the verdicts in the cases of two young labor rights activists charged with "conspiracy to subvert the government" who had been detained since May 1994 and brought to trial only in November 1996. Li Wenming, a journalist from Hunan, and Guo Baosheng, a former philosophy student from Beijing University, both received prison terms of three and a half years—a relatively light punishment.

At the same time, attempts during the year by jailed Chinese dissidents, including Liu Nianchun, Zhou Guoqiang, Bao Ge, the Yao brothers, Liu Xiaobo and others, to appeal their punishments or pursue lawsuits protesting ill-treatment in prison through domestic legal channels were rejected by the courts. In the case of several Shanghai-based dissidents, the local court even claimed it had no jurisdiction in the matter since the sentences in question had been imposed by the police.

In March and August, the security authorities placed veteran dissident Ren Wanding, released from jail in June 1996 after completing a seven-year sentence, under close house arrest throughout the respective visits to Beijing of U.S. Vice-President Al Gore and U.S. National Security Adviser Sandy Berger.

Despite the inhospitable climate, political dissent continued to surface. On the eighth anniversary of the Tiananmen Square crackdown, Shen Liangqing, a state prosecutor-turned-dissident from Anhui province and a former political prisoner, sent a petition to the National People's Congress (NPC) demanding an official reassessment of the 1989 crackdown, the release of all political prisoners, and permission for the return to China of exiled prodemocracy activists. Two months later, the government responded by ordering Shen to evacuate his private residence and surrender it to the local authorities. The following month, Shen was taken into police detention after he signed a letter expressing solidarity with demonstrating workers in Mianyang, Sichuan province (*see* below); as of October he was still being held incommunicado.

In August, prior to the landmark Fifteenth Congress of the Chinese Communist Party, the veteran Wuhan dissident Qin Yongmin issued an open petition to President Jiang calling for wide-ranging democratic reforms. In September, Lin Mu issued a public appeal to senior delegates to the congress urging them to introduce freedom of the press, publication and speech, a reversal of the official verdict on the June 1989 protests, and an end to one-party rule in China. A few days later, another dissident, Lin Xingshu, sent an open letter to congress delegates raising similar demands and stressing that the congress should serve as a platform for the public debate of urgent social issues. And when the former detainee Bao Ge petitioned the congress to show its opposition to "despotism and the cult of personality" by cremating the mummified corpse of Mao Zedong, his telephone line was cut off, and he was placed under intense police surveillance. Around the same time, supporters of ousted former party chief Zhao Ziyang issued an unprecedented appeal to government leaders calling for Zhao's release from eight years of house arrest ahead of the forthcoming congress. In the event, the congress made no discernible progress towards the introduction of democratic political reform.

Several dissidents and others jailed for exercising their rights to freedom of expression and association were freed during the year, mostly after having completed their prison terms in full. One of the most notable early releases was that of Xi Yang, a journalist on Hong Kong's *Ming Pao* newspaper who had been sentenced to twelve years of imprisonment in March 1994 for allegedly leaking state secrets in articles about the Chinese economy. His release in late January was an apparent gesture to Hong Kong public opinion in advance of the former British colony's return to Chinese sovereignty.

The releases in May of labor activists Tang Yuanjuan and Li Wei were also noteworthy. In a significant departure from previous judicial practice, the court authorities quashed one of the two principal counts ("organizing a counterrevolutionary group") on which the men had originally been convicted; the other main charge ("counterrevolutionary propaganda and incitement") was upheld, but the surprise move paved the way for the two dissidents' release from prison in July.

The year brought news of two unannounced releases that had occurred several years ago. Ding Junze, a fifty-five-year-old former lecturer in philosophy at Shanxi University, who had been serving a twelve-year prison term for his involvement in the 1989 prodemocracy movement, was released on medical parole in 1994. Suffering from high blood pressure, heart disease and arteriosclerosis, he reportedly had been close to death on several occasions over the past few years. Chen Zhixiang, a former teacher at the Guangzhou Maritime Transport Academy who had been sentenced to ten years in prison in 1990 for writing "reactionary" speeches and around the time of the June 1989 crackdown, was also released, apparently in 1996.

Dissidents freed from untried detention after completing their administrative sentences of labor reeducation in full included Zhang Lin, a labor-rights activist; Tong Yi, Wei Jingsheng's former secretary, who had suffered numerous harsh beatings at the hands of fellow prisoners during her incarceration in Wuhan; and Bao Ge, a founder of the unofficial Shanghai-based Association for Human Rights and a longtime campaigner for Japanese war reparations to China. Both described punishingly long hours of work in prison.

In August, Bao Tong, former chief aide to ousted party leader Zhao Ziyang, was finally released from de facto detention in a government compound in western Beijing to which he had been consigned immediately after his completion in May 1996 of a seven-year prison term imposed for his alleged role in the 1989 protests; Bao's freedom was made conditional upon his family agreeing to evacuate their government-supplied residence in central Beijing and relocate to a closely monitored apartment in the far western suburbs of the city.

In several reported cases, the authorities denied Chinese citizens the right to return to their own country, in violation of Article 13 of the Universal Declaration of Human Rights. The government appeared to have expanded an internal blacklist of overseas-based Chinese activists officially barred from reentering China. In April, Han Xiaorong, wife of exiled dissident Liu Qing, was refused permission by mainland immigration officials to enter China from Hong Kong. The following month, Hou Xiaotian, the wife of U.S.-based dissident Wang Juntao, was also denied entry to China from Hong Kong. Dissidents who did succeed in reentering China were subjected to various forms of harassment. The U.S.-based poet Bei Ling endured surveillance, detention and interrogation by the police; Liu Hongbin, a London-based poet, was expelled. In addition, numerous prodemocracy activists and politicians in Hong Kong, including leading members of the Democratic Party, continued to be denied permission to enter mainland China for any purpose.

A series of major protests by workers and other disaffected urban residents occurred during the year in a number of Chinese cities. The root cause appeared to be layoffs at state-owned enterprises that have left an estimated 25 percent of the urban industrial workforce (or roughly thirty million people) actually or effectively unemployed, compounded by the influx of as many as 130 million migrants from the countryside and the lack of a social security or welfare system.

In May, the official *Workers Daily* newspaper reported that "in theory" the urban unemployment rate stood at 24 percent, although the official unemployment rate in the cities was said to be in single digits. In October 1996, when the magazine *Chinese Writers* tried to publish its own unemployment figures, the magazine was promptly closed down by the authorities, and 100,000 copies of the issue were reportedly destroyed. According to several reports, internal decrees issued during 1997 ordered a media blackout on incidents of unauthorized labor unrest and reiterated a government ban on the formation of unofficial trade unions.

The most serious of large-scale worker demonstrations erupted in the first half of the year in a number of cities in Sichuan. Other provinces experienced similar unrest. In March, in Nanchong, more than 20,000 workers from the city's largest silk factory took the factory manager hostage, paraded him through the streets, and besieged the city government hall for thirty hours until local leaders pledged that the workers would be paid. Four of the demonstrating workers were detained, one of whom was reportedly released. Several weeks later, a large pipe bomb was exploded in the city hall by someone believed to be an unemployed worker. (The same month, unemployed workers were officially blamed for setting off bombs on two buses in central Beijing, injuring around a dozen people.)

In July, upwards of 4,000 workers from three bankrupt textile plants in the city of Mianyang, Sichuan, staged a demonstration outside the city government office, demanding jobs. When city officials refused to meet with the workers, the protests became more heated and the government sent in People's Armed Police officers to break up the gathering. Several dozen demonstrators were reportedly injured in the ensuing confrontation, and a similar number of arrests were made. The following month, in the Sichuan city of Dujiangyan, a crowd of several hundred demonstrators, comprising both unemployed workers and retired elderly people who had not received their pensions or were demanding overdue cost-of-living increases, staged a sit-in protest outside the government offices for several days. Meanwhile, Li Bifeng, a former tax officer who had faxed reports about the protests to overseas human rights groups and sent appeals to the central authorities in Beijing, went into hiding in late July after learning that the security authorities were searching for him. Li's girlfriend, Zhang Jian, and two of his other friends were detained and interrogated several times by the police in an attempt to ascertain his whereabouts. Zhang was released after three days.

In May, when laid-off workers from the Zhongyuan Oilfield in Henan province reportedly organized an unofficial union and sent delegates to Beijing to plead their case, the delegates disappeared and were feared to have been arrested, with no further word on their fate.

Freedom of expression and association remained tightly constrained. In January, the Ministry of Civil Affairs imposed an indefinite nationwide moratorium on the creation or registering of any new "social bodies," a broad and inclusive category encompassing all non-governmental organizations as well as academic societies, business associations and social pressure groups.

The government devoted particular attention to controlling organized religious activities. Local officials redoubled their efforts to implement regulations issued by the government in 1994 requiring all "unofficial" Christian, Muslim, Daoist, Buddhist, and other religious congregations to register with the Religious Affairs Bureau or face dissolution. In December 1996, some eighty members of the underground Catholic church near Linchuan city in Jiangxi province were reportedly detained, beaten and fined by the police, apparently in an attempt to dissuade them from carrying out plans to hold a large outdoor mass at Christmas. Around the same time, CCP officials in Jiangxi reportedly issued an internal directive on registering such persons and forcing them to write letters denying their faith and pledging to join the official church. Similarly, an internal document issued by the authorities in Zhejiang province's Tongxiang municipality in February 1997 outlined a three-stage "special campaign" against all unauthorized religious activities by local Christians, including Catholics. A new requirement that all religious groups and organizations undergo annual government inspections was instituted during the year.

In March, eight public security officers conducted a night-time raid at the home of Bishop Joseph Fan Zhongliang, leader of the city's underground Catholic diocese, and confiscated Bibles, medals, rosaries and cash amounting to 20,000 *yuan* (around U.S. $2,500); no receipt was issued, and the goods and money were subsequently not returned. The following month, police ransacked the home of another local underground Catholic priest, Rev. Zen Caijun, and seized religious articles, cash, a telephone and a video-recorder.

In April, eight Protestant house-church leaders, including Peter Xu Yongze, leader of the Zhengzhou-based "Born Again" evangelical group, were detained by police in Henan province after a meeting. On September 25, the Zhengzhou Intermediate Court reportedly sentenced Xu to a ten-year term for "disturbing public order." The sentence is believed to be the longest meted out to a religious dissident since 1983.

In November 1996, a peasant named Jiang Fenglan and other prominent members of a Sichuan-based chapter of the Asia-wide sect devoted to the worship of a charismatic woman known as the "Qinghai Master" were arrested; by the end of the year, there had been no further word on the detained sectarians.

Freedom of expression suffered further assaults. New government press regulations introduced in February stipulated that publishing houses were forbidden to publish anything that opposed China's constitution, revealed "state secrets," "harmed national security," or jeopardized "socialist public morality or the people's fine cultural traditions." New controls on the Internet were introduced in June, requiring all Internet service providers to apply for licenses from the authorities and provide data on the scope and nature of their activities. Meanwhile, dozens of World Wide Web sites that had been proscribed and electronically blocked by the government in 1996, including those of overseas-based dissident groups and human rights organizations, remained inaccessible to the country's estimated several hundred thousand Internet users. Also in June, academics in Beijing were ordered to inform the police in advance if they planned to hold conferences attended by more than twenty participants, in or out of the capital, and scholars wishing to engage in exchange programs or joint activities with foreign and Taiwanese institutions were required to secure prior permission from the Ministry of State Security, the Ministry of Public Security and the State Education Commission, in addition to that from their college party committees.

Censorship of books continued, the most notable being *Wrath of Heaven,* a novel by Chen Fang that was a thinly disguised fictionalized account of the saga of disgraced former mayor of Beijing, Chen Xitong, charged with corruption.

The human rights picture in Inner Mongolia, Xinjiang and Tibet remained bleak. On February 5 and 6, the city of Yining in northwestern Xinjiang was shaken by large-scale riots after local people tried to prevent police from arresting an ethnic Uighur. Uighurs, a predominantly Muslim people, form the core of several separatist movements in Xinjiang. The authorities responded by sending in armed police to quell the protests. According to official reports, ten people were killed, 198 injured, and about 500 were arrested. (Exiled Uighur opposition sources claimed far higher figures.) On the afternoon of February 25, at least three homemade bombs exploded on crowded public buses in the regional capital of Urumqi, killing nine people. The Chinese authorities later blamed these incidents on "outside instigation" by foreign radical Muslim groups, in particular by the Pakistan-

based "Tableeghi Jamaat" sect. An underlying factor, however, was rising tension over dominance by Han Chinese of what was formerly a Uighur majority region, home in 1944 to the short-lived Republic of East Turkestan. The collapse of Communism in Eastern Europe and the subsequent emergence of the independent republics of Kazakhstan, Kyrgyzstan and Tajikistan gave considerable impetus to pro-independence sentiment in Xinjiang.

Few details have come to light regarding the many Uighurs reportedly arrested in the crackdown that followed the incidents described above. Those known include: Abudu Heilili, twenty-nine, reportedly the "ringleader" of the Yining riots; Abu Khair and Abdu Medchit, both said to be students and around twenty-five years old; and Abdukhalil Abdulmedchit, whom Uighur exiles claimed had swiftly been executed by the authorities. In late March, the Urumqi People's Procuratorate announced that nine people had been arrested in connection with the incidents, including one ethnic Han and eight Uighurs, and the group included people who had allegedly sold and supplied weapons and explosives to the separatist groups concerned. Reuters news agency reported that three men were executed in April and twenty-seven others had been sentenced to prison terms ranging from seven years to life, and that another eight were executed in May in connection with the Urumqi bus bombings.

In response to the unrest, the government carried out a major purge of local officials and targeted "underground" Muslim religious activities, including banning the construction or renovation of 133 mosques. Altogether forty-four "core participants in illegal religious activities" were arrested in the Yili region. In addition, more than one hundred "illegal classes" teaching the Koran were broken up by security authorities, five school principals were sacked and numerous teachers threatened with dismissal for allegedly stirring up separatist sentiment.

In Inner Mongolia, two Inner Mongolian activists, Hada and Tegexi, were sentenced to fifteen and ten years of imprisonment respectively for helping to form the pro-autonomy Southern Mongolian Democratic Alliance.

In Tibet, a government-orchestrated campaign against the Dalai Lama continued throughout the year. In mid-April 1997, the party school in Tibet announced a meeting had been held to "expose the crimes" of the Tibetan leader. A ban on possession and sale of photographs of the Dalai Lama continued to be in force.

The campaign included a reeducation program for monks and nuns. Beginning in 1996 at Tibet's three most famous monasteries, Sera, Drepung, and Ganden, it had reached some fifty monasteries and nunneries by June and over 900 by September. Monks were supposed to denounce the Dalai Lama, accept that Tibet had been a part of China for centuries, and acknowledge the legitimacy of the Chinese government's selection of the new Panchen Lama, or resign.

Monks who refused to cooperate with reeducation officials faced punishment. In Gongkar county, Jampel Tendar, a twenty-year-old from Choede monastery, was arrested during the year after several monks refused to denounce the Dalai Lama in writing. In Nyemo county monks were locked in their rooms for at least three weeks for their intransigence, and in Tsethang county, Tandruk Samdrubling monks walked out *en masse* on June 18 after reeducation began. Refusing to comply with instructions to denounce the Dalai Lama, they opted to close the monastery and go home. At Terdrom nunnery in the Drigung area, some fifty miles northeast of Lhasa, over half the 240 residents nuns were expelled after reeducation ended in December 1996.

The issue of the Panchen Lama (*see* World Report 1997) remained unresolved. The Chinese government finally acknowledged that Chadrel Rinpoche, the abbot who had headed the committee to select the child later acknowledged by the Dalai Lama to be the reincarnation of the tenth Panchen Lama,

had been sentenced on April 21, 1997 to a six-year term and three years' subsequent deprivation of political rights. He was charged with "conspiring to split the country," "colluding with separatist forces abroad," "seriously jeopardizing the national unification and unity of ethnic groups," and "leaking state secrets." Authorities did not disclose his whereabouts, and his trial was closed because "state secrets" were involved.

It was not until September 9, 1997 that Human Rights in China reported that Chadrel Rinpoche was being held under horrendous conditions in a secret compound in Chuangdong No. 3 Prison, Dazu county, Sichuan province. Located behind an isolated "strict observation brigade," as the special section which houses recalcitrant prisoners is called, it is forbidden to all but three people, two commissars who report directly to the Ministry of Justice and a prisoner who acts as a guard and a cook. Chadrel Rinpoche was reportedly taken there shortly after sentencing. He is reported to be denied all outside contacts and to be restricted to his cell.

The child selected as the Panchen Lama, Gendun Choekyi Nyima, now eight years old, remains in state custody in an undisclosed location.

A comprehensive revision of the 1979 Criminal Law had little immediate impact on the human rights situation. Counterrevolutionary offenses abolished by the NPC in March were merely replaced by a new, largely identical set of offenses called "crimes of endangering state security." The changes opened the way for virtually any type of dissident activity to be judicially branded as criminal and those responsible sentenced to terms of up to life imprisonment. Nor would the reforms result in any kind of review of the cases of more than 2,000 sentenced "counterrevolutionaries" still officially said to be held behind bars in China.

The implementation in January of a revised Criminal Procedure Law (CPL), enacted by the NPC at its previous session in March 1996, somewhat strengthened the rights of suspects on paper but brought little in the way of enhanced legal safeguards for the rights of detained dissidents. Announcements by the government during the year that it planned to maintain the country's system of "reeducation through labor" ended hopes for an end to the use of such arbitrary forms of detention in China.

In July, the Ministry of Public Security called for teams of inspectors to be set up at all levels of China's police force to investigate the endemic problem of torture and ill-treatment in the country's prison and detention facilities.

The nationwide anti-crime campaign known as "Strike Hard" resulted in the highest number of judicial executions (more than 4,000) and suspended death sentences since the first such campaign in 1983.

The government's chief response to continuing foreign criticism of the conditions in state orphanages was to continue to restrict access for foreign volunteers and aid agencies. It also announced that rather than allocating any additional state funds toward the upkeep of these institutions, it would seek to raise money from the public through a state-sponsored charitable lottery.

Virtually the only bright spot on China's human rights front were the release of Wei Jinsheng and its signing of the U.N. International Covenant on Social, Economic and Cultural Rights in October. The undertaking did not include any pledge to ratify the covenant, however, thus relieving the Chinese government of becoming legally bound by its provisions.

The Right to Monitor

No independent human rights advocacy organizations were allowed to operate in China or Tibet. In September, China prevented two nongovernmental organizations highly critical of its human rights record, Human Rights in China and the Hong Kong Human Rights Monitor, from attending the annual meeting of the World Bank in Hong Kong by denying them accreditation on the grounds that their work was not relevant.

The emergence of quasi-nongovernmental organizations on the mainland, some of them dealing with women's rights and community empowerment, continued, although such groups were subject to strict surveillance. They did not monitor human rights abuses by the government.

A meeting between the International Committee of the Red Cross (ICRC) and Chinese officials took place in May, resuming long-stalled negotiations over access to Chinese prisons, although China continued to maintain that it could not accept the ICRC's conditions for such access.

The Role of the International Community

China escaped serious international pressure on its human rights record during the year, with its key trading partners continuing either to trade silence on human rights for commercial contracts or to express concern that too much emphasis on rights would lessen their leverage on security issues.

United Nations

By delaying a final decision on sponsoring a resolution on China at the U.N. Commission on Human Rights until after U.S. Vice-President Albert Gore Jr. visited China in late March, the Clinton administration joined the European Union (E.U.) in handing China another major victory at the commission's meeting in Geneva. China succeeded in splitting the E.U., normally the lead sponsors of a resolution, by promising to sign contracts with French companies and the Airbus consortium during a visit by President Jacques Chirac in May. France was joined by Germany, Spain, Italy and Greece in failing to sponsor the resolution. When President Chirac went to Beijing, he reportedly raised the cases of seventeen political dissidents, although their names were never made public, and he was praised by Jiang Zemin for the "wise and far-sighted" decision to sabotage action in Geneva. The Chinese authorities also persuaded other key governments such as Japan, Canada and Australia to abandon their sponsorship in exchange for bilateral human rights "dialogues" and a promise to sign the International Covenant on Economic, Social and Cultural Rights before the end of the year. The Chinese government signed the covenant in late October. Denmark, under U.S. pressure, put forward a measure at the last minute despite threats of trade retaliation by China. However, a Chinese no-action motion was adopted (27 to 17) on April 16, keeping the resolution off the agenda and preventing a debate or vote.

In October, the U.N. Working Group on Arbitrary Detention visited China.

United States, European Union, and Canada

In addition to defeating a resolution at the U.N. Commission on Human Rights, President Jiang Zemin scored a huge diplomatic triumph as the first Chinese leader to be hosted for a state visit to Washington since the June 1989 crackdown. The late October summit went forward without any human rights preconditions although human rights concerns were clearly addressed privately and publicly by President Clinton. President Clinton announced plans to visit China in 1998. Jiang Zemin was also scheduled to visit Canada for a state visit in late November, in conjunction with the Asia-Pacific Economic Cooperation (APEC) forum in Vancouver.

The U.S. State Department's annual report on human rights practices, issued on January 30, declared that in 1996 "all public dissent against the government and the party was effectively silenced" in China. This was preceded by a stunning admission by President Clinton in a nationally televised news conference that his "constructive engagement" policy had failed to produce any significant human rights progress.

Vice-President Gore's visit to China was largely a wasted opportunity to press for concrete rights improvements. Gore signed $685 million worth of contracts for Boeing Corporation in a high-profile ceremony with Premier Li Peng while saying nothing publicly about human rights and bypassing Hong Kong altogether just months before the July 1 handover. Following his meetings, Gore proclaimed that China's leaders had "a more

receptive ear" to concerns about human rights and cautioned that results might take time.

International concern during the first half of the year was mostly focused on Hong Kong, and the Group of Eight (G8) leaders of industrialized nations at their summit meeting in Denver on June 20-23 did include in their final communique an appeal to China to fulfil its promises to protect Hong Kong's "fundamental freedoms and the rule of law" after July 1. However, the G8 failed to discuss or adopt any long-term strategy for promoting human rights and the rule of law in China during the crucial post-Deng Xiaoping transition.

Just weeks before the July 1 handover, a report of Wei Jingsheng's beating by other inmates provoked expressions of concern by some officials, including U.S. Secretary of State Albright, who met with Chinese Foreign Minister Qian in Hong Kong. Other governments, including Japan, were silent.

U.S. Congressional concern was also focused on the President's decision to renew Most Favored Nation (MFN) trading status. A coalition of religious and labor groups led a campaign for revocation of MFN. But the debate, focused on a broad range of issues including religious persecution, China's family planning practices, and repression in Tibet, was countered by a business and a White House-led lobbying effort to maintain unconditional MFN. A House motion of disapproval, to revoke MFN, was defeated (259 to 175) on June 24.

In mid-July, the first of a series of human rights exchanges between China and Canada took place in Ottawa. A combined Ministry of Justice and Foreign Ministry delegation discussed a wide range of concerns, including political prisoners and treatment of minorities, but made no new commitments. A second session was scheduled for Beijing in October.

A parliamentary delegation from Germany visited Tibet in late August and was given a guided tour of detention centers and monasteries.

On September 22, foreign ministers of the E.U. *troika* (from the United Kingdom,

Netherlands and Luxembourg) met with Chinese Foreign Minister Qian Qichen at the U.N. in New York and agreed to resume the E.U.-China human rights dialogue, with talks scheduled to take place in Brussels. The question of E.U. sponsorship of a 1998 resolution in Geneva next year was left unresolved. However, during its October session the European Parliament passed an urgent resolution urging E.U. member states to jointly sponsor a China resolution in Geneva.

Asia

Australian Prime Minister John Howard's visit to China in late March focused almost exclusively on solidifying commercial relations. He was accompanied by a large business delegation. In mid-August, Australian Foreign Minister Alexander Downer went to Beijing for four days of talks on human rights issues and pledged $300,000 (Australian dollars) to support "policy development, research, training and administrative resources" for China's criminal and judicial systems. Downer also urged ICRC access to Chinese prisons.

Japan's prime minister, Ryutaro Hashimoto, visited China in early September, mainly to promote Japanese investment and stable diplomatic relations. Hashimoto raised concern about human rights with Premier Li Peng and other leaders only in the most general terms in the context of "global issues." The trip ended with no date set for the first Sino-Japanese bilateral dialogue on human rights, agreed to when Foreign Minister Yukihiko Ikeda went to Beijing on March 30, and Tokyo said it would drop its cosponsorship of the Geneva resolution.

The World Bank

The World Bank, in a prominent report on China's future economic development issued at the opening of its annual meeting in Hong Kong in late September, warned that continued growth would be hindered by the lack of the rule of law and by corruption. But the bank in 1997 gave more funds to China than any other government; during fiscal year 1997 China received a total of $2.8 billion in World Bank loans. Legislation introduced in the U.S. Congress aimed to cut off China's access to multilateral funds, but absent a coordinated effort with other donors, passage of such a law was unlikely to produce any change in current bank policy.

Relevant Human Rights Watch reports:

State Control of Religion in China, 10/97
"State Security" in China's New Criminal Code, 4/97
Chinese Diplomacy, Western Hypocrisy and the United Nations, 3/97

HONG KONG

The transfer of sovereignty over Hong Kong from Britain to China on July 1 and the installation of the new Special Administrative Region (S.A.R.) government were arguably the most important events in the territory's history, but the political changes produced no dramatic crackdowns, no arrests, and no bans on demonstrations by late October. Journalists pointed to many instances of self-censorship on the part of their editors, but the S.A.R. government itself did not censor the print or broadcast media. The worrisome changes were almost all on the legal front, where China's concerns about security and stability took precedence over civil rights protections. Tung Chee-hwa, a businessman appointed S.A.R. chief executive in December 1996, showed himself to be a proponent of the "Asian values" school of thought and in August, he endorsed Malaysian Prime Minister Mahathir's suggestion that the Universal Declaration of Human Rights be reviewed.

Human Rights Developments

Assaults on the legal foundation of civil liberties proceeded steadily throughout the year. In December 1996, the Preparatory Committee, a body handpicked by China to handle transition matters, authorized the appointment of a provisional legislature that was to remain in place for one year. The appointed body replaced the elected Legislative Council (Legco) on July 1, but it in fact began meeting in China long before then.

In early 1997, the Preparatory Committee submitted proposals to China's National People's Congress (NPC) to repeal or amend twenty-four Hong Kong laws, on the grounds that they had been passed after the 1984 Sino-British Joint Declaration had been signed and were therefore in violation of the Basic Law, the document that has become the S.A.R. constitution. Among the laws affected were several provisions of Hong Kong's Bill of Rights, adopted in 1991, and two British colonial laws, the Societies Ordinance and the Public Order Ordinance, that had been amended after 1991 to bring them into conformity with the Bill of Rights. The Bill of Rights had been adopted in an attempt to ensure that the provisions of the International Covenant on Civil and Political Rights (ICCPR) were implemented in Hong Kong; the repealed section, arguably the most important part of the bill, gave the bill's guarantees of rights precedence over past and future Hong Kong laws that might be in conflict with them.

The proposed changes generated strong opposition in Hong Kong. On February 19, a Legislative Council motion, endorsed by both the Democratic and Liberal parties, urged the NPC not to accept the proposals. On February 26, however, the NPC approved them.

The proposed amendments of the Societies and Public Order Ordinances would have made it possible for the S.A.R. to ban demonstrations or dissolve associations on broadly defined political grounds in the interests of "national security." After a much-publicized "consultation" process through which Tung Chee-hwa invited public comment on the laws, some of the most egregious provisions in the draft were dropped. But even in their final form as passed by the provisional legislature on June 14, the laws have disturbing elements.

Whereas, before, groups organizing protests had merely to notify the police of their plans, they now must receive permission from the police, which may be denied in the interests of national security. On July 18, the commissioner of police issued a document titled "Guidelines on 'National Security' in the Public Order Ordinance" in which he cited "advocacy of independence for Taiwan or Tibet" as grounds for refusing permission to demonstrate.

Likewise, in the final version of the Societies Ordinance, the government can deny registration to a society; before it was passed, societies simply had to notify the government of their formation to have a legal existence. "National security" is again grounds for denying registration, and societies deemed to be "political organizations" are barred from receiving funds from abroad. The consultation process did result in narrowing some of the definitions used. "Political organization," for example, was defined to mean only those organizations which put up candidates for election to public office.

In the final days of the elected legislature, the British administration pushed a heavily opposed Official Secrets Ordinance through the Legislative Council on June 4, 1997, a day when most members of the pro-democracy parties were absent commemorating the anniversary of the Tiananmen crackdown. The government argued that such a law was needed to "localize" colonial legislation into domestic law and to satisfy the requirements of key provisions of the Basic Law. The resulting act, modeled on much-criticized British legislation, criminalizes a broad range of activity, such as being "in the neighborhood of...a prohibited place" for "a purpose prejudicial to the safety or interests" of Hong Kong. It is not even necessary to show that the act did in fact jeopardize Hong Kong's interests if the "known character" of the accused would indicate that such was his or her intention. The law does not allow certain common defenses for the disclosure of official information, such as prior publication of the information.

On July 16, the provisional legislature suspended four labor laws passed by the elected legislature in the days leading up to the handover. The laws would have brought Hong Kong into compliance with standards set by the International Labour Organisation. They explicitly guaranteed the right to union representation and collective bargaining, the right to conduct union activity on an employer's premises, and the right to be compensated for union work done during the course of the normal work day. The laws had also altered previous legislation restrictive of union sovereignty and would have allowed unions to act without governmental approval on certain internal issues. Three and a half months later, in late October, the Provisional Legislative Council would move to dismiss much of the legislation entirely, voting to remove the suspended legislation on collective bargaining and anti-union discrimination.

The continued independence of the courts remained cause for concern, although that concern was somewhat eased by the appointment in late May of Andrew Li, a widely respected barrister, as head of the Court of Final Appeal, the S.A.R.'s highest court.

But in mid-July, in the case of *Ma Wai Kwan*, the Hong Kong Court of Appeals made a landmark decision on the legality of the provisional legislature that seemed to give license to China's legislature to violate Hong Kong's Basic Law at will. A criminal defendant had argued that laws and indictments in force prior to the transfer no longer existed, because the provisional legislature had provided for their continuation and the legislature itself was in violation of the Basic Law. In ruling against the defendant, the court acknowledged that the provisional legislature was nowhere described by the Basic Law but opined that Hong Kong courts could not judge it illegal because it was established by a body authorized by the NPC. S.A.R. courts, the court said, had no power to examine either the decisions or institutions created by the NPC.

Finally, under the terms of new voting laws presented to the public on August 15, two-thirds of the legislature's sixty seats are to be filled by "functional constituencies," many with a heavy business and corporate focus. The remainder are to be elected not through the "one person, one vote" system that allowed pro-democracy candidates to sweep the polls in the 1995 elections, but in one of two possible systems, variations on proportional representation, that would reduce the number of seats held by the most popular pro-democracy groups.

In early September, Andrew Li and Lord Irvine, Britain's lord Chancellor, met to discuss possible British assistance to the Hong Kong judiciary, and it was announced on September 8 that two British judges would be made available to the Court of Final Appeal.

In April, the outgoing government allowed Human Rights Watch and the Hong Kong Human Rights Monitor to conduct the first-ever international investigation of the territory's prison system. The investigation was undertaken as a way of establishing benchmarks against which to measure changes that might take place after the transition. (Given China's notoriously poor prison conditions and its frequent use of capital punishment, some of Hong Kong's 12,000 prisoners expressed grave apprehensions regarding their treatment under Chinese rule.) In light of these concerns, the investigation was also meant to establish a precedent of independent monitoring of the territory's prisons, to encourage future monitoring. In general, the delegation found the prisons to be administered by an extremely competent and professional staff, the physical infrastructure to be in very good shape, and the prisons themselves to be relatively safe and secure. On the negative side, the delegation found that many of the prisons were seriously overcrowded and the controls on contact with the outside world were unnecessarily stringent.

Human rights groups had raised concerns during the year about two particularly vulnerable groups, Chinese dissidents who had fled to Hong Kong, and Vietnamese asylum-seekers who remained in detention camps in Hong Kong. All of the dissidents at risk who wished to leave Hong Kong were successfully resettled in third countries before the reversion. In the case of the Vietnamese, the determination of both the Hong Kong government and the United Nations High Commissioner for Refugees (UNHCR) to respond to Chinese pressure to get all of the boat-people home before July 1 led to a single-minded focus on repatriation efforts and an effort to "push" the Vietnamese out by making conditions in the camps increasingly intolerable.

Some 525 stateless ethnic Chinese formerly resident in Vietnam, whom the Vietnamese government refused to take back on the grounds that they were not Vietnamese citizens, remained in Hong Kong as of October. All either had fled Vietnam in the late 1970s during an anti-Chinese campaign— their family members had Taiwanese passports after 1949—or had fled to mainland China at various times and had been refused entry.

The Right to Monitor

No human rights organizations based in Hong Kong, domestic or international, reported significant hindrance of their activities, either before or after the handover. A policy institute linked to Paul Yip, a close adviser of Tung Chee-hwa, did conduct a survey of nongovernmental (NGOs) early in the year, however, asking for information on legal status and sources of funding. It was not clear how the results of the survey were going to be used.

In September, two NGOs, the Hong Kong Human Rights Monitor and Human Rights in China, were denied accreditation to the World Bank annual meeting in Hong Kong at China's request. China had argued that the organizations' work had no relevance to the meeting.

The Role of
the International Community

So much concern was expressed internationally about the transition that there was little for the international community to say or do in the immediate aftermath of July 1. The U.S. government repeatedly criticized the rollback of civil liberties in strong terms and said it would not consider "legitimate" any laws passed by the provisional legislature. In March, the U.S. House of Representatives adopted the 1997 Hong Kong Reversion Act, augmenting the U.S.-Hong Kong Policy Act of 1992, spelling out additional benchmarks and reporting requirements to determine whether the S.A.R. is "sufficiently autonomous" to justify separate treatment by the U.S. As of October the Senate had not taken up the bill.

In June, leaders of eight major industrialized nations meeting in Denver, Colorado, included an appeal to China in their final communique, urging it to meet its commitments to protect Hong Kong's "fundamental freedoms and the rule of law."

In a final pre-handover report, the British government repeated its position that replacing the elected legislature was entirely unnecessary and reaffirmed the need for continued monitoring of the situation.

The transition was watched closely around the world. Most countries sent high-level officials to observe the ceremonies surrounding the July handover, but both U.S. Secretary of State Madeleine Albright and British Prime Minister Tony Blair refused to attend the swearing-in ceremony of the provisional legislature, in protest of the dissolution of the elected Legco.

Tung Chee-hwa visited the U.S. in September. President Clinton, following a brief meeting with Tung on September 12, expressed his "disappointment" at the decision to reverse Hong Kong's legislative electoral reforms. Earlier in the year, Clinton had also met with Martin Lee, head of the Democratic Party in Hong Kong. Many members of Congress and senior State Department officials who saw Tung remained unconvinced that the changes in the electoral laws were warranted or necessary.

Japan generally refrained from public criticism of the changes in civil liberties laws or the abolition of the elected legislature. It did state firmly that it would not tolerate a severe crackdown in Hong Kong along the lines of the Tiananmen Square killings of

1989, although such a crackdown was generally considered unlikely in the immediate future.

Relevant Human Rights Watch reports:
Hong Kong: Prison Conditions in 1997, 6/97

INDIA

Preoccupied with its own political survival, India's United Front (UF) government made little progress in advancing human rights in 1997. Although India signed the Convention against Torture and other Cruel, Inhuman or Degrading Treatment or Punishment in October, the U.N. special rapporteur on torture in a 1997 report noted with regret "the reluctance of the government to invite him to visit the country." India's long-delayed report on compliance with the International Covenant on Civil and Political Rights (ICCPR) also downplayed a number of serious violations, and India was one of the most prominent nations to state that it would not sign a new global treaty banning the use of anti-personnel mines.

Military operations against insurgent groups in Jammu and Kashmir and India's northeast resulted in many of the worst abuses, as federal forces engaged in extrajudicial executions and torture, and armed opposition groups carried out attacks on civilians. Outside these areas of conflict, the most serious abuses were the result of local police practices that had the sanction of state officials. Deaths in police custody and custodial abuse remained a major problem throughout the country. Police also threatened and assaulted human rights activists and routinely beat and jailed demonstrators protesting against development projects. They were also complicit in incidents of communal violence against low-caste or tribal activists. On a positive note, a December 1996 Supreme Court ruling marked a serious step forward in enforcing laws banning bonded labor. Following a shake-up in India's United Front coalition government in May, Prime Minister H. H. Deve Gowda was replaced by Indrajit Gujral, whose reputation for promoting better relations with neighboring countries raised hopes for a rapprochement with Pakistan. By year's end, however, there had been no major breakthrough in relations between the two countries, and artillery exchanges across the border had resulted in a number of civilian casualties.

Human Rights Developments
The restoration of an elected government in Jammu and Kashmir in October 1996 did not translate into improved human rights conditions. Three human rights groups who conducted a fact-finding mission in June documented a large number of extrajudicial executions that had occurred in the year since Farooq Abdullah's government took power. In one case in early March, suspected militants Mohammed Yusuf Ganai, Manzoor Ahmad Khan, Firdous Ahmad Kirmani, and Abdul Majid Wani were killed in custody by the Special Operations Group (SOG) of the Jammu and Kashmir state police. On October 27 the bodies of two teenaged boys who had been detained by the SOG in Srinagar on August 5 were exhumed in Pampore, some twenty miles south of the city. State-sponsored paramilitary groups working with Indian security forces also committed serious human rights abuses. Imtiyaz Ahmed Wani, a hospital employee, reportedly died in police custody in May after he was abducted by members of the pro-government militia, Muslim Brotherhood (Ikhwan-ul-Muslimoon). Wani had organized a protest against army harassment of medical employees the day of his abduction.

Indian human rights groups also documented an increase in reports of rape by Indian troops. In one incident, members of an Indian army unit, the Rajputana Rifles, reportedly raped six women in the village of Wawoosa on the night of April 22-23. The women, whose ages ranged from about thirteen to thirty, filed a complaint with the police on April 24, but the latter declined to register a case, according to human rights activists who interviewed five of the women. After the local community protested, the state government and army initiated a joint investigation. As of October, no findings had been made public.

On August 8, the Jammu and Kashmir state government appointed a human rights commission to investigate complaints of abuse but gave it no jurisdiction over the army or other federal forces. Although the government claimed to have prosecuted security personnel in a number of human rights cases, it continued to refuse to make public the nature of both the abuses and the punishments, despite requests by human rights groups that it do so.

Abuses by militant groups in Kashmir also continued. On March 21, seven Hindu villagers in Sangrampora were murdered by a militant group which reportedly had close links to Pakistan. On October 31 a car bomb in Srinagar killed three and injured at least thirty. On March 29, a car bomb in Jammu killed sixteen civilians and injured more than seventy. Militants also assassinated members of the state's governing National Conference party and other officials. In Punjab, Sikh separatist groups launched a number of surprise attacks. One of the bloodiest occurred on July 8 when an unidentified militant group detonated a bomb on a train in the state, killing at least thirty-eight passengers.

Civilians continued to be victims of Indian military operations against armed opposition groups seeking autonomy in India's northeastern states. Security forces, who were granted extraordinary powers under the Armed Forces (Special Powers) Act, engaged in arbitrary arrests and detentions, extrajudicial executions and torture, including rape. On the night of February 8, 1997, Junmoni Hangique, sixteen, sister of a member of the armed opposition United Liberation Front of Assam (ULFA), was reportedly raped by officers from the 79th Sikh regiment. The family filed charges, but as of October, none of the officers had been prosecuted.

Armed opposition groups in turn carried out attacks on security personnel and government officials and engaged in arbitrary killings of noncombatants. Bodo separatists in Assam were accused of train bombings that killed over one hundred civilians in 1997. Armed opposition groups in Assam, Tripura and Manipur were all accused of attacks on villagers of rival ethnic groups. Kidnapping and extortion also remained hallmarks of militant operations in the region; managers and laborers on tea estates were particular targets. In August, police in Assam began an unprecedented crackdown on persons thought to be providing logistic or financial support to ULFA, and charged senior tea industry executives with supporting ULFA through the payment of protection money.

A three-month cease-fire between Indian forces and the National Socialist Council of Nagaland (Isak-Muivah) (NSCN-IM) went into force in Nagaland on August 1. It was later unilaterally extended to other Naga groups but did not include Manipur. Despite the truce, the chief minister of Nagaland, S.C. Jamir, and former government ministers Rajesh Pilot and Pawan Singh Ghatowar were the targets of a September 27 assassination attempt when unidentified gunmen fired at their convoy near the town of Kohima.

Progress in prosecuting police responsible for abuses in some states was offset by official indifference or endorsement of abuse in others. In Punjab, the courts continued to hear evidence in cases of custodial torture, killings and "disappearances" by senior police officers. Prosecutions of senior officers continued despite protests by police following the suicide in June of Superintendent Ajit Singh Sandhu, who had been charged in a number of human rights cases. As of October, cases were pending against 123 police officers.

In October forty-three policemen in Uttar Pradesh were indicted in connection with the 1996 murder of two young men. In Maharashtra, meanwhile, state Home Minister Gopinath Munde vowed that a policy of "encounters," that is, extrajudicial executions, would be followed to restore law and order. Human rights groups documented a surge in police "encounter" killings of suspected criminals in the Maharashtra state capital, Bombay. On July 10, India's official National Human Rights Commission (NHRC) issued a notice to the Maharashtra director-general of police asking for information on the increase in encounter killings in Bombay. In July, Bombay police opened fire on low-caste protesters who had organized a demonstration against discriminatory state policies, killing ten.

A reported increase in deaths in juvenile custodial facilities prompted the NHRC to launch a nationwide investigation in May. In an attempt to address increasing complaints of custodial violence, on August 10 the NHRC announced that it would initiate visits to police lock-ups throughout the country.

Detention of persons under the notorious Terrorist and Disruptive Practices (Prevention) Act (TADA) continued for offenses allegedly committed before the law lapsed in 1995—a practice that authorities have reportedly abused through the spurious backdating of violations. Those detained joined more than 3,000 TADA detainees who were held under a provision authorizing their continued detention, even though the law itself was no longer in force.

Police in Maharashtra arrested and beat demonstrators protesting against the construction of the Dabhol power plant, a joint venture involving U.S.-based multinational corporations. Protesters were held for periods ranging from five to ten days, apparently in an effort to prevent further demonstrations of dissent. Women and young girls were reportedly singled out for arrest. In June, some one hundred demonstrators staging a peaceful protest against a World Bank-financed power project in Singrauli, Orissa, were beaten and detained by police.

On December 10, 1996, India's Supreme Court reached a landmark decision aimed at freeing child laborers from hazardous industries by promoting compulsory education through the creation of a trust fund from employers and the government. It also recommended a program of job replacement aimed at providing jobs to adult family members instead of children. The decision had broad implications for India's bonded child laborers, estimated to number about fifteen million or from one-fourth to one-eighth of the total child labor force. Under the court's plan, offending employers were to be fined for each child worker, and the funds collected would be used for the child's education and welfare. Employers would remain liable to contribute to the fund even if they dismissed their child workers.

In another ruling on December 11, 1996, the Supreme Court prohibited shrimp farming along coastlines protected under India's environmental laws. The ruling served as an indictment of the shrimp industry and effectively put an end to abuses by shrimp company employees and the local police who had engaged in beatings and arrests of local villagers and activists organizing protests against the shrimp farms.

In accordance with the 1993 Chemical Weapons Convention, India acknowledged that it possessed chemical weapons, but declined to make public any information about its program.

The Right to Monitor

Human rights groups who operated in major cities or enjoyed an international reputation continued to operate fairly freely, although some were obstructed from investigating specific incidents of abuse. For example, in June, members of the Committee for Initiative on Kashmir were prevented from visiting Pahalgam, the site of widespread abuses by Indian troops.

A pattern of state-tolerated intimidation against civil liberties lawyers and other political activists continued in Andhra Pradesh, where the state government has been engaged in a longstanding conflict with armed Maoist groups collectively known as Naxalites. In April and May a group calling itself the "Green Tigers"—a reportedly fictitious name used by a police counter-insurgency unit—claimed responsibility for assaults on two senior members of the Andhra Pradesh Civil Liberties Committee (APCLC) and a protest singer, and threatened to attack four other prominent civil liberties activists. In June, the Andhra Pradesh government ordered state colleges and universities to take disciplinary action against any academic with ties to APCLC. Several universities responded by sending letters to APCLC office holders ordering them to disassociate themselves from the human rights group.

In September, a police official entered the offices of the South Asia Human Rights Documentation Centre (SAHRC) in New Delhi and questioned the director, Ravi Nair, about the group's activities. When Nair requested that the official provide proper identification, he left. Subsequently, Nair received a call from the deputy commissioner of police who threatened to arrest Nair and give him "special treatment" if he did not cooperate.

In October, R. N. Kumar, an activist from the Committee for Initiative and Action in Punjab, received anonymous death threats over the telephone. Kumar had been instrumental in bringing about investigations into the "disappearances" of over 980 people in Punjab between 1984 and 1994. Also in October, Babloo Singh Loitongbam of the Committee on Human Rights in Manipur was interrogated by police in Imphal, Manipur, after he criticized India's human rights record at the U.N. Human Rights Committee's hearings in Geneva in the last week of July.

Progress was slow in the investigation of the 1996 murder of Jalil Andrabi, a prominent human rights lawyer and political activist associated with the pro-independence Jammu and Kashmir Liberation Front. A special investigation into Andrabi's killing was launched under the direction of the Jammu and Kashmir High Court. As of October, the army major who arrested Andrabi had been indicted but remained at large, although the NHRC had called on the army to disclose his whereabouts.

Attacks on activists by non-state actors also posed special problems for Indian non-

governmental organizations (NGOs). On October 27, the decapitated body of Father A.T. Thomas, a Jesuit priest who together with other priests had worked on development issues among low caste communities, was found in the Hazaribagh district of Bihar. The murder followed other attacks on Christian and low caste communities in the region which are believed to have been carried out with the sanction of police and local officials. In July, Indian social worker Sanjoy Ghose, head of the Association of Voluntary Agencies for Rural Development (AVARD), was abducted and killed by members of ULFA who were unhappy with his rural organizing efforts. The abduction galvanized the Indian NGO community, and a global campaign was launched to call for Ghose's release. Critics believe, however, that Ghose was killed soon after his abduction.

In August, police in Assam arrested six prominent human rights activists and journalists for alleged links with ULFA, including Ajit Kumar Bhuyan, editor of *Pratadin*, a popular Assamese daily, and chairman of the Organization for the Struggle for Human Rights (Manab Adhikar Sangram Samiti, MASS), a local human rights organization, and Ashish Gupta, secretary general of the North East Human Rights Coordination Committee (NECOHR). Although Bhuyan had been vocal in his criticism of the abduction of Sanjoy Ghose, he was charged by authorities with complicity in Ghose's murder and held in virtual incommunicado detention for almost three weeks.

Human rights organizations concerned about deteriorating conditions in India's northeast launched a country-wide campaign in April calling for the repeal of the Armed Forces (Special Powers) Act. The law gives sweeping powers to the security forces operating in the northeast and in Kashmir. The campaign, based on an earlier fact-finding mission to all seven northeastern states by fourteen prominent Indian activists, significantly raised the profile of human rights concerns in the region. On August 20, the Supreme Court reserved judgment on a petition brought by a participating organization, the Naga People's Movement for Human Rights, challenging the act on the grounds that it provided no procedure to file complaints about violations of the right to life or indiscriminate use of the law in conflict areas. The court was expected to frame rules for application of the act, but as of October, no date had been set for a final hearing.

The Role of the International Community

United Nations

In July, the U.N. Human Rights Committee considered India's long-overdue report on compliance with the ICCPR. In its concluding observations, the committee, while commending India for some initiatives, including the establishment of a national human rights commission, criticized the government for its use of special powers legislation in disturbed areas, including continued use of laws permitting preventive detention, and for its failure to adequately prosecute security personnel for abuses.

European Union

As the E.U. continued to expand trade relations with India, few human rights issues attracted international attention apart from child labor, although a number of countries expressed concern about the need for progress in talks between India and Pakistan on Kashmir.

At the beginning of September, representatives of the past, present and future chairs of the E.U. (the so-called *troika*) met with representatives of India in Luxembourg to discuss improving relations between the E.U. and India, the situation in Kashmir, including the unresolved case of Western hostages, and human rights, including forced child labor. The E.U. and India also decided to elevate relations from a twice-yearly ministerial meeting to an ongoing dialogue that would involve more regular meetings of senior officials. They also discussed India's potential membership in the Asia Europe Meeting (ASEM), which in 1997 included only nations from East and Southeast Asia

and the E.U. A working group was established within the E.U. on strengthening democracy in the region and tackling child labor issues.

United States

The U.S. State Department's 1997 report on human rights was a notable improvement over the 1996 report and reflected better consultation with local and international NGOs. The report, however, relied on inaccurate government statistics on bonded labor and ignored the fact that existing laws prohibiting bonded labor were seldom enforced.

In September, Assistant Secretary of State Karl R. Inderfurth visited India in the first of a series of high-level visits designed to enhance trade relations and boost discussions between the two countries on disarmament and other security issues; Secretary of State Albright was due to follow in mid-November and President Clinton in early 1998. Also in September, U.S. President Bill Clinton and Indian Prime Minister Gujral at the U.N.

In October, the U.S. Congress introduced a bill to ban the import of goods made by forced child labor.

World Bank

In June, pressure on the World Bank by well-coordinated networks of Indian and international NGOs concerned about the use of child and bonded child labor in World Bank-funded projects led the bank to convene meetings with Indian NGOs to determine means by which it might address child labor issues in India. The bank agreed to canvas existing projects to determine if they employed children and to ensure that social assessment work be carried out for projects under preparation that posed a strong risk of employing child labor. The overall response of NGO participants in these meetings was cautiously positive. They urged the bank to continue and expand its efforts to consult with nongovernmental organizations on child labor issues and to encourage India's government to do likewise. NGOs stressed the need for the bank to emphasize prevention through quality primary education as well as the need for law enforcement.

INDONESIA AND EAST TIMOR

In Indonesia, the year was marked by serious communal clashes, the most violent election campaign in the history of President Soeharto's thirty-one-year-old government, harsh treatment of political dissidents, ongoing labor rights problems, and harassment and intimidation of non-governmental organizations. In East Timor, the human rights situation deteriorated dramatically during the year as the armed conflict heated up. And the forest fires in Kalimantan and Sumatra that by September had the makings of an international environmental disaster were attributed by many to the absence of checks on the executive branch of government that restrictions on freedom of association and expression have perpetuated.

Internationally, while Indonesia took the lead in getting an ASEAN delegation to try to mediate the Cambodian crisis, it also took a leading role in ASEAN in pressing for admission of Burma (*see* Burma chapter). Indonesia's enthusiasm for Burma's membership was not unrelated to the Soeharto family's extensive investments in Burma. Indonesia sent an observer to Oslo but did not sign the new treaty banning anti-personnel mines, and it joined a number of other countries with poor human rights records to take steps that could weaken the U.N. Human Rights Commission.

Human Rights Developments

To no one's surprise, the ruling party Golkar won the May 29 parliamentary elections by over 74 percent, an even bigger than usual margin in the exercise that takes place every five years. The government allows only two opposition parties to field candidates in what it calls the "festival of democracy:" the Indonesian Democratic Party, known by its Indonesian initials PDI, and the United Development Party, PPP. As a result of the government ouster in June 1996 of the popular Megawati Soekarnoputri as head of PDI and a ruling on January 20 blocking both Megawati and her supporters from running as candidates, popular support for that party evaporated. The strongest critics of the government then either advocated a boycott of the vote or joined forces with the strongly Muslim PPP.

Restrictions on freedom of expression and association increased as the election approached. On January 14, Aberson Marle Sihaloho, a fifty-eight-year-old member of parliament from the PDI and a close adviser to deposed PDI leader Megawati Soekarnoputri, went on trial in Central Jakarta District Court on charges of insulting Indonesian authorities in public. The charges stemmed from a speech he had made in July 1996, a tape of which was presented as evidence, in which he accused President Soeharto of recolonizing the Indonesian people, using the public's money to buy military weapons that were used against the people themselves, and turning the Indonesian parliament into a body representing big conglomerates. He was also accused of indirectly implying that he wished Soeharto's death by saying, "If you want to change Soeharto, that's easy. There is no need to pray or to burn incense, God will turn Soeharto into soil later." On July 21, he was sentenced to nine months in prison.

On January 18, five Indonesian students in Purwokerto, Central Java were arrested and accused of incitement after they distributed stickers advocating a boycott. All faced up to four years in jail.

On January 27, the attorney general issued an order to South Jakarta police to investigate Megawati herself as a suspect in what the authorities claimed was the holding of an illegal political meeting at her house on January 10 related to the twenty-fourth anniversary of PDI. After refusing several summonses, she finally agreed to appear for questioning on February 20; no further legal action against her was taken.

On March 5, an outspoken former parliamentarian named Sri Bintang Pamungkas was arrested and charged with subversion, a capital offense, for urging a boycott of the elections in a card he sent around to Indonesia's political elite to mark the end of the Muslim fasting month, Ramadan. At the time, he was free pending the outcome of an appeal to the Supreme Court after having been sentenced to thirty-four months in prison for insulting the president, in a lecture he had given in Berlin, Germany in April 1995. The subversion charge was also related to Sri Bintang's establishment of a political party called the United Indonesian Democratic Party (Partai Uni Demokrasi Indonesia, PUDI), in violation of a law restricting the number of parties to the two mentioned above, PPP and PDI, in addition to Golkar. In September, press reports suggested that PUDI, along with a number of other organizations, was going to be formally banned by the Ministry of Home Affairs. As of this writing, Sri Bintang was still awaiting trial. On April 7, Andi Syahputra, printer of an underground magazine called *Suara Independen* (Voice of Independence), was sentenced to two years and six months in prison for defaming President Soeharto and distributing material hostile to the head of state. He had been arrested in October 1996. The offending issue of the magazine contained an interview comparing Soeharto to the king in the fairy tale "The Emperor's New Clothes." On the same day, a two-day training workshop in election monitoring organized by the Committee for Independent Election Monitoring (KIPP) in the South Sulawesi capital of Ujung Pandang, was broken up by security forces halfway through the first day, despite the fact that all necessary permits had been secured and the meeting was fully in accordance with Indonesian law.

On April 28, Jakarta courts issued the harshest sentences handed down for peaceful political dissent in more than a decade against a group of students active in a left-wing political organization, the People's Democratic Party (PRD), and arrested following a riot in Jakarta in July 1996. Budiman Soedjatmiko, head of the PRD, was sentenced to thirteen years in prison, and Garda Sembiring, head of the group's student affiliate, to twelve. Seven others were sentenced to prison terms ranging from eighteen months to eight years. In Surabaya, East Java, three other students associated with the same organization—Dita Indah Sari, Coen Husein Ponto, and Mohamed Soleh— were also sentenced to heavy terms. Dita's sentence of six years was reduced on appeal to five; the four-year terms of the two others were reduced to three and a half years. The government accused the PRD of being the latest manifestation of the banned Communist Party of Indonesia. It also accused the students, correctly, of organizing worker rallies, calling for a referendum on East Timor, and campaigning for a more open political system. The PRD was formally banned on September 30.

A demonstration outside the courts on the opening day of the PRD trials led to the arrests of two more students, Anom Winanto and Aris, of an organization called the National Committee for Democratic Struggle (Komite Nasional Perjuangan Demokrasi). As of September, they remained in detention, and it was unclear when their trials would begin. They were accused of "spreading hatred" toward the Indonesian government by holding up a pro-Megawati banner.

On May 26, the PPP complained to the National Human Rights Commission that over one hundred of its supporters in the central Javanese town of Jepara had been arbitrarily arrested from their homes.

Among the many outbreaks of election-related violence, two were particularly noteworthy. On May 24, PPP supporters in Banjarmasin, Kalimantan, led an attack on the local Golkar office after Golkar supporters tried to ride by a mosque during Friday prayers. The attack turned into a riot marked by burning, looting, and destruction of homes, shops, and vehicles belonging to ethnic Chinese. Several churches and a temple were also burned. The death toll from a fire in one large shopping mall alone was 123; two other people were stabbed to death. Rumors that some of the victims had been shot could not be verified because the dead, many of whom were said to be burned beyond recognition, were buried before an adequate forensic investigation or attempt at identification was undertaken. A brief investigation by the National Human Rights Investigation was insufficient to shed much light on what happened. As of June, families reported 197 people still missing. Over one hundred people were brought to trial on relatively minor charges such as looting; only one person was tried for incitement, a man named Tohar who had appeared on a silent police videotape. The only witnesses against him were police who said he had been urging a holy war against Golkar.

On May 29, a crowd in Sampang, Madura rioted after alleging that election officials had tampered with ballots to ensure a Golkar victory in what was traditionally a PPP stronghold. At least three people died in unexplained circumstances. The family of one victim, Wafir, who disappeared during the violence and whose body was found in a rice field a week later, believed he was killed by security forces.

At least five editors were demoted or suspended for election-related coverage in cases of direct or indirect government pressure. In early March, Kafil Yamin, political editor of the English-language newspaper, *Indonesian Observer*, was dismissed from work for one month after his paper published a photograph of Megawati and one of Indonesia's most important Muslim leaders, Abdurrahman Wahid. The photograph was construed as supportive of Megawati. Four editors were dismissed or demoted following a meeting of top army commanders on June 3 where media coverage of the elections was deemed injurious to national stability. The Jakarta-based Alliance of Independent Journalists said twenty journalists were beaten, harassed and/or had their films seized while covering the election campaign.

On July 29 began the long-awaited trial of the man suspected in the August 1996 murder of Fuad Muhammad Syafruddin,

known as Udin, a journalist for the Yogyakarta, central Java newspaper, *Bernas*. Udin was widely believed to have been killed for his investigations into corruption by the district head of Bantul, outside Yogyakarta. The prosecution claimed that Dwi Sumaji, the accused, had killed Udin in a fit of jealous rage; Dwi Sumaji claimed he had been framed by police. Police investigators filed the case five times before it was accepted for prosecution by the Bantul district court. It was rejected the first four times for lack of evidence.

Indonesia was struck during the year by many instances of communal violence, not so clearly linked to the elections, which were spawned by or resulted in human rights violations, although there was no evidence that the government was directly involved in the initial outbreak. On December 26, 1996, violence broke out in the West Java town of Tasikmalaya following police detention and torture of Muslim teachers who had disciplined the police chief's son. The son had been accused of petty theft. Reports of the torture led to a mob attacking and setting fire first to police stations and guardposts across the city, then to shops and homes of ethnic Chinese. Four churches, three Protestant and one Catholic, were also badly damaged. At least four people died in the violence, including a sixty-two-year-old Chinese woman and a fourteen-year-old year old student. Over 160 people were arrested and interrogated at the district military command, including many who said they were only bystanders. A veteran rights activist named Agustiana, aged thirty-two, was taken into custody on January 8, held in two different hotels by police and military intelligence without ever being informed of the charges against him, and was finally given a formal detention order and moved to a normal pretrial detention facility on January 29. When he refused to countersign the order, saying he wanted to know first what he was being accused of, he was put in solitary confinement for three days. Eventually charged with subversion for being the "intellectual mastermind" behind the violence, he went on trial in August. The prosecution's charges focused heavily on his contacts with other activist organizations and appeared to be based primarily on tapped telephone conversations. As of this writing, the trial is still ongoing.

On January 30, in Rengasdengklok, a village in Krawang district, West Java, a riot broke out after an ethnic Chinese woman complained about the recording coming from a nearby mosque that was intended to wake up Muslims for their pre-sunrise meal during the fasting month. Her husband, Tjio Kim Tjon, allegedly threw a stone at the mosque. In the anti-Chinese riots that ensued, three churches and several vehicles belonging to Chinese were burned. The government filed charges against twenty-one of the rioters who were later sentenced to terms ranging from two to four months. Tjio Kim Tjon, who was arrested and charged with blasphemy, received a sentence of three years and six months. The relative harshness of his sentence compared to those of the rioters, indeed the fact that Tjio Kim Tjon was arrested at all, appeared to be evidence of anti-Chinese discrimination. Another major anti-Chinese riot erupted on September 15, this time in Ujung Pandang, Sulawesi, after a disturbed man of Chinese origin stabbed a nine-year-old Muslim girl to death. Some 500 Chinese shops were burned in the violence that followed. President Soeharto's close association with Chinese financiers, combined with a policy of official discrimination that restricts the number of Chinese in state universities, bans the use of Chinese characters, and with few exceptions bans Chinese from the civil service and military, makes the Chinese population a convenient target for expressions of political and economic discontent.

Communal violence also broke out in Banti, Irian Jaya between the Amungme and Dani people in late January, not far from Timika where the mining operations of the U.S. corporation Freeport McMoRan are based, and again between Amunge and Dani in Timika itself in March. It was the fourth major outbreak of communal violence in the area since March 1996. In late August, four more people were killed near Timika, two teenagers in an incident apparently involving a Freeport vehicle, and two men after the military opened fire on a group of tribes people, some of whom were allegedly armed with bows and arrows. A National Human Rights Commission delegation, after visiting the site, blamed the troubles on inefficient local government, but local activists said the commission's investigation was wholly inadequate.

In West Kalimantan (Indonesian Borneo) from late December 1996 through late February, an outburst of violence by indigenous Dayaks against immigrant Madurese resulted in a death toll of over 500; the army admitted to 300 dead. The Indonesian government did not instigate the initial clash, but its efforts to ban news coverage and discourage any investigation served to fuel rumors that exacerbated the conflict. Moreover, hundreds of people were later arbitrarily arrested under an anachronistic law banning possession of sharp weapons in a part of the country where virtually every family owns them.

In terms of labor rights, the government of Indonesia continues to allow only one officially recognized trade union federation. A ministerial regulation issued in early 1994 did allow workers to organize plant-level unions for collective bargaining; if they sought to federate with other workers beyond the plant, however, they could only do so through the official union. The government claimed that over 1,400 plant-level agreements had been reached; as of this writing, no one, from nongovernmental organizations (NGOs) to Jakarta-based diplomats, has been able to obtain a list of the 1,400 plants. Of the few such agreements known to have been concluded, many appear to have been effectively designed and drafted by management without real worker representation.

Muchtar Pakpahan, the founder of Serikat Buruh Sejahtera Indonesia (Indonesian Prosperous Workers Union, SBSI), the only independent trade union to constitute a challenge to the government federation and a man who for many has come to symbolize the struggle for worker rights, remained on trial in Jakarta on subversion charges at the end of the year. He was arrested shortly after the July 27, 1996 riots. In its formal charge-sheet, the prosecution cited a book Pakpahan had written in August 1995 that noted increasing social injustice and feelings of hatred toward the family of President Soeharto. The book also called for a referendum on independence to be held in East Timor. The prosecution also cited Pakpahan's signing of a statement in June 1996, together with representatives of thirty human rights, development, and pro-democracy organizations, that rejected the government's efforts to oust Megawati and called for democracy and for Soeharto to be put on trial. For most of the year, Pakpahan was hospitalized with what was reported to be a tumor in his lung, and the trial was put on hold; it resumed in September.

While the SBSI itself was not formally banned, its meetings were regularly broken up by security forces. On July 29, a joint military team closed down an SBSI training seminar in the town of Pringsewu, Lampung province and confiscated all documents and a computer. All twenty-six participants were arrested without warrant and interrogated for three days. The questioning initially focused on the lack of a permit for the meeting, then shifted to the content of the seminar, implying that it served to "spread hatred" and discredit the government.

On September 19, SBSI tried to hold its second congress at the SBSI headquarters in Tebet, South Jakarta, only to have police and military arrest eight SBSI members and four foreign observers after a verbal confrontation. All were released after questioning.

A major new draft labor law submitted to the Indonesian parliament during the year drew heavy criticism from local NGOs and international labor groups for not meeting international standards in terms of freedom of association and the right to strike.

In East Timor, the human rights situation worsened. Tensions escalated as the army continued efforts to "Timorize" the security forces, with a heavy reliance on unemployed young people as informers, and as socioeconomic problems (a high unemployment rate; development policies seen as favoring non-Timorese; and an increasing number of Indonesian migrants) fueled resentment of the Indonesian presence. A series of guerrilla attacks around the time of the Indonesian elections in May killed dozens of soldiers and police and brought a predictable response from the army: widespread arbitrary detention, with torture used to force detainees to produce names of possible perpetrators. The May attacks were preceded by a series of violent outbreaks, each of which led to mass arrests and accompanying human rights violations. They included the demonstration in Dili on December 24, 1996 when Bishop Carlos Ximenes Belo returned to Dili from Norway after receiving the Nobel Peace Prize. Hundreds of thousands lined up along the road to welcome him from the airport, but in several places, people suspected of being intelligence agents were set upon by East Timorese youth who believed they were planning to assassinate the bishop. An army corporal was killed, and the police commander of Dili and several others were beaten. A massive manhunt took place in the aftermath of the violence; sixteen people were eventually arrested, tried, and received light sentences in July. One reason for the leniency, according to their lawyer, may have been the evidence of torture produced at their trials.

Between February 6 and 10, more than thirty people were arrested in Viqueque after armed members of the youth militia, Gardapaksi, together with the counter-insurgency forces, mounted an operation in Uai-Tame and Nae-Dala, two villages suspected of being logistical supply bases for the guerrillas. Villagers were terrified by the operation, saying it was as bad as anything they had seen since 1975, the date of the Indonesian invasion. The leader of the Gardapaksi unit that led the operation, Eugenio da Costa Soares, was later killed in an ambush by guerrilla forces in April.

On February 21, a riot erupted in Oecusse, Ambeno district, involving more than 600 youths started after a parish priest, attending the first-ever celebration there of the end of the Muslim fasting month at the district military command on February 19, was served a meal that had been tampered with beforehand, making it look like he was getting leftovers. Despite apologies from the military commander, word of the incident leaked out and led to a riot in which one man was killed and several kiosks were destroyed. Dozens were arrested by armed troops from the mobile police brigade (Brimob). Seven were later charged with a variety of criminal offenses.

On March 23, a group of young protestors held a demonstration at the Mahkota Hotel in Dili where U.N. Special Envoy Jamsheed Marker was staying. The demonstration was forcibly broken up and led to the arrests of thirty-three people, several of whom were tortured in custody. Nineteen had been convicted by September and sentenced to one-year prison terms on charges of "spreading hatred"; fourteen remained to be tried, apparently on assault charges.

Several of the guerrilla attacks in May involved clear violations of international humanitarian law. On May 27, a group of unidentified youths attacked a number of election officials in the village of Nunira, subdistrict Laga, Baucau, killing two sergeants. The next evening in West Dili, guerrillas attacked the headquarters of a mobile police brigade company, wounding five police. The same day in a village outside Los Palos, in Lautem district, guerrillas shot an elementary school teacher named Castelo whom they suspected of being an informer, together with three of his children and a group of other teachers. In a separate attack the same day in Baucau, guerrillas shot and killed Miguel Baptismo da Silva, aged fifty-four, and his wife. On May 31, several men wearing Indonesian army uniforms threw a grenade into a truck carrying twenty-six policemen and two soldiers in Quelicai, Baucau. An oil drum of gasoline in the back of the truck exploded, and in the resulting inferno, thirteen of the people in the truck were burned to death and four were shot as they tried to escape. The dead included sixteen policemen and one soldier. It was unclear if there were any casualties among the attackers.

A massive manhunt was launched in retaliation, leading to hundreds of arrests across the territory. A guerrilla commander named David Alex was shot in an army ambush on June 25 near the town of Baucau. He was taken into custody and, after an inexplicable delay, was flown to the Indonesian military hospital in Dili, where he died. The military later announced that his family had attended his burial, which was not true.

The Right to Monitor

The Indonesian government generally did not prevent the formation of human rights organizations, but constant surveillance, telephone taps, dispersal of meetings, and other forms of intimidation made it very difficult for some of them to function. In late September, the Indonesian press reported that the Ministry of Home Affairs was about to ban several politically active groups, including SBSI (which the government has always considered an NGO, not a trade union); PUDI, the party of Sri Bintang Pamungkas; and PRD, the party to which the students sentenced in April belonged.

On March 22, police and military broke up the national meeting of Indonesia's largest human rights organization, the Indonesian Legal Aid Foundation (Yayasan Lembaga Bantuan Hukum Indonesia or YLBHI) at the Graha Asri Hotel in Bandung, West Java, on the grounds that YLBHI had not applied for an official permit to hold the meeting. Two local organizers, Wirawan and Hemasari, as well as the hotel manager, were taken to the local police station in Cidadap (Kapolsek) around 11:00 a.m. and were later transferred to the regional police office (Kapolwiltabes) in Bandung, where they were interrogated that evening.

On April 11, security forces in Brastagi, North Sumatra broke up an advocacy training seminar on agrarian issues carried out by the Study and Research Group on Community Development (Kelompok Studi, Penelitian dan Pengembangan Masyarakat or KSPPM). The security forces confiscated identity cards and bags of all of the participants, then interrogated them for fifteen hours at the local police headquarters before releasing them without charge.

On June 19, the annual meeting of a Medan-based organization, the People's Information Network (Wahana Informasi Masyarakat or WIM), in the North Sumatran village of Haranggaol was broken up by the police also on the grounds that the organizers did not have a permit. The meeting had been scheduled for the beginning of April, but WIM had been urged by local security officials to delay it until after the elections.

The official Indonesian National Human Rights Commission in general continued to do a creditable job of pressing the government for answers when human rights violations occurred, but it had neither the resources nor, in some cases, the inclination to pursue investigations beyond brief one- or two-day visits where commission delegations were almost always accompanied by senior officials from the local government. With respect to the communal violence in West Kalimantan, the head of commission rejected suggestions that his organization should probe the violence more deeply, saying in effect that the violence was over and trying to find out more would only stir things up.

The East Timor office of the commission was widely recognized to be a failure. On the other hand, the Justice and Peace Commission of the Catholic church in East Timor improved its documentation capacity during the year and became an important source of information on human rights abuses. No international human rights organizations had access to East Timor.

The Role of the International Community

The international community kept its attention during the year primarily on East Timor, arms sales to Indonesia, the rigged May election, and the ongoing labor rights problems.

Response on East Timor

The awarding of the Nobel Peace Prize to José Ramos Horta and Bishop Carlos Ximenes Belo of East Timor in late 1996 gave both men greater access to world leaders and raised the profile of the East Timor issue. In February, U.N. Secretary-General Kofi Annan appointed former Pakistani diplomat Jamsheed Marker as his special representative on East Timor, a sign of greater U.N. interest in moving ahead with long-stalled talks between Indonesia and Portugal. Beginning in July, an initiative by South African President Nelson Mandela to help resolve the conflict was welcomed by all parties, although the prospect of any breakthrough in the political stalemate seemed slim.

Human rights violations in East Timor led to an international effort to stop arms sales to Indonesia. The U.S. Senate included in the fiscal year 1998 foreign aid bill a provision stating that in any "sale, transfer, or licensing of any lethal equipment or helicopters" to Indonesia the agreement should state that these items would not be used in East Timor. A debate in the U.S. Congress over the proposed sale of F-16 fighter planes led President Soeharto to send a letter to President Clinton on May 26, saying that, given the "unjustified criticism" from Congress about Indonesia's human rights record, he had decided to forego both the F-16s and U.S. training of Indonesian officers under the International Military and Education Training (IMET) program. In the U.K., Foreign Secretary Robin Cook decided to let arms contracts signed by the previous U.K. government proceed, but in September he canceled two contracts with British firms to supply armored personnel carriers and sniper rifles to Indonesia. In doing so, he cited his party's May 1 manifesto not to sell arms to governments that might use them for internal repression. In the U.S. initiatives were underway in the Massachusetts legislature to ban the state from purchasing the goods and services of any corporation that did business with Indonesia because of human rights violations in East Timor.

In April, the U.N. Human Rights Commission in Geneva passed a resolution calling on the Indonesian government, among other things, to ensure the early release of East Timorese detained for their political views; to invite the commission's special rapporteur on torture to East Timor; to facilitate the stationing of a program officer from the office of the High Commissioner for Human Rights in Jakarta and allow him or her unhindered access to East Timor; to encourage the secretary-general of the U.N. to continue to use his good offices to achieve a just and internationally acceptable solution in East Timor; and to provide access to East Timor for human rights organizations.

European Union and the United States

Both E.U. countries and the U.S. were critical of the electoral process in Indonesia. On May 15, the European Parliament adopted a resolution condemning the harsh sentences given to the student dissidents and requesting independent monitors observe the Indonesian elections. Just prior to the elections, nine members of the U.S. House of Representatives wrote to President Clinton expressing concern about the pre-election violence and urging the administration to assess the conditions in the lead-up to the elections with a view to providing observers. On May 30, the U.S. State Department issued a sharply worded statement, citing reports from independent local monitors that the elections had been marked by intimidation, multiple voting, and numerous procedural irregularities. Shortly after the elections were held, the European Parliament passed a resolution deeming them undemocratic. It also urged the Indonesian government to throw out legislation restricting popular political participation.

Much attention around the world focused on the detention of independent labor leader Muchtar Pakpahan and the situation of labor rights more generally. Pakpahan

received regular visits from U.S. and European embassy officials; the U.S. tried unsuccessfully to secure his exit abroad for medical treatment. In February, the U.S. trade representative (USTR) sent an official to meet with the government, labor rights organizations, and others to assess progress on the benchmarks agreed to in 1994 by then-USTR Mickey Kantor and Indonesian Foreign Minister Abdul Latief. The agreement resulted from U.S. pressure on Indonesia to improve its labor rights practices or lose tariff benefits for Indonesian exports under the Generalized System of Preferences (GSP) program. As of October, a petition filed with the USTR in 1995 by Human Rights Watch urging a formal resumption of the worker rights review remained pending.

World Bank

The annual meeting of Indonesia's major donors, called the Consultative Group on Indonesia, took place in Tokyo in July. The donors together pledged $5.3 billion for Indonesia's development, but more than half brought up the need for transparency, implying the need to end corruption, and for strengthening the rule of law. Several donors expressed concern about harassment of NGOs; only the U.S. mentioned East Timor in its formal statement. The World Bank's total lending to Indonesia in fiscal year 1997 totalled $914.6 million, mainly for infrastructure and rural and social development.

Relevant Human Rights Watch report:

Deteriorating Human Rights in East Timor, 9/97

JAPAN

Human Rights Developments

Prison conditions in Japan, compensation for "comfort women," the coverage of World War II in school textbooks, and treatment of foreign workers continued to be major issues in Japan during the year.

Japan's treatment of some 200,000 "comfort women," compelled by the Japanese army to provide sexual services during World War II, continued to generate criticism, especially for the government's refusal to provide individual compensation to victims as recommended by the U.N.'s special rapporteur on violence against women in her 1996 report. Instead, a voluntary fund was established. Lawsuits for compensation filed in 1993 in Tokyo district court in the case of comfort women from the Philippines were expected to be concluded by the end of the year, and cases on behalf of South Korean women sometime in 1998. Nongovernmental organizations (NGOs) working with comfort women in Indonesia objected to Japan's giving a block grant from the fund to the Indonesian Ministry of Social Affairs, rather than directly to the women themselves.

In September, the Japanese government also announced it would not issue an apology or provide compensation to more than 16,000 mentally or physically disabled Japanese women who were forcibly sterilized under a government program that began in 1948.

In an important civil liberties case, the Supreme Court ruled on August 29 that the Education Ministry must cease the use of censorship in school textbooks. The ministry had deleted references to abuses committed by Japanese forces during World War II. Though the court did not strike down all use of censorship by the ministry, it declared that the power had been abused in expunging cases of well-documented atrocities from school books. For years the issue had generated widespread controversy throughout Asia, where Japan was often criticized for not directly confronting its war record, and civil liberties advocates in Japan hailed the court's decision.

Other human rights abuses continued in the areas of treatment of foreign workers and trafficking of women into Japan for prostitution, with questions raised about failure to provide adequate interpretation for foreigners accused of violating Japanese law, treatment of inmates in immigration detention centers, and failure of Japanese officials to make any distinction between illegal immigrants and trafficking victims.

On August 29, Bahman Daneshian Far, an Iranian prisoner detained in Fuchu prison, filed a lawsuit against the Japanese government for discrimination and physical abuse. He claimed that prison officials had made derogatory remarks about Iranians and when he protested, he was beaten, kicked repeatedly in the groin, placed in solitary confinement, and punished by being forced to wear leather handcuffs which the guards could tighten to cause pain. The lawsuit is only the second brought by a foreign prisoner in Fuchu.

At the United Nations, the government of Prime Minister Ryutaro Hashimoto played a more constructive role in the preparatory discussions on the creation of an International Criminal Court (ICC) while reiterating its opposition to the ICC being used to punish transgressions committed during World War II. Tokyo participated in the Oslo process on the banning of anti-personnel land mines, and provided demining assistance in Cambodia and other countries. In late October, Japan announced it would sign the treaty banning anti-personnel mines.

With the World Bank, Japan continued to co-host donor consortium meetings, convening the Indonesia donor meeting in July and preparing to host the annual donor meeting on Vietnam in December. Ironically, Tokyo's higher profile in the international donor community coincided with an unprecedented decision by the government during the year to cut back the level of Official Development Assistance (ODA) funding, with a 10 percent reduction authorized in fiscal year 1998. Meanwhile, the level of foreign aid funding declined in 1996 approximately 35 percent from the previous year, partly due to foreign exchange rates: worldwide ODA declined from U.S. $14.4 billion in 1995 to only $9.4 billion in 1996. But according to the Foreign Ministry's annual report on ODA in 1996 (published in February 1997), Japan still maintained its position as the top global aid donor.

An interagency panel was formed in April to discuss ODA reform, and the government took more aggressive steps to promote its aid program with the Japanese public, calling for a "people-centered" development strategy in the twenty-first century and beginning a pilot program to include NGOs in official delegations abroad to formulate ODA projects. On the other hand, the government's implementation of the ODA Charter's principles on human rights and democratization continued to be inconsistent and sporadic, for the most part sparing Japan's most important economic and trading partners from threats to cut or actual reductions in ODA because of their human rights practices. The Foreign Ministry's annual ODA report argued against "mechanical application of a set of uniform standards" and seemed to accept arguments offered by some of Asia's authoritarian governments that stronger action to exert pressure for human rights improvements through aid sanctions might be seen as "a unilateral imposition of values" that would "provoke a backlash and delay improvements in the situation."

Indonesia (receiving $965.5 million in 1996) and China ($867 million in 1996) remained the top two ODA recipients, despite their poor human rights records; Indonesia was promised a total of $1.88 billion in ODA for fiscal year 1997. Japan's close economic and trade relationship with Indonesia affected its overall approach to Jakarta, as reflected in its failed effort to negotiate a chairman's statement on East Timor at the U.N. Commission on Human Rights in April (instead of the much stronger resolution that was eventually passed); its reluctance to criticize abuses committed in the run up to the May elections; and its hesitancy to directly raise human rights questions at the Indonesia donor meeting in Tokyo in July.

Japan's reluctance to use economic leverage was apparent outside Asia as well. It continued to provide ODA and balance of payment support assistance to Kenya, for example, despite the Kenyan government's failure to keep its promises of political reform. Japan did co-sign several strongly worded statements with twenty-two other foreign embassies protesting the deteriorating situation in Kenya during the year. Aid also flowed to Peru and to Egypt, with Cairo receiving praise for its "political stability and democratization, as seen in the operations of the democratic legislature." Egypt received more ODA than any other Middle Eastern country ($243 million in 1995, the latest figures available) and was the eighth largest recipient worldwide.

Tokyo's most controversial aid decision during the year was its move to resume assistance to Cambodia approximately a month after the coup. At a donor conference in Paris in early July, Japan had pledged $69.6 million in aid to the Cambodian government in fiscal year 1997, plus $1 million in demining assistance, continuing its role as Cambodia's leading aid donor. Following the July 5-6 coup, Japanese aid workers were withdrawn from Cambodia and ODA effectively suspended, and the government announced four principles for resumption of aid, including respect for the 1993 elections and restoration of "fundamental human rights and freedoms." But as early as July 17, Prime Minister Hashimoto signaled that aid would soon flow again despite reports of extrajudicial executions and other abuses. When U.S. special envoy Stephen Solarz visited Tokyo in late July to coordinate U.S. Cambodia policy with other countries in the region, Foreign Minister Yukihiko Ikeda refused to criticize the appointment of Ung Huot as the new Cambodian first prime minister to replace the deposed Prince Ranariddh, urging the U.S. to take a "realistic approach." When Ikeda met Ung Huot at an ASEAN conference in Kuala Lumpur later in July, he announced that ODA would be resumed despite the fact that the four conditions were not being met, and shortly thereafter aid workers began returning to Cambodia.

Japan closely followed plans for elections in May 1998 and indicated it would consider sending election observers. In April,

Hashimoto had sent a letter to the two Cambodian prime minsters condemning political violence and calling for free and fair elections in 1998.

Relations with China were a key foreign policy issue in 1997, marked by Prime Minister Hashimoto's visit to Beijing from September 4 to 7 to commemorate the twenty-fifth anniversary of the normalization of relations between the two countries. A visit to Tokyo by Li Peng was scheduled for early November. Foreign Minister Ikeda visited Beijing in late March in order to smooth relations, officially resuming grant assistance cut off in 1995 because of China's nuclear testing program, and also seeking to ease tensions over regional security issues and the Diaoyu Islands. In a highly controversial move, Ikeda acceded to a request from Beijing that Japan drop its annual cosponsorship of a resolution on China at the U.N. Commission on Human Rights. In return, China reversed a decision made during a February visit by a senior Foreign Ministry official denying Japan's request to open a bilateral human rights dialogue. By the time of Hashimoto's September trip, however, the date and agenda for the dialogue had yet to be negotiated. Hashimoto brought up human rights in his meetings with Li Peng and other officials but only in general terms in the context of "global issues." The Chinese government later informed Japan that it would send some "human rights experts" to Tokyo from October 21-23. Meanwhile, economic relations continued to boom reaching $60 billion in bilateral Sino-Japanese trade in 1996, and Japan pursued its active lobbying for China's early entry into the World Trade Organization.

On Hong Kong, Japan agreed to inclusion of an appeal for human rights and the rule of law in the communique issued at the summit of the Group of Eight (G8) industrialized nations meeting in Denver in June, but in general it took a low-key approach, refusing to publicly criticize actions by the new Hong Kong government to roll back civil liberties protections, while privately urging Beijing to honor its commitments to Hong Kong's autonomy. Foreign Minister Ikeda attended the swearing-in of the Hong Kong provisional legislature on July 1.

In its policy on Burma, Japan continued to refrain from resuming ODA suspended since 1988, although in May it did offer to resume at least one key ODA project, involving some $60 million for expansion of the Rangoon airport, as an incentive to encourage an end to harassment and the beginning of a dialogue with the National League for Democracy (NLD). The Burmese government, however, rejected the overture, and the offer was withdrawn. During a visit to Indonesia in January, Hashimoto told President Soeharto that he supported Burma's prospective membership in ASEAN, but he warned that Burma's admission should "not become a cover for oppression." Ikeda repeated this message during the ASEAN conference in Malaysia in July, stressing that democratization and national reconciliation in Burma were essential. Just days after ASEAN had announced its formal decision to admit Burma, Keidanren, the powerful Japanese business association, dispatched a major trade mission to Rangoon in early June. The government took no action to discourage or delay the mission.

Separately, Keidanren announced in December 1996 a new "charter for corporate good behavior." Among its provisions was a stipulation that corporations should "stand firm against antisocial forces and organizations that threaten the order and security of civil society," and in their operations abroad, they should "respect the cultures and customs of the hosting society."

In August, the highest-ranking delegation to visit Burma in five years arrived in Rangoon for talks with senior SLORC officials just as heavy prison terms for NLD members were announced. But Parliamentary Vice Foreign Minister Masahiko Komura did not bring up these cases in his discussions, nor did he meet with Aung San Suu Kyi. For the first time, Japan gave humanitarian assistance in 1997 to Burmese refugees on the Thai border through a consortium of NGOs.

Throughout Southeast Asia, Japan focused on upgrading its commercial and political relations, sending two ODA missions to Vietnam and planning to maintain its high level of aid to Hanoi ($830 million was pledged in 1996), while generally avoiding explicit criticism of human rights problems. In a prominent policy speech delivered in Singapore at the conclusion of an ASEAN-wide tour in January, Prime Minister Hashimoto emphasized Tokyo's interest in developing a "broader and deeper partnership" with ASEAN. This became known in the region as the "Hashimoto doctrine" and was taken to mean that Japan would take a higher-profile interest in political affairs of the region. It was also widely interpreted in the region as a way of solidifying links between Japan and ASEAN at the expense of China.

In South Asia, Japan focused on nuclear proliferation, pressing both India and Pakistan to join the non-proliferation treaty. No human rights issues were explicitly on the agenda with either country, and Japan attempted to address child labor concerns in India mainly as a poverty reduction issue. In Sri Lanka, Japan provided $264 million in ODA in 1995, recognizing Colombo's efforts to improve human rights, while "continuing to observe the situation in the north and east, where human rights are still being violated in strife-torn regions," according to the Foreign Ministry's ODA report.

The Right to Monitor

Human rights groups in Japan faced no legal restrictions on their activities.

The Role of the
International Community

Most of the international action with respect to human rights in Japan took place within the United Nations. Japan's human rights record came under international scrutiny as the government provided its report to the U.N. Human Rights Committee monitoring compliance with the International Covenant on Civil and Political Rights. The last such report, submitted in 1993, triggered recommendations from the committee dealing with the death penalty, interrogation methods, inadequate protection of suspects' rights, treatment of women and refugees, and other concerns. In the 1997 report, the government vigorously defended the continued use of the death penalty, tight restrictions on condemned prisoners' contacts with outsiders, and refusal to give family members advance notice of executions. The government also denied that the pretrial detention system violates the rights of detainees by subjecting them to prolonged interrogation without counsel. Japanese lawyers and civil liberties groups criticized the report for failing to adequately address the Human Rights Committee's earlier findings and recommendations.

At its meeting in August in Geneva, the U.N. Subcommission on the Prevention of Discrimination decided not to recommend that the Human Rights Commission take up Japanese prison conditions under a confidential review procedure. The subcommission did convey concerns about the issue to the Japanese government, however.

The U.S. and Japan cooperated on promoting democracy and civil society through the G8 initiative announced in June, as well as the "Common Agenda," a program of cooperation on global issues initiated when President Clinton was in Tokyo in 1993. On specific issues, however, there were notable differences, such as resumption of aid to Cambodia after the July coup and sponsorship of a resolution on China at the U.N. Commission on Human Rights.

PAKISTAN

Human Rights Developments

Sectarian violence and the government's harsh response to it dominated Pakistan's political landscape in 1997, leaving little scope for improvement in human rights. Although violence in Karachi dropped considerably following the brutal 1996 crackdown against the armed opposition Immigrants' National Movement (Mohajir Quami Movement or MQM), clashes continued between the MQM and federal security forces. Sectarian violence between Sunni and Shi'a political groups also escalated dramatically in Punjab, leaving at least 200 dead. In August, in a misguided effort to quell the violence, the Nawaz Sharif government enacted the Anti-Terrorism Act (ATA)—a hastily conceived law suspending constitutional safeguards and giving increased power to police and other security forces. At the same time, the government made no progress in curbing rampant police abuse or in addressing statutory discrimination against women and religious minorities. The government took some steps to respond to international pressure to end child labor but without seriously enforcing legislation prohibiting bonded labor.

In February, the Pakistan Muslim League (PML), led by Prime Minister Nawaz Sharif, swept the national and Punjab assembly seats in elections triggered by the November 1996 dismissal of Benazir Bhutto, leader of the Pakistan People's Party (PPP). The grounds for Bhutto's dismissal included corruption and human rights abuses committed in the course of the crackdown on the MQM in Karachi. A judicial inquiry into extrajudicial executions of some MQM militants was begun in June; its report was due in October.

The change of government did not herald an end to human rights violations in Karachi. At least 400 persons had been killed in the city between January and November, victims of extrajudicial executions by police and federal security forces or retaliatory killings by the MQM. Several children were counted among the victims, including a twelve-year-old whose corpse was found on a garbage dump with a note accusing him of being a police informer. The MQM has claimed to represent mohajirs, Urdu-speaking migrants who fled India after the 1947 partition and who compose 60 percent of Karachi's population of twelve million. Following a government crackdown in July, involving 8,000 paramilitary police in Karachi, the MQM changed its name to United National Movement (Muttahida Quami Movement, still with the initials MQM) and raised demands for free education and an end to discrimination against the Ahmadiya religious minority (see below) in an apparent bid to attract other ethnic groups. It remained to be seen whether the move would result in an end to the group's campaign of political violence. Meanwhile, hundreds of MQM activists and supporters remained in prison without trial.

In Punjab, at least 200 people were killed in sectarian clashes. Police blamed the surge in violence on escalating strife between the militant Sunni Sipah-I-Sahaba Pakistan (SSP) and its Shi'a counterpart, Sipah-I-Mohammad Pakistan (SMP). Founded in the early 1980s, the SSP has demanded that Shiites be declared a non-Muslim minority in Pakistan. The murder of Sunni leader Zia ul-Rehman in Lahore in January and the February killing of Muhammed Ali Rahimi, head of an Iranian cultural center in the southern Punjab city of Multan, provoked further retaliatory attacks between members of the two sects during the year. In July, police launched a crackdown on religious militants aimed at stemming sectarian violence in Punjab province. Over forty people were picked up in police raids in the cities of Rawalpindi, Jhelum, Chakwal, and Attock. Meanwhile, in the northwestern city of Peshawar, police set on fire more than fifty homes and shops of suspected criminals in an effort to curb crime in the tribal area and break up a kidnapping ring.

On August 6, nine people were killed in an attack on the Sunni Ziaul Uloom Mosque in the Gujjarpura area of Lahore, the capital of Punjab. The same day, three worshippers were killed when a bomb exploded in a Sunni mosque in Multan. The attacks were believed to be in retaliation for the killing of a Shi'a shopkeeper earlier in the day. Following the incidents, mosques in Lahore began posting private armed guards to protect against random attacks.

Sunni Islamic schools, many under SSP

control, have operated as recruiting centers for soldiers fighting in Afghanistan, including those associated with the Taliban, a movement of conservative students whose forces took control of much of Afghanistan in 1996 with Pakistan's support. Because of the SSP's role in the Afghan conflict, officials have often looked the other way and allowed it and other such groups to operate with impunity. In August, however, police began investigating charges against an Islamic school accused of forcibly sending thirteen-year-old Maroof Ahmed to join the Taliban in Afghanistan. The case prompted a number of other investigations into such schools.

Claiming that the violence in Punjab and Karachi represented an "extraordinary situation" requiring an "extraordinary measure," in August the government introduced the Anti-Terrorism Act, a law which authorized law enforcement personnel to open fire on anyone "committing a terrorist act" or "likely to commit a terrorist act." The ATA also authorized police to arrest and search without a warrant and take possession of any property or weapon "likely to be used" in any act of terrorism. A provision allowing confessions to the police, even those made under duress, to be admissible as evidence contradicted constitutional protections against self-incrimination and the use of torture. Eleven special courts were set up under the ATA to carry out summary seven-day trials for those charged with acts of terrorism. Within days of the ATA becoming law, more than 3,000 lawyers in Punjab staged a protest strike, demanding its repeal. As of October, the new law had been challenged in three high courts.

Despite protests by medical practitioners, ordinary criminal courts and Shari'a (Islamic) courts continued to award sentences of *qisas*, punishment equal to the injury caused, and *diyat*, blood money. Human rights groups have complained that the Qisas and Diyat Ordinance has effectively enabled wealthy and influential people to escape punishment even for crimes as serious as murder or assault and has been discriminatory toward non-Muslims who do not have the option of paying diyat for the murder of a Muslim.

In April, the National Assembly amended the Offence of Zina (Enforcement of Hudood) Ordinance 1979 to award the death penalty to persons convicted of gang rape. At the same time, the government made no move to amend provisions of the Zina Ordinance that have been interpreted in such a way that rape victims may be charged with adultery if they are unable to prove rape. In August, the government-appointed Commission on the Status of Women, an advisory body which included a number of prominent human rights activists, recommended that the Hudood Ordinances (of which the Zina Ordinance is a part) be repealed. The report also recommended that marital rape be considered a crime; that women be given the right to seek an abortion within 120 days of pregnancy; and that 33 percent of seats in each elective body, from the local to national level, be reserved for women. As of November, the government had yet to react to the Commission's recommendations.

On March 10, the Lahore High Court handed down a landmark decision in the much-publicized Saima Waheed case, upholding the validity of the twenty-two-year old Pakistani woman's marriage, which had been challenged by her father. Many women's rights activists remained cautious about the judgment which also called for basic amendments to family laws to enforce parental authority and discourage courtships and extramarital relationships. The Supreme Court was to hear an appeal on the High Court decision by the end of the year. Waheed remained in hiding because of threats from religious organizations opposed to the court's decision.

Pakistan's so-called blasphemy laws and other legislation regulating religious practice were used to harass, intimidate and punish religious minorities, particularly Christians and Ahmadis. As of July, more than 2,000 Ahmadis had been charged with various offenses under the laws. The laws contributed to a climate of violence against these groups. On June 19, Ateeq Ahmad Bajwah, an Ahmadi lawyer and local leader of the Ahmadiyya community, was shot and killed in broad daylight in Vihari, Punjab. At this writing, no one has been arrested for the murder. On October 10, retired High Court Justice Arif Iqhal Bhatti was shot and killed in his Lahore office. The murder was reportedly committed by a member of a militant Sunni Muslim organization who was enraged by Justice Bhatti's 1995 decision to acquit two Pakistani Christians accused of blasphemy.

Despite repeated assurances that freedom of the press would be respected under the Sharif administration, a number of journalists were attacked and newspaper offices ransacked in 1997. Reporters working in remote areas and for smaller publications were most vulnerable. The attacks were instigated predominantly by political parties angered by reporting critical of their members or activities.

The year began on an ominous note when the Peshawar Press Club was attacked during a New Year's eve function by armed workers of two Islamist parties, the Jamaat-e-Islami and the Jamiat Ulema Islam. The two religious parties later apologized to journalists and promised to take disciplinary action against those responsible. In February, the Rawalpindi offices of the Urdu daily *Assas* were ransacked and staff members attacked by over one hundred armed persons reportedly angered by the paper's refusal to publish a political candidate's statement containing unconfirmed allegations against his opponent. In the same month, Sailab Meshud, president of the Tribal Union of Journalists and correspondent for the daily *The News* was severely beaten by a police officer when he attempted to obtain information on a detainee held at a police station in the Punjabi town of Tank. In March, a bomb exploded in the office of the Urdu evening newspaper *Qaumi Akhbar.* Although no one was injured, the office sustained extensive damage.

In August, Shakeel Naich, chief reporter for *Awami Awaz,* was brutally assaulted by political activists angered by an interview Naich had published critical of Mumtaz Bhutto, former caretaker chief minister of Sindh and chief of the Sindh National Front (SNF) party. Naich sustained serious head injuries as a result of the attack. Workers for SNF later obstructed distribution of the paper in numerous cities by seizing bundles and setting them on fire. The bureau office of the newspaper *Kawish* in Larkana, Sindh, was ransacked and burglarized the following month, apparently because of its extensive coverage of the assault on Naich. A similar incident took place in May when copies of the English daily *Dawn* were confiscated and burned, reportedly in retaliation for the publication of an article critical of the chief minister of Sindh, Liaquat Ali Khan Jatoi.

The year was further marred by the deaths of two journalists and the court martial and conviction of a third. On January 18, one press photographer was killed and five others were injured in a bomb blast at a Lahore Sessions Court. The bomb was intended for leaders of the Sipah-I-Sahaba party who had been brought to the court for a hearing. On June 9, Shamsuddin Haider, a program producer for Radio Pakistan, was shot in his home by two gunmen in the southern Punjab town of Bahawalpur. For only the second time in Pakistan's history, a civilian journalist was tried in a military court. Humayun Fur, Peshawar bureau chief of the daily *Mashriq,* was detained in June and charged with "anti-state" activities. On September 9 he was sentenced to five years in prison. The Human Rights Commission of Pakistan expressed serious concern over Fur's conviction and predicted that it would have a chilling effect on freedom of the press in the country. On October 7 Fur was pardoned on medical grounds soon after he was hospitalized for hepatitis C and jaundice. Fur's condition had reportedly deteriorated in jail, where repeated requests for medical attention were ignored.

The Right to Monitor

As had been the case in previous years, human rights activists in 1997 continued to receive more threats from religious groups than from government agents. Asma Jahangir, a prominent human rights lawyer and chairperson for the Human Right Commission of Pakistan, continued to receive threats from religious organizations opposed to the Lahore High Court's decision in the Saima Waheed case.

The Role of the International Community

The international community's concerns focused largely on child labor to the exclusion of most other human rights concerns.

United Nations

After a ten-year lapse, Pakistan resumed dialogue with the U.N. Committee on the Elimination of Racial Discrimination upon the country's submission of its tenth, eleventh, twelfth, thirteenth and fourteenth periodic reports (pursuant to Article 9 of the International Convention on the Elimination of All Forms of Racial Discrimination). At a meeting in March, the committee commended Pakistan for establishing a Ministry of Human Rights in 1995 and particularly noted the active role played by the nongovernmental Pakistan Human Rights Commission. The committee noted that Pakistan's definition of minorities was based on religious affiliation and not on ethnic, racial or linguistic grounds, and recommended that Pakistan extend its legal protections to all minority groups. Further information on the right to equal treatment before tribunals and on protection by the state against violence or bodily harm (whether inflicted by government officials or by any individual group or institution) was also requested.

European Union and the United States

In December 1996 the European Commission and representatives of the government of Pakistan met in Brussels for the first round of negotiations for a new, third-generation agreement between the European Community and Pakistan. The agreement covers cooperation in development, trade and commerce, economics, and science and technology. The parties met again in April 1997 and continued to face a deadlock on issues relating to human resource development. Pakistan refused to include any specific reference to International Labour Organization (ILO) principles, particularly those relating to child labor, in the text.

Any progress by the Pakistan government to address the problem of child labor was due in large part to increased international pressure. Although enforcement of relevant laws, particularly the Bonded Labour (Abolition) Act, remained grossly inadequate, the government took some positive steps during the year. On February 15, under an accord signed with the ILO, Pakistan agreed that children under fourteen would no longer be employed in the stitching of soccer balls. Nike, Reebok and several other sporting goods companies simultaneously announced their decision not to buy soccer balls made in Pakistan using child labor. The project was set to be phased in over a period of eighteen months. Pakistan, the European Union, and the ILO's International Programme for Elimination of Child Labour (IPEC) launched two additional programs targeting child labor. On May 31, officials announced that U.S. $1.5 million would be spent on rehabilitating 7,000 children employed in the football stitching industry in Sialkot. Another $2.2 million, two-year program was launched to target bonded child labor in carpet and brick factories.

The moves should be seen in the context of a petition filed with the European Commission which could eventually trigger the withdrawal of tariff benefits under the E.U.'s Generalized System of Preferences (GSP) program if Pakistan failed to begin to address the problem of forced labor. The United States had already partially suspended Pakistan's preferential trade benefits under the GSP program in March 1996. The suspension, which affected trade in surgical instruments, sporting goods, and certain carpets, was due in part to Pakistan's inadequate efforts to address the problem of bonded and child labor. As of October 1997, the U.S. had not reinstated those benefits.

In May, members of the European Parliament proposed that India and Pakistan use the International Court of Justice in the Hague as a forum to resolve their disputes over Kashmir. U.S. President Bill Clinton met with Indian Prime Minister Inder Kumar Gujral and Pakistani Prime Minister Nawaz Sharif in September and renewed the United States' offer to help the two countries settle their differences.

SRI LANKA

Political violence continued to plague Sri Lanka, both in the lead-up to local elections in late March and in the ongoing war with the separatist Liberation Tigers of Tamil Eelam (LTTE). Politicians from mainstream political parties and members of LTTE both stood accused of political assassinations in 1997. Efforts to account for past abuses made some progress as the government vowed to make public the reports of three presidential commissions that concluded investigations into nearly 17,000 reported "disappearances" dating back as far as 1988, but attempts to prosecute abuses proceeded haltingly, and new violations continued. Arbitrary arrests, torture, rape, extrajudicial executions and some new "disappearances" of Tamil civilians by members of the security forces and armed groups working alongside the military were reported in 1997. The LTTE was also accused of arbitrary killings of civilians and of taking hostages. The government made little progress toward resolving its war with the LTTE or gaining wider acceptance for a new proposed constitution aimed at devolving more power to minorities through regional councils defined in part along ethnic lines.

Human Rights Developments

On February 11, one day before the deadline for filing nominations in the March 21 local elections, People's Alliance (PA) Member of Parliament (MP) Nalanda Ellawalla was assassinated by prominent members of the United National Party (UNP). The murder sparked a rampage in southern Sri Lanka, as PA supporters burned scores of UNP homes and buildings. A special police unit set up to monitor campaign and election violence recorded 369 complaints in February alone, including many incidents of threats and assaults on UNP and other opposition party members by PA supporters. In an effort to contain the violence, President Kumaratunga ordered the confiscation of arms owned by political party members and declared an amnesty until March 15 for those who voluntarily turned in their weapons. Some took advantage of the amnesty, but many did not. Two citizens' groups monitoring the vote, the Movement for Free and Fair Elections and the Movement against Political Violence, reported 1,836 incidents of political violence during the elections, including murder, assault, voter intimidation and impersonation, theft of polling cards, and abduction and intimidation of opposition polling agents. The government was accused of using state-owned media to influence the election, and international observers were denied visas.

In July, the LTTE was implicated in the assassinations of two popular politicians, both in Trincomalee district. On July 5, Arunasalam Thangathurai, Tamil United Liberation Front (TULF) MP for Trincomalee District, and five others were killed in a grenade attack as Thangathurai left the premises of a school where he had addressed a public meeting. Thangathurai was known to be critical of both government and LTTE abuses in his constituency. On July 20, Mohammed Mashroof of the UNP together with five others, including Mashroof's driver and the driver's four-year-old son, was killed when gunmen thought to be LTTE forces opened fire on his jeep. The UNP group had been on its way to meet the families of forty-one villagers from Irakakkandy who had been abducted by the LTTE on July 2.

Fighting between the LTTE and government forces was fierce in 1997. On May 13, Sri Lankan armed forces launched the largest military operation of the year in northern Sri Lanka. In a massive offensive which continued through October, some 20,000 troops backed up by artillery, armored vehicles, and air support were deployed to recover rebel-held territory and reopen a supply route to the Jaffna peninsula across the LTTE-controlled Vanni region. At the outset, an estimated 20,000 to 30,000 civilians fled the offensive, adding to the hundreds of thousands already displaced in the area. There were reports of civilian casualties, and many suffered from periodic shortages as restrictions were placed on the movement of food and supplies. In August, Tamil politicians charged that indiscriminate attacks on civilian areas not under government control had resulted in civilian deaths and injuries and had damaged homes, schools and places of worship.

Conflict-related violence was not limited to the country's north and east. Some eighteen people died on October 15 in a bombing of Colombo's World Trade Center and gun battles in the city's business district. At least 110 people were wounded. The government blamed the LTTE for the violence; a London-based spokesman for the group denied involvement.

Journalists continued to have great difficulty filing independent stories on the war, as they have had since 1995 when the Defense Ministry introduced regulations barring the press from visiting the north except during infrequent visits organized under military escort. The result has been a massive propaganda battle of claims and counterclaims regarding combatant and noncombatant casualties, attacks on civilians, and delivery of humanitarian assistance to persons displaced by the conflict, and journalists have been censured for inaccurate war reporting. In July, well-known war correspondent Iqbal Atthas made several complaints to the police about harassment by

persons thought to be connected to the security forces who had placed him under surveillance.

In reporting unrelated to the war, *Sunday Times* editor Sinha Ratnatunga was convicted in July, and three other editors faced criminal defamation charges for publishing articles critical of President Kumaratunga.

Constraints on freedom of movement remained a serious problem for Tamil civilians fleeing the violence in the north. Tens of thousands of displaced persons seeking to travel south during the year were involuntarily detained for months in crowded "welfare centers" in Vavuniya pending rigorous government security clearance. Civilians wishing to travel to Jaffna were stranded in July when passenger service to the northern peninsula was suspended after the LTTE attacked ships transporting civilians. In Colombo and other towns under government control, police enforced often contradictory registration requirements for Tamil newcomers and their hosts, contributing to harassment of Tamil civilians, arbitrary arrests and increased likelihood of mistreatment in custody. Police in Colombo looking for LTTE suspects conducted frequent cordon and search operations and mass roundups, sometimes picking up hundreds of suspects at a time.

Reported rapes by security personnel escalated in early 1997, particularly in Jaffna and in eastern Sri Lanka, but it remained unclear whether the numbers reflected an actual increase in incidents, since rapes have been notoriously underreported. Several of these cases received extensive publicity, including the alleged rape and murder by police officers of Murugesupillai Koneswary, a mother of four children, who was killed by a grenade explosion on May 17. As of October, the case was under investigation, but any evidence of rape was destroyed by the explosion. Joseph Pararajasingham, an MP for Batticaloa district who has documented human rights abuses provided details in July of six other rapes by police and army personnel, but he estimated that there had been many more in his constituency since 1995. Pararajasingham also claimed that extrajudicial killings and "disappearances" had occurred at a combined rate of about seven per month in Batticaloa district since January 1997.

The government continued to make efforts to investigate "disappearances," that occurred under previous administrations as well as abuses reported under its own watch, but it was less vigorous in its pursuit of prosecutions. By August 1997, the Sri Lankan government had initiated investigations into some 760 complaints of "disappearances" that had occurred in the Jaffna peninsula during the previous year—the highest reported figure since 1992. In August, hearings into "disappearances" in Jaffna were conducted by the Defense Ministry within the perimeter of an army camp, a move that drew criticism from observers who reported that the venue was causing difficulties for witnesses.

Progress was slow in the prosecution of important cases of extrajudicial killings by state forces. As of October, there had been no movement towards reopening the notorious Bolgoda Lake case, which the chief magistrate ordered off the court's docket in March after members of the prosecuting team failed to appear for two consecutive court dates. The case dates from mid-1995, when some twenty-one bodies, many of them young Tamil men abducted from local guest lodges, were found in and around Bolgoda Lake near Colombo. Some showed signs of starvation, strangulation or torture. Twenty-two officers of the Special Task Force (STF), a police counterinsurgency agency, were arrested and charged in the case. They were later released on bail. Calling the prosecution's absence "an obstruction of justice," the judge refused to continue the trial. Sri Lankan Ambassador to the United Nations Bernard Gunatilleke vowed that the case would continue, telling the U.N. Human Rights Commission in Geneva on April 9 that the government had "decided to file indictments directly against the STF personnel in the High Court without going through a non-summary inquiry to avoid delay." The

attorney general claimed to be awaiting further forensic evidence before filing the case against the accused.

In April, Sri Lankan courts dismissed two important "disappearance" cases dating back to 1989, allegedly for lack of evidence. On April 4, a Colombo magistrate ordered the releases of Assistant Superintendent of Police Sumith Edirisinghe and Chief Inspector Anton Sisira Kumara. They were accused of abducting and murdering a number of people in the Hokandara area in 1989 and having them buried along a roadside. The site was later excavated and skeletal remains found, some of which were sent for forensic examination. On April 5, charges were also dropped against suspects in the Wawulkeley murder case in which six persons including four police officers were accused of abducting and murdering six youths in 1989.

Hearings proceeded intermittently in the trial of eight soldiers charged with the murder of twenty-five Tamil civilians including women and children in a massacre in the village of Kumarapuram in Trincomalee district on February 11, 1996. At a hearing in April, a surviving witness, Arunasalam Paramarani, identified two of soldiers accused of the killings.

In June human rights organizations in Sri Lanka and elsewhere voiced concern over the government's decision to dismantle the Human Rights Task Force (HRTF), a government body established in 1991 to monitor the welfare of detainees held under emergency regulations. All HRTF assets, including their extensive data files on detainees, were to be transferred to the newly established National Human Rights Commission, which finally received its government appointees on March 17. Bowing to pressure from human rights organizations, the government agreed to allow the HRTF's regional offices to operate for another month. No arrangements were made regarding the HRTF staff, some of whom had built up significant expertise in human rights investigation and also risked possible retaliation from army and police personnel they had encountered while investigating abuses. At the time of the decision, the National Human Rights Commission was not yet operational and lacked staff to do systematic monitoring and intervention. Human Rights Watch joined Sri Lankan and international human rights organizations in urging the government to ensure that the functions of the HRTF were not allowed to lapse even temporarily and that its expertise did not go to waste.

On August 8, the government announced a long-awaited plan to establish citizens' committees to monitor arrests and detentions at police stations.

In September the government announced that both the final and interim reports of the three presidential commissions of inquiry into past "disappearances," which were delivered to the president on September 3, would be made public. The president also announced that the government would pursue prosecution of those against whom the commissions found prima facie evidence of wrongdoing. The commissions were established in late 1994 to investigate "disappearances" and abductions by non-state agents reported in the country since January 1988. They heard evidence in some 16,750 cases out of 19,079 complaints and were to identify those responsible, recommend legal action, and suggest relief and preventive measures. In September President Kumaratunga also announced plans for a new commission to examine complaints that had not been addressed by the three commissions before their terms ended.

In October, Sri Lanka notified the U.N. of its ratification of the Optional Protocol of the International Covenant on Civil and Political Rights. The protocol allows individual complaints about violations to be taken to the U.N.'s Human Rights Committee.

The Right to Monitor

Although Sri Lankan human rights organizations continued to operate without legal restrictions, international relief agencies and nongovernmental organizations faced obstacles when attempting to operate in conflict areas. Both Quaker Peace and Peace Brigades International, organizations which had carried out important relief and monitoring efforts in eastern Sri Lanka, were barred from operating in Batticaloa district in April. The restrictions, which did not appear to be motivated by security concerns, were lifted later in the year. International relief agencies were also permitted to operate in areas outside government control, but pulled out when military operations intensified. Agencies did not receive permission to work with independent local nongovernmental organizations (NGOs) in Jaffna; if allowed to work at all, they were required to do so with state-linked institutions. This policy discouraged some organizations from seeking permission to work in Jaffna and caused others to withdraw.

In the lead-up to local elections in late March, a broad-based network of citizens' groups and NGOs launched a massive campaign against political violence, undertaking voter education, organizing rallies and calling on voters to shun candidates linked to violence. Despite the campaign's success in raising the issue of political violence, international observers who were invited by these groups to attend an NGO workshop on election monitoring were denied visas.

In July, media freedom groups called for the repeal of laws governing criminal defamation as well as the Press Council Law, which appoints a council to regulate newspapers, and to censure journalists for professional misconduct, and makes it an offense to publish a false report about issues under consideration by members of the Cabinet. On September 11, in response to NGO pressure, Sri Lanka repealed the Parliamentary Privileges Special Provision Act, a law that gave parliament the right to fine and imprison journalists for defamation.

The Role of the International Community

Most governments and international NGOs that raised concerns about Sri Lanka's human rights record focused on abuses linked to the ongoing war. Many governments denounced LTTE violence and called for a political solution to the conflict. They also gave some attention to the need for humanitarian relief, accountability for past violations, and the plight of Sri Lankan refugees.

United Nations

In August, Bacre Waly N'diaye, the U.N.'s special rapporteur on extrajudicial, summary or arbitrary executions, undertook a twelve-day visit to Sri Lanka. N'diaye expressed concern over the high numbers of unresolved "disappearances" and stated that "the gap between those who have disappeared and the number of people whose whereabouts have been finally discovered is too huge, too important." He noted that Sri Lanka had the second-highest number of cases pending with the U.N. Working Group on Enforced or Involuntary Disappearances, some 10,000 since the 1980s, and that reports of "disappearances" in Jaffna had also increased since 1996.

Japan

In its 1996 annual report on Overseas Development Assistance (ODA), published in February 1997, Japan noted in connection with the human rights clause of the ODA charter that while the Sri Lankan government was "making efforts to protect and improve human rights," instability and ongoing human rights violations persisted in "strife-torn regions." Japan pledged to "continue to observe the situation in the north and east."

European Union

On April 2, the Sri Lankan government announced that with the assistance of British Undersecretary of Commonwealth and Foreign Affairs Liam Fox, an agreement had been reached between Sri Lanka's ruling People's Alliance and the opposition UNP to work together to end the war with separatist Tamil rebels. Sri Lankan Foreign Minister Lakshman Kadirgamar added, however, that "the government was not contemplating mediation or facilitation by any foreign government or third party at this point of time."

Also in April, Also in April, German State Minister in the Foreign Office, Dr.

Werner Hoyer vowed during a state visit that his government would not provide any support to the LTTE, directly or indirectly, and that Germany was "ready to ban" the group or deport its members if there was evidence that they were engaged in terrorism.

United States

In July, following a number of LTTE attacks on noncombatants, including the burning of an Indonesian passenger ferry, the seizure of a North Korean cargo vessel and the killing of one of its sailors, and the assassination of the two MPs in Trincomalee, the U.S. called on the LTTE to "cease all acts of terrorism" and expressed unconditional support for the Sri Lankan government's proposals for a political resolution of the ethnic conflict. During a visit to Colombo that month, Australian Foreign Minister Alexander Downer expressed similar views.

On August 29, 1997, the U.S. promised Sri Lanka U.S. $1 million for humanitarian assistance for war victims and displaced children. The USAID grant is in addition to $1 million that the U.S. granted to the Citizens' Participation (CIPART) project in Sri Lanka, a program designed to strengthen democratic institutions. In September, the new U.S. Assistant Secretary of State for South Asian Affairs, Karl R. Inderfurth, visited Colombo on his first trip to the region. Inderfurth told journalists that President Kumaratunga had once again urged the U.S. to designate the LTTE as a terrorist organization but said that the U.S. was still examining the legal ramifications of such a decision. On October 8, the Clinton administration included the LTTE on a list of thirty organizations banned under a 1996 anti-terrorism law. The law bars LTTE members from the United States, prohibits fund-raising for the organization, and permits the freezing of members' bank accounts.

THAILAND

Thailand's economic crisis, culminating in the collapse of its currency in July, pushed all other developments out of the headlines, but the full extent of the social and political repercussions of the crisis remained unclear at the end of the year. A new constitution, passed in September in the wake of the crisis, promised more protections for human rights and greater government accountability, offsetting efforts by the government earlier in the year to place restrictions on Thailand's traditionally free press. In the meantime, however, the paramount human rights problem, the government's treatment of refugees and migrants, deteriorated steadily during the year with massive forcible returns of refugees into Burma and denial of entry into Thailand of would-be refugees from both Burma and Cambodia. (The government eventually admitted tens of thousands of Cambodians fleeing the violence that followed the July 5-6 coup in Phnom Penh.) Although Thailand's economic growth in recent years was built on a supply of cheap migrant labor, largely from Burma, the economic crisis resulted in an immigration crackdown, leading to summary deportations and filling immigration detention centers that already had a reputation for overcrowding and abuse. Thailand had a mixed record in support for human rights in the international arena. It became a full party to the International Covenant on Civil and Political Rights (ICCPR) in January and indicated that it would sign the multilateral treaty to ban anti-personnel mines. However, its officials wavered but ultimately supported Burma's admission as a full member of the Association of South East Asian Nations (ASEAN), thus giving up an important source of leverage on Burma's leaders to improve their human rights practices.

Human Rights Developments

Prime Minister Chavalit Yongchaiyudh, a former commander of the Thai army who took office in November 1996, presided over a weak six-party coalition, characterized by frequent shifts in policy and paralyzing infighting, until his resignation in November after months of escalating economic pressures. The weakness of his government contrasted sharply with his own desire to play the role of strongman, resulting in a heavy reliance on military advisers, the blurring of military and civilian roles, especially in the intelligence field, and more government supervision of the generally free Thai press. Chavalit was also responsible, however, for unprecedented cuts in the defense budget.

Signs of Thailand's economic slide were apparent early in the year. While the immediate causes were bad debts, irresponsible borrowing, and a property boom gone bust, many Thais attributed the problem to corruption, political favoritism and generally bad governance. One result was the drafting of a new constitution by a specially elected ninety-nine-member assembly focusing on political reform, with protection of civil liberties, a strengthened judiciary, fairer voting practices, and government accountability high on the agenda. The reforms were given only a slight chance of surviving undiluted until the economy hit bottom in July; by August, when the parliament began active consideration of the draft, it was widely expected to pass and in September did so, becoming the sixteenth constitution since 1932.

The Chavalit government took several steps to control the media. In late 1996, Chavalit had appointed the supreme commander of the Thai military as chairman of the Mass Communications Authority, and in early 1997 he installed the former editor of a pro-army magazine as head of a key state-run television network. But the most worrisome move came on June 11 when a media monitoring committee, called the News Analysis Centre, was set up under the Ministry of Interior to analyze media reports for the prime minister's office in an effort to ensure "accurate" reporting. While the government denied the move was an effort to restrict freedom of the press, it came at a time when some officials were blaming critical press reporting for the country's economic woes.

Thailand's security forces increasingly resorted to the use of excessive force and summary executions of suspected criminals in 1997. Some twenty-nine people were shot by the security forces between November 1996, when six suspected drug traffickers who had surrendered and had been handcuffed were shot dead by police, and April 1997; by the end of the year, none of the investigations into these killings had been completed. In January Thai security forces shot dead three minors from Cambodia as they were crossing the border from Sa Kaew Province in Thailand to Poipet town in Cambodia. Thai authorities have not clarified the circumstances of these shootings, and no investigation took place. In June, in an apparent attempt to crack down on illegal immigration, police in Sangkhlaburi district opened fire on a truck containing civilians from Burma. At least one person in the truck was killed and a number of others injured.

The Thai government's treatment of refugees along the Thai-Burmese and Thai-Cambodian borders was a major concern. In February, Burma's armed forces launched an offensive in areas controlled by the Karen National Union (KNU) in Burma's Tenasserim Division and Karen State, driving an additional 20,000 refugees from Burma into Thailand and swelling to 117,000 the number residing in camps along the Thai/Burmese border. In a reversal of its previous policy of allowing asylum-seekers from Burma temporary refuge, the Thai Army and Border Patrol Police either denied entry to or in some cases pushed back some 8,500 refugees, violating international strictures against forced returns or *refoulement*.

In one incident on February 25, 230 men who had fled into Bong Ti, a Thai village were separated from the women, children, sick and elderly with whom they had fled, and trucked to Pu Nam Rawn, a point on the Thai-Burmese border in Kanchanaburi Province. From there the Thai authorities repatriated the men to Burma,

directly into an active conflict zone. The remaining 900 refugees were trucked to a point further south and repatriated. The previous day, Thai Border Patrol Police at Pu Nam Rawn had refused entry to some 500 men, including minors.

In February, there were multiple repatriations from Htee Hta Baw and Htee La Pah from a group of refugees that had originally numbered 2,300. In March, in Sangkhlaburi District, 2,000 people at Tho Kah were repatriated. In May some 430 civilians who had fled into Mae Hong Son Province from Shan State were forcibly returned; they had fled their homes after Burmese soldiers had accused them of harboring rebels. The soldiers had beaten some of the villagers and taken others away as porters.

On two occasions in June, the Thai authorities repatriated a total of 1,700 refugees from Huay Satu in Prachuap Khiri Khan Province. The same month, 400 ethnic Mons who had fled into Thailand in April were sent back, with personnel from the office of the United Nations High Commissioner for Refugees (UNHCR) observing their return. The Thai government maintained that the refugees had indicated their desire to go back, but a number of international nongovernmental organizations (NGOs) questioned the voluntariness of the repatriation. They also criticized UNHCR for lending legitimacy to the return by having staff present as observers.

From the beginning of June, the Thai government refused to allow new refugees from Burma to enter Thailand, with the result that thousands of people massing on the Burmese side of the border were left vulnerable to attack.

Thailand's failure to provide adequate security for camps close to the border, sometimes even straddling it, left refugees vulnerable to cross-border raids by Burmese troops or forces backed by the Burmese government. Attacks in January on three refugee camps in Thailand— Huay Kaloke, Don Pa Kiang and Mae La—resulted in at least three deaths and left 7,000 homeless. Despite the obvious danger, Thai authorities refused to allow the refugees to move. Again in April, Burmese troops attacked the Ta Per Poo refugee camp, razing eighteen houses. The international outcry that followed the instances of refoulement in February prompted Thai authorities to move some of the camps away from the border, but most of the approximately twenty-five camps remained where they were. Thailand continued to refuse formal permission to UNHCR to work in the region bordering Burma.

Conditions remained poor in the refugee camps newly established during the year, as the Thai authorities permitted only temporary structures constructed very close together, in breach of the World Health Organisation's minimum guidelines. They also refused to allow schools to be established in the camps.

Thailand continued to block the establishment of camps for refugees fleeing worsening human rights abuses in Burma's Shan state, driving many from Shan state to join the estimated one million migrant workers in Thailand who risk harassment, arrest and deportation by the Thai authorities in addition to abuse by their employers. A 1996 program permitting employers in designated industries in forty-three provinces to register illegal foreign workers for two years offered some protection to the migrants, but authorities often did not distinguish in arresting and harassing foreign workers between the registered and unregistered. In June it was reported that a twenty-two-year-old registered seaman from Burma, working out of the port of Mahachai in Sumut Sakhon province, was beaten to death by a Thai police officer while trying to hide from the police to escape harassment.

Conditions in immigration detention centers continued to be cause for concern. In June, Mahachai police station reportedly held up to 400 nationals from Burma in severely overcrowded and unsanitary conditions. Officials reportedly accepted bribes to transfer detainees to Bangkok's Immigration Detention Center where conditions were somewhat better, but even there conditions were harsh, with serious overcrowding and juveniles and adults being held together.

Refugees from Cambodia also faced problems. In August some 30,000 civilians fleeing in the aftermath of the July coup (*see* Cambodia chapter), entered Thailand from the border town of O'Smach, and another 7,000 came in from the Cambodian town of Poipet. Although the Thai authorities facilitated their entry, Prime Minister Chavalit made it clear that the Cambodians would not be accorded refugee status and would be returned once the fighting subsided. As with Burmese refugees, the Thai government operated on the inaccurate assumption that fear of persecution was solely related to armed conflict and not to other forms of human rights abuses.

In early August the Thai embassy in Phnom Penh stopped issuing visas to Cambodians, effectively preventing them from traveling legally into Thailand. This was consistent with Thailand's position that all asylum-seekers are illegal immigrants, subject to arrest, detention, and deportation, even when they are deemed by UNHCR to be in need of international protection. Indeed on September 15, three ministers of the National Coalition Government of the Union of Burma, Burma's government-in-exile, were arrested from their office in Bangkok. Thai police said they would be deported to Burma, but the three were eventually released just inside the Thai border at Mae Sot after international protests.

No progress was made during the year toward enforcement of laws banning forced and child prostitution and trafficking of women or protection of the women and children caught up in trafficking networks.

The Right to Monitor

Provision was made in the new constitution for the establishment of an independent National Human Rights Commission and creation of three ombudsmen empowered to examine complaints of human rights violations. Their powers will depend on an implementing law which must be finalized within two years of the passing of the constitution.

The number of local NGOs increased during the year, and Thailand continued to be an important center for regional and international NGOs as well. Generally both domestic and international NGOs were able to operate without obstruction. NGOs organized a large number of protests throughout the year against the construction of the Yadana gas pipeline from Burma to Thailand's Kanchanaburi and Ratchaburi provinces. Groups working on issues considered to be politically sensitive, however, were closely monitored and, on occasion, restricted by the government. In May four Burmese students were detained by Thai intelligence officials for holding a peaceful demonstration outside the Malaysian embassy in Bangkok to demand that Burma not be admitted into ASEAN. Four Burmese students who were detained during U.S. President Clinton's visit to Thailand in 1996 while trying to stage a demonstration remained in Bangkok's Special Detention Center during the year, despite being recognized as persons of concern to UNHCR.

The Role of the International Community

Several governments, including the United States and the European Union, responded promptly to the refoulement of refugees and called on Thailand to halt the practice. In the first half of the year, fourteen foreign embassies sent visitors to refugee camps along the Thai-Burmese border. Only the U.S. embassy, however, visited the more isolated camps.

In February, the UNHCR in Bangkok issued a press release seeking clarification from the Thai government about reports of refoulement of nationals from Burma and expressing concern for the lives of those who were returned. UNHCR officials also made numerous visits to refugee camps along the Thai-Burmese border. The organization, however, did not make any further public statements about instances of refoulement which occurred after February or about Thailand's policy of denying entry to new refugees from Burma.

At the end of January, the European Commission approved a package of humanitarian aid worth ECU2 million for Burmese ethnic minorities living in Thailand or recently returned to Burma. The aid, managed by the European Community Humanitarian Office (ECHO), allowed European NGOs and their local partners to carry medical and food aid to refugees.

The U.S. Congress continued to appropriate funds to support work by Burmese student groups and other NGOS along the Thai-Burmese border. In legislation passed in July, the Senate earmarked $5 million for fiscal year 1998 and specified that $2 million of those funds should be used for humanitarian assistance to displaced refugees. The Senate also required, sixty days after enactment, a report from the secretary of labor on forced labor practices in Burma, including details on forced relocations and forced labor used "in conjunction with, and in support of" the Yadana gas pipeline being built through Burma to Thailand.

Relevant Human Rights Watch report:
No Safety in Burma, No Sanctuary in Thailand, 7/97

HUMAN RIGHTS WATCH

HELSINKI

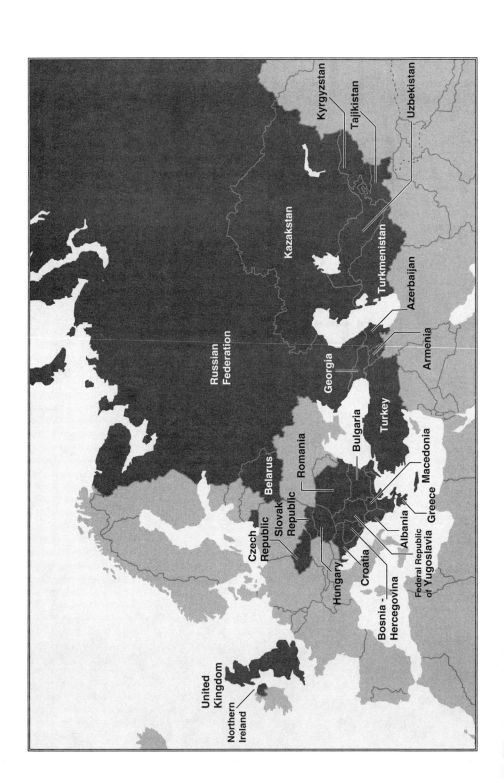

Human Rights Developments

The Helsinki region comprises the fifty-three countries of Europe and North America that are signatories to the 1975 Helsinki accords. Here we cover twenty-three of those countries (For discussion of the United States, *see* separate section, below), as well as a thematic section on asylum policies in the European Union.

The changing and expanding role of regional institutions—the North Atlantic Treaty Organization, the European Union, the Organization for Security and Cooperation in Europe, and the Council of Europe—has been a dominant theme in the Helsinki region in recent years, with potentially significant implications for human rights. During 1997, this process culminated in the decision by the North Atlantic Treaty Organization (NATO), the quintessential post-World War II security institution, to invite three former members of the Warsaw Pact—the Czech Republic, Hungary, and Poland—to join the organization in its first round of expansion. From a human rights perspective, NATO enlargement and the anticipated parallel expansion of the European Union (E.U.), as well as the growing involvement in human rights monitoring by the Organization for Security and Cooperation in Europe (OSCE) and the Council of Europe, offered a unique opportunity for these institutions to emphasize their common principles of democracy, rule of law and human rights, and to insist that these principles be the minimum criteria for membership. But in 1997, as in previous years, regional bodies were too often willing to compromise their core values, dispensing with human rights principles for short-term gains. As the debate raged in Russia, the Caucasus, Eastern Europe, the Balkans and Turkey about the criteria for "entering Europe," it was increasingly unclear which minimum human rights standards these institutions and their member states were willing to uphold.

Although for NATO, security concerns remained paramount, during 1997 the alliance's leadership explicitly acknowledged that regional security was intrinsically linked to the rule of law and respect for human rights. The carrot of possible E.U. and NATO membership has contributed to the resolution of tensions among several states: Poland and Romania finally signed friendship treaties with neighboring states that addressed minority rights issues. Both organizations also took the opportunity to raise human rights concerns that would, if unresolved, be obstacles to future admission. However, critics noted that NATO had a double standard, tolerating oppressive minority policies, the systematic use of torture, and other serious human rights abuses among some of its current members, most notably Greece and Turkey.

While NATO pressed for human rights improvements in the context of its expansion, in Bosnia over 30,000 NATO-led troops were all but paralyzed by U.S. fears of casualties. After British Special Air Service troops' efforts to arrest two indicted war criminals in Prijedor in July, there was reason to hope that NATO finally understood the important role it could play in establishing individual accountability for genocide and war crimes as an essential component of any lasting peace. Unfortunately, as of this writing, no further arrests have been made.

During the year, the E.U. identified specific human rights concerns in Bulgaria, the Czech Republic, Romania, and Slovakia that would be obstacles to ultimate membership, and resolutely condemned Slovakia's human rights record. Although the E.U. continued to express concern about Turkey's human rights record, it undermined this legitimate expression of concern during 1997 when the Dutch foreign minister, in his capacity as E.U.-term president, questioned whether a Muslim country such as Turkey had any place in Europe. The E.U. later stated that

Turkey would be judged by the same criteria as other potential members.

In Bosnia, the OSCE—dominated as it was by the U.S. government's determination to define the Bosnia mission as a success—continued to downplay human rights abuses in order to further its primary goal of municipal elections. It refused to publicize some human rights abuses for fear of offending abusive officials and violated its own electoral regulations prohibiting the participation of political parties in the municipal elections if they maintain indicted persons in a party position or function. However, some OSCE field staff—often under difficult and even dangerous conditions—actively monitored human rights abuses and pressed local authorities to address human rights concerns, sometimes despite pressure from the regional or national OSCE leadership. In countries such as Belarus, the OSCE was more willing to condemn human rights violations.

In recent years, the Council of Europe has admitted several new members without first insisting that they meet the council's own human rights standards. The benefits of constructive engagement appeared speculative, at best, on the first anniversary of Russia's admission to the council in February, when incontrovertible evidence was presented that Russia's human rights record had deteriorated in the intervening year. Similarly, the council was unable to wrest any significant human rights improvements from the Croatian government in the year following its November 1996 admission. However, in the Caucasus—with Armenia, Azerbaijan, and Georgia being the only countries currently under consideration for admission—the council appeared to be taking a more principled stand, and it suspended Belarus' guest status in January because of that country's human rights record.

The devastating consequences of ignoring human rights abuses to achieve strategic goals were abundantly clear in the case of Albania, where the international community had offered unconditional support and substantial economic aid to the government of Sali Berisha despite mounting evidence of human rights violations. Sparked by the collapse of high-interest-bearing investment companies in early 1997, but fomented by Berisha's complete disregard for human rights, angry protests became violent, and anarchy gradually spread throughout the country. A state of emergency was declared on March 3, the OSCE helped to broker a government of national reconciliation in March, international peacekeeping troops were sent to the country in April, and early elections in July resulted in Berisha's ouster.

In 1997, fewer areas in the Helsinki region were plagued by armed conflict than in previous years. Over 30,000 NATO troops kept the peace in Bosnia, and cease-fires negotiated in previous years continued to hold in Abkhazia and South Ossetia (Georgia), Nagorno-Karabakh (Azerbaijan), and Moldova. There was progress even in some of the region's most entrenched conflicts: in June, the inter-Tajik talks brought a formal albeit extremely fragile end to the five-year civil war in Tajikistan. The new Labour government in Britain was able to reinvigorate the Northern Ireland peace process in the second half of 1997, facilitated by a renewed cease-fire by the Irish Republican Army (IRA) in July. Despite these gains, however, the need to address human rights concerns and issues of accountability in order to create a stable, longterm peace in many former areas of conflict remained an unanswered challenge.

Persons responsible for abuses during armed conflicts continued to exert political and economic control in Bosnia, Croatia, the Federal Republic of Yugoslavia (FRY), Georgia, Tajikistan, and Chechnya, and their ongoing influence hampered efforts to return displaced persons to their homes, as well as to create state institutions to protect human rights. British SAS troops arrested one indicted person and killed another who resisted arrest in Prijedor in July, and because of intense international pressure, ten Bosnian Croats turned themselves over to the International Criminal Tribunal for the former Yugoslavia (ICTY) in October.

Although there appeared to be a lower level of fighting in the thirteen-year conflict in southeastern Turkey, security forces continued to commit serious human rights abuses especially against the Kurdish minority. The Workers' Party of Kurdistan (PKK) continued to commit extrajudicial killings, kidnapping, extortion, and destruction of property. The IRA continued to carry out acts of violence against civilians and police until it renewed its cease-fire in July. Non-state actors attempting to influence politics and post-war settlements in Chechnya and Tajikistan continued to commit humanitarian law violations, including summary executions, hostage-taking, and torture.

Torture and other inhumane treatment remained common practice in Armenia, Azerbaijan, FRY, Georgia, Russia, Turkey, and Uzbekistan. Little progress was made in eradicating torture, in large part because torturers were rarely punished and confessions extracted under torture were frequently admitted into evidence by national courts. Such practices were all the more troubling in those countries that continued to enforce the death penalty, such as Kazakstan and Turkmenistan.

Police brutality and violations of due process continued to be a chronic problem. During 1997, police used excessive force to break up peaceful demonstrations in Albania, Belarus, Bulgaria, FRY, Georgia, and Macedonia, and deaths due to ill-treatment in custody were reported in Bulgaria and FRY. Police harassment and brutality were often directed at the region's most vulnerable groups, such as ethnic and racial minorities, the homeless, refugees and homosexuals. Before Moscow's 850th anniversary celebration, for example, police violence and predatory behavior increased noticeably against Caucasians, Central Asians, refugees from poorer countries, and the homeless. Roma continued to suffer pervasive mistreatment by the police and racially motivated attacks by private individuals with state complicity, as well as discrimination in Bulgaria, the Czech Republic, Hungary, Romania, FRY and Slovakia.

Overcrowding and substandard facilities, as well as poorly trained staff, contributed to abysmal prison conditions. Ill-treatment and the excessive use of force by prison officials were also reported in many countries, including Azerbaijan, Georgia, Tajikistan, and Uzbekistan. In one of the worst cases of 1997, security forces in Tajikistan quelled a prison riot in the northern city of Khojand, killing at least twenty-four prisoners and wounding thirty-five others.

In recent years, there has been an escalation in reports of racial and ethnic intolerance and discrimination in the region, as citizens and governments alike have sought scapegoats for the social and economic ills produced by the transition from communism—in the countries of the former Soviet Union and of Eastern and Central Europe—and by the growing number of legal and/or illegal migrants and asylum seekers, especially in the countries of Western Europe. In addition to rampant persecution of ethnic and racial minorities throughout the region, discrimination and police abuse against homosexuals was reported in Bulgaria and Romania, and women faced widespread discrimination and were routinely denied the equal protection of the law. Women victims of crime, such as domestic violence, rape, and forced prostitution, faced obstacles in trying to obtain justice for the crimes against them. Women also faced severe abuses in conflict and post-conflict situations. Refugees and asylum seekers often existed in a bureaucratic limbo without a concrete legal status, making them more vulnerable to police abuse, harassment, and discrimination in host countries. In Russia, for example, police refused to register refugees from outside the Confederation of Independent States, exposing them to routine beatings, extortion and eviction by police. E.U. member states continued to enforce ever more restrictive asylum policies, leading, in some cases, to *refoulement*, in contravention of international law.

Religious persecution was increasingly frequent, as so-called "traditional" religions attempted to protect their privileged position from the influx of "new" religious groups. A disturbingly vague and discriminatory law was signed by Russian President Boris Yeltsin, revoking almost all rights from "minority" religious groups existing in Russia for less than fifteen years. In Bulgaria and Greece, the government refused officially to register certain religious groups, who, in some cases, reported discrimination and attacks by police.

In other countries in the region, governments took steps to counter the perceived threat of Islamic "fundamentalism." In Turkey, the civilian government, under severe pressure from the military, sought to close controversial state-supported religious schools and took steps to ban the Islamist Welfare Party (Refah).

The independent media were the targets of systematic government harassment. Pressure from various governments amounted to a tacit acknowledgment of the growing power of independent media which, bolstered by advanced technology, are increasingly difficult to silence. Journalists were harassed, ill-treated by the police, and sometimes arrested, in Albania, Armenia, Belarus, Bosnia, Bulgaria, Croatia, FRY, Turkey, Turkmenistan, and Uzbekistan. Strict libel laws were often used to intimidate government critics, the politically motivated misuse of criminal statutes was also common. State-controlled media not only denied citizens access to diverse views, but were sometimes used by governments to incite violence and ethnic hatred. State control over the broadcast media also had negative implications during elections in Bosnia, Croatia, and FRY, where opposition candidates were at an overwhelming disadvantage in getting their message out to the electorate.

The Right to Monitor

In many countries in the Helsinki region, human rights organizations—both domestic and international—were able to work without governmental interference. More importantly, in much of the region, the vibrant community of nongovernmental organizations (NGOs) increasingly represented a check on official conduct. During 1997, NGOs formed coalitions to ban anti-personnel landmines, to call for an international criminal court, to insist that indicted persons from the former Yugoslavia be arrested, as well as to raise other human rights concerns. In several countries, local human rights organizations became increasingly expert at using international mechanisms to pursue remedies for human rights abuses.

However, in several countries, human rights activists continued to face governmental repression. Although Turkey has a dedicated and vocal human rights community, human rights activists were arrested during the year and human rights publications were banned. The leaders of two of Turkey's most prominent human rights groups faced criminal prosecution during 1997. Local authorities in the Russian provinces carried out a wave of repression against human rights activists during late 1996 and 1997; at least four activists were arrested, and the charges against them were believed to be motivated solely by local officials' desires to silence their most forceful critics. In countries such as Albania, Bosnia, FRY, Greece and Uzbekistan, human rights monitors were subjected to police surveillance and various forms of official harassment. In the ethnic Albanian region of Kosovo, FRY, human rights activists were often detained and occasionally ill-treated. The conditions in Turkmenistan remained so repressive that no groups or even individuals were able to monitor human rights violations. The precarious security situation in Tajikistan created severe obstacles for both domestic and international human rights monitors.

Human Rights Watch honored Fatos Lubonja, a co-founder and member of the Albanian Helsinki Committee who had been imprisoned from 1974 to 1991 for his writings, at our annual human rights monitors event in November.

The Role of the International Community

There was ample proof during 1997 that investments of financial, human and military resources were no substitute for a clearly articulated human rights policy and the political will to back it up. NATO's refusal to order the arrests of persons indicted for war crimes in Bosnia, continued to impede most other efforts to obtain civilian compliance with the

Dayton agreement. By year's end, economic aid and human resources that had been poured into Bosnia had achieved only modest compliance with the Dayton agreement. International leaders were determined to call the Bosnian peace effort successful—often narrowly defined as the completion of elections and the maintenance of a cease-fire—and therefore were often reluctant to take any concrete action that might affect the perception of a foreign policy success. Human rights in Albania deteriorated dramatically in early 1997, despite the enormous political and financial support given to the Berisha government from 1992-1996.

United Nations

United Nations peacekeepers and military monitors continued to play an important role in maintaining security and, to a lesser extent, monitoring human rights in the region. The very presence of the United Nations Transitional Authority in Eastern Slavonia (UNTAES) was widely recognized as having prevented a massive exodus of ethnic Serbs from the region during the year. UNTAES continued to take an active role in monitoring human rights, and its troops carried out the first arrests of indicted war crimes suspects by international forces in the former Yugoslavia. In Georgia, the U.N. Observer Mission in Georgia (UNOMiG) was largely unsuccessful in fostering the return of refugees and displaced persons from Abkhazia, although it continued to monitor the peace settlement in that region. Although the U.N. Preventive Deployment Force (UNPREDEP) in Macedonia contributed to short-term regional and domestic security concerns, but gave little attention to the human rights developments in the country that present a risk to long-term stability. The U.N. Mission of Observers in Tajikistan (UNMOT) and the office of the U.N. secretary-general played an important role in the conclusion of a peace accord ending the five-year civil war. However, UNMOT's reduced presence in Tajikistan during the year precluded it from actively deterring abuses.

In Bosnia, the U.N. International Police Task Force (IPTF) achieved only modest results in restructuring the local police forces in the federation; in the RS, it did not even obtain the agreement of the local authorities to carry out its restructuring mandate until late September. Although in late 1996 the IPTF was given an expanded mandate to investigate human rights violations by local police, its 120-member human rights investigative unit was not fully operational as of October 1997. Follow-up in serious cases of human rights abuses remained inconsistent, and the results of independent investigations were often delayed or never reported publicly. The IPTF did conduct thorough investigations in a few prominent cases, but generally failed to take full advantage of its new powers.

U.N. human rights bodies, including the Human Rights Committee, the Committee Against Torture, the Committee on Elimination of Religious Discrimination, and the special rapporteur on the independence of lawyers and judges, were active in the Helsinki region during 1997, highlighting serious human rights abuses in several countries, including in Bulgaria, Georgia, the U.K. (Northern Ireland), and Russia.

European Union

The European Union's human rights record was mixed during 1997. On the one hand, it was critical of Croatia's failure to cooperate with the ICTY and to comply with its human rights obligations, and threatened trade sanctions for 1998 if the situation did not improve. However, in April, the E.U. granted FRY preferential trade status despite President Milosevic's attempts to annul the Serbian opposition's electoral victory and ongoing human rights violations in FRY. It later announced that the preferential trade status would be revoked if the FRY did not improve its human rights record by the end of the year and sent a delegation to the country in October to assess progress in this regard. The E.U. did criticize ongoing human rights violations against ethnic Albanians in Kosovo.

European institutions and governments remained content, during 1997, to allow U.S. interests to dominate Bosnia policy. In one commendable step, British special forces carried out an arrest effort—the only one to date—in the Bosnian Serb town of Prijedor, arresting one indicted person and killing another during a shoot out. But U.S. pressure prevented other such initiatives. Instead, Europe concentrated on providing financial incentives for compliance with the Dayton agreement. Even this policy was ambiguous, however, despite the E.U.'s professed commitment to conditionality of aid, the E.U. neglected to create mechanisms to help distribute aid at the micro-level, opting instead to suspend all non-humanitarian aid to the Republika Srpska.

During 1997, the E.U. was a vocal critic of the Belarusian government's human rights record. During its review of potential candidates for future E.U. membership, it raised concern about specific human rights abuses in Bulgaria, Croatia, the Czech Republic, Hungary, Romania, and Slovakia. The E.U. continued to insist on provisions relating to human rights and democratization in its partnership and cooperation agreements (PCAs) with non-member states. But it undercut these positive standards in some cases. For example, although the E.U. had not yet ratified PCAs with Uzbekistan and Kyrgyzstan because of human rights concerns, interim agreements with these countries lessened its leverage for obtaining human rights improvements. The European Parliament was more consistent: it continued to block payment of adjustment fees related to its 1995 customs union agreement with Turkey on human rights grounds and issued a strongly worded resolution condemning, among other things, torture, ill-treatment and prison conditions in Russia.

Organization for Security and Cooperation in Europe

In recent years the OSCE has expanded its human rights monitoring efforts in several countries in the region, devoting large numbers of staff and resources especially in Bosnia. While the OSCE's increasingly active role could have been a positive development, to date its work has often been compromised by the political interests and goals of the OSCE and its most powerful member states. In Bosnia, the OSCE refused to publicize some human rights abuses, defended its own performance, and sometimes tried to undermine the credibility of independent monitors, often to the dismay of its own human rights staff. Given this record, there was little reason to celebrate the organization's decision to send 250 human rights monitors to Eastern Slavonia. The OSCE also failed to exploit key opportunities to raise human rights concerns in Azerbaijan and Uzbekistan.

By contrast, in Belarus, the OSCE forcefully condemned the human rights record of President Aleksandr Lukashenka's government and initiated negotiations to open a permanent OSCE office in Minsk, while in Tajikistan its field offices played a significant role in monitoring human rights abuses. In Albania, the OSCE helped broker a deal between the government of then president Sali Berisha and the opposition to form a reconciliation government until new elections could be held in June. The OSCE helped organize and monitor the elections, which went off relatively peacefully. The OSCE planned to establish permanent representatives in Belarus and Georgia (Abkhazia), and its representative in Chechnya criticized human rights developments during the year. In response to large-scale demonstrations to protest election violations in FRY, the OSCE sent a mission, which confirmed massive electoral fraud and pressed the government to accept the electoral results.

Council of Europe

Consistent with its previous decisions to admit countries that clearly did not comply with the organization's most basic human rights tenets, the Council of Europe admitted Croatia as a member in November 1996. The council monitored respect for human rights in Russia during the year, but its assessment remained confidential. In 1997, Armenia, Azerbaijan, and Georgia were being considered for membership. However, the council accurately concluded that Armenia did not yet meet its human rights standards, and an assessment of human rights in Azerbaijan was pending as of this writing. It also suspended Belarus' guest status in January, reflecting the widespread violations of human rights in that country. The council ended its special monitoring of Romania in April, but warned that such monitoring would resume if the government did not address certain human rights concerns.

NATO

On July 10, NATO undertook its first action to arrest indicted war crimes suspects in the former Yugoslavia. NATO's actions in Prijedor quieted any doubt that the arrest and surrender of indicted persons by international troops in Bosnia could be carried out in accordance with the current mandate of the Stabilization Force (SFOR) and that any reprisals could be contained. Disappointingly, however, no further arrests were made by SFOR. Instead, SFOR resorted to its previous and now well-worn excuses for inaction. Throughout the year, there were repeated and credible reports that SFOR troops failed even to uphold their mandate—to arrest indicted persons only when encountered—as they narrowly defined it.

United States

There was a noticeable contrast between the U.S. government's forceful condemnation and effective strategies against human rights abuses in some countries and its subversion of human rights concerns to strategic and economic interests in others. The U.S. remained highly engaged in Bosnia during 1997, but its policy continued to be driven by U.S. domestic political considerations. Although the Clinton administration voiced its strong support for the British SFOR arrest action in Prijedor in July and continued to insist on its firm commitment to bring war criminals to justice, the U.S. worked behind the scenes to prevent further such arrests in the follow-up to municipal elections in September. The U.S. also continued to advocate for human rights conditionality of economic aid to the region, but the administration did not create the mechanisms to ensure that aid would not enrich those indicted for war crimes or those who obstructed the Dayton agreement.

Although critical of human rights abuses in Armenia, the U.S. failed to use the significant leverage that it had—due primarily to massive, long-term U.S. aid to that country—to obtain concrete improvements. U.S. oil interests took precedence over human rights concerns in Azerbaijan, and although the U.S. government reportedly expressed concern about the country's poor human rights record to government officials, no public condemnation was issued. Largely motivated by regional security concerns, the U.S. failed to criticize human rights abuses in Macedonia, especially those against the ethnic Albanian population. Although it did openly criticize the Turkish government's human rights record, this criticism was often tempered by its strategic interests in that country.

By contrast, the U.S. was the main force behind the maintenance of economic sanctions in FRY, forcefully condemning abuses in Kosovo, as well as violations in Serbia proper, and refusing to restore full diplomatic relations unlike the E.U. member states. Similarly, the U.S. took a leading role in raising human rights concerns in Croatia. In June, the U.S. blocked a World Bank loan to Croatia and, in September, called on the Council of Europe to suspend Croatia because of its human rights record. The Clinton administration was also a vocal critic of abuses in countries such as Belarus, Kazakstan, Kyrgyzstan, Slovakia, and Uzbekistan, and raised human rights concerns in Bulgaria and Romania as part of the debate on NATO expansion. After six years of unequivocal support, the U.S. government criticized Albanian President Sali Berisha's violent suppression of civic protest and supported new elections.

The Work of Human Rights Watch

Convinced that the failure to arrest indicted persons would have long-term repercussions for human rights in the Balkans and beyond,

Human Rights Watch continued to give top priority to the arrest of indicted war crimes suspects during 1997. Other priorities in the region included: insisting on conditionality of aid to Croatia and FRY, challenging xenophobia and the mistreatment of migrants in Russia, building respect for human rights and democratic principles in Albania, Belarus and FRY, exposing severe abuses in Central Asia and the Caucasus to international scrutiny, opposing torture and restrictions on freedom of expression in Turkey, ensuring that human rights were a component of peace negotiations in several countries in the region, and urging the European Union not to undermine refugee protection.

Human Rights Watch employed a three-pronged strategy for its work in Bosnia: systematic documentation and exposure of human rights violations by all sides, a focus on the failure of international actors to stop abuses, and a campaign for the arrest and prosecution of persons indicted for war crimes. In an effort to highlight the continuing influence of indicted war crimes suspects, we concentrated our research on key cities and towns where abusive local officials who were responsible for atrocities during the war exert ongoing political and economic control, making an effort to investigate human rights violations by all ethnic groups. In a December 1996 report, we showed that underground Bosnian Serb paramilitary organizations led by the ruling nationalist-based Serbian Democratic Party (SDS), continued to destabilize the peace process and obstruct implementation of the Dayton agreement by IFOR and other international bodies. In a follow-up report issued in January 1997, we demonstrated that the same warlords who had "ethnically cleansed" the town of Prijedor retained total control in the post-war period over key economic, infrastructure, and humanitarian sectors of the community. Two of the individuals featured prominently in our report were later indicted by the tribunal and were the subject of the first arrest efforts by SFOR in July. The third report in this series, issued in August, documented the systematic persecution of those who are not members of

Alija Izetbegovi's Party of Democratic Action (SDA), particularly those who fought on the Bosnian-Serb side during the war, by local authorities in the Una Sana canton. During the year, we also conducted a fact-finding mission to Croat-controlled areas in and around Mostar; investigated the human rights concerns of Bosnian women in the post-conflict period; and conducted an evaluation of the role played by the IPTF in vetting the police force in Bosnia.

We continued to make accountability for war crimes and crimes against humanity during the war a priority of our work in the former Yugoslavia. Through our reports, numerous articles in the press, and in a broad-based international NGO coalition, we maintained pressure on Western leaders to order SFOR troops in Bosnia to arrest the remaining war crimes suspects. The *Arrest Now!* campaign was launched on July 10, to coincide with the second anniversary of the fall of Srebrenica. A press briefing was conducted in Madrid (at the time of the NATO summit), and press conferences were held in Washington, D.C., London, Paris and Sarajevo by Human Rights Watch and its partners on the campaign. We released an open letter— signed by more than 130 prominent individuals and ninety organizations from throughout Europe— to European political leaders on September 9 calling for NATO action to arrest war crimes suspects.

In Croatia and FRY, Human Rights Watch focused on the governments' crackdown on civil society, as well as ongoing discrimination against ethnic minorities, and pressed for all financial assistance to be linked to respect for human rights. In an effort to highlight human rights concerns that needed addressing before the transfer of authority in the only remaining Serb-controlled region of Croatia, in an April report we warned that unless the international community pressured Croatia to fulfill its human rights obligations, the transition could bring more violence and displacement to the region. In June, we successfully urged the United States government to use its influence to block a U.S.$30 million loan to Croatia because of that country's human rights record and failure to cooperate with the ICTY. In an effort to prevent a mass exodus of ethnic Serbs at the time of the transfer of authority in Eastern Slavonia, we met with Croatian government officials and senior representatives of the international community to urge respect for human rights guarantees; we also monitored the treatment of ethnic Serbs in the Krajina. Before the Serbian elections in September 1997, we released a report analyzing electoral violations during the November 1996 municipal elections and documenting police abuse during mass demonstrations in Belgrade to protest those violations. We conducted detailed investigations into minority rights in Sandzak and Vojvodina, as well as Kosovo. A report on violations against ethnic Albanians in Kosovo was released in December 1996. In statements and reports, we also criticized Milosevic's failure to cooperate with the ICTY.

To keep the legacy of abuse committed during the war in Chechnya a vital issue in Russia and among international institutions, we published two reports about the war's aftermath: one addressed to the OSCE Review Conference in November 1996, the other timed for the January 27 presidential elections in Chechnya. In February, the first anniversary of Russia's membership in the Council of Europe, we issued a report enumerating Russia's failure to implement Council of Europe requirements, including its conduct during the Chechnya conflict and continued use of the death penalty. Building on our research and advocacy— locally and among the international community—on xenophobia, refugee rights and residence restrictions, we documented the Moscow residence permit system and the predatory and racist way in which it is enforced. Our Moscow office intervened in several specific cases and conducted regular advocacy to stop the extradition of refugees to other CIS countries. In an effort to secure a veto on the discriminatory law on religion, we urged the international community through numerous letters, briefings and other advocacy efforts to register concern about the deeply flawed law and

issued a series of letters to President Boris Yeltsin, the Council of Europe, and individual European leaders about our concerns. As provincial authorities attempted to silence local human rights activists and public defenders, we petitioned the Russian procurator general's office to secure their release.

Due to the deteriorating human rights situation in Belarus and Albania, our work in these countries took on a new urgency during 1997. Beginning soon after the crisis erupted in early 1997, three separate field missions to Albania allowed Human Rights Watch to document and publicize violations—such as the banning of demonstrations, police brutality, and the harassment of key opposition politicians, journalists, and government critics by the secret police—as they were taking place and to provide information to policymakers and the public. We followed up our field work with numerous statements and letters of concern addressed to the Albanian government and the international community. After the June elections, we worked to make international aid to Albania conditional on respect for human rights. In September, Human Rights Watch representatives met officials of the new government to discuss human rights concerns, including judicial reform, depoliticization of state institutions, and government respect for a free press.

Based on an April mission to Belarus to investigate the government's crackdown on civil society, we issued a severely critical report in August at press conferences in Minsk and Moscow and met with Belarusian government officials to present our findings and recommendations. As follow-up, we urged the Clinton administration, the OSCE and the E.U. to censure and isolate the regime of Aleksandr Lukashenka if human rights violations continued. We also pressed the Russian government to use its influence in Belarus to obtain human rights improvements.

The countries of Central Asia and the Caucasus suffer from numerous human rights violations, including to varying degrees torture and other mistreatment in detention, pervasive disregard for due process, strict control of the mass media, police brutality, and abysmal prison conditions. To highlight and expose human rights abuses there to greater international scrutiny, in light of the Council of Europe's review of human rights conditions in Armenia, Azerbaijan and Georgia for possible membership, as well as the growing international business interest in the region, Human Rights Watch began the process of establishing a permanent field office in Tbilisi, Georgia from which to monitor human rights in the Caucasus. During 1997, we made submissions to the U.N. Committee Against Torture (October) and the U.N. Human Rights Committee (March) highlighting ongoing concerns in Georgia. In March, we also made a submission to the U.N. Commission on Human Rights regarding serious human rights violations in Tajikistan, Turkmenistan, and Uzbekistan. A mission is underway in Azerbaijan as of this writing. In Uzbekistan, police brutality and the government's backtracking on its commitments to respect the independence of the press were the primary themes in our work.

In Turkey, we continued to press the government to put a stop to torture, including by holding abusive police accountable. We issued a report in March that exposed the systematic pattern of torture and other abuse by anti-terror police units, which have methodically incorporated torture and abuse into their daily operations, utilizing special equipment, including special straps to bind detainees, high-pressure hoses, racks for suspending suspects by their arms, and instruments to apply electric shock. We also conducted a fact-finding mission to the country in September to investigate ongoing violations of freedom of expression.

During 1997, Human Rights Watch attempted to make constructive recommendations related to cease-fires and peace talks in Bosnia, Northern Ireland, and Tajikistan. Taking lessons from other peace processes, we worked throughout the year to identify human rights concerns —most importantly, accountability for abuses committed during the conflicts, confidence-building measures such as the vetting of abusive military and police forces, and the creation of institutions to address the complaints of civilians— that would be essential to any successful peace process. We were intensely engaged in Northern Ireland during the year and worked with a coalition of human rights groups to monitor police action during the 1997 marching season. We issued a report analyzing police practices in Northern Ireland in May, at press conferences in London and Belfast, and met with government officials in Belfast, Dublin and London to discuss our findings. In Tajikistan, our field office monitored human rights during the peace negotiations, investigated the political crackdown in the Leninabad region, and raised our concerns about the treatment of Tajik refugees and returnees in numerous international fora.

Human Rights Watch continued to highlight the human rights implications of the European Union's increasingly restrictive asylum policies, believing that E.U. policies not only increased the risk of refoulement in individual cases, but also ran the risk of undermining internationally guaranteed refugee rights worldwide. In 1997, we continued to monitor asylum policies at the E.U. level, as well as in Sweden, the U.K., Germany, France, and the Netherlands, issuing reports on the Netherlands and on France during the year. In February, we called on E.U. member states to reject Spain's proposal to eliminate the right of E.U.-member-state nationals to seek asylum in the E.U. and, in April, we cosponsored a meeting of nongovernmental organizations, parliamentarians, and representatives of the European Commission and Council of Ministers to discuss the commission's proposed joint action on temporary protection.

In 1997, we remained committed to documenting human rights abuses against Roma and pressing governments to address the difficult problems of racially motivated violence both by private and state actors. Following up on a 1996 report on police abuse against Roma in the Czech Republic, we issued a translation of the report in 1997 and conducted numerous meetings with Czech government officials to urge progress on specific recommendations contained in the report.

For a listing of relevant reports and missions see page 459 at the end of this report. Partial listings also follow each country chapter.

ALBANIA

Human Rights Developments

1997 was a tumultuous and tragic year for Albania, in which approximately 2,000 people lost their lives during a popular revolt, the government's violent response, and the chaos that ensued. As discontent with the government spread, the state arrested and beat demonstrators, muzzled the press, and ordered the secret police and army to quell the uprising through all means. The ruling Democratic Party (DP) armed its supporters to defend the embattled president Sali Berisha, who ultimately lost power in an election monitored by the international community.

The spark for the mass protests was the collapse of criminally linked high-risk investment schemes in November and December 1996, in which large sections of the population lost their life savings. Many believed that Berisha's government was tolerating, if not directly involved in, the schemes. However, underlying the protests was dissatisfaction with Berisha's increasing authoritarianism and the fact that, by the end of 1996, Albania had become a one-party state based on fear and corruption. The DP controlled the executive, judiciary, and legislative branches of government, as well as the police, security service (SHIK), and electronic media.

In January 1997, the government responded to the growing protests with repression and force. Demonstrations were banned and the police beat and detained hundreds of protestors, especially in the south where the dissatisfaction with Berisha was most intense. On television, Berisha accused the protesters of being "red bandits" working in collaboration with "Albania's traditional enemies." The secret police harassed key opposition politicians, journalists, and government critics, whom the state-run media were blaming for inciting the crisis. At least eight people were physically attacked by unknown assailants believed to be the secret police during January and February, including the independent writer Edi Rama (January 22) and Socialist Party activist Ndre Legisi (January 27), both of whom were seriously injured. In all cases, the police failed to conduct an adequate investigation.

The government undertook increasingly repressive measures in January and February as the demonstrations grew more violent, and angry mobs ransacked the DP headquarters and municipal buildings in towns across the south. From January 26-30, the police and SHIK made wide-scale arrests in the southern towns of Lushnje, Berat, and Korça. Many people were taken from their homes in the middle of the night without an arrest warrant and held for three to four days in unspecified locations. Upon their release, many reported physical abuse and torture.

Journalists also came under increasing attack, especially Albanians working with foreign news agencies. Correspondents with Reuters, Associated Press, and the BBC were followed and received threatening phone calls from unidentified persons believed to work for the state. Some of them were detained by the police or had their equipment and notebooks confiscated during demonstrations. A number of them fled the country out of fear for their lives.

Violent protest erupted into open fighting with the SHIK in the southern city of Vlora on February 27, one day after approximately one hundred secret police forces were sent south from Tirana. The violence quickly spread to other cities in the south, where insurgents overran police stations and army bases, arming themselves with automatic weapons, grenades and anti-aircraft guns.

Berisha mobilized the army, and parliament declared a state of emergency on March 2, which included a shoot-to-kill policy on armed insurgents and a curfew. The emergency legislation also placed restrictions on public gatherings and required that newspapers be cleared by a government censor. Article 3 of the emergency law stated that investigations would begin immediately against those who had "organized or instigated the revolt," which allowed the government to intimidate those who had peacefully expressed their opposition to the government and had not been involved in the violence. The day the state of emergency went into effect, a rubber-stamp parliament re-elected Berisha to another five-year term as president.

That night the office of the largest opposition newspaper, *Koha Jone*, was destroyed by arsonists believed to be members of the secret police. On three occasions during the night, groups of armed men fired automatic rifles at the paper's office and, during their last visit, set the building on fire. The police never conducted an investigation. That night, two *Koha Jone* employees were detained by plainclothes policemen in Tirana; Alfred Peza, a journalist, was detained in the police station in Fier on March 4. All three were held for one day and beaten.

Meanwhile, DP "volunteers" were armed by the party with assistance from the secret police. Local DP branches handed out weapons to their supporters throughout the country, especially in Tirana and the north. These armed civilians, together with SHIK, comprised Berisha's defense in the capital.

On March 6, after an E.U. and OSCE delegation visited Tirana, Berisha withdrew the armed forces from the south, leaving the population free to commandeer army, navy, and air force bases across the region. By this time, many of the young conscripts had already defected, and large sections of the population, including children, became heavily armed. Prisoners broke free from the state's prisons; criminals and armed gangs took advantage of the chaos to loot businesses and terrorize the local population. There were many reports of rapes and murders.

Increasingly isolated in Tirana and under pressure from the international community, on March 9 Berisha agreed to form a Government of National Reconciliation with representatives from all the Albanian political parties, although the DP maintained control of the all-important Ministry of the Interior. The transitional government, headed by a Socialist, was mandated to restore order and prepare the country for new parliamentary elections that were scheduled for June 28. But Berisha maintained control of the secret police and broadcast media.

Outside the capital, "salvation committees" were formed. In some places they were local attempts to restore order; in other places they were run by gangsters intent on profiting from the chaos and Albania's lucrative trade in cigarettes, arms, drugs, and the trafficking of women. The DP claimed that some of these committees were supporting the Socialist Party.

On March 28, the U.N. Security Council authorized an eight-country military force, led by Italy, to secure the delivery of humanitarian aid, even though humanitarian organizations said that such protection was not required. Most observers believed the unspoken reason for the intervention was to stem the flow of Albanian refugees to Italy and other neighboring countries.

The elections on June 28 were monitored by the OSCE with assistance from the multi-national military force, which escorted foreign observers. Despite anarchic conditions that created obstacles to the electoral process, such as the Democratic Party's inability to campaign in the south and Berisha's strict control of the state media, the elections proceeded in a surprisingly fair manner. The international community deemed them "adequate and acceptable."

The Socialist Party (former Communists) won more than two thirds of the seats in the new parliament, compared to 25 percent for the Democratic Party. Six other parties also won seats in the 140-seat assembly. After some delay, Berisha resigned, and Fatos Nano, who had been imprisoned by Berisha for four years following an unfair trial in 1993, was elected prime minister. A five-party coalition government was formed, and a physicist, Rexhep Mejdani, was chosen president.

At the end of 1997, it was still too early to evaluate the new government's human rights record. Nano had condemned political revenge and promised to return Albania to a state governed by the rule of law. Some signs were promising: in September a repressive press law, enacted by Berisha in 1993, was abrogated, and the state television, radio, and press agency (ATA) became more open to a diversity of political views, although they were still subject to political pressures. The government was attempting to collect arms from the population, and a commission to draft a constitution had been formed.

However, the now-opposition Democratic Party, headed by Berisha, was complaining of politically motivated purges of state employees. DP deputies staged hunger strikes to protest what they viewed as biased coverage in the state television and radio against the DP. On September 20, a well-known DP deputy, Azem Hajdari, was shot by a Socialist deputy inside the parliament building. Hajdari claimed it was a political attack, but evidence suggests that it was an individual act of revenge. The government condemned the attack, arrested the attacker, and charged him with attempted murder.

The Right to Monitor
The general atmosphere of fear during the 1996-97 crisis restricted the work of domestic human rights organizations, but there were no direct attempts by the government to hinder their work. Before and during the crisis, however, critical human rights groups came under constant attack in the state-run media for being "communists" or "enemies of the state." The June 28 elections were monitored freely by local and foreign organizations, both governmental and nongovernmental.

Since the elections, Human Rights Watch/Helsinki is not aware of any government attempts to restrict local or international human rights groups. However, on June 30, a Human Rights Watch representative was struck once during a press conference of the Democratic Party by an unidentified person believed to be a supporter of the DP. In early July, a member of the British Helsinki Human Rights Group, an organization that

has supported Berisha and the DP, was reportedly shot at by an unknown assailant as he sat in a cafe with Tritan Shehu, the former foreign minister and DP secretary general.

The Role of the International Community

Europe
The international community bears some responsibility for the crisis in Albania. Eager for an ally in the region during the war in Bosnia, the United States and West European governments, especially Italy, provided high levels of political and economic support to Berisha's government from 1991-96 despite the human rights abuses and corruption that were taking place. The European Union provided more aid per capita to Albania (U.S. $560 million since 1990) than to any other East European country, even though the E.U.'s Trade and Cooperation Agreement with Albania was conditioned on "respect for democratic principles and human rights." The Council of Europe, especially the head of the Parliamentary Assembly, Leni Fischer, failed to criticize the government—and even praised Berisha—despite the ongoing violations. Such unqualified support, without regard for the Albanian government's human rights record, helped Berisha dismantle all viable political forces in the country, some of which were more moderate and democratic minded.

The European community reversed its one-sided position once the crisis began to have international ramifications. An OSCE mission, headed by former Austrian Chancellor Franz Vranitzky, was instrumental in brokering the creation of the reconciliation government and organizing the June elections. The multi-national military force escorted foreign election monitors during the elections and helped stabilize the country. However, on March 28, approximately eighty Albanians drowned in the Straits of Otranto when an Italian military ship collided with an Albanian ferry packed with refugees heading to Italy. At year's end, the circumstances of the accident remained unclear.

After the elections, the European community pledged its support for the new government, as long as it undertakes the necessary economic and political reform, such as cleaning up the pyramid schemes and initiating legal reform. At a donors' conference in Brussels, the international community, including the World Bank and International Monetary Fund, pledged U.S. $600 million in support without articulating clear human rights conditions.

United States

From 1991-1996, the United States was one of Berisha's most fervent supporters; it provided Albania with U.S. $236 million in aid, making the U.S. the second largest bilateral donor (following Italy). In return, Berisha opened Albania's ports and airstrips for NATO use and allowed C.I.A. spy planes to be based in the country. Despite this, the U.S. was the first country publicly to express dissatisfaction with Berisha's authoritarianism, although it did so long after ample evidence of serious human rights violations had mounted. More than other countries, the U.S. criticized the fraudulent parliamentary elections that took place in May 1996, as well as other human rights violations.

In 1997, the U.S. played a central role in supporting the reconciliation government, facilitating the elections and encouraging Berisha to accept the results. According to the Department of State, future aid will be conditioned on human rights, although no detailed plan was devised. In October, Prime Minister Nano met Secretary of State Albright in Washington.

ARMENIA

Human Rights Developments

In 1997, the government of Armenia showed tentative signs of easing some of the restrictions on political activity and freedom of the press imposed in the wake of the severe crackdown on the opposition that followed

the September 22, 1996, presidential elections. But despite these limited measures, the results were often uneven and did not lead to substantial improvements in human rights conditions.

Notably, the government kept in place the December 1994 ban on the Armenian Revolutionary Federation, or *Dashnaktsutiyun*, a prominent opposition party. At that time, the government banned the Dashnak party and party-affiliated newspapers after accusing several individuals of membership in Dro, a secret terrorist organization within the party whose alleged goal was overthrow of the government.

During the year the government carried out negotiations with Dashnak party leaders aimed at reinstating the party. However, the discussions yielded no tangible results and the government cited what most observers note are easily surmountable technical difficulties for continuing the ban, originally slated to last six months. The government did allow party members access to previously confiscated equipment thereby allowing for publication of a Dashnak-affiliated newspaper, *Hoyots Ashkhar*. However, the authorities did not officially lift the ban on other Dashnak-affiliated newspapers.

In 1997, there were three separate sets of trials in which the government prosecuted members of the opposition alleged to have participated in three attempted coups, including those accused of membership in Dro. Three of eleven defendants found guilty of involvement in activities associated with Dro were given death sentences in December 1996. In July a Supreme Court appeals council reduced the death sentence to fifteen years of imprisonment for one of the defendants, Arsen Grigorian, convicted of murder and of drug trafficking. The appeals council denied the clemency petitions of two other defendants in the case who were similarly convicted of murder and drug trafficking.

President Ter-Petrossian indicated that executions will not be carried out in Armenia during his term, and no official executions were reported. However, the president has not commuted the sentences of those currently under the death sentence. In April, the National Assembly favorably reported a bill on the first reading that would abolish the death penalty. A second reading of the bill was expected later in the year.

The government continued prosecuting thirty-one defendants in a second Dashnak-related set of trials. The defendants stand accused of involvement in a July 1995 coup attempt that the government alleges was intended to disrupt by-elections. The trial of the lead defendant, Dashnak party chief Vahan Hovannisyan, charged with organizing activities aimed at the overthrow of the government and terrorism, dragged on through 1997. Throughout the proceedings Hovannisyan alleged, with good reason, that deliberate delays and postponements in the trial were intended to hinder the defense, that witnesses had been pressured into providing false evidence they later recanted, and that on several occasions he was refused access to his attorney. Earlier in the year Hovannisyan and other defendants on trial complained of pressure and beatings of some of their family members by Interior Ministry personnel.

In February prosecution began of individuals charged with involvement in disturbances in the wake of the September 1996 presidential elections, when demonstrators entered the National Assembly building and beat parliamentary speaker Babken Araktsyan and deputy speaker Ara Sahakyan. In a positive development, Armenia's new prosecutor general, Genrik Hachatryan, was reported to have acknowledged in May that legal proceedings in the Dashnak-related trial of thirty-one were unjustifiably dragged out. One of the September 1996 defendants, Manik Sagsyan, convicted of engaging in an act of terrorism and organizing mass disturbances, stated that she was tortured during the investigatory phase of her detention. Her five-year prison sentence was reduced to three years of probation on the grounds that she lacked a prior record and was responsible for the care of her mother and son. As of this writing the prosecutor's office has not investigated Sagsyan's torture charges.

Other defendants, including Vage Varsanyan, who served as a member of the Yerevan electoral commission representing the opposition National Democratic Union; Onik Unanyan; and Seryezha Melkonyan, were convicted after having charges against them reduced from organizing mass disturbances to a lesser charge of disturbing public order, and received suspended sentences in June. The defendants alleged that they were severely beaten subsequent to their September arrests and later in court withdrew their initial testimony after stating that it had been gained under duress.

Kim Balayan, a member of the Dashnak party leadership and a former member of parliament, was convicted of organizing mass disturbances and was given a suspended sentence of two years of imprisonment in June. Balayan claimed that he was singled out for prosecution due to past animosities with Armenia's prosecutor general related to Balayan's former position as chairman of the National Assembly's justice commission.

In addition to outright bans on Dashnak-affiliated newspapers imposed in December 1994, the government continued to exercise control over the media through through its monopoly ownership of printing equipment and the newspaper distribution system, *Haimamul.* The government also maintained a capricious and arbitrary system for licensing television stations that limits the media's ability to broadcast information critical of the government.

Moreover, local reporters stated that security forces confiscated broadcast journalists' equipment and used arbitrary detention and threats during questioning to discourage the broadcast or publication of information it deemed embarrassing or critical of the government or of officials. The result has been to encourage journalists to engage in self-censorship, especially on topics related to government corruption and national security issues. Three reporters from Noyan Tapan news service were reported to have been detained for seven hours and pressured during questioning by Interior Ministry personnel in June after printing articles on Nagorno

Karabakh deemed to infringe on national security. On March 7, unidentified attackers broke into the offices of *Yerevan Orer* newspaper, demanding that the editor, Mikael Hairapetyan, erase the newspaper from the computer's memory. Hairapetyan's attackers beat him when he did not comply, and he stated that their demands that he cease to publish the newspaper led him to believe that the incident was politically motivated.

The Right To Monitor

Human Rights Watch is not aware of instances of restrictions on the monitoring of abuses. However, the ransacking of a library in August maintained by the Constitutional and Human Rights Center in Vanadzor, a partner organization of the Armenian Helsinki Association, raised concerns.

The Role of the International Community

Council of Europe

The Council of Europe continues to evaluate Armenia's application for membership. Lawyers advising the Parliamentary Assembly of the Council of Europe (PACE) rightfully concluded in a May 1997 report that Armenia's judicial system is currently incompatible with council standards for human rights protection. The report noted that although provisions to protect basic human rights are spelled out in Armenian law, the court system lacks the necessary independence from the executive and legislative branch to guarantee them in practice.

The report characterized Armenia's political system as in crisis and noted that the crisis had to be resolved in such a way as to ensure pluralism and give meaning to the institutions of parliamentary democracy already established. Further reports by members of PACE committees overseeing the application process, including the subcommittee on human rights, are expected following visits scheduled for October and November.

United States

The State Department's *Country Report on Human Rights Practices for 1996* presented an accurate portrait of Armenia's human rights situation in 1996. The report characterized the September 1996 presidential elections as flawed and added that the Constitutional Court's handling of a case brought by opposition parties protesting the results did not assuage doubts about the credibility of the official election results. It also drew attention to violence by security forces immediately after the elections and to the beating of detainees during arrest and interrogation.

The State Department's report is comprehensive in its treatment of human rights abuses, and U.S. Embassy staff in Yerevan are well informed about violations through regular meetings with individuals and opposition groups. Moreover, U.S. Ambassador Peter Tomsen identified assistance with development of democratic institutions as an important U.S. policy priority in Armenia and has favored increased U.S. spending for such projects.

Armenia received an earmark of U.S. $95 million in the Fiscal Year 1997 foreign operations appropriations bill, and it may receive funding at similar levels in FY 1998, making it one of the highest per capita recipients of U.S. foreign assistance in the world. Given the government's heavy reliance on funds provided by the U.S. and the international community, the U.S. failed to use its influence on the government to the fullest extent possible to further lift restrictions on political activity and to halt abuses by Interior and Security Ministry personnel. Further, the U.S. Embassy failed to make public statements on breeches of due process associated with ongoing trials during the year.

AZERBAIJAN

Human Rights Developments

Azerbaijan's human rights record in 1997 continued to be dismal but had no perceptible impact on the unprecedented level of involvement by the international community and international business in the country. International investment activity in the petroleum sector was feverish: two new consortia were formed for Caspian sea oil, President Heydar Aliyev signed agreements with U.S. oil companies totaling U.S.$10 billion, and drilling began in some fields. The international community largely glossed over Azerbaijan's poor human rights record in order to protect oil interests.

In 1997 (January 9 and 16, March 19) the Supreme Court of Azerbaijan convicted fifty-six individuals implicated in the March 1995 uprising by the Special Task Force Police (OPON) in Baku. In the January 9 trial, several individuals who had given testimony against the lead defendant later retracted it in court, claiming police had extracted it using torture. In December 1996, the court for the second time had refused to order forensic evidence in the cases of defendants convicted on January 16—evidence that might have supported their seemingly credible claims of the torture endured during the investigation.

The Supreme Court convicted all twenty-one defendants in the so-called Case of the Generals, in which four generals and one civilian were charged with planning coups in April and August 1995. In December 1996 nineteen of the defendants wrote to Amnesty International claiming they were tortured.

The treason trial of five members of the Islamic party of Azerbaijan, for allegedly spying for Iran, ended in lengthy prison sentences for four. In 1996, police released two other suspects in arrested in the same case to the custody of their families: one died as a result of injuries he had sustained during police torture.

Against this backdrop, the chair of the parliamentary human rights commission in January acknowledged that prison conditions in Azerbaijan were poor, but claimed that there were no political prisoners in Azerbaijan. Regarding torture of OPON defendants, he acknowledged that "sometimes there were mistakes," but he discounted even this by suggesting that, since the OPON members were found guilty, they had brought the ill-treatment upon themselves.

Political arrests on alleged coup and treason charges continued in late 1996 and in 1997. On November 25, 1996, police arrested Rasim Agayev, press secretary to former president Ayaz Mutalibov, on charges of high treason in connection with yet another alleged coup attempt. On March 18, police confiscated Mr. Agayev's academic works, claiming they contained coup plans. On January 13, police arrested Akhad Mamedov, assistant to the chair of the opposition party Musavat, allegedly because his telephone number was in the phone book of a man charged with espionage. Two Musavat officials remained under police investigation for their role in attempting to prevent the June 1993 coup that eventually brought President Aliyev to power.

In a positive move, on January 29, the procuracy released former Prime Minister Panah Huseinov after nine months in detention, although it did not drop the corruption charges against him.

Media censorship continued in 1997, despite government claims to the contrary, especially on such "sensitive" issues as criticism of President Aliyev's policy on Nagorno Karabakh, on oil, and on human rights, including critical thought about Azerbaijan's entry to the Council of Europe. In January, the opposition daily *Azadlyg* (Independence) reported that in 1996, 105 issues were censored in some way, including twenty-seven articles and three caricatures that were completely banned and seventy-six articles that were partially banned. A Baku district court fined an *Azadlyg* journalist for insulting the honor and dignity of the Milli Majlis (parliament) for commenting that one member, a former teacher, treated the parliament like a school auditorium, and its deputies like school children. The Ganja local government confiscated all 2,400 copies of a book about the 19th century Russian occupation of Ganja.

A Baku police station chief beat journalist Tapdyg Farkhadoglu on November 17 after his interview with an opposition leader. The government closed its investigation of the beating on January 28, allegedly because the suspect could not be located, and re-opened it under pressure in April, with no results.

The government sought to maintain a virtual information blockade on the Nakhchivan Autonomous Republic, accessible to the rest of Azerbaijan only by air. In a move to isolate former president Abulfaz Elchibey, who resides in the Nakhchivan village of Keleki, and to prevent his return to Baku, police repeatedly prevented him from meeting with journalists and opposition leaders. On May 4, Nakhchivan police questioned an *Azadlyg* journalist, held him for eleven days (for allegedly resisting police officers), and fined him 22,000 manat. In July, police at the Nakhchivan airport questioned Irene Lasota, editor of the U.S. publication *Uncaptive Minds*, and attempted to confiscate materials from her interview with Mr. Elchibey; on September 6 two politicians and two journalists attempted to visit Mr. Elchibey, but were turned back to Baku at the Nakhchivan airport; similar incidents occurred September 11 and October 6. On October 30, however, Mr. Elchibey returned to Baku on a plane provided by the Azerbaijani government.

Police harassed opposition political parties mostly by preventing local party conferences and other gatherings. This harassment is significant in its own right, and also given the likelihood of presidential elections in 1998. In January, Salyan district police prevented the Party of Civic Solidarity from staging a meeting between activists and residents. Police dispersed members of the Azerbaijani Popular Front Party (APFP) as they attempted to hold a conference on June 3 and forbade the APFP from meeting in Lerik district. On June 28 police in the Qebele district broke up a Musavat conference. In February, a court ruled illegal the Ministry of Justice's persistent refusal to register the Democratic Party of Azerbaijan, yet as of this writing the party remained unregistered.

The Right to Monitor

Verbal attacks by members of parliament and in the state-run press against the human rights movement in 1997 targeted individual activists rather than organizations. Two deputies to the Milli Majlis unleashed a veritable witch hunt in the state-owned media against Arzu Abdullayeva, head of the Azerbaijani National Committee of the Helsinki Citizens Assembly, Leyla Yunusova, chair of the Institute for Peace and Democracy (a human rights advocacy group) and co-chair of the Vahdat political party, and Lala Gajiyeva, of the Liberal Party. The unfounded smear campaign against Ms. Abdullayeva criticized her defense of the rights of ethnic Armenians in Azerbaijan and branded her an Armenian spy; the campaign painted Ms. Yunosova, who has spoken out frequently against government abuse, as a spy for the Russian military.

The Ministry of Justice arranged for at least two visits by non-governmental human rights organizations to post-conviction labor camps, but continued to refuse access to pretrial facilities.

The Role of the International Community

Europe

As part of its procedure for considering Azerbaijan's membership application, the Council of Europe sent a team of attorneys to Baku to evaluate the degree to which the country's legal system met Council standards; as of this writing the report has not been made public. During their visit the team spoke frankly to the press about Azerbaijan's human rights problems.

In November, the OSCE's Office for Democratic Institutions and Human Rights (ODIHR), organized a conference for government officials on the role of the judiciary in the rule of law. Ambassador Audrey Glover, head of ODIHR, limited her public remarks on the human rights situation in Azerbaijan. In a meeting with journalists she stated, "Azerbaijan is in first stage of transition from totalitarianism to democracy and we want to help it along this path," a lost opportunity for the OSCE to acknowledge the country's poor record.

United States

President Aliyev made the first state visit ever to the U.S. by an Azerbaijani head of state, a clear sign of the Clinton administration's desire to promote U.S. oil interests. Human rights concerns were eclipsed by the overwhelming business and political concessions President Aliyev gained during the visit, including $10 billion in contracts with U.S. oil companies; administration pledges to overhaul or circumvent Section 907 of the Freedom Support Act, legislation that bans direct U.S. assistance to the Azerbaijani government; and a joint statement with the Department of Defense indicating the Pentagon's desire to deepen its relationship with the Azerbaijani military through education and training. Both President Clinton and Secretary of State Madeline Albright raised human rights issues; however since no information about such conversations was made public, President Aliyev was able to claim later that the Clinton administration approved of Azerbaijan's progress on rule of law.

Draft foreign trade legislation would circumvent Section 907 by authorizing operations by the Overseas Private Investment Corporation and the Trade Development Agency. As of this writing legislation had not been adopted.

REPUBLIC OF BELARUS

Human Rights Developments

The Belarusian government stepped up its campaign to crush civil society and opposition activities in 1997 and ignored international pressure to restore respect for human rights and the rule of law. In the first half of the year, the government sought to silence opposition by sanctioning police violence to break up opposition demonstrations; detaining and fining opposition leaders, demonstrators, and passers-by; harassing journalists; and threatening newspapers and nongovernmental organizations with closure. In the second half of the year, the government's campaign targeted several journalists and political opponents of the president with politically motivated criminal charges.

The new constitution, adopted in a highly controversial referendum in November 1996, subordinated the legislature and judiciary to the executive, thereby significantly broadening President Lukashenka's powers. President Lukashenka disbanded the Supreme Soviet (the old parliament) and hand-picked a new parliament (the National Assembly) from deputies who had remained loyal to him. He also altered the Constitutional Court making more than half of its members presidential appointees.

The referendum, the union treaty with Russia, and Lukashenka's repressive policies triggered a series of street protests by the Belarusian opposition in the first months of 1997. Seeking to end what he called an "orgy of street democracy," on March 5 President Lukashenka issued a decree restricting demonstrations that, among other things, forbade the use of unregistered flags, as well as posters and other objects deemed to insult the honor and dignity of officials of the state. The decree also established a system of exorbitantly high penalties for violations of the decree, especially by participants and organizers of demonstrations. As of this writing, the National Assembly was working on a draft law on demonstrations containing the same provisions as the presidential decree.

Police regularly broke up demonstrations, arbitrarily arresting both participants and bystanders and using excessive violence that seemed aimed more at spreading terror than at restoring or protecting public order. Police also beat up and detained numerous journalists during demonstrations in early 1997. On March 14, police prevented a demonstration altogether, arresting scores of bystanders, including elderly women and children as young as fourteen years old, who later faced trial on fabricated charges. Almost all court hearings in cases related to demonstrations were blatantly unfair. Judges refused to allow testimony by defense witnesses and based their decisions on testimony from police officers. Hundreds of people were sentenced to between three and fifteen days of administrative detention and fines from U.S.$100 to U.S.$800. (The average monthly salary in Belarus is less than $100.)

The Belarusian government used arbitrary rent increases and audits to intimidate nongovernmental organizations (NGOs), and in particular targeted Children of Chernobyl, a humanitarian NGO that helps victims of the 1986 Chernobyl disaster. In late 1996, the government raised the organization's rent twenty-fold and conducted an audit in March. A preliminary report of the audit, issued in May, contained highly speculative accusations against the founder of the organization, Gennady Grushevoy. On the basis of the report, a Minsk prosecutor announced on public television that criminal proceedings had been instituted against Grushevoy, who was in Germany at the time of writing as he feared immediate arrest upon return to Belarus.

In an apparent attempt to deprive Belarus' nascent civil society of one of its main sources of financial assistance, the Belarusian authorities ordered an audit of the Belarusian Soros Foundation and subsequently imposed a U.S.$3 million fine for alleged currency exchange violations. After unsuccessfully attempting to find a compromise with the Belarusian government, the Soros Foundation closed its office in Belarus on September 3.

President Lukashenka eroded the independence of lawyers in a decree obliging all lawyers to become member of lawyers' collegia, which are tightly controlled by the Ministry of Justice. The decree also established that lawyers could receive a required license only after passing an exam with a qualification commission, which is headed by the Minister of Justice. In an act of political harassment, the ministry stripped Mechislav Grib, a deputy of the disbanded Supreme Soviet, of his license on July 7, claiming it had a right to do so because a court had convicted him for organizing an opposition rally in violation of the March 5 decree.

The crackdown on the independent media intensified in 1997. Having banned public discussion from the pages of the state-owned press, the Belarusian government moved its campaign of harassment to the independent print media. The authorities audited several independent newspapers in late 1996 and handed down punitive and disproportionate fines on grounds of questionable validity. The State Committee on the Press issued warnings and threatened to close various newspapers for their publication of articles that allegedly violated the press law but fell well within the limits of freedom of speech. In August, the Minsk prosecutor's office opened criminal investigations against *Izvestiya* (a leading Russian newspaper) correspondent Alexander Starikevich and the newspaper *Svaboda* for an article the correspondent wrote in that newspaper, which called for mass protests against Lukashenka's government. The Belarusian government considered the article to be libelous and to call for the violent overthrow of the government.

On several occasions, the Belarusian government used legislation to attack freedom of the press. On March 18 it issued a decree banning the import and export of information deemed to threaten "the national security, rights and freedoms of individuals, health and morale of the population, and environmental protection." On June 25, the lower house of the National Assembly approved draft amendments to the press law that would codify the decree into law. The law would also empower the State Committee on the Press to close media outlets, should they violate the press law, and to ban publications deemed libelous of the Belarusian president and other state officials. Finally, foreign media could distribute their products only with the approval of the State Committee on the Press and could only set up representative offices with approval of both the committee and the Ministry of Foreign Affairs.

In an apparent attempt to block the wide circulation of information critical of his government, President Lukashenka specifically attacked Russian television transmissions, which can be received in most of Belarus. The authorities several times forbade Russian television journalists to transmit video materials of opposition rallies and, on March 24, 1997, stripped Alexander Stupnikov, correspondent for Russian independent television, of his accreditation and expelled him from the country for alleged systematic distortion of information about events in Belarus. On July 7, Pavel Sheremet, Russian Public Television (ORT) Minsk bureau chief, was stripped of his accreditation for similar reasons.

On July 26, several days after they filmed a program intending to demonstrate the transparency of the Belarusian-Lithuanian border, Belarusian police arrested Pavel Sheremet and two of his crew members on charges of having "unlawfully crossed the border." President Lukashenka—making far-fetched claims that new, high technology border security equipment was being tested in the area—charged that Sheremet was working not for ORT but for a foreign intelligence agency. Belarusian police arrested yet another ORT crew on August 16. Like Sheremet's crew, the journalists had also intended to film the border but were arrested a short distance from their destination. They were charged with "attempted border violations" and held in detention. After pressure from Russia, Belarusian authorities released all the journalists relatively quickly, with the notable exception of Sheremet, who was finally released on October 8, having spent seventy-four days in custody. ORT correspondent Anatoliy Adamchuck (of the second crew) and Sheremet's cameraman, Dmitri Zavadsky, were pressured into writing letters to President Lukashenka requesting their release. After his release, Zavadsky claimed that the letter circulated by the Belarusian authorities, which contained his confession and apologies, significantly differed from what he indeed had written. On August 20, the Belarusian government announced that ORT's accreditation had been annulled and accused ORT of organizing "a political provocation against the country's leadership." As of this writing, the trials of the journalists had yet to begin.

Members of the disbanded Supreme Soviet and of political parties, among the main organizers of protest rallies, came under constant government attack. Numerous deputies were detained and beaten during demonstrations, and sentenced to administrative detention and fines, and one of them was beaten up by unknown men in his home. The prosecutor's office launched criminal investigations against at least three deputies. One of them, Vladimir Kudinov was charged with giving a bribe of U.S.$500 and sentenced to seven years of imprisonment in August, a case that Belarusian human rights activists claim was political rather than criminal. On August 29, deputy Viktor Gonchar, head of the Supreme Soviet committee that investigated unlawful actions by the Belarusian president, was forcibly taken to the prosecutor's office in Minsk and charged with libeling President Lukashenka. He was released after questioning. Similarly, political motives seemed apparent in criminal proceedings against former Central Bank director Tamara Vinnikova, who was arrested in early 1997 on economic charges.

The Right to Monitor

In 1997 the government targeted the Belarusian Helsinki Committee (BHC). Several BHC members were arrested during demonstrations in March, April and June. One of them was acquitted in court while the others received warnings, fines or sentences of administrative detention. Police beat up two monitors of the organization during demonstrations on March 14 and April 2. The BHC came under renewed attack on October 20, when twenty-one-year-old Nadezhda Zhukova, a trial and demonstration observer, was assaulted and threatened with reprisals after leaving the Leninsky District Court by three men who identified themselves as "young Belarusian patriots," which raised suspicion that they were members of the pro-presidential Belarusian Patriotic Youth Movement that openly advocates violence. Further evidence suggested police collusion in the assault. In a clear case of harassment, on October 23, Tatiana Protko, the head of the BHC, while interviewing a dismissed collective farm manager in Mohilev region, was arrested on charges of obstructing the work of local officials who had arrived to "measure" the farm manager's home. The charge was later changed to "illegal personal assumption of government authority." However, at her trial the following morning, the case against her was dismissed.

Government policies aimed at marginalizing the independent press seriously limited the circulation of information on the human rights situation in Belarus. Human Rights Watch was not aware of restrictions placed on monitoring by international human rights groups.

The Role of the International Community

The international community responded swiftly to the sharp decline in the human rights situation in Belarus. In October, Belarus reported to the U.N. Human Rights Committee (HRC) on its implementation of the International Covenant on Civil and Political Rights. As of this writing, the HRC has yet to issue its final recommendations, but in its preliminary concluding observations the committee noted that Belarusian citizens seem to be under "police pressure reminiscent of the era of the former Soviet Union" and urged the Belarusian government to lift its restrictions on a variety of civil and political rights.

European Union

The European Union (E.U.) reacted to the November 1996 referendum by sending a fact-finding mission to Belarus to investigate the circumstances of the referendum in January. Based on the conclusions of this mission, the E.U. Council of Ministers conditioned economic cooperation programs with Belarus on concrete steps to establish the rule of law. With this aim, a working group—involving E.U. mediators and representatives of the Belarusian government and the opposition—was created to discuss a new constitution that would guarantee a true separation of powers and human rights. On September 15, the E.U. Council of Ministers suspended the dialogue indefinitely, stating that President

Lukashenka had not acted in good faith and had obstructed the dialogue.

Council of Europe and the Organization for Security and Cooperation in Europe

The Parliamentary Assembly of the Council of Europe suspended Belarus' special guest status in late January 1997 in reaction to the November 1996 referendum. The Organization for Security and Cooperation in Europe (OSCE) sent a fact-finding mission to Belarus from April 15 to 18 which concluded that "there is every indication that the [Belarusian] authorities are constructing a system of totalitarian government." The OSCE delegation recommended that a permanent OSCE representation be established in Minsk to monitor the human rights situation and advise the Belarusian government on promoting democracy. Although the Belarusian government agreed to the presence of such an OSCE representation, it obstructed the establishment of the office by suspending negotiations on July 18, 1997. Only on September 18, after the E.U. had suspended its dialogue with the Belarusian government, did Belarus agree to resume negotiations.

Inexplicably, the Inter-Parliamentary Union, having suspended Belarus in April for establishing the National Assembly "through a process whose legality is questioned," promptly reinstated the country just before the September Inter-Parliamentary Conference in Cairo. Belarus authorities exploited this move in their attempts to reinstate Belarus as a special observer in the Council of Europe.

United States

Following the November 1996 referendum, the United States reassessed its policy toward Belarus. Considering that Belarus' poor human rights record had reduced the framework for constructive relations, the Clinton administration adopted a policy of selective engagement, limiting government contacts to a minimum while continuing to work with democratic institutions, such as the independent media and NGOs.

Relations were strained further when, first, Peter Byrne, Executive Director of the Belarusian Soros Foundation, was refused entry into Belarus on March 16, and a week later Serge Aleksandrov, the U.S. Embassy's first secretary, was expelled from the country for his alleged participation in an opposition demonstration. The Clinton administration protested the expulsion, expelled a Belarusian diplomat and requested that the new Belarusian ambassador to the U.S. delay his posting.

Relevant Human Rights Watch report:
Republic of Belarus: Crushing Civil Society, 8/97

BOSNIA AND HERCEGOVINA

Human Rights Developments

A fragile peace, established by the U.S.-brokered Dayton Peace Agreement (DPA), held Bosnia and Hercegovina throughout 1997. Persons indicted for war crimes continued to exert political and economic control in the region and used their power to obstruct the implementation of the civilian components of the DPA. Their ongoing influence contributed to an overall poor human rights situation throughout the country. During 1997, few displaced persons were able to return to their prewar homes, ethnically-motivated expulsions and evictions remained common, and freedom of movement remained limited. Police on both sides of the Inter-Entity Boundary Line (IEBL) served as instruments of the dominant political parties and were responsible for some of the worst abuses. Ethnic minorities, the independent media, and members of political opposition parties were particularly vulnerable to harassment and ill-treatment. The absence of a functioning, independent judiciary meant that such groups were especially unlikely to enjoy equal protection under the law or access to remedies for abuses suffered at the hands of the state. Media was often times another means for hard-line nationalists to incite violence, including against international monitors, and to encourage the obstruction of the DPA. Grave concerns were raised about the integrity of the September 1997 municipal elections which were carried out under the auspices of OSCE. An overall atmosphere of impunity prevailed.

To varying degrees, all three dominant ethnically-based political parties continued to resist integration. The process of establishing common institutions following the September 1996 national elections progressed slowly. The Bosnian Serb authorities, in particular, boycotted meetings of joint institutions. Similarly, despite claims by the Bosnian Croat authorities that they had dissolved the self-proclaimed "Croat Republic of Herceg-Bosna," the political goal of a separate Croat entity was perpetuated by the formation of the "Croat Community of Herceg-Bosna."

War criminals

While the primary responsibility for the arrest and extradition of war criminals lies with the regional governments, few were willing to fulfill their obligation. This was particularly true of the local authorities in the Republika Srpska (RS) who resolutely refused to turn over to the International Criminal Court for the Former Yugoslavia any of the thirty-eight indicted persons still believed to be in RS territory. RS President Biljana Plavsic informed U.N. Secretary General Kofi Annan by letter in January that the Republika Srpska would not hand over Radovan Karadzic and Ratko Mladic (the former commander of the Bosnian Serb Army) to the ICTY, a decision supported by Republika Srspka Prime Minister Gojko Klickovic only a few days later. During most of 1997, the Bosnian Croat authorities refused to cooperate with the ICTY. However, under intense pressure from the international community, on October 6, ten Bosnian Croat indictees were handed over and transferred to the Hague. Nevertheless, as of this writing, the

Bosnian Croat authorities continued to harbor four other indicted persons.

There appeared to be a shift in the international community's policy regarding arrests during June and July, when troops of the United Nations Transitional Authority in Eastern Slavonia (UNTAES) detained Slavko Dokmanovic, the former Serb mayor of Vukovar, and handed him over to the Hague. This arrest was followed by an arrest effort by British SFOR (Stabilization Force, successor to IFOR) troops on July 10 of two persons indicted by the ICTY in and near Prijedor, in the northwestern part of the Republika Srpska. Milan Kovacevic, the town's hospital director and formerly a municipal official, was detained by British troops. Simo Drljaca, the town's former chief of police and ongoing de facto leader of the town, was killed during a shoot-out with British soldiers when he resisted arrest. While the arrest of Kovacevic and the attempted arrest of Drljaca seemed to indicate a changed policy concerning the apprehension of persons indicted by the ICTY, no further arrests were made by SFOR.

Although fully authorized by the Dayton agreement and various Security Council resolutions to arrest persons indicted by the ICTY, SFOR chose to interpret its mandate narrowly, insisting that it was not obliged to search for and apprehend persons indicted by the tribunal and that it could only detain indicted persons who were encountered during the course of normal duties—and even then, only if "feasible." U.S. President Clinton reinforced this position in February by stating that U.S. troops in Bosnia and Hercegovina should not be used for police functions such as the apprehension of indictees.

Thus, persons indicted for war crimes continued to exert economic and political control in the country, using their influence to obstruct the DPA. Bosnian Serb indictee Radovan Karadzic remained the de facto political leader of the Srpska Demokratska Stranka party, evidenced by the fact that his picture appeared on SDS posters during the municipal elections in September. Karadzic— in collaboration with Momcilo Krajisnik, the Serb member of the joint Presidency of Bosnia and Hercegovina, RS Prime Minster Gojko Klickovic, and former RS Minister of the Interior Dragan Kijac—obstructed and undermined all efforts toward peace and democracy in the entity of RS.

Further complicating the political landscape, in early summer, a power struggle broke out between two factions in the leading Bosnian Serb party, the Serbian Democratic Party (Srpska Demokratska Stranka, SDS). Despite the international community's support for RS President Biljana Plavsic in her confrontation with Karadzic, he continued to wield considerable power and violate OSCE election rules and regulations and a July 1996 agreement brokered by U.S. envoy Richard Holbrooke to stay out of public life.

Ethnically motivated violence and evictions

Although a clear goal of the Dayton agreement was to reestablish a multi-ethnic, united Bosnia and Hercegovina, little progress was made toward that end. Due largely to obstruction by local authorities (the overwhelming majority of whom are members of the nationalist parties), few were able to return to their prewar homes during 1997. Of the more than two million Bosnians who were displaced by the war, only approximately 250,000 had returned to the country by November; but very few to their pre-war homes in areas that are now controlled by another ethnic group. What is more, during the two years since Dayton, another 80,000 individuals were displaced due to transfers of territory between the two entities.

As in the previous year, during the first months of 1997, evictions of Bosniaks from Bosnian Croat-controlled west Mostar continued. In a particularly violent incident in February, a group of Bosnian Croats, including both uniformed and plain clothes police, attacked Bosniaks from east Mostar who were attempting to visit a graveyard in west Mostar during the Muslim holiday of *Bajram*. The Bosnian Croats fired as the Bosniaks fled the scene; one person was killed and over twenty persons were seriously injured. In the once Serb majority town of Drvar (now controlled by Croats), in May, twenty-five Bosnian Serb houses were destroyed by arson when Serb displaced persons attempted to return. Displaced Bosniaks were prevented—both by physical and bureaucratic means—from returning to pre-war homes in Stolac, Capljina, and other parts of the Croat-controlled Hercegovina. Houses of would-be returnees were burned and dynamited, despite months of effort by the international community to institute orderly returns to the area.

In one of the most serious cases of ethnically motivated evictions and violence, in early August, more than 400 Bosniaks who had just returned to villages surrounding Bosnian Croat-controlled Jajce were again expelled from their homes by a crowd of Bosnian Croats. International monitors in the region reported that local police used the media to incite protests and violence prior to and during the expulsions and that off-duty local police officers were spotted among the crowds. During the events, a dozen Bosniak houses were set on fire, and a Bosniak returnee was murdered. International observers, including SFOR troops and International Police Task Force (IPTF) monitors, failed to anticipate or respond to the expulsions. During the second half of August, on the basis of an agreement brokered by the international community, 474 families were finally reinstated to their houses. The events in Jajce had repercussions in Bosniak-controlled Bugojno, where Bosnian Croats were expelled and Bosnian Croat houses were severely damaged in late August. In Bosniak-controlled Travnik, a crowd of local Bosniaks prevented a group of Bosnian Croats from visiting their houses. In a separate incident in September, two Bosnian Croat returnees, a father and son, were murdered in Travnik.

Freedom of Movement

While there was limited progress in freedom of movement across inter-entity lines during 1997, widespread obstruction of this right continued on all sides, especially in the Serb and Croat controlled areas. In March, a bus with Bosniaks traveling through the Republika Srpska from Sarajevo to the Bosniak enclave of Gorazde was stopped, the passengers robbed and beaten, and a hand grenade thrown into the bus. Fortunately, it did not explode. On the same road, a Swedish journalist was shot by armed civilians during election weekend in September. Displaced persons attempting to visit their prewar houses were stopped by local crowds in Stolac, Travnik, Gajevi, Brcko, and elsewhere. During the Jajce events described above, Bosnian Croat crowds set up road blocks in preparation for the violent expulsion of recently returned Bosniaks. In Stolac, the Bosnian Croat authorities set up a permanent checkpoint near the Inter-Entity Boundary Line (IEBL) and continued to collect money from travellers despite protests to SFOR and IPTF by international monitors regarding the illegality of the checkpoint. Republika Srpska authorities continued to require "visas" for travel of non-residents through the RS, charging fees of various amounts. On the positive side, UNHCR's bus service continued to serve an important role in encouraging inter-entity travel.

Media

The media in Bosnia and Hercegovina continued to be tightly controlled by the three nationalist political parties, and the work of independent media was often obstructed during 1997. On February 2, a group of thugs attempted to evict staff from the offices of the independent monthly *Dani* ("Days") in Sarajevo, throwing tear gas into the building and physically attacking the deputy editor-in-chief. In June, the police in Sarajevo tried to block the sales of *Polikita*, an independent Bosnian Serb bimonthly magazine, arguing that the magazine was "vulgar and insensitive." The magazine's editors, however, claimed that they were attacked because of their criticism of Alija Izetbegovic, the Bosnian president. In September, the offices of the Bosnian Serb alternative newspaper *"Alternativa"* in Doboj were destroyed by a bomb. "Alternativa" had been the target of similar attacks in the past. Bosnian Serb hardline television transmissions continued to broadcast discriminatory and inflammatory statements against non-Serbs, NATO troops, and the international community, ignoring repeated protests by international monitors.

Politically-Backed Violence

Individuals linked to war crimes suspects—often accompanied by local officials or operating with their tacit approval— engaged in attacks against ethnic groups and members of the political opposition, human rights activists, and the independent media. They also used the media to threaten or incite violence against international representatives. In Brcko in August, an angry mob of armed civilians threw stones at SFOR and IPTF, slightly injuring three IPTF monitors. The crowd also heavily damaged and looted one IPTF station, overturned about thirty vehicles, and vandalized sixty-five to seventy other vehicles. As a result, eighty-six IPTF monitors were evacuated from Brcko, and SFOR was forced to pull out at gunpoint. Robert Farrand, supervisor of IPTF in Brcko, stated that the attacks were "part of a deliberate, orchestrated plan to discredit the efforts of the International Community...[and] were clearly orchestrated and planned from the outset."

Members of opposition parties in areas controlled by any one of the three ethnic groups experienced harassment and discrimination. In Bihac, supporters of Fikret Abdic's DNZ party were dismissed from official and professional posts because of their political affiliation. In a number of towns across the RS under the control of the hardline Karadzic supporters, non-SDS members were removed from their positions as directors of commercial enterprises. In west Mostar, the voices of opposition members were largely silenced because of threats and harassment by organized crime and supporters of the HDZ.

There were widespread reports of due process and other procedural violations during arrest and detention in 1997. In August, the IPTF discovered two Bosnian Serbs held in secret detention, when they paid an unannounced visit to the prison in the Bosniak majority town of Zenica. In previous scheduled visits, these prisoners had been hidden from the IPTF by Zenica prison authorities, in blatant violation of the Dayton agreement and international human rights standards.

In the Stranka Demokratske Akcije stronghold of Bihac, twelve persons (both Bosniaks and Bosnian Serbs) were arrested in 1996 and detained on charges of war crimes. They continued to be held well into 1997. These arrests were in violation of the Rome Agreement of February 1996 (also known as "Rules of the Road"), which established that evidence for war crimes charges would be submitted to the International Criminal Tribunal for the Former Yugoslavia (ICTY) for review before any arrests on charges of war crimes could be made. The twelve were arrested without prior authorization by the ICTY, and their cases were not submitted to the ICTY until ten months after the signing of the Rome Agreement. IPTF confirmed that a number of the detainees were beaten or tortured while in police custody and were forced to sign confessions.

The judiciary frequently functioned as a tool of political interests, failing to provide an independent and impartial forum for review of complaints. In one case, seven Bosniaks, who became known as the Zvornik Seven, were tried by the court in Zvornik (Republika Srpska) on charges of murder and weapons possession. The Zvornik judicial authorities refused to allow the defendants' chosen lawyers from the Federation to try the case in the RS. After court proceedings, in which the court-appointed defense lawyers were given only five minutes to speak, three of the accused were sentenced to twenty-one years of imprisonment and the others to one year of imprisonment each. The case drew considerable attention due to confirmed reports of police ill-treatment and violations of due process. In Mostar, three Croat police officers arrested in connection with the murder of one and wounding of several Bosniaks visiting the West Mostar cemetery in February were found guilty, yet all three received suspended sentences of from six months to one year of imprisonment in a trial deemed a "farce" by international observers.

Elections

As in the 1996 national elections, the Organization for Security and Cooperation in Europe (OSCE) ignored the absence of adequate conditions for municipal elections (including freedom of movement and access to the media for opposition parties and candidates). The integrity of the September municipal elections was further severely compromised by the OSCE, which struck deals with Bosnian Croat and Bosnian Serb officials in order to guarantee a non-violent election. For example, the OSCE agreed to cancel the voting in the central joint-administration district of Mostar after the Hrvatska Demokratska Zajednica (Croat Democratic Union, HDZ) threatened to boycott the elections. In Brcko, the OSCE authorized the last-minute admission of some 2,660 individuals whose names, for unexplained reasons, did not appear on the voter registration list. The organization also allowed Brcko's tendered ballots to be counted in Brcko instead of in a central location near Sarajevo, where all other ballots from the rest of the country were to be counted. In another outrageous decision, Ambassador Robert Frowick agreed to the SDS demand that no individuals on the sealed indictment list be arrested over election weekend.

In clear violation of the OSCE's elections regulations, SDS election posters with pictures of war crimes suspect Radovan Karadzic appeared in the RS capital of Pale and in villages in the eastern areas of Republika Srpska. The Election Appeals Sub Commission (EASC), an independent organ of the OSCE mission with final judicial authority, ruled that these posters violated the electoral rule prohibiting the participation of political parties in the municipal elections if they maintain indicted persons in a party position or function. On the basis of this ruling, the EASC decertified the SDS from the ballot in Pale. However, Ambassador Frowick, in an unprecedented step, overruled the EASC's decision to decertify the SDS, citing security reasons. In response to Frowick's decision regarding Pale, two EASC judges resigned in protest. Ambassador Frowick also reinstated SDS candidates in Bosanski Brod and Prijedor who had been stricken by the EASC because of their involvement in election fraud. To compound the error, he disparaged the EASC by stating that it was not a legal body. These deals struck by the OSCE and the lack of transparency of Frowick's decision-making process, combined with the fact that the conditions for elections fell far short of international standards, seriously undermined the integrity of the election process. Doubts were raised about the integrity of the results and of the certification process. In towns such as Zepce, Drvar, and Srebrenica, the pre-war ethnic majority, which had been "ethnically cleansed" during the war and unable to return to their homes, won the majority in the municipal governments. As of this writing it remained unclear how the results of the elections would be implemented.

The Right To Monitor

Under the Dayton agreement, nongovernmental human rights organizations must be granted "full and effective access" for investigating and monitoring human rights conditions. The OSCE and other intergovernmental and regional human rights missions must be provided with the opportunity to establish local offices to monitor human rights developments. In general, international human rights organizations were able to carry out their activities without interference during 1997. However, the authorities in both entities harassed local human rights activists; some even received death threats. The Federation Human Rights Ombudsmen persevered in their courageous work against ongoing human rights abuses in the Federation, but they and a newly active local human rights organization in the RS were in dire need of international support and protection.

The Role of the International Community

More than 30,000 SFOR troops remain in Bosnia and Hercegovina (down from approximately 60,000 IFOR-soldiers initially stationed in the country after the signing of the DPA). Yet despite the huge international commitment of troops and other personnel, as well as the billions of U.S. dollars invested in the peace process over the past two years, the US and Western Europe waivered in their commitment to the human rights provisions of the DPA. Intent upon defining the peace effort in Bosnia as a success, the Americans and Europeans often appeared unwilling to take the difficult steps—in particular the apprehension of indicted persons such as Radovan Karadzic and Ratko Mladic—that would have increased the prospects for long-term peace and respect for human rights in the region. As in previous years, the stated human rights objectives of the international organizations such as the OSCE were severely compromised by the influence of powerful member states such as the United States. Simultaneously, European institutions often remained too willing to take a back seat to the United States. Washington and Paris— two important contributors to SFOR in Bosnia— pointed to each other to justify the decision not to apprehend war criminals.

United Nations and NATO
In December 1996, the Implementation Force (IFOR) was replaced by SFOR; the number of soldiers deployed decreased from more than 60,000 to around 33,000. The current mandate of SFOR is scheduled to expire in June 1998. SFOR played a major role in the municipal elections process, taking control of radio transmitters in order to block the broadcasting of incitement to violence by local authorities. SFOR also conducted crucial de-mining activities, contributed to reconstruction efforts, and gave limited back-up support to the IPTF in the performance of its tasks. In December 1996, the international community finally decided to treat paramilitary forces as military forces, and thus SFOR began confiscating the weapons of Bosnian Serb police since the RS authorities refused to sign a mandatory restructuring agreement with IPTF. However, except in isolated cases, SFOR generally refused to protect returnees or to prevent ethnically motivated expulsions. SFOR continued to interpret its

mandate in the narrowest possible terms— especially as it related to protecting victims of abuse and arresting indicted persons— thereby missing valuable opportunities to make a much larger contribution to the peace process in Bosnia and Hercegovina.

The International Police Task Force
Under Annex 11 of the Dayton agreement, the U.N. International Police Task Force (IPTF) has responsibility for monitoring and inspecting the activities of the local police, in addition to advising and training local police forces in the execution of their tasks. IPTF was also assigned the difficult task of restructuring the police, which includes the screening of all police for past involvement in human rights violations. In the territory of the Federation, IPTF started restructuring the local police forces during 1997 and completed the preliminary screening in several cantons including Gorazde, Neretva, Sarajevo, and Central Bosnia. Although no exact figures are known, as of this writing only approximately twenty police officers had been removed from the police forces because of their suspected involvement in human rights abuses or non-compliance with the DPA (this figure does not include police officers fired by the authorities prior to the screening, or officers still under investigation). In September 1997, a Security Council resolution granted IPTF a wider mandate to investigate human rights violations.

The authorities of the Republika Srpska, however, had resisted the restructuring process throughout 1996 and most of 1997. However, on September 26, the authorities in both Pale and Banja Luka agreed in principle to the restructuring plans. The activities of the IPTF were also hampered by the refusal of the RS authorities to hand over a complete list of persons employed in the police forces.

The International Criminal Tribunal for the Former Yugoslavia
In 1997, the International Criminal Tribunal for the Former Yugoslavia delivered its first verdict. On May 7, Dusan Tadic, a Bosnian Serb from the area around Prijedor, was found

guilty on eleven counts of persecution of persons based upon their ethnicity and beatings of Bosniaks interned in concentration camps in 1992. Tadic was acquitted on nine counts of murder. In July, Tadic was sentenced to twenty years of imprisonment. The trial of Tihomir Blaskic, a one time commander in the Bosnian Croat Army (later promoted to a general in the Croatian Army), began on June 23. Blaskic was indicted on twenty counts involving atrocities against Bosniaks in the Lasva valley during the Bosniak-Croat war in 1993. The arrests of Slavko Dokmanovic in Eastern Slavonija and of Milan Kovacevic in Prijedor, as well as the attempted arrest of Simo Drljaca in Prijedor, revealed that the official ICTY list of indictees was supplemented by a sealed list of indictments.

The work of the ICTY continued to be seriously hampered by the failure of the Bosnian Serb, and to a lesser extent Bosnian Croat authorities and SFOR to arrest indictees. Most of the persons indicted by the ICTY were still at large during 1997, and local authorities who are primarily responsible for arresting the indictees, showed little interest in cooperating with the tribunal. Croatia had long refused to comply with a subpoena from the ICTY for documents relevant to investigations into war crimes committed by Bosnian Croats in Bosnia and Hercegovina. However, on October 6, ten Bosnian Croat indictees surrendered to the ICTY after being promised speedy trials.

European Union

The European Union used primarily financial incentives to influence the political situation. However, it also gave insufficient care to monitoring the distribution of financial aid, leading to serious concerns that the assistance was ending up financing the separatist nationalist structures. Perhaps out of a lack of willingness to conduct investigations into funding recipients in the RS, on July 10, 1997, the European Union took a radical step in announcing that it would suspend all non-humanitarian aid to the Republika Srpska.

The United Kingdom's decision to order British troops to arrest Milan Kovacevic and Simo Drljaca in Prijedor represented a welcome change in European policy, but was unfortunately not followed by further arrests. In the meantime, Germany and Switzerland began to demand that Bosnian refugees return to Bosnia, although the vast majority could not return to their pre-war homes.

United States

Throughout the year, the United States stressed the importance of accountability for wartime atrocities, yet failed to order U.S. troops to arrest any indicted persons. In fact, following the arrest initiative by British SFOR troops in Prijedor in July, the U.S. government worked behind the scenes to prevent further arrests.

The U.S. attempt politically to isolate or "sideline" Radovan Karadzic was a dramatic failure, yet the U.S. continued to pursue this policy throughout the year. U.S. policy continued to be dictated by the fear of retaliation against American SFOR troops and the anticipated political costs of casualties that might result from an apprehension attempt. Instead of arresting Karadzic, the U.S. opted to provide military and financial support to RS President Plavsic to bolster her in her power struggle with Karadzic; yet Plavsic failed to demonstrate in any concrete way her stated support for implementation of the DPA.

Meanwhile, the United States continued its "Equip and Train" program for the Bosnian Army. On January 2, SFOR troops confiscated a large amount of tank ammunition that was donated to the Bosnian Army by the U.S. because the ammunition had not been registered according to the requirements of Dayton.

The U.S. government also paid lipservice to the need for economic aid to be linked to the parties' compliance with the DPA. However, it failed to set clear conditions for such aid and, most importantly, failed to establish guidelines to avoid enriching and strengthening existing nationalist power structures that continue to obstruct the most crucial provisions of the Dayton agreement.

Relevant Human Rights Watch Reports:
Bosnia and Hercegovina—Politics of Revenge: The Misuse of Authority in Bihac, Cazin, and Velika Kladusa, 8/97
Bosnia and Hercegovina—The Unindicted: Reaping the Rewards of "Ethnic Cleansing," 1/97
Bosnia and Hercegovina: The Continuing Influence of Bosnia's Warlords, 12/96

BULGARIA

Human Rights Developments

Bulgaria experienced significant political and economic upheaval in 1997. In February, the Socialist government agreed to early elections after more than a month of strikes and mass demonstrations against corruption and economic mismanagement. Elections on April 19 installed a coalition government led by the Union of Democratic Forces. While the new government pledged greater respect for human rights, serious violations continued: police brutality, violence and discrimination against minorities, especially Roma Gypsy, and government interference in religion and the media were of particular concern.

Police brutality continued to be a major human rights problem during 1997. Several individuals died in suspicious circumstances involving the police, and numerous cases of excessive use of force were reported. Complaint procedures were inadequate, with police undertaking initial investigations themselves, and many investigations pending for extended periods. Moreover, persons bringing complaints were often subsequently charged with criminal offenses.

Three persons died during or immediately after leaving police custody during 1997. A detainee died in police custody in Popovo on January 7, and the subsequent military investigation had yet to report its findings at the time of this writing. A criminal suspect, Georgi Biandov, died in hospital under suspi-

cious circumstances on March 26 following his arrest and possible mistreatment at the hands of police in Burghs. On June 5, Petar Karandzha was shot in the head while allegedly attempting to escape from a detention facility in Sofia. A subsequent investigation by the military prosecutor's office exonerated the officers involved in the killing, despite the lack of evidence that Karandzha's actions threatened the life or security of anyone present at the time.

The amendment to the penal code adopted on August 12 guaranteeing trial within one year of incarceration (two for serious cases) was a positive development. Regrettably, the Parliament decided in September that the law would only apply to those sentenced after August 12, offering no hope to prisoners already in custody, some of whom have gone without trial for more than three years. Bulgaria's moratorium on executions remained in effect in 1997, although death sentences were issued by the courts as recently as September.

One of most blatant abuses of police power occurred during a peaceful anti-government protest on January 11. A large police contingent clubbed and kicked demonstrators, including several opposition members of parliament. The action resulted in approximately 300 injuries; eleven people were hospitalized. The incident was not an isolated one: on February 4, Roma demonstrated in Pazadijk and threw stones at several food stores. Special police responded with indiscriminate violence, beating approximately sixty Roma, some inside their homes. In June, a special police unit raided a nightclub in Sofia, beating or harassing many of its patrons, resulting in fifty-one formal complaints by victims.

Violence and discrimination against Roma in Bulgaria was not limited to police action. Attacks on Roma by other Bulgarians were common. On April 6, five Roma were reportedly beaten in front of the mayor's office in Sredno Selo by a crowd of between one hundred and one hundred and twenty people after the theft of some cattle from a neighboring village. The most serious incident took place on July 20 in Sliven. Nedka Tsoneva, a forty-one-year-old Roma woman and her twelve-year-old son were assaulted by four teenage boys. The son watched as the boys beat the woman to the ground and repeatedly kicked her. Mrs. Tsoneva fell into a coma during the attack and died the following day. The boys reportedly cursed "the Gypsies" as they beat Mrs. Tsoneva, and the oldest is alleged to have told investigators that he killed the woman "because he hated Gypsies."

The Bulgarian president told the Council of Ministers in Strasbourg on April 22 that there was no Macedonian minority in Bulgaria. Expressions of Macedonian culture were frequently suppressed: on May 5, police arrested fifteen ethnic Macedonians to prevent a cultural celebration. On October 9, however, the Bulgarian president signed the Council of Europe Framework Convention on the Protection of National Minorities, signaling a new commitment to uphold minority rights.

The gay community was also the target of official discrimination. On March 5, police raided the Flamingo gay bar in Sofia, beating up and harassing several people, some of whom were taken to the police station and handcuffed for as long as twenty hours. On August 29, police raided a gay bar in Sofia and assaulted and harassed its patrons.

State intervention in religious matters continued in 1997, despite the change in government. The government refused to register Fikri Sali as chief mufti of the Muslims in Bulgaria, despite a Supreme Court order to do so. Religious minorities also fared badly: non-Orthodox Christian groups including the Jehovah's Witnesses and Word of Life were refused official recognition, and along with Mormons, were the subject of public attacks and official discrimination.

A member of a Protestant evangelical group had custody of her child taken away from her by a court, reportedly on religious grounds. A campaign organized in April against evangelization by several recognized Protestant churches included the patriarch, who called the evangelicals "traitors of faith and nation" and the chief prosecutor, who warned

of possible revocation of the churches' official legal recognition by the state. In August 1997, municipal authorities in Haskovo prohibited a meeting by Baha'is and evicted them from property they occupied in the town.

Five journalists covering the demonstration on January 11 were beaten by police, marking the start of a bad year for press freedoms. Major issues included violence against journalists and the use of courts to suppress reporting. The effect of Bulgaria's strict libel laws became clear in March when a court handed Yovka Atanssova, a journalist with *Starozagorksy Novini* (Stara Zagora), three consecutive sentences totaling eight months and a 710,000 lev fine (about U.S.$410) for a series of articles about secret service informants who have become prominent business and political figures.

The Right to Monitor

Human Rights Watch received no reports of interference with the right to monitor.

The Role of the
International Community

Although the new government made contradictory statements regarding its commitment to human rights and in many cases failed to change existing policy, the response of the international community to Bulgaria's applications to NATO and the European Union, appeared to have little to do with the country's human rights record.

In April, however, the U.N. Committee on the Elimination of Racial Discrimination met to discuss Bulgaria's progress in meeting its obligations under the Convention on the Elimination of all Forms of Racial Discrimination (CERD). Although it noted the current difficulties faced by Bulgaria, the committee expressed concern over Bulgaria's failure adequately to address continued discrimination against racial and ethnic minorities in the country, especially those of Roma origin.

In July, the European Commission issued its opinion on Bulgaria's fitness to begin E.U. membership talks. The report concluded that Bulgaria is not ready for membership, primarily for economic reasons. The report pointed to "too frequent abuses by the police and secret services" and problems with the integration of Roma as concerns, but concluded that "Bulgaria is on the way to satisfying the political criteria" for membership.

Although Bulgaria's application for membership in NATO failed to win acceptance at the July 8 NATO summit in Madrid, it received positive support from the United States. On a July 14 visit to Sofia, U.S. Defense Secretary William Cohen said that Bulgaria would be a "very strong contender" for membership in the future if it remained committed to democracy and the promotion of human rights. This position contrasts with the generally accurate assessment of human rights in the U.S. State Department's *Country Reports on Human Rights Practices for 1996.*

CROATIA

Human Rights Developments

International pressure induced a modest turnaround in Croatia's human rights record in 1997. The Croatian government's desire for financial aid and political recognition led it to take some steps toward the political and social integration of Eastern Slavonia, Baranja, and Western Sirmium with the rest of Croatia. However, Serbs continued to face discrimination and ill-treatment by representatives of the state, leaving many anxious about their future prospects in the country. As in previous years, the government of President Franjo Tudjman cracked down on all political dissent and criticism, putting pressure on the independent press and domestic political opponents. Croatia also failed to use its considerable influence over Bosnian Croat communities to encourage the protection of human and minority rights in regions under their control. In October, however, Croatia did appear to reverse its long-standing policy of opposing the work of the International Tribunal for the Former Yugoslavia (ICTY) by helping to broker the surrender and extradition of ten Bosnian Croats indicted for war crimes by the tribunal.

Eastern Slavonia, Baranja, and Western Sirmium (hereafter referred to as "Eastern Slavonia") remained under the jurisdiction of the U.N. Transitional Authority for Eastern Slavonia (UNTAES) throughout 1997, with turnover now scheduled for January 15, 1998. Massive protests and violence in late 1996 and early 1997—including the bombing of a Catholic church and Croatian government offices—reflected the anxiety of Serb residents of Eastern Slavonia over the area's imminent reversion to Croatian rule. Many Serbs, however, have pledged to remain in the region after the turnover date.

Official discrimination against Serbs in Eastern Slavonia took a variety of forms in 1997, with Serbs facing obstacles to obtaining citizenship papers and receiving pensions. A 1996 amnesty law was shrouded in confusion and thus accorded no security to thousands of Croatian Serb combatants. In early 1997, the Croatian government circulated a list of thousands of Serbs suspected of committing war crimes, although the list was reduced first to 150 following international pressure, and later down to twenty-five. Police, nevertheless, arrested hundreds of Serb "suspects" on war crimes and other criminal charges. Croatia's constitutional court upheld a law allowing Croat refugees and displaced persons "temporarily" to occupy "abandoned" Serb property, though it did repeal articles prohibiting the exchange and sale of homes.

After repeated urging by the U.N. and assurances from Croatian government and social leaders, some Croatian Serbs did briefly appear to reconsider the possibility of reintegration. Though a successful referendum was held in early April on the creation of Eastern Slavonia as a politically autonomous region, Serb groups nonetheless decided to participate in national elections and a new moderate Serb political party, the SDSS (Independent Democratic Serb Party), won seats in Eastern Slavonia in the Croatian local elections held on April 13. On the other hand hundreds of Croatian Serbs were unable to vote when their names were mysteriously struck from voter registration lists, and thousands more were disenfranchised as a result of the dragged-out procedure of obtaining citizenship.

Through the first half of 1997, the Croatian government hampered attempts by non-Croats to return to Croatia, however, by the fall the government was allowing limited return. In May, around one hundred Serb refugees were expelled after an attempt to return to homes near Sisak. President Tudjman announced in the same month that it was "unreasonable" to expect that all of the 200,000 Serbs exiled from Croatia would be able to return and later claimed that such return would inevitably lead to renewed conflict—that Croatia's first priority must be to bring "home" all ethnic Croat refugees. Local newspapers have quoted officials as saying that the equivalent of only 5 percent of the prewar Serb population would be allowed to stay in Croatia. By October, however, international pressure had prodded the government into allowing 5,000-7,000 Serbs to return to their homes in the Krajina and Western Slavonia.

The government continued to exert strong control over the media, harass opposition politicians, and severely limit freedom of expression, despite repeated promises to open public dialogue to opposition views. In December 1996, the Croatian Journalists' Society declared that pressure on Croatian journalists had actually increased since Croatia joined the Council of Europe. Both the April 13 local elections and the June 15 presidential election suffered seriously from media bias toward the ruling HDZ (Hrvatska Demokratska Zajednica). An American study found that Tudjman was given 300 times the airtime as that of his nearest opponent, and the Organization for Security and Cooperation in Europe declared the presidential elections flawed on the basis of unequal access to the media.

In May, two journalists from the independent *Feral Tribune*, charged under an internationally-criticized law forbidding defamation of top government officials, again faced trial after an appeals court overturned their September 1996 acquittal. The Feral Tribune was also subjected to a U.S.$7,000 fine for printing a "pornographic" cover. Independent Radio 101, another frequent target of state harassment, was threatened with non-renewal of its broadcasting license; although the government bowed to pressure from the European Union and public protests in November 1996 and did ultimately extend the license.

Democracy suffered further setbacks in Croatia throughout 1997. President Tudjman was re-elected in a presidential election described by the OSCE as seriously flawed. In addition to the impact of media bias described above, the presidential election was also compromised by an eleventh-hour assault on candidate Vlado Gotovac, who was beaten so badly by a Croatian army captain that he was forced to spend the days leading up to the election in the hospital. Gotovac's subsequent request that the election be postponed was rejected by the government.

President Tudjman and the ruling HDZ party continued to suppress opposition in 1997, after having Interior Minister Ivan Jarnjak removed in December 1996 for failing to quell anti-government protests. Following its wide success in the April elections, the HDZ succeeded in placing enough members on the Zagreb city council to elect a mayor from the HDZ, ending an eighteen-month standoff during which time Zagreb was essentially without a mayor, as President Tudjman had vetoed the installation of one opposition-party mayor after another.

Intolerance to opposition reached absurd heights in May, when Croatian opposition politician Stipe Mesic was accused of treason for allegedly providing ten pages of testimony to the ICTY on conversations between President Tudjman and then-President of Serbia Slobodan Milosevic on the partition of Bosnia and Herzegovina prior to the war. Such conversations were widely believed to have taken place. Mesic, the last president of federal Yugoslavia, has never testified before the tribunal. Ivan Zvonimir Cicak, president of the Croatian Helsinki Committee, is currently under investigation for discussing the same conversations in an August interview with the Feral Tribune. The newspaper was the subject of bomb threats following publication of the interview.

Croatia failed to secure compliance of ethnic Croats in Bosnia in accordance with its promise under the Dayton Peace Accords to "guarantee" their compliance with the agreement. Instead, Croatian officials frequently appeared to support divisionist tactics by Bosnian Croats. In May, Defense Minister Gojko Susak indicated his support for the illegal nationalist attempt to create a Croatian state within the Bosnian Federation and attended a "state" meeting in which "Herceg-Bosna" adopted a coat-of-arms, flag, and national statute. Susak also gave a funeral oration for Bosnian Croat leader Mate Boban, head of the HDZ during the height of wartime abuses against civilians, in which he praised Boban for creating "the framework of statehood," and swore that Croats must not "betray what he began."

Providing a clear indication of the Croatian government's influence over the Bosnian Croats, a threatened boycott of the September Bosnian municipal elections by Bosnian Croats led OSCE Chief Ambassador Robert Frowick to ask for Tudjman's assistance in convincing the Croats to accept the election. Tudjman's intervention in this case resulted in the immediate suspension of the boycott. By contrast, Croatia failed to intervene in West Mostar, where Bosnian Croats, through mass evictions, bombings, and killings, successfully "cleansed" their town of its small minority of Bosniaks.

Until October, the Croatian government voiced frequent and heated opposition to the work of the ICTY—in violation of its numerous promises to support the Dayton agreement. In December 1996, President Tudjman decorated indictee General Tihomir Blaskic *in absentia* for retaking the Knin region in 1995—the very operation that was the subject of Blaskic's indictment by the tribunal. Croatia has persistently refused to supply official transcripts, memos, and recordings solicited by the ICTY as evidence in the Blaskic case. Defense Minister Susak called the ICTY's demands inappropriate, saying that turning over these documents would "jeopardize national security," and also repeatedly refused the ICTY's request that he come to provide testimony before the court. Justice Minister Miroslav Separovic echoed these statements in May, charging that the ICTY "violated Croatian sovereignty" by conducting investigations in Croatia without the government's approval. Then, in a surprising about-face, Croatian authorities played a major role in the October surrender of ten Bosnian Croat indictees to the ICTY. It remains to be seen, however, whether Croatia similarly will refuse to provide important documentation in these cases, which would significantly handicap their prosecution.

The Right to Monitor

Human rights monitoring by domestic and international organizations generally proceeded unhindered, though the threat of lawsuits under Croatia's excessively restrictive government defamation laws and harassment by extremist groups inevitably resulted in a certain degree of self-censorship among domestic monitors.

The Open Society Institute (OSI), a democracy-building initiative of the U.S.-based Soros Foundation, was singled out for particular attention from the Croatian authorities this year. In December 1996, Croatian customs confiscated U.S.$65,000 from OSI on the grounds that it was not properly declared, and then detained three staff members on related charges. The organization was later accused of tax evasion and forced to pay $500,000 in order to be able to stay in the country.

The Role of the International Community

United Nations

Though the transfer of Eastern Slavonia was scheduled to have taken place on July 15, the Security Council resolved on July 14 to extend UNTAES' mandate for an additional six months, expressing "grave concern" over the lack of necessary conditions for refugee return to Eastern Slavonia, the lack of improvement in the area of civil and political rights, and the government's failure "to cooperate fully" with the ICTY. The secretary general added in his October 2 status report that "Croatia's insistence and pressure for the termination of the UNTAES mandate has increased, but the progress achieved to date does not give confidence that the peaceful reintegration of the people of the region is as yet self-sustainable and irreversible."

It was generally believed that the presence of UNTAES was the only reason Serbs have felt comfortable staying as long as they have in Eastern Slavonia during 1997. Croatia was adamant that the mandate of UNTAES finally end in January 1998, though it expressed a willingness to accept the presence of international monitors in a reduced capacity.

Organization for Security and Cooperation in Europe

On June 26, the OSCE decided to broaden the mandate of its mission to Croatia, increase the number of personnel on the ground to 250 from fourteen, and extend the stay of its mission from June 30, 1997, to December 31, 1998. Expressing concern over the status of refugee return and the protection of national minorities, it declared its intention to monitor legislation and official actions pertaining to these issues, as well as to continue to monitor human rights and assist the Croatian government with the development of democratic institutions and processes.

European Union

The European Commission did not recommend that Croatia be invited to begin talks on accession into the E.U. Croatia received a "no compliance" rating with regard to the E.U.'s conditions for Croatia's membership, including cooperation with the ICTY, facilitation of refugee return, ethnic reintegration, political cooperation in Mostar, and national reconciliation. Both the E.U. as a body and individual European governments expressed deep concern over Croatia's intransigence in these areas, and the E.U. threatened to place trade sanctions on Croatia in 1998 if improvements did not occur. The European Commission did

continue, however, to provide financial support for de-mining efforts and reconstruction of infrastructure.

United States

The U.S. remained one of the most active monitors of the Croatian government's activities, exerting substantial pressure on Croatia throughout 1997 to resettle refugees and cooperate with the ICTY as promised under the Dayton agreement. A number of visits from U.S. officials brought renewed pledges from officials but appeared to generate few tangible results. Frustrated with Croatia's lack of progress, in June, the U.S. blocked a $30 million World Bank loan to Croatia that was to be the second installment in a three-year $486 million package. In September, the U.S. also issued a paper to the Council of Europe calling for Croatia's suspension from that body on the basis of its noncompliance with commitments to improve, among other things, freedom of expression, discrimination against minorities, and resettlement of refugees. The U.S. withdrew the suspension recommendation after the ten indictees' turnover, though its fundamental criticism was unchanged. Croatia's November 1996 admission to the Council of Europe was conditioned on its agreement to respect the rights of minorities and to promote reconciliation and return.

Relevant Human Rights Watch Report:

Croatia: Human Rights in Eastern Slavonia During and After the Transition of Authority, 4/97

CZECH REPUBLIC

Human Rights Developments

Although the Czech government maintained a generally acceptable level of human rights protection for most ethnic Czechs during 1997, human rights abuses persisted for members of the sizable Roma (Gypsy) minority. Despite some positive steps, the state did not do enough to combat the serious problem of racially motivated violence against Roma. Many Roma who claimed the Czech Republic as their country, and were nationals of Czechoslovakia prior to its breakup in 1993, could not acquire Czech citizenship because of a discriminatory citizenship law enacted that year.

Denied rights in their own country, many Roma fled abroad, encouraged by some local government officials to do so. A television program broadcast in August on the private station TV Nova showed Romani families from the Czech Republic living well in Canada with Canadian government support. The program sparked an exodus of hundreds of Roma from the Czech Republic to Canada, forcing Canada to reimpose a visa requirement for Czech citizens. A similar exodus occurred two months later to England. The mayor in Ostrava, a town with a large Roma population, offered to pay Romani families two-thirds of their travel costs. (Prime Minister Vaclav Klaus condemned her statement.)

Embarrassed by the negative world attention, the government began to address the problems that the Roma community, human rights groups, and certain organizations, like UNHCR and the OSCE, had been complaining about since 1993. In August, a report from the government's Council on Nationalities said that the government had failed to bridge the ever-growing gap between Roma and ethnic Czechs. Prime Minister Klaus initially rejected the report but, on October 29, the government approved a resolution "On the Situation of the Roma Community in the Czech Republic," which proposed concrete ways to address discrimination in housing, education, employment, and the work of the police.

A fundamental problem remained the alarming number of racially motivated attacks against Roma, usually by "skinheads" or other extremist groups. As in previous years, Czech police were sometimes hesitant to respond to Romani calls for help or to make arrests. Courts did not always consider such attacks to be racially motivated, which carries a stiffer penalty under Czech law.

Despite government statements to the contrary, there were still many Roma who were not able to obtain Czech citizenship in 1997, even if they were citizens of the former Czechoslovakia and born in the Czech Republic or had lived there most of their lives. The problem stemmed from a 1992 citizenship law, enacted when Czechoslovakia split into two countries. The law appeared discriminatory in intent and application: its requirements concerning permanent residence and five years of a clean criminal record were clearly aimed at the Roma minority and served to deny many the possibility of obtaining Czech citizenship. In addition, some Romani applicants who met all of the requirements were arbitrarily denied citizenship by local officials.

An amendment from 1996 allowed the Interior Ministry to waive the clean criminal record requirement. But insufficient efforts were made in 1997 to inform Roma about the possible waiver, and some local officials deliberately misinformed Roma about the amendment. Still, according to the government, 1,175 people were granted citizenship under the amendment.

The undetermined number of Czech Roma still without Czech citizenship, however, were unable to vote or run for office, and many had difficulty receiving permanent residence, which is necessary to receive social benefits from the state. In addition, non-citizens may be expelled from the country if they commit a crime, which happened to an undetermined number of people in 1997. In one highly publicized case, a Romani man was sentenced to expulsion from the country for stealing five dollars' worth of beets, although this judgement was later reversed.

The citizenship status of orphans, many of whom are Roma, also remained a major concern. A large number of these children were considered Slovak citizens, even if they were born in the Czech Republic and had no ties to Slovakia. Once released from state institutions at age eighteen, they have an undetermined legal status in the Czech Republic and face possible deportation. According to the Czech Helsinki Committee, there may be as many as 1,400 such children in Czech institutions today.

The Right to Monitor

The offices of the Czech Helsinki Committee were broken into in December by unknown individuals, who searched files and damaged the office. The police opened an investigation into the incident but, to date, no one has been charged. Otherwise, Human Rights Watch was not aware of any interferences with the right to monitor in 1997.

The Role of the International Community

Both the European Commission and the U.S. Helsinki Commission voiced serious concern over the continued negative impact of the citizenship law and urged the Czech Republic to repeal those sections that had a discriminatory impact on Roma. There was also strong international condemnation of attempts by local Czech authorities to encourage the emigration of Roma to Canada. Nonetheless, relations between the U.S. and the Czech Republic remained friendly, and the U.S. unequivocally supported the Czech Republic's admission into NATO. The E.U. was also sufficiently satisfied with the Czech Republic's performance to begin negotiations on membership in the E.U.

FEDERAL REPUBLIC OF YUGOSLAVIA

Human Rights Developments

The government of the Federal Republic of Yugoslavia (FRY), comprised of Serbia and Montenegro, demonstrated a blatant disregard for human rights throughout 1997. In November 1996, it annulled the results of local elections won largely by the opposition in Serbia and then beat those who protested; ethnic minorities suffered discrimination, imprisonment and torture because they are non-Serbs; the independent media was harassed; and, in violation of the Dayton Agreement, the government refused to hand persons indicted for war crimes over to the International Criminal Tribunal for the former Yugoslavia.

On November 17, 1996, the opposition coalition Zajedno fared surprisingly well in municipal elections, winning in fourteen of Serbia's nineteen largest cities. The government annulled the results, citing "unspecified irregularities," which sparked massive demonstrations in Belgrade and other Serbian cities. A delegation from the Organization for Security and Cooperation in Europe (OSCE) confirmed the opposition's victory, and the peaceful and creative demonstrations continued for eighty-eight days, demanding respect for the election results, media freedom and political pluralism in Serbia.

Beginning on December 26, the government used violence and arrests to silence the demonstrators. Although random incidents of police violence also took place at other times, it was especially at the end of December and again in the beginning of February that hundreds of peaceful demonstrators were beaten by the police or special riot forces, some of them seriously. Clearly identifiable journalists were sometimes targeted by the police. From late December to February, at least fifty people were arrested and convicted on charges of "destroying state property" or "disturbing the peace" in trials that did not comport with international standards.

At the same time, the Serbian government took steps to prevent the public from finding out about the demonstrations. The state-run television and radio—the main source of information for those outside of Belgrade—either ignored the demonstrators or referred to them as "hoodlums" and "vandals." On December 3, the government ordered Serbia's two main independent radio stations, Radio B-92 and Radio Index, to close because they did not possess the proper broadcasting license. The stations reopened after substantial international pressure, but a number of smaller independent stations remained closed. At the same time, the government harassed the independent print media by limiting print runs and restricting newsprint supplies.

The relentless public protest and substantial international pressure finally forced the government to recognize the opposition's victory on February 22, 1997. As of November, however, no one had been held accountable for the human rights abuses that occurred during the elections or the ensuing demonstrations, even though more than sixty criminal charges had been filed in Serbian courts against Belgrade policemen for using excessive force.

The state continued its harassment of the independent media throughout 1997, especially in the period leading up to the September 21 elections for a new Serbian president and parliament (former president of Serbia, Slobodon Milosevic, was elected president of the FRY in August). In a coordinated action in July involving the Yugoslav Ministry for Transport and Telecommunications, the criminal police, the financial police, and various state agencies, the government temporarily shut down more than seventy-five private television and radio stations that, it claimed, were operating illegally. Many of the stations did not possess the proper broadcast license, due primarily to the government's unwillingness to grant licenses to stations that broadcast critical views of the state. The government consistently used the FRY's complex and contradictory broadcast laws and licensing procedures to deny licenses to the media outlets it considered "disloyal."

As the above events demonstrate, all citizens of the FRY suffered human rights violations, regardless of their ethnicity, if they criticized or opposed the rule of Slobodon Milosevic. Throughout 1997, however, minority populations (non-ethnic Serbs and Montenegrins) continued to be especially susceptible to abuse. Ethnic Albanians, Hungarians, Muslims, Turks, and Roma were subjected to varying degrees of persecution, as in previous years, ranging from discriminatory legislation to arbitrary arrests, torture,

and deaths in detention.

The most severe abuse occurred in the southwest region of Kosovo, inhabited by 1.8 million ethnic Albanians, who comprise 90 percent of the local population. Serb authorities continued to use political trials, police violence, and torture to repress ethnic Albanians, sometimes resulting in death.

In January 1997, the police arrested approximately one hundred ethnic Albanians accused of working with the Kosova Liberation Army, an underground organization that had taken credit for killing a number of Serbian officials and policemen since February 1996, as well as two ethnic Albanians it accused of collaborating with the Serbian government. On July 11, the district court in Priština, Kosovo, sentenced fifteen of the detainees to combined prison terms of 264 years for terrorist activity. Serious violations of due process and the use of torture to extract confessions prevented the defendants from obtaining a fair trial. In October, another nineteen Albanians went on trial, including Nait Hasani, who was held in unacknowledged detention for one month and reportedly tortured. Jonuz Zeneli, who was scheduled for trial, died in a prison hospital on October 17, reportedly due to ill-treatment at the hands of the police.

The Serbian authorities also continued to deny Albanians in Kosovo their right to free association and speech. Albanian organizations, from political parties to sports clubs, were often harassed by the police and security forces, and activists were taken in for "informative talks," which sometimes led to beatings in detention. No Albanian-language television or radio were allowed to broadcast from Kosovo, and the print media faced economic restrictions imposed by the state, such as high rents and an expensive distribution system, as well as ongoing harassment in the form of "informative talks" and identity checks.

On September 1, 1996, Milosevic signed an agreement with the Kosovar Albanian leader Ibrahim Rugova to reopen Albanian-language schools that had been closed in 1990; but, by the start of the 1997 school year, the agreement had not been implemented. Instead, students and teachers were still detained and, on occasion, beaten for trying to study or teach in their native language. In October, ethnic Albanian students held two peaceful demonstrations to demand the implementation of the education agreement. On October 1, the police forcibly dispersed the crowd in Prishtina and beat many of the demonstrators.

In neighboring Sandzak, with a large Muslim Slav population, there was similar discrimination, if not as intense as in Kosovo. The wave of state-sanctioned violence that swept through Sandzak during the war in Bosnia abated, but there was continued intimidation, harassment, and violence by the police in 1997.

On July 10, special police forces overtook the city hall in Sandzak's capital, Novi Pazar, and ousted the local Muslim-led government headed by Sulejman Ugljanin, on the charge that it was about to declare the autonomy of Sandzak. The local government was replaced with members of the ruling Socialist Party of Serbia and its coalition partner Yugoslav United Left (headed by Miloševic's wife, Mira), and criminal proceedings were opened against Ugljanin for threatening the FRY's territorial integrity, a charge often used against leaders of the FRY's ethnic minorities.

Open violence and repression against minority groups (Hungarians, Croats and Roma) in the northern region of Vojvodina were not as pronounced as in other parts of the FRY. But the perception and reality of a system uniformly and consistently biased against minorities continued to encourage their emigration from the country. The large influx of refugees—ethnic Serbs from Bosnia, and Croatia—into Vojvodina, especially since 1995, continued to have a deleterious impact on the local minorities, with cases of coerced land swaps and state-sponsored seizures of homes.

In late June, the municipal assembly of Zemun (near Belgrade), headed by the ultra-nationalist leader of the Radical Party, Vojislav Šešelj, ordered the eviction from their homes of some ethnic Croat families who had lived in Zemun for up to three generations. The Belgrade District Court overturned the eviction order on July 10, but the police did not implement the order to evict the new tenants.

On October 19, a group of skinheads in Belgrade clubbed a thirteen-year-old Roma boy, Dušan Jovanovic, to death. Five suspects were arrested.

Domestic human rights organizations continued to criticize the government's inconsistent and discriminatory policy toward the estimated 600,000 refugees from the former Yugoslavia living in the FRY. The FRY's Law on Refugees, which does not comply with international standards, prohibited large numbers of refugees from obtaining refugee status, thereby limiting the amount of humanitarian aid they could receive and threatening them with possible repatriation. Some refugees were registered to vote in the September 1996 elections under conditions that strongly suggested coercion, intimidation, and fraud.

The Dayton Agreement, signed in 1995, obliged the Yugoslav government to cooperate with the International Criminal Tribunal for the former Yugoslavia (ICTY), specifically by handing over persons indicted for war crimes. Despite this, a number of indicted individuals, such as Miroslav Radic and Slobodon Miljkovic, resided in the FRY in 1997. Veselin Šljivan anin, indicted for the murder of more than 200 hospital patients in the Croatian city of Vukovar in 1991, taught military tactics at the military academy in Belgrade. One of the most notorious indictees, Bosnian Serb Army Gen. Ratko Mladic , visited Belgrade in June for his son's wedding and was then seen vacationing on the coast of Montenegro. Although not yet indicted by the ICTY, the notorious war crimes suspect Zeljko "Arkan" Raznatovic maintained a public persona in Belgrade.

The Right to Monitor
Domestic human rights groups like the Helsinki Committee for Human Rights in Serbia and the Humanitarian Law Center were regularly kept under police surveillance but were generally allowed to perform their duties in 1997.

One incident involved the well-known human rights lawyer, Nikola Barovic, who was assaulted by the bodyguard of Radical Party leader Vojislav Šešelj after Barovic and Šešelj got into an argument during a televised interview. Human rights groups in minority-inhabited areas experienced more constant harassment. Activists for the Council for the Defense of Human Rights and Freedoms in Kosovo, for example, were often detained and, on occasion, beaten. International human rights groups, while also under state surveillance, were generally free to conduct their investigations without interference, although on one known occasion, an ethnic Albanian family was interrogated by the police after they talked to a foreign human rights monitor.

The Role of the International Community

United Nations and Europe

Despite the plethora of violations in 1997, there was only one period of unambiguous condemnation and action by the international community against the government in the FRY. This occurred during the post-election demonstrations, albeit only after foreign governments realized that the demonstrations were gaining momentum and Miloševi had resorted to threats of violent suppression and bans on the independent media. An OSCE delegation to Serbia, headed by Spain's former Prime Minister Filipe Gonzalez, confirmed that electoral fraud had occurred and presented recommendations to promote democracy and respect for human rights, known as the "Gonzalez report." European governments appropriately condemned the arrest of demonstrators, police violence, and restrictions on the independent media.

As soon as Milošević recognized the election results, however, European governments resumed welcoming him and the abusive Yugoslav government back into the international community. In April 1997, the E.U. granted the FRY preferential trade status, although, according to the agreement, the status will "be reviewed" if there is no progress in a number of human rights related areas, such as improvements in Serbia's media laws, reform of the judicial system, and improvements in Kosovo. An E.U. delegation visited the FRY in October to determine whether the status would be extended. The E.U. and the U.N. did, however, condemn the ongoing violations and persecution of ethnic Albanians in Kosovo, especially the political trials in 1997 and the police violence against the peaceful student demonstrations in October.

An outer wall of sanctions remained in place throughout 1997, which kept the FRY out of international lending institutions like the World Bank and the International Monetary Fund, but this was mostly due to the unilateral resolve of the United States.

United States

In contrast to Europe, the U.S. government took a more principled stand regarding human rights abuses in the FRY. Unlike most European countries, the U.S. did not reestablish full diplomatic relations and was the main force keeping the outer wall of sanctions in place. Top government officials, including the president and secretary of state, repeatedly stressed their disapproval of human rights violations in Kosovo, although making clear that there was no support for an independent Kosovar state. In Serbia proper, the U.S. government maintained good relations with the political opposition. When Radio B-92 was closed in December 1996, the U.S. government offered temporary use of the Voice of America frequency.

Relevant Human Rights Watch Reports:
Serbia and Montenegro—Discouraging Democracy: Elections & Human Rights, 09/97
Clouds of War: Chemical Weapons in the Former Yogoslavia, 3/97
Serbia and Montenegro— Persecution Persists: Human Rights Violations in Kosovo, 12/96

GEORGIA

Human Rights Developments

As Georgia's human rights record has come under increasing scrutiny by the international community—notably by the United Nations and the Council of Europe—the government took steps in 1997 to indicate that it is making human rights a priority. However, Georgia's rapidly improving image as a reforming post-Soviet country far outpaced its actual performance in human rights. In its most progressive move, the government instituted a de facto ban on capital punishment. However, most chronic problems persisted, principally torture and police abuse, refusal to prosecute war crimes committed during its civil wars in South Ossetia in 1991 and Abkhazia in 1992-94, and violations of the rights of refugees and the internally displaced. Most alarming, the government continued to obfuscate and discount many of these problems.

This year Georgia underwent its first reviews by the United Nations Committee Against Torture (October 1996) and the U.N. Human Rights Committee (March 1997). In its initial reports to these committees, the Georgian government was candid about the appalling conditions of its prisons and acknowledged the existence of serious problems like torture. However, it generally under-reported the true, horrifying scope of torture and police brutality, as documented by independent observers. For example, the Initial Report on compliance with the International Covenant on Civil and Political Rights (November 21, 1995) stated that only two cases of torture had taken place during the four-year period Georgia had been party to the Convention; nongovernmental organizations, however, documented scores of cases during that same period.

Symptomatic of the government's unwillingness to disclose the scale of the problem was its selection of Deputy Prosecutor General Anzor Baluashvili as a delegate to defend Georgia's record before the Human Rights Committee. Extensive circumstantial evidence suggests that Mr. Baluashvili had prosecuted numerous criminal suspects who were coerced into admitting guilt through physical and psychological abuse, and that Mr. Baluashvili condoned, if not ordered, the brutal treatment. Although the government was aware of these allegations, it has refused to investigate them. Closing its eyes to brutality within its own ranks, on the one hand, and pledging to curb torture, on the other, greatly undermined the government's credibility during the review process.

This year Georgia took welcome steps toward the abolition of the death penalty, one of the principal preconditions to membership in the Council of Europe. On December 10, 1996, President Eduard Shevardnadze issued a moratorium on capital punishment pending the reduction from thirteen to seven of the number of capital offenses in the Georgian Criminal Code. (The amended Code entered into force on February 1, 1997.) In July, President Shevardnadze instituted a de facto ban on executions by commuting the death sentences of the existing fifty-four death-row inmates to twenty years of imprisonment.

A presidential decree issued in June, inter alia, called for punishing violations of the rights of suspects and prisoners and the broad dissemination of pertinent international human rights standards to government agencies. Although the decree may in time result in improved protections, the government's failure to enforce the human rights protections already enshrined in Georgia's existing legal obligations suggests the decree may have only symbolic significance.

The cease-fires that ended the fighting in Georgia's South Ossetia and Abkhazia regions several years ago continued to hold in 1997, despite sporadic fighting in the Abkhazian border region of Gali, which abuts Georgia. Wide scale attacks on civilians were averted this year, overwhelmingly thanks to continued mediation by the Russian Federation and the U.N. and to the continued presence of Confederation of Independent States (Russian) peacekeeping troops and of U.N. military observers in the region. However, according to UNHCR figures from December 1996, some 272,400 internally displaced persons remained unable to return safely to Abkhazia, in violation of their rights.

The government squandered another year by not moving closer to prosecuting the massive war crimes that characterized the internal conflicts in South Ossetia and Abkhazia, including the murder of civilians, widespread looting, and "ethnic cleansing." Instead, the government called on an international court to take the responsibility. This strategy allows the government publicly to condemn war crimes without punishing violators, including combatants under its own command. Although landmines remained a crippling humanitarian problem that was at least partially responsible for the inability of displaced persons to return to Abkhazia, Georgia did not sign onto the international landmine ban treaty in Oslo, Norway, in September 1997.

Such fundamental civil rights as freedom of speech and of assembly were generally well protected in Georgia. However, special forces reportedly broke up a peaceful march by the political opposition in Tbilisi on May 26, beating participants and reporters with truncheons and arbitrarily detaining several dozen, according to Iprinda News Agency. In June, a parliamentary investigating committee revealed that the Ministry of State Security had illegally tapped the telephones of Nodar Grigolashvili, the editor-in-chief of the newspaper *Sakartvelo* (Georgia). The extent of unsanctioned government wiretapping in Georgia is unclear, but the work of the committee is encouraging, and the attention generated by its findings may help deter future abuse.

The Right to Monitor

By and large, domestic human rights activists enjoyed broad freedom to work this year. However, in at least one case of harassment, Elena Tevdoradze, chair of the parliamentary subcommittee for penitentiary reform, reportedly suffered several death threats in connection with her work on behalf of prisoners, according to *Droni* (Time) of September 4-6. Many activists reported that their work was stymied by lack of government cooperation in accepting and acting on their information. International monitors generally received greater government attention than did their domestic counterparts. In March, for example, Russian human rights activist Sergei Kovalev and his colleagues were given full access to prisoners they wished to meet, and Mr. Kovalev was able to convey his findings and recommendations to the president in person.

The Role of the International Community

United Nations and the Organization for Security and Cooperation in Europe

As discussed above, the U.N. Committee against Torture and Human Rights Committee worked actively this year to evaluate Georgia's human rights record and urge improved compliance with international standards. The United Nations continued to mediate a settlement of the Abkhaz conflict and to secure the safe return of refugees and displaced persons from that region; on both counts, its efforts were fruitless. Its most positive contributions to the human rights situation there appeared to be extending the mandate for the Observer Mission in Georgia (UNOMiG) and the posting of a human rights representative based in Sukhumi, Abkhazia. Under the terms of a joint agreement, an OSCE representative is also monitoring the situation in the field. To date, however, there was no noticeable improvement in reporting or prosecuting human rights violations.

Council of Europe

Since July 14, 1996, when Georgia applied to the Council of Europe to upgrade its status from special guest to full member, the Council worked to identify Georgia's human rights problems and craft recommendations for achieving adequate compliance with the Council's standards. Credit for Georgia's rapid progress toward a de jure moratorium on the death penalty this year was due overwhelmingly to the Council's membership review process. In light of Georgia's overall human rights record, one hopes the Council of Europe will issue rigorous recommendations for compliance with European Convention human rights standards and, should Georgia accede to the Council, that it will enforce them strictly.

GREECE

Human Rights Developments

Greece, a member of the European Union (E.U.) since 1981, continued to experience persistent human rights abuses, especially related to ethnic minorities and migrants. Other areas of concern included restrictions on freedom of expression and freedom of worship. The government of Prime Minister Costas Simitis, whose Pan-Hellenic Socialist Movement (PASOK) won parliamentary elections in September 1996, took some positive steps, including working to legalize the presence of an estimated 500,000 illegal Albanian migrants and to increase infrastructure investments in Turkish villages in Thrace. In February, Prime Minister Simitis openly acknowledged the problem of racism in Greece, a first for a Greek prime minister.

In 1997, Greece finally ratified the International Covenant on Civil and Political Rights and signed the Council of Europe's Framework Convention for the Protection of National Minorities. Nevertheless, the government of Greece continued to recognize only one minority, the "Muslim" minority protected under the 1923 Treaty of Lausanne. The government refused officially to acknowledge the existence of a Turkish minority, although today the vast majority of the "Muslim" minority identify themselves as Turks, regardless of their Turkish, Pomak, Roma or other origin. Other ethnic minorities legally denied recognition included Slavic-speaking Macedonians. Ethnic minorities that are not officially recognized often suffered restrictions on their freedom of expression and association.

The Greek government appeared to take a dual policy toward the Turkish minority in 1997: it continued to deny its identity—including forbidding the use of the word "Turkish" in official titles of organizations—while at the same time increasing funding for infrastructure in ethnic Turkish areas. The government also continued its policy of affirmative action for Turkish students applying to universities. But few ethnic Turks were employed by municipalities, and none in senior positions. Despite being guaranteed by the Lausanne Treaty, Turkish-language secondary schools remained few in number and of poor quality, there were inadequate numbers of translators for court proceedings, and repair of some mosques was problematic. What is more, although the Simitis government pledged to amend article 19 of the citizenship law, which is sometimes used arbitrarily to deprive non-ethnic Greeks of their citizenship, 7,000 non-ethnic Greek citizens lost their citizenship between 1981 and 1996. While the apparent intent of article 19 was to force those deprived of citizenship to migrate to Turkey, some stayed in Greece. Some estimate that as many as 1,000 stateless persons who were formerly Greek citizens still reside in the country. They have difficulty receiving social services like health care and education and are even denied the rights of the 1954 U.N. Convention Relating to the Status of Stateless Persons ratified by Greece in 1975.

Another area of concern is a 1990 law that gave the state the right to appoint the mufti; previously muftis were appointed following consultation with community leaders, although this contravened a 1920 law requiring that they be elected. Currently, there are two muftis in Xanthi and Komotini—one appointed and one elected. The elected mufti has been repeatedly prosecuted for "pretense of authority" for using the title of mufti.

In Florina, capital of the Florina district of northern Greece where most ethnic Macedonians live, four Greek Macedonians were put on trial in October 1997 for "inciting citizens to commit acts of violence." In

September 1995, a mob led by the Florina mayor had attacked and ransacked the offices of the ethnic Macedonian Rainbow Party after the four men hung a sign in Greek and in Macedonian stating "Rainbow-Florina Committee." No charges were filed against those who attacked the offices. However, the party was prosecuted for using the Macedonian language on the sign in a clear violation of the right to free expression. At an October 1997 hearing, the trial was postponed until September 1998.

Ethnic Macedonians who fled Greece as a result of the 1946-49 civil war were more easily able to visit Greece during 1997 than in previous years: throughout 1996, such individuals—who number in the tens of thousands—were not allowed to enter Greece, even briefly to visit relatives or attend funerals. Ethnic Greek political refugees, on the other hand, were regularly allowed to return to the country. Greece's Roma (Gypsy) minority, estimated at some 350,000, continued to be the most marginalized societal group, subject to discrimination in employment and housing and to police abuse. In April, municipal authorities forcibly removed Roma living in the Ano Liosia area. Reportedly, inhabitants lost personal possessions when bulldozers raised their settlements. Roma having valid residence permits were moved to a new settlement, surrounded by a wire fence and guarded by a armed watchman. Throughout 1997, Roma were expelled or threatened with expulsion in many other sites by the municipal authorities and sometimes the courts, while the often announced plan to find appropriate living quarters for them was never implemented.

While Greece's varied and lively press is largely free, there were violations of freedom of the press in 1997. Mr. Abdulhalim Dede, the director of a Turkish-language radio station, Radio Light (Radio Isik), and a newspaper, Voice of Thrace (Trakya'nin Sesi), had criminal charges brought against him on four occasions in 1997. On two occasions he was charged with "defamation" and "dissemination of false information;" in each of the remaining two cases, he was charged with "broadcasting without a license." Although most private radio stations in Greece operate without a license, Radio Isik was the only one charged. The director was convicted of aggravated defamation and sentenced to six months of imprisonment. In July, two journalists of the newspaper *Niki* were sentenced to thirty-three months for "defamation" of the justice minister.

Migrant workers in Greece—the majority of whom are illegal immigrants from Albania—continued to suffer police abuse and discrimination. Sentences meted out to ethnic Albanians were excessively harsh when compared with those given to Greeks: in February, for example, an Albanian illegal immigrant received six and one-half years for theft of a wallet and illegal entry; in March, a Greek citizen received three and one-half years for attempted manslaughter against four Albanian immigrants. Despite promises by the Greek government, migrant workers from Albania were still not able to obtain legal status in Greece.

The Greek constitution gives the Eastern Orthodox church the status of an official religion, relegating other religions to a disadvantaged status. In September 1996, the European Court criticized Greek legislation, noting " a clear tendency...to use these provisions to restrict activities of faiths outside the Orthodox Church." The constitution also prohibits proselytism, but does not define the term. In December 1996, the Greek Helsinki Monitor reported that the closing of the Church of Scientology also violated freedom of religion.

The Right to Monitor

In August and September, state security forces openly followed a joint Greek Helsinki Monitor/Human Rights Watch mission in Thrace. The delegation met with many people whose phones appeared to have been tapped. After complaining to authorities, however, the tailing ceased. In June, the Greek Helsinki Monitor reported that its mail had been tampered with, reportedly by state authorities.

The Role of the International Community

United States

Relations between Greece and the United States were good in 1997, although the State Department's *Country Report on Human Rights Practices for 1996* was frank about human rights violations by Greece. For FY 1997, Greece received U.S.$3.23 million in loan subsidies and $122.5 million in Foreign Military Financing (FMF) loans. The U.S also appointed former Bosnia negotiator Richard Holbrooke to work toward a settlement on the divided island of Cyprus.

HUNGARY

Human Rights Developments

Hungary maintained a generally acceptable level of human rights protection for many of its citizens in 1997. Despite Hungary's acceptance into NATO and a decision by the European Union to begin membership talks, both decisions reflecting the general perception that Hungary had made significant strides toward democracy and the protection of human rights, a number of human rights violations continued to plague the country during 1997. The Roma minority continued to face widespread discrimination, especially in housing, education, and employment, as well as ill-treatment by the police. In addition, reports of police brutality and violations of due process continued to surface during the year. The Hungarian government's efforts to address these violations were only minimally effective.

In 1997, the Roma (Gypsy) continued to encounter both governmental and societal discrimination. Most Roma continued to live in ghettoized communities segregated from the majority of Hungarians. This situation reflects the consequences of housing and settlement policies during the communist era, but it is also the result of ongoing discrimination in housing and employment. The Parliamentary Commissioner for National and Eth-

nic Minority Rights reported that from July 1, 1995, until the time of this printing, about 68 percent of all complaints submitted to the ombudsman were complaints filed by Roma. Many of these complaints focused on housing discrimination by the local self-governments.

Roma also continued to face pervasive discrimination in employment and education. In some areas of eastern Hungary, the unemployment rate among Roma men reached 80 percent. In many school districts, Roma children continued to attend separate classes. In June 1997, in the town of Tiszavasvári, Roma and Hungarian graduating students held separate graduation parties because the Roma children were considered by the parents to be lice-infested, misbehaved, and dirty. The minister of culture and education, Balint Magyar, initiated an investigation, but as of this writing had issued no findings.

Numerous racially motivated attacks against Roma were reported in 1997. On April 26, 1997, thirty Roma teenagers accompanied by three adults were attacked by skinheads during a trip to Kismaros. One young Roma was hospitalized. The investigation by the Vác police turned up no suspects. In another incident in Satoraaljaujhely, in northeastern Hungary, the local authorities decided to force Roma to leave the town. Using euphemisms such as "certain people" who are "unable to live in towns" to denote the Roma, the local authorities announced that they would force these people to leave the town even if it required using illegal means. Jeno Kaltenbach, the ombudsman for minority rights, investigated the matter and, on September 26, 1997, asked the local authorities to withdraw their decision. The local authorities unanimously rejected his request.

Roma continued to report being excluded from some public establishments. However, in a landmark case, the Hungarian courts for the first time found in favor of a Roma man who was discriminated against in a public establishment. Mr. Gyula Goma, a Roma man, who had been refused service in a bar because he was a "Gypsy," sued the owners of the establishment. In January

1997, he won both a criminal and civil case against the bar. At the time of this printing, the civil case was on appeal.

In late July 1997, the government approved a comprehensive plan—developed jointly with Roma associations—intended to improve welfare and health conditions, provide work, and increase the number of young Roma in education.

Police abuses remained a serious problem throughout Hungary. Despite the government's public condemnation of police brutality and its promises to prosecute such abuses, reports of physical violence by the police, of interrogation under duress, and of illegal arrests remained high. Although regulations applying to police lockups comply with European standards, the regulations were often ignored. For example, detainees were often denied adequate medical treatment, suspects were often not allowed to use the phone to call lawyers or families, and suspects' correspondence was monitored.

Human rights organizations reported that Roma were particularly likely to be the victims of police abuse. There were numerous cases of Roma being subjected to longer periods of detention and sentenced for longer periods of time than non-Roma. Victims of police abuse were often unable to obtain an adequate remedy for such abuse. Only 3 percent of cases brought against the police led to a conviction. In those few cases in which the police were convicted, the penalty was usually a fine, probation, or a suspended sentence, and the police officer typically remained on the force.

In May, the parliament passed a law on the processing and protection of medical and related personal data. This bill, which allowed the police to examine individuals' medical records in the name of crime prevention, was criticized by NGOs for violating the right to privacy.

The Right to Monitor

Human rights monitoring was generally unimpeded, although some human rights organizations reported attempted intimidation and harassment by the police. Police occasionally used their authority to search premises for illegal workers and to enter into the offices of human rights organizations and disrupt their activities.

The Role of the International Community

Europe

In recognition of the important steps Hungary has taken to build a strong democracy based on the rule of law and protection of human rights, it was admitted into NATO during the first round of expansion. In July, the European Commission also recommended starting E.U. membership talks with Hungary. The European Commission, however, also pointed out that in order for Hungary to become a full member of the E.U., it had to improve minority rights for the Roma population, including better judicial recourse for abuses.

In December 1996, the Hungarian parliament ratified its treaty with Romania to permit the development of friendly relations and full respect for the minorities of each country. This was followed by the two countries exchanging consulates, numerous visits of high ranking officials between each country, and a growing atmosphere of cooperation and reduction of tensions between the two countries.

United States

Relations between Hungary and the United States remained good in 1997. The Hungary chapter of the U.S. State Department's *Country Reports on Human Rights Practices for 1996* was accurate, and the United States was a leading force behind Hungary's admission into NATO.

KAZAKSTAN

Human Rights Developments

In general, the government of Kazakstan continued to observe the rule of law and most civil and political rights in 1997. There were still major areas of concern, however, including prison conditions, continuing use of the death penalty, diminishing possibilities for free assembly, resulting in part from the implementation of a new criminal code, and the apparent reduction in media choice through the government's redistribution of broadcasting rights which excluded independent voices.

Parliament adopted a new criminal code on July 16, replacing the Soviet code in use in Kazakstan since 1959. Positive aspects include a reduction in the application of the death penalty to murder and crimes such as terrorism, eliminating its use for crimes such as receipt of bribes and aggravated rape. It will no longer be applied to women (formerly only pregnant women were excluded) or men over sixty-five. Also—and importantly, given the imperfect nature of the country's judicial system—it extends to two years the time between sentencing and execution to allow for final appeals. Previously this period was on average one year, including final appeal and a request for clemency. On the negative side, however, the new code criminalizes the activity of nongovernmental organizations (NGOs) that have not been granted formal registration by the government and the organization of unsanctioned public meetings and demonstrations.

Use of the death penalty continued in 1997, although no figures were available for the number of people executed. Government actors, especially President Nazarbaev's legal affairs advisor, Igor Rogov, displayed an openness to dialogue on the issue when they attended a seminar on the death penalty organized by the nongovernmental Kazakstan-American Bureau for Human Rights and Rule of Law on January 22-23. They indicated a readiness to reduce application of the death sentence and, according to Mr. Rogov, eventually to abolish it. Yet it was shortly after this, in the last week of April, that the authorities, ignoring repeated pleas from Amnesty International and other groups, executed Oleg Gorozashvili. The execution went ahead despite doubts about his guilt, concerns about a serious miscarriage of jus-

tice, and an apparent commitment from state investigators to delay execution pending further examination of the case.

A perverse argument for retaining the death penalty, advanced by government officials at the January seminar, was that prison conditions were so atrocious that few prisoners would survive a long sentence anyway. In July the Interior Minister was quoted as saying 1,122 people had died in prison as of that date, 770 of them from tuberculosis. This was roughly the same level as in 1996, when 2,531 prisoners had died, according to government officials. The Interior Minister also said that Kazakstan had 83,000 prisoners in July, a figure that included 15,000 released on parole. Officials said one in five prisoners had tuberculosis.

A variety of legal sanctions continued to be applied to individuals who were punished for their political activity rather than for any crime. In June the authorities in Almaty held the sixty-year-old leader of a pensioners' action group called Generation (Pokolenie), Nina Savostina, in custody for seven days and held the deputy head of the Workers' Movement, Yury Vinkov, for fifteen days for participating in a May 30 rally of pensioners. Madel Ismailov, chairman of the Workers' Movement, was held in custody until late July on charges of organizing the demonstration. He was tried on September 17 and sentenced to one year of corrective labor; he will be allowed to serve the sentence at his own place of work with a portion of his salary deducted. The authorities' determination to prevent even such basic rights of assembly indicated an extremely alarming intention to stamp out political opposition.

Another source of opposition to government policies, the independent labor movement, was also subjected to government harassment this year. The leader of the Independent Trade Union Federation, Leonid Solomin, was charged with financial irregularities on March 13 after a long-running investigation. Although the charges were dropped in September for lack of evidence, the accusations had isolated Mr. Solomin as a political figure and seriously hampered his work. Another prominent opposition figure, Petr Svoik, co-leader of the Azamat opposition movement, faced criminal charges relating to alleged improprieties during his time as head of the State Antimonopoly Commission. The case had not been tried as of this writing. Again, raising these accusations at a time when Azamat was gaining authority, and the subsequent prolonged, inconclusive investigation, point to an attempt to discredit and isolate a powerful political figure.

The year 1997 saw no recorded politically motivated convictions in the context of ethnic relations. The last case, a trial ending December 25, 1996, involved Nina Sidorova, chair of the Russian Center, who was given a two-year suspended prison sentence for contempt of court and resisting police authority. The charges had been brought against her in 1996, months after the alleged crimes and only when she attempted to register the Russian Center as a public association.

A reduction in the public's access to Russian-language media—the most important outside source of information in Kazakstan—came when the authorities cancelled rebroadcasts of the Russian Federation national TV station RTR. The Russian station announced on January 27 that its programs had not been shown in Kazakstan since December 5. Since 1995, rebroadcasts of its programs had been reduced to two and a half hours a day. The Kazakstan authorities said the move was not political but rather the result of the Russian station's nonpayment of rebroadcasting fees, although some observers saw it as yet another step to diminish the presence of Russian-language media and alternative viewpoints generally.

The domestic media underwent great change as existing broadcasting frequencies were put up for tender, first in Almaty and the surrounding region and then in the rest of the country. Opponents of the scheme said it was designed to weed out and close stations seen as hostile to the government. The government claimed it was acting purely out of commercial interest, but even if this was true the inordinately high initial fees of up to the equivalent of U.S.$111,000 effectively barred free expression. At least thirty-one TV and radio stations were forced off the air after failing to win broadcasting rights between January and May. An employee of one of them, TV "M", was reportedly told by a member of the presidential administration that it was being shut down because its output was "too politicized."

The Right to Monitor

Local and international human rights groups operated unhindered. The government showed itself generally receptive to the human rights agenda. However, deputy head of the presidential Human Rights Commission Zhumabek Busurmanov appeared on Kazakstan national television on February 12 to attack local human rights NGOs. He accused them of working with "certain international human rights organizations of a dubious nature" and described some of those whose rights they defended—principally activists in the Russian community—as "odious." His attack revealed an attitude toward human rights and NGOs that was unchanged from Soviet times. It is unclear to what extent his statement reflects official views.

The Role of the International Community

European Union

On March 13 the European Parliament gave its assent to ratification of a Partnership and Cooperation Agreement (PCA) with Kazakstan. One of the basic conditions that the E.U. sets out in the PCA is that human rights and democratic principles be observed in the partner country. Ratification had been delayed because of E.U. concerns about the suspension of the Kazakstan parliament in 1995.

United States

The United States government conducted a number of high level interventions in which it raised concerns about specific individual cases. In addition, its *Country Report on Human Rights Practices for 1996* presented an unbiased view of human rights problems in Kazakstan.

KYRGYZTAN

Human Rights Developments

In 1997, the Kyrgyz government put unrelenting pressure on the independent or critical media and on opposition figures. This stood in stark contrast to President Askar Akaev's remarks in July to the U.S. government proclaiming respect for democracy and freedom of speech. In a disturbing trend, the government increasingly leveled criminal charges against opposition figures, newspapers, journalists, interest groups, and demonstrators for what should be civil offenses, on grounds of questionable validity under both domestic and international law. Kyrgyzstan continued to apply the death penalty, widening its application to include drug offenders.

On January 8, Topchubek Turgunaliev, a leader of the opposition Erkin Kyrgyzstan Party, was sentenced to ten years of imprisonment for the alleged embezzlement of $10,000 in 1994 from a Bishkek university. Turgunaliev's former colleague at the university, Timur Stamkulov, was sentenced to six years in a prison colony. Turgunaliev was sentenced despite overwhelming evidence that he had borrowed the money by agreement, and after investigators had, on six occasions, argued that it be adjudicated in a civil court. That the Procuracy succeeded in holding a criminal trial can be explained only by the government's desire to silence Mr. Turgunaliev's reinvigorated political dissent at the time of his arrest. Turgunaliev's arrest, on December 17, 1996, followed his participation in a peaceful public protest that sought to highlight the plight of pensioners and his founding of "For Deliverance from Poverty," a new political movement that publicly challenged government economic policies. Turgunaliev and Stamkulov's sentences were reduced on appeal on February 18 to four and three years respectively, which they were permitted to serve at home. However, in March, following participation in political rallies, Turgunaliev was taken to a remote settlement colony in Leylek in southern Kyrgyzstan, a center with appalling conditions, no medical facilities, and poor nutrition for the convicts, where he fell extremely ill and was hospitalized.

On May 23, Zamira Sydykova, editor of the influential weekly *Res Publica*, and Aleksandr Alyanchikov, a journalist on the same newspaper, were convicted of libel under Article 128 (2) of the criminal code and sentenced to eighteen months of imprisonment. Their conviction on criminal charges related to articles published in *Res Publica* said to have contained defamatory remarks about the wealthy and influential chair of Kyrgyzstan's state-owned gold company. Together with two other *Res Publica* journalists, Marina Sivasheva and Bektash Shamshiev, they were fined $120 each and banned from doing journalistic work for an eighteen-month period. On June 10, Sydykova's sentence was reduced to eighteen months in a lower security prison, where conditions were appalling; Alyanchikov's sentence was suspended and later reduced. The Supreme Court released Sydykova on August 6, ostensibly due to time already served, but likely in response to international attention to her case. The charges against Sivasheva and Shamshiev were dropped.

An amnesty, announced by Akaev on August 11 for sick or disabled prisoners and those prosecuted for libel under the criminal code, failed to address the most egregious cases of prosecution for criminal libel. The amnesty did not reinstate those independent newspapers forcibly closed, such as *Kriminal,* shut down in February, and others in 1995 and 1996 for allegedly breaching the libel law.

On March 24, another *Res Publica* journalist, Yrysbek Omurzakov, was arrested on charges that stemmed from his January article criticizing government privatization policy and detailing state-owned factory workers' complaints about the proposed privatization of factory-owned housing. Charged with criminal libel, Omurzakov spent seventy-four days in pre-trial detention before being released by the Municipal Court on August 12. The trial resumed on September 18, with disturbing reports that the court claimed to have lost witness testimony essential to the defense, and that factory workers had been threatened with the loss of their factory-owned housing if they testified on Omurzakov's behalf. The court sentenced Omurzakov to six months in a prison colony on September 29. The ruling was upheld, but Mr. Omurzakov was released on November 4 under the law on amnesty, which went into force in July 1997 and, in part, covers individuals charged with violating Articles 128 and 129 of the Kygyzstan Criminal Code. Two co-defendants Dzhybek Akmatova and Gulina Ibraimova, also received six-month sentences, but were pardoned as "first-time offenders" under an August 11 amnesty.

Key opposition figure Kubanichbek Apas, who resides now in Moscow due to government harassment, returned to Bishkek in August to visit his wife and two young children. During Apas' stay, an interview with him was published in the weekly youth newspaper *Asaba*, in which he implicated the president in impropriety and corruption concerning gold-mining operations and condemned government treatment of journalists and excessive state control over the media. On September 12, the night after Apas returned to Moscow, KGB officers ransacked his wife's apartment, severely frightening his family. Apas believes the officers were looking for his opposition articles and publications and sought to curtail his political activities through the intimidation of his family.

Freedom to receive and impart information was dealt a serious blow when the government issued Resolution 320 of September 2, limiting the import of all forms of information that ". . . may damage the political [or] economic interests of the Republic, its national security, public order, health protection and public morals." The list of goods that may be prohibited include books, printed materials, films, film negatives, audio-and video materials, records, tapes, discs, and hand-written materials.

In 1997 the Uighur organization, Ittipak, which advocates establishing an independent Uighur homeland in the neighboring western Chinese province of Xinjiang, was allowed to function unhindered. This was a marked im-provement over 1996.

The Yntymak Society, an organization that advances the housing concerns of migrant workers in Bishkek, came under attack by the government following peaceful demonstrations outside the government building in Bishkek. On July 7, twelve demonstrators, including human rights activist Tursunbek Akhunov, were arrested by police while picketing the building. Credible reports cite excessive police violence against the demonstrators, causing at least one woman to be hospitalized. All twelve were barred from future demonstrations, and the Bishkek police public order department warned the society that they would arrest all participants of any further rallies.

Thirteen members of Yntymak, including the group's leader, Nurlan Alymkulov, currently face criminal charges for "unsanctioned occupation" of land in Bishkek where they built their homes. The use of criminal law to prosecute an essentially civil matter appears unduly punitive and linked to the group's political activities.

The Right to Monitor
There were no reported violations of the right to monitor.

The Role of the International Community

European Union
The E.U. made no known interventions on human rights abuses in Kyrgyzstan in 1997. It continued to channel to Kyrgyzstan substantial amounts of aid in the form of its TACIS and ECHO programs. In anticipation of the ratification of the Partnership and Cooperation Agreement (PCA), initialed in November 1995, the European Parliament gave its assent to an Interim Agreement that brought into effect the trade provisions of the PCA, despite the fact that the PCA hinges on respect for human rights and democratic principles.

United States

The United States Embassy in Bishkek closely monitored the cases of journalists facing libel charges, and, along with the case of Turgunaliev, sent observers to their trials. The State Department made public and private demarches, in particular during President Akaev's July visit to the U.S., criticizing the Kyrgyz government for treating libel cases against journalists and opposition figures as criminal rather than civil matters. The U.S. distributed economic and humanitarian aid, including substantial amounts under the Freedom Support Act Funding program and funds for democratic reform. The State Department's *Country Reports on Human Rights Practices for 1996* provided a comprehensive analysis of the human rights situation in Kyrgyzstan.

MACEDONIA

Human Rights Developments

During 1997, the government in Macedonia made some progress toward consolidating democracy. But human rights violations persisted, especially against non-ethnic Macedonians, placing the government's commitment to international law in question and shaking the country's already fragile ethnic balance.

The most serious issue was the discriminatory treatment of ethnic Albanians who, according to the Macedonian government, make up 23 percent of the population. Albanians, like ethnic Turks and Roma, are grossly underrepresented in state structures such as the police, even in areas where they constitute a clear majority of the local population.

An unresolved point of contention was the right to higher education in languages other than Macedonian. An Albanian-language private university in Tetovo was allowed to operate during 1997, although the government refused to recognize its diplomas. Rector of the university, Fadil Sulejmani, was released from prison on February 1, after serving ten months of a twelve month sentence for resisting the police when the university first opened in 1995. A draft law on higher education under consideration in 1997 would prohibit higher education in any languages other than Macedonian.

Another controversy involved the public display of foreign flags in Macedonia, particularly the state flags from neighboring Albania and Turkey. In early 1997, newly-elected local governments run by ethnic Albanians in the western towns of Tetovo and Gostivar hoisted the Albanian and Turkish state flags outside their municipal halls. The Macedonian constitutional court prohibited the action, but its decision was ignored by the local governments, despite many warnings.

On July 8, parliament passed a law on the use of flags in Macedonia that allowed the flags of other states to be flown at any time on private property or during sporting events and alongside the Macedonian state flag on state buildings during national holidays. The next day the Ministry of Interior ordered the police to remove the Albanian flags from the Tetovo and Gostivar town halls. An estimated 10,000 ethnic Albanians attempted to hinder the police and violent clashes ensued. According to the government, the police came under attack, fired in the air and then used force where necessary to subdue the crowd and perform their duties. However, according to ethnic Albanian leaders, witnesses, and local human rights organizations, such as the Helsinki Committee for Human Rights of the Republic of Macedonia, the police used excessive force against individuals who were not offering any resistance, or had ceased to resist, resulting in the death of three ethnic Albanians, Shpend Hyseni, Nazmi Salihu, and Milaim Dauti. At least one hundred other people were treated for injuries in the local hospital, mostly for wounds on the head and shoulders. During and after the clash, the police searched homes in the area without a warrant, arresting approximately 300 people. Many of the detained were denied their constitutional rights, such as access to a lawyer or information on the reason for their arrest.

The mayor of Gostivar, Rufi Osmani, was arrested and charged with ignoring a court ruling, organizing armed guards and inciting national and racial hatred. After fifty-three days in pre-trial detention, he was sentenced to thirteen years, eight months in prison. The head of the Gostivar city council, the mayor of Tetovo, and the head of the Tetovo city council received sentences ranging from two and a half to three years in prison. According to the Greek Helsinki Monitor, which observed the Osmani trial, due process irregularities violated the defendant's right to a fair trial, most seriously the court's unwillingness to admit any witnesses on behalf of the defense. The thirteen-year, eight-month sentence for Osmani also struck many observers as exceedingly high. By contrast, earlier in the year, ethnic Macedonian students had used highly aggressive and xenophobic slogans during demonstrations against the expanded use of the Albanian language at the Pedagogical Faculty in Skopje, but they had not been charged with inciting racial hatred.

Other criminal proceedings in 1997, including those against ethnic Macedonians, were marked by irregularities and violations of due process. A new code of penal procedure came into effect on April 11 that brought Macedonian law up to European standards, but local human rights groups still reported cases in which a person's period of detention exceeded the twenty-four hours allowed by law, the police failed to inform a detainee of the reason for his or her arrest, or the police denied the defendant access to a lawyer.

Police abuse was a problem against all Macedonian citizens, regardless of their ethnicity, although non-ethnic Macedonians were especially susceptible to abuse. Most allegations were of ill-treatment during the time of arrest or in police stations. The Albanian Party of Democratic Prosperity complained that its members were harassed and, on occasion, detained and abused by the police.

As in previous years, the fairness of elections in Macedonia was questioned in late 1996 and 1997. According to local human rights organizations, there were incomplete voting lists in the local elections in November and December 1996. In some polling stations,

the number of unregistered voters was as high as 20 percent. The state-financed media, both electronic and print, was biased in favor of the ruling Social Democratic Union, which won the elections.

A proposed law on religion also came under criticism for distinguishing between the major "traditional" religions and "new" religious groups. In 1997, the Macedonian government continued to deny recognition of the Serbian Orthodox Church in Macedonia. Two clergymen from the Serbian Orthodox Church in Serbia, Bishop Irinej Bulovic and Archdeacon Radovan Bigovic, were refused entry into Macedonia to attend an international conference in Skopje on October 26.

The Right to Monitor

Human Rights Watch is not aware of any government attempts to restrict or hinder the work of human rights monitors in Macedonia.

The Role of the International Community

United Nations and the Organization for Security and Cooperation in Europe

The international community's priority was to maintain the territorial integrity and political stability of Macedonia. Toward this end, a United Nations Preventive Deployment Force (UNPREDEP) and the Organization for Security and Cooperation in Europe (OSCE) mission continued to monitor and report on the internal and external threats to the country. While providing a necessary element of security, in the name of stability, both organizations voiced little public criticism of human rights violations committed by the Macedonian government. The UNPREDEP mission, whose mandate was extended until November 30, was scaled down in 1997 from 1050 to 750 members, mostly from Scandinavian countries and the United States. During the crisis in Albania, it helped monitor the border and avert potential clashes. The U.N. special rapporteur on the former Yugoslavia, Elizabeth Rehn, criticized certain violations in 1997, especially the use of excessive force by the police in Gostivar, but praised the Macedonian government's "considerable progress in the protection of human rights." She proposed that Macedonia be removed from her mandate.

European Union
A Cooperation Agreement between Macedonia and the European Union came into effect on December 1, 1996. The agreement provides an a ECU 150 million credit line to Macedonia for infrastructure projects and is a step toward Macedonia's associate membership in the E.U.

United States
The United States repeatedly stressed its support for the territorial integrity and multi-ethnicity of Macedonia, making clear to ethnic Albanian leaders that it encouraged cooperation within government rather than the establishment of parallel structures. The U.S. considered Macedonia a vital buffer between the competing interests of Bulgaria, Albania, Serbia, and Greece. In order to support the government of Kiro Gligorov, however, the U.S. failed strongly to criticize human rights abuses that took place in 1997, such as the police abuse in Gostivar. Close military cooperation within the framework of NATO's Partnership for Peace continued throughout the year.

ROMANIA

Human Rights Developments
The Romanian government took steps to improve Romania's human rights record during 1997, reflecting newly-elected President Emil Constantinescu's electoral promise to make human rights a priority for his administration. However, while progress was made in addressing the concerns of the ethnic Hungarian minority, serious human rights abuses, especially against Roma, homosexuals and prisoners, persisted, and accountability for police ill-treatment and excessive use of force remained rare.

On a positive note, the government made an effort to improve the status of the ethnic Hungarian minority. Its new coalition government is the first since World War I to include an ethnic Hungarian party; additionally, the government appointed three Hungarian prefects and in July allowed a Hungarian consulate to be opened in Cluj, satisfying several long-held demands of the Hungarian minority. However, the Hungarian flag on the front of the consulate was stolen soon after it opened and, when the consulate replaced the flag, Mayor Gheorghe Funar himself arrived with a crane to remove it, announcing that he would make the thieves honorary citizens of Cluj.

The Roma minority continued to face significant discrimination and ill-treatment in 1997, including high levels of police brutality. Although to a lesser extent than in previous years, Roma villages continued to be attacked by their Romanian neighbors, and the state's response remained inadequate. On January 16-17, 1997, for example, between fifty and one hundred ethnic Romanians, reportedly armed with pistols and shotguns, chased Roma out of the town of Tanganu near Bucharest and vandalized their homes. Although three individuals were arrested in connection with the attack, no charges were filed against them, and they were soon released. Two police officers who allegedly did nothing to halt the violence were cleared of any wrongdoing.

Contrary to the Romanian government's assertion that it swiftly and even-handedly responded to racially motivated attacks on Roma, there was little evidence in 1997 of a more aggressive effort by the government to prosecute police or private individuals accused of committing such crimes. As in previous years, police officers or individuals accused of ill-treating Roma were rarely charged with a crime. In the few cases where charges were brought, the cases dragged on in the judicial system.

Article 200 of Romania's penal code, which previously outlawed all homosexual acts, was amended slightly in September 1996 to punish only homosexual acts "committed in public, or which cause public scandal." However, the vague wording of the amended article remained of concern in 1997 because private homosexual conduct that becomes publicly known may still be prosecuted. In a number of cases reported during 1997, such "private" conduct was made public by a private informant, an individual who witnessed or even participated in a homosexual act and then gave this information to the state. The vague wording of article 200, which criminalizes homosexual conduct that "incit[es] or encourag[es]... sexual relations between persons of the same sex, along with propaganda or association or any act of proselytism committed in the same scope," may also be employed to limit expression, assembly, and association.

Homosexuals also continued to be the victims of widespread police brutality. In a case from June in which three men from Constanta were arrested on charges of having sex in a deserted storage cabin, all three complained of being beaten by civil guards and by a major in the municipal police. One of the three men has not been allowed to see his family since the time of his arrest; one man also said that, under threat of further beatings, he was coerced into signing three statements—the contents of which were unknown to him. Gay men also reported that police often waited in known "cruising areas" in order to extort money in return for not arresting them.

There continued to be a lack of accountability for law enforcement officials accused of using excessive force. In one such case, a policeman who was accused of the 1994 murder of Ioan Rus was finally brought to trial after international organizations protested the early closure of the murder investigation. He was acquitted in December 1996 after trial by a military tribunal. This acquittal is currently under appeal.

From February 7-11, 1997, prison inmates in nine Romanian cities went on a hunger strike to protest poor conditions within the prisons. For the most part the protests were peaceful, but some violence did erupt.

The Right To Monitor

There were no reported violations of the right to monitor.

The Role of the International Community

Europe

In 1997, Romania pressed to be included in the first round of NATO expansion and to begin talks with the European Union about future membership. Romania was not successful on either count during the year. However, Romania's goal of integration with Western Europe gave European governments and institutions significant leverage to influence human rights developments. The European Commission, for example, praised Romania for the strides it was making, but underscored the necessity for it to improve its treatment of the Roma minority before it would be ready to begin membership talks with the European Union. On April 29, 1997, the Council of Europe's Parliamentary Assembly announced that Romania "honored the most important obligations" with regard to human rights and that it would end its special monitoring of Romania. It did warn, however, that monitoring would be resumed if the Romanian government did not fulfill its pledges to amend the penal code provisions related to homosexuality and to continue to fight discrimination.

Romania also improved its relations with two of its neighbors, Hungary and the Ukraine. A friendship treaty was signed last year between Hungary and Romania, which included significant provisions for the protection of minorities. On July 23, 1997, Hungary was allowed to open a consulate in Cluj. There were numerous visits of high ranking officials between Romania and Hungary including visits between the prime ministers and presidents of both countries, which showed the desire of each country's government to have friendly relations.

United States

In July 1997, the United States said that Romania needed to improve its human rights record in order to join NATO. The United States recognized the important steps Romania had made in the field of human rights and said that if Romania's record continued to improve, it would be selected in the next NATO expansion. The U.S. State Department's *Country Report on Human Rights Practices for 1996* was largely accurate in its portrayal of the human rights situation in Romania.

THE RUSSIAN FEDERATION

Human Rights Developments

In 1997, the Russian government again neglected the country's many human rights problems—appalling prison conditions, rampant police brutality toward ethnic minorities and criminal suspects, and persecution and harassment of human rights activists. This lack of reform contrasted starkly with the efforts to promote economic reform by the new government, appointed by a reinvigorated President Boris Yeltsin after a long absence due to a quintuple by-pass operation. However, several government interventions favoring human rights were made in response to public pressure, contributing to a mixed record in 1997.

The government presided over a newly emerging pattern of harassment and persecution of human rights and other activists in the Russian provinces. The Russian authorities enacted a new law on religion that severely restricted religious rights and equality between religious denominations. The government did not take any measures to put an end to police brutality, both against ethnically non-Russians and criminal suspects. In Moscow, a clear increase of police violence against Caucasians, Central Asians, third-world refugees, and the homeless preceded the 850th anniversary of the city. The government took no steps to abolish the propiska system and guarantee freedom of movement in practice, despite yet another Constitutional Court

decision reinforcing the constitutionally guaranteed right. Detention centers remained severely overcrowded, and ill-treatment in these centers, as well as in police custody and the army, continued with almost complete impunity. Russia failed to introduce a formal moratorium on executions but did not carry out any executions and signed Protocol Six to the European Convention on Human Rights on abolishing the death penalty, Russia had not yet ratified the European Convention on Human Rights at the time of this writing, nor complied with many other obligations related to its accession to the Council of Europe in February 1996. In a positive development, on June 14, President Yeltsin rescinded two unconstitutional presidential decrees, which allowed the police to detain people without presenting charges for up to 30 days.

One of the most disturbing developments in 1997 was a rise in the harassment of human rights activists in the Russian provinces, and the inadequate prosecutor general's response to it. Beginning in November 1996, regional authorities arrested and charged at least four human rights activists in an attempt to silence their critical voices and prevent them from serving as public defenders (*See* Right to Monitor). Throughout 1997, the Federal Security Service (FSB) continued to pursue outrageous espionage charges against environmentalist Alexander Nikitin for co-writing a report by the Norwegian environmental group, Bellona, on nuclear pollution from Russia's Northern Fleet nuclear submarines. After releasing Nikitin from FSB detention in St. Petersburg in December 1996, the Procurator General's office failed to drop the charges and chose instead to prolong the term of investigation several times. On September 9, the FSB issued its fifth indictment, which was, like those before, based on secret legislation. During this time, the FSB had only conducted a third expert assessment of the Bellona report, which was as deeply flawed as the previous ones, meanwhile the FSB forbids Nikitin from traveling outside St. Petersburg.

On September 26, President Yeltsin signed a highly discriminatory law on Freedom of Conscience and Religion Associations, making it the first piece of restrictive legislation that Russia has introduced to replace a federal law that adequately protected the rights and freedoms of its citizens. According to the law, religious associations that local authorities deem to have existed on Russian territory for less than fifteen years would lose virtually all their rights, making their work and development in Russia all but impossible. The law contains numerous vague provisions allowing local authorities to further restrict the rights of "minority" religious groups and arbitrarily to close religious associations.

On July 22, President Yeltsin vetoed a draft of the law, arguing that it violated a range of constitutional rights and freedoms. A compromise version, proposed by the presidential administration to the State Duma on September 3, granted some property rights to religious groups, but retained the original draft's discriminating approach and draconian registration requirements. Representatives of many religions claimed they were pressured into approving the presidential proposal without having seen the final version, and several of them withdrew their support for the draft. Restrictive laws on religion already exist in about twenty-five of Russia's eighty-nine regions, including Sverdlovsk, Arkhangelsk and Buryatia. Federal authorities made no effort to challenge the constitutionality of such laws. Harassment of religious groups under the new law had already started in October 1997, within weeks after the law entered into force.

Regional governments continued to restrict freedom of movement by enforcing a registration system that is of a licensing, rather than of an informative, nature. In Moscow, a set of local ordinances allow only those with close relatives in Moscow and owners of dwellings to become permanent residents of the city and oblige the city's visitors to go through highly bureaucratic registration procedures within 24 hours of their arrival. In a positive move, on December 17, 1996, the Moscow government complied with an April 1996 Constitutional Court ruling by cancelling the prohibitive fee for a permanent residence permit. On July 2, the Constitutional Court ruled unconstitutional a similar fee levied in Moscow Province, which the provincial government had instituted after the court's April 1996 decision. Also to its credit, the Moscow city government attempted to simplify the bureaucratic procedures for citizens of the former Soviet Union to register their temporary stays of up to six months. Discriminatory regulations continue to oblige such visitors to pay higher fees for temporary registration in Moscow than Russian citizens. Moscow city police strictly but highly selectively enforced this registration system, especially prior to the city's 850th anniversary celebrations. They stopped overwhelmingly people with dark hair and skin, people from the Caucasus, Central Asia, refugees from the third world, and the homeless for identity checks on the streets, at metro stations and in private apartments. According to Moscow police statistics, police officers carried out more than 1.4 million registration checks, including police visits to more than 1.3 million private apartments, over the first five months of 1997. The police regularly beat those stopped for passport checks, set fines arbitrarily, and appeared to pocket the money themselves.

The situation of asylum seekers was especially grave since police routinely refuse to acknowledge their UNHCR and migration service registration cards as adequate documentation for registration. Police detained and threatened to deport at least ten asylum seekers; thirty others were deported without the opportunity to apply for asylum. Detained asylum seekers have no access to the outside world. In one egregious case, on January 6, Moscow police took Badai Galalia—an Iraqi Kurd married to a Russian woman who was not registered—from his home into custody without explanation and detained him for 111 days, during which he was not permitted to shower, see a lawyer, or phone his wife. When a despairing Galalia attempted suicide toward the end of the 111 days, police sent him to a psychiatric hospital (without informing his wife) where he stayed until June 16.

As in 1996, Russia not only failed to grant proper protection and asylum to dissidents and opposition politicians from countries of the former Soviet Union, its law enforcement agencies harassed several of them and extradited one. On February 21, Albert Musin, a formerly Moscow-based human rights activist, was stopped by the police during a routine identity check and detained when a computer check indicated he was wanted by the Uzbek authorities. Following an international protest campaign the Russian government released him and Uzbekistan dropped the extradition request. On June 25, four armed police officers entered the building of the Moscow Helsinki Group (a leading Russian human rights organization) and took Abdulfattakh Mannapov, another Uzbek dissident who had just obtained Russian citizenship, to the police station because of his alleged lack of registration. Immediate action by the Moscow Helsinki Group and *Express Khronika* (a human rights newspaper) secured his release. On August 18, Ayaz Akhmedov, an Azerbaijani dissident poet, was visited by unknown men and a woman at his home who eventually left as Akhmedov refused to open the door. Several days later, Akhmedov was beaten up in Moscow by two unknown men. Unable to turn to the police for protection, Akhmedov left Russia and was granted political asylum in Norway.

Police arrested Akhmadjon Saidov, former deputy chairman of the Supreme Soviet of Tajikistan, on February 7 at the request of the Tajik government. The office of the procurator general extradited him to Tajikistan on June 27, ignoring the possible political motives behind the case. Extradition requests were reviewed on the basis of the Minsk Convention of 1993, which does not allow for access to a lawyer nor to judicial review of the legality of detention. The procurator general's office also selectively refused to subject the charges of the requesting side to critical review to exclude political motivations.

Comprehensive amendments to the 1993 Law on Refugees entered into force on July 3, 1997. The amendments improved the 1993 law by clarifying some procedural matters and introducing terminology consistent with the 1951 Convention, but otherwise left the refugee determination procedure intact. Importantly, the law allows for asylum seekers to register with police on the basis of migration service identification cards.

Despite these improvements, the situation of refugees remained highly problematic. The Federal Migration Service (FMS) had not issued instructions to its local branches on how to implement the new law, and consequently migration services throughout Russia were unable to process new asylum claims. In 1997, the FMS began reviewing the merits of a number of asylum claims filed in 1993 and 1994. Judicial review of denials continued to be extremely slow. Most refugees arriving at Moscow's international airport were sent back to their country of origin without being given a chance to file an asylum claim.

A new presidential decree "On the manner of granting political asylum in the Russian Federation," which replaced a 1995 decree, did nothing to improve the plight of ordinary asylum seekers, nor did it correct any of its predecessor's problematic provisions; indeed to the contrary, it introduced some additional restrictions on the right to asylum. Most disturbingly, it grants local officials great discretion over whether an asylum claim is reviewed on merit, fails to provide for an appeal procedure, and categorically rules out asylum claims from countries Russia deems "democratic."

Human rights violations continued on a massive scale in the criminal justice and penitentiary system, despite structural reforms required by the Council of Europe. The government did not strip the FSB of its right to run detention centers or reform the procurator's office, as required by the Council. The State Duma adopted a draft criminal procedure code on June 6, which failed to establish a criminal law system based on the equality of parties, in violation of article 123(3) of the Russian constitution, and which contained many of the flaws of the 1960 criminal procedure code. In a positive move, President Yeltsin signed a decree ordering the transferal of the penitentiary system from the Ministry of Interior to the Ministry of Justice.

Law enforcement agencies continued the large scale use of torture during criminal investigation. Torture occurred mostly in the first hours or days of detention, when detainees were completely isolated from the outside world by police refusal to grant suspects access to a lawyer of their own choice or to allow them to contact their relatives. In numerous cases, testimony received from tortured suspects was used in court and accepted as evidence by judges while procurators failed to investigate or open criminal proceedings against the police officers involved. In a symptomatic case, on November 21, 1996, police officers in Yekaterinburg tortured fifteen-year-old Oleg Fetisov when he refused to confess to a crime he claims he did not commit. Police beat and kicked Fetisov, forced a gas mask on his head and then cut the oxygen flow until he lost consciousness. Fetisov promised to sign the confession but quickly jumped from the fourth floor window, and as a result suffered a concussion and broken ribs. Although criminal proceedings were instituted against the police officers, they were dropped in May on unclear grounds. As of this writing, Fetisov's trial was scheduled to begin in November.

The rescinding of two notorious presidential decrees marked significant improvements. On Immediate Measures for the Protection of the Population Against Banditry and Other Manifestations of Organized Crime" had allowed police to detain people suspected of ties with organized crime for up to thirty days without presenting charges. Various police officers had used this decree widely and arbitrarily, especially in connection with the war in Chechnya. Presidential Decree 1025, of 1996, On Urgent Measures on Strengthening Law and Order and Intensifying the Fight Against Crime in Moscow and Moscow Region, which singled out "vagrants and beggars" and allowed police to hold these persons in "social rehabilitation centers" for up to thirty days and to remove the homeless forcibly from Moscow, was also rescinded.

The Moscow city implementing decree remained in force.

Severe overcrowding made conditions in pre-trial detention facilities torturous and fatal. According to figures provided by the Ministry of Interior to the Moscow Center for Prison Reform, on July 1 some 275,567 people were being held in detention centers intended for a maximum of 182,358 detainees. Sanitary conditions were extremely poor, as was medical care. Increasing numbers of detainees and prison inmates suffered from tuberculosis, which caused the death of seventy-four per 100,000 prisoners in 1994, and 178 in 1995. (The total prison population in Russia as of July 1 was 1,017,848). On July 1, according to official figures, 67,151 convicted prisoners were ill with the disease. Overall, 676 of every 100,000 prisoners died in 1994 and 720 in 1995.

Neither the government nor the procurator general took any steps to discourage the almost automatic use of custody as a measure of restraint, nor to promote the use of bail. As a result, many procurators continued to issue sanctions to arrest suspects without properly reviewing the necessity of custody. The draft criminal procedure code would continue the widespread application of custody, even though it would limit its use to some extent.

Although in 1997 Russia observed a de facto moratorium on executions and signed Protocol Six to the European Convention on Human Rights on April 17, courts continued to sentence people to death. According to official figures, as of February some 900 people remained on death row, 680 of whom were still in the appeal process.

For the second year in a row a draft law on domestic violence failed to reach the Duma for debate. A draft circulated this year would have limited the right to many such benefits as places in government-run shelters only to those women who were financially dependent on their partners. The draft also failed to require the police and procuracy to gather statistics on domestic violence. Reported rapes fell thirteen percent in 1996—the result, no doubt, not of improved crime prevention but of survivors' increased reluctance to report rapes. Rape crisis counselors estimate that fewer than five percent of rape survivors report the crime.

In 1997, assassinations and frequent kidnappings shattered hopes of post-war stability in the Chechen Republic. Unidentified gunmen murdered a group of six delegates of the International Committee for the Red Cross on December 17, 1996; several elderly Russians suffered the same fate later that month. Throughout 1997, well over fifteen journalists and many other aid workers and other people were taken hostage by unknown groups motivated by ransom. Among them were Yelena Masyuk and two colleagues working for Russia's independent television network (NTV), who were taken hostage on May 10. They were released on August 18, apparently only after NTV paid a large sum to the kidnappers. Numerous others remained hostages.

In an apparent attempt to end rampant crime, the Chechen government publicly executed convicted prisoners on at least two occasions in 1997. In April, a man from the settlement of Bachi-Yurt was executed, and on September 3 a man and a woman who had been convicted for premeditated murder were executed by firing squad on a central square in Grozny, in the presence of some 2,000 people. The execution was televised. Two more executions, which had been planned for the following week, were postponed after international protests. Under the Chechen criminal code at least eight crimes carried capital punishment. Some punishments involve the infliction of terrible pain, such as decapitation and stoning. The criminal code also provided for caning for at least eleven crimes.

The Right to Monitor

In late 1996 and 1997, local authorities in the Russian provinces arrested at least four human rights activists and brought charges against them involving such things as libel, contempt of court, making death or other threats, and having sexual intercourse with a minor. All activists had provided free legal advice to people in their regions and acted as public defenders at court hearings. They were pre-

sumably arrested to silence their often harsh criticism of the work of local procurator's offices, judges, and the police. Even though the procurator general's office apparently played a role in the release of some of the human rights activists—albeit under concerted pressure from Russian and international human rights groups—it did nothing to end the upsurge in repression of human rights activism.

Yury Shadrin from Omsk was arrested on November 29, 1996, following a decision by the provincial procurator of Omsk to combine three old and unrelated charges, involving death threats, a car accident, and contempt of court, into one case. Shadrin was released on December 31 following a public outcry but the charges have not been dropped. Magadan police arrested Rafael Usmanov on March 25, 1997, while on his way to a court hearing on a case for which he had been serving as public defender, and charged him with libel, presumably in relation to his severely critical article about the Russian Constitutional Court. Usmanov was released on April 10, and the charges were dropped. Criminal proceedings against Yury Padalko from the town of Irkutsk on presumably trumped-up charges of libel, hooliganism, and other offenses instituted in 1992 continued to be pursued. Murmansk police arrested Mr. Pazyura on May 26, 1997, and charged him with libel, contempt of court, and death or other threats. Shortly before, Pazyura had sharply criticized the chair of the Murmansk provincial court in a telephone conversation with her. At a September 9 court hearing, Pazyura made an emotional verbal attack on the judge, who subsequently appointed yet another assessment of his mental health. Vasily Chaykin from Krasnodar was arrested on April 17 1997, and charged with having had sexual intercourse with a minor. However, there was sound reason to believe that these charges had been fabricated as a form of revenge for his public criticism. At this time, Chaykin remained in detention.

The Role of the International Community

United Nations

In November 1996, the U.N. Committee against Torture considered Russia's second periodic report. The committee expressed concern at widespread allegations of torture and ill-treatment of suspects, persons in custody, and in the army. It also deplored the absence of effective machinery for prompt examination of complaints about ill-treatment and the serious overcrowding in Russian prisons. The committee further noted with concern the extradition of individuals who are at risk of torture and ill-treatment in their home countries. The committee's recommendations included introducing torture as a criminal offense and establishing an effective institution to monitor conditions of criminal investigation and custody. It also urged the Russian authorities to improve conditions in prisons radically and to introduce a training program for law enforcement agencies.

European Union

The European Union (E.U.), Russia's largest trading partner, engaged Russia on several high-profile human rights issues. E.U. ambassadors to Russia expressed concern about the draft Law on Freedom of Conscience and Religious Associations after it had been adopted by the Russian parliament. However, the E.U. inexplicably failed to protest the equally bad proposal issued by the presidential administration after President Yeltsin vetoed the original bill.

European Commissioner Hans van den Broek wrote to Alexander Nikitin and his attorney on January 31, stating that the European Union will follow "with particular interest" further developments in the criminal case against him and expressed willingness to raise his case with the Russian authorities in case such a necessity would arise.

On April 10, the European Parliament adopted a resolution condemning torture and ill-treatment practiced by Russian law enforcement agencies, violence and other arbitrary treatment against ethnic minorities, and inhuman conditions in prisons. In June, the parliament expressed concern about the use of registration permits in Moscow to deny street children access to municipal services and about police harassment of a nongovernmental organization working with these children.

Council of Europe

The Council of Europe's overall assessment of Russia's compliance with council obligations and membership conditions remain in a confidential report by Rudolf Bindig, a Council of Europe Rapporteur. As part of the Order 508 procedure, under which the Council monitors certain new member states, Mr. Bindig visited Russia in late 1996 and wrote a report on its compliance. At this time, the Council of Europe was waiting for the Russian government's comments on the report.

In February, Council of Europe rapporteur on the Nikitin case Erik Jurgens visited in St. Petersburg to express concern about the use of secret legislation in the case, as well as other issues. In a report to the Legal Committee of the Parliamentary Assembly of March 11, Jurgens wrote he was "shocked" by the gross violations of the presumption of innocence in the Nikitin case.

The Parliamentary Assembly Legal Committee discussed the draft law on Freedom of Conscience and Religious Associations at its sessions in June and September and expressed concern about the law to the Russian delegation.

On September 5, Leni Fischer, president of the Parliamentary Assembly, condemned a public execution, that was carried out in Chechnya two days earlier.

Organization for Security and Cooperation in Europe

In February, after the OSCE had observed and declared free and fair the January presidential elections in Chechnya, the outgoing government ordered the OSCE's representative, Tim Guldimann, to leave the country, as Guldimann had stated that Chechnya is a part of the Russian Federation. He was later permitted to return.

On September 10, the head of the OSCE Assistance Group in Grozny, Mr. Thorning Petersen, expressed his deep concern to President Maskhadov about the use of public executions by the Chechen authorities. The executions that had been planned for that day were later postponed.

United States

The Clinton administration and the U.S. Congress vigorously opposed the new religion law. At the G8 meeting in Denver in June, President Clinton expressed concern to President Yeltsin while the draft was under consideration by the State Duma. In July, the U.S. Senate approved an amendment that would cut about US$ 200 million in aid to Russia in 1998 if Yeltsin signed the religion law. In September, after the Duma adopted the revised law, Vice President Gore publicly expressed doubts about the law after a meeting with Prime Minister Chernomyrdin.

On June 17, President Clinton wrote to Alexander Nikitin and his fellow Goldman Environmental Prize Winners, stating the U.S. government's deep concern about the serious procedural irregularities in the Nikitin case and promising to monitor further developments in the case.

Relevant Human Rights Watch reports:

Moscow: Open Season, Closed City, 9/97
First Anniversary of Its Accession to The Council of Europe, 2/97

SLOVAKIA

Human Rights Developments

Slovakia's human rights record continued to deteriorate in 1997, despite pressure from the European Union and North Atlantic Treaty Organization countries to improve efforts towards full democratization and the protection of minorities in order to be considered for admission into the E.U. and NATO. A number of troubling developments—including the illegal ousting of a Slovak parliamen-

tarian, refusal to enact a law to protect minority languages, official inaction in the face of skinhead violence against Roma, and continuing police brutality—led to wide international criticism of Slovakia's human rights record. On December 4, 1996, the Slovak parliament stripped deputy Frantisek Gaulieder of his mandate after he left the ruling Movement for a Democratic Slovakia (HZDS) for membership in an opposition party. Claiming to have received a letter announcing Gaulieder's resignation from the parliament, Parliamentary Chairman Ivan Gasparovic refused to reinstate Gaulieder despite Gaulieder's protestations that the letter was a forgery and that he would go to court to recover his mandate. On December 6, a bomb exploded outside of Gaulieder's home, demolishing the front of the house; the investigation into this incident was later "closed for lack of evidence."

The E.U. immediately issued a resolution demanding that Gaulieder be reinstated, and thirty-seven opposition party deputies lodged a complaint with the Slovak Constitutional Court, demanding that it call for his reinstatement. Gaulieder, however, was not reinstated. On July 25, the Constitutional Court announced that Gaulieder had been illegally removed from his position; however, it stopped short of demanding his reinstatement as it concluded it had no legal basis to do so. Opposition parties then introduced a bill in parliament to return him to his position. Through September, however, members of the ruling coalition routinely left the chamber whenever the bill was up for a vote, thus effectively blocking a vote on the bill for lack of a quorum. Though this obstructionism brought wide international criticism, as of this writing Gaulieder has not yet been reinstated.

In the first half of 1997, an opposition-proposed referendum on the direct election of Slovakia's president was first the subject of delaying tactics and then finally subverted through the misprinting of referendum ballots. As the president is elected by the parliament under Slovakia's current constitution, the referendum's success would have constituted a loss of power for the sitting parliamentarians and particularly for Prime Minister Vladimir Meciar, who will be responsible for performing presidential functions in the event that a new president is not elected immediately after President Michal Kovac's term expires in March 1998. In response to the opposition's successful fulfilment of an election petition, Prime Minister Meciar insisted that there was no constitutional basis for a referendum on this question and asked the Constitutional Court to rule on its constitutionality. However, Meciar continued to oppose the referendum even after the Constitutional Court declared that the referendum was indeed constitutional and the government's own Central Referendum Commission declared the referendum legal. The referendum on presidential elections was to take place on May 23-24, at the same time as a previously-scheduled referendum on membership in NATO. While the government wrangled over the legality of the referendum, Interior Minister Gustav Krajci declared his intention to print ballots with only the questions related to NATO. Despite the government's final decision to proceed with the referendum on presidential elections, many ballots containing only questions relating to NATO membership were distributed at polling stations. This provoked a boycott of the poll in which voter turnout was so low that the results of all of the referenda were ultimately invalidated. On June 8, 8,000 people demonstrated against the government's interference in the referendum, and opposition leaders demanded Krajci's dismissal; Krajci, however, survived several attempts by the opposition to achieve a no-confidence vote on his performance as interior minister. Foreign Minister Pavol Hamzik did resign, as he viewed the government's blockade of the referendum to be fatally damaging to his attempts to bring Slovakia into NATO.

On a positive note, the Slovak parliament ultimately failed to approve penal code amendments that would have criminalized speech uttered with "the intention of subverting the country's constitutional system, territorial integrity, or defense capability." A more restrictive version of this amendment nearly passed into law in 1996; the amended version passed the parliament in 1997 but was vetoed by President Kovac, and the parliament failed to pass the bill over his veto.

Slovakia's record on other issues related to free expression was poor. Journalists, international organizations, and even President Kovac continued to complain about the government's pervasive control of state media. Slovakia's first private news agency, SITA, was burglarized a week before it opened and lost computers and supplies; rather than displaying any support for the agency, the Slovak Ministry of Culture just one week later urged government institutions not to use the independent SITA. In September, long-running anonymous threats against Peter Toth, a journalist for the independent paper *Sme*, culminated in the bombing of his car; to date, no one has been charged in the case. On October 16, the state telecommunications company cut the independent radio station Radio Twist off its main frequency for twenty-five hours, claiming that it had not paid for use of its transmitter in Bratislava, though the station maintained that it had paid the bill days before.

Slovakia's ruling coalition continued to draw criticism in 1997 for its treatment of national minorities, particularly Hungarians, Roma, and Jews. In September, Hungarian Prime Minister Gyula Horn revealed that, during their August meeting, Prime Minister Meciar proposed a "population exchange" of ethnic Hungarians living in Slovakia for ethnic Slovaks living in Hungary. This outrageous suggestion followed a year of controversy over Slovakia's language law, which currently outlaws the use of Hungarian for, among other things, printing bilingual school report cards in Hungarian minority-dominated areas. At least one school teacher, Alexander Toth, was fired for violating this law. In April, the Ministry of Education also proposed that certain subjects be taught only by "native" ethnic Slovaks in minority school districts, but no action was taken on this proposal.

Jewish groups were outraged over the Ministry of Education's unqualified endorsement of Milan Durica's *The History of*

Slovakia and the Slovaks, a primary school textbook that justifies Slovakia's mass deportation of Jews during the Holocaust . Because the book was published using funds from the E.U. PHARE program intended to help Slovakia prepare for admission to the E.U., the European Commission immediately issued a stern rebuke to the Slovak government and demanded that it withdraw the book from the country's schools.

The situation of Roma in Slovakia did not improve in 1997. After the brutal murder of a Romani man by a skinhead teenager on December 22, Romani leaders accused the government of indifference to the growing intolerance and later announced the formation of ethnic militias to protect Roma against high levels of skinhead and police brutality. In a report released by the European Roma Rights Center in February, a quote from a young Romani man encapsulated the pervasiveness of anti-Roma prejudice in both the public and private sectors: "If I am attacked again, I won't call the police. It would be like calling the skinheads." Roma also continued to face discrimination in education, housing, and employment.

The Right to Monitor
Human Rights Watch was not aware of any attempts by the Slovak government to impede the monitoring of human rights in 1997.

The Role of the International Community
The international community's most effective condemnation of Slovakia's human rights practices came through its refusal to issue Slovakia membership into NATO and the E.U. The E.U. and the U.S. were particularly disapproving of the Slovak government's unwillingness to reinstate Gauleider, its ongoing failure to protect minority languages, and its obstruction of the presidential election referendum. The Human Rights Committee of the U.N. High Commissioner for Human Rights released a report in August, which noted that "the remnants of the former totalitarian rule have not yet been completely overcome" and that Slovakia needed to improve its response to discrimination, independence of the judiciary, and free expression, among other issues. In April, the E.U. also released a report critical of prison conditions in Slovakia. The Commission for Cooperation and Security in Europe (CSCE) released a 40 page report in September criticising Slovakia's human rights record.

TAJIKISTAN

Human Rights Developments
Tajikistan's fragile human rights situation appeared ripe for improvement following a June 27, 1997, peace accord between the government and the United Tajik Opposition, which formally ended five years of civil war. In August, however, fighting erupted between rival government groups in the capital, Dushanbe, and in the southern and western regions of the country, resulting in at least thirty summary executions, abductions, rapes, and widespread looting. In early September, further fighting broke out between government militia and opposition forces in the east of Dushanbe in clear violation of the newly-signed peace accord. As the peace agreement began to be implemented in September and October, the capital witnessed at least seventeen explosions by unidentified perpetrators, brutal murders of ethnic Russians, the assassination of the son of the procurator general, and retaliatory kidnappings of family members of the commander of the presidential guard and rogue rebel leader Rizvon Sodirov. On October 16, fourteen members of the presidential guard were assassinated in their Dushanbe barracks by eighty armed and masked men, and at the end of that month, one of the groups defeated in the August combats conducted an armed attack on government forces on the Tajik-Uzbek border 80 kilometers west of Dushanbe. In the ensuing breakdown in law and order, human rights suffered a serious setback, as paramilitary groups and independent warlords continued to loot, threaten and harass civilians, and renewed hostage-takings; con-

sequently, widespread fear and insecurity pervaded the country's population.

The government was unwilling or unable to control such activity and also arrested individuals on political grounds. Notably, it presided over the June peace agreement, and created a Commission on National Reconciliation, composed of twenty-six government and opposition members, to foster an atmosphere of trust and forgiveness and to facilitate conditions suitable for July 1998 national elections. The commission prepared a general amnesty, which the Majlisi Oli (the parliament) adopted into law on August 1, and oversaw the exchange of 167 government and 133 opposition detainees by by the end of October. However, the indefinite suspension of the commission's activities—due to the August and September hostilities—seriously undermined public confidence in the peace process and contributed to the persistent climate of insecurity.

The atmosphere of insecurity and violence severely disrupted the work of international organizations throughout 1997. In February 1997, a rogue rebel group led by the warlord brothers Bahrom and Rizvon Sodirov took seventeen people hostage in Obigarm, about eighty kilometers east of the capital, and in downtown Dushanbe. Among those kidnaped were five UNMOT (The U.N. Mission of Observers in Tajikistan), four U.N. High Commisioner for Refugees (UNHCR), and two International Committee of the Red Cross (ICRC) staff, as well as the Tajik Minister of Security. The hostages were released after two weeks; some had been beaten and abused. Non-essential staff from UNMOT and the other U.N. agencies were relocated to Uzbekistan until the end of April, and the U.N. suspended some programs for six months due to the security crisis.

On February 18, the day following the release of the hostages, unidentified gunmen assassinated seven people, including two ethnic Russian off-duty U.S. embassy guards, in Dushanbe. After opposition and warlord groups shot at the ICRC twice in June and July, the latter suspended its operations in Garm and the Tavil-Dara area.

Civil rights were severely repressed in the north. In April security forces stormed a prison in Khojand to quell a riot, killing at least twenty-four and wounding thirty-five others; unconfirmed reports indicated a substantially higher number of casualties. An assassination attempt on President Imomali Rakhmonov in Khojand at the end of that month, possibly linked to the prison riot, led to widespread arrests and persecution of political opponents. Among them was the May 23 arrest of Abdukhafiz Abdullaiev, the brother of the leader of the National Revival Movement, one of the main opposition movements in Tajikistan. Although originally arrested on charges of possession of narcotics, Abdullaiev was soon after charged with conspiring to assassinate the president. Suffering from cancer, Abdullaiev as of early November remained in detention, although the charges against him had not yet been confirmed.

UNHCR's activities in 1997 were significantly limited by security conditions inside and outside the country; however, large numbers of refugees and all but a few internally displaced persons were able to return to their homes in safety. In February, because of the hostage crisis, UNHCR suspended its program to repatriate Tajik refugees in camps in Afghanistan, and it did so again at the end of May, following the Taliban advance on northern Afghanistan. In mid-July, repatriation was underway again despite logistical and security problems resulting from the volatile situation in northern Afghanistan and the closure by Uzbek authorities of Termez and the Afghan-Uzbek border, ostensibly in reaction to the fighting in northern Afghanistan. At the beginning of October, renewed fighting between Taliban and anti-Taliban coalition forces spilled over into Sakhi camp close to Mazar-i-Sharif, resulting in at least two deaths, up to forty wounded, and serious shortages of food, water, and fuel in the camp. Following intense international pressure, Uzbekistan in late October agreed to open its border with Afghanistan to allow for the passage of the Sakhi refugees through Termez to Tajikistan. As of early November, close to 7,000 refugees from camps in northern Afghanistan had been repatriated. Although some returnees reported that other people illegally occupied their houses, refugee return operations for the most part were smoothly carried out. At this writing, however, large numbers of returnees in the south were without adequate winter shelter.

Some 23,000 internally displaced persons who fled Tavil-Dara during fighting in 1996 were able to return home safely by mid-July. Also in July the International Organization of Migration (IOM) completed its program to return 1,896 internally displaced persons from Gorno Badakhshan to Dushanbe and Khotlon province. In the wake of the August fighting in the capital, nonetheless, some of the displaced elected to return permanently to southeastern Gorno Badakhshan.

Hostage-taking, practiced throughout the past four years, persisted during the year, keeping the population in the grip of insecurity. Government militia forces, opposition commanders, and rogue rebel groups kidnapped one another at regular intervals, requiring the constant mediation of the Joint Commission and UNMOT. During the February hostage crisis, in a blatant mockery of the government's lack of authority, the Minister of Security himself was captured by the rogue Sodirov group. The Sodirov group in July and August again kidnapped nine people, among whom were Amonullo Negmatzoda, Tajikistan's chief mufti, his brother, and two of his sons. Although the government had pledged on several occasions to provide secure working conditions for international personnel, as of this writing Rizvon Sodirov and many of his supporters were still at large.

Security concerns kept the international community out of Garm and the Karategin Valley. Accurate and comprehensive information on the human rights situation was thus difficult to obtain. In Tavil-Dara and Garm, credible reports surfaced of increasing restrictions on dress for women and other restrictions linked to Islamic practice.

Chaos prevailed over law enforcement. The government admitted that criminal elements riddled its security forces and most citizens opted to keep silent in the face of mistreatment rather than risk retaliation by the police themselves. At road checkpoints throughout the country government, opposition, and independent armed groups regularly harassed, beat, and threatened the civilian population.

The government controlled the majority of the country's television and radio stations and newspapers, and most journalists continued to exercise careful self-censorship. In February, authorities denied accreditation to *Nezavisimaya gazeta* (Moscow) journalist Igor Rotar on the grounds that he had been "unscrupulous and biased" in his reporting on certain events that took place in Tajikistan. In the wake of the May 30 assassination attempt against President Rakhmonov, Russian journalist Aleksey Vasilivetsky was arrested and detained—allegedly on charges of possession of narcotics—following unpublished interviews with members of opposition political parties and dissident government employees. In late May, a journalist working for the Moscow-based newspaper Pravda-V had her accreditation confiscated following the publication of articles said to be critical of the president. Later that month a Russian team of journalists investigating the Khojand prison riot and the assassination attempt received threats from local authorities and was advised to leave because the team allegedly had not obtained appropriate accreditation. In July, a ruling issued by the Ministry of Culture ordered the temporary closure of nongovernmental television stations that did not possess an operating license, although no government body had established such a procedure.

Nonetheless, several new newspapers emerged with the founding of new political parties. The formerly dissident newspaper *Charogi Ruz* made its appearance in Tajikistan after an absence of five years.

The Right to Monitor

Almost no monitoring was carried out by local groups in 1997. Severe security restraints placed upon international personnel, particularly the U.N. and ICRC, limited their ability to monitor. International personnel throughout 1997 were shot at, robbed, and otherwise hampered in their humanitarian aid and information-gathering activities. The government continued to deny the ICRC access to prisons in accordance with the organization's standard procedures, while insufficient security guarantees prevented it from operating in the Tavil-Dara and Garm regions from July to early November. Although the government committed itself to establish a national civil rights institute, it had failed to do so as of this writing.

The Role of the
International Community

UNMOT's limited field presence in 1997 prevented it from monitoring and deterring abuse. The Organization for Security and Cooperation in Europe, through its field offices in Shaartuz, Dusti, and Kurgan-Tiube and through its head office in Dushanbe, conducted ongoing interventions. As in 1996, the Russian-led Confederation of Independent States' troops continued to be the target of criminal and political attacks, mostly in Dushanbe, and were accused of supporting the central government's forces during the August fighting. The World Bank once again approved more than U.S.$100 million for, among other things, privatization and land reform without taking into account corruption and serious abuses of human rights. An international donors' conference scheduled for mid to late November was to solicit U.S. $64 million to aid in the implementation of the peace accord.

United Nations

UNMOT, and in particular the Special Representative of the secretary-general, was widely regarded as key to the successful completion of the inter-Tajik talks. Human rights issues, while not directly part of UNMOT's mandate, figure prominently among the factors that impede the peace process. UNMOT's overall impact on the country's human rights and security situation, however, was otherwise negligible in 1997. The decision to maintain only a headquarters based in Dushanbe and a liaison office in Khojand for most of the year limited UNMOT's ability to obtain and provide firsthand and precise information on country conditions. In addition, although under its mandate UNMOT is to facilitate humanitarian assistance efforts by the international community, its military personnel on more than one occasion gave contradictory and scanty security advice to aid groups. UNMOT's mandate was extended until November 15, 1997.

Representatives from the U.N. Centre for Human Rights conducted a needs-assessment mission to Tajikistan in June, visiting Dushanbe, Kurgan-Tiube, Khojand, and Garm, and meeting with government and international agencies, including Human Rights Watch. The team concluded that a lasting peace in Tajikistan was threatened by serious human rights abuses at all levels and recommended deploying by the end of September one to two human rights experts to work with the Special Representative of the Secretary-General. As of early November, however, the experts had not arrived in the country.

UNHCR carried on with successful repatriation efforts despite daunting security and logistical impediments.

Organization for Security and
Cooperation in Europe

The OSCE played an important role in monitoring human rights abuses in the south through its field offices in Kurgan-Tiube, Shaartuz, and Dusti. Although plans were under way to open additional field offices in Garm and Khojand early in the year, as of this writing the OSCE had failed to gain the necessary governmental clearance to do so. OSCE was named in the peace agreements as a principal guarantor of the development of human rights and legal and democratic institutions; however, as of November, this role in practice remained unclear.

OSCE organized conferences on the socio-economic aspects of the peace process and the rule of law, as well as police and prison officer training programs, had either been postponed or were pending at the time of this writing.

TURKEY

Human Rights Developments

In power just under a year, Turkey's first Islamist-led government, the Welfare/True Path Party *(Refahyol)* coalition of Prime Minister Necmettin Erbakan resigned on June 18 after an intense public and private campaign headed by the military and the General Staff. One editorial writer dubbed the act the country's "first post-modern coup" as the military was able to force the government from office without taking power directly or putting troops in the streets. The minority three-party coalition (ANASOL-D) of Prime Minister Mesut Yilmaz took office in July after the resignation of Refah. The new Prime Minister and many of his ministers have made positive statements about improving the human rights situation and instituting reform, though only time will tell if these will translate into structural, far-reaching improvements. The conflict in southeastern Turkey between security forces and the Workers' Party of Kurdistan (PKK) continued into its thirteen year, with both sides committing serious abuses, though at a level in line with a sharp reduction in fighting inside Turkey. Although a lively, if small, civil society was active and there was both progress and setbacks with regard to prosecuting police, lowering detention periods for security detainees, and releasing jailed editors, persistent human rights abuses continued. They included restrictions on free expression, torture, death in detention, and police abuse and maltreatment. Prisons continued to be a problem, with poor administration and excessive use of force during unrest. Militant left and right-wing groups continued to commit abuses, such as bombings and assassinations.

1997 witnessed a continual back-and-forth between signs of improvement and abuse. The former Erbakan government lowered detention periods for security detainees and ordered increased oversight of police, but reports of torture and maltreatment by police continued. The Yilmaz government quickly passed a law in August resulting in the release of at least ten editors jailed on free expression charges. Unfortunately, other laws continued to punish freedom of thought. In October, for example, Esber Yagmurdereli, a respected lawyer and human rights activist, was remanded into custody to start serving a twenty-two-year sentence on free expression charges. On November 10, using legal sleight of hand, the local prosecutor released him for a period of one year to be renewed upon review. There appeared to be an increase in the prosecution of abusive police, especially in cases involving the January 1996 death of journalist Metin Goktepe in police custody and the death of ten inmates in the September 1996 riot in Diyarbakir prison, but in the case of the torture of teenagers in Manisa in December 1995, there was a serious setback when the court did not order police charged in the case to appear in court so their accusers could identify them. It took the direct intervention of Mr. Yilmaz, a commendable effort in itself, to arrest the relatively low-ranking police officers charged in the Goktepe case; later, four of the men were released on bail. In September, State Minister Salih Yildirim announced the need for Kurdish-language television broadcasts in southeastern Turkey. In Istanbul, however, the governor's office blocked the Kurdish Culture and Research Foundation *(Kurt-Kav)* from conducting Kurdish-language courses. Finally, the investigation into the Susurluk scandal, an auto accident in November 1996 that pointed toward "illegal gangs" in the security forces, proved disappointing, despite an immense public outcry and a parliamentary investigation that issued a report which, though not perfect, called for serious reform. The parliamentary immunity of those believed to be the key figures in the scandal, among them former Interior Minister Mehmet Agar, was not lifted, and only eleven low-ranking security officials were brought to trial. They were released from custody in September, though three are still held in another case.

Mr. Erbakan's hapless *Refahyol* coalition, beset by internal conflict with his secular coalition partner and by scandal, had infuriated the military by its attempt to legalize certain aspects of Islam at odds with Turkey's constitution, such as the right of female civil servants to wear head scarves. Turkey's military establishment, which views itself as the ultimate guardian of the secular, Kemalist state, also grew wary of Refah's attempt to pack the bureaucracy with its supporters and of intemperate statements by some Refah leaders. The military declared "fundamentalism" Turkey's number one threat and sought closure of state-supported religious schools (*Imam-Hatip*), schools that had been opened by every government since 1950—including the military after the 1980 coup. At the end of February, the military presented Mr. Erbakan's government with an eighteen point program to rein in Islamist activity, and in May, the government took legal action to ban Refah (Welfare Party) for threatening the secular character of the state, though the case as presented in the indictment was largely based on free expression charges. The final blow came in a June 11 statement from General Staff headquarters threatening that "weapons would be used if necessary in the struggle against fundamentalism." The government resigned a week later. It was also reported that the military sought to reinstate article 163, which banned fundamentalist activity and had been abolished in 1991.

Although the military consistently tops the polls as the most respected institution in Turkey and was supported in its anti-Refah campaign by trade unions, some business groups, and most of the press establishment, its interventionist proclivity is sharply at odds with the role the military plays in most democratic countries. The military exerts its influence through the National Security Council (MGK), a half-civilian/half-military body chaired by the president and provided for under the 1982 constitution, a restrictive document written after the 1980 coup. Law No. 2945 gives the *MGK* a broad and poorly-defined sphere of responsibility that includes protecting the state "against any foreign or domestic threat to its interests...including political, social, cultural, and economic...." A report on democratization in Turkey issued in January *1997 by* The Turkish Industrialist's and Businessmen's Association (TUSIAD) stated that, "If Turkey wishes to move in the direction of modern democracy, the issues of domestic and foreign security and national defense must be differentiated, and the Turkish armed forces' sphere of interest must be restricted to national defense."

The conflict in southeastern Turkey with the Workers Party of Kurdistan, continued into its thirteenth year, albeit at a much reduced level of intensity. Small scale incidents were also reported in mountainous regions south of the Black Sea. As in the past, most abuses committed by government forces and the PKK continued to occur in the southeast. Abuses included torture, extrajudicial killings, and indiscriminate fire. Much of the fighting moved to remote mountain areas or to northern Iraq, from which the PKK launched raids into Turkey. In mid-May, Turkey launched a large-scale incursion into northern Iraq in pursuit of PKK insurgents, and there was talk of setting up a buffer zone. Another cross-border operation commenced in September. Though not independently confirmed, in October the government reported that 28,000 individuals had been killed since the start of the conflict.

The Yilmaz government's coalition protocol stated that, "The reasons for the problems of the southeast are not ethnic, but geographical, social, and economic, stemming from the region's feudal structure..." In July, Deputy Prime Minister Bulent Ecevit led a delegation to Diyarbakir, the center of Turkey's ethnically-Kurdish regions, to announce job creation programs, increased education opportunities, and housing for the forcibly displaced.

A state of emergency remained in force in nine provinces of the region for most of 1997, though in October emergency rule was lifted in Batman, Bingol, and Bitlis provinces with promises to abolish emergency rule at the end of 1997. After the abolishment of emergency rule in Mardin province in early 1997, local human rights groups reported little change because a 1996 amendment to the provincial administration law gives extended and restrictive powers to provincial governors.

Parties that made demands for legal recognition of Turkey's Kurdish minority continued to face criminal prosecution. In May, the party chair, Murat Bozlak, and other administrators of the People's Democracy Party (HADEP), the top vote-getter in southeastern Turkey, were found guilty of aiding the PKK in a trial based on weak and questionable evidence; it appears that a case will be opened to ban the party. In June, the Democratic Mass Party (DKP) of Serafettin Elci, a former minister, was prosecuted under article 81 of the Political Party Law entitled, "Preventing the Creation of Minorities."

The most serious consequence of the fighting in the southeast has been the forced evacuation of villages and hamlets in the region. The majority were forcibly evacuated between 1993-1995; while large-scale evacuations have ceased, some smaller operations continued during 1997. In July, Deputy Prime Minister Bulent Ecevit announced that 3,185 villages and hamlets—home to an estimated 370,000 individuals—had been evacuated during the conflict. The United States State Department cited 560,000 as a "credible estimate." Little state aid or compensation was given to the displaced, and few were able to return to their homes. According to Interior Ministry figures released in March 1997, approximately 20,000 individuals had returned to their homes in 108 villages and ninety hamlets over the past year. In addition, a food "embargo" that limited the amount of staple food villagers could purchase was in effect in Tunceli province, allegedly to cut off the PKK's ability to receive or steal supplies.

While the government claimed that individuals left voluntarily under pressure from the PKK, it appeared that a conscious military strategy aimed at denying the PKK logistic support and recruiting opportunities forced the majority of evacuations. The PKK, however, continued to pressure villages to give logistic support and to burn pro-state villages run by village guards. According to a Turkish Union of Architects and Engineers (TMMOB) study based on 689 households that had migrated to Diyarbakir since

1976 (369 between 1990-96), 38.46 percent reported that their villages had been burned, while 25.54 percent left because of "events in the region." Another 30.04 percent left because of an inability to make a living, while 12.48 percent had no land. Upon the request of Reublican People's Party (CHP) deputy Algan Hacaloglu, a former state minister for human rights, a parliamentary committee was formed to investigate the cause of displacement and to provide aid to the displaced. It began work in July.

The village guard system (Koruculuk) continued to raise human rights concerns. Approximately 50,000 ethnic Kurdish villagers functioned as a civil guard force in remote areas in the southeast. On the whole poorly-trained and disciplined, village guards continued to be implicated in a variety of crimes including smuggling, kidnaping, and abuse of authority. According to Interior Ministry figures, between 1985-1996, village guards were involved in 296 murders. In February, Unal Erkan, a True Path Party (DYP) deputy and former governor of the emergency rule region, stated that village guards often operated outside the control of the gendarmerie. While some join willingly, either out of economic need or because their tribes are pro-state, many villages face pressure to enter the system. In January, there were reports of large-scale detentions by the gendarmerie in the Lice district of Diyarbakir based on the refusal of villagers to become village guards.

For its part, the PKK continued to commit human rights abuses such as extrajudicial killings, kidnaping, extortion, and destruction of property. Attacks are often targeted against those whom the PKK charges with "cooperating with the state," such as civil servants, teachers, and village guards' families. In April, PKK leader Abdullah Ocalan warned that he would not take responsibility for "the death of your children and families." In March, an official of the ERNK, the political wing of the PKK, threatened attacks against civilian targets, including tourists; in July, a female suicide bomber accidentally killed herself in a bathroom in the resort town of Bodrum as she prepared her attack.

In 1996, the PKK carried out suicide bomb attacks that took the lives of both civilians and soldiers. In May, it was reported that PKK fighters murdered five workers at a water drilling site in the hamlet of Cardakli, Hani district of Diyarbakir. In July, PKK militants raided a village in the Eruh district of Siirt province and murdered a villager on the basis that he was an "informer." In August, PKK members attacked a postal vehicle in Van province, killing four individuals. In Ordu, fighters murdered a policeman in a minibus stopped at a PKK roadblock.

While lively expression and debate existed in a wide variety of newspapers and private television stations, a number of laws, including articles 312 (inciting ethnic hatred) and 159 (insulting the parliament, army, republic, judiciary) of the Turkish penal code, article 8 of the Anti-Terror Law (separatist propaganda), the Law to Protect Ataturk (No. 5816), and article 16 of the Press Law, were employed to punish, fine, and imprison journalists and writers, and to confiscate and ban publications. Subjects that were sometimes punished included the Kurdish question, the role of the military, and political Islam, and newspapers most affected include leftist dailies like *Emek* (Labor) or Kurdish nationalist publications like *(Ulkede) Gundem* (Agenda in the Land).

In addition, a vaguely-worded law (no. 3984), which regulates Turkey's sixteen national and 360 local television stations—the vast majority private—was used to fine and temporarily close stations (usually for one day.) The government discussed amending the law to change closure penalties into fines, but as of this writing, no new law had been passed.

The case of three journalists arrested in June 1997 exemplifies the arbitrary and contradictory nature of repression of free expression. Two journalists from the now defunct *Demokrasi* newspaper and the Diyarbakir correspondent from ATV television station were arrested in June for interviewing two former PKK members alleged to have taken part in killings and illegal activities on behalf of the state. The three journalists were charged with forcing the pair to make the statements "in accord with the goals of the PKK." The men, however, made the same statements without incident to other newspapers, two television programs, including Mehmet Ali Birand's *32nd Day*, and to a Turkish parliamentary commission investigating the 1993 death-squad-style death of journalist Ugur Mumcu. A similar case occurred with the Turkish-language edition of Leo Muller's book *Gladio: Das Erbe des Kalten Krieges* (Gladio: The Legacy of the Cold War), originally published in Germany. While Pencere publishing, a small Istanbul publishing house, released the first edition without incident, the second edition of the book published in February was confiscated and both the publisher and translator were tried under article 312 and the Anti-Terror Law. In September, they were given a suspended sentence on the article 312 charge and an a fine under the Anti-Terror Law. Both sentences are under appeal.

Torture in pre-trial detention and police abuse continued, though the Refahyol government reduced detention periods for those held for crimes under the jurisdiction of State Security Courts, and the present government of Mesut Yilmaz vowed to end police abuse. The outcome of both these actions was unclear, however, and credible accounts of abuse appeared frequently in the press in 1997. In December 1996, the Council of Europe's Committee for the Prevention of Torture (CPT) issued a "Public Statement on Turkey" that condemned "flagrant examples of torture encountered by CPT delegations." Electric shock, squeezing of testicles, suspension by the limbs, blindfolding, and stripping naked were often used as a method of interrogation, especially by the Anti-Terror police. It was also reported that police continued to flout regulations requiring the immediate registration of detainees to avoid compliance with the March 1997 law reducing maximum detention periods for security detainees, which dropped from fifteen to seven days, and from thirty to ten days in the state of emergency region.

Police discipline and control was often lacking during crowd control duties, especially those involving leftists and Kurds. In February, an individual in Antalya died in police detention of a heart attack after being beaten with walkie-talkies. In July, four cameramen covering an Islamist demonstration in Istanbul were beaten so badly by the police that they needed hospitalization; in September, some participants in the "Musa Anter Peace Train" were beaten by police and had their banners burned. A report prepared by a private U.S. consulting firm noted the lack of adequate oversight of police by supervisory officers, especially during crowd control, as well as the inadequacy of the government response to allegations of torture.

Overcrowding, under-funding, and bad conditions continued to plague Turkey's prison system; 562 prisons held 56,000 prisoners, including 9,241 security detainees. The Justice and Interior Ministries' split jurisdiction over prisons, lax oversight, and poorly trained and easily bribed warders (*gardiyan*) further exacerbated an already explosive situation. Convicts were housed in large open wards, which allowed prisoners, especially in political cases, to enforce discipline and punishment—including executions—among themselves. There were credible reports of the gendarmerie beating prisoners while transporting them to court or to the hospital. In suppressing prison unrest, the gendarmerie often used excessive and deadly force. Six inmates charged with criminal offenses died in July during a riot in Istanbul's Metris prison. Turkish television broadcast footage of gendarmerie brutally beating inmates with rifle butts and batons while attempting to restore order. While it is still unclear whether security forces or prisoners were responsible for the six deaths, Yucel Sayman, the chair of the Istanbul bar who investigated the incident, put ultimate blame on "the order of vested interests in the prisons."

Far-left armed groups, such as Revolutionary Left (Dev Sol/DHKP-C) and Turkish Workers' and Peasants' Liberation Army (TIKKO), continued to commit abusive, violent acts. In August, it was reported that *Dev-Sol* launched an unsuccessful attack in an attempt to kill eight Islamists charged in the 1993 fire that killed thirty-seven intellectuals in Sivas. In May, TIKKO members reportedly killed four civilians at a flour mill in Tokat. In September, a radical Islamist group, *Vasat*, a splinter of The Islamic Great Eastern Raiders Front (IBDA-C), killed one and wounded twenty-four others in a grenade attack during the Gaziantep trade fair.

Civil society played an increasingly important role, a bright spot in the year. A lively if sometimes sensationalist press aggressively pursued the Susurluk story, and the Press Council lobbied for the August law freeing journalists. Peaceful demonstrations dubbed "A minute of darkness for light" spread over Turkey as households turned off the lights to protest Susurluk and corruption. The Turkish Industrialist's and Businessmen's Association (TUSIAD) continued its call for greater democratization with the release of a 204-page report, *Perspectives on Democratisation in Turkey*. Individuals also spoke out. A state security court prosecutor during a television talk show questioned the independence of the judiciary. He was later charged with insulting the judiciary. Esber Yagmurdereli ran a campaign to gather 1,000,000 signatures to draw attention to the conflict in the southeast and handed them to the Speaker of the Parliament in mid-1997. Yagmurdereli, recently remanded into custody on free expression charges, commented that, "People are much more aware of the restrictions of their freedom than in the past...Policies which limit the practice of politics in this country cannot survive much longer."

The Right To Monitor

Turkey's three main human rights groups, the Human Rights Foundation of Turkey (HRFT), the Human Rights Association (HRA), and the Islamist-based *Mazlum-Der*, continued their vocal and active monitoring. The government's behavior was contradictory. It appeared to recognize the legitimacy of the groups' activities, evidenced by it allowing all three to participate in an August meeting of the government's newly-created

"Human Rights High Council." On the other hand, there were arrests and criminal prosecutions of human rights activists, and human rights publications were banned. In August, a criminal trial began to close the HRA on grounds of "disseminating separatist propaganda" and "inciting the people to enmity through racial and regional discrimination" during Human Rights Week in December 1996. Between May and August, the Diyarbakir, Izmir, Malatya, Konya, Urfa, Mardin, and Balikesir branches of the HRA were ordered closed by state authorities; as of this writing, only three have been allowed to reopen. In May, Dr. Tufan Kose was found guilty of "negligence in denouncing a crime" and Mustafa Cinkilic, a lawyer, was acquitted of "disobeying the orders of authorities." The case against both men, representatives of the HRFT Adana branch, stems from their refusal to provide authorities with the names and records of 167 victims of torture who sought treatment in Adana. As revealed in foreign ministry documents leaked in 1996, the trial was opened because the HRFT reports were widely used and quoted by news agencies and foreign embassies and governments.

Foreign human rights groups were generally able to travel to Turkey to conduct research and observe trials. Amnesty International's researcher for Turkey remained banned from entering the country, though Amnesty was able to send other researchers and trial observers. In September, the Yilmaz government lifted the entrance ban against twenty-one German citizens, including an Amnesty consultant deported in June 1995. No journalists, foreign or domestic, were allowed free access to northern Iraq during Turkey's May incursion; select foreign correspondents were taken under military supervision in a one-time press pool. In general, access for journalists and human rights observers to rural areas of southeastern Turkey under emergency rule is limited, and it has proven difficult to enter Tunceli province, scene of heavy fighting between security forces and the PKK. Steven Kinzer, the *New York Time's* Istanbul bureau chief, was de-

tained overnight and questioned near Batman province in February 1997.

The Role of the International Community

Europe

Turkey continued to have tense relations with the European Union over a number of issues, including human rights and possible E.U. membership for Turkey. On December 13, 1995, the European Parliament ratified a customs union agreement intended to reduced trade barriers and tariffs between Turkey and the E.U. The parliament, however, continued to block payment of some U.S.$470 million in adjustment funds because of human rights concerns. Greece—an E.U. member— had also opposed releasing the funds to Turkey.

The E.U. sent mixed signals to Ankara concerning future E.U. membership. While Brussels continued to raise concerns over democratization, respect for human rights, and economic development, in 1997 Turkey's Muslim identity also became an issue. In February, Dutch Foreign Minister and E.U. term president Hans Van Mierlo stated that, "There is a problem of a large Muslim state. Do we want that in Europe? It is an unspoken question." Eventually, the E.U. lowered its cultural hurdle and stated that Turkey would be judged under the same criteria as other applicants.

The European Commission of Human Rights, which acts as a gatekeeper for the European Court of Human Rights, continued to review applications—primarily allegations of arbitrary detention, torture, forced village evacuations, disappearances while in custody, and unlawful death—brought by Turkish citizens under the right of individual petition. Between 1990-96, the commission registered 1,389 applications; it declared 133 admissible and 274 inadmissible. In September 1997, the Court ruled that in 1993 the Turkish gendarmerie had raped and tortured an ethnic Kurdish woman in custody.

United States

The U.S. government maintained its policy of keeping human rights issues on the agenda while stressing the overall importance of Turkey as a strategic U.S. ally. During his July confirmation hearings as Secretary for European and Canadian Affairs, Marc Grossman, the previous U.S. ambassador to Turkey, stated that U.S. policy toward Turkey contained three dimensions: promoting democracy, getting "the right kind of a security relation," and expanding trade. The Clinton administration at times did openly criticize the Turkish government: in February, Secretary of State Madeline Albright stated that, "there are things going on there which we do not approve of, certainly in the area of human rights." In June she spoke against any direct intervention by the military. The embassy was active in monitoring human rights, including trials, and the State Department's *Country Report on Human Rights Practices for 1996* was candid and well-informed.

The level of U.S. military loans (FMF) and economic support funds (ESF) remained steady. In 1997, U.S. $22 million in ESF and $175 million in FMF were appropriated for Turkey. The Turkish government had earlier rejected the ESF funds because of a dispute over two amendments passed by Congress. An additional $1.5 million was appropriated under the International Military Education and Training program; much of that was used to conduct human rights training among Turkish forces.

The issue of weapons transfers again proved to be a controversial topic, especially in light of a Congressionally-mandated report prepared by the Departments of State and Defense on the use of U.S. weapons in the conflict with the PKK. Released in July, it charged that the Turkish government had conducted a conscious policy of forced village evacuations.

Relevant Human Rights Watch report:

Turkey: Torture and Mistreatment in Pre-Trial Detention by Anti-Terror Police, 3/97

TURKMENISTAN

Human Rights Developments

The rigidly authoritarian government in Turkmenistan continued to prevent the exercise of virtually all civil and political rights in 1997. Turkmenistan's autocratic ruler, President Saparmurad Niyazov, used security forces and heavy censorship to repress the citizens of Turkmenistan. As a result, with almost no information on human rights abuses, no opposition, no possibility of public debate, no freedom of assembly, no foreseeable movement toward democratization, and omnipresent security services to maintain repression, there was, ironically, a sense of public calm. This allowed human rights to be effectively removed from the agenda in Turkmenistan's dialogue with outsiders keen to benefit from its hydrocarbon wealth.

One of the few documentable cases of abuse, reminiscent of the Soviet-era abuse of the psychiatric system, was that of Durdymurad Khojamuhammedov, co-chair of the banned Party of Democratic Development of Turkmenistan. He has reportedly been in mental hospitals since February 23, 1996, with no medical justification. Eight prisoners of conscience, arrested in Ashgabat on June 12, 1995 in connection with a march protesting deteriorating economic conditions, remained in jail in 1997. Their names are not known, except for Charymurad Amandurdyev. The authorities showed no signs of releasing two men serving long sentences for an alleged, but as yet unproven, plot to assassinate President Niyazov. Two men associated with the exiled opposition— Muhammedkuli Aymuradov and Khoshali Garaev, who were sentenced in 1995 to fifteen and twelve years, respectively, in strict-regime labor camps—remained in prison. There is no information about their current conditions of detention.

Turkmenistan's rubber-stamp parliament approved a new criminal code on June 12. The death penalty is provided for seventeen crimes, and the maximum custodial sentence is twenty years.

No official moves toward a general overhaul of the police, judicial and penitentiary systems were reported. In one move reflecting apparent dissatisfaction with the prosecution service, the president replaced the prosecutor general, Bayrammurad Ashyrlyev, on April 3 with Deputy Prosecutor Gurbanbibi Atajanova. In firing Ashyrlyev, President Niyazov launched an attack on prosecution officials, accusing them of incompetence and corruption and of prosecuting the innocent instead of criminals. Three days later, he chastised police and security forces for failing to understand the requirements of building a "law-governed democratic state"—without defining how he himself planned to move in that direction. By the year's end it was unclear whether his criticisms had effected any improvements.

In an apparent attempt to alleviate overcrowding in the prisons, the president reportedly released at least 5,000 prisoners in two amnesties in December 1996 and June 1997. Under the June amnesty, death sentences passed on 222 prisoners were also reportedly commuted to sentences of between ten and twenty years. No figures for the number of executions carried out in 1997 were available; there were an appalling 400 in 1996, making Turkmenistan a world leader in per capita state executions.

A death penalty case that highlighted the arbitrary and biased methods of Turkmenistan's criminal justice system was that of Ashirgeldy Sadyyev. Sadyyev was sentenced to death for drug trafficking on May 21. Amnesty International and other sources familiar with the case reported that the case against him was fabricated.

The Right to Monitor

The harsh oppression that pervades Turkmenistan society made comprehensive monitoring of human rights virtually impossible. There are no known local groups documenting violations of civil and political rights. It is almost impossible for foreign groups to contact locals without endangering the latter with grave consequences, such as harassment by security forces or arrest. The government established an Institute for Democratization and Human Rights in October 1996, but so far no evidence suggests that it has even the most limited mandate to seek the truth or effect change.

The Role of the International Community

There was virtually no public criticism of Turkmenistan's human rights record by international actors. In one exception, the U.S. Department of State's *Country Report on Human Rights Practices for 1996*, provided a comprehensive and highly critical overview of abuses. Foreign governments made no known demarches on human rights matters. This is no doubt in part due to the lack of new individual cases in such an atmosphere of total repression. However, their silence and that of international donors creates a sense of impunity among Turkmenistan's already insulated leadership.

UNITED KINGDOM

Human Rights Developments

Northern Ireland

The election of a new Labour government in May 1997 and the renewal of the Irish Republican Army (IRA) cease-fire on July 20, 1997, revived a moribund Northern Ireland peace process. The cease-fire afforded Sinn Féin, the political arm of the IRA, a seat at the negotiating table for peace talks that resumed on September 15, 1997. Despite threats by the Ulster Unionist Party (UUP), the largest Protestant political party, to withdraw from the negotiations, the UUP has remained at the table. A car bomb explosion in the village of Markethill on September 16, 1997, threatened to derail talks before they had even begun, but the IRA immediately issued a statement denying responsibility for the attack. A fringe republican paramilitary group, the Continuity IRA, claimed responsibility

·for the bombing. As of this writing, substantive talks are under way, with local and international human rights groups pressing for integration of human rights concerns into the peace process. The treatment of prisoners, police abuse, the use of plastic bullets, unresolved miscarriages of justice, and delayed government response to fresh evidence in the Bloody Sunday killings by security forces remain outstanding human rights concerns.

On November 20, 1996, Roisin McAliskey, the twenty-five-year-old daughter of civil rights activist Bernadette McAliskey, was arrested and detained under Northern Ireland's emergency laws. McAliskey was four months pregnant, asthmatic, and suffering from an eating disorder at the time of arrest. The arrest was made allegedly on the basis of an extradition warrant issued by German authorities in connection with an IRA mortar attack on a British army base in Osnabruck, Germany, in June 1996. McAliskey was interrogated at the notorious Castlereagh Holding Centre in Belfast; she alleges that the mortar attack was not mentioned by Royal Ulster Constabulary (RUC) detectives until the sixth day of interrogation. She was remanded in custody to London and placed in Holloway Prison, a women's prison. On November 30, 1997, McAliskey was transferred to Belmarsh Prison—an all-male, high security detention facility—and kept in isolation. After an international outcry, McAliskey was transferred back to Holloway and placed in solitary confinement as the only Category A high security risk inmate. McAliskey was prohibited from association with other prisoners, subjected to frequent strip searches, and permitted "closed" visits only—visits where no physical contact between prisoner and visitor is permitted. Most disturbing were credible reports that McAliskey was denied appropriate obstetric care despite medical reports that her fetus was underweight. After international protests against the U.K. government for violations of the prohibition against cruel, inhuman or degrading treatment, McAliskey's classification was changed

and her conditions of detention improved. After repeated denials of bail, McAliskey was released on bail to a London hospital where she gave birth to a baby girl on May 26, 1997. On June 3, she was granted conditional bail on medical grounds and transferred to a hospital with a mother and baby unit. McAliskey's extradition hearing has been adjourned repeatedly because she is too ill to attend, and the judge refuses to hold the hearing in her absence. The next hearing is scheduled for November 10, 1997. Disturbing questions have arisen about the quality of the evidence that the German authorities possess allegedly connecting McAliskey with the Osnabruck attack, including an admission on German television by an alleged government witness that he had never seen McAliskey.

IRA violence, which resumed in February 1996 after a seventeen-month cease-fire, continued into 1997. In December 1996, an IRA gunman shot and injured an RUC officer guarding a unionist politician visiting his son in the hospital. An IRA sniper shot and killed a twenty-three-year-old British infantryman at a checkpoint in the village of Bessbrook in February 1997. In April 1997, a part-time policewoman was shot by an IRA sniper while on guard duty outside the London/Derry Crown Court. These attacks culminated with the murders of two police officers in Lurgan on June 16, 1997, by two masked IRA gunmen in the presence of several eyewitnesses.

On June 23, 1997, Colin Duffy—who had publicly accused the RUC of collusion with loyalist paramilitaries in the past—was arrested for the murders of the Lurgan police officers. Duffy had been acquitted on appeal for the murder of a former soldier in September 1996 after it was discovered that the key prosecution witness, Lindsay Robb, had been convicted for illegally procuring arms for a loyalist paramilitary group. Duffy won his appeal based on Robb's inherent unreliability as a witness. The case strongly suggested that the RUC knew about Robb's paramilitary associations and was complicit when Robb testified under oath that he had no connections with loyalist paramilitaries. After Duffy's arrest for the murders of the police officers, numerous witnesses stated that he was not at the scene of the crime. Eyewitness descriptions of the gunmen did not match Duffy's physique, and there was no forensic evidence connecting Duffy to the murders. The only witness against Colin Duffy—a woman held in protective police custody—was described by those who know her well as a habitual liar and emotionally unstable. Other eyewitnesses claim that she was not present when the murders occurred, but arrived on the scene after the gunmen fled. Duffy was denied bail three times. Human rights organizations made representations to the police, the director of public prosecutions (DPP), and the U.N. Working Group on Arbitrary Detentions seeking Duffy's immediate release. On October 3, 1997, the charges against Colin Duffy were dismissed for lack of evidence and he was released after spending four months in custody. Colin Duffy has been harassed routinely by the police since his release. The Duffy case is a focal point for human rights advocacy efforts to reform the highly abusive features of the criminal justice system in Northern Ireland.

In July 1997, government-sponsored negotiations aimed at reaching a compromise between nationalist residents of the Garvaghy Road and members of the Protestant Orange Order seeking to march down the predominantly Catholic road failed, resulting in a decision by Marjorie Mowlam, secretary of state for Northern Ireland, to allow the July 6 Orange march to proceed under heavy police and military guard. RUC Chief Constable Ronnie Flanagan claimed that allowing the march to proceed was the lesser of two evils, indicating that the government and police submitted to threats of violence from supporters of the Orange Order, resulting in a breakdown in the rule of law. A police operation commenced on the Garvaghy Road in the early hours of July 6 during which residents and international monitors reported that police and British soldiers used excessive physical force to clear peaceful protesters from the road. Nationalist outrage was exacerbated by a confidential government memo dated June 20 and leaked to the press on July 7 which stated that, in the absence of local accommodation between the Garvaghy Road residents and the Orange Order, allowing the march to proceed was "the least worst outcome." Violence expected to erupt the following week during July 12 marches was eclipsed by an announcement by a number of Orange lodges that many contentious marches would be canceled or rerouted.

Approximately 2,500 plastic bullets were fired by the police and army in the aftermath of the Garvaghy Road march. Numerous people were seriously injured , including a thirteen-year-old girl who was hit in the mouth by a plastic bullet on her way home from a disco and a fourteen-year-old boy who was in coma for several days due to a head wound from a plastic bullet. The European Parliament, and numerous human rights groups, including Human Rights Watch, have called for a ban on plastic bullet use in Northern Ireland. Arguments for a ban were fortified by U.K. Ministry of Defense revelations in June and August 1997 that defective plastic bullets were deployed during civil disturbances arising from the 1996 and 1997 marching seasons, increasing their inaccuracy and the likelihood of injury. Moreover, important disparities in the guidelines for plastic bullet use among the RUC, the British army in Northern Ireland, and British police forces have led to criticism of the weaknesses in the current mechanisms for accountability.

On June 20, 1997, Patrick Kane, one of the Casement Three convicted in 1989 for the murders of two British army corporals, was released after serving eight years in prison. The Court of Appeal described Kane's conviction as "unsafe" because the trial judge did not have access to medical evidence concerning Kane's diminished mental capacity at the time he was interrogated by police in the absence of a guardian or legal counsel. Sean Kelly and Michael Timmons remain incarcerated despite strong evidence that their convictions were the result of inadequate or faulty legal procedures including trials in juryless Diplock Courts, violation of the right to remain silent, reliance upon poor-quality video footage for identification purposes, and confused application of the doctrine of common purpose. The Northern Ireland secretary of state refused to send the two cases back to the Court of Appeal for review, but the cases have been submitted to the Criminal Case Review Commission, established in 1997 to evaluate and make recommendations regarding miscarriage of justice cases. On October 27, 1997, the Northern Ireland Life Sentence Review Board (LSRB) held that Timmons and Kelly would be permitted leaves from prison for weekend and holiday visits with family and that the two men would be allowed to work outside the prison beginning in the spring of 1998.

New revelations regarding the conduct of British paratroopers and soldiers who opened fire on unarmed civilians killing thirteen people on Bloody Sunday, January 30, 1972, and the tampering with evidence submitted to the Widgery Tribunal—tasked with investigating the events of that day—have led to renewed calls for a fair and transparent public inquiry. The British government is currently considering whether to quash the findings of the original tribunal.

Positive developments during 1997 include government plans to introduce legislation to incorporate the European Convention on Human Rights into British law and the repeal of internment legislation.

Racially-backed Violence

The U.K. had one of the highest levels of racially-motivated violence and harassment in Western Europe in fiscal year 1995-96. Between 1989 and 1996, the number of racially-motivated attacks increased by 275 percent, from 4,383 to 12,199, suggesting an ongoing crime wave perpetrated by some British whites, including members of radical nationalist parties, against ethnic minority groups. Most disturbing are numerous reports of police brutality—resulting in deaths in custody and severe physical and psychological ill-treatment of non-white detainees— that itself appears to be racially-motivated. Despite the introduction in October 1997 of a new government policy of longer sentences for racially-motivated crimes, there is widespread evidence that police and investigators fail to investigate effectively racially-motivated crimes and that mechanisms for police accountability, such as the police complaints system, are ineffective checks on police misconduct.

The Right to Monitor

Government and law enforcement officials cooperated with the efforts of local and international human rights organizations to monitor police action during the 1997 marching season in Northern Ireland. There were no reported violations of the right to monitor in the U.K.

The Role of the International Community

United Nations

In response to concerns raised by human rights groups about the persistent harassment and intimidation of defense lawyers by RUC detectives and allegations of police collusion in the loyalist paramilitary murder in 1989 of Catholic defense lawyer Patrick Finucane, the U.N. Special Rapporteur on the Independence of Lawyers and Judges made an official visit to the U.K. and Northern Ireland in October 1997. The special rapporteur publicly called for an independent inquiry into the murder of Catholic defense lawyer Patrick Finucane and criticized the RUC for failing to address the serious issue of lawyer intimidation and harassment in Northern Ireland's holding centers. The special rapporteur's report will be submitted to the U.N. Human Rights Commission in March 1998.

United States

The Subcommittee on International Operations and Human Rights of the House Committee on International Relations held congressional hearings on "Human Rights in Northern Ireland" on June 24, 1997. The Clinton administration was criticized by members of the subcommittee for failing to send an invited representative to the hearing, signaling a failure on the part of the U.S. government to highlight the critical importance of human rights guarantees and accountability for past abuses to a just and lasting peace. On June 27, the subcommittee sent a letter calling on the RUC to ban the use of plastic bullets. Representative Chris Smith, chairperson of the subcommittee, led a human rights fact-finding mission to Northern Ireland in August 1997. The subcommittee sponsored an open meeting on October 9, 1997, at which nongovernmental organizations briefed House members on the human rights dimension o the Northern Ireland peace process.

The U.K. section of the U.S. State Department's *Country Reports on Human Rights Practices for 1996* cited numerous human rights concerns with respect to Northern Ireland including international criticism of plastic bullet use, restrictions on due process rights arising from emergency legislation, serious irregularities in the investigations into the murders of Patrick Finucane and Patrick Shanaghan, U.N. treaty bodies' concerns about the mistreatment of detainees in Northern Ireland's interrogation centers, and abusive police action during the 1996 marching season which "damaged the RUC's reputation as an impartial force."

The report also noted the concern of the U.N. Committee on the Elimination of Racial Discrimination (CERD) that a disproportionate number of minorities in the U.K. were victims of deaths in police custody and that police brutality also appeared to affect racial and ethnic minorities disproportionately.

Relevant Human Rights Watch Reports:
To Serve Without Favor: Policing, Human Rights and Accountability in Northern Ireland, 5/97
Racist Violence in the United Kingdom, 4/97

UZBEKISTAN

Human Rights Developments

Human rights observance in Uzbekistan in 1997 was marked by a sharp departure from government promises made in 1996 to improve its performance. Initial hopes were confounded by a series of retrograde actions by the government, and some recent improvements, such as the release of twelve prisoners of conscience under amnesty in 1996, were not repeated in 1997. The government continued to violate most civil and political rights and actively harassed or prosecuted Islamic figures and human rights activists. (The government had liquidated the political opposition by 1995.) In light of this, the introduction of new legislation covering various aspects of human rights this year appeared more symbolic than designed to yield actual improvements.

The media remained suffocated by state controls, in violation of the constitution's ban on censorship. Hopes were raised in January by the publication of a new newspaper, *Hurriyat* (Freedom), under an editor, Karim Bahriev, who defied official displeasure by publishing uncensored material. However, by the time the newspaper's sixth issue came out on February 12, mounting pressure from senior media and government officials had forced Bahriev out of his position, and the newspaper was transformed into yet another tame, censored voice of officialdom.

Nongovernmental human rights activists struggled to organize, but the government refused to grant them registration. The improved atmosphere surrounding an Organization for Security and Cooperation in Europe-sponsored human rights seminar in September 1996 had led many to believe that the government would finally register the nongovernmental Human Rights Society of Uzbekistan; indeed, President Islam Karimov invited the Society's chairman Abdumannob Polat to visit the country after three and a half years in exile. However, the Justice Ministry rejected the Society's application in January 1997, citing a number of technical problems in the submitted documentation, but a duly revised application met a final rejection in July. The Independent Human Rights Organization held a founding meeting in Toshkent on August 2, 1997. The Toshkent city council refused even to respond to the group's application to hold this small public gathering, a legal stipulation that in itself indicates how little freedom of assembly exists in Uzbekistan. Nevertheless, it held the meeting and lodged an application for registration with the Justice Ministry on August 29.

By 1995, the government had ceased the arbitrary arrest of political opponents and independent Islamic figures on the almost standard charges of illegal possession of arms and narcotics. But the lull in arrests was broken this year with two new arrests on precisely these charges. Rahim Otoqulov, who appears to have been targeted because he taught Islam to pupils at home, was convicted on June 10 and given a three and a half year sentence for possession of drugs and pistol cartridges. Almost a textbook case of politically motivated arrest, his trial in the town of Margilan raised considerable questions of due process. In a very similar case, on June 19, a court sentenced Olimjon Ghofurov, a teacher of Islam from Namangan, to one year in prison for arms and drugs possession.

A leading Islamic figure, Toshkent teacher Obidkhon Nazarov, was subjected to constant pressure from state security agents through the first half of 1997. Beginning in 1996, local authorities repeatedly attempted to evict his family from their home, and on April 23 the city prosecutor brought criminal charges against him for alleged slander, based on the flimsy evidence of one cassette recording of unknown provenance and authenticity. As of this writing, no further action had been taken against him, but the charges appeared to be designed to deter him from further exercising his free speech rights.

The Muslim community as a whole was affected by restrictive moves undertaken by the authorities, including curbs on the use of loudspeakers for the call to prayer, steps to prevent female students from wearing Islamic headscarfs in schools and colleges, and the closure of official as well as unofficial Islamic teaching establishments (*madrasas*). Although government officials claimed these closures were temporary measures pending a legal reorganization, none had reopened as of this writing.

Muslims were not the only community to suffer from government curbs on their right to worship. A Baptist preacher in the region of Karakalpakistan, Rashid Turibaev, was charged with conducting illegal church services, facing a possible sentence of three years. His congregation, the Full Gospel Christians, was prevented from holding further meetings and was reportedly placed under surveillance. In a move to counter what they regard as illegal proselytizing by predominantly Protestant groups, the Uzbekistan authorities announced in January that they had confiscated 25,000 copies of the New Testament in Uzbek translation, seized while being imported by rail the previous month.

The Law on Political Parties, passed on December 23, 1996, came into effect on January 7. According to the law, a party must submit the signatures of at least 5,000 members across eight or more of the country's thirteen regions, an almost impossible task, given the repressive atmosphere in which few would dare label themselves as potential opposition members. Other more liberal legislation introduced in the course of 1997 included laws upgrading the parliamentary commissioner for human rights into an ombudsman, enshrining the public's right to access information, and securing journalists' rights (all three passed on April 24). These laws could potentially strengthen citizens' rights, but, since positive aspects of previous legislation are routinely ignored by the highest authorities in Uzbekistan, these new laws look suspiciously like windowdressing to please western donors and investors.

After fighting around the Afghan city of Mazar-i-Sharif, where a camp for refugees from Tajikistan is located, Uzbekistan closed its border with Afghanistan in May and refused to allow through its territory the repatriation of refugees to Tajikistan. Following high-level interventions from U.N.

officials, including Secretary General Kofi Annan, the Uzbekistan authorities eventually allowed some of the refugees passage, but closed the border again in September.

Human Rights Watch received scores of reports of police abuses this year. Victims reported systematic physical mistreatment and torture to obtain confessions. In one of the few cases to be raised by a local organization, a lawyer reported being attacked and beaten up in her home in June by uniformed and plainclothes police of Hamza district, Toshkent. Although such cases are rarely pursued, in this case, the regional attorneys' association to which the lawyer belongs lodged a complaint with the Justice Ministry. As of this writing they had received no reply.

Prison conditions continued to be atrocious; former inmates and their relatives described overcrowding, unchecked disease, and violence by wardens as some of the problems in the prisons. Kahraman Hamidov's death from tuberculosis in prison on June 12 suggested appalling conditions of detention as well as the frequently arbitrary and unjust reasons for incarceration. Hamidov was leader of Humanity and Human Values (Odamiylik va Insonparvarlik), a Muslim-oriented popular movement operating in Kokand from 1988 until his arrest and conviction in 1992 on apparently fabricated charges of assault.

The Right to Monitor

There was no reported interference in monitoring activities carried out by foreign observers, including a Human Rights Watch representative. However, perhaps the most outspoken and active local human rights advocate, Mikhail Ardzinov, was subjected to overt police surveillance on at least two occasions. In addition, when he applied for an exit visa in December 1996, the Interior Ministry confiscated his passport without explanation. Compounding these actions, the Ministry of Foreign Affairs sent Mr. Ardzinov a letter informing him that he was on an official list of mentally disturbed persons and must undergo psychiatric testing in order to receive a visa. Police made Mr. Ardzinov's passport available to him only after a delegation from the European Parliament raised the matter with Foreign Ministry officials in May. Ardzinov received neither a visa nor a reason for its refusal.

While refusing to register the Human Rights Society of Uzbekistan, in violation of its pledges to do so, the government nevertheless did not actively impede its monitoring activities.

The Role of the International Community

United Nations

On July 12, 1997, the United Nations Development Agency and the Uzbekistan government formally agreed to implement a Program on Democratization and Governance, although in reality some elements of the program began in 1996. The effort emphasizes assistance to law enforcement agencies and other areas of government that have an impact on human rights. Unfortunately, the U.N. has not incorporated any effective means of accounting publicly for the way these organizations use the assistance. For instance, substantial funding has gone to the office of the new ombudsman and to the National Center for Human Rights, neither of which can or will pursue policies independent of the official government stance.

Organization for Security and Cooperation in Europe

The OSCE mission gained a new officer concerned purely with human dimension issues. It held a human rights training session in May and invited official organizations, including the National Security Service, the prosecutor's office, the police and the Justice Ministry, as well as two of the three nongovernmental human rights groupings. The OSCE, however, made no known interventions on any human rights cases in Uzbekistan. By ignoring specific human rights abuses and assisting the organizations that commit them without calling them to account, the OSCE is effectively condoning such behavior.

European Union

After the European Union signed a Partnership and Cooperation Agreement (PCA) with Uzbekistan on June 22, 1996, the European Parliament and its Committee on Foreign Affairs, made serious efforts to ensure Uzbekistan was honoring the PCA's provisions on democratization and human rights. A delegation of Foreign Affairs Committee members visited Uzbekistan in May, met with government and NGO actors in the human rights sphere, and concluded that ratification of the PCA should be suspended until the end of 1997, by which time it hoped to observe some improvement in human rights. The Parliament will reevaluate the situation in the spring of 1998, although an interim agreement will go into effect before that, rendering the temporary suspension of ratification a symbolic and thus ineffective gesture.

United States

The U.S. government was, as in previous years, the major source of pressure on the Uzbekistan government. It also offered direct assistance to nascent human rights bodies. In June the U.S. embassy and the U.S. Information Service disbursed $10,000 each to four organizations—the official parliamentary Commission for Human Rights, the National Center for Human Rights, the nongovernmental Human Rights Society of Uzbekistan and the Committee for the Protection of Personal Rights. The grants were given in the form of computer and Internet equipment and had no strings attached.

Embassy officials raised a number of individual cases of abuse with senior government officials. The Commission for Security and Cooperation in Europe published a letter on June 12 condemning the trial of pastor Turibaev and the confiscation of 25,000 Bibles. The State Department produced a highly critical assessment of the human rights situation in Uzbekistan in its *Country Report on Human Rights Practices for 1996*. However, the U.S. government failed to match its condemnation with sanctions or otherwise insist on compliance with its demands and therefore won almost no concessions from the Uzbekistan authorities.

Relevant Human Rights Watch Report:

Uzbekistan—Violations of Media Freedom: Journalism and Censorship in Uzbekistan, 7/97

THE RIGHT TO ASYLUM IN THE EUROPEAN UNION

Human Rights Developments

The trend toward increased restrictions on the right to asylum in European Union (E.U.) member states continued in 1997. After several years of steady decline, the number of asylum applications stabilized and even grew in some states. Meanwhile, the percentage of asylum seekers recognized as refugees under the 1951 Convention relating to the Status of Refugees (refugee convention) remained low, as many E.U. member states implemented new restrictions on the rights of asylum seekers and refugees.

In most E.U. member states, asylum seekers were given only limited access to asylum procedures once their asylum claims were deemed either "manifestly unfounded" or the responsibility of a "safe third country," defined as any country where the asylum seeker would be admitted and protected against persecution or *refoulement*. Inspired by resolutions adopted by E.U. member states in 1992, these policies gave immigration officials substantial discretion to deny asylum after little or no substantive review of the asylum claim. Moreover, the right to appeal a negative decision was in many such cases rendered meaningless because the asylum seeker had no right to remain in the country while the appeal was pending.

"Safe third country" rules posed an especially acute problem, subjecting many asylum seekers to a chain of deportations from one country to another. Even the most cautious E.U. states can be complicit in chain deportations when they deport an asylum seeker to a "safe third country," which may then deport him or her to yet another country, safe or not, without any prior review of the merits of the asylum claim. The risk of chain deportations grew in 1997 as E.U. member states negotiated an ever-widening web of readmission agreements, committing their eastern and southern neighbors to readmit illegal aliens, without any specific provisions for the protection of asylum seekers and refugees.

Several E.U. member states continued to apply an unduly strict interpretation of the refugee convention, especially as it related to persecution by non-state actors. Of particular concern was jurisprudence concluding that an asylum seeker may only acquire refugee status if he can show that his government's authorities are complicit in the feared persecution. Some states gave temporary protection or residence permits on humanitarian grounds to asylum seekers who fell afoul of this restrictive interpretation of the refugee convention. In France, for example, many Algerians fleeing persecution by Islamist groups received temporary residence permits in lieu of refugee status. These permits, however, were valid only for renewable three- or six-month periods and often provided no right to work. Such policies reflected a growing inclination to substitute limited, temporary solutions for the traditionally more complete and durable protection mandated by the refugee convention.

The inadequacy of temporary protection was illustrated by the hundreds of thousands of Bosnians who remained in E.U. member states for more than five years after having fled hostilities in the former Yugoslavia. Ongoing human rights abuses in Bosnia prevented most refugees from returning home (see section on Bosnia-Hercegovina). The United Nations High Commissioner for Refugees reported that 28,000 voluntarily returned in the first quarter of 1997. A total of 200,000 returns were expected by year's end,

leaving another 600,000 still displaced outside of Bosnia. Despite repeated threats from host states, forced repatriations were limited in 1997; Germany, for example, forcibly repatriated approximately 650 Bosnian refugees in the twelve months previous to this writing. Some E.U. member states gave up on repatriation altogether and gave Bosnians permanent residence permits.

Detention of asylum seekers was widespread in E.U. member states in 1997. Detention of rejected asylum seekers and illegal aliens awaiting deportation was particularly prevalent. Because of difficulties many member states experienced in enforcing deportation orders, many foreigners languished in European detention centers for months. Too often they were held intermingled with common criminals or under a remand regime inappropriate to their status as administrative detainees.

The Role of the International Community

Many of the asylum policies pursued by E.U. member states in 1997 were inspired by resolutions, recommendations, and joint decisions adopted at the E.U. level in recent years. The E.U. effort to harmonize asylum policies continued in 1997 and the restrictive trend showed little sign of abating.

The most significant development at the E.U. level was the October 2, 1997, signing of the Amsterdam Treaty, revising the 1992 Maastricht Treaty that established the E.U.. According to the new treaty, the E.U. will adopt key asylum and immigration measures within five years of the treaty's entry into force, expected in 1999. The agenda includes establishing criteria for determining which state will have responsibility for an asylum application; defining the scope of refugee, humanitarian, and temporary protection; and identifying minimum standards for asylum procedures and reception conditions. Because measures must be adopted unanimously, advocates for refugees and asylum seekers fear that this new initiative will only result in further codification of the lowest common denominator of member states' policies and practices.

In a widely criticized move, E.U. member states adopted a Spain-sponsored protocol to the Amsterdam Treaty. The protocol asserts that, with some narrow exceptions, member states will not accept asylum applications from nationals of other member states. Recognizing that this rule would violate their obligations under the refugee convention, officials from several member states asserted that they would continue to accept all asylum applications. However, only Belgium appended a declaration to the protocol making explicit its commitment, in accordance with the refugee convention, to carry out an individual examination of all asylum claims submitted by member state nationals.

In a significant development for E.U. "safe third country" policies, the Dublin convention came into effect on September 1, 1997. The convention establishes rules and procedures for determining one and only one member state that will be responsible for adjudicating each asylum claim. It replaced the similar asylum-related provisions of the Schengen agreement, which had been in effect among a subset of E.U. member states for nearly three years. The Dublin convention represents an improvement in that it provides an institutional framework for ensuring that asylum seekers sent from one E.U. member state to another will actually be admitted to the asylum procedure in the receiving state. On the other hand, nothing in the agreement prevents the receiving state from concluding in the course of its asylum procedure that the asylum seeker should be sent to a "safe third country" outside the E.U. Moreover, a 1992 E.U. resolution commits member states to look outside the E.U. for a responsible "safe third country," before considering a potentially responsible E.U. member state under the Dublin rules. The Dublin convention also risks dividing families while their asylum claims are pending, sending, for example, a woman to one member state and her father, husband, and children to another. Faced with similar problems under the Schengen agreement, in 1997 signatories of that agreement adopted guidelines to keep families together during the procedure. These guidelines limit the definition of family to spouses and dependent children, however, and fail therefore to meet the needs of, for example, aged parents.

In another important E.U. development, the European Commission submitted a draft joint action on temporary protection of asylum seekers to the Council of Ministers and the European Parliament. The commission's proposal would give beneficiaries of temporary protection a high level of social rights. On the other hand, it also called for the suspension of refugee determination proceedings for up to five years of temporary protection, sparking criticism that temporary protection was being designed to supplant rather than complement refugee protection under the refugee convention. At this writing, the temporary protection proposal was still under debate in the Council of Ministers and parliament.

E.U. member states also moved toward a common policy on treatment of unaccompanied foreign children present in their territories. A non-binding resolution adopted in May 1997 established guidelines for special accommodation and procedural arrangements for minor asylum seekers. The resolution provided further that unaccompanied children with no legal right to remain in an E.U. member state, should not, in principle, be deported unless there will be adequate reception and care available upon the child's arrival in the receiving country.

In another non-binding resolution, the E.U. committed to an annual review of implementation of its policies in the asylum field. The resolution foresees contributions from UNHCR and nongovernmental organizations, promising an opportunity for those groups to point out problems encountered with restrictive asylum policies adopted in recent years. Many of these problems were also cited in a critical resolution adopted by the Parliamentary Assembly of the Council of Europe in April 1997.

Relevant Human Rights Watch reports:
France: Toward a Just and Humane Asylum Policy, 10/97
Uncertain Refugee: International Failures to Protect Refugees, 4/97

HUMAN
RIGHTS
WATCH

MIDDLE
EAST

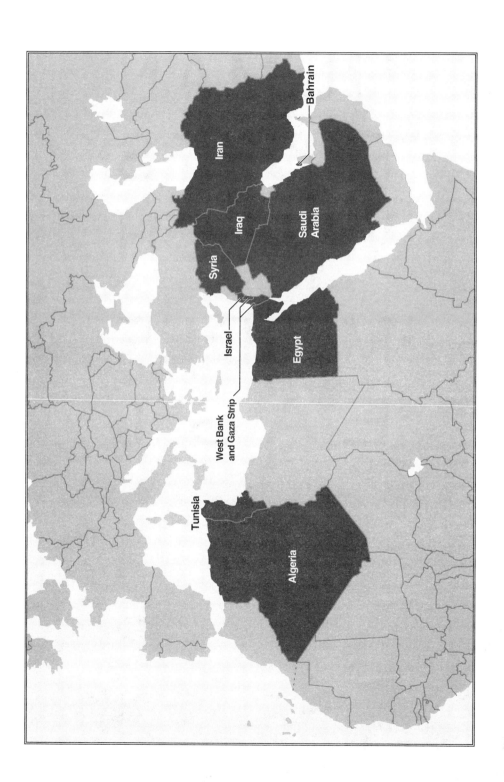

HUMAN RIGHTS WATCH/MIDDLE EAST OVERVIEW

Human Rights Developments

In the Middle East and North Africa, the overwhelming majority of people lived in countries where basic rights were routinely violated with impunity and where open criticism of the authorities knew sharp limits. This picture changed little during 1997, despite a few hopeful developments that included the Iranian presidential election, the region's first, excluding Israel, in which the outcome was not known in advance.

The battle against "terrorism" was invoked by several governments of the region to justify curbs on rights. Without exception, governments that invoked that struggle, including Tunisia, Algeria, Egypt, Israel, and Bahrain, went well beyond justifiable security measures to violate the rights not only of suspected militants but also of peaceful critics and of the population as a whole. All of these governments except Bahrain have ratified the International Covenant on Civil and Political Rights and the Convention against Torture. Yet all violated core rights that are considered nonderogable even in times of national emergency.

Religion provided another mantle for the violation of rights. In Iran, an official council of clerics and jurists limited the pool of candidates eligible to run for public office by vetting them for "piety." Pursuant to its interpretation of Islamic (shari'a) law, Saudi Arabia conducted trials in a manner that deprived defendants of their due process rights, while in both Saudi Arabia and Iran courts imposed death by stoning and other forms of severe corporal punishment on offenders. Shari'a-based family and personal status law were used in Iran, Saudi Arabia, Algeria, Egypt, Jordan, Lebanon, Morocco, and Syria, among others, to discriminate against women, notably in the matters of child custody and in the freedom to marry and to divorce.

Several armed opposition groups invoked religion to justify their own abuses of human rights, including the deliberate and indiscriminate killing of civilians in Algeria, Egypt, and Israel. In 1997, armed groups in Algeria targeted civilians on a scale and with a savagery that was unprecedented in that country's six years of civil strife. They slaughtered scores and in some incidents more than a hundred unarmed men, women and children in numerous nighttime raids carried out on villages not far from Algiers. The Algerian security forces, for reasons that remained unclear, often did little to intervene, and were themselves implicated in torture, "disappearances," and summary executions

The Algerian tragedy was held up by some governments as a reason to "go slow" on democratization. In neighboring Tunisia, going slow was a euphemism for going backwards, toward intolerance of all forms of political dissent. Across the region, those in power employed common methods to suppress or limit opposition, whether peaceful or violent:

Direct government control over the content of television and radio broadcasts was the norm. Lebanon, with scores of privately owned but unlicensed stations, was an exception, until that country's media diversity was dramatically reduced when the cabinet began in September 1996 to license the audiovisual media pursuant to a 1994 broadcasting law. By July 1997, the number of private television and radio stations in Lebanon was reduced to six and fifteen, respectively, and unlicensed stations were forced to suspend operations. In addition, content bans imposed by the 1994 law curtailed free expression on the airwaves.

In the Palestinian self-rule areas, an effort to bring to viewers live coverage of the outspoken Palestinian Legislative Council was suppressed, at least temporarily, by the Palestinian Authority (PA). In Algeria, where all media faced strict censorship of coverage of the internal strife, state television and radio gave some coverage in 1997 to opposition politicians during the parliamentary election campaign and the sessions of the new national assembly. While Algerians supplemented the local coverage by watching foreign television via satellite, in Tunisia and some other countries the purchase and use of satellite dishes was heavily restricted, and in Iraq they were banned outright.

Newspapers in most of the Gulf states, Iraq, Syria and Tunisia, whether governmental or private, could not print news or commentary on political affairs that displeased the authorities. The print media in Morocco, Kuwait, Algeria, Egypt, Lebanon, and Yemen fared better, although journalists and publications that crossed certain lines in their criticism of authorities or of government policy risked harsh punishment. In Iran, small independent magazines have proliferated since the early 1990s. However, journalists affiliated with them ran enormous risks that included imprisonment and court-sanctioned whippings. In 1997 independent publisher Ebrahim Zolzadeh was at least the third writer to die since November 1994 in suspicious circumstances that suggested government complicity.

The government of Jordan took a step backward in May by enacting, while parliament was in recess, draconian amendments to the 1993 press and publications law. These amendments considerably broadened existing content bans and specified extremely high capital requirements for newspapers, steep fines, and suspension and closure of publications for infractions of the content bans. The amendments greatly diminished press freedom and self censorship increased. Six weeks before the parliamentary elections on November 4, authorities suspended thirteen weekly newspapers, some of which had developed reputations for independent, critical reporting.

Governments also moved to control the flow of information via the Internet. For this reason, few Tunisians enjoyed Internet access during 1997. The Bahraini authorities, who also closely monitored net access, arrested in March 1997 an engineer employed by the state telecommunications company, reportedly because of information he was transmitting abroad via the Internet. As of October, he remained in detention without charge. The police chief of Dubai, in the United Arab Emirates, stated in 1996 that the Ministry of Interior and the police had to license all subscribers before they could receive Internet services.

Countries including Bahrain, Iraq, Kuwait, Saudi Arabia, continued to allow no political parties or associations. In Kuwait, however, the sometimes-fractious parliament housed different political tendencies.

Governments that allowed some space for opposition politics continued to outlaw certain political groups—often Islamist ones—and prosecute their suspected members. Egypt continued to target members of the country's leading political opposition movement, the Muslim Brotherhood. Since 1995, members of this officially banned but long tolerated group—including elected leaders of professional associations, ex-parliamentarians, and academics—were imprisoned following unfair military court trials for their peaceful political activity. The government of Algeria, which tolerated two legal Islamist parties despite a new law outlawing parties based on religion, continued to ban the Islamic Salvation Front, which was dissolved in 1992 after winning a plurality in the first round of parliamentary voting. Tunisia tolerated no party that genuinely challenged the positions of the ruling party, and held hundreds of men and women behind bars for membership or political activity in the once-tolerated Islamist Nahdha movement, along with a smaller number of nonviolent leftists. The Israeli military government in the West Bank continued to imprison or administratively detain Palestinians for affiliation with political groups that opposed the Israeli-PLO accords.

The plight of Palestinians living in the Gaza Strip and the West Bank, including Israeli-annexed East Jerusalem, worsened in many respects during 1997. The Palestinian Authority protested Israel's continued construction and expansion of settlements, in violation of international law, in the occupied West Bank, including East Jerusalem, and its delays in redeploying troops from the territories. A series of bombings were carried out inside Israel and claimed by the Islamic Resistance Movement (Hamas), and Israel charged that the PA was not doing enough to combat anti-Israel violence. In an act of collective punishment against more than 1.5 million Palestinians, Israel imposed the tightest restrictions since the Gulf War on the movement of people and goods in the West Bank and Gaza Strip, with devastating consequences for the daily life and economy of Palestinians. The closure, imposed on the grounds that it helped to prevent further attacks inside Israel, blocked movement not only out of the West Bank and Gaza Strip, but internally as well: Israeli Defense Force checkpoints in the West Bank kept most of the area's Palestinians under de facto town arrest, preventing many from reaching their workplace or fields, visiting relatives, obtaining medical attention, or traveling abroad, to list but a few hardships.

As noted above, religion was invoked to justify a wide range of abuses, from legal discrimination to acts of violence. The government of Iran considered Baha'ism a heretical sect and singled out its members, as well as evangelical Christians, for harsh persecution. In Saudi Arabia, public worship by non-Muslims was prohibited, and as in Bahrain, the sizable Shi'a community charged discrimination in the fields of education and public-sector employment, as did the Coptic Christian minority community in Egypt. The Shi'a government of Iran restricted the growth of Sunni mosques and seminaries, and held in detention Sunni religious leaders, reportedly because of their demands for parity for the large Sunni minority.

The Christian minority in Egypt continued to suffer from state-sponsored discrimination as well as acts of violence by armed militants in which Coptic Christians and other civilians lost their lives. Two particularly heinous massacres occurred in Upper Egypt, in February and March, in which twenty-four people, twenty of them Copts,

were killed. Egyptian Muslims who converted to Christianity were unable to obtain legal recognition of their new religion; the children of converts could not be registered in the religion of their parents; and the marriages of Christian men to Muslim women were not recognized. Church construction and repair continued to require a presidential decree, pursuant to a 19th century Ottoman law.

In Algeria, there was religious persecution of another type: Islamist armed groups waged a campaign of violence against their Muslim compatriots who deviated from the militants' own view of the righteous path, in terms of personal conduct, appearance, or interpretation of religion. Since 1993, many Algerians falling into these categories have been assassinated by armed groups, although the precise reasons for specific killings and authorship have been difficult to establish. This type of persecution, moreover, was distinct from the large-scale massacres of villagers in 1997.

Most governments in the region practiced torture but either flatly denied it or conceded only isolated abuses. Israel admitted to putting Palestinian suspects from the West Bank and Gaza Strip through various forms of physical and psychological pressure, but claimed to ensure these did not reach the threshold of torture. During 1997, Israel's highest court continued to refrain from challenging this claim, by ruling against Palestinian petitioners when they sought court orders barring the General Security Service from using physical force against them. In May, the U.N. Committee against Torture rejected the government's position, calling Israel's interrogation techniques "torture."

Several governments of the Middle East, including those of Iran, Iraq, and Israel, were linked to political assassinations or attempted assassinations on foreign soil over the last decade. While none of these governments has formally admitted to these acts, the evidence linking Iran and Israel to killings on foreign soil was dramatically strengthened during 1997. In April, a German court, after a lengthy investigation and testimony from former Iranian agents, ruled that "the Iranian political leadership" was responsible for the murder of four activists from Kurdish armed opposition groups in Berlin in 1992. It was the first time a court had held Iran's leaders responsible for some of a number of killings of Iranians that have taken place on European soil since the Islamic revolution.

The government of Israel all but officially admitted that its Mossad agency had carried out on September 25 a botched attempt in Jordan on the life of Hamas official Khaled Meshal. After strong pressure from King Hussein, Israel provided an antidote to the fatal toxin its agents had administered to Meshal outside the Hamas office in Amman, and he recovered. The suspected perpetrators were allowed to return to Israel as part of an Israeli-Jordanian deal that included Israel's release of Sheikh Ahmad Yassin, Hamas' spiritual leader, and other Jordanian and Palestinian prisoners. Israeli leaders defiantly refused to rule out such operations in the future; a government spokesman vowed that Israel's "long arm will reach terrorists wherever they are." Israel was reportedly responsible for a series of assassinations that included Islamic Jihad leader Fathi Shikaki in Malta in 1995.

Amidst this gloomy picture of human rights in the region, some of the elections that took place during 1997 provided a basis for cautious optimism. In Oman's Shura Council elections in October, women were permitted to vote and run as candidates nationwide for the first time. In Iran, Mohamed Khatami scored a surprise victory in May over the presidential candidate favored by the ruling religious establishment. The election was not free: an official body had pruned the would-be list of candidates down to four, all of whom came from within the religious establishment. But Khatami's campaign promises to institutionalize the rule of law inspired hope that Iranians would enjoy more freedom of expression and less intrusion in their private lives.

While Jordan's November parliamentary election was preceded by mounting restrictions on freedom of expression and assembly, Algeria's parliamentary elections in June presented a mixed picture. Constitutional and legal reforms put in place since late 1996, and measures taken during the campaign to promote pro-government candidates, ensured that the resulting National Assembly would pose no serious challenge to the power of the executive. Nevertheless, for the first time since independence, a multiparty parliament was in place, one that included secular and Islamist critics of government policies. It remained to be seen whether the assembly, despite its limited powers, could contribute to more accountable government and to ending the horrific strife in the country.

The governments of Yemen and Qatar committed themselves to signing the international treaty banning landmines when it is opened for signatures in December 1997, and other governments in the region indicated their intention to follow suit. In the negotiations on establishing the International Criminal Court (ICC), Egypt played a positive role by supporting provisions that would empower the court to prosecute those accused of genocide, crimes against humanity, and serious war crimes.

There was also encouragement to be drawn from the persistence of independent human rights and women's rights organizations, in approximately half the countries of the region, in documenting and publicizing abuses and lobbying for reforms. In several countries that did not tolerate human rights organizations on the ground, such as Bahrain and Iran, information got out—and in—often aided by foreign broadcasts and the new information technologies.

The Right to Monitor

Throughout the region, supporters of human rights struggled to create, maintain, or expand the space inside their countries for independent monitoring and reporting. In many countries, however, lack of access to the countries themselves or to information about the situations there complicated the tasks of both international and domestic human rights activists.

In several parts of the region, notably Egypt, Israel, Jordan, Palestinian self-rule areas, and Yemen, human rights remained a growth industry as local activists expanded existing organizations, launched new ones, and increasingly reached out to their counterparts elsewhere in the region and internationally. The dissemination of information was enhanced by new information technologies, with electronic mail and Internet sites enabling local organizations to provide timely reports of human rights developments and violations in a speedy manner that was unthinkable several years ago. In an important sense, the globalization of accurate information, the basis of the human rights craft and rights-related advocacy, made important inroads in the region in 1997, and held future promise as models for emerging NGOs.

Government policies, however, still regulated and for the most part restricted the extent to which human rights activists enjoyed internal operating space and access to information. At one extreme the complete lack of freedom of association in Saudi Arabia, Syria, and Iraq, for example, meant that no locally based organizations could monitor and report on human rights conditions. This, combined with these states' denial of access to international human rights organizations, kept the flow of information about abuses there to a trickle. Iran also did not allow human rights organizations to function, but did tolerate monitoring within certain bounds and did not impose controls so draconian as to prevent some courageous Iranians from documenting information abroad about human rights conditions.

At the other end of the spectrum, in Egypt, Israel, and areas under the Palestinian Authority, human rights communities thrived, and the work of locally based groups gained increasing international recognition and media coverage. The situation in Israel and Palestine was particularly acute during protracted periods of closure of the occupied territories that kept human rights workers from moving freely within and between the West Bank and Gaza Strip. In Egypt, groups had to find creative ways to circumvent the restrictive 1964 associations law, and still were forced to operate under constant monitoring by internal security forces operatives and an ever-present risk of possible closure by authorities.

The government of Tunisia conditionally released from prison one human rights activist, Khemaïs Chammari, but detained another, Khemaïs Ksila, on the day he launched a hunger strike to publicize the persecution he had suffered for pursuing human rights work. In Algeria, human rights lawyer Rachid Mesli was sentenced to three years in prison after an unfair trial on charges of aiding "terrorist" groups. During the trial the judge questioned him about his contact with Amnesty International's research team on Algeria. It was in Syria that human rights monitors paid the highest price; there five activists from the Committees for the Defense of Democratic Freedom and Human Rights in Syria continued to serve prison sentences of up to ten years.

The Role of the International Community

Governments of the larger industrialized countries generally paid scant public attention to human rights issues in the Middle East. Their chief interests were access to oil, natural gas, and export markets; promoting Israeli-Arab accords; and combating, or at least containing, the violence committed by armed opposition groups. Western inaction on human rights was sometimes justified with reference to the violent and intolerant nature of some opposition groups; on other occasions, inaction was dressed up as deference toward Islamic sensibilities or cultural traditions-usually as defined by those holding power.

United Nations

In September 1997, both Secretary-General Kofi Annan and High Commissioner for Human Rights Mary Robinson publicly challenged the Algerian government's insistence that the country's human rights problems were strictly an internal affair. The United Nations continued to maintain peacekeeping forces in the region, including southern Lebanon and the Syrian-Israeli demilitarized zone, and to aid Palestinian refugee communities through the U.N. Relief and Works Agency (UNRWA). In September, former US Secretary of State James Baker, as the special representative of the secretary-general, brokered an agreement between Morocco and the Polisario Front on a pro-posed code of conduct for a referendum over the future of the Western Sahara. In Iraq, the U.N. continued to monitor the status of nuclear, chemical and biological weapons development, and the distribution of food and other relief goods under the post-Gulf War sanctions regime. The humanitarian crisis in Iraq was not ended by the Security Council-authorized purchase by Iraq of humanitarian goods in 1997. Special rapporteurs continued to cover human rights developments in Iran, Iraq and the Israeli-occupied territories, but did not visit those countries in 1997.

European Union

In April the foreign ministers of the European Union member states and the twelve Euro-Mediterranean partners, from Morocco to Turkey, held a second summit in Malta. However, unlike the Barcelona Declaration of 1995, the communique from the meeting was issued only several months later—report-edly on account of disagreements over lan-guage referring to human rights—and con-tained only passing reference to "the rule of law, democracy and human rights" as com-mon objectives.

During 1997, many E.U. member state governments took up ratification of the Euro-Mediterranean Association Agreements that the E.U. had initialed earlier with Tunisia, Israel, and Morocco. During this process, parliamentarians and others raised the issue of human rights compliance-particularly with regard to Israel-which is specified in common Article 2 of the Association Agreements. Several governments indicated they would seek to have the European Commission set up a human rights monitoring mechanism as part of the implementation process. However, no European government demanded human rights improvements from the governments of Is-rael, Tunisia, or Morocco as a condition for its ratifying of the Association Agreement. Dur-ing 1997 the E.U. signed an interim associa-tion agreement with the Palestinian Author-ity, and was scheduled to sign one with Jordan in late November. Negotiations continued on the terms of agreements with Egypt and Algeria. As E.U. and Syrian officials prepared to open negotiations on an agreement, the E.U. Council of Ministers continued to sup-press a November 1995 report on human rights in Syria that the European Parliament had mandated as a condition for economic assistance.

United States

The U.S. continued to play the largest role of any outside government in the Middle East in terms of trade, economic and military assis-tance, and arms sales. In its *Congressional Presentation for Foreign Operations* for fis-cal year 1998, the Clinton administration identified U.S. interests in the Middle East as promoting a comprehensive Arab-Israeli peace settlement, containing threats to en-ergy supplies and regional stability posed by Iran, Iraq and Libya, maintaining full and secure access to Persian Gulf energy re-sources, expanding trade and investment opportunities for the U.S. private sector, and encouraging democracy and sustainable de-velopment.

Israel and Egypt accounted for U.S.$5.3 billion, or 91 percent, of the $5.8 billion requested by the Clinton administration for foreign military and economic support assis-tance globally. U.S. arms accounted for just under $24 billion worth of weapon deliveries to the countries of the Middle East in the 1993-1996 period, or 47 percent of the total, according to the U.S. Congressional Research Service. Saudi Arabia was the leading arms purchaser.

Despite the potential leverage this role provided, and despite high-level declarations of the centrality of human rights to U.S. policy, Washington did and said little pub-licly to promote human rights in the region. Israel, Egypt, Bahrain, and Saudi Arabia, all close U.S. allies, engaged in grave and system-atic human rights abuses as matters of state policy, without any public indication from

Washington that these violations had or would have consequences for relations.

The severity of abuses, as well-documented in the State Department's *Country Reports on Human Rights Practices for 1996*, was almost never reflected in the public responses of President Clinton, Secretary of State Albright, or other high officials to developments in the region. Assistant Secretary for Democracy, Human Rights and Labor John Shattuck and his top aides passed another year without visiting the Middle East or North Africa.

On her first trip to the region, in September, Secretary of State Madeline Albright called on Israel to ease its blockade of the PA-controlled areas, and to refrain from "land confiscations, home demolitions and confiscation of I.D.s." These recommendations, however welcome, were made explicitly as means to improving the climate for negotiations with the Palestinian Authority. Israeli abuses were never publicly characterized by Albright or any other senior official as violations of human rights or humanitarian law. During her stops in Egypt, Syria, Lebanon, Jordan and Saudi Arabia, and during her meetings with foreign ministers from the region at the U.N. General Assembly sessions, she made no public comments about human rights practices in any of these countries.

In July the State Department issued a congressionally-mandated report, *Religious Freedom: Focus on Christians*. The entries included all Middle East countries, in some cases elaborating on information contained in the *Country Reports* and noting U.S. government responses to instances of persecution or discrimination against Christians on the basis of religious belief.

U.S. foreign assistance in the region included funds for UNRWA and the Israel-Lebanon Monitoring Group. The U.S. also continued a military air patrol of northern Iraq, discouraging a major Iraqi military incursion into that mainly Kurdish-populated area.

The $5 million U.S. Middle East Regional Democracy Fund supported the dispatch of election observers to Yemen and Algeria. The U.S. also provided funds to the Palestinian Authority and the Palestinian nongovernmental sector to promote democracy and rule of law, but undermined these objectives by demanding a crackdown on suspected militants without demanding that the PA avoid the abusive methods that had accompanied such crackdowns in the past.

In his confirmation hearings, Assistant Secretary of State for Near Eastern Affairs Martin Indyk said "In cases where 'quiet' diplomatic efforts are unsuccessful in addressing human rights abuses" a more effective approach would be sought, "but the approach we take depends on the nature of our relationship with the country involved."

The Work of Human Rights Watch

In 1997 Human Rights Watch placed a priority on exposing human rights abuses in the Gulf states; providing in-depth analyses of human rights conditions in Algeria, Iran, and Jordan on the eve of elections; exposing human rights abuses in Lebanon in a fashion that highlights the responsibility of the Lebanese, Israeli and Syrian authorities; and increasing our work with the European Union, in the context of the negotiation of Association Agreements with several Middle Eastern countries and growing European interest in the countries on its southern flank as well as Iran.

Iran and the Gulf states were largely closed to human rights monitoring. The authorities in Teheran did not approve our requests to return, following our first-ever authorized mission to Iran in early 1996, and permission to send fact-finding missions to Saudi Arabia and Bahrain was not granted.

Research and action continued, however, on countries that did not give access to human rights monitors. In May we issued a report before Iran's presidential elections that described the means by which the religious establishment used arbitrary criteria to disqualify candidates from outside its own ranks, as well as other impediments to free and fair polling. A second report, issued in September, exposed discrimination in law and practice against the country's religious and ethnic minorities. We gave priority to communicating our findings on Iran via scores of Farsi-language interviews with radio stations broadcasting to that country.

In April, following a German court verdict that implicated Tehran's top leadership in the 1992 assassinations of four Kurdish Iranian leaders of armed opposition groups in Berlin, Human Rights Watch called on the E.U. foreign ministers to condition the resumption of normal political and commercial relations with Iran on that government investigating extrajudicial executions and holding accountable any officials found to have been involved in them.

In July we published a report on Bahrain that highlighted measures against activists in the Shi'a community and in the broad-based movement seeking the restoration of the dissolved parliament and suspended rights. The report refuted the government's claim that it repressed only participants in "a campaign of disturbance orchestrated by foreign backed terrorist groups."

Repression and controls on the flow of information made Saudi Arabia one of the world's countries most closed to human rights monitoring. During 1997, we obtained information about a Syrian who was executed on charges of practicing witchcraft, but whose real "offense" appears to have been incurring the wrath of his wealthy and well-connected Saudi employer. After Saudi authorities ignored our inquiries on the case, we issued a report describing the flaws in the Saudi justice system that this case revealed.

Many of Lebanon's human rights problems were linked to the continuing foreign intervention in that country. Israel continued to occupy 850 square kilometers of southern Lebanon. We issued two reports during the year on abuses stemming from Israel's conflict with Lebanese guerrillas, based on two missions each to Lebanon and Israel. The first documented laws of war violations committed by Israeli military forces and Lebanese guerrillas in April 1996, causing civilian casualties on both sides of the border, although it was only in Lebanon where civilians were killed. On the first anniversary of the Israeli

artillery shelling of the U.N. base at Qana, in which over one hundred Lebanese civilians perished, the Arabic-language daily newspaper *al-Hayat* (London) published a two-part Human Rights Watch report on the attack. A full report on the conflict followed in September that showed the attack on the U.N. base was only the most calamitous in a series of incidents in which Israel's military did not take precautions to spare Lebanese civilians from harm during attacks and fired at or near U.N. peacekeeper vehicles and bases. The report also criticized Hizballah's indiscriminate attacks on civilians in northern Israel and its firing of weapons from positions near the civilian-filled U.N. base at Qana.

In September we reported on a forgotten aspect of the conflict: Israel continued to hold twenty-one Lebanese prisoners in long-term detention. Two of the detainees-Sheikh Ahmad Hikmat Obeid and Mustafa al-Dirani -continued to be held in utter secrecy and isolation, in undisclosed locations, since 1989 and 1994 respectively. Others among these prisoners completed prison sentences in Israel up to nine years ago but orders for their deportation upon release were suspended without explanation and their long imprisonment under administrative orders has continued. Our report built on and supported the work of nongovernmental organizations in Lebanon, the West Bank, and Israel that have been working for years on behalf of these prisoners.

While Syria did not formally occupy any part of Lebanon, it maintained an estimated 30,000 troops as well as intelligence operatives on the ground. The Syrian role in carrying out arbitrary arrests, abductions, and "disappearances" in Lebanon was first documented in our 1990 report. In May 1997 we published a report showing that Lebanese authorities acquiesced and sometimes directly collaborated in this practice. The report was disseminated in Arabic in the region, encouraging families of the "disappeared" to provide information about their relatives to international organizations. Neither the Syrian nor the Lebanese government commented officially on its findings.

Following the government's decision in September 1996 to license only four television and eleven radio stations, and impose content restrictions, we dispatched a fact-finding mission to Lebanon. In a report issued in April, we argued that the state's legitimate interest in regulating airwaves must not become a pretext for restricting the political content of broadcasts and limiting dissenting viewpoints.

Working with the Ramallah-based Centre for International Human Rights Enforcement (CIHRE), we concentrated on pressing the international community to end its acquiescence in Israeli abuses. We campaigned in several European capitals where the European Union's Association Agreement with Israel was up for ratification. These efforts helped to provoke discussion within parliaments and questioning directed at government ministers, as well as Israeli responses to these initiatives. We suggested to parliamentarians ways to give substance to the human rights clause common to the agreements with Israel, and also with the governments of Tunisia, Morocco, and the Palestinian Authority.

In April, prior to the Euro-Mediterranean ministerial conference in Malta, Human Rights Watch urged the foreign ministers of the attending governments to address a number of human rights issues. These included discrimination and xenophobic violence directed at migrant workers and their families, and the need to make a public and unconditional commitment to end the practice of torture. At a European Parliament hearing devoted to human rights in Tunisia in June, we outlined a framework for the role that the international community should play in promoting human rights in that country.

We joined with Israeli human rights organizations to campaign to block legislation that would prevent Palestinian victims of Israeli human rights abuses from seeking compensation in Israeli courts. The government ended up submitting a toned-down but still objectionable version of the bill to the Knesset, which had not acted on the bill as this report went to press.

In October, as the Palestinian Authority resumed rounding up suspected Islamist militants in response to outside pressure, we issued the findings of research into abuses under the PA. In addition to condemning the pattern of arbitrary arrests of suspected militants as well as other critics by the PA, we criticized foreign powers, including the U.S., for demanding a crackdown without insisting that the PA avoid the pattern of abuse that accompanied its previous crackdowns. During the year we also issued statements condemning the suicide bombings inside Israel and the punitive closures that Israel imposed on Palestinians in their wake.

Although Human Rights Watch does not monitor elections per se, we frequently strived to demonstrate how their fairness can be judged only against a full picture of prevailing human rights conditions. This was the goal of our report issued prior to Iran's presidential election in May (*see* above) as well as the report issued before parliamentary elections there in early 1996. A mission to Algeria in March and April yielded a report placing the June parliamentary elections in the context of the civil strife, controls on free expression and assembly, and constitutional amendments that barred certain political parties. We also worked with human rights lawyers in Algiers who collected hundreds of dossiers on "disappeared" persons. In October, together with three other international human rights organizations, we called on the United Nations to conduct an inquiry into the massacres taking place in Algeria. In October, in advance of Jordan's parliamentary elections, we issued a report documenting the effect of curbs on press freedom—the subject of a Human Rights Watch report in June—and other restrictions on freedom of expression and assembly that compromised the fairness of the electoral contest.

We issued a series of statements on the arrest of activists who were peacefully protesting implementation of new land tenancy laws in Egypt and visited the country twice. In April, we testified before the U.S. House of Representatives on human rights in Egypt and in June expressed alarm over the impact of an Egyptian court decision rejecting a government ban on female genital mutilation.

As always, we responded on many occasions where local lawyers, activists, journalists and others were being pressured or persecuted because of their efforts to expose human rights abuses. Letters were sent to governments in support of lawyers in Algeria, Lebanon and Tunisia, activists and journalists in Egypt, Jordan, Bahrain, and the West Bank, to name but a few.

For a listing of relevant reports and missions, see page 459 at the end of this report. Partial listings also follow each country chapter.

ALGERIA

Human Rights Developments

The year was marked by the first legislative and local elections since the last round of voting was cancelled in 1992. Algeria had been governed without an elected parliament since elections were halted in January that year to prevent a victory by the Islamic Salvation Front (Front Islamique du Salut, FIS). Since then, political strife has become endemic. 1997 appeared to be the bloodiest year yet and, more than ever, civilians bore the brunt of the violence.

The main adversaries were armed Islamist groups on the one hand and, on the other, the security forces and armed civilian groups allied with them. Assaults on civilians included an unprecedented wave of massacres in farming and semi-rural communities, mostly in the Mitidja region southwest of the capital. The assailants indiscriminately killed and maimed men, women, children and infants in the communities they attacked by beheading them, hacking them to death or mutilating them and leaving them to die. Some women were abducted and reportedly raped and then killed.

Observers attributed the attacks to motives that included reprisals by armed groups against villagers who had retreated from their one-time support of the rebels;

feuds between armed groups; vendettas between competing armed Islamist groups and government-backed "self-defense" militias; and disputes over land ownership.

The shadowy Armed Islamic Group (known by the acronym GIA) was blamed for much of the carnage and claimed responsibility for some of the killings. For example, on September 26, after attacks on the Algiers suburbs of Rais and Bentalha on August 29 and September 22 respectively that, according to press reports, left more than 500 dead, the GIA issued a statement in London saying it was behind the recent massacres, according to the Agence France-Presse.

Many of the massacres occurred in districts that had voted overwhelmingly for the FIS in the 1990 and 1992 elections. According to press reports, several of the massacres targeted villages whose inhabitants had, since 1993, reportedly given provisions and money to the armed groups, but had since withdrawn their support and in some cases had sought weapons from the authorities to defend themselves.

The security forces often reportedly did not try to halt the massacres or apprehend the killers, even when the slaughter took hours to complete and occurred less than a mile from their barracks and installations. According to survivors interviewed by Amnesty International, armed forces units with armored vehicles stationed just outside Bentalha did not intervene even though it was clear they were aware of the situation, and even stopped some villagers trying to flee from doing so. The army also did not allow neighboring local militia to enter Bentalha in response to the attack. After massacring over two hundred persons over the course of several hours, the attackers fled without being stopped.

Algerian newspapers and others expressed skepticism toward the semi-official explanations of security force inaction, which focused on the dangers to soldiers posed by land mines and ambushes.

Various factors impeded identification of the perpetrators of specific atrocities. These included both government censorship of security-related information (*see* below) and the physical risks of conducting on-site investigations in conflict zones. In addition, criminal trials shed little light on specific incidents since they tended to focus only on such general charges as membership in "an armed group."

The government largely denied the existence of a human rights problem other than the "terrorism" it attributed to armed Islamist groups. However, security forces were responsible during 1997 for summary executions and "disappearances," most of them carried out against suspected Islamists and their sympathizers. Human Rights Watch is unaware of a single instance in which security force members were punished for their role in these grave abuses.

Police commonly detained suspects without identifying themselves and without warrants. Persons detained on suspicion of links to "terrorism" and "subversion" often remained in incommunicado custody beyond the twelve-day limit stipulated by the penal code, and without their families being informed of their whereabouts, as required by law. Dozens of persons arrested in 1997 remained unaccounted for as this report went to press, adding to the hundreds of cases of "disappearances" reported by human rights lawyers since 1993. When confronted with inquiries on cases of "disappearances," authorities have either not responded or stated that the missing person is not in their custody, even when eyewitnesses testified to having seen the person being taken away by security force members.

Government-backed militia were also reportedly responsible for "anti-terrorist" operations that went beyond self-defense and the limits of the law, including killings of suspected Islamists or their families in reprisal for acts attributed to armed groups, according to Amnesty International. The government issued a decree in March intended to bring the militia under closer supervision by the defense and interior ministries but did not refer to basic human rights standards.

On June 5, parliamentary elections took place under the eyes of national and international observers. The elections produced the country's first-ever multiparty National Assembly. Pro-government parties won a solid majority. While the outlawed FIS was barred from participating, two other Islamist parties won 27 percent of the seats.

The election stakes were determined in part by a referendum in November 1996 under unfair conditions in which the government secured voter approval for amendments to the constitution that enhanced the powers of the executive branch at the expense of the National Assembly. The constitutional amendments, along with new election and party laws passed in March 1997, restricted Algerians' right to freedom of association by banning parties based on religion and ethnicity.

In local elections on October 23, a pro-government party won more than half the seats, triggering street marches in Algiers in which more than 15,000 supporters of the other major parties protested alleged fraud. The interior ministry banned further "unauthorized public demonstrations" and police in some instances prevented protestors from gathering.

Following the June elections, authorities released from prison FIS chief Abbasi Madani, who was in the middle of a twelve-year sentence for subversion, and another senior FIS figure, Abdelqader Hachani, who had been held for over five years without trial. In July he was tried and sentenced to five years in prison—time already served—for incitement against state security. Meanwhile, the whereabouts of deputy FIS chief Ali Belhadj, who also had been imprisoned for subversion, remained unknown since his transfer in 1995 to secret detention.

FIS representatives in exile repeatedly disassociated their party from the massacres and other deliberate killing of civilians. "The FIS condemns all of these terrible killings," said Abdelkrim Ould Adda, FIS executive committee in exile spokesman in April. "Let me say it very clearly: The FIS has no links with the GIA. We firmly condemn these barbarous acts committed by these terrorist groups against the civilian population." A unilateral cease-fire declared for October 1 by the FIS's armed wing, the Islamic Salvation Army (AIS), was denounced by the GIA and did not stem the massacres taking place.

Algeria's private press enjoyed some freedom to criticize government policies. State-controlled television opened up a bit during the election campaigns, providing air time for all parties running parliamentary candidates, and later aired debates in the National Assembly. However, authorities censored the speeches of opposition candidates that referred to the military-backed cancellation of the January 1992 elections as a "coup."

Although private newspapers reported on the massacres in the second half of 1997, what they could say about them was limited by censorship, restriction on access to massacre sites and witnesses, and the armed security forces who accompanied most Algerian and foreign journalists, whether they wanted them or not. Any reporting on governmental abuses carried out in connection with the internal strife was liable to be deleted. Algerian television offered only the official line on the conflict, generally playing down the scope of violence, in an apparent effort to buttress the government's case that "terrorism" was only residual.

The government allowed many foreign journalists in at the time of the two election campaigns, but throughout the year denied visas to certain reporters without explanation, including those of the French daily *Libération*. On September 29, the authorities withdrew the accreditation of an Agence France Presse (AFP) correspondent, one of the few foreign news bureaus remaining in the country. A Foreign Ministry official did not provide a reason except to say that AFP had been "warned" about its coverage of the unrest, the agency reported.

Journalists, intellectuals, artists and political figures continued to be assassinated in 1997, in attacks attributed by the authorities to armed groups. The best-known figure to be slain was Abdelhaq Benhamouda, leader of the country's main labor syndicate, the General Union of Algerian Workers. A group calling itself the Islamic Front for the Armed Jihad claimed responsibility for his killing in January. At least three political party activists were killed in the days leading up to the June 5, 1997 elections, and ten party officials were killed ahead of the municipal elections.

Human Rights Watch investigated, while in Algiers in April, the apparent execution in custody of Rached Medjahed, the alleged mastermind of the assassination of Benhamouda. Medjahed was arrested a few days after the killing and was shown "confessing" on Algerian national television. But when his family requested permission from an investigating judge to visit him, they were told he had died. Authorities claimed that he had died from wounds incurred during his arrest, but the information collected by Human Rights Watch cast doubt on this claim. Medjahed's death in custody fueled suspicion about who was behind the killing of Benhamouda.

The Right to Monitor

Two independent human rights organizations functioned openly in Algeria, although neither the Algerian Human Rights League nor the Algerian League for the Defense of Human Rights produced much documentation of abuses. Defense lawyers played a key role in aiding victims and disseminating information about their plight. They sometimes paid a price for their activism. The office of lawyer Mohamed Tahri, whose clients include relatives of "disappeared" persons, suffered a suspicious burglary during the weekend of June 12-13, in which the only items missing were personal documents and correspondence with clients. The break-in occurred only days after Tahri was featured speaking about human rights in *Le Monde* (Paris) and on French television. On October 20, Tahri was arrested and held for seven hours after demonstrating in Algiers with about fifty women seeking information about missing relatives.

Rachid Mesli, an Algiers lawyer who had been openly helpful to Amnesty International during and since its 1996 mission to Algeria, was sentenced after an unfair trial to three years in prison, on charges of "encouraging" and "providing apologetics" for "terrorism." During his initial interrogation and trial, the judge questioned Mesli about his contacts with Amnesty International.

The Human Rights Monitoring Body (Observatoire National des Droits de l'Homme, ONDH), which reports to the president's office, continued to serve as a conduit between the government and persons lodging complaints of human rights abuses. While it made some general criticism of government abuses, in its annual report for 1996 and elsewhere, the ONDH publicly defended the government's record against criticism from international human rights organizations. The ONDH's president immediately rejected a joint call by international human rights organizations on October 15 for an international inquiry into the human rights situation in Algeria, saying it showed "a deliberate willingness to spread misunderstanding about those responsible for the latest massacres of civilians in Algeria," according to Algerian radio.

Several international organizations were granted permission during 1997 to investigate abuses in Algeria. However, applications to visit from Amnesty International, an organization that has persistently documented abuses in Algeria, were refused. The Human Rights Watch delegation was assisted by the ONDH and received by the ministers of interior and justice. However, the delegation was accompanied by government security personnel during half the visit, despite the organization's strong protests. Although imposed ostensibly for the delegation's protection, this unwanted escort severely hampered the delegation's ability to meet freely with Algerians.

The Role of the
International Community

United Nations

Following a series of massacres U.N. Secretary-General Kofi Annan issued a public appeal on August 30 for an "urgent solution" to the bloodshed. "As the killing goes on," he said, "it is extremely difficult for all of us to pretend that it is not happening, that we do not know about it and that we should leave the Algerian population to their lot."

Annan's comments were echoed on September 30 by the new U.N. Human Rights Commissioner, Mary Robinson. After meeting with Algerian Foreign Minister Ahmed Attaf that day, she commented, "When there are serious violations of civilians' rights, and when a situation is as bad as in Algeria, I do not consider that—and I cannot consider that—to be internal." Following a meeting late October with Mohamed-Salah Dembri, Algeria's representative to the U.N. in Geneva, Robinson said they had "discussed Algeria's cooperation" with U.N. human rights mechanisms, which include the Working Group on Enforced or Involuntary Disappearances and various rapporteurs. Algerian authorities publicly rejected any outside intervention in the crisis, however.

Earlier in the year, the U.N. secretary-general had played a more considered role than his predecessor when asked by President Zeroual to send U.N. election observers. For the presidential elections of 1995, then-Secretary-General Boutros Boutros-Ghali had sent a team of observers who had then made no public statements on voting conditions, thereby giving the government the right to boast of the international presence without having to face public reporting. In 1997, Annan did not send observers but deployed a team of four officials who only coordinated the efforts of observers from some twenty countries who could speak freely of their findings. Thus the secretary-general provided a gesture of support for the holding of elections while making it difficult for that gesture to be exploited.

On August 13, the U.N. Commission on Human Rights' Subcommission on Prevention of Discrimination and Protection of Minorities defeated by secret ballot a draft resolution that Algerian authorities had lobbied against. While critical of "armed groups of religious extremists, who...are terrorizing civilian population," the draft had also expressed concern at reports "indicating that, going beyond the requirements of the fight against terrorism, violations of human rights are being committed more and more frequently by certain sectors of the security forces."

In a statement issued on September 18, the United Nations High Commissioner for Refugees (UNHCR) urged governments to refrain from the "hasty deportation of rejected Algerian asylum seekers in the midst of an upsurge of violence in Algeria." UNHCR defined those at risk as coming from both sides of the conflict: "Algerians who have close links with the government" as well as "members or perceived members of Islamic groups."

European Union

The European Parliament passed a resolution on December 12, 1996, criticizing the constitutional referendum held in November for "concentrat[ing] power in the hands of the president" and thus being "likely to make it more difficult to establish democratic and cultural pluralism." The resolution urged the European Commission "to take into account developments with regard to democratization and respect for human rights" in upcoming talks regarding a Euro-Mediterranean Association Agreement. Article 2 of the trade agreement stresses "respect for human rights and democratic principles... constitute an essential element." Negotiations commenced in March, and at the time of writing had not concluded.

Manuel Marin, vice president of the European Commission, urged adoption of the Association Agreement as a means to democratic reform. Following Algeria's parliamentary elections, Marin on June 24 urged the Foreign Affairs Committee of the European Parliament to take a "pragmatic" and "realistic" attitude regarding Algeria in order to encourage it to complete its "democratic transition."

On September 18, the European Parliament passed a resolution urging the Algerian government to "deepen the dialogue with all the political forces and democratic elements...who reject the use of violence...and allow the rule of law and respect for human rights, including the freedom of the press and the right to demonstrate, to be reestablished." The resolution also called on European Union member states "not to repatriate Algerian nationals residing in their territory whose safety would be endangered if they are forced to return to Algeria."

E.U. foreign ministers met on October 26, at a time of mounting calls for international involvement in the crisis in Algeria. But the ministers limited themselves to a general condemnation of the violence, with some explaining that without the Algerian authorities' consent they could play no role in ending the country's crisis.

France

France, Algeria's former ruler and largest trading partner, remained quietly supportive of the government while insisting that Algerians alone could solve the country's problems. It extended annual assistance worth nearly U.S.$1.2 billion, mostly in the form of government-backed credits to purchase French goods. About a third of the sum was not renewed in 1997 due to administrative problems. Viewed generally as the Western state with the greatest interest in developments in Algeria, France actively lobbied international financial institutions in 1995 to provide debt refinancing to Algeria on favorable terms, and sought to set the course of Western policy toward Algeria.

French authorities tended to condemn atrocities attributed to armed Islamist groups while remaining circumspect on government repression. Indications of a shift in approach came in the fall, after the election of a Socialist-led government and an unchecked streak of massacres that shocked French opinion. Prime Minister Lionel Jospin suggested, on September 29, that the violence did not have a single address: "We can see there is a terrible reign of terror...but it is extremely difficult to make out what is happening." He referred not only to "a fanatical and violent opposition" but also to "a State which is in a way imposing its will with violence and force."

In high-level consultations in September and October with the U.S. and European governments, France reportedly argued against international initiatives on Algeria as long as Algiers opposed them. Foreign Minister Hubert Vedrine told the Paris weekly *L'Express* in October that France can show its willingness to "support any form of action undertaken by the international community if it were accepted or requested by all the parties, starting with the authorities." Premier Jospin indicated that France should respond at home by opening its doors toward Algerians seeking safety. "I am in favor of ... relaxing the visa policy for all who fear for their lives in Algeria," he said on September 29.

The National Consultative Council on Human Rights, an advisory commission attached to the prime minister's office, adopted a resolution in October urging that the question of human rights in Algeria be placed on the agenda of the U.N. Commission on Human Rights, and that U.N. missions should be dispatched as soon as possible to investigate torture, summary executions and arbitrary detentions.

United States

U.S. government influence on Algeria remained limited. The U.S. provided no direct economic or military assistance other than an annual U.S.$75,000 military training program. Cognizant of human rights concerns, Washington maintained a policy of rejecting licenses sought by U.S. companies for the sale to Algeria of equipment that could be used by the security forces in an offensive capacity. However, U.S. engagement in Algeria appeared to increase during the year, as U.S. private investment in Algeria's energy sector soared to nearly $2 billion. The U.S. Export-Import Bank (Eximbank) resumed activity in Algeria in 1996 after a two-year halt. It set a ceiling of $150 million for new projects and financially backed U.S. corporations selling to Sonatrach, Algeria's state-run oil and gas company. As of September 30, Eximbank's exposure in Algeria totaled $2.1 billion.

With the holding of parliamentary elections, the U.S. seemed to regard the government-led political process as worthy of encouragement, despite its limitations. The U.S. stopped calling publicly for a national political dialogue that included "pragmatic elements of the FIS," the banned Islamist party that the government had excluded from the elections. In gestures of support for the vote, the U.S. financed thirteen election observers and openly encouraged other countries to send teams. On June 9, four days after the polling, State Department spokesman Nicholas Burns described the election as a "positive" move but acknowledged, "I would not use the words free and fair to describe the Algerian elections, simply because the international monitors ... did not use these words....We do think it's positive, however, that people voted in great numbers; and it's positive that the government was able to open up television and radio to political debate." He urged the Algerian government to take into account the "issues raised by international observers and political parties" about flaws in the election process.

On September 10, at a time of almost daily reports of massacres, outgoing U.S. Ambassador Ronald Neumann said after a farewell audience with President Zeroual that the U.S. backed "military measures, consistent with the rule of law, to protect civilians" and "the policy spelled out by President Zeroual of economic and political reforms, freedom of the press, and development of the rule of law. We encourage national reconciliation and the inclusion in the political process of all who reject violence."

In light of the U.S. support for the parliamentary elections, the lack of U.S. comment on the government's shocking failure to intervene to protect the population from a steady succession of massacres, some observers interpreted the ambassador's statement as a signal of a new pro-government tilt in U.S. policy. Denying this, officials told the press that the ambassador's comments were merely an attempt "to give a gentle push to the army to do its job."

Neumann told a U.S. Senate Foreign Relations Subcommittee on October 1 that human rights problems remained an impediment to better relations. In his prepared remarks, Neumann praised the convening of a multiparty parliament but cautioned that the election was "only a modest, first step towards representative institutions." He added that while the unity of the military was important to Algeria's stability, "We must continue to be cautious in our dealings as doubts linger about the military's respect for the rule of law and their willingness to allow parliament to develop real power." He continued, "Sometimes security forces themselves have been guilty of excesses....There are also credible reports of torture...and the Algerian government refuses to allow observers to inspect prisons."

The Clinton administration's nominee to replace Neumann, Cameron Hume, said at his Senate confirmation hearing on October 28 that Washington could not intervene directly in what "all Algerians feel is an internal conflict." But he noted the U.S. actively promoted press freedom for Algerian journalists, through diplomatic demarches and bringing Algerian journalists to the U.S. He added that the U.S. supported the work of nongovernmental organizations, including international human rights groups.

The U.S. condemned "terrorism" in Algeria on numerous occasions during the year and maintained the Armed Islamic Group on its official list of terrorist organizations worldwide.

Relevant Human Rights Watch Report:
Algeria—Elections in the Shadow of Violence and Repression, 6/97

BAHRAIN

Human Rights Developments
The human rights situation in Bahrain showed no improvement in 1997 and in some respects worsened. Street protests and clashes between security forces and demonstrators calling for political reform, which had first erupted in December 1994, continued throughout the year, intensifying in June 1997. Shaikh Abd al-Amir al-Jamri and seven other Shi'a community leaders, arrested in January 1996, remained in detention without charge. The government continued to prosecute persons on security-related charges in the State Security Court, where procedures did not meet basic fair trial standards and whose verdicts were not subject to appeal. The exercise of the freedoms of assembly and political association remained effectively outlawed under the terms of the penal code and the law of societies and clubs.

The year saw further arrests and harassment of individuals for writing or possessing written materials which the government considered hostile. On June 14, 1997, six young men in detention for the previous fourteen months were found guilty by a State Security Court on charges of possessing leaflets that according to the Interior Ministry contained "false news and unfounded statements." They were sentenced to time already served plus fines of 200 Bahraini dinars (BD; approximately U.S.$530). In March 1997, Sayyid Jalal Alawi Sharaf, an engineer employed by the state telecommunications company, was arrested in a dawn raid on his home, and his home computer equipment was confiscated, reportedly on the grounds that he was transmitting information abroad via the Internet. He remained in detention without charge or trial as of early October. In February, Ali Hasan Yusif was dismissed from his job with the Ministry of Information and subsequently arrested and detained without charge for several months in connection with a volume of poems he had published, some of which referred in very general terms to conditions of censorship and oppression. Yasir al-Sayigh was detained for months without charge and beaten after a coworker had thrown a leaflet in his office wastebasket.

The government also moved to prevent information about the situation in the country from reaching the outside world through the media. In late September 1996, Abbas Salman, a Bahraini reporter working for Reuters for nearly twenty years, was detained for more than twenty-four hours and interrogated about a story he had filed before being released without charge. In early 1997, the government issued a regulation restricting Bahraini journalists employed by local media from also working for the international press. The government was thus able to force Ismat Moussawi, a reporter with *Al-Ayyam*, a daily close to the government, to cease her work as the BBC Arabic Service stringer, thus effectively stifling an important source of uncensored news for many Bahrainis.

In June 1997 the government closed the office and expelled the correspondent of the German Press Agency (DPA), the last Western news agency with a bureau in Bahrain. The correspondent, Ute Meinel, told Human Rights Watch that her expulsion followed her eyewitness accounts of three days of intense clashes in the town of Sanabis in June, and dispatches regarding several unrelated cases of Bahrainis who had died after being beaten by security forces. On the night of June 24, she was summoned by a senior interior ministry official and interrogated about a recent dispatch. The next day she was shown a charge sheet accusing her of "spreading lies, harming the welfare of the state, insulting the ruling family." Two days later, the Interior Ministry official told her that she would have to leave Bahrain immediately.

In July 1997, ten leaders of the People's Petition Committee prepared a letter to the amir, Shaikh Isa bin Salman, requesting a meeting to discuss political reform issues raised in a 1994 petition which the organizers claimed had been signed by 21,751 Bahrainis. These issues included restoring the partially-elected National Assembly, which was disbanded by decree in 1975, freeing political prisoners, and allowing the return of persons forcibly exiled by the government. An official in the prime minister's office telephoned several committee members to warn them against delivering the letter. On July 29 a high Interior Ministry official summoned two of them, Ahmad al-Shamlan, a defense lawyer and veteran opposition activist, and Ibrahim Kamal Eddin, a businessman, and warned them to cease their efforts. When the men declined, the official told al-Shamlan, who suffers from a heart ailment, to "think of your health." The next day the official phoned al-Shamlan to say that he would not be allowed to leave for Europe that evening as planned for medical tests and a vacation. Several hours later al-Shamlan suffered a serious stroke from which he had not recovered as of October 1997.

The government provides virtually no information regarding numbers of persons arrested, tried, convicted, acquitted or released in political or security-related cases. The exception concerned the high-profile March 1997 security court trials of fifty-nine Bahrainis whom the government charged in June 1996 with planning and carrying out acts of sabotage on behalf of "Hizballah Bahrain-Military Wing." Thirty-six of the defendants were convicted and sentenced to prison terms ranging from three to fifteen years plus large fines, and twenty-three were acquitted. Based on information made available by Bahraini defense lawyers, Human Rights Watch estimates that at least 600 persons were taken into custody for political or security-related offenses over the past year, and at least seventy-one were convicted by state security courts. Bahraini lawyers told Human Rights Watch that the number of persons in prolonged detention without trial was around 1,500 in late September 1997—approximately the same number as were being held a year earlier—and that beatings and other forms of physical abuse were commonly used to secure confessions and information.

In late October 1996, the government signed an agreement with the International Committee of the Red Cross (ICRC), allowing that organization access to persons held for security-related offenses. There were reports that the ICRC had visited over one thousand detainees in more than twenty detention centers. In keeping with ICRC policy, its findings were communicated directly to the government and not announced publicly.

During the year, three persons died in detention or very shortly after being released from detention, prompting allegations of medical neglect and mistreatment. Shaikh Ali al-Nachas, a blind cleric about fifty years old, had been imprisoned without charge or trial from January 1996 until February 1997, reportedly on grounds that his sermons were "political." Shortly after his release he was rearrested on similar grounds, and died in custody on June 29.

The death of al-Nachas followed the deaths in late May and early June of two young men, reportedly after beatings at the hands of security forces. Bashir Abdallah Ahmad Fadhil died following an assault by security forces in the village of Daih on May 18. According to the Bahrain Freedom Movement, an opposition organization, Fadhil was among some thirty persons beaten and arrested then, and two days later his body was returned to his family for burial. The government claimed he died of "natural causes" associated with his having been a drug addict. An independent journalist told Human Rights Watch that Fadhil's history of addiction may have contributed to his death, but that witnesses saw him being beaten severely by security forces. On June 6, Abd al-Zahra Ibrahim Abdallah, twenty-seven, died after his arrest five days earlier during clashes with security forces in the village of Sanabis. The government claimed that Abdallah had been released from custody on June 3 and "later died in a hospital from a blood disease." According to the Bahrain Freedom Movement, Abdallah was beaten at the time of his arrest and transferred to Salmaniyya hospital, where he died.

The unrest has been marked by increased violence against persons and property. Independent journalists confirmed to Human Rights Watch that security forces, in suppressing gatherings deemed illegal, increasingly resorted to smashing automobiles and other property, including Shi'a assembly halls (ma'tams) and mosques. Protesters sabotaged power generators and attacked other public property as well as individual shops. There were arson attacks on stores and residences that killed six South Asian workers over the past year. No group or individuals claimed responsibility for any of these attacks. Three men who were sentenced to die in 1996 for their alleged role in a firebomb attack that killed seven foreign nationals remained in prison as of October 1997.

The government routinely attributed attacks and the unrest generally to Iranian-backed "terrorists," a term it applied to the opposition without distinction, including such groups as the London-based Bahrain Freedom Movement, which asserted that it is committed to a strategy of nonviolent civil resistance. On July 9 Shaikh Isa Qasim, a prominent opposition leader now living in Iran, condemned "all the fires and sabotage that destroy properties and that cause death."

The Right to Monitor

No local human rights organizations were permitted to operate in Bahrain, and the government continued to deny requests from international human rights organizations to conduct official visits. Over the past year, the government increased pressure on Bahraini defense lawyers to refrain from providing information about arrests and security court trials to the press, and threatened some lawyers with disbarment if they continued to do so. Close government monitoring of telephone, fax and Internet links made most Bahrainis afraid to discuss the situation with Human Rights Watch.

The Bahrain Human Rights Organization (BHRO) and the Committee for the Defense of Human Rights in Bahrain (CDHRB), operating abroad, compiled information on detainees and other issues. In responding to questions from Human Rights Watch in March 1997, Bahrain's ambassador in Washington, Dr. Muhammad Abdul-Ghaffar, charged that "the BHRO is not a bona fide Human Rights Organization" and that its director, Abdul-Hadi Abdallah al-Khawaja, "is a trained terrorist and a fugitive from the 1981 failed armed coup." He provided no evidence for these allegations, and in a letter to Human Rights Watch al-Khawaja noted that he had flown back to Bahrain in February 1994 in an effort to return home—hardly the step of a fugitive from an armed coup attempt. At that time, according to a letter al-Khawaja submitted immediately afterwards to the U.N. Human Rights Center, the authorities interrogated him at the airport for eleven days about his human rights activities and finally denied him entry, but at no point mentioned the ambassador's subsequent allegations about the attempted coup.

Following the July publication of Human Rights Watch's report *Routine Abuse, Routine Denial: Civil Rights and the Political Crisis in Bahrain,* Ambassador Abdul-Ghaffar wrote to Human Rights Watch that "the majority of the information upon which the report has been based is neither credible nor accurate" but provided no specifics. The ambassador continued, "There is no deterioration of the human rights situation in Bahrain and the government has, through its legitimate police forces and the rule of law, dealt with the situation in an entirely fair, sensitive and proper manner balancing the requirements of public order and individual rights."

The Role of the International Community

United Nations

The 49th Session of the United Nations Subcommission on Human Rights, meeting in Geneva in August, passed a resolution expressing "deep concern about the alleged gross and systematic violations of human rights" in Bahrain and urging the government "to comply with international human rights standards and to ratify the international covenants on human rights and the Convention Against Torture and Other Cruel, Inhuman, or Degrading Treatment or Punishment." The resolution also requested the Commission on Human Rights to consider Bahrain's human rights situation at its next session. Bahrain, in an unsuccessful effort to persuade some of the subcommission experts to vote against the resolution, offered to ratify the Convention Against Torture and to donate $100,000 to one of the working groups of the Subcommission.

Bahrain was also cited for reported human rights violations in the reports of the special rapporteur on the independence of judges and lawyers (February 1997) and the special rapporteur on torture and other cruel, inhuman or degrading treatment or punishment (January 1997).

The Arab World

Bahrain's government continued to enjoy the support of most Arab governments for its policies, and a number of the Gulf Cooperation Council states provided financial aid. No Arab government except Qatar (*see* below) publicly criticized any aspect of Bahrain's human rights record. Algerian President Liamine Zeroual visited Bahrain in mid-October 1996, where he was quoted as saying, "There will be coordination between Bahrain and Algeria to wipe out terrorism in the Arab world." In March 1997, Kuwaiti state security officials detained thirteen Bahraini nationals for "gathering donations without permission and distributing illegal literature," according to the Kuwaiti daily *Al-Watan,* and four remained in detention in early October 1997. In May 1997, the special operations commander of the Jordanian armed forces visited Bahrain, and the next month the director of Jordan's General Intelligence Department led a delegation to Bahrain to discuss "issues of common concern," according to the official Bahraini news agency.

In December 1996, Bahrain announced it would try two Qatari nationals on charges of espionage in connection with a long-running dispute between Qatar and Bahrain over ownership of the uninhabited Hawar islands. Qatar charged that its two nationals had been tortured, which Bahrain denied. The two were convicted by the State Security Court on December 25, 1996, but were promptly pardoned by the amir.

European Union

In September 1997 the European Parliament passed a resolution on human rights abuses in Bahrain, calling on the government to release political prisoners, to open negotiations with the opposition with a view to scheduling democratic elections, and to allow monitoring of human rights conditions by international and local organizations. The resolution also requested that the fifteen member states "refrain from supplying arms or security support" to Bahrain and "take initiatives in order to obtain similar restraint at the international level until democratic conditions have been restored."

The United Kingdom's policy toward Bahrain was generally uncritical with regard to human rights, although the election of a Labour government in March did lead to some critical public remarks. Derek Fatchett, the new minister of state responsible for the Middle East, responding to questions on Bahrain in a parliamentary debate on June 3, stated that he had raised human rights concerns in a recent meeting with the Bahraini ambassador and urged the ambassador to invite "Amnesty International or any similar organization to be involved in monitoring the situation closely." Fatchett also characterized the Bahraini opposition based in London as "moderate people with a moderate set of demands."

United States

Bahrain serves as headquarters for the U.S. Fifth Fleet, comprising some fifteen warships and approximately 1,500 on-shore U.S. military personnel and dependents. During the year the U.S. Air Force also deployed some twenty fighter aircraft and, for a time, several B-1 bombers in Bahrain as well, and U.S. and Bahraini forces conducted joint exercises.

The State Department congressional presentation for Fiscal Year 1998 estimated that U.S. military sales would total U.S.$201.2 million, and that fiscal year 1997 sales were $78.8 million. In July the Department of Defense notified Congress of the intent to sell Bahrain twenty F-16 fighter jets at an estimated cost of $303 million. Under the Excess Defense Articles program, which allows for free or reduced-price transfers of "excess" U.S. weapons inventory, the U.S. provided Bahrain with Hawk anti-aircraft missiles, howitzers, and a former U.S. Navy frigate. The Clinton administration also requested $175,000 in International Military Education

and Training (IMET) funds for training Bahraini armed forces in fiscal 1998.

Several high-level U.S. military officials visited Bahrain in the course of the year. In June Defense Secretary William Cohen delivered a letter from President Clinton to Shaikh Isa, the amir, inviting him to visit Washington later in the year. Secretary Cohen did not comment publicly on Bahrain's internal security policies, confining his remarks to Bahrain's military cooperation with the U.S. in the Persian Gulf.

State Department officials avoided public comment on the human rights record of this close ally. In September, Secretary of State Madeleine Albright, commenting during her visit to Saudi Arabia on the recent election of Muhammad Khatami as president of Iran, said that the U.S. would continue to support "the UAE and Bahrain against Iranian intimidation," but made no mention of human rights in either country. The emphasis on security without regard for human rights was reaffirmed by President Clinton's nominee as ambassador to Bahrain, Johnny Young, who in his Senate confirmation hearings in September stated, "The United States supports fully the Government of Bahrain's efforts to maintain order and stability in the face of periodic outbreaks of violence." Other than a pro forma qualification that "this objective must be pursued in a manner consistent with international standards of human rights," Young avoided mention of the severely repressive situation inside the country.

The Bahrain chapter in the Department of State's *Country Reports on Human Rights Practices in 1996* was comprehensive, but continued to understate the government's hostility to human rights monitoring and made a point of denigrating gratuitously the human rights work of the BHRO and the CDHRB, commenting that they "reportedly receive funds from sources hostile to the government" and "are viewed by many local observers as espousing a political, rather than a purely human rights, agenda."

Relevant Human Rights Watch Report:

Routine Abuse, Routine Denial: Civil Rights and the Political Crisis in Bahrain, 6/97

EGYPT

Human Rights Developments

Conflict continued in Egypt between institutions of civil society and the government; security forces and suspected Islamist militants; and Islamist activists and proponents of intellectual freedom and a secular state. Facing a new political challenge from the countryside in 1997, the government clamped down well in advance of the October implementation of sweeping changes in the rent and tenure system regulating agricultural land, pursuant to a reform law passed in 1992 and due to take effect after a five-year grace period. Citizens uninvolved in politics suffered torture and ill-treatment at police stations around the country, abuses to which criminal suspects and sometimes their male and female relatives fell victim. On the positive side, Egypt's independent human rights community continued to flourish and new organizations were launched, despite the restrictive and much-criticized 1964 law that regulates the formation and activities of nongovernmental organizations (NGOs). Women's rights groups actively campaigned against gender-based discrimination and female genital mutilation, a widespread practice in Egypt (*see* Women's Rights Project).

In February, the state of emergency was extended until May 31, 2000. Emergency law, in effect for almost thirty years except for an eighteen-month hiatus during the rule of Anwar Sadat, permits arrest and detention on the basis of suspicion or because individuals are considered a danger to security and public order; these powers continued to be widely abused. Emergency law also provides the legal basis for trials of civilians in military courts and exceptional state security courts, whose verdicts cannot be appealed to higher tribunals as required by international law, and allows the retrial of defendants previously acquitted by security courts.

The state maintained its strategy of undermining politically the long-banned but also long-tolerated Muslim Brotherhood, the most well-entrenched political group in the country. Prominent members were serving prison sentences of three to five years following military court trials in 1995 and 1996 in which they were prosecuted for peaceful political activities. These included elected leaders of professional associations and former members of parliament such as physician Eissam al-Erian and university professor Muhamed al-Sayed Habib. Other Muslim Brothers detained in 1997 for peaceful political activities included thirty-four men, teachers and engineers among them, who were arrested on August 9 for allegedly planning to recruit new members at Alexandria University. A prosecutor ordered their detention pending investigation for possession of anti-government leaflets and membership in a "banned organization" whose goal is to seize power, according to legal sources cited by Agence France-Presse.

The Interior Ministry claimed repeatedly in 1997 that it had vanquished Egypt's armed Islamists, who are affiliated with Jihad, the Islamic Group, and other small, clandestine organizations. Interior Minister Gen. Hassan al-Alfi, in an interview with the weekly *Rose al-Yusef* (Cairo) published on April 21, said that political violence had been "reduced to limited random incidents." Violent incidents in 1997 included a series of attacks in Upper Egypt in February and March in which twenty-two villagers were killed by suspected militants who went unapprehended. Christians clearly appeared to be the intended targets, one of the patterns that has marked the bloodshed of the 1990s.

In one such incident on February 12, four masked gunmen entered St. George Church in Fikriyah village near Abu Qurqas in Minya province, where a weekly youth meeting was in progress. According to the Cairo-based Egyptian Organization for Human Rights (EOHR), which interviewed eyewitnesses, three of the gunmen "closed the door and fired for some sixty to ninety seconds at a group of young people sitting on the left hand side of the hall." Eight were killed and five wounded; they ranged in age from thirteen to twenty-six years old, and most were students. The assailants fled into nearby fields, killing a farmer en route. On February 14, the bodies of three Copts—a sixty-year-old fisherman, his son, and a police officer—were found in a field near Abu Qurqas.

An unnamed Islamic Group official, quoted in the Arabic daily *al-Hayat* (London) on February 17, claimed responsibility for both attacks. Referring to the three men who were found dead, he said: "The [Group] was convinced they were collaborating with the police." Regarding the slaughter in the church, he noted that "our policy is not to kill Christians wherever they are, nor to attack places of worship, unless plots are being hatched there against Islam."

In a March 27 report, EOHR expressed alarm about unconfirmed reports that in Upper Egypt "security forces have trained popular militias in the use of weapons and assigned them to guard some public buildings, set up ambushes and search suspects." EOHR warned that a cycle of violence could be set in motion if the Interior Ministry used armed civilians as substitutes for or supplements to police and security forces. It stressed that the state was responsible for protecting citizens, and that the rule of law was best upheld if trained law enforcement officials were "subject to supervision and accountability."

Armed militants, many of them wanted by authorities, were shot dead in security force operations, although few details were available about the circumstances of these killings. Between June and August, for example, at least twenty-three suspected militants, some reportedly senior leaders in the Islamic Group's armed wing, were killed, according to information provided to the press by unnamed Egyptian security sources. This included a report in the semi-official daily *al-Ahram* (Cairo) on August 17 that thirteen Islamic Group militants had been killed in a major operation in the Minya region.

In July, imprisoned founding members of Jihad and the Islamic Group appealed "to all our brothers to halt military operations inside and outside the country." The highly publicized signed statement was read at the July 5 opening session of a military court trial of over ninety civilians, including five women. The government was reportedly unresponsive to this call for a unilateral cease-fire, and it was not heeded by some cadres on the ground, as violence intensified. Suspected militants mounted several attacks in Upper Egypt, killing policemen and in some circumstances civilians. For example, on October 13, gunmen, some wearing police unifoms, killed nine policemen and two civilians in two separate but simultaneous operations near Abu Qurqas and Mallawi. The victims were forced out of cars at roadblocks and executed, some of them after being bound at their hands and feet. The Islamic Group later claimed responsibility for these attacks.

Military and state security courts handed down death sentences against alleged militants convicted of acts of violence, bringing to eighty-two the number of death sentences issued by military courts since President Mubarak began referring civilians to these courts in 1992; of these, fifty-eight had been carried out as of October 22, according to Amnesty International. Criminal courts also sentenced men and women to death in 1997 for nonpolitical offenses.

Thousands of suspected Islamist militants, as well as some of their defense lawyers and suspected supporters, remained detained—without charge or awaiting trial—under grossly substandard conditions which caused or contributed to a number of deaths. In a February report, EOHR documented wholly inadequate medical care, including the cases of twenty-five prisoners who died between 1994 and 1996, the majority of them in Wadi al-Gedid, Liman Tora, Fayoum, and Wadi al-Natroun prisons, and thirty-two cases of seriously ill inmates whose poor health, EOHR said, merited release or transfer to specialized medical facilities. Among them were men in their twenties and thirties whose official causes of death had been noted as tuberculosis, heart or circulatory failure, and pneumonia. Prisoners in need of urgent medical attention included men suffering from cancer, partial paralysis, cardiac problems, tuberculosis, detached retinas, and asthma.

Shortly after the EOHR report's release, two more political detainees died in prison apparently due to inadequate medical attention. One of them, Bekheit Abdel Rahman Salim, a thirty-eight-year-old teacher who was partially paralyzed and had severe bed sores on his buttocks, was seen by an EOHR representative in Tora Istiqbal prison on March 12, so weak "that he was unable to speak and fainted during the visit." He was transferred shortly thereafter to Liman Tora prison hospital and then to a regular cell in Fayoum prison, where he died on March 26.

Egyptian rights groups increased the focus in 1997 on the routine nature of torture and ill-treatment in police stations. In a March report, EOHR stated that torture was "widespread," and was used on suspects to coerce confessions and on their relatives to obtain information or force suspects to surrender to authorities. In one case, eighty-five-year-old Ahmed Abdel Halim al-Zeini was held for one week in Meit Ghamr station in Dakahliya, in Lower Egypt, for a minor offense, kicked in the genitals by an officer, and died in early June 1996 from what a June 3 forensic medical report said was injury to the testicles that led to cardiac arrest. EOHR's report profiled the cases of fifty-seven citizens who were tortured in police custody between December 1993 and September 1996, twelve of whom died. It said the most common abuse was cuffing victims' hands behind the back and suspending them "in a slaughtered animal position," which "is usually accompanied by beatings, punching or electric shocks."

These findings were reinforced by a report of the Nadim Center for the Management and Rehabilitation of Victims of Violence, another Cairo-based NGO. Nadim maintained, too, that torture by police was a nationwide phenomenon, and described various methods of torture that had been used on its clients including: beating with sticks and whips; kicking with boots; electric shocks;

and suspension from one or both arms. Nadim noted that in all cases victims had been threatened, insulted and humiliated, and in some cases, particularly those involving women, victims had been stripped, exposed to "verbal and tactile sexual insults," and threatened with rape.

Passions ran high in the countryside as grass-roots organizing proliferated in advance of the implementation in October of the agricultural reform law (Law No. 96 of 1992) that lifted rent controls and protections against eviction put place during the Nasser era in the 1950s. Protests, some of them violent, erupted nationwide. The independent, Cairo-based Land Center for Human Rights (LCHR) documented how security forces intervened to prevent conferences and meetings that had become increasingly popular mechanisms during the year for bringing together farmers to discuss concerns about the law. On May 14, for example, violence broke out when security forces forcibly dispersed participants at a peaceful conference in Nazlit al-Ashter village in Giza, near Cairo. On June 25, security forces prevented farmers in Saft al-Arafa village, south of Cairo, from holding a meeting, and twenty were arrested after the village farming cooperative was burned down. LCHR reported that 176 conferences had been held on the land law since the beginning of the year through August 20; forty-three had been cancelled, and thirty-one people arrested. Authorities also arrested farmers after peaceful protest marches were dispersed. In one incident on August 4, sixty-three farmers were arrested in the Salihiya area of Ismailiya after police broke up their march. Farmers interviewed by Human Rights Watch in July said that security forces had also arrested local activists in advance of planned protest demonstrations and forced farmers to remove black flags that flew in symbolic opposition to the law.

Authorities also targeted supporters of the farmers. For example, four activists were arrested on June 17, including journalist Hamdin Sabbahi, a prominent Nasserite. Prosecutors accused them of "promoting ideas intended to incite a social class to use violence against other classes," "acquiring printed materials prepared for distribution" to further those ideas, and related charges. They were detained until September 25. As of October 5, at least five other activists remained in detention, according to EOHR, along with some 182 of the 822 farmers arrested during the year, according to LCHR. As of September 29, fifteen had been killed and 238 injured in rural unrest related to the land law since the beginning of the year.

Freedom of expression, including press freedom, faced challenges during the year from several quarters. Scholars at al-Azhar, the state-funded university which has served as an authoritative center of Sunni Islamic scholarship for 1,000 years, continued to take actions that fueled a climate of intimidation and physical danger for Egyptian intellectuals. For example, Dr. Hassan Hanafi, a professor of philosophy at Cairo University, was singled out as an apostate in an April 29 statement issued by Dr. Yehia Ismail, secretary general of the Azhar Scholars Front (ASF). He called for Dr. Hanafi's expulsion from the university, and claimed that his work in Islamic studies "scorned, mocked and derided every feature of the nation's religion." The independent, Cairo-based Center for Human Rights Legal Aid (CHRLA), condemning initiatives of this sort in a press release it issued the next day, stated that "such allegations, coming from respected institutions such as al-Azhar, will be like a license for armed Islamic organizations to kill, especially in the current atmosphere where fanatical religious intolerance is rampant."

A 1992 court sentence of one-year imprisonment for writer Ala' Hamed, because his novel *The Bed* was judged immoral pursuant to vaguely worded penal code provisions, was upheld on appeal on May 25. The court also supported the lower court's order that the book be confiscated. Public prosecutors filed the original complaint against Hamed in 1991, charging that his book showed "disrespect for religious clerics," and advocated "immorality" and "sexual freedom." CHRLA, while acknowledging that the exercise of free expression should not conflict with the protection of public morals, pointed out that the penal code provisions used to prosecute Hamed were "imprecise," and served to intimidate writers and "create an atmosphere in which the exercise of freedom of opinion and expression becomes a risky adventure fraught with danger [of imprisonment.]"

The government moved a step closer to its goal of controlling the content of sermons delivered in Egypt's tens of thousands of private mosques. In December 1996, with the amendment of Law. No. 272 of 1959, parliament required mosque preachers to obtain permits from the Ministry of Awqaf (religious endowments) or face fines and possible one-month jail terms. Under the law, four-member committees (two representatives from the ministry and two from Al-Azhar) in each province were assigned the task of vetting applications. "Preachers who have personal ambitions or seek popularity should not have a place in the propagation of Islam," said Awqaf minister Hamdi Zaqzug after the measure was passed. The minister reported in June 1997 that 15,000 permits had been issued.

Outright censorship by authorities and criminal prosecution of journalists compromised press freedom for Egyptian and foreign newspapers alike. For example, in August the interior minister charged that the opposition biweekly *al-Sha'b* (Cairo) was "the organ of the Moslem Brotherhood and the terrorists," adding that "everything that is printed in this newspaper is a lie." His complaint led to the initiation of legal proceedings that month against editor-in-chief Magdi Hussein and five other journalists for a series of allegedly libelous articles about corruption and abuse of power by the minister and his associates. The prosecutor general subsequently banned Egyptian and foreign media from any reporting about the lawsuit, and later ordered that *al-Sha'b* suspend publication of its next three issues because it had defied his ban. The trial against the *Sha'b* six began on October 15, and the next session was set for November 10; the journalists faced up to three years in prison if convicted.

Authorities also prevented the printing in Cairo of 5,000 copies of the September 17 issue of *al-Hayat* because a front-page article about the Halaib triangle, the long-disputed border area between Egypt and Sudan, was deemed biased. On September 14, two publishers and three editors with the weekly *al-Jadida* magazine and its parent—the London-based, Saudi-owned *al-Sharq al-Awsat* daily—were convicted of libeling President Mubarak's sons Ala' and Gamal for an article that was never published but had been advertised on May 27 in *al-Sharq al-Awsat*, concerning the sons' alleged corrupt business practices. The five, tried in absentia, were fined, and sentenced to one-year prison terms. The Egyptian who wrote the unpublished article, Sayyed Abdel Ati, was fined and sentenced to six months in prison.

The Right to Monitor

The number of Egyptian human rights organizations continued to expand and gain increasing international exposure and recognition, but the government remained hostile to their wide-ranging work and members of leading organizations told Human Rights Watch that internal security agents continued to monitor closely their activities. EOHR, which was founded in 1985, continued its legal battle to have overturned the decision of the Ministry of Social Affairs denying it registration under the associations law (Law. No. 32 of 1964) on the grounds that there was another group carrying out similar work. EOHR maintained that Law No. 32 was an unconstitutional infringement on freedom of association and, along with other Egyptian NGOs, has long advocated its repeal. In the past, the law has been invoked to dissolve NGOs and seize their assets. The law constitutes unwarranted interference with free association by preventing openly functioning NGOs from securing legal status and unreasonably forcing these groups to operate under the constant threat of closure.

A Human Rights Watch researcher was refused entry into Egypt on the night of June 19, despite the fact that Human Rights Watch had notified the Egyptian government well in advance of his visit. He was detained for ten hours at Cairo International Airport, refused permission to make any phone calls, and forcibly placed on the next return flight on June 20. Some Human Rights Watch publications were confiscated from his luggage. He was subsequently allowed to return to Egypt and conduct his research, although his movements and contacts were openly monitored by SSI officers in plainclothes.

The Role of the International Community

European Union

Negotiations continued between the European Commission and the Egyptian government over the text of an Euro-Mediterranean Association Agreement, similar to those already concluded with Israel, Tunisia and Morocco. Article 2 of each agreement states that "respect for human rights and democratic principles...constitute an essential element" of the agreement. Egypt reportedly objected to having to accept an accompanying joint declaration, identical to one accompanying the Morocco agreement but not those with Israel and Tunisia, which specifies that breaches of the "human rights" and "democratic principles" conditionality could trigger suspension of the agreement.

United States

Egypt continued to enjoy a strong bilateral relationship with the U.S. in areas of trade, aid and military cooperation. As in past years, the Clinton administration also relied on Egyptian officials as intermediaries in ongoing negotiations between the Israeli government and the Palestinian Authority. Egypt's annual $2.1 billion package of U.S. aid, second only to Israel's, included $1.3 billion in Foreign Military Financing and $815 million in economic support funds. Egypt was also a major market for U.S. products, importing some $3 billion annually.

Secretary of State Madeleine Albright articulated the basis for the long-standing bilateral ties at a joint press conference following her September 13 meeting in Alexandria, Egypt, with President Mubarak. She said that the U.S.-Egyptian relationship "has grown in importance and scope every year," praised Egypt as "a vital force for moderation in a region where violent extremists have inflicted enormous suffering," and added that "the United States considers Egypt a valuable partner in the quest for peace and stability, especially in the Middle East and Gulf." Citing bilateral efforts "to bring the peace process back to life," she said: "The United States cannot forget that without Egypt there would have been no peace process; without Egypt there would have been no Camp David Accord, no Madrid Conference, no Oslo process, and no handshake on the White House lawn." The secretary omitted mention of human rights when identifying common interests of the two countries—which she identified as "a joint commitment to peace, security and development," and "a rapidly increasing exchange of business people, students and tourists traveling back and forth between our two nations"—and did not make references to human rights elsewhere in the text.

The State Department, in its 1997 report "United States Policies in Support of Religious Freedom: Focus on Christians," stated that the U.S. embassy in Cairo "maintains a continuous dialogue with the Government of Egypt on all human rights issues." More specific information about the nature and substance of this dialogue was not publicly disclosed. The U.S. embassy in Cairo told Human Rights Watch in September that the only high-level demarches during the year focused on female genital mutilation and religious persecution.

IRAN

Human Rights Developments

The upset victory of Mohammad Khatami, a presidential candidate disfavored by much of the clerical establishment, changed the nature of the human rights debate in and about Iran. In May elections, Iranian voters gave Khatami more than twenty million votes compared to the seven million for Majles speaker Ali Akbar Nateq Nouri. Human rights discourse then turned on a new question: Would the new president have the power and the will to fulfill campaign promises to guarantee the rights of citizens and institutionalize the rule of law?

The violations of human rights that continued in the months leading up to Khatami's inauguration on August 3 underlined the challenge facing him in this realm. Executions after unfair trials proliferated, protesters were arbitrary detained, and religious minorities, government critics, and independent thinkers were targeted for persecution. The authorities carried out mass arrests in response to popular unrest over economic problems in different parts of the country. Elements within the government continued to tolerate or encourage the activities of violent religious zealots known as Partisans of the Party of God (Ansar-e Hezbollah or Hezbollahi), who continued to assault and intimidate writers and intellectuals, disrupt gatherings critical of government policies and carry out violent raids on the offices of magazines and newspapers with which they disagreed.

The challenges facing Khatami were compounded by competition among centers of political power within the government. While the presidency is accorded considerable power under the constitution, he is subordinate to leader of the Islamic Republic Ayatollah Khamene'i. In addition, Khatami's predecessor as president, Hojatoleslam Rafsanjani, did not withdraw from the political scene. He was appointed head of the Council for the Determination of Exigencies, a body with loosely defined power to determine policy "in the best interests of society." Originally created in 1988 by Ayatollah Khomeini to override legislative gridlock between the parliament and the Council of Guardians, the Council for the Determination of Exigencies expanded its powers to take unilateral action on a number of occasions. In addition to the competition between these three centers of executive power, the parliament (Majles) and the Council of Guardians also exercised powers under the constitution.

The Council of Guardians, an appointed body responsible for upholding Islamic principles in government policy, vetted candidates wishing to run in the presidential elections. In all, of the 238 candidates who sought to run, the council approved only four, all from the country's clerical leadership. The council is charged, under the constitution, with assessing such factors as a candidate's wisdom and piety. It is not required to give reasons for excluding candidates, and those rejected have no right of appeal.

The constitution requires that the president be a Shi'a Muslim, thereby excluding the approximately 20 percent of the population who are Sunni Muslims or members of other religious minorities. Women are also ineligible to run for president.

Khatami's election campaign was itself disrupted by sometimes violent mobs of religious conservatives who created disturbances at rallies, shouting down speakers and beating those in attendance. Moreover, there were reports that hundreds of election workers were detained by elements within the security forces opposed to his platform.

The government repeatedly showed its intolerance of public gatherings critical of its policies. Following the death in disputed circumstances on December 2, 1996 of a prominent Sunni cleric, Mollah Mohammed Rabi'i, in Kermanshah, the major city in the province of Kurdestan, security forces broke up his funeral procession, sparking three days of violent clashes between Sunnis and the security forces. A police colonel was killed in these clashes. Accounts of the number of civilians killed range from an official count of four to a claim by a Kurdish opposition group of scores of civilian deaths. The demonstrators blamed the government for Mollah Rabi'i's death.

Even wholly peaceful memorial ceremonies to mark the anniversary of the death of the first prime minister of the Islamic Republic, Mehdi Bazargan, were banned or disrupted. On January 31 a Hezbollahi-led group released ammonium chloride gas in a hall in Tehran where Bazargan's supporters

had gathered. Attempts to hold similar gatherings in Hamadan, Qazvin and Zanjan were blocked by security police. Javad Ghanbari, one of the organizers of the Zanjan memorial ceremony, wrote an open letter to the Iranian authorities protesting his detention and ill-treatment by the security forces, who he said shot at him when arresting him.

On February 16, riot police broke up a protest by striking refinery workers outside the Oil Ministry in Tehran. The workers were protesting what they said was the government's failure to make good on promises to provide pay raises, food coupons and housing loans for workers. Detainees held after such incidents could be held indefinitely with no access to lawyers or family. While most were released quickly, some were held for longer periods and faced accusations of political offenses carrying heavy penalties. It was reported by opposition sources inside and outside Iran that four participants in the February oil workers demonstration were executed. Authorities did not release the names of those arrested or details of trials and sentences.

On August 14 clashes between demonstrators and police were reported in Neyriz, east of Shiraz. According to eyewitness reports the clashes erupted when police broke up a peaceful demonstration over administrative redistricting and arrested more than ninety demonstrators. Dozens of the protesters suffered injuries.

The government continued to make prominent announcements of the discovery of plots and espionage activities directed against it, thus seeking to discredit political criticism as hostile foreign interference. On January 16 the security forces announced the arrest of six "spies" in west Azarbaijan province. On March 3 fifty people were arrested in Orumieh in Western Azarbaijan and accused of espionage. On August 9, Mohammad Assadi, a seventy-year-old lawyer accused of involvement in a 1980 coup plot, was executed as a spy. Evidence cited in his trial included his having traveled to Israel before the 1979 revolution, when the two countries had diplomatic relations. He had been in prison for four years. His execution just days after President Khatami's inauguration was seen by many as an assertion of independence by the cleric-dominated judicial branch and a challenge to the new president's vows to protect rights. In September Siavash Bayani, a former army colonel who served in the Iran-Iraq war, was executed as an American spy. He had returned to Iran in 1995 after living for several years in the United States.

All espionage cases are tried before Revolutionary Courts, in which procedures fall far short of international standards for a fair trial. Defendants are denied access to legal counsel and may be held indefinitely incommunicado in pre-trial detention. Political offenders and accused drug traffickers are also tried before Revolutionary Courts. Scores of persons convicted for drug trafficking were executed in 1997, many in public.

Grand Ayatollah Hossein Ali Montazeri, the former designated successor to Ayatollah Khomeini as leader of the Islamic Republic, and several other senior Shi'ite clerical leaders in Qom and Mashhad, were constrained from expressing their views openly and subjected to restrictions on their movements and access to the outside world. Score of followers of clerical leaders critical of the government remained in prison, although the legal basis for their detention was not clear.

On March 14 the parliament approved a ten-year extension of the Law of Hodoud and Qissas, originally approved for a five-year trial period. The law provided for corporal punishments such as lashing and amputation as well as particularly cruel methods of execution like stoning. In August, the Iranian press reported that Zoleykhah Kadkhoda, a twenty-year-old woman, survived an attempt to stone her to death after she was convicted of adultery in Boukan. She was buried in a ditch from the waist down and pelted with stones, but revived after being carried unconscious to the morgue. Judicial authorities were deciding whether to reimpose the penalty on her, according to the press reports.

The banning of newspapers and magazines critical of the government and the prosecution of independent writers continued. In January, Karamollah Tavahodi, a Kurdish writer in Mashhad, was arrested and sentenced to one year in prison because of official objections to the content of volume five of his *Historical Movement of Kurds in Khorasan.*

On February 12, the 15 Khordad Foundation, an organization with close ties to the clerical leadership, announced an increase to U.S.$2.5 million in the reward for the murder of the British novelist Salman Rushdie. There was no official repudiation of this announcement, although President Rafsanjani did stress that the foundation was "nongovernmental," and that government policy remained "unchanged." The government did not condemn the threats to Mr. Rushdie's life stemming from the pronouncement by Ayatollah Khomeini that he should be killed for insulting Islam in his novel *The Satanic Verses.*

Faraj Sarkouhi, the editor of *Adineh* magazine, was arrested in February on charges of attempting to leave the country illegally. He was held for months without access to family members or his lawyer. Controversy surrounded his whereabouts during the six weeks preceding December 13, 1996, when Sarkouhi was presented at an unusual press conference at Tehran's Mehrabad airport in an apparent attempt by the authorities to refute accusations that they had been holding him during this period. At the press conference, Sarkouhi declared that he had been in Germany during this six-week period. This version of events was undermined by the publication abroad of a letter smuggled out of Iran in which Sarkouhi claimed that he was the victim of an elaborate plot orchestrated by the authorities, who had held him in detention during the period in question. In the letter, he claimed that throughout this period he had been subjected to interrogation and torture. In June, 1997 authorities announced that Sarkouhi was on trial for espionage, an offense that carried the death penalty. They seemed at the time to be seeking to use Sarkouhi as a bargaining chip with Germany following the May verdict of a Berlin court implicating the

Iranian government in the killing of four of its political opponents in Berlin in 1992. The German authorities appeared to corroborate Sarkouhi's version of events by stating that he had not entered the country in late 1996 and that the German entry visa stamped in his passport appeared to be forged. In September, after the case had attracted concern internationally, it was reported that Sarkouhi had been sentenced to one year of imprisonment for circulating harmful propaganda, a charge that had not been mentioned prior to his trial. Although the sentence was unexpectedly light in view of the original espionage charge, the fact remains that Sarkouhi was the victim of arbitrary detention and unfair trial simply for exercising his right to peaceful expression. He was denied access to his lawyer, and his trial took place in secret, in violation of international standards.

Cases in addition to that of Sarkouhi cast a long shadow over the freedom of editors and writers throughout the year. In January, Professor Ahmad Tafazzoli of Tehran University was found dead in Punak, a suburb northwest of Tehran. He was known to have contacts with many Iranian academics working abroad, and many of his colleagues believed that the authorities were behind his death. While the precise circumstances remained unclear, Tafazzoli's death created a climate of fear at the university and discouraged criticism of the government.

In February, Ebrahim Zalzadeh, publisher of the independent magazine *Mayar,* "disappeared." His body was discovered in the Tehran morgue on March 29. Members of his family accused the authorities of responsibility for his death. Zalzadeh was one of eight writers and publishers who had offered to share in the punishment of Abbas Maroufi, editor of *Gardoun* magazine, who was sentenced to receive twenty-five lashes in February 1996 for writing an article critical of the government.

In April, Mohammad Sadegh Javadi-Hessar, the editor of *Tous* magazine, was convicted of "causing public confusion." He was banned from journalism for ten years and fined the equivalent of U.S. $1,000 for an article critical of higher education policy.

The program presented by President Khatami promised a brighter future for freedom of expression. Ata'ollah Mohajerani, his nominee for the key post of minister of culture and Islamic guidance, told the Iranian parliament prior to his confirmation, "I am in favor of cultural tolerance....We must create a climate in the Islamic Republic in which individuals will be able to express their views on various issues." He also condemned the activities of the Ansar-e Hezbollah, stating, "We must ultimately decide whether we are going to live under a system of law and order or not."

However, in an indication that writers' problems continued after Khatami's election, Hezbollahi militants ransacked the offices of *Iran-e Farda* magazine in August. Although no action was taken against the perpetrators, the Ministry of Islamic Guidance issued an unprecedented condemnation of the attack, stating, "This kind of action will lead to anarchy....All protests against the contents of a publication must be done through legal channels and in a rational manner." In September, the editor of *Iran News*, an English-language daily, Morteza Firouzi was arrested, following publication of articles advocating the release of foreign nationals held in Iranian prisons. He remained in detention and was accused of being a United States spy.

Iran's constitution provides only qualified commitments to the principle of non-discrimination on the basis of religion or ethnic identity. In practice, discrimination is widespread and institutionalized, and, in the case of Baha'is and evangelical Christians, amounts to outright persecution. In February, death sentences against Musa Talebi and Zabihollah Mahrami, two Baha'is convicted as spies by Revolutionary Courts, were approved by the Supreme Court. Allegations of espionage for Israel were often used by the government as a pretext for persecuting Baha'is. The headquarters of the Baha'i World Community was situated in Haifa, in Israel.

The Martyr Qudusi Judicial Center in Tehran, which handles prosecutions for dress code violations, issued new guidelines in

February providing that women who wore a "thin or short scarf" or who otherwise violated the requirement to cover the hair and the back of the neck, would be subjected to fines, prison terms of up to three months, or up to seventy-four lashes. Security forces carried out mass arrests of violators of dress and other moral codes. For example, in December 1996 police in north Tehran announced the arrest of 130 young people who had participated in mixed-gender parties in private houses.

The Right to Monitor

There were no independent nongovernmental human rights organizations operating inside the country, although several semi-official organizations published mild criticism of government policies, indicating a slight opening in the public human rights debate. The government denied access to all independent international human rights organizations that applied to conduct field research, including Human Rights Watch. In June Human Rights Watch asked to send an observer to attend the trial of Faraj Sarkouhi but this too was denied. Maurice Copithorne, the U.N. special representative on the human rights situation in Iran, applied unsuccessfully to visit the country during 1997.

Government critic Habibullah Peyman was denied permission to attend an International environmental conference in Germany in February. Abbas Amir-Entezam, a former deputy prime minister who was sentenced to life imprisonment in 1979, continued to speak out on human rights issues after he was released from prison. His movements continued to be restricted, and the authorities made clear that charges of espionage on which he had been convicted still stood. Prominent philosopher Abdol Karim Soroush, who speaks openly about the need for respect of basic freedoms, was denied permission to travel to numerous international conferences to which he had been invited after his return to Iran in April. His speaking and teaching in Iran was curtailed by threats from Hezbollahi mobs.

The Role of the International Community

United Nations

Maurice Copithorne, the U.N. special representative on the human rights situation in Iran, submitted his third report to the Commission on Human Rights in April, concluding that "violations of generally accepted human rights norms are occurring in Iran and that in some cases, by act of commission or omission, the government must be responsible for them."

In April, the commission again condemned Iran for gross and systematic violations of human rights. The resolution emphasized government involvement in the killing of dissidents abroad and the continuing threats to the life of Salman Rushdie.

European Union

The European Union (E.U.) officially suspended its policy of "critical dialogue" with the Iranian government in April, following the verdict of a German court holding "the Iranian political leadership" responsible for the murder of Sadeq Sharifkandi, the leader of the Kurdish Democratic Party of Iran, an armed opposition group, and three companions in Berlin's Mykonos restaurant in 1992. While E.U. member states, with the exception of Greece, withdrew their ambassadors from Tehran, European leaders showed no eagerness to recast their relations with Tehran over the Mykonos verdict or other human rights issues.

Human rights was one area of Iranian policy that the "critical dialogue" explicitly aimed to improve. But commercial interests remained paramount both before and after the dialogue was suspended, and there was little evidence of European initiatives on human rights. German Foreign Minister Klaus Kinkel made clear that for Germany there would be "no economic sanctions and no severing of relations." Following the election of Khatami as president, the E.U. reportedly initiated discussions with Tehran regarding the possible return of their ambassadors.

In July, the French government announced that it would insure a $500 million export loan provided to Iran by a French bank. In September, the French oil company Total announced a $2 billion dollar investment, in partnership with a Russian and a Malaysian firm, in the development of the Iranian off-shore gas industry. The French company had the explicit support of its government and the E.U. in its decision to invest.

United States

The U.S. had no diplomatic relations with Iran, and maintained unilateral sanctions imposed in 1995 because of what the Clinton administration termed Iranian policies of "supporting international terrorism,"and "pursuing the creation of weapons of mass destruction." The Iranian government continued to deny these accusations.

The E.U. decision to suspend "critical dialogue" and the election of President Khatami were conducive to narrowing the gap between U.S. and E.U. policy toward Iran. While the E.U. signaled displeasure with Iran after the Mykonos verdict, prominent voices in the U.S. advocated reevaluating its call for multilateral economic sanctions against Iran in light of evidence that they had won scant international support and had achieved little in the areas of policy that the sanctions had been designed to change, including human rights. At the June summit of the group of eight industrialized countries in Denver, the U.S., Russia, Japan, Canada and the major European powers were able to agree on common language "noting with interest" the election results and the "constructive role" of Iran in U.N. peace efforts in Tajikistan. These rare positive comments on Iran were coupled with a call for the Iranian government, "to respect the human rights of all Iranian citizens and to renounce the use of terrorism, including against Iranian citizens living abroad."

In June in a speech to the National Arab-American Association in Washington, D.C., Acting Assistant Secretary of State for Near Eastern Affairs David Welch reiterated the five areas, including "lack of respect for international standards of human rights," in which the U.S. is demanding progress as a condition for improved relations. Welch welcomed "the sign that Iran will permit democratic expression," and noted that the U.S. "will continue to work with our allies to bring our approaches on Iran closer together." Also in June, appearing at a press conference with British Prime Minister Tony Blair, President Clinton referred to Khatami's election as "interesting and hopeful." On September 30, with reference to the French oil company Total's decision to lead a multi-billion dollar investment project in Iran despite U.S. sanctions, State Department spokesperson James Rubin said that Washington might forego moves to impose penalties on Total if France agreed to increase pressure on Iran to halt what he referred to as its support of terrorism and its accumulation of weapons of mass destruction. Many in the U.S. Congress, however, opposed any relaxation of the U.S. embargo of Iran. On July 23, for instance, 222 members of the House of Representatives wrote to President Clinton urging that sanctions against Iran be toughened.

The Iran chapter in the State Department's *Country Reports on Human Rights Practices for 1996* was generally accurate and comprehensive. But throughout the year human rights took a back seat to other issues in Washington's relations with Iran, including Iran's opposition to the Israeli-Palestinian peace process and concern that Iran was developing a mid-range ballistic missile capacity.

Relevant Human Rights Watch reports:

Iran—Religious and Ethnic Minorities: Discrimination in Law and Practice, 9/97
Iran—Leaving Human Rights Behind: The Context of the Presidential Elections, 5/97

IRAQ AND IRAQI KURDISTAN

Human Rights Developments

The government of Iraq continued to engage in a broad range of gross human rights abuses, including mass arrests, summary executions, extrajudicial executions with no pretense of due process, and "disappearances." Armed Kurdish political parties and Iraqi security forces continued to be implicated in abuses in the portions of northern Iraq under Kurdish control. In May, Turkey launched a major military campaign against bases of the Workers Party of Kurdistan (PKK, see chapter on Turkey) in northern Iraq, adding to the large numbers displaced by ongoing fighting among armed Kurdish political parties in that region. Iranian airstrikes against an Iraqi-based Iranian opposition group reportedly resulted in civilian injuries.

The United Nations maintained its economic sanctions against Iraq, now in their eighth year. The implementation of U.N. Resolution 986 allowed Iraq to sell limited amounts of oil and use the revenues to purchase goods to meet humanitarian needs. These goods began arriving in March, but malnutrition and shortages of medicines and spare parts for sanitary infrastructure continued to cause hardship among the Iraqi people.

Human Rights Developments in Government-Controlled Iraq

Opposition groups in exile reported mass arrests and summary executions, many in conjunction with the December 12, 1996 attempted assassination of President Saddam Hussein's son Uday. For example, the Tehran-based Supreme Council for the Islamic Revolution in Iraq (SCIRI) and the Amman-based Iraqi National Accord (INA) both reported arrests of between 600 and 2000 people in the period immediately after the assassination attempt. The London-based Worker Communist Party of Iraq reported mass executions during February and March of 250 prisoners with life sentences or suspended

death sentences at Abu Ghraib prison. These and similar reports were difficult to verify due to Iraq's tight controls on travel, free expression and contacts with foreigners (see below).

Press freedom and freedom of expression and belief remained severely constrained. Iraq's main media outlets were government-owned, and foreign newspapers and magazines were banned. In April the government increased the punishments for ownership of satellite dishes, which have been banned since 1994. The new penalties reportedly included the confiscation of all household furniture, a 1 million dinar fine (approximately U.S. $660 at black market rates), and imprisonment. As in previous years, the government interfered with Shi'a religious observances in Karbala. In June Iraqi forces set up roadblocks outside the city, turning back some Shi'a pilgrims making the annual walk to the tomb of Imam Husayn. Some Shi'a opposition groups also reported clashes between pilgrims and security forces resulting in many arrests.

Despite repeated inquiries by the U.N. Working Group on Enforced or Involuntary Disappearances, the Iraqi government failed to clarify the fate of over 16,000 individuals reported "disappeared" in Iraq. These cases are in addition to those of over 600 persons reported "disappeared" during the Iraqi invasion of Kuwait.

Kurdish and Turkomen families reportedly continued to be forced to leave the economically and strategically important Kirkuk and Khanaqin areas as part of what observers have described as a policy of Arabization in these areas. It is impossible to verify exact numbers, but U.N. sources involved in food distribution in northern Iraq said at least 500 families displaced from their homes during the first six months of 1997 had registered in areas under their supervision. Those displaced suffered delays in obtaining rations, because they had to reregister in a new district. Some were reportedly unwilling to do for fear of undermining their claim to residence in their home districts.

The U.N. Security Council kept in place economic sanctions against Iraq, which were originally imposed in response to Iraq's 1990 invasion of Kuwait. The sanctions block all Iraqi exports, freeze Iraqi assets abroad, and thereby constrain Iraq's ability to pay for goods to meet the population's basic needs, which are excepted on humanitarian grounds from the prohibition of exports to Iraq. The sanctions have contributed since 1990 to a massive public health crisis marked by malnutrition and increasing levels of infant mortality. Resolution 687 (1991) conditioned the lifting of this embargo on a determination by the Security Council that the Iraqi government had complied with demands made in that resolution, including the destruction of its chemical, biological, and nuclear weapons programs and the payment of reparations to Kuwait. In late October Iraq ordered U.S. members of the U.N. Special Commission's arms inspection team to leave the country, and barred other U.S. team members from entering Iraq.

Security Council resolution 986 (1995) allowed the sale of U.S. $2 billion in oil during a 180-day period, but implementation did not begin until December 1996. Resolution 986 allowed Iraq to use $1.3 billion of the oil proceeds to purchase humanitarian supplies, including $260 million in supplies for Kurdish-controlled northern Iraq, which was administered separately. Although the sale of Iraqi oil proceeded relatively smoothly, the purchase and distribution inside Iraq of the humanitarian goods were delayed by disputes over distribution plans, monitoring, and processing of contracts. The first shipments did not begin to reach Iraq until March and the first shipment of medical supplies did not arrive until May. Iraq suspend oil exports from mid-June to mid-August in protest of the ongoing delays. The Iraqi government increased ration amounts for some foodstuffs after the arrival of food shipments. However, with only a small number of U.N. monitors allowed into Iraq it was difficult to determine if distribution was equitable, and whether the quantities of humanitarian supplies reaching the Iraqi people were sufficient to produce significant health improvements. After a week-long visit to Iraq in May, Yasushi Akashi, the head of the U.N. Department of Humanitarian Affairs, said that he and his team of experts saw "clear evidence of prevailing humanitarian suffering which is unmistakable." Resolution 986 was renewed for an additional six-month period in June 1997.

In September Iranian planes bombed bases of the People's Mojahedine Organization, an Iranian opposition group based in Iraq. The group reported that bombs destroyed Mojahedine buildings in Kut and Jalula in southern Iraq, and injured civilians in residential areas of Jalula.

Human Rights Developments in Iraqi Kurdistan

Iraq continued to station ground forces along the border of the Kurdish-controlled region created in the north of the country. The region was located within the "no-fly zone" imposed on Iraq in the aftermath of the Gulf War and Iraq's brutal suppression of an uprising by Kurds and Shiites in March 1991. The zone's airspace was policed by the U.S. and the U.K. from Turkish bases. Iraqi military forces briefly returned to the region in 1996 at the invitation of Kurdish Democratic Party (KDP) forces in fighting against rival Patriotic Union of Kurdistan (PUK) forces and they reportedly engaged in arbitrary arrests and executions of dozens of opponents of the Iraqi government and the KDP at that time. Although Iraq quickly withdrew its uniformed forces after the 1996 invasion, it is reported to have significantly expanded its security presence in areas under KDP control, and in late 1996 the U.S. conducted a mass evacuation of Kurdish and Iraqi personnel who had been employed by the U.S. or U.S. funded humanitarian agencies because of fear for their safety. In January Iraq announced a month-long amnesty for "Iraqis who committed the crime of giving information or communicating with foreign sides," which may have been intended to apply to the thousands who had been in contact with foreigners prior to August 1996. In previous government amnesties individuals who turned themselves in were latter arrested and in some cases executed.

Despite ongoing efforts by the U.S., Turkey and Iran to broker a cease-fire, fighting among rival Kurdish political parties continued throughout the year, with clashes between the KDP and the PUK causing significant displacement of civilians. Both parties have been implicated in a wide array of abuses, including arbitrary arrest of suspected political opponents; torture and ill-treatment of detainees; evictions of supporters of rival parties, and extrajudicial executions of dissident political activists. The KDP alleged PUK responsibility for the assassination of its officials Sirwan Nawroli (January), and Mouhiddin Rahim (March), and the attempted assassination of KDP governor of Irbil Francois Hariri (February). The PUK denied the charges, and alleged the KDP arbitrarily detained its civilian supporters and indiscriminately shelled civilian areas. In April the two parties reportedly exchanged 131 prisoners of war as part of an agreement signed in October 1996.

In May thousands of Turkish forces launched a major offensive against the Workers Party of Kurdistan (PKK), which had bases in northern Iraq. Turkey had launched similar invasions in previous years. The KDP's forces supported the Turkish offensive and some reports linked the KDP to executions of PKK members and civilian supporters, especially in Irbil. On June 15 Turkey announced a partial troop withdrawal, but then launched a second major incursion in late September. In October the PUK alleged that Turkish air and artillery support for KDP attacks on PUK positions resulted in civilian casualties. According to journalists, both the KDP and Turkey have restricted access to the border region since the beginning of the invasion.

Fighting among Kurdish parties and between Turkish and Kurdish forces aggravated an already serious problem of internally displaced people. The U.N. Center for Human Settlement estimated that "more than one third of the population [of the three northern governorates] . . . are internally displaced persons," of whom over 500,000 are in need of assistance. Many have been expelled from their homes in northern Iraq because of presumed support for rival Kurdish

parties, while others fled north after Iraq expelled them from their homes in the Kirkuk and Khanaqin areas (see above). The U.N. High Commission for Refugees' decision in January to close the Atroush camp on the Iraqi/Turkish border uprooted once again that camp's population of approximately 14,000 Turkish Kurdish refugees.

The Right to Monitor

No human rights organizations functioned in government-controlled Iraq. The August 1996 return of Iraqi security forces to portions of northern Iraq under KDP control resulted in the closure of the few small, predominantly Kurdish human rights organizations that had functioned in northern Iraq, as activists either fled the region or were unable to work openly out of fear of retaliation by Iraqi security agents.

The government continued to refuse to grant a visa to the U.N. special rapporteur on Iraq, and to reject repeated requests by the U.N. Commission on Human Rights to station human rights monitors on its territory. Iraq allowed U.N. monitors access to northern and government-controlled Iraq, but they were few in numbers and their mandate was strictly limited to observing and reporting on the implementation of Resolution 986 (1995). Iraq imposed severe penalties for unauthorized contact with foreigners, adding to a climate of fear that discouraged citizens from reporting abuses to international human rights organizations or foreign reporters.

In February Iraq announced that it was willing to allow the International Committee of the Red Cross (ICRC) to visit political prisoners in Iraq, but as of early November agreement on such visits had not been reached.

The Role of the International Community

European Union

The European Union (E.U) is the largest provider of humanitarian assistance to Iraq. European Commissioner for Humanitarian Affairs, Fisheries and Consumer Policy Emma Bonino said in August that she had returned from her trip to Iraq "with a number of doubts" about the embargo, noting that "we have still not found the most effective way of combating a dictatorship." While Bonino said that she did not "feel able to say the suffering of the population today is due to the embargo" alone, she described the humanitarian situation she observed as "serious, especially in the center and south of the country." "The 'food' aspect [of Resolution 986] is being fulfilled in Kurdistan as well as in Iraq. However the medicine side of the contract has been delayed significantly," and the sanitation infrastructure program "has not yet begun," she said.

In July the European Parliament adopted a joint resolution demanding an immediate withdrawal of Turkish troops from northern Iraq and calling upon the PUK and KDP to resolve their differences in a peaceful fashion.

United States

The U.S., in conjunction with Turkey and the U.K., continued to police a "no-fly" zone in northern Iraq, while maintaining a similar zone in southern Iraq in conjunction with the U.K. and Saudi Arabia. France ended its participation in policing the northern no-fly zone in December 1996. The northern zone was designed to provide its predominantly Kurdish population with protection from Iraqi air attacks and to discourage Iraqi ground attacks. However, it did not prevent Turkish ground and air strikes against PKK bases in northern Iraq.

Turkey supplied bases for the "no-fly" zone patrols, and the U.S. worked closely with Turkey in efforts to negotiate a cease-fire between the KDP and the PUK, sending U.S. diplomats into northern Iraq via Turkey for meetings with KDP and PUK leaders. The U.S. declined to express reservations regarding Turkey's invasion of northern Iraq, with State Department spokesman Nicholas Burns saying on June 12, "Turkey's an ally, and we have no reason to question the need for an incursion across the border." The U.S. did condemn Iran's September airstrike against Mojahedine bases in southern Iraq, and State Department spokesman James Rubin said the U.S. would take "whatever action necessary" to prevent both Iraqi and Iranian entry into the no-fly zone.

The U.S. continued to strongly support U.N. sanctions against Iraq and to deny any responsibility for the humanitarian costs of the embargo. In September Under Secretary of State Thomas Pickering denied allegations by Iraq and some Security Council members that the U.S. was delaying delivery of humanitarian goods, saying "It is the *Iraqi* regime which continues to bear the responsibility for the suffering of its people. It is the *Iraqi* regime which cynically causes delays in the distribution of humanitarian goods by refusing to sell oil for two months."

ISRAELI-OCCUPIED WEST BANK AND GAZA STRIP

Human Rights Developments
The Palestinian Authority (PA), established in 1994 pursuant to the Oslo Accords, exercised authority over internal security and other spheres in those areas of the West Bank and Gaza Strip in which the vast majority of Palestinians resided. Israeli military authorities continued to exercise direct authority over a minority of West Bank Palestinians, mostly those living outside the major cities. Israeli civilian authorities exercised authority over Palestinians living in Israeli-annexed East Jerusalem. In addition, Israel exercised extensive control over the freedom of movement of all West Bank and Gaza Palestinians, and over those rights that depended on it.

Tension remained high throughout the year. In March, the PA suspended talks with Israel in protest over Israeli settlement construction in annexed East Jerusalem. A series of deadly bombings were carried out inside Israel and claimed by the Islamic Resistance Movement (Hamas). Israel, in a crippling act of collective punishment against more than 1.5 million Palestinians, imposed the tightest restrictions since the Gulf War on the movement of people and goods in the West Bank and Gaza Strip.

On March 21, a Palestinian suicide bomber killed three Israelis in a cafe in Tel Aviv. A second suicide bombing occurred in the West Jerusalem Mahane Yehuda market on July 30, killing fourteen in addition to the bombers. A third suicide attack, in a West Jerusalem street mall on September 4, killed five passersby and wounded more than 150.

Israel's response to the attacks included a tightening of the existing closure of the West Bank and Gaza Strip. It blocked the flow of goods and of Palestinians into and out of the West Bank and Gaza Strip, and also between the Palestinian-controlled cities of the West Bank. Thus, most West Bank Palestinians except Jerusalem residents were confined to their home towns, regardless of whether they worked or had pressing business elsewhere. Although the official policy was to exempt from the restrictions relief supplies, ambulances, medical professionals and patients, there were numerous reports of their being delayed or turned back at military checkpoints, and of hospitals struggling with reduced staffs. According to hospitals and local human rights organizations, including the Ramallah-based Al-Haq, two Palestinians died after encountering long delays at checkpoints while en route to hospitals.

The Israeli Defense Force (IDF) gradually eased its internal closure of the West Bank after September 14, but kept in place the general closure, in effect since March 1993, which barred Palestinians who lacked hard-to-obtain Israeli permits from entering or transiting through Israel or East Jerusalem. In addition to impairing economic activity, permit denials disrupted family life for the thousands of families whose members lived in different parts of the territories, prevented over one thousand Gazans from reaching the West Bank universities in which they were enrolled, and kept worshippers from the holy sites in Jerusalem, to list but a few of the obstacles created.

Israeli authorities claimed the closure was a justified security measure intended both to assist the investigation of the bombings and to prevent future attacks, and that during closures "every effort is made to ensure that normal life for the Palestinians should continue as far as is possible." In fact, few official mechanisms functioned efficiently and responsively to mitigate the hardships. Despite its stated security grounds, the closure amounted to an act of collective punishment because of its imposition in an indiscriminate fashion on an entire population.

According to local human rights groups, such as the Palestinian Society for the Protection of Human Rights and the Environment (LAWE), there were at least 500 Palestinians in administrative detention held in jails within Israel at the end of October, some 200 of them detained since the July 30 bombing. Administrative detainees were held without charge or trial for renewable periods of up to six months each and were denied their right to a meaningful appeal. The Israeli human rights group B'Tselem, in a May 1997 report, reported that since the signing of the Israeli-PLO accords, Israel had administratively detained Palestinians for longer periods than previously, with over half of the detainees having had their orders extended at least once. The longest-held administrative detainee, Ahmed Qatamesh, entered his sixth year in custody without charge.

The Israeli General Security Service (GSS) continued to torture while interrogating Palestinian security detainees. The standard methods involved a prolonged regimen of confinement in painful and unnatural positions, hooding, exposure to incessantly loud noise, sleep deprivation, and in some cases, vigorous shaking of the head back and forth during questioning. Israeli authorities did not deny using these methods, but stated that they were carefully regulated to ensure that physical pressure remained "moderate" and never amounted to torture. Virtually all human rights organizations and the U.N. Committee against Torture (see below) insisted that these practices, used in combination and over time, constituted torture.

The Israeli Supreme Court continued to abstain from ruling whether GSS interrogation methods violated domestic or international law. During 1996 and 1997 it ruled against Palestinians under interrogation who petitioned the court to bar the use of physical force against them. In those cases in which the GSS contested the petition, the court accepted its arguments that intensive interrogation was required to obtain from the detainees crucial and urgent information affecting Israeli security. The court merely warned that GSS interrogators were bound by Israeli law—which prohibits "the use of force or violence" during interrogation—without commenting on the tension between this law on the one hand and, on the other, the GSS internal guidelines permitting the use of "moderate physical pressure" and the physical methods being consistently alleged by the petitioners.

Violent clashes continued to erupt between Palestinian stone—and bottle—throwers and Israeli soldiers, notably in the Hebron area. Although the security forces relied more on rubber-coated bullets than in previous years, they killed fourteen Palestinians between January and July, according to B'Tselem, and inflicted many serious injuries, including loss of eyesight, by firing these bullets at close range.

Israel stepped up the bulldozing of houses built or expanded without permits in East Jerusalem and the West Bank, demolishing more than one hundred houses, according to local human rights groups. While Israel asserted that it was merely enforcing building codes, the fact that the demolitions surged after the July suicide bombing gave a blatantly political coloring to the practice. Shlomo Dror, spokesman for the Israeli civil authority in the occupied territories, alluded to this in September. "We had delayed [demolitions]," he said, "to try to give some chance to the negotiations between us and the Palestinians and to try to stop tension between us." After the July attack, "everything changed, all the reasons we had before did not exist anymore."

Many Palestinians built without permits because Israeli authorities in the West Bank and the Jerusalem municipality rarely issued permits to Palestinians seeking to construct or enlarge their homes. Jewish homeowners with the same aspirations were granted permits more easily and with extremely rare exceptions, did not risk the razing of their property if found to have built without a permit.

Israel also continued its policy of collective punishment by demolishing the family homes of militants suspected of killing Israelis, even when the militant was himself already dead. At least four family residences were destroyed on these grounds during 1997.

In July, Israel's parliament gave its initial approval to a draft law limiting the right of Palestinians to seek compensation for wrongful injury or death caused by Israeli soldiers. The legislation would disqualify most suits by unduly broadening the definition of "combat activity"—situations for which no compensation could be sought—and by exempting from consideration injuries that are not serious and permanent. If enacted, this bill would eviscerate what has been one of the few means of holding the Israeli army accountable for abuses: civil suits in Israeli courts.

Since 1996, the right of East Jerusalem Palestinians to reside in their native city came under direct threat from a policy apparently designed to further Israel's objective of limiting the Palestinian population of the contested city. These 170,000 Palestinians had overwhelmingly elected not to accept citizenship after Israel annexed the eastern portion of the city. Israel classified these Palestinians as "permanent residents" of Israel. This status was subject to revocation, whether or not a person was born in the city, if the Interior Ministry determined that he or she had established a primary residence elsewhere. Over 1,000 adults had lost their right to legal residence since 1996, and with them, several times that number of dependents. They also lost their health insurance and social benefits, and risked being barred from reentry if they ever ventured out of the city. The appeals process placed the burden of proof on the residents to show through written documentation that Jerusalem remained their "center of life." Meanwhile, Israel did not subject to the same scrutiny and tests the status of Jewish Jerusalem residents who were not citizens. The Interior Minister declared his determination to continue the policy in spite of a promise by Prime Minister Benjamin Netanyahu early in 1997 to review it.

The Palestinian Authority

The Palestinian Authority (PA) failed during 1997 to institutionalize important safeguards against patterns of human rights abuses that included arbitrary detentions without charge or trial, sometimes without disclosing the detainee's whereabouts; mistreatment of detainees under interrogation; and persecution of those who criticized or challenged the authorities. The PA continued to refer cases to the State Security Court, where defendants received almost none of the basic due process rights. The preeminent forum for airing human rights issues remained the Palestinian Legislative Council, but its influence was diminished by the dismissive attitude of the executive branch toward its activities and resolutions.

In August, Palestinian human rights groups, including LAWE, estimated the total number of detainees being held by the PA without charge or trial at between 200 and 300. The following month, at least eighty suspected Hamas activists were rounded up and held without charge, following Israeli and U.S. pressure for a crackdown in the wake of the September 4 bombing in Jerusalem.

The independent Palestinian Human Rights Monitoring Group (PHRMG) issued a report on May 27 alleging "widespread" torture of detainees under interrogation, based on a study of forty-two West Bank and Gaza residents who underwent interrogation since 1996. The report stated that, according to their testimony, "all suspects were beaten, over half with the aid of a weapon or while tied in a painful position." Nine were either subjected to immersion in cold water or exposed to cold weather or burns from cigarettes or other hot objects, PHRMG reported.

One of the five suspicious deaths in

custody between January and September resulted in a criminal trial by the time this report went to press. A military court was convened one day after the June 30 death of Nasser Abed Radwan from blows to the head. It sentenced three officers to death and three others to prison terms. As in other cases that caused an uproar, the announcement of a trial, conviction and sentencing so quickly after the death suggested an effort by the authorities above all to mollify critics, with little regard for ensuring that the defendants enjoyed their rights in court. None of the death penalties handed down by Palestinian courts had been carried out as of this writing.

There were some gestures by the PA in response to human rights criticism. In July, Fayez abu Rahmeh was named to replace Attorney General Khaled al-Qidra, who had gained notoriety for ordering the arrest of several critics of the PA and other measures that undermined the rule of law. And on July 1, Police Chief Ghazi Jabali warned the security services to curtail abuses and violence among their ranks. "We will not be tolerant of anyone, no matter what their rank, if there is a complaint about him from a citizen who was beaten," he announced in advertisements in Palestinian newspapers in which he urged people to voice their complaints.

Soon after becoming attorney general, Abu Rahmeh promised to examine the cases of some 180 detainees that he said were being held without charge or trial, and to try or release them "as soon as possible." But after he ordered the release of ten detainees for lack of evidence on August 15, Palestinian security forces promptly rearrested the men.

At least three men reputed to have sold land to Israelis were murdered in circumstances that strongly suggested official tolerance if not involvement in the killing. They were killed shortly after the PA announced in early May that it would seek the death penalty for Palestinians convicted of selling land to Jews, pursuant to Jordanian law, which remains in effect in the West Bank. Justice Minister Freih Abu Medein made inflammatory statements at the time that seemed to give a green light to violence against suspected land dealers. For example, after the May 9 murder of land dealer Farid Bashiti, Abu Medein told the press, "As I have said before, expect the unexpected for these matters because nobody from this moment will accept any traitor who sells his land to Israelis." The PA made no arrests in any of the killings.

After two years in which newspapers were confiscated and journalists threatened and arrested, the local Palestinian press generally avoided direct criticism of President Arafat, although criticism within certain limits of lower PA officials was tolerated. While public dissent was not systematically suppressed, critics of the PA continued to be at risk of arrest. Gazan lawyer Jameel Salameh was detained on April 26 in connection with an article he wrote that compared the PA unfavorably with the government of Israel in its handling of corruption. He was released after one week without charge. On July 2, Palestinian Preventive Security forces arrested Fathi Subuh, a professor of education at al-Azhar University in Gaza, shortly after he had given his students an examination containing a question on corruption at the university and within the PA. The official claim that "security reasons" were behind the arrest was undermined when security forces confiscated the students' examination booklets from his home. Subuh was allowed no contact with his family or lawyer for more than a month. Petitions to secure his release from detention in October, at which time he had still not been charged, were rejected by the Palestinian High Court of Justice on the grounds that the case was before the State Security Court and therefore beyond its jurisdiction, according to the Gaza-based Palestinian Centre for Human Rights.

In the face of PA intimidation of critics, the Palestinian Legislative Council was the preeminent forum for debating and exposing issues of human rights and corruption. When live coverage of the council's stations proved popular among West Bank viewers, the PA responded by jamming the signal and detaining Daoud Kuttab, the journalist responsible for arranging the broadcasts. Kuttab was released on May 27 after one week in detention without charge. Although the PA had not, as of early November, permitted the resumption of extensive live coverage of the council's sessions, the West Bank's local television stations continued to offer talk and call-in shows that provided a lively contrast to the staid PA-controlled station.

The Right to Monitor

Israel permitted human rights organizations to collect and disseminate information in the areas under its control. However, closures kept human rights workers, like other Palestinians who did not hold Jerusalem identity cards, from moving freely among regions within the West Bank and Gaza Strip. Palestinian lawyers were frequently unable to reach clients in jails inside Israel.

On July 27, Israel renewed for six months the administrative detention of Sha'wan Jabarin, fieldwork coordinator at Al-Haq. He has been held off and on for a total of nearly five years since 1989, all of that time without charge or trial.

The PA allowed human rights organizations to operate in the territory under its jurisdiction. For a variety of reasons, including pressure on those who publicly criticized the PA, some of these groups opted for tactics other than public denunciation to make known their concerns about PA practices.

On October 26, Palestinian security forces arrested Khaled Amayreh, a journalist and human rights activist, after he published a report on the torture of Hamas detainees in a PA center near Hebron. Amayreh said later that he was held for almost two days and verbally abused by Jibril Rajoub, head of the Preventive Security Service in the West Bank. He was released without charge.

The PA continued to deny to rights groups regular access to prisons, although ad hoc visits were granted to lawyers and human rights workers in their individual capacities. The human rights group LAWE stated on October 20 that the head of General Intelligence in the West Bank, responsible for detainees under investigation, had barred its staff from any visits to prisons under its authority. LAWE linked the move to its exposure of torture by Palestinian security forces.

The Role of the International Community

United Nations

The U.N. Committee Against Torture, on May 7, 1997, following its review of Israel's report of February 17, found that Israel's methods of interrogation, as documented by human rights organizations, "constitute torture as defined in article 1 of the Convention." The committee recommended that methods that are in conflict with the Convention "cease immediately" and urged Israel to incorporate the Convention's provisions into domestic law. In its report, Israel did not dispute the charges made by human rights organizations but instead defended the use of "a moderate degree of pressure, including physical pressure," during interrogation of "dangerous terrorists who represent a grave threat."

European Union

In December 1996, the Council of Ministers cited Israel's commitment under the Euro-Mediterranean Association Agreement "to promote compliance with the basic norms of democracy, including respect for human rights and the rule of law." The E.U.-Israel Association Agreement was ratified by most E.U. member states during 1996-1997. Ireland, Netherlands, Denmark and the United Kingdom added ministerial statements or parliamentary resolutions that underscored the human rights dimension of the agreement, in some cases stating that the persistence of abuses such as torture would place Israel in violation of the agreement.

The European Union was the largest single donor to the PA. By 1996 it had provided the PA with U.S.$404 million, and pledged to provide an additional $63 million annually until 1998. In 1997 a preliminary agreement was reached that would promote trade cooperation and development of the PA areas and pave the way for a Euro-Mediterranean Association Agreement. According to

press reports, when President Arafat came to Brussels to sign the interim agreement, E.U. officials cautioned him that the agreement could be jeopardized by a persistent pattern of human rights abuses.

United States

Israel remained the largest recipient of U.S. bilateral aid, with over $3 billion in economic and military assistance. As in past years, there were no indications that the U.S. was prepared to link continued aid to curtailing human rights abuses.

The U.S. remained the principal third party in the Israeli-PLO negotiations. With that process stalemated during much of the year amid mutual recriminations, the Clinton administration publicly pressured the PA to crack down on Hamas and Islamic Jihad. It also broke its customary silence on Israeli abuses on a few occasions when it believed that Israeli practices were complicating the negotiations. Settlement construction was the most frequent but not the only human rights topic mentioned. During Secretary of State Madeleine Albright's first visit to the region in September, she called on President Arafat to fight harder against terrorism while urging Israel to take a "time out" on settlement construction, ease its blockade of the PA-controlled areas, and refrain from "land confiscations, home demolitions and confiscation of I.D.s." It was probably the strongest public statement on human rights uttered in Israel by a U.S. secretary of state in several years. While such public demarches were infrequent, diplomats at the Tel Aviv embassy and Jerusalem consulate actively followed human rights developments throughout the West Bank and Gaza Strip and made numerous demarches both with the Israeli and Palestinian authorities.

U.S. policy toward the PA was dominated by pressure on the PA to act decisively against anti-Israeli violence, one of Israel's conditions for continuing the negotiating process. U.S. pressure was often applied in a manner that, in light of the past record of the PA, condoned arbitrary arrests and other abuses in the name of containing anti-Israeli violence. For example, on August 5, Secretary Albright told reporters, "What we would like is as robust a reaction to the terrorists as [Arafat] took in March 1996, where he undertook a series of very specific steps to deal with the terrorist threat," an apparent reference to the roundup of several hundred suspected Islamists who were then held without charge or trial, and the summary closure of charitable organizations affiliated with Hamas and Islamic Jihad. The U.S. applauded when the PA began rounding up suspected Hamas activists in September—again, without charges being filed—and closing Hamas-affiliated charitable organizations. State Department spokesman James Foley said on September 8, "We think any step in the direction of an active, relentless effort to dismantle the security infrastructure [of the extremist groups] in the territories under the Palestinian Authority's control is a positive step...."

Following the failed assassination attempt by Israeli intelligence agents of Khaled Meshal, a Hamas official in Amman, Jordan, the U.S. obliquely criticized the Israeli operation while urging the PA to continue its crackdown on that organization. Referring to the Hamas institutions the PA shut down as having supported "the terrorist infrastructure that we're trying to eliminate," State Department spokesman James Rubin said on October 6, "We want them shut down. Those people who support them ought to be arrested and ought to stay in jail."

When the PA committed abuses that fell outside the context of the fight against anti-Israel violence—such as by jailing secular critics and journalists, and when a detainee died under suspicious circumstances—the U.S. was more willing to speak out and make demarches. The U.S. took a strong public stance over the arrest of Palestinian-American journalist Daoud Kuttab. And following the death of detainee Yousef al-Baba in February, U.S. Consul in Jerusalem Edward Abington declared, "Too many Palestinians have died while in [PA] custody. Palestinians must not suffer at the hands of other Palestinians. Those who break the law must be held

accountable." He also told Reuters, "Security is important but it can't come at the cost of human rights," a laudable maxim that did not characterize U.S. policy overall toward the PA during 1997.

The U.S. provided an annual $100 million to the West Bank and Gaza Strip, most of it toward programs administered by U.S. Agency for International Development (AID). The self-described goals of AID programs included strengthening democracy and civil society and increasing the flow and diversity of information to citizens. One recipient was the project to provide live televised coverage of the sessions of the Palestinian Legislative Council (*see* above). In August 1997, U.S. assistance to the self-ruled areas was held up following Congress's failure to re-certify, within a deadline provided by legislation, that the PA was doing enough to curb anti-Israeli violence.

Relevant Human Rights Watch reports:

Israel—Without Status or Protection: Lebanese Detainees in Israel, 10/97
Israel/Lebanon: "Operation Grapes of Wrath," 9/97
Palestinian Self-Rule Areas: Human Rights under the Palestinian Authority, 9/97
Israel—Legislating Impunity: The Draft Law to Halt Palestinian Tort Claims, 7/97

SAUDI ARABIA

Human Rights Developments

The government of Saudi Arabia, an absolute monarchy, continued to violate a broad array of civil and political rights, allowing no criticism of the government, no political parties, nor any other potential challenges to its system of government. The use of arbitrary arrest and incommunicado detention, torture, and corporal and capital punishment was common in both political and common criminal cases, and the judicial system failed to provide the most basic fair trial guarantees.

Women faced institutionalized discrimination affecting their freedom of movement and association and their right to equality in employment and education. Muslim religious practices deemed heterodox by government-appointed Islamic scholars, and all non-Muslim religious practices, were banned and subject to criminal prosecution. Labor organizing and collective bargaining were also illegal. Saudi labor law gives employers tremendous control over foreign workers' freedom of movement, control that was often used to force workers to accept oppressive labor conditions or forgo legitimate claims to compensation. Labor protections did not extend to domestic workers, and labor courts rarely enforced the few protections provided by law, such as when workers sought to have the terms of their contracts honored.

Saudi law granted the king broad powers to appoint and dismiss judges and create special courts, undermining judicial independence. Detainees had no right to legal counsel, to examine witnesses, or to call witnesses in their own defense. The law also allowed for unlimited pre-trial detention, and conviction on the basis of uncorroborated confessions. Article 4 of the Basic Law of 1992 waived, for cases of "crimes involving national security," the few protections Saudi law did offer detainees. In this article, these crimes are so broadly defined as potentially to extend to nonviolent opposition to the government.

The Saudi government has not published or disseminated a penal code, code of criminal procedure, or code of judicial procedure. Only a limited number of laws existed in published form. Principles of Islamic law were subject to reinterpretation by government-appointed religious leaders. Judges enjoyed broad discretion in determining which witnesses would be called to testify, and in defining criminal offenses and setting their punishments. These factors encouraged arbitrariness in sentencing and allowed great scope for manipulation of the justice system by well-connected interested parties.

The case of 'Abd al-Karim al-Naqshabandi, a Syrian worker executed on witchcraft charges in December 1996, illustrated how defendants' rights were violated and decisions regarding arrest, trial and sentencing were vulnerable to outside intervention. According to al-Naqshabandi's written testimony, he was arrested in 1994 at the behest of his employer, a nephew of King Fahd. The primary evidence against him appears to have been his alleged possession of religious amulets. Denied access to a lawyer and physically abused in police custody, al-Naqshabandi signed a confession that he attempted to retract during the trial. Although he provided names of twenty-three individuals who could have given testimony on his behalf, the judge called only prosecution witnesses. Friends and family members who visited al-Naqshabandi in prison three days before his execution said that he had no knowledge he had even been convicted, and his family only learned of his execution when they read about it in the newspaper. As of October his body had not been returned to his family for burial, despite an official request from the Syrian embassy. The case was featured in a Human Rights Watch report issued in October.

Two British nurses employed in Riyadh who were charged with murdering an Australian colleague were, in a highly unusual development, allowed access to legal counsel during their trial. British consular officials also received permission to attend the hearings. Deborah Parry and Lucille McLauchlan both attempted to withdraw confessions obtained from them, saying they confessed under duress after being subjected to psychological, physical and sexual abuse during their interrogation. Their lawyers reported that they were not allowed adequate opportunity to review the prosecution case or to submit evidence, and charged that "all they [the judges] looked at were the two confessions, which had been retracted. Never once did they examine how flimsy and circumstantial the evidence is." Verdicts were apparently reached in August but lawyers for McLauchlan were only notified of the sentence of 500 lashes and eight years imprisonment in late September. Parry was believed to be facing a death sentence but as of late October her sentence had not been announced. A death penalty in a murder case can be commuted if the victim's family agrees to commutation in exchange for compensation, and on October 15 the victim's brother agreed to the commutation in exchange for U.S.$1.2 million. Both Parry and McLauchlan's sentences must undergo additional review, and may be reduced in light of the settlement.

In January a group of nineteen Pakistanis, including seven children, were arrested on drug smuggling charges on their arrival in Jeddah. Drug smuggling carries a death sentence in Saudi Arabia. In August Saudi ambassador to Pakistan Asad Abdul Aziz al-Zuhair denied press reports that he had promised Pakistani officials that the children would be returned to Pakistan, saying that "the case is before the court and [the children] may be released afterwards." Islamic law sets puberty as the age of criminal responsibility, raising the possibility that at least one of the older children, a thirteen-year-old girl, could be convicted. Although Saudi Arabia in 1996 ratified the Convention on the Rights of the Child, which prohibits sentences of capital punishment or life imprisonment for minors, it entered formal reservations exempting itself from the obligation to comply with "all such articles as are in conflict with the provisions of Islamic law."

Shi'a citizens of Saudi Arabia faced widespread government discrimination, including unequal access to social services, education, and government jobs, especially those in the national security sector. The government rarely permitted private construction of Shi'a mosques or community centers, and even books on Shi'ism were banned. In its 1996/97 annual report, the al-Haramain Islamic Information Center, a London-based Shi'a organization, published the text of a December 1996 court ruling against Mohammad Hussayn Mohammad al-Tawil and 'Abdullah 'Ali Hassan al-Jatil on charges of bringing 1,313 Shi'a religious books into Saudi Arabia from Kuwait. Describing the books as constituting "a definition of the doctrine of this corrupt sect," the judge sentenced Al-Tawil to one year in prison and 240 lashes, and al-Jatil to eighteen months in prison and 300 lashes.

Widespread arrests of Shi'a suspected of political activities continued throughout 1997, and were especially frequent in Eastern province, where the majority of Shi'a reside. A number of those arrested were Shi'a clerics, including Hassan Muhammad al-Nimr, who was arrested on March 25. Individuals in custody were frequently subject to threats and abuse during interrogation, according to Shi'a organizations in exile. In December 1996 Al-Haramain reported the death in police custody of twenty-one-year-old Haytham 'Ali Bahr, apparently as a result of torture. Human Rights Watch received reports that at least two other individuals were hospitalized as a result of torture in police custody during 1997.

The government owned all domestic radio and television stations, and exerted tremendous influence over other domestic and international media outlets. Several important foreign-based print and broadcasting media were owned by members of the Saudi royal family or their associates, and according to the Committee To Protect Journalists, the domestic media was subject to close supervision by the king, who had to approve senior staffing decisions. Foreign publications were often censored or banned. In January the Egyptian literary magazine *Akhbar al-adab* was banned, apparently because its cover featured a drawing of Jesus. A May issue of *al-Hayat* newspaper containing an interview with Osama bin Ladin, an exiled Saudi financier known for backing radical Islamic groups, was confiscated before reaching newsstands.

Saudi Arabia's accession in September to the Convention on the Elimination of All Forms of Racial Discrimination (CERD) and the Convention against Torture and Other Cruel, Inhuman or Degrading Treatment or Punishment was undercut by the formal reservations it registered. The government exempted itself from the obligation to implement CERD provisions it deemed "in contradiction with the Shari`a," and rejected Article 22's provision allowing any State Party to bring disputes over interpretation or application of the convention to the International

Court of Justice. Its reservation to the Convention against Torture rejected the provision of Article 3, which forbids turning over a person to another state where he or she may be at risk of torture, and Article 20, which provides a mechanism for monitoring and reporting on patterns of torture. Saudi Arabia has on several occasions deported or extradited individuals to countries where they were at risk of torture.

In July King Fahd expanded the all-male Consultative (Shura) Council from sixty to ninety members, including two Shi'a members. The first appointments to the council, in 1993, included only one Shi'a member, although the Shi'a community is believed to comprise about 10 percent of the Saudi population. The council is an appointed advisory body with no legislative functions. Its meetings are closed to the public and members are forbidden to take any documents relating to the council's work out of the council offices.

The Right to Monitor

Saudi controls on information and its harsh suppression of freedom of conscience and expression made it impossible for human rights organizations to operate in Saudi Arabia. Government monitoring of telephone and mail communications made Saudis reluctant to comment on human rights conditions there, and even those who lived abroad often requested anonymity when providing human rights information, so as to avoid reprisals against themselves or their families.

No international human rights organization has received authorization to conduct a mission to Saudi Arabia for several years. In 1995 Human Rights Watch received a verbal invitation to visit the country from Prince Bandar, the Saudi ambassador to the U.S., but subsequent inquiries to follow up on the invitation have gone unanswered.

Foreign journalists needed visas to enter Saudi Arabia and were often refused access.

The Role of the International Community

United Kingdom

Saudi Arabia remained a major U.K. trading partner and market for arms exports. British firms were in competition for arms contracts worth several billion dollars. Secretary of State Robin Cook announced in July that the new Labour Party government policy would reflect a commitment to human rights, and promised a review of British arms sales and military training assistance programs to ensure that they were consistent with human rights objectives. As of October the results of such a review had not been made public.

British courts in May allowed three domestic workers, all Philippines nationals, to sue their employers, one of whom belonged to the Saudi royal family, for physical abuse, forced confinement, and breach of contract. The abuses allegedly were suffered both in Saudi Arabia and when they were brought to work for the couple in London. British law since 1980 allowed foreigners to bring domestic staff with them to Britain on the condition that these workers not change jobs while in Britain, a condition that forced some workers to submit to abuse or accept deportation. Geraldine Juralbal and Josephine and Slordeliza Mabanta had contested their employers' arguments that the case should be heard in Saudi Arabia, saying they would not be able to get a fair hearing in Saudi Arabia and they would be at risk if they were returned there. Lawyers for the women expected the case to go to trial in early 1998. In August Immigration Minister Mike O'Brian said that he was "very concerned by repeated allegations of ill-treatment of domestic workers allowed temporary entry into Britain to work for their foreign employer," and promised that "the Government intends to tackle this."

In September Secretary Cook broke a long British tradition of "quiet diplomacy," to publicly denounce the sentence of 500 lashes against British citizen Lucille McLauchlan (*see* above), calling it "wholly unacceptable in the modern world."

United States

Saudi Arabia continued to enjoy close relations with the U.S. in a strategic partnership. It provided a major market for U.S. arms and civilian goods, a base for over 5,000 U.S. troops and for U.S. planes patrolling the "no-fly zone" in southern Iraq, and remained a major force in the oil industry. In 1996 U.S. exports to Saudi Arabia reached U.S.$7.31 billion, while Saudi petroleum exports to the U.S. totaled U.S. $8.16 billion.

Although the State Department's *Country Reports on Human Rights Practices for 1996* provided a fairly comprehensive overview of the range of human rights abuses in Saudi Arabia, such criticisms seemed to have little or no impact on U.S. policy, and public statements on Saudi Arabia throughout the year rarely included human rights concerns. One exception was the issue of religious freedom, which was the subject of congressional hearings and proposed legislation providing for sanctions against governments engaged in religious persecution. Assistant Secretary of State for Democracy, Human Rights, and Labor John Shattuck said in January, "We have been very concerned and have raised both privately and publicly the issue of freedom of religion and particularly the question of free exercise of religion by United States personnel when they are in Saudi Arabia . . . I think our engagement on this subject is very important in terms of presenting a climate in which individuals from overseas are able to practice their faiths." At his confirmation hearing in September, however, Wyche Fowler, the new U.S. ambassador to Saudi Arabia, raised the issue of that country's prohibition against Christian worship, but he made no criticism of Saudi policy and appeared to dismiss it as a matter of concern. "The strong emphasis that is placed on the privacy of the individual's home," Fowler stated, allowed "many Americans [to] express their religious faith privately or in the company of close friends and associates. In fact, many Americans have developed personal networks that allow them to exercise their faith in a manner which they find personally satisfactory." And the U.S. took no public stance during the year in defense of the rights of Saudi or other non-U.S. nationals who were discriminated against because of their religious beliefs, including the indigenous Shi'a minority.

Saudi Arabia's human rights record may have been cited by U.S. Justice Department officials in efforts to gain custody of Shi'a dissident Hani 'Abd al-Rahim al-Sayegh after his arrest in Canada. After transiting the U.S. al-Sayegh had sought asylum in Canada, where he was arrested in March, apparently on the basis of Saudi reports implicating him in the June 1996 al-Khobar bombing that killed nineteen U.S. soldiers. Al-Sayegh did not contest Canada's decision to return him to the U.S. in June, after seeking guarantees that he would not be refouled to Saudi Arabia. Al-Sayegh's lawyer alleged the American authorities threatened al-Sayegh with return to Saudi Arabia if he refused to plead guilty to charges that he participated in planning an attack prior to the al-Khobar bombing that was not carried out. On his return he pleaded not guilty. The U.S. moved to dismiss the case for lack of evidence in September, and said it would "respond appropriately" to Saudi requests for extradition. In a letter to Attorney General Janet Reno, Human Rights Watch voiced concern about the U.S.'s alleged use of a credible fear of torture and severe mistreatment to pressure al-Sayegh, and warned that the extradition of al-Sayegh to Saudi Arabia would violate the U.S.'s obligation as a party to the Convention against Torture to refrain from extraditing persons to a country where they would be at risk of torture. The Justice Department responded on October 18 that "[a]uthorities in both this Department and the State Department are cognizant of their responsibilities relating to human rights issues, and such issues will be carefully evaluated in the event the point is reached at which they are pertinent." The letter also stated that al-Sayegh "has not been subjected to coercion by U.S. authorities."

Relevant Human Rights Watch report:
Saudi Arabia—Flawed Justice: The Execution of 'Abd al-Karim Mara'i al-Nashquabandi, 10/97

SYRIA

Human Rights Developments

The dual legacy of decades of one-party rule and state repression continued to cripple independent political life in Syria. With emergency law in effect since 1963, peaceful political expression and association criminalized, and all independent institutions of civil society long ago dismantled, citizens were unable to exercise basic civil and political rights guaranteed under international human rights law. The government-controlled print and broadcast media and the quadrennially elected parliament provided no opportunities for independent or opposition voices to be heard. Hundreds of members of unauthorized political opposition groups, imprisoned in the 1980s for nonviolent activities, languished in prison. Many of these long-term detainees, university students at the time of their arrest, were only sentenced in the mid-1990s by the Supreme State Security Court in proceedings that did not meet international fair-trial standards. Barring amnesties, some of these political prisoners, serving terms as long as fifteen years, will not be eligible for release until 2002.

The absence of freedom of expression and association made systematic and timely monitoring of information about human rights developments virtually impossible. The families of victims of human rights abuse often dared not provide detailed information to human rights organizations, consent to publicize cases internationally, or even grant permission to raise individual cases with Syrian authorities. This remained the norm not only for past abuses, but for violations that occurred in 1997.

One family in Aleppo, for example, suffered a "disappearance" in silence for almost twenty years. Their son, whose name Human Rights Watch was asked not to disclose, was detained in late 1979, when he was a university student in his twenties. He was held for the first six months in a prison in Aleppo, then transferred to Damascus. From that time, the family had no further information concerning his whereabouts and did not know if he was dead or alive. Despite the time that had passed, the family in 1997 remained afraid to publicize the case for fear of retribution by state agents against family members in Aleppo. In a recent case, news of the arrest in June and subsequent incommunicado detention of three peaceful political activists reached a family member in the United States, who provided details to Human Rights Watch. Because of fear of worsening the situation for the detainees and putting the family at risk, the details of this case cannot be published. The absence of an independent human rights community inside Syria, coupled with the lack of regular and unrestricted access to the country by international human rights monitors and journalists, served to isolate victims of abuse and their families and deny them sources of support and advocacy at the local and international levels.

There were no reports in 1997 of government initiatives to address patterns of discrimination against Syrian Kurds, who comprise from 8.5 to 10 percent of the population and form the largest non-Arab ethnic minority in Syria. By the government's own count, the Kurdish minority included over 142,000 stateless Syrian-born Kurds, including children. A 1996 Human Rights Watch report documented such discriminatory practices as the prohibition of Kurdish private schools; the denial of Syrian citizenship to Syrian-born Kurds and their children; lack of legal recognition of the marriages of certain Syrian-born Kurds; and the refusal of the state to register and grant Syrian nationality to the children born of marriages between stateless Syrian-born Kurdish men and women who were Syrian citizens, and of stateless Syrian-born Kurdish couples.

In written replies to questions from the U.N. Committee on the Rights of the Child, which the committee received on December 11, 1996, the Syrian government did not acknowledge discriminatory state policies and practices against the Kurdish minority. The government maintained, for example, that "in Syria there is no child who does not have a specific name and nationality." Ignoring the stateless status of tens of thousands of Syrian-born Kurdish children due to its own policies, the government merely noted: "A refugee to Syria may be accorded Syrian nationality through naturalization, whereupon nationality is also acquired as a consequence by his minor children." In another reply to the committee, the government dodged the issue of the state's refusal to recognize the marriages of stateless Kurds: "The legislative enactments in force in Syria recognize the marriage deeds of all minorities when they are duly issued both legally and systematically, whether in Syria or elsewhere," the government wrote.

The strong presence of Syrian military and security forces inside Lebanon did not diminish in 1997, and Syria continued to play a dominant role, particularly in areas related to political and security affairs, and foreign policy. The bilateral May 1991 Treaty of Brotherhood, Cooperation and Coordination provided for joint initiatives in a variety of fields, ranging from commerce and industry to agriculture and transportation, as well as special efforts in the fields of defense and security affairs. A separate Defense and Security Agreement, concluded in September 1991, created a bilateral defense affairs committee, composed of the interior and defense ministers of both countries. Clause 2(a) of the agreement required that Syrian and Lebanese military and security authorities "[b]an all military, security, political and media activity that might harm the other country." Clause 2(b) specified that the authorities of both states must "[r]efuse to give refuge to, facilitate the passage of, or provide protection to persons and organizations that work against the other state's security. If such persons or organizations take refuge in either of the two states, that state must arrest them and hand them over to the other side at the latter's request."

One manifestation of Syria's role in Lebanon was the continuing "disappearances" of Lebanese citizens and Palestinian refugees at the hands of Syrian security forces, and the officially unacknowledged transfer of these "disappeared" persons to prisons and detention centers in Syria. There were at least four confirmed "disappearances" in Lebanon in 1997, in addition to cases that remained unsolved from 1996 and previous years. One such case was that of Lebanese citizen Gabi 'Akl Karam, who was taken from his mother's home in the Sinn al-Fil section of Beirut on January 6 by two men in plainclothes who said that they were members of Lebanese Military Intelligence. Karam was detained at the Lebanese Ministry of Defense headquarters, and the next day he was handed over to Syrian security forces and transferred to the Palestine Branch of Military Intelligence in Damascus. Karam was held there incommunicado until March 27, when he was returned to Lebanon and held in Lebanese army custody until his release on April 3. There was no official acknowledgment of Karam's detention by Lebanese or Syrian authorities, and there was no written reply to the abduction and unlawful detention complaint filed by Karam's lawyer on March 12 with Lebanon's chief public prosecutor Adnan Addoum.

The Syrian government did not reply to a recommendation by Human Rights Watch, in letters sent to President Hafez al-Asad in November 1996 and March 1997, to halt the "disappearances" and disclose fully the names and other information about non-Syrians held in custody in Syrian prisons and detention centers. According to an Amnesty International report issued on October 9, at least 200 Lebanese citizens were imprisoned in Syria, following their detention in Lebanon by Syrian intelligence forces and subsequent transfer to Syria; most of them were held incommunicado, and without charge or trial.

The Right to Monitor

Syrian citizens were unable openly to monitor human rights developments and abuses, report such information openly inside Syria, and communicate it to the outside world. The last known organized initiative of this kind inside Syria, by activists associated with the nascent nongovernmental Committees for the Defense of Democratic Freedoms and Human Rights in Syria (known by the acronym CDF), was suppressed harshly by authorities. Beginning in December 1991, authorities rounded up and detained suspected CDF members and supporters, and in March 1992 seventeen of them were tried by the Supreme State Security Court in Damascus. The court sentenced ten of the activists to prison terms ranging from five to ten years. Five were released in 1997, after serving their full terms, and five remained in prison.

Those still behind bars, and their sentences, were: writer Nizar Nayouf (ten years); lawyer Aktham Nuaissa, Muhammed Ali Habib, and Afif Muzhir (nine years); and Bassam al-Shaykh (eight years). Nayouf remained in Mezze military prison in Damascus, while the others were held in Sednaya prison. Both Nayouf (aged thirty-five) and Nuaissa (aged forty-six) were reportedly in urgent need of specialized medical care. Syrian authorities ignored repeated appeals from international human rights organizations for the release of the CDF members and other Syrians imprisoned for the peaceful exercise of their right to freedom of expression and association.

An Amnesty International delegation visited Syria in March, and met with government officials and the prosecutor and judges serving on the security court, among others. Following the mission, Amnesty issued a press release on March 25, calling for the immediate release of prisoners detained solely for their political beliefs. "We welcome the government's willingness to continue dialogue and cooperation with the organization for the protection of human rights in Syria, but we would like this translated into action," Amnesty wrote, noting that it had submitted the names of over 500 political prisoners to the authorities. Amnesty added that its delegation had "asked the authorities to review the cases of hundreds of political prisoners convicted and sentenced after unfair trials, to release everyone not charged with a recognizably criminal offense and to clarify the fate and whereabouts of the 'disappeared.'"

Human Rights Watch continued to wait for an affirmative response from the Syrian government to a long-standing request to visit the country again following its first officially approved fact-finding mission, undertaken from March to May 1995. The request for a follow-up mission was first made to Syrian authorities in July 1995, and was subsequently raised repeatedly with the government.

United Nations

The U.N. Committee on the Rights of the Child considered the initial report of Syria at the committee's meeting in January in Geneva. The committee's concluding observations, published on January 24, included criticism of the government's discriminatory policies toward Syrian-born Kurdish children: "The situation of refugee and Syrian-born Kurdish children is a matter of concern to the Committee in the light of article 7 of the Convention [on the Rights of the Child]." (Article 7 requires, among other provisions, that children should be registered immediately after birth and have the right to acquire a nationality.) The committee continued: "In this regard, the Committee notes the absence of facilities for the registration of refugee children born in Syria, and that Syrian-born Kurdish children are considered either as foreigners or as *maktoumeen* (unregistered) by the Syrian authorities and face great administrative and practical difficulties in acquiring Syrian nationality, although they have no other nationality at birth." The committee stressed that "the right to be registered and to acquire a nationality should be guaranteed to all children under the Syrian Arab Republic's jurisdiction without discrimination of any kind, irrespective, in particular, of the child's or his or her parents' or legal guardians' race, religion or ethnic origin."

On April 4, the U.N. Human Rights Committee met in New York to consider the second periodic report submitted by Lebanon under Article 40 of the International Covenant on Civil and Political Rights. The committee examined Lebanon's violations of civil and political rights, and heard presentations by local and international human rights organizations concerning the Syrian role in Lebanon and the continuing problem of "disappearances." During its meeting in New York on May 15, the Working Group on Enforced or Involuntary Disappearances of the U.N. Commission on Human Rights received information about "disappearances" in Lebanon by Syrian security forces.

European Union

Human Rights Watch is unaware of any European Union (E.U.) rights-related initiatives with respect to Syria in 1997. The E.U., like the U.S. (see below), appeared preoccupied with diplomatic activity aimed at reactivating the Israeli-Syrian negotiating track. The Council of Ministers failed to forward to the European Parliament the report on human rights conditions in Syria that it received in November 1995 from the European Commission, a report it had committed itself to prepare as part of the December 1993 decision to extend Fourth Protocol assistance to Syria, which amounted to U.S. $178 million over five years. Human Rights Watch urged in May that the Council of Ministers instruct the Commission to prepare an update to this report, and submit it to the parliament prior to the August recess, and that the original report and the update be made public.

United States

U.S. policy toward Syria again was almost entirely drive by efforts to revive the stalled Israel-Syria peace talks, suspended since February 1996, in order to accomplish one of the administration's long-sought objectives, a peace treaty between the two countries. Although Syria once again appeared on the State Department's 1997 list of state sponsors of terrorism, the Clinton administration exempted Syria from the Antiterrorism and Effective Death Penalty Act of 1996, which prohibited, as of August 22, 1996, all financial transactions by U.S. persons with govern-ments on the terrorism list.

In 1997, the Clinton administration opposed efforts by members of congress to have the 1996 law fully applied to trade with Syria. R. Richard Newcomb, director of the Treasury Department's Office of Foreign Assets Control, explained to the Senate Foreign Relations Subcommittee on African Affairs on May 15 that new Treasury Department regulations, based on State Department guidance, authorized "financial transactions with the Governments of Syria and Sudan except for (1) transfers from those governments in the form of donations and (2) transfers with respect to which the U.S. person knows or has reasonable cause to believe that the financial transaction poses a risk of furthering terrorist acts in the United States." Philip Wilcox, the coordinator for counterterrorism at the State Department, told the House of Representative Judiciary subcommittee on June 10 that the additional sanctions against Syria could put the Israel-Syria peace process at risk. He added that "there were other reasons why imposing more sanctions on Syria would be counter-productive but could not discuss them at an open public hearing," according to a report of the hearing published by the U.S. Information Agency.

Secretary of State Madeleine Albright, in her first visit to Syria on September 12, met in Damascus with President Asad for four hours and then left the country without making any public comments. There were no indications that the secretary used the occasion of the meeting to raise privately any U.S. concerns about human rights conditions in Syria. Human Rights Watch is unaware of any public statements by Clinton administration officials in 1997 that highlighted or criticized specific aspects of Syria's human rights record, and there was no public evidence that U.S. diplomats engaged their Syrian counterparts in discussions aimed at improving the country's dismal human rights situation through specific and measurable reforms. Despite this public silence, the State Department's assessment of human rights conditions in Syria remained, as in past years, condemnatory in its *Country Reports on Human Rights Practices for 1996.*

Relevant Human Rights Watch report:
Syria/Lebanon—An Alliance Beyond the Law: Enforced Disappearances in Lebanon, 5/97

TUNISIA

Human Rights Developments

In December 1996, four political prisoners who had been the subject of international campaigns were released conditionally before the end of their sentences. Their release prompted hope that, as Zine al-Abidine Ben Ali headed toward the tenth anniversary of his presidency on November 7, 1997, Tunisia would once again know a small measure of tolerance for those who peacefully challenged the government's policies and rights record.

Those hopes were soon dashed. Not only were the ex-prisoners—Mohamed Mouada, Khemaïs Chammari, Nejib Hosni, and Mohamed Hedi Sassi—subjected to harassment and restrictions of their rights throughout the year, but the overall climate in Tunisia remained one of fear and intimidation. Repressive laws were invoked to arrest those who protested the lack of freedoms or who were accused of belonging to "unlicensed" political groups. An omnipresent police force kept dissidents, ex-prisoners, and the families of prisoners and of exiled activists under constant surveillance and harassment. The press, private and official, avoided all criticism of the government. Foreign newspapers were banned from circulation whenever their coverage of Tunisia displeased the authorities.

Authorities, exploiting domestic and international concern over a spillover of the conflict from Algeria, have since 1990 prosecuted and jailed thousands of suspected members and sympathizers of the banned Renaissance (an-Nahdha) party on charges relating to nonviolent expression and association. The repression continued despite the absence of political violence in Tunisia since the early 1990s.

The largest category of victims of abuse consisted of the wives and children of members of imprisoned or exiled Nahdha members. Police searched family homes at all hours; wives were summoned for questioning about their financial resources and were pressured to cease contact with their husbands. Some were threatened sexually, according to a detailed report by Amnesty International issued in June. Many of those who sought to emigrate to join husbands in exile were denied passports, although no charges were pending against them. As these families struggled financially, authorities prosecuted those found to have collected or provided money for them.

Toward the end of the year, the government gave passports to the wives and children of thirty-five exiled dissidents, and allowed them to be reunited with their husbands abroad. This welcome breakthrough raised hopes that the government would soon resolve additional cases of this nature.

Prisons were severely overcrowded, a condition that was not dictated by economic constraints; Tunisia boasted the highest per capita income in North Africa. Released political prisoners faced a range of harassing and punitive measures, some of them extrajudicial. These included for most a ban on travel abroad and requirements to register with the police one or more times daily. Some were dismissed from their public-sector jobs and for years were subjected to such heavy police surveillance that acquaintances were intimidated into curtailing contact with them.

The four activists freed in December 1996 were subjected to harassment, despite a statement by the Tunisian embassy in Washington that their early release reflected "a policy animated by a humanist spirit of pardon and clemency." The embassy added that their offenses were "common criminal offenses, tried in Tunisian court and in perfect harmony with international instruments to which Tunisia is a signatory." But the political nature of their prosecution was echoed in their post-release mistreatment. Mouada, leader of the legal opposition Movement of

Democratic Socialists (MDS), was placed under de facto house arrest. Visitors, including foreign journalists and diplomats, were barred from seeing him. Human rights lawyer Hosni was prevented from resuming his profession and his phone service was cut. Both Hosni and Moada were denied passports and prevented from accepting invitations to participate in the European Parliament's hearing on human rights in Tunisia in June. However, human rights activist Khemaïs Chammari was able to testify at the hearing.

The government introduced new directives in 1997 that showed its determination to restrict the exercise of the freedom of association and assembly. In January, the Ministry of Higher Education ordered that anyone organizing a meeting or conference in Tunisia submit in advance to the Ministry of Interior a list of participants, a copy of the agenda, and the text of any speeches or conference papers. A March directive from the Ministry of Tourism stated that police authorization was necessary for all gatherings and required hotel managers to inform police of the name of the organizer, the number and nationality of the participants, and other details.

Radio and television, both state-run, were government mouthpieces. None of the many privately owned newspapers and magazines could be considered independent. All evidently took instructions, reportedly from the president's office, on whether and how to cover developments the least bit sensitive. Newspapers also printed scurrilous attacks on persons in disfavor with the government, thereby contributing to the climate of intimidation.

In June 1997, the World Association of Newspapers (WAN), a trade association of publishers, expelled its Tunisian affiliate, the first time that the WAN had expelled a member for having failed to fulfill the requirement that members work to defend freedom of the press. The WAN rejected the case made by the Tunisian association that its silence simply reflected the fact that press freedom was alive and well in Tunisia.

Authorities sought to toughen the legal tools to punish Tunisians engaged in political or human rights activities outside the country. Past prosecutions under a "terrorism" article of the criminal code undermined the government's claim that article "does not in any way target peaceful political activities and does not aim to intimidate Tunisians abroad who are concerned with human rights." In September, the government introduced draft legislation that would extend the scope of the criminal code's article concerning the offense of harming Tunisia's external security (Article 61) to include the act of "establish[ing] wilfully relations with agents of any foreign state or foreign body or international body in order to expose or disseminate erroneous information likely to harm Tunisia's vital interests."

The level of education and workforce participation for Tunisia's women was high by regional standards, and its code of family and personal status, promulgated in 1956, excluded the more discriminatory norms found in some of the legal codes of the region based on Islamic law. Against this impressive record were set the practices that egregiously violated the rights of women, including the systematic harassment of the wives of imprisoned and exiled Islamists (see above), and restrictions on women's rights organizations (see below).

The Right to Monitor

The government boasted incessantly of its human rights record and initiatives to deepen political pluralism. But human rights critics faced restrictions ranging from a black-out in the government-controlled press to imprisonment on trumped-up charges.

Khemaïs Ksila, a vice president of the Tunisian Human Rights League, was arrested on September 29, the day he launched a well-publicized hunger strike to dramatize the price he himself had paid for his human rights work: dismissal from his public-sector job, ban on travel abroad, and police surveillance. He was accused of "disseminating false news" and inciting others to disturb the public order, and was still in detention as of early November. Human rights lawyer Radhia Nasraoui reported that her clients were questioned by police about how much they were paying her and where they got the money to do so. On April 29, her office was the scene of a suspicious break-in; it was not the first time that her property had been stolen or vandalized. Hachemi Jegham, a lawyer and president of the Tunisian section of Amnesty International— which does not work on human rights in Tunisia—was detained twice in March by police and questioned about a legal conference scheduled for later that month.

The independent Tunisian League for Human Rights celebrated its twentieth anniversary. While government pressures made it more cautious than in the past, it continued to speak out against human rights violations. The league's communiques were ignored by the Tunisian press except when they praised a step taken by the Tunisian government or criticized violations by a foreign government. In September, the LTDH noted that an ongoing dialogue it had sought with the Interior Ministry had gotten under way, and that it was presenting its concerns and individual cases to the ministry. The LTDH also praised President Ben Ali for consenting to prison visits by the organization, an agreement that, if implemented, could be an important breakthrough.

The LTDH continued to face obstacles to holding public meetings, particularly for its branches located outside the capital. In December 1996, authorities prevented the LTDH from holding a conference and reception to mark the anniversary of the Universal Declaration of Human Rights. One month earlier, the minister of interior blocked at the last moment an LTDH seminar on various forms of detention, which was scheduled to take place at a Sousse hotel. Authorities also blocked a January 1997 meeting organized by Collectif 95 Maghreb Egalité, a regional women's rights group.

Beyond the small circle of individual human rights activists, a wider circle of Tunisians signed petitions demanding greater freedoms. Two hundred and two Tunisians signed an April 9 petition calling for respect of basic liberties, revisions of the electoral code to broaden pluralism and an amnesty for all

Tunisians prosecuted or convicted for their opinions and political activities. Several union activists who organized petitions demanding labor and other rights were arrested early in the year and questioned about the documents they had prepared.

The government effectively prevented all but one of the Tunisian invitees from addressing a European Parliament forum on human rights in Tunisia on June 11 in Strasbourg. The two independent organizations that were invited, the LTDH and the Tunisian Association of Democratic Women, succumbed to government pressure not to send representatives.

The Role of the International Community

European Union

Except for some initiatives by its parliament, European Union (E.U.) institutions, including the Council and the Commission, missed opportunities to press Tunisia on its human rights record during 1997. By October, the Association Agreement between Tunisia and the E.U., which was initialed in 1995 and which lowers trade barriers in both directions and provides financial assistance to Tunisia, had been ratified by all but one of the parliaments of the E.U. member states. These parliaments showed little interest in using Article 2, which makes human rights an essential element of the agreement, to make explicit demands on Tunisia to improve in its human rights record. However, the president of the German parliament traveled to Tunisia in May and, according to reports, raised human rights concerns in high-level meetings. She hosted a reception at the German embassy to which independent political figures and human rights activists were invited.

On June 11 in Strasbourg, the delegations of several liberal, green and left-wing political groups in the European Parliament sponsored a forum on human rights in Tunisia in the context of the Association Agreement. Despite the Tunisian governments brazen attempt to stifle the discussion by pressuring the invited Tunisians not to attend or preventing them from traveling, the European Parliament narrowly failed to adopt a critical resolution the following month on human rights in Tunisia. In a possible indication of the weight that Tunisia gives to scrutiny by the European Parliament, authorities restored the passports of four dissidents just before the vote.

A six-member parliamentary delegation raised human rights issues during an official visit to Tunisia in October. French MEP Marie-Arlette Carlotte said that the group submitted a list of cases to the justice minister and raised with the prime minister proposed revisions to the penal code (*see* above). She added, "A policy of opposing fundamentalism must not be an excuse not to provide space for freedoms."

Throughout the year, the E.U. promoted European investment in Tunisia. In September, the European Commission and Tunisian government co-sponsored in Tunisia a forum on Euro-Mediterranean cooperation, attended by hundreds of businesspersons from both sides of the Mediterranean.

France

France is Tunisia's leading trade partner and source of foreign investment. In 1996, French bilateral aid to Tunisia doubled to the equivalent of U.S. $220 million.

President Jacques Chirac's embrace of President Ben Ali in 1995 as "leading his country ever further down the road of ... democratic progress" remained emblematic of French policy after the election of a Socialist-led government in France in June 1997. The year's highlight was the state visit by President Ben Ali to Paris on October 20-21, at which time accords on French bilateral aid and investments were signed. Both President Chirac and Prime Minister Lionel Jospin showered praise on President Ben Ali for Tunisia's economic performance and opening toward Europe, each making only a single, oblique public reference to Tunisia's human rights problem.

Toasting Ben Ali at a state dinner in his honor, Chirac said that in Tunisia's climate of economic growth, the temptation to violence disappears and "the rule of law, democracy can progress more easily, and a culture of liberty can blossom more easily." Jospin told Ben Ali in his own toast the following day that he took pleasure in knowing that Tunisia's economic opening Europe will "lead you toward an ever-greater opening toward the values of democracy and pluralism." Chirac's spokeswoman pointed out that Chirac had raised human rights in his private meetings with Ben Ali, including individual cases and the issue of press freedom, but she provided no details.

Ben Ali's human rights record proved more of a hindrance to his reception at the National Assembly. The Tunisian president had reportedly sought to deliver an address before the assembly, as King Hassan II of Morocco had done, but human rights concerns prompted the French to offer instead a reception hosted by the assembly's president. Several parliamentarians boycotted that reception to protest repression in Tunisia.

Ben Ali's state visit to France had been postponed three times between October 1996 and June 1997. The press speculated that French discomfort over Tunisia's rights record played a role in some of the postponements, but neither side said anything publicly to confirm this.

In November 1996, the National Consultative Commission on Human Rights, a French semi-official advisory body, issued a damning summary of Tunisia's human rights record and called on the French government to "urge the Tunisian authorities to release all prisoners of conscience, end torture and mistreatment, and break the cycle of impunity that encourages the continuation of human rights violations." Throughout 1997, however, no French official publicly reaffirmed the commission's concerns or commented on the arrests and harassment of dissidents and other troubling developments taking place in Tunisia. In a typical formulation, the Foreign Ministry spokesperson omitted human rights when describing the agenda of Hubert Vedrine's first visit to Tunisia as foreign minister in August, but responded when asked, "The French government follows with attention the situation of human rights everywhere in the world. There is no subject that our Tunisian friends and we bar from considering when we meet."

United States

The U.S. was openly critical of Tunisia's human rights record, while reaffirming that other factors—notably Tunisia's support for Israeli-PLO negotiations, economic liberalization, and military cooperation with the U.S.—reinforced warm relations between the two countries. The U.S. provided no economic aid in 1996 but awarded Tunisia about U.S.$6 million in excess defense articles and $816,000 under the International Military Education Training program.

U.S. embassy staff maintained contacts with human rights activists and political opposition figures in Tunisia. On March 7, two political officers attempted to meet with Mohamed Moada, leader of the opposition Democratic Socialist Movement, who had been released from prison in December. Outside his home, the two were blocked by plainclothes guards who identified themselves.

At her confirmation hearing before the U.S. Senate Foreign Relations Committee on September 18, Ambassador-designate Robin Raphel stated, "Nonviolent political groups which oppose the policies of the government should be free to speak without fear of reprisal, the press should be free to publish the full range of political debate, and people should know they are free to participate in opposition politics without government harassment. We have an ongoing dialogue with the Tunisian government on the need for a more open and inclusive democratic process."

U.S. activism on human rights tended to focus on the rights to political participation, press freedom, and the plight of secular dissidents. This laudable engagement was not accompanied — at least publicly — by comparable advocacy on behalf of the largest and most vulnerable victims of abuse in Tunisia, persons in any way connected to the Islamist Nahdha party. This included prisoners, ex-prisoners, and family members who were subjected to severe harassment and deprivation of their right to travel.

HUMAN
RIGHTS
WATCH

UNITED STATES

Human Rights Developments

During the year, human rights violations relating to immigration practices, police abuse, custodial treatment and conditions, the death penalty, and issues of discrimination continued in the United States. The effects of new laws restricting the rights of asylum seekers arriving in the country, prisoners seeking to challenge unconstitutional treatment or conditions, and defendants in capital cases became apparent. Meanwhile, a torture allegation made by a Haitian immigrant against New York City police officers in August alarmed city residents, with even the most stalwart supporters of the police acknowledging abuse and accountability problems within the force. And, for the first time since four Vietnam anti-war protesters were shot and killed at Kent State University in 1970, a U.S. citizen was shot dead on U.S. soil by on-duty military personnel—this time by Marines on anti-drug patrol near the U.S.-Mexico border.

Immigration Policy and Practice

Implementation of the Illegal Immigration Reform and Immigrant Responsibility Act (IIRIRA) of 1996 began in April, causing widespread confusion. The law's new expedited removal provisions hindered the ability of asylum seekers to exercise their internationally protected right to seek and enjoy asylum and undermined the prohibition on the expulsion or return (*refoulement*) of refugees as set out in international human rights treaties and U.S. law. Individuals arriving at a port of entry during 1997 with fraudulent documents, or none, were questioned by immigration inspectors to ascertain whether they should be allowed to make cases of credible fear of return to their countries. The asylum seeker was not allowed access to legal counsel at the time of this determination, which took place on the spot after typically long international flights and, in some cases, immediately following traumatic experiences. Despite requests from several nongovernmental organizations and the United Nations

High Commissioner for Refugees, the U.S. Immigration and Naturalization Service (INS) did not allow access or independent monitoring during this critical decision-making process.

If asylum seekers were allowed to make a credible-fear claim, they were required to prepare their cases in a very short time (sometimes days) while in detention, without essential documentation or guarantees of legal advice. During the credible-fear interview, asylum seekers have a right to counsel, but in many instances these representatives were not allowed to participate. Human Rights Watch learned of individuals with credible claims who had been returned to their countries of origin following these determinations. If an individual was successful in the credible-fear hearing, he or she would usually be detained for an undetermined time pending an asylum hearing.

During the year, Congress considered legislation to focus on the plight of religiously persecuted groups around the world, and the bills included provisions to allow those persecuted on religious grounds to bypass the new expedited removal proceedings, thus apparently acknowledging the lack of appropriate protections for those seeking asylum under the new law. Critics of the legislation also opposed its preferential treatment for one group of asylum seekers over all others.

The 1996 immigration law also promoted the use of detention of immigrants and refugees as a central aspect of U.S. policy. The bill provided for the detention of most individuals arriving at ports of entry without proper documentation, and created new categories of immigrants with criminal backgrounds whose detention was mandatory. The increased numbers of detainees strained existing detention facilities, leading the INS to house almost half of all its detainees in local jails.

The increasing reliance on privately run contract facilities or local jails to hold individuals in INS custody raised serious questions about INS oversight and standards required of the facilities. Human Rights Watch visited jails holding INS detainees, and among their complaints were poor physical conditions, inadequate access to legal assistance, inadequate information from the INS regarding their status, mixing with criminal populations in the jails, poor health care, physical mistreatment, and isolation from families as they were often detained in remote areas thousands of miles from where they were originally apprehended.

Treatment of minors in INS custody raised human rights concerns, as the rights of hundreds of detained children in California and Arizona were violated. Human Rights Watch found that INS treatment of minor children detained with no responsible adult present ignored both international law and INS regulations and policy by its failure to inform detained children of their legal rights, interference with children's attempts to obtain legal representation, and long-term detention of children in high-security facilities with prison-like conditions.

Human rights violations, such as unjustified shootings, sexual assaults, and beatings, continued to be committed by the U.S. Border Patrol and other immigration officials along the U.S.-Mexico border. A Citizens' Advisory Panel was appointed by the Justice Department to recommend long-overdue reforms and monitor implementation, yet after more than two years of existence, the panel failed to submit a report to the U.S. attorney general with its recommendations, although in October the INS claimed that a report would be issued shortly. It was not clear whether the panel, or a similar yet differently staffed advisory committee, would continue to meet to hold more hearings or make recommendations for reform on this issue. The panel's inability to complete its task confirmed the view of many human rights groups that external, independent citizen review of complaints against INS personnel was the only way to gauge the extent of abusive conduct and to ensure accountability when violations occur.

In the meantime, the number of Border Patrol agents increased dramatically during 1997, from approximately 3,400 agents in fiscal year 1993 to a force of 6,000; the force was projected to grow to 10,000 agents by the year 2001. This was cause for some concern, as hiring surges in the past had resulted in the rushed recruitment of individuals unsuitable for any law enforcement work, and in long delays in checking recruits' qualifications and background; under such circumstances, ill-qualified or violent recruits remain undiscovered until beyond the probationary period and become almost impossible to dismiss later. Furthermore, as thousands of new agents were quickly put in place, INS officials acknowledged that agents being promoted to supervisor positions were not receiving adequate training.

As a result of policy-reform suggestions from Human Rights Watch and others, the Justice Department stated that it was considering hiring an undisclosed number of new Office of the Inspector General investigators (who are responsible for investigating some abuse allegations) whose staff had not increased as the Border Patrol grew exponentially for years. And in response to Human Rights Watch's request for information on disciplinary actions taken against Border Patrol agents, the Justice Department disclosed that thirty INS employees, including Border Patrol agents stationed along the southwest border, had been disciplined during a twenty-eight month period, with punishments ranging from counseling to termination. While the disclosure of even this limited amount of disciplinary information was unprecedented, it remained impossible to assess whether disciplinary actions were taken in deserving cases.

On May 20, eighteen-year-old high school student Esequiel Hernández was shot dead by U.S. Marines patrolling the border near Redford, Texas as he tended his family's goats. Texas Rangers investigating the shooting complained that the Marines failed to provide investigators with even basic information about what had taken place, and noted that the physical evidence did not support the Marines' accounts. The shooting sparked community criticism of military deployment in populated areas and led to a temporary suspension of anti-drug border operations by the Marines, working in conjunction with the Border Patrol along the U.S.-Mexico border. In August, a grand jury (which reportedly included a Border Patrol supervisor on duty the night of the incident, the wife of a Border Patrol agent, and a retired Border Patrol agent) chose not to indict the Marine who shot Hernández; in August, a similar consent degree was reached with the Steubenville, Ohio police force

Police Abuse

Incidents of police abuse continued unabated during the year; the torture allegations by Haitian immigrant Abner Louima against officers of the New York City Police Department renewed calls for effective oversight of that police force. Observers questioned whether the signals sent by high-level police and city officials regarding "zero tolerance" for criminals had encouraged officers to engage in brutal treatment. Among the troubling facts surrounding the case were: the habitual "code of silence" among police officers who refused to cooperate with investigators even after the police commissioner and the city's mayor publicly urged them to do so; the force's internal affairs unit's improper handling of the timely complaint filed by a nurse at the hospital where Louima was taken; and the apparent nonchalance displayed by the involved officers on the night of the incident, indicating that they felt they had little to fear for even this egregious act.

The problems identified in New York following the Louima case were evident throughout the country. Weak civilian review, flawed internal investigations, and rare criminal prosecutions by local and federal prosecutors combined to create an atmosphere in which brutal officers had little reason to fear punishment of any type. One positive development during the year was the use of new federal civil "pattern or practice" power to compel particularly troubled police departments to make reforms. In Pittsburgh, Pennsylvania, the Justice Department was so concerned by a "pattern or practice" of brutality and poor response to such incidents that it entered into a consent decree with the city and its police force in February, and required major reforms in the way misconduct allegations were handled. Among the other police forces under investigation using the Justice Department's new civil powers were Los Angeles, New Orleans, New York, and Philadelphia.

Custodial Conditions

The United States continued to incarcerate a greater proportion of its people than almost any other country in the world, with one of every 163 U.S. residents behind bars. At the end of 1996, the number of prisoners and jail inmates reached a new high of approximately 1.7 million, representing a doubling of the incarcerated population since 1985. Notably, racial disparities in the rate of incarceration continued to worsen. African-Americans, who made up 51 percent of the national prison population, were incarcerated at a rate 7.5 times that of whites. Women prisoners—including many mothers of small children—constituted a small minority of the inmate population, but their numbers continued to grow quickly: by the end of 1996 there were at least 75,000 women confined in U.S. federal and state prisons. According to a U.S. Department of Justice analysis, if current rates of incarceration continued, one in twenty Americans would go to prison at some point in his or her life.

Overcrowding in U.S. prisons contributed substantially to violence and abuse among inmates, and between guards and inmates, as well as to the inadequate provision of medical and mental health care services in many prison systems. According to a Justice Department report released in June, state prison populations significantly exceeded state prison capacities. California, with the most crowded prison system, was operating at over twice its capacity. Because of the space shortage, over 31,000 prisoners had to be placed in local jails lacking appropriate facilities, services and programs.

The burgeoning prison population reflected less on the crime rates than on changes in incarceration and sentencing practices: more nonviolent offenders were being incarcerated and the actual time served by prisoners was increasing because of "truth in sentencing" laws and diminished parole release rates. According to official figures released in 1997, drug offenders accounted for 23 percent of the state prison population and 60 percent of the federal prison population. Many of them faced remarkably harsh sentences. In New York, for example, nonviolent drug offenders convicted of the possession or sale of relatively small amounts of drugs faced the same felony sentences as murderers and rapists. (see Drugs and Human Rights discussion in Special Issues section).

Despite the increasing numbers of people in prison, "rehabilitative," educational, and vocational programs got scant support. Some politicians and prison officials even decided that confinement in prison was not punishment enough, and began, as of 1995, reintroducing prison chain gangs—euphemistically referred to by corrections officials as "secured work groups." The first state to institute roadside work crews of prisoners was Alabama, followed by Arizona, Florida, Iowa, Indiana, Illinois, Wisconsin, Montana, and Oklahoma. After an Alabama prisoner, released from his shackles, attacked another chain-gang member with his bush axe and was subsequently shot dead, states modified their systems from group shackling to individual leg shackles. Two states, Arizona and Indiana, had women chain gangs. Officials stated that their goal in using chain gangs was to humiliate prisoners so as to deter them and onlookers from committing crimes in the future. During the year, many institutions considered using—and in some cases, started to use—stun belts instead of chains, allowing correctional officers to shock prisoners from a distance of 300 feet, for up to ten minutes; once shocked, a prisoner loses bladder and bowel control.

Prison systems continued to construct super-maximum security facilities in which prisoners deemed particularly disruptive or dangerous were confined for years in small, often windowless cells for twenty-three hours a day, subjected to extremely restrictive controls and denied educational, vocational and social programs that would promote their successful reintegration into the general prison population. Of particular concern were super-maximum security facilities where there was often a lack of programming and services for inmates; the psychological impact of prolonged solitary confinement; and the absence of adequate mental health screening, monitoring and treatment. Excessive isolation, controls and restrictions without adequate penological justification and insufficient mental health care are inhumane. While such conditions pose mental health risks for inmates generally, they may constitute such cruel treatment as to be considered torture under international human rights standards for the many mentally ill inmates or those with pre-existing psychiatric disorders.

Correctional officials too often responded with inhuman and dangerous disciplinary measures to the unruly behavior of the increasing number of mentally ill individuals confined in U.S. prisons. At Utah State Prison, a mentally ill young man died in April after prison officials strapped him to a restraint chair for sixteen hours. Blood clots formed in his legs during the prolonged continuous restraint, then triggered a fatal pulmonary embolism. After having first claimed the chair was rarely used, state corrections officials admitted that 150 inmates had been restrained in the chair a total of 200 times during the previous two years. Some inmates were strapped in the chair for up to five days. One mentally ill inmate was strapped to a steel plank for twelve weeks; he was let up twice a day. In April, a Utah professional review panel determined that the doctors who ordered such treatment had violated basic standards of care.

In their quest to develop quick and effective methods to control resisting prisoners and suspects, law enforcement and correctional officials have developed technologies that can prove fatal. In June, a prisoner died of shock from an allergic reaction to pepper spray after California correctional officers used the chemical irritant to permit them to forcibly extract him from his cell in San Quentin prison. Two months later, a young man died in police custody in Colorado after being pepper-sprayed and then handcuffed with his legs and hands behind his back, a practice which has been shown to cause positional asphyxia by restricting breathing after a suspect is sprayed. More than thirty-two people died in California alone from 1993 to 1997 after being sprayed with the chili pepper extract.

Conditions in some states' juvenile detention facilities were appalling. Human Rights Watch findings on treatment of juveniles in Louisiana and Georgia spurred Justice Department investigations: in Louisiana, the Justice Department found "life-threatening" abuses and documented extreme brutality by guards, as well as a failure to protect children from sexual and physical abuse. A Justice Department investigation in Georgia is ongoing at this writing. Eight Colorado institutions, investigated by Human Rights Watch, were overcrowded (some at 2.5 times capacity) and unsafe, with excessive use of restraints and punitive segregation; there were complaints of chronic hunger; and incidents of physical abuse by staff.

Meanwhile, legislation was debated in Congress that would allow juveniles to be held in adult facilities, ignoring international standards prohibiting this practice. The proposed law would make youths vulnerable to violence by adult prisoners and would isolate them from necessary educational and other programs.

Widespread sexual abuse of women prisoners, exposed by Human Rights Watch in 1996 and documented by local advocates in many states, continued as corrections officials did little to curtail the abuse. In one positive development, the Justice Department acted on its threat to sue the states of Michigan and Arizona in 1997 for violating women's constitutional rights by allowing prison staff to sexually abuse female prisoners with impunity. And legislation to require improved accountability for abusive correctional officers was introduced in Congress in October. The bill would require that states receiving federal funding criminalize sexual contact between correctional officers and prisoners; it would also require that the Justice Department set up a tracking system to prevent officers found criminally or civilly liable in sexual misconduct incidents from being re-hired, and to assist prisoners in filing complaints about sexual misconduct by guards.

Death Penalty

Ignoring the international trend away from capital punishment, U.S. states carried out executions at a record pace in 1997, with fifty-four men executed as of the end of September. Executions in Texas made up half of the total. In March, Pedro Medina was executed in Florida using an electric chair which malfunctioned, setting his head ablaze. Florida courts held that executions should continue, despite the repeated malfunctions. During the year, two Mexican nationals were put to death in Texas and Virginia, and in both cases notification to the Mexican government was delayed in contravention of the Vienna Convention, which requires that defendants' governments be notified promptly.

At this writing, several states are moving toward reintroduction of capital punishment. Iowa, Massachusetts, and the District of Columbia—which are all traditionally anti-death penalty—typified this trend. In Iowa, the state legislature delayed a vote on the issue until early 1998. In Massachusetts, a last-minute vote switch by a House member blocked passage of legislation to reinstate the death penalty in November 1997. And in the District of Columbia, a U.S. Senator introduced a bill to allow capital punishment in the federal capital. In most cases, the proposals to reinstate the death penalty were in reaction to particularly brutal murders.

The United States is one of only six countries in the world that execute people for convictions based on acts committed before the age of eighteen; the other five are Iran, Nigeria, Pakistan, Saudi Arabia, and Yemen. At present, fifty-eight people are on death row for such acts.

Defending individuals in capital cases became more difficult during the year, as the effects of habeas corpus changes and cutbacks in funding for legal service centers left defender organizations and attorneys scrambling to assist those facing execution. In February, the American Bar Association (ABA) called for a moratorium on executions until policies and procedures could be established to ensure fairness and due process and to minimize the risk of executing innocent persons. The ABA called the current administration of the death penalty a "haphazard maze of unfair practices with no internal consistency." And in July, a report by the Death Penalty Information Center showed that since 1973, sixty-nine prisoners had been released from death row on grounds of innocence, and warned that the new obstacles in defending capital defendants would make mistakes more likely.

Free Expression

In June, the U.S. Supreme Court strongly affirmed the right to free speech on the Internet. In *Reno v. ACLU*, the court ruled that the federal Communications Decency Act placed unconstitutional restrictions on protected speech. This landmark ruling affirmed the earlier decision of a trial court. The Supreme Court found that the "the vast democratic fora of the Internet" merit full First Amendment protection — the same degree of protection afforded the print medium, not simply the more limited protection given to broadcasting.

Race

President Clinton engaged in welcome, high-profile efforts to improve race relations, including a call for national debate on race relations (the Initiative on Race and Reconciliation) through town hall meetings. At the same time, however, the U.S. failed to submit a long-overdue compliance report on an international anti-racism treaty and did not support a proposed World Conference on Racism at the United Nations, calling instead for a special session of the General Assembly to examine the issue. Critics contended that the U.S. position diminished the importance of the problem of racism.

Critics of anti-crime policies point out that blacks and Hispanics were arrested, convicted, and received higher sentences than whites for the same crimes. Perhaps the major cause of this disparity continued to be the country's "war on drugs." For many African-Americans, the symbol of disparate treatment at the hands of the criminal justice system was the much harsher sentencing for crack than for powder cocaine offenses under federal law. Compliance with the International Convention on the Elimination of All Forms of Discrimination (CERD) requires revision of the drug sentencing laws to ensure that blacks—convicted more frequently of crack offenses—and whites—convicted primarily of powder cocaine offenses—receive equivalent sentences for equivalent crimes.

Compliance with International Standards

The low priority given to international human rights treaty compliance and human rights monitoring mechanisms by the U.S. became increasingly apparent during the year. Since 1994, the U.S. has been party to the Convention Against Torture and Other Cruel, Inhuman or Degrading Treatment or Punishment and CERD. Both treaties require reports to the United Nations, describing the nation's treaty compliance. The U.S. compliance reports on both treaties were due in November 1995, but as of October 1997, neither had been submitted. Submission of such reports should be timely, and the reports should cite specific practices or incidents relevant to the treaty's provisions, rather than mere recitation of U.S. law that ought to, but does not always, protect U.S. inhabitants from treatment prohibited under international standards.

Other important human rights treaties, including the International Covenant on Economic, Social and Cultural Rights, the Convention on the Elimination of All Forms of Discrimination Against Women (CEDAW), and the Convention on the Rights of the Child, remained unratified. (Only two countries in the world have not ratified the Convention on the Rights of the Child: Somalia, which has no internationally recognized government, and the United States.) The administration took no action toward signing or ratifying core International Labour Organisation conventions intended to protect basic labor rights, while the administration and members of Congress pursued fast-track authorization for trade agreements that would remove labor rights standards from bilateral treaty negotiations.

The U.S. Commonwealth of the Northern Mariana Islands (CNMI) received heightened scrutiny by Congress, the administration, and human rights monitors due to continuing reports of abuse of thousands of migrant laborers. The laborers, primarily from China, the Philippines, and Bangladesh, are essentially treated as indentured workers by garment manufacturers. The CNMI authorities are exempt from normal federal immigration, trade, and worker protection statutes. According to a July 1997 inter-agency report by the Clinton administration to Congress, "allegations persist regarding the CNMI's inability to protect workers against crimes such as illegal recruitment, battery, rape, child labor, and forced prostitution....Some workers labor under 'shadow' or secondary contracts signed in their home country that subvert their rights under the U.S. Constitution, such as their right to engage in political and religious activities while on U.S. soil." Legislation was introduced in both houses of Congress to address these concerns, including a Senate bill backed by the Clinton administration, but not acted upon as of November. Human Rights Watch joined other nongovernmental organizations in calling for federal action.

The Role of the International Community

The United States agreed to a mission by the United Nations' special rapporteur on extrajudicial, summary, or arbitrary executions, yet provided little assistance in facilitating the inquiry. The rapporteur examined the application of the death penalty and deaths in police custody; he traveled to five states, interviewing officials, prisoners on death row, and human rights advocates. Senator Jesse Helms, chair of the U.S. Senate's Committee on Foreign Relations, protested the visit in a letter to the U.S. ambassador to the United Nations, calling the special rapporteur's visit an "absurd U.N. charade." Nevertheless, the mission served several functions, by reminding federal and local officials of their obligations under international human rights treaties, by acquainting local human rights activists with the United Nations' procedures, and by publicizing international concern over U.S. practices relating to the death penalty and police killings. A report on the mission is due to be submitted to the United Nations Commission on Human Rights during its March/April 1998 session.

Relevant Human Rights Watch reports:

Cold Storage: Super-Maximum Security Confinement in Indiana, 10/97
High Country Lock-Up: Children in Confinement in Colorado, 8/97
Slipping Through the Cracks: Unaccompanied Children Detained by the U.S. Immigration and Naturalization Service, 4/97
Cruel and Unusual: Disproportionate Sentences for New York Drug Offenders, 3/97
All Too Familiar: Sexual Abuse of Women in U.S. State Prisons, 12/96

THE ARMS PROJECT

In 1997, only eight years after the collapse of the Berlin Wall, the political map of state relations, conflict management and arms control had changed radically. During the Cold War, most conflicts were fueled by superpower rivalry and massive state-to-state military assistance. The U.S. and U.S.S.R. intervened directly in wars or fought them by proxy, but nearly all armed conflicts, whatever their origins in local or regional disputes, had a decidedly East-West cast. As manager of global affairs, the United Nations was paralyzed by political gridlock. During periods of detente, attempts were made to check arms proliferation, which was understood to mean only the proliferation of weapons of mass destruction.

This Cold War order of stability through mutually assured destruction (as long as the other guy didn't pull the nuclear trigger, everything was okay) was largely replaced—from a global perspective—with a disorder of manageable instability (all kinds of triggers are being pulled, but wars are contained) in the first half of the 1990s. A single superpower remained, but its reach was limited, and global power became more decentralized. Conflicts lost their ideological hue: they tended to reflect the real interests of the local, and sometimes regional, actors involved (even if ethnicity and religion were used to mask contests over power and resources). Privatization became one of the mantras of this new order; focused initially on rendering state enterprises more efficient and profitable, the drive to privatize industry began to affect even the realm of national security and military assistance (goods and services). Other key factors affecting this new order were initiatives to promote conflict prevention/resolution, peace building, civil society, democracy, development, and human rights.

Although the United Nations has continued to be hamstrung by bureaucratic inertia in the post-Cold War years, the political deadlock at the top has been broken, and as a result the world organization has begun to take a more activist role, if not always successfully so. Nongovernmental organizations like Human Rights Watch have found that it has become possible to generate political will and mobilize state actors in support of limited reform agendas. In the areas of conflict management, human rights protection and democracy promotion, for example, we have witnessed activities ranging from efforts toward establishing an international criminal court to election monitoring, peacekeeping operations and humanitarian interventions in situations of genocide or other forms of mass slaughter. In the field of arms control, we have seen efforts to eliminate weapons of mass destruction through inter-

national treaties and to contain the proliferation of conventional weapons through codes of conduct, weapons registers and new initiatives like the Wassenaar Arrangement on Export Controls for Conventional Arms and Dual-Use Goods and Technologies, the Organization of American States (O.A.S.) draft treaty designed to control illicit arms trafficking in the Americas, and the European Union Program for Preventing and Combating Illicit Trafficking in Conventional Arms, which has similar objectives in Africa.

Comprehensive Landmines Ban

The most important development in 1997 in the field of arms control was the adoption of a comprehensive treaty banning antipersonnel landmines in Oslo in September. This profoundly humanitarian treaty, which was scheduled to be signed by more than one hundred governments in early December, promised to put a stop to the terrible havoc this indiscriminate weapon has caused in civilian communities around the world. Some 26,000 civilians are estimated to be killed or maimed by landmines each year, and in 1997 the toll continued to climb—in Afghanistan, Angola, Bosnia, Cambodia, Iraq, Mozambique, Somalia and other areas that have seen violent conflict.

The signing of the landmines ban treaty was a historic event. It marked the first time that states outlawed an entire weapon system that has been in widespread use. The treaty prohibits, in all circumstances, the use, production, stockpiling, and transfer of all antipersonnel mines (a minimal number may be kept solely for demining and other training purposes), and requires that all stockpiled mines be destroyed within four years and all emplaced mines within ten years of the treaty's entry into force. It also calls on governments to provide for the care and rehabilitation of mine victims. It is a truly comprehensive treaty that clearly creates a new international norm.

Perhaps as important as the treaty itself has been the process bringing it about, often called the "Ottawa Process." This can be seen as a new, post-Cold War model of innovative diplomacy, driven not by the "big" powers but by middle and smaller states, including those from the developing world. Governments set several highly significant precedents. First, they abandoned the notoriously laborious and consensus-bound approach of the United Nations in favor of an independent fast-track approach. The traditional U.N. approach had encouraged the exercise of veto power by the most abusive nations, permitting the lowest common denominator (in the case of landmines, the no-ban policies of China, Russia, India, and Pakistan) to reign supreme. When it became clear in 1996 that the U.N.-sponsored review of the Convention on Conventional Weapons (CCW) would not soon lead to a meaningful ban on landmines, a core group of nations—most notably Austria, Belgium, Canada, Mexico, Norway, and South Africa—decided to draft a treaty and negotiate it outside the U.N. framework. The principal idea behind this approach was that rather than seeking to bring everyone on board from the beginning, thereby allowing recalcitrant states to hijack the entire process, core states would establish an unequivocal norm and then haul in the stragglers as international moral momentum built.

The second convention-shattering precedent was the extraordinary role played by nongovernmental organizations (NGOs), without whom this treaty would not have come into existence. The ban effort was driven by a large coalition known as the International Campaign to Ban Landmines (ICBL). In 1997 it had a membership of more than 1,000 NGOs in more than fifty countries and included groups in the areas of human rights, arms control, development, humanitarian assistance, the environment, peace and conflict prevention, veterans' affairs, women's rights, and children's rights, as well as religious and medical groups, and organizations specializing in mine clearance and mine-victim assistance. While putting pressure on states to join the effort to ban landmines, this coalition enjoyed unprecedented access to the circles of power, coordinating closely with the key governments, and playing a critical role in drafting the final treaty. In

another first for both arms-control and humanitarian treaties, the ICBL had official observer status during the Oslo negotiations, with access to all deliberations and the right to make interventions. This newly forged ad hoc relationship between states and NGOs augured well for future negotiations on other treaties. On October 10, the ICBL was awarded the 1997 Nobel Peace Prize.

The treaty conference in Oslo in September was preceded by a series of events that were important building blocks. These included government-sponsored treaty preparatory conferences in Vienna in February, Bonn in April, Johannesburg in May, and Belgium in June, NGO conferences in Maputo in February, Tokyo in March, and Stockholm in May, and International Committee of the Red Cross (ICRC) conferences in Harare in April and Manila in July. In each case, NGOs played a prominent role in the government conferences, and vice versa. The success of the ban movement was due to this close partnership between governments, NGOs and the ICRC, and the ground-breaking treaty is accurately described as a collaborative effort that had the potential to save millions of lives and change the face of international diplomacy as well.

Chemical and Biological Weapons

The year 1997 was significant for another reason as well. On April 29, the 1993 Convention on the Prohibition of the Development, Production, Stockpiling and Use of Chemical Weapons and Their Destruction (the CWC) entered into force after the sixty-fifth signatory nation deposited its instrument of ratification. As of October 31, 103 states had either ratified or acceded to the CWC, including the Russian Federation, which had already declared it had a stockpile of 40,000 tons of chemical agent. Another sixty-five signatory states had yet to ratify. The CWC represented an improvement over the 1925 Protocol for the Prohibition of the Use in War of Asphyxiating, Poisonous or Other Gases and of Bacteriological Methods of Warfare (the Geneva Protocol) as it explicitly prohibited the development, production and stockpiling of chemical weapons, in addition to their use, and created an intrusive verification regime to ensure compliance. The verification provisions include detailed declaration requirements, routine inspections of declared facilities, and short-notice challenge inspections of undeclared, suspected facilities.

Once the CWC came into effect, the monitoring organization established under its terms, the Organization for the Prohibition of Chemical Weapons (OPCW), was activated. The OPCW, charged with ensuring State Party compliance with the treaty, began its important work of conducting inspections of declared facilities of States Parties. Member states were required to submit, within thirty days of entry into force of the convention, initial declarations about their possession of chemical weapons and past or existing chemical weapons production facilities. As of October 1997, about a third had not yet done so. Meanwhile, the OPCW reported in September that it had already carried out seventy inspections around the world in the first four months of its existence.

In an effort to meet requests by NGOs and the media, the OPCW's director-general requested the permission of member states to release information of a general nature about the States Parties' declarations and OPCW inspections. Of those states that submitted initial declarations, five did not consent to the release of this limited information. Three states declared that they possessed functional chemical weapons, and seven states declared that they had either existing or former chemical weapons production facilities; of these seven states, five—China, France, Japan, the United Kingdom, and the United States—consented to the release of this information. In a move that was praised widely in the media, India also disclosed to the OPCW that it had been involved in the development of chemical weapons—something it had denied repeatedly over the years—but unfortunately declined to allow the OPCW to make this information formally public.

There were also further developments with respect to the 1972 Convention on the Prohibition of the Development, Production and Stockpiling of Bacteriological (Biological) and Toxin Weapons and on their Destruction in 1997. That treaty explicitly banned the production and use of biological weapons but lacked a mechanism to monitor States Parties' compliance with the convention. Official admission by two States Parties, the Russian Federation and Iraq in, respectively, 1992 and 1995, that they had breached the convention by developing, producing and stockpiling biological weapons induced the international community to begin negotiations to strengthen the Convention. Although progress was limited in 1997, these negotiations took at least one big step forward when the Ad Hoc Group charged with this task issued a rolling text in June that was to form the basis of a future verification protocol.

Conventional Weapons

According to figures released by the U.S. Congressional Research Service in 1997, the value of worldwide arms transfer agreements increased in 1996 for the first time since 1992. The United States continued to be the world leader in arms sales. In 1996, the value of arms transfer agreements worldwide was U.S.$31.8 billion. The U.S. share was 35 percent ($11.3 billion). The United Kingdom was second with 15 percent ($4.8 billion) and the Russian Federation third with 14 percent ($4.6 billion). Of these agreements, $19.4 billion were sales to the developing world. Here, too, the U.S. was the leader, with agreements valued at $7.3 billion (38 percent). The Russian Federation ranked second (20 percent with $3.9 billion) and the U.K. third (9 percent with $1.8 billion).

The U.S. also ranked first in arms deliveries made in 1996, with 46 percent of the market ($13.8 billion, of which $9.5 billion went to the developing world). The U.K. again came in second, with 20 percent ($5.9 billion, of which $5.4 billion went to the developing world). France and the Russian Federation were third globally with 10 percent ($2.9 billion) each, though France shipped more arms to the developing world ($2.4 billion).

These formal transfers of arms by governments directly or by commercial companies with government approval, were supplemented by the extensive illegal trade in arms, i.e., smuggled weapons. To contain both flows again posed a major challenge to the international community and NGOs in 1997.

Arms continued to be provided by states to forces that were involved in abuses of international human rights or humanitarian law. Whether primarily pursuing geostrategic interests or propelled by the profit motive, these states fueled the abuses that were committed through the weapons and other forms of military assistance they provided. Among the notable recipients of arms which were involved in abuses of human rights or the laws of war in 1997 were the governments of Angola, Burundi, Colombia, Indonesia, Israel, Rwanda, Sudan, Turkey and Zaire, and a number of rebel movements, including the CNDD in Burundi, the ex-FAR and the ADFL in Rwanda and Congo/Zaire, Hezbollah in Lebanon, the PKK in Turkey, the SPLA in Sudan, the Tamil Tigers in Sri Lanka, and UNITA in Angola. (According to the Stockholm International Peace Research Institute, there were twenty-seven major armed conflicts in the world in 1996, only one of which—India-Pakistan—was of an international nature.) The principal suppliers were the U.S., the Russian Federation, the U.K., France and China—not coincidentally the five permanent members of the Security Council—but also regional powers like Brazil, Egypt, Iran, Israel and South Africa.

Nongovernmental organizations continued to put pressure on multilateral organizations to establish mechanisms that would limit the flow of arms to the countries that are most repressive and the most abusive of human rights. One such proposed mechanism was a code of conduct, with efforts focused at the level of the United Nations, the European Union and individual governments. In May, twelve Nobel Laureates gathered to endorse the International Code of Conduct on Arms Transfers, which had gained the support of a large international network of NGOs. Moreover, seven European Union member states agreed to an E.U. Code of Conduct which included a set of eight Common Criteria for Arms Exports that E.U. governments must take into consideration in deciding to issue licenses for the export of arms and ammunition. One of these criteria was "the respect of human rights in the country of final destination," while others related to the overall protection of human rights. These criteria are not binding; a Council Working Group ("COARM") began the work of examining how E.U. Member States should implement them.

On June 10, the U.S. House of Representatives approved an amendment to the State Department Authorization bill entitled the "Arms Transfers Code of Conduct." The amendment required the president to identify those countries that are either undemocratic, abusers of human rights, involved in acts of armed aggression, or that are not members of the U.N. Register on Conventional Arms. If passed, Congress would then have the option to enact legislation disapproving certain countries for U.S. weapons transfers. In October, the fate of the U.S. Code remained unclear as it became caught up in partisan wrangling in Congress over passage of the Authorization Act.

In July, the newly elected Labour government of Prime Minister Tony Blair announced new criteria that, he said, the U.K. would start applying to all licenses for arms exports. He specified that "Labour will not permit the sale of arms to regimes that might use them for internal repression or international aggression." Lamentably, the government failed to withdraw any of the more than 21,000 existing defense licenses, including one for the sale of sixteen Hawk jets and armored vehicles to Indonesia, but it did block the new but small sale to Indonesia of six armored Land Rovers and a shipment of sniper rifles, at a total value of $1.6 million, in September. In August, the French prime minister, Lionel Jospin, also freshly elected, declared French support for Blair's initiative, and said that he would study turning it into a European or world code of conduct. Then in October, the Belgian foreign minister expressed his government's support for the initiative. The movement toward a European code of conduct appeared to be undermined that same month, though, when the government of Tony Blair announced that it had approved eleven new contracts for equipment under the so-called military list, worth millions of dollars, to Indonesia.

Another mechanism to control the flow of arms was the (voluntary) United Nations Register on Conventional Arms, which in 1997 was in its fifth year. The register uses transparency as a method of arms control by encouraging states to be open about their arms sales and purchases. On August 29, the U.N. published the register for calendar year 1996, which showed that eighty-five states had provided information on their exports and imports during that year. This was a slight decrease from the 1996 register when ninety-one governments made submissions. In the new report, all the major exporters of defense equipment provided information, and more states supplied detailed descriptions of their exports and imports. Noticeably absent from the register were two major recipients of U.S. military assistance, Egypt and Turkey. Efforts to improve the register this year were unsuccessful. When the Group of Government Experts on the U.N. Register of Conventional Arms met in August to discuss measures to expand and strengthen the register, it failed to agree on proposals to include new categories of weapons, to change the definitions of existing categories, to require states to indicate the specific types of weapons transferred, or to require countries to provide information on procurement through national production and weapons holdings.

The Wassenaar Arrangement on Export Controls for Conventional Arms and Dual-Use Goods and Technologies, established in 1996, had thirty-three members and a small secretariat in Vienna in 1997. The principal goal of the Arrangement was to promote transparency with respect to transfers of conventional arms and dual-use goods and technologies for military uses, and to prevent the accumulation of arms and military capabilities in areas of instability. In 1997, the secretariat was developing guidelines and procedures for member states, a number of which had not previously been involved in an export control regime. Member states had begun reporting on their exports of munitions and dual-use goods and technologies, and the first semi-annual meeting was held in June.

A final mechanism designed to prevent weapons from creating humanitarian havoc, the 1980 Convention on Conventional Weapons (the CCW), has been in force for a number of years but was awaiting state ratifications following the changes made to the treaty by the Review Conference that ended its work in May 1996. The Conference amended Protocol II on landmines and added Protocol IV on blinding laser weapons. As of October 15, 1997, ten states had ratified the amended Protocol II while thirteen had ratified the new Protocol IV. Both protocols require twenty ratifying states before entry into force.

New efforts were made in 1997 to stem the flow of smuggled weapons. In 1997, out of concern about the increase in the illicit manufacturing and trade of small arms in the western hemisphere, the Permanent Mechanism of Political Consultation and Consensus (aka the Rio Group) introduced a draft Inter-American Convention Against the Illicit Production of and Trafficking in Firearms, Ammunition, Explosives and Other Related Materials to the O.A.S. The draft convention recognized that the rise in arms manufacturing and trafficking was fueling problems, including political violence, drug trafficking, organized crime and other related offenses, that were increasingly coming to be seen as threats to national and international security, as well as posing a danger to the social and economic development of the people in the region and their right to live in peace. In order to achieve its goals at both the regional and international levels, the draft convention set out specific guidelines and obligations for each State Party. These included, but were not limited to: the adoption of legislative measures; the creation of registers of manufacturers, traders, importers and exporters of the said materials; the adoption of a standardized import/export system; and the guaranteed access to relevant information by the participating States Parties. In addition, a consultative committee, consisting of representatives from each State Party, was to be set up to monitor progress on the international level, foster international cooperation in the region, and promote the exchange of information, the standardization of laws, the development of communication, an increase in training and technical assistance related to the issues, and the unification of administrative procedures to ensure that uniform standards would be upheld. A final draft treaty was negotiated in October, and a special session of the O.A.S. general assembly was scheduled for mid-November during which the treaty was expected to be approved and opened for signature. The treaty appeared to enjoy widespread support.

During the Dutch Presidency of the E.U. in the first half of 1997, the E.U. adopted the "E.U. Program for Preventing and Combating Illicit Trafficking in Conventional Arms," an initiative that had developed out of discussions begun in the above-mentioned Council Working Group (COARM). This program envisaged a number of measures to strengthen cooperation among European customs and law enforcement agencies at the national and international levels, and was expected to focus initially on the light weapons trade in Africa.

Arms Transfers to Abusive End-Users

In 1997, the flow of arms—primarily small arms, light weapons, explosives, and ammunition—continued to fuel abuses of international human rights and humanitarian law around the globe, especially in Africa, but received little attention compared to weapons of mass destruction. In one positive development, in August, a U.N. Panel of Governmental Experts on Small Arms produced a consensus report on the worldwide problem of small-arms proliferation despite serious disagreements among panel members on a number of issues. Important recommendations that survived the various versions of the report included a call for a global conference on illicit arms transfers and a recommen-

dation to destroy surplus weapons and weapons that remain after a conflict's end. On the other hand, success in increasing transparency in the light weapons trade, a highly controversial topic of debate, remained lamentably elusive. The report also reflected the bias of its authors in focusing on the activities of nonstate actors while playing down the role of governments in supplying weapons and committing abuses of human rights. The U.N. displayed a further sensitivity to the importance of the trade in conventional weapons in October, when the U.N. secretary-general, Kofi Annan, told the Conference on Disarmament that the absence of norms governing conventional weapons was of particular concern to him, and that in his view little had been done to curb their rapidly escalating proliferation, a situation that had created "perverse chains of events."

One of the most powerful tools the international community had to control the flow of arms to abusive end-users—international arms embargoes—remained largely ineffective in 1997. The reason was the absence of the embargoes' active implementation and enforcement, with the exception of punitive sanction regimes imposed on Iraq and Libya. Reporting on the implementation of all other embargoes remained minimal, and no actions were taken against violators. In Africa, arms embargoes were observed solely in the breach, circumvented by arms traffickers operating on the territories of nations that kept their eyes shut or even facilitated arms flows in an effort to assist allies and defeat enemies.

The Great Lakes Region

The only ray of hope in 1996, already dimming in 1997, was the work of the U.N. Commission of Inquiry in the Great Lakes region, also known as UNICOI, which had been established in 1995 in the wake of a Human Rights Watch report on arms supplies to the perpetrators of the Rwandan genocide and was charged with investigating violations of the international arms embargo on Rwanda. UNICOI carried out its investigation during a period of twelve months, issuing two preliminary reports. Unfortunately, its third and final report, submitted to the U.N. secretary-general at the end of October 1996, though promptly leaked to the press, was never made public, and the U.N. Security Council failed to give the commission a new mandate. As a result, the important investigative work UNICOI had been able to carry out was abruptly halted at year's end, and the recommendations it made were ignored. These recommendations included: the creation of an office, at the time of the imposition of an international arms embargo, that would monitor, implement and enforce the operation of the embargo on the territory of each neighboring state, collect evidence of violations, and make regular reports to the Security Council; the creation of voluntary regional registers or data banks of movements and acquisitions of small arms, ammunition and materiél; the encouragement for regional governments to ratify the Convention on Conventional Weapons; the establishment, on an ad hoc basis, of commissions of inquiry to investigate reported violations of arms embargoes; and the request that states producing arms and materiél take any measure necessary under their domestic law to implement the provisions of international arms embargoes, and in particular to prosecute their nationals who are found to be in violation of such provisions, even if they conduct their illegal activities in third countries.

The U.N.'s motives in failing to release and act upon UNICOI's report remained obscure, but the commission's very existence had a number of salutary consequences: It provided the means to investigate and verify some specific allegations of serious violations of an international arms embargo; it allowed for the consideration of new, more effective ways of dealing with the problem of weapons proliferation in Africa, if not by the Security Council, then by other U.N. bodies and NGOs; and it put those involved in arms trafficking on notice that they could no longer operate with complete impunity, that they were being watched. It is possible even that the commission's work during its brief tenure had a deterrent effect on those most closely involved in the lethal trade.

Absent a serious effort to strengthen the effectiveness of arms embargoes, the imposition of such embargoes by the United Nations, the European Union and, in the case of Burundi, regional coalitions of states remained wholly symbolic. In October, the U.N. Security Council imposed an arms embargo on Sierra Leone, authorizing the Economic Community of West African States (ECOWAS) to ensure strict implementation of the arms embargo but failing to establish specific mechanisms designed to assist ECOWAS in doing so. Also in October, the Security Council put fresh sanctions on the National Union for the Total Independence of Angola (União Nacional para a Independência Total de Angola, UNITA), on top of an earlier arms embargo, in an attempt to force the rebel movement to join Angola's peace process by prohibiting, inter alia, foreign air traffic—including planes carrying supplies of arms—into UNITA-controlled territory.

The situation in Burundi continued to be cause of grave concern in 1997, and evidence emerged that external actors were instrumental in fueling the highly abusive civil war through their direct transfers of arms to parties to the conflict or their failure to prevent such transfers by private arms dealers. A number of countries, including China, France, North Korea, the Russian Federation, Rwanda, Tanzania, Uganda, the United States, and Zaire/Congo, directly provided military support to abusive forces engaged in the fighting, although France and the United States stated that their assistance had ceased in mid-1996. Other states, most notably Angola, Kenya, Rwanda, Tanzania, Uganda, and Zaire/Congo permitted the transshipment of weapons through their territories. Tanzania and Zaire/Congo allowed insurgents to establish bases on their territory, while Kenya served as a headquarters for the various Hutu rebel organizations. Most commonly, private arms merchants took advantage of loose restrictions on arms transfers, poor controls at border points, and/or corrupt officials in South Africa and Europe to ship arms from former East Bloc countries to the Great Lakes region. Belgium and South Africa were particularly viable transshipment countries and bases of activity for arms traders, who have operated with impunity. Using these weapons, the Burundian armed forces and allied Tutsi civilian militias and gangs, and Hutu guerrilla groups have killed tens of thousands of unarmed civilians, often solely because of their ethnicity, and forced hundreds of thousands from their homes during the war. The sanctions, including an arms embargo, that neighboring states imposed on the government of Burundi—but not on opposition forces—in 1996 remained in force in 1997, even if they did not appear to be actively enforced.

In 1997, some of the governments implicated in the illicit trade of arms took small steps to rein in the activities of arms traffickers and mercenaries, who continued to cater to violent conflicts around the world, seemingly unhampered by the few national and international restrictions that do exist on such activities. The Belgian government, for example, announced that it had opened an investigation into the use by arms traffickers of Ostend Airport, a prime transshipment point for arms from the former Warsaw Pact countries to African conflict zones, especially the Great Lakes region. In another example, the U.K. government undertook an investigation of a company registered on the Isle of Man that was implicated in repeated violations of the international arms embargo on Rwanda, after reporters found a series of arms sales contracts in a cache of documents left behind by retreating Rwandan Hutu rebel forces in eastern Zaire/Congo in November 1996. The documents showed that the company had supplied more than $5.5 million worth of weapons and ammunition to the perpetrators of the 1994 genocide in Rwanda. It soon became clear that the company had been able to do so after the U.K. government had failed to request the Isle of Man, a crown dependency, to incorporate the international arms embargo on Rwanda into its domestic law, as the U.K. itself had done in 1994. The government subsequently claimed that this failure was "just an oversight" and that the matter would be rectified. Human Rights Watch called upon the United Kingdom to identify and prosecute violators of international arms embargoes, and to execute stricter oversights over companies registered there and in its offshore dependencies.

The Role of South Africa

Whereas the post-apartheid government of President Nelson Mandela has tried to leash South Africa's aggressive arms-export industry since it came to power in 1994, elements of the old regime continued to ferry weapons illegally to conflicts in Africa in 1997, and arms industry pressures on the government led to a series of controversial official sales as well. The National Conventional Arms Control Committee (NCACC), headed by the minister of water affairs and forestry, Kader Asmal, in July approved the sale of what it termed "nonlethal" military equipment to the government of Rwanda. The sale had been suspended for almost a year because of concerns in South Africa over the unstable situation in the Great Lakes region. Asmal justified the weapons sale to Rwanda by stating, in October 1996, that "a void [was] more dangerous"; that "the U.N. [had] lifted the arms embargo" on the Rwandan government; that the Rwandan government "is a legitimate government"; that the weapons constituted "self-defense equipment"; and that the value of the sale, 68 million South African Rand (about U.S.$14 million), was "very small compared to what South Africa [under apartheid] used to send to [the previous government of] Rwanda." Human Rights Watch pressed the government of South Africa to reconsider the decision to give the green light to the sale, which came at the time when the Rwandan government publicly admitted the role of its military forces in the campaign to oust Zaire's president, Mobutu Sese Seko, from power earlier in 1997, and evidence emerged of the involvement of these forces in mass killings of Hutu civilians.

In October, the government's primary arms broker, Denel, announced that it was negotiating with the government of Algeria the sale of Rooivalk attack helicopters and Seeker unmanned reconnaissance aircraft. The situation in Algeria had just marked a sharp deterioration, with unidentified armed groups carrying out brutal massacres of civilians on the outskirts of the capital. Earlier, though, in August, the South African government vetoed the sale of twelve Rooivalk attack helicopters to Turkey on the grounds, in part, of Turkey's poor human rights record. At the end of August, South Africa's minister of defense, Joe Modise, announced that his government was seeking to sell excess antiaircraft weapons, infantry vehicles, helicopters, and other war materiél. This announcement came in the wake of media reports that South African weapons had turned up on both sides of the war in Sudan, and raised concerns that excess weapons sold to unscrupulous buyers might also find their way to conflict zones—in Sudan and elsewhere. Human Rights Watch pressed the government of South Africa for guarantees that the excess weapons would not be used in the conflict in Sudan.

In late July, the government announced its new policy on transparency regarding the export of South African arms. Around the same time, it became known that the government had suppressed information about a proposed sale of military hardware to Saudi Arabia. Unable to prevent publication of the recipient country's name, despite having threatened South African newspapers with legal action, the government proceeded to negotiate the $1.5 billion oil-for-arms deal with the Saudi Kingdom, while claiming that transparency in its view did not include naming recipient countries if the latter preferred to remain anonymous.

Finally, the government in 1997 also took one further step in reining in the activities of South African nationals who, marketing themselves as private security consultants, have operated as mercenaries in several African countries. In July, the government submitted legislation to Parliament that would force South African mercenaries to obtain a license to provide military-related services abroad, and that provided for penalties of a one million Rand fine (about $213,000) or ten years in jail, or both. In October, the draft legislation was still being debated.

Sudan

The war in southern Sudan was in its fourteenth year in 1997. More than a million people have died and millions more have been forcibly displaced, many seeking refuge in neighboring countries, since 1983. In 1997, the war continued to spread to other regions of the country, and threatened to spill across Sudan's borders, as government military support of opposition groups in Eritrea, Ethiopia and Uganda was matched by these governments' military aid of Sudanese rebel groups. A steady flow of sophisticated arms into the region over the past decade and continuing in 1997 has fueled the escalation of the fighting and multiplied its lethal impact on the civilian population.

In 1997, the government of Sudan continued to enhance its conventional arms capability through the acquisition of large quantities of light and medium arms and ammunition, medium and heavy armor and artillery, and air power. Its suppliers in 1997 included China, some of the former East Bloc states, and Iran and Iraq, although Sudan also continued to use weapons dating from previous decades. These weapons appeared to be of Western manufacture, and were likely to have been provided to Sudan when it was ruled by a government friendly to the West. The main rebel groups, the Sudan Alliance Forces (SAF) and the Sudanese People's Liberation Army (SPLA), had a substantial fleet of tanks and armored vehicles in 1997, many captured from government forces but some also provided by neighboring states. The announcement by the government in June that it would sign the treaty to ban antipersonnel landmines in Ottawa in December came as evidence emerged of the government's use of antipersonnel landmines in the war, and the supply of mines to allied opposition forces in neighboring countries.

Turkey

The war in Turkey's southeast between government forces and fighters of the Kurdish Workers Party (known as the PKK) also continued in 1997, with Turkish security forces making repeated forays into northern Iraq, ostensibly in pursuit of PKK units. To support their war effort, both sides have made arms acquisitions. The PKK, at times supported by Syria, Iran and Kurdish parties in northern Iraq, has bought weapons on the open market, financed primarily by supporters in western Europe. As for the government, an estimated 80 percent of Turkey's military arsenal consisted of U.S.-made or -designed hardware. In early 1997, the Turkish government announced its intention to make further military hardware purchases abroad, including attack and transport helicopters, battle tanks, armored vehicles and assault rifles, as well as fighter jet upgrades. The U.S., France, Germany, Britain, Israel, and Italy jostled to win multi-million dollar contracts, with no human rights conditions attached, for their industries to upgrade, design, co-produce, and sell military equipment to Turkey.

U.S. arms sales to Turkey continued to be controversial in the wake of the scuttling of a sale of Super Cobra attack helicopters in late 1996, on the grounds of Turkey's human rights record. Despite the apparent reluctance by the U.S. government to rubber-stamp arms sales to Turkey, it made no serious attempt to monitor the use of its weapons by Turkey nor to attach human rights conditions to any arms transfer in 1997. The State Department had provided Congress with an end-use monitoring report in 1995 that was unsatisfactory in a number of respects, and Congress had subsequently requested an updated report by July 1997. The second report better reflected the human rights impact of the use of U.S. weapons by Turkish security forces, but continued to ignore the role of these forces in the forcible displacement of the population of Kurdish villages, and tried to shift the blame for the most egregious abuses to gendarmerie and police "special operations teams" which, the report implied, are not directly under the command of the U.S.-supported military.

In March, the trial of the Turkish translator and publisher of the 1995 Human Rights Watch report on arms transfers and human rights violations in Turkey came to an end. Ertu rul Kürkçü and Ay enur Zarakolu had been accused of "defaming and belittling the state military and security forces" for having translated and published the report in Turkish. The state prosecutor in particular had seized on a reference in the report to the special police teams as "brutal thugs," a term used, as it turned out, by an official at the U.S. embassy in Ankara who was quoted in the report. On March 14, a three-judge panel found the translator and publisher guilty of the charge of defamation, giving Kürkçü a ten-month prison sentence, suspended for two years, and fining Zarakolu the largely symbolic amount of 1.5 million Turkish Lira, about $12. The verdict was a violation of Turkey's obligations under Article 10 of the European Convention on Human Rights, and could intimidate journalists, writers, peaceful protesters, and others concerned with the conflict in southeastern Turkey. Kürkçü and Zarakolu both appealed the verdict; the appeal was still pending in late October. Human Rights Watch, the Belgium-based Reporters Without Borders, and the U.S. government all sent observers to the trial.

United States Policy

Figures released in 1997 indicated that the U.S. was the largest exporter of military equipment in 1996, the most recent year for which data were available (see above). In the most important step forward in transparency regarding U.S. arms exports in a decade and a half, a new congressionally mandated report was issued by the State Department in September. Known as the "Section 655" report (after the section of the Foreign Assistance Act requiring it), this document provides a very detailed breakdown of U.S. arms exports through both government and private channels, including types of weapons and dollar value, on a country-by-country and program-by-program basis. Among other things, it reveals that in FY 1996 the State Department approved licenses for private commercial firms to export $27 billion in weapons. The report was in essence a reinstatement of a reporting system discontinued by the Reagan administration in 1981; the Human Rights Watch Arms Project, joined by other NGOs, initiated the effort to reinstate the report in 1993 by calling on Congress to write the appropriate language into the Foreign Aid Authorization Bill.

Commercial imperatives continued to guide arms transfer policy, while U.S. participation in multilateral efforts at curbing arms proliferation was lukewarm at best. It took serious backroom bargaining and arm-twisting before the Clinton administration was able to garner enough support in the Senate to secure ratification of the Chemical Weapons Convention in April, just days before the treaty was scheduled to enter into force. Failure to ratify would have excluded the U.S. from a number of benefits accruing from participation in this international regime and, by depriving the CWC's monitoring group, the OPCW, of a significant financial contribution, would have rendered the treaty's effective implementation unlikely.

Support for the international effort to ban landmines was similarly reluctant, despite the fact that President Clinton had shown leadership on this issue in years past. In 1997, the U.S. at first refused to join the Ottawa Process to ban landmines, launching an ill-conceived effort at the U.N. Conference on Disarmament (CD). Both the ICBL and the ICRC condemned the U.S. move as diversionary and counterproductive to rapid achievement of a global ban. As it turned out, the sixty-one-member CD was unable even to agree on a mandate to discuss landmines, and could do no more than appoint a special coordinator to try to reach agreement. The CD adjourned amid bitter recriminations on September 9 without even setting a timetable for serious discussion of landmines or any other arms control initiative.

As newspaper editorials in the U.S. started challenging the Clinton administration's handling of the landmines issue, grass-roots activists began bombarding the White House with letters, postcards and a petition with over 100,000 signatures calling for a ban, and protesters organized vigils outside the White House and the offices of landmine producers. In August, under intense public pressure, the president finally agreed to send a negotiating team to Oslo. However, he did so without any change in U.S. policy on mines and as a result the U.S. delegation in Oslo insisted on a handful of amendments that would have gutted the treaty. In a testament to the Ottawa process, each of the U.S. demands was rejected due to strong leadership by the International Campaign to Ban Landmines and key governments such as Norway, Canada, Austria, and South Africa. Anticipating defeat in a formal vote, the U.S. withdrew its amendments and later indicated it did not intend to sign the treaty in December. In an effort to ease the embarrassment of Oslo, the U.S. promptly announced that it would continue to pursue a ban in the CD, and that it was now committed to banning the weapon by the year 2006. Left out of the announcement was the fact that the U.S. intended to rename approximately one million of its "smart" antipersonnel mines as submunitions, thus exempting them from the ban. Having failed to convince other governments in Oslo with its attempt to relabel these mines, the Clinton administration was now trying its deception on the U.S. public.

At the end of 1997, the United States had yet to ratify the amended Protocol II to the Convention on Conventional Weapons (concerning landmines) or the new Protocol IV (banning the use and trade of blinding laser weapons). Even though it signed Protocol IV in October 1995, the U.S. was continuing in 1997 to pursue research on tactical lasers that have the capacity to blind.

The Work of
Human Rights Watch

The Human Rights Watch Arms Project was established at the end of the Cold War to tackle the problems and exploit the opportunities that the new world order/disorder was expected to present. In the five years of its existence, it has brought a novel approach to both arms control and human rights advocacy, seeking to set new international norms and effect positive change in the behavior of international actors. In 1997, the strategy continued to be to investigate, to expose, to articulate new norms, to mobilize, to stigmatize, and to effect change, concentrating our efforts on the campaign to ban landmines, exposing the presence of chemical weapons in the former Yugoslavia, and highlighting the role of international actors in fanning the flames of conflict and human rights abuses in the Great Lakes region of Africa.

Banning Landmines

Only twice has the international community brought itself to ban a whole class of conventional weapons. One was blinding lasers, the use and trade of which were banned in 1995, and the other was antipersonnel landmines, with the comprehensive ban treaty of 1997. On both occasions Human Rights Watch played an instrumental role. As a founder of the International Campaign to Ban Landmines and a member of its steering committee, and as chair of the U.S. Campaign to Ban Landmines, the organization's Arms Project was in the forefront of efforts to reach consensus on a comprehensive landmines ban under the Ottawa Process. On October 10, the ICBL and its coordinator, Jody Williams, were jointly awarded the 1997 Nobel Peace Prize.

Human Rights Watch participated in all major conferences addressing this issue in 1997, and served as an ICBL representative and spokesperson at the government-sponsored treaty preparatory conferences in Vienna in February, Bonn in April, Johannesburg in May, and Brussels in June, as well as at the treaty-negotiating conference in Oslo in September. It had a prominent role in the organization of and region-wide build-up to the ICBL's conference held in Mozambique in February aimed at fostering the creation of a mine-free zone in southern Africa—a goal achieved just a few months later. In the U.S., Human Rights Watch engaged in regular dialogue with U.S. military and political officials in an ultimately futile bid to find common ground. The organization also visited a number of other national capitals to discuss our landmines concerns in an

effort to bring stragglers on board and urge supporters to adhere to a comprehensive ban without reservations. Human Rights Watch was deeply involved in the unprecedented NGO role in drafting and negotiating the treaty, and worked in close cooperation with the key governments in the Ottawa Process.

The Human Rights Watch Arms Project published four reports on landmines in 1997. The first comprehensive exposé of U.S. companies involved in manufacturing antipersonnel mine components was published in April, identifying forty-seven U.S. corporations. Following correspondence with Human Rights Watch, seventeen of these companies agreed to renounce all future landmine production—startling evidence of the power of the mine ban campaign. The devastating legacy of three decades of rampant landmine use in the southern part of the African continent was described in a report released in May, and provided African pro-ban activists with a powerful advocacy tool. It was presented at the mine conference in Johannesburg which led to the de facto creation of a "mine-free zone" in southern Africa. An analysis of the Pentagon's own archives on the use of landmines in the Korean and Vietnam wars was published in July. Evidence culled from these archives that tens of thousands of U.S. soldiers were killed and maimed by their own landmines in the wars in Korea and Vietnam made headlines and undercut one of the U.S. government's principal contentions, that landmines protect U.S. forces. The positions of the members of the British Commonwealth on antipersonnel landmines were elaborated in a report published at the Commonwealth meeting in Edinburgh in October.

Monitoring the Prohibition on Chemical Weapons

In March, less than two months before the Chemical Weapons Convention was to enter into force and its ratification by the U.S. Senate appeared to be blocked, Human Rights Watch sent a letter to Senate Majority Leader Trent Lott urging an early scheduling of a Senate vote on the issue in light of the CWC's hopeful promise to rid the world of this most insidious of weapons. In April, Human Rights Watch sent a statement, co-signed by twenty-six other U.S. NGOs—including human rights, relief, arms control, religious, peace and veterans' groups—urging all one hundred members of the U.S. Senate to vote in favor of ratification of the CWC.

At the end of March, the organization released a report based on a year of research on the existence of chemical weapons in the former Yugoslavia. The continued presence of a chemical weapons production capability in the region posed a potential threat to the fragile peace established under the Dayton accords. Members of the international community, especially the United States, who are aware that the republics of the former Yugoslavia are capable of producing chemical weapons, were shown to have been reluctant to make this information public. In 1997, the investigation continued of the alleged use of chemical weapons by Bosnian Serb forces around Srebrenica at the time of the collapse of this U.N. safe haven in July 1995.

Part of the interest in pursuing investigations of chemical weapons production, trade, and use was to encourage governments' transparency about existing capabilities so as to stave off a dangerous proliferation and possible use of these weapons in times of conflict. Following research based on documents obtained under the U.S. Freedom of Information Act, Human Rights Watch published an article in the *Bulletin of the Atomic Scientists* in September disclosing that the U.S. government has only selectively revealed what it knows about the chemical weapons capabilities of other states—protecting its allies as it fingered some of the so-called "rogue" nations. The article named over twenty countries in Europe, Asia, the Middle East and Africa that, according to U.S. assessments, had chemical weapons programs in various stages of development.

Monitoring Arms Transfers to Abusive End-Users

In 1997, Human Rights Watch continued to monitor arms flows to forces that were involved in serious abuses of international hu-

man rights or humanitarian law. In particular, we monitored conflicts in Turkey, Sudan, Angola, and the Great Lakes region in Central Africa, while keeping an eye on the principal arms suppliers: the United States, the Russian Federation, China, the United Kingdom, France, and, especially in Africa, South Africa. Research on Burundi and Sudan was completed in November.

In early 1997, Human Rights Watch drew attention to reported attempts by the Turkish government to make fresh purchases of military hardware abroad. We urged potential supplier governments to refrain from transferring weapons until the Turkish government showed concrete progress to end abuses and bring its military into line with international and North Atlantic Treaty Organization norms and guidelines; and made recommendations to the U.S. concerning end-use monitoring and regular reporting of its findings to the U.S. Congress.

The Great Lakes remained an important area of focus for Human Rights Watch in 1997 as well. The Arms Project initiated communications with governments involved in the supply of weapons to parties in the conflict in Burundi with a view to stemming the flow of arms into the area. We also urged the U.N. Security Council to revive the International Commission of Inquiry (UNICOI) in Rwanda, implement the important recommendations it made in 1996, and provide it with a new mandate to investigate arms trafficking in the Great Lakes region, including Rwanda, Burundi, and the Congo. Human Rights Watch published an article in the *Bulletin of the Association of Concerned Africa Scholars* in the fall, analyzing the work of the commission and the reasons for its untimely demise.

An important component of efforts to stem the flow of weapons to abusive end-users is the creation of mechanisms that control the export of arms by manufacturing states. Human Rights Watch has supported the campaign to institute an international Code of Conduct on arms transfers, at the United Nations and the European Union, as well as in the United States. In July, as a U.S. Code of Conduct for conventional arms transfers was moving slowly through Congress, Human Rights Watch wrote to Senator Jesse Helms, chairman of the Senate Foreign Relations Committee, as part of a coalition of three hundred arms control, human rights, women's professional, development and religious organizations. The Code had been included in a State Department Authorization Act which was approved by the House of Representatives in June. The Arms Project urged Senator Helms to keep the Code provision in this Act as it was debated in conference committee. In October, the Senate had yet to vote on the Act and its various provisions, including the Code.

Relevant Human Rights Watch reports:

Stoking the Fires: Military Assistance and Arms Trafficking in Burundi, 12/97

Killers in the Commonwealth: Antipersonnel Landmine Policies of the Commonwealth Nations, 10/97

Antipersonnel Mines in The Korean and Vietnam Wars, 7/97

Still Killing: Landmines in Southern Africa, 5/97

U.S. Companies and Production of Antipersonnel Mines, 4/97

Chemical Weapons in Former Yugoslavia, 3/97

THE CHILDREN'S RIGHTS PROJECT

Developments in Children's Rights

Abuses that uniquely affect children pose particular challenges for human rights action. Research requires new and specialized methodology; the assessment and development of policy options must address the special circumstances and vulnerabilities of children in need and the problems they confront; and to raise awareness, build coalitions, and bring about change, unique campaigning initiatives are needed. The range of abuses requiring attention include those carried out by governments as well as those in which governments do not exercise due diligence in protecting the rights of the child. Abuses by armed opposition groups are also crucial children's right issues, not least the use of children as soldiers.

Effective work toward an end to the abuses that expressly affect the rights of children requires devising innovative research and advocacy strategies, drawing on strong partnerships with local activists world-wide in their formulation and implementation. A crucial goal of an effective program for the rights of children is to bring international and national children's groups together with the larger human rights community.

In 1997 children continued to be victimized and exploited around the world. In some countries, eight-year-old children were forced to become child soldiers; some were forced to beat or hack other children to death. In other countries, five and six-year-old children worked as bonded laborers, laboring in dreadful conditions for long hours to try to pay off loans made to their families. In many countries, children were routinely beaten by police officers, arbitrarily detained, and sent without due process to appalling institutions that provided no education or rehabilitation, while governments and the general public ignored their distress.

These are just some of the children's rights issues that required research and action for change in 1997. The sections that follow examine some of the unique human rights dimensions of the issues of child labor, child soldiers, street children, and juvenile justice, drawing from the work of Human Rights Watch in these areas over the past year.

Child Labor

My sister is ten years old. Every morning at seven she goes to the bonded labor man, and every night at nine she comes home. He treats her badly; he hits her if he thinks she is working slowly or if she talks to other children he yells at her. He comes looking for her if she is sick and cannot work. All I want is to bring my sister home. For 600 rupees I can bring her home. But we will never have 600 rupees.

— Lakshmi, a nine-year-old beedi (cigarette) roller in Tamil Nadu in

India, in an interview with Human Rights Watch. Six hundred rupees is the equivalent of about U.S. $17.

The International Labor Organization (ILO) has estimated that 250 million children between the ages of five and fourteen worked in developing countries—at least 120 million full time. Sixty-one percent of these were in Asia, 32 percent in Africa, and 7 percent in Latin America. Most working children in rural areas were found in agriculture; urban children worked in trade and services, with fewer in manufacturing, construction and domestic service. Bonded child labor, a form of slavery, is the part of this larger picture upon which Human Rights Watch has focused its efforts.

Children who work long hours, often in dangerous and unhealthy conditions, are exposed to lasting physical and psychological harm. Working at looms, for example, has left children disabled with eye damage, lung disease, stunted growth, and a susceptibility to arthritis as they grow older. They are denied an education and a normal childhood. Some are confined and beaten, reduced to slavery. Some are denied freedom of movement—the right to leave the workplace and go home to their families. Some are even abducted and forced to work.

Child labor is not a simple issue. Even nongovernmental organizations (NGOs) and others concerned with child labor are sharply divided on how to proceed, arguing variously that all child labor be eliminated immediately; or that the conditions in which children work be reformed with a view toward ultimate elimination; or even that working at a young age may play an important and positive role in children's lives and in their relations with their families, and that it should be reformed but not abolished.

Simply demanding the discharge of child workers can lead to devastating results for the children. In Bangladesh in 1993, for example, garment manufacturers discharged thousands of child workers, believing that proposed legislation prohibiting the importation into the United States of any product made with child labor had been enacted into law. Subse-

quent studies found that none of the children discharged ended up in school, that many ended up on the street in prostitution or crime, and that the rest were working in worse conditions and for less pay.

The trade sanction approach—seeking boycotts of employers who use child workers in order to eliminate child labor—is, in its seeming simplicity, appealing; it has been used in the carpet industry and with soccer ball manufacturers. In theory, consumers can discourage child labor by not buying products made by children, and feel content to have played a part in reform. Unfortunately, employers' assurances that they have not used child labor cannot be verified without the presence of independent monitors and it is impossible at present to monitor manufacturing workplaces worldwide. No such mechanisms exist today. At any rate, the ILO estimates that only about 5 percent of child laborers work in export industries and the Bangladesh example shows that there are no guarantees that children affected by a boycott will necessarily be better off.

Conditions of child labor range from that of four-year-olds tied to rug looms to keep them from running away, to seventeen-year-olds helping out on the family farm. In some cases, a child's work can be helpful to him or her and to the family; working and earning can be a positive experience in a child's growing up. This depends largely on the age of the child, the conditions in which the child works, and whether work prevents the child from going to school.

Forced and bonded child labor stand out in that the rights abuses entailed are clear and acute. Tackling these aspects of the complex and troubling child labor issue can serve to draw attention to the plight of bonded and forced child laborers and help to end these appalling practices, while contributing to the debate on the rights dimension of the larger issue of children and work. Both forced labor and bonded labor are viewed in international law as forms of slavery; legislation in many countries forbids these practices, but is frequently unenforced. Forced or bonded child laborers are denied the rights to freedom from slavery, freedom of movement, freedom from violence and abuse, and the right to an education and a normal childhood.

Bonded labor takes place when a family receives an advance payment (sometimes as little as U.S. $15.) to hand a child—boy or girl—over to an employer. In most cases the child cannot work off the debt, nor can the family raise enough money to buy the child back. In some cases, the labor is generational—that is, a child's grandfather or great-grandfather was promised to an employer many years earlier, with the understanding that each generation would provide the employer with a new worker—often with no pay at all. In India alone, 15 million children work as bonded laborers.

Child Labor in India

Bonded child labor exists throughout India, with the vast majority found in industries that produce products for domestic consumption, although bonded children are also to be found laboring in some export industries. Bonded child laborers in six industries in India—silk, beedis (hand-rolled cigarettes), leather, silver, gemstones, and carpets—have been found by Human Rights Watch to involve similar practices, in which the lives and labor of children as young as five were mortgaged to private employers. The children were bound by this form of slavery to work long hours, to perform tasks that resulted in lasting physical injury, in conditions that were often unsafe, for periods that were in effect limited only by the child's capacity to continue completing the tasks required. They lose their health, their right to receive an education, and their futures: many of the children now in bonded servitude have inherited the debts of parents' who themselves lost their childhoods as bonded laborers. Unless broken, this cycle of bondage offers little hope for their own children.

The Indian government's failure to enforce its own laws against bonded labor had condemned millions of children to lives of grueling labor in unsafe conditions, and prevented them from receiving the education to which they were entitled. Pressure to this end, led by Indian nongovernmental organizations, some parts of the Indian judiciary, and supported by international nongovernmental organizations led to some movement toward reform in late 1996 and 1997. A report prepared by Human Rights Watch, in consultation with Indian counterpart organizations, appeared in October 1996. A series of recommendations agreed by these partner organizations centered on the importance of India's implementation of its own laws that outlaw bonded labor, while providing a remedy for injustices done to the children freed from bondage that would look to their future. The principal proposal to this end was that the government provide education, in compensation for, and as a measure of rehabilitation for the wrong done these children and to prevent their return to bondage—and that the guilty employers contribute to this.

The Indian Supreme Court in December 1996 ordered child laborers to be freed from hazardous industries and promoted compulsory education for children through the creation of a trust fund from employers and the government. It also recommended a program of job replacement aimed at providing jobs for adult family members who would replace the freed children. The court also ordered state labor ministries to complete surveys of child labor. In January 1997 the Karnataka State Labor Department raided five establishments that employed child labor and filed a total of twenty-five cases against their owners. Similar raids in Tamil Nadu in April 1997 and in Gudiyatham in November 1996 resulted in the identification of bonded child laborers.

In another promising development, the Karnataka State High Court ruled in 1997 that children in the sericulture (silk) industry must be taken out of work and that their educations must be provided for by employers under the directives of the December Supreme Court ruling. NGOs in partnership with Human Rights Watch said that the decision gave them a useful tool in eradicating child labor in the silk industry.

Research revealed that the silk industry, which was heavily supported by the World Bank, employed many bonded child laborers.

The World Bank, embarrassed by this disclosure, chose to include NGO monitoring of projects for child labor as a condition of support on future projects. The bank has now acknowledged that child labor was used in its projects and, in cooperation with the government and nongovernmental organizations, was exploring pilot programs that would remove children from the workplace, rehabilitate them, and provide them with education. It has also begun the process of developing a policy on child labor that could be reflected in its lending agreements with countries.

The Swiss Development Corporation, which also funded sericulture projects in India, convened an NGO working group to develop programs aimed at curbing the use of child labor in Swiss Development Corporation/World Bank funded programs. The working group met regularly to design approaches to alleviate the human rights abuses resulting from child labor in sericulture.

Child Soldiers

I was good at shooting. I went for several battles in Sudan. The soldiers on the other side would be squatting, but we would stand in a straight line. The commanders were behind us. They would tell us to run straight into the gunfire. The commanders would stay behind and would beat those of us who would not run forward. You would just run forward shooting your gun. . . . I remember the first time I was in the front line. The other side started firing, and the commander ordered us to run towards the bullets. I panicked. I saw others falling down dead around me. The commanders were beating us for not running, for trying to crouch down. They said if we fall down, we would be shot and killed by the soldiers. In Sudan we were fighting the Dinkas, and other Sudanese civilians. I don't know why we were fighting them. We were just ordered to fight.

— Fourteen-year-old boy, abducted by the Lord's Resistance Army, interviewed by Human Rights Watch in Gulu, Uganda in May 1997.

One of the most alarming trends in contemporary armed conflicts is the reliance on children as combatants. An estimated quarter of a million children under the age of eighteen serve as soldiers in government forces or armed opposition groups around the world. Children as young as eight are being forcibly recruited, coerced, or induced to become combatants, targeted to become soldiers because of their unique vulnerability as children. Their emotional and physical immaturity make them particularly malleable and easily susceptible to psychological and physical control. Manipulated by adults, children are drawn into violence that they are too young to resist, while they are too young to appreciate and cope with its consequences.

Children are recruited in a variety of ways. Some are conscripted, others are forcibly recruited, press-ganged or kidnaped and literally dragged from their homes, schools, and villages. Some families offer their children for military service, driven by poverty and hunger, and sometimes children become soldiers simply in order to survive, when their families are dead or the children have become lost or separated from their families. Without other means of support, for some children becoming a soldier may be a means of guaranteeing meals, clothing, and security in troubling times.

Child soldiers perform a variety of duties, ranging from support functions as cooks, porters, messengers and spies, to actually fighting as combatants—due in part to the increased availability of lightweight, simple to operate, and inexpensive automatic weapons. Girls are also often forced to provide sexual services to other soldiers. Whether serving in support functions or as combatants, all children are likely to find themselves at times in the midst of heated battle, where their inexperience and physical immaturity make them particularly vulnerable to injury and death.

Even after children are demobilized, their future is often tragically bleak. Effective planning and long-term support for demobilized children is essential for the meaningful reintegration of children into their families and into civilian society. In addition to meeting children's immediate physical, emotional, and psychological needs, children must be equipped with the skills and education necessary in order for them to survive and live productively as civilians. This is true for all children, but especially so for those who remain separated from their families or whose families have been killed or whose whereabouts are unknown. Without families that are able and willing to accept, support and nurture the children upon return, prospects for their future are especially grim without strong government and community support.

Children were used as soldiers by all of the warring factions in Liberia's long civil war, including the National Patriotic Front, led by Charles Taylor, whose election to the presidency in July 1997 appears to have brought an end to the conflict. In 1994, UNICEF estimated that some 10 percent of the 40,000 to 60,000 fighters were children under the age of fifteen. A major challenge in the rebuilding of Liberia will be the rehabilitation of tens of thousands of children— traumatized by their experiences as child soldiers and cut off from any access to education in their formative years—so they can become a part of civil society. In southern Sudan, the long war between the (Muslim) Khartoum government in the north and (non-Muslim) southern secessionist movements continued. The southern rebel movements, in particular the Southern People's Liberation Movement (SPLA), continued their longstanding practice of mass abductions of young boys, for indoctrination and mobilization as child soldiers, and the employment of children in combat. At the same time, the abduction of children by Sudanese government troops and government-backed militia, for child soldiers or sale as slaves, continued to be reported.

The abduction of children by the northern Ugandan opposition group calling itself the Lord's Resistance Army (LRA) is only the most recent situation of the exploitation of child soldiers to be the object of intensive human rights field research and international attention. Over the past two years, between three and five thousand children have escaped from LRA captivity; a total of between six and ten thousand children were estimated to have been abducted. Former child captives who had managed to escape said that heavily armed LRA rebels abducted children as young as eight from their schools and homes, and forced children to march to rebel base camps in southern Sudan, carrying heavy loads, without rest and with very little food and water. Children who protested, or who could not keep up or attempted to escape, were killed, often by other child captives who were forced to participate in killings as a means of breaking their spirits and initiating them into the ways of the LRA. In Sudan the children received rudimentary military training and were armed and sent into combat. The children were forced to fight against the Ugandan government army and against an armed Sudanese rebel group. They were forced to loot and destroy villages and to abduct other children, during the course of which they often became involved in combat. Abducted girls, in addition to performing duties as servants, cooks, and sometimes fighters, were also given as "wives" to LRA soldiers. The abducted children became virtual slaves; their labor, their bodies, and their lives were all at the disposal of their captors.

Those who were lucky enough to escape or be captured alive by the Ugandan government soldiers faced a harsh reality upon their return to civilian life in Uganda. With many of their family members dead, displaced, unlocatable, or fearful of having the children return home, many children found that they had nowhere to go and no means of supporting themselves. In addition to dealing with severe emotional and psychological trauma, malnourishment, disease and physical injuries suffered while in captivity, many children faced worries about their basic survival— how they would feed, clothe, and shelter themselves.

Street Children

We didn't sleep at all last night. That's why we're sleeping now, during the day. Night is the most dangerous for us. The police come while we're sleeping and catch you off guard, and grab and hit you. They'll take you to Makadara court and then you'll be sent to remand [detention] for months. Last night there was a big roundup and we had to move so many times to avoid being caught. There was a large group of police in a big lorry, driving around, looking for kids. They're cleaning up the streets now to prepare for the Nairobi International Show [an annual international commerce and trade fair held in Nairobi].

—Moses, a Nairobi street boy, interviewed by Human Rights Watch in Nairobi, Kenya in September 1996.

Street children throughout the world have been subjected to physical abuse by police or been murdered outright, as governments have treated them as a blight to be eradicated—rather than as children to be nurtured and protected. They were frequently arbitrarily detained by police simply because they were homeless, or charged with vague offenses such as loitering or vagrancy, or petty theft. They have been tortured or beaten by police and often held for long periods in poor conditions. Girls were sometimes sexually abused, coerced into sexual acts, or raped by police. Few advocates have spoken up for these children, and few street children have had family members or concerned individuals willing and able to intervene on their behalf.

The term street children refers to children for whom the street more than their family has become their real home. It includes children who might not necessarily be homeless or without families, but who live in situations where there is no protection, supervision, or direction from responsible adults.

While street children have received a fair amount of national and international public attention, that attention has been focused largely on social, economic and health problems of the children—poverty, lack of education, AIDS, prostitution and substance abuse. With the exception of the massive killings of street children in Brazil and Colombia, often by police, which Human Rights Watch reported in 1994, very little attention has been paid to the constant police violence and abuse

from which many children suffer. This often neglected side of street children's lives has been a focus of Human Rights Watch's research and action.

The public view of street children in many countries has been overwhelmingly negative. Police round ups—or even murder—of the children, as means to get them off the street, have had public support. There has been an alarming tendency by some law enforcement personnel and civilians, business proprietors and their private security firms, to view street children as almost subhuman. In several countries, notably Brazil, Bulgaria, and Sudan, the racial, ethnic, or religious identification of street children has played a significant role in their treatment. The disturbing notion of "social-cleansing" has been applied to street children even when they were not distinguished as members of a particular racial, ethnic, or religious group; branded as "anti-social," or demonstrating "anti-social behavior," street children have been viewed with suspicion and fear by many who would simply like to see street children disappear.

In India, Kenya and Guatemala, police violence against street children was pervasive in 1997, and impunity was the norm. The failure of law enforcement bodies promptly and effectively to investigate and prosecute cases of abuses against street children allowed the violence to continue. Establishing police accountability was further hampered by the fact that street children often had no recourse but to complain directly to police about police abuses. The threat of police reprisals against them served as a serious deterrent to any child coming forward to testify or make a complaint against an officer. In Kenya, Human Rights Watch worked with NGOs and street workers to encourage the establishment of a network for documenting and reporting police abuses against street children, and to follow up on individual cases. Yet even in Guatemala, where the organization Casa Alianza has been particularly active in this regard and has filed approximately 300 criminal complaints on behalf of street children, only a handful have resulted in prosecutions.

Clearly, even where there are advocates willing and able to assist street children in seeking justice, police accountability and an end to the abuses will not be achieved without the commitment of governments.

Street children make up a large proportion of the children who entered the criminal or juvenile justice systems and who end up being committed, often without due process, to correctional institutions. Street children who entered the criminal or juvenile justice systems often ended up adjudicated "delinquent" and confined in institutions which did little to assist and rehabilitate children, even when optimistically called "schools." While it may sometimes be necessary and in the interests of the child to commit a child to institutional care, the conditions in such institutions should always be aimed at promoting the rehabilitation, education, and welfare of the child, rather than punishment.

Conditions in Children's Institutions

E.B.T.R.. [East Baton Rouge Louisiana Training School], that's a messed up place. The guards will beat you. One of them named Mr. O, he has a thing called a 'house party'; if you work on weekends, he wake you up at 5 a.m. He calls you in the back where we take showers and beats you for a whole hour. When we go to mess hall to eat we have to count, and he tells you to come see, then he calls you into the washroom and beats you up and another sergeant comes to beat you. It has only happened two times to me . . . . 'New jacks' come in talking, and they beat them up for nothing. This boy at EBR with me, a guard broke his arm with a broom . . . if you tell a counselor, all it's going to do is make it worse.

—Fifteen-year old boy to Human Rights Watch in 1995.

In 1997, throughout the world, children were confined in correctional institutions—sometimes adult prisons, sometimes juvenile "training schools"—in conditions that hindered their development and damaged their health. The general public was rarely concerned about these children, viewing them as "predators,"

or particularly vicious criminals. Few voices were raised in concern for these children's human rights. Children in confinement rarely received education, vocational training, psychological treatment or other forms or rehabilitation. They were often held in filthy, unsanitary conditions with no privacy. All of these children eventually return to society; failure to prepare them for their return was not only cruel but shortsighted—the social costs were enormous.

Children in confinement have often suffered doubly, having been taken into custody only after having previously suffered abuse at the hands of their families or in the streets they have made their homes. Police violence against street children in Bulgaria, India, Kenya and Guatemala (discussed above) was accompanied by appalling conditions of confinement. In Guatemala, for example, abused or neglected children (including rape victims), runaways, and others were mixed in with violent offenders. Eight-year old abuse victims were locked up with seventeen-year-old convicted murderers. Children received no formal education, psychological treatment, or vocational training. These conditions contravened international standards as set forth in the U.N. Convention on the Rights of the Child (Article 40), a binding treaty to which Guatemala is party, and norms such as the Standard Minimum Rules for the Administration of Juvenile Justice, the U.N. Rules for the Protection of Juveniles Deprived of their Liberty, and the U.N. Guidelines for the Prevention of Juvenile Delinquency.

Shockingly poor conditions for children in correctional institutions existed in the United States as well. State and federal legislators have enacted laws that required trying children in adult courts at younger and younger ages: twelve years old in Colorado, for example. Exaggerated fears of youthful crime led to the incarceration of more and more children and extremely overcrowded institutions in many states, in spite of the FBI's finding that only 7 percent of the juvenile arrests in the U.S. in 1994 were for violent crimes. Legislators were willing to provide money for bricks and mortar, but reluctant to provide money for education, rehabilitation and treatment of children in their care.

Conditions for children in correctional institutions in the three U.S. states of Louisiana, Georgia, and Colorado, have been the object of Human Rights Watch inquiries and reports. There was pervasive brutality by guards against children in Louisiana's four secure institutions. Children were handcuffed and then beaten by guards; children were put in isolation for long periods. These findings, published in 1995, led the U.S. Department of Justice (DOJ) to investigate these four facilities. In 1997 the DOJ issued a damning report: it referred to "life-threatening" abuses, and documented extreme brutality by guards, as well as a failure to protect children from sexual and physical abuse. The DOJ threatened to sue the state, and was negotiating with the state to ensure significant reforms.

In Georgia's children's correctional institutions many children were held in overcrowded, squalid, and unsanitary institutions with inadequate programming. Children were held in four-point restraints, tied by wrists and ankles to a bed, a technique used as a punishment and also for children considered possibly suicidal. Isolation was used as punishment (one child was held this way for sixty-three consecutive days), although international standards forbid isolating children at all. These findings were set out in a 1996 Human Rights Watch report. Again, the DOJ took on the case, and in 1997 opened a formal investigation into the Georgia institutions; that investigation is ongoing.

Research in eight Colorado institutions in 1996 found that virtually every incarceration facility for children was seriously overcrowded (some at two-and-a-half times capacity) and unsafe. The staffs used restraints excessively and punitive segregation; children who could learn and be supervised within the community and presented no threat to public safety were routinely committed; children were sent to facilities out of state, away from their families, or to private contract facilities where the state exercised little control over day-to-day operations or the quality and training of staff. Children complained of chronic hunger; and in several facilities incidents of physical abuse by staff were reported.

The Role of the International Community

The U.N. Committee on the Rights of the Child, UNICEF, and the U.N. Commission on Human Rights were the international governmental bodies which were at the forefront of work for children's human rights.

The U.N. Committee on the Rights of the Child, the treaty body charged with monitoring enforcement of the U.N. Convention on the Rights of the Child, was particularly effective, urging governments, for example, to set up juvenile justice systems where none existed. The U.N. secretary-general also acted upon the committee's recommendations that he institute a two-year study on the impact of armed conflict on children. The committee also prevailed upon U.N. member states to set up a working group to draft an optional protocol to the Convention on the Rights of the Child to raise the minimum age for combat—that working group was next to meet in January 1998.

In March 1997 Human Rights Watch submitted to the committee a report on the Czech Republic's denial of citizenship to Roma (Gypsy) children who had spent their entire lives there, thus denying them their right to acquire a nationality, a guarantee set forth in the U.N. Convention on the Rights of the Child (Articles 7 and 8), which has been ratified by the Czech Republic. Of particular concern was the situation of orphans who faced possible deportation as a result. The Czech government considered many of them to be Slovak, even if they had been born in the Czech Republic and had no ties to Slovakia.

The two-year U.N. Study on the Impact of Armed Conflict on Children (known as the Machel study for the chair of the group, Graca Machel) concluded its work. Human Rights Watch had assisted by providing information, suggestion, and proposing language for the final report that was presented to the General Assembly in November 1996.

A major recommendation of the study was that an expert, responsible directly to the secretary-general, be appointed to follow up on the study's recommendations. That special representative, Olara Otunnu, was appointed in September.

United Nations Children's Fund (UNICEF) was active in addressing questions of bonded child labor, child soldiers, police violence against street children, and other issues of concern to nongovernmental organizations working for children's rights. Children's issues to be incorporated into the draft legislation to establish an international criminal court and plan complementary advocacy steps were the object of consultation between Human Rights Watch and UNICEF officials in August 1977. In September, UNICEF head Carol Bellamy issued a press release on the Lord's Resistance Army's treatment of children citing the findings of Human Rights Watch and Amnesty International.

In March 1997 Human Rights Watch submitted to the U.N. Commission on Human Rights a statement on worldwide police violence against street children, and on bonded child labor. The safety and well-being of the two boys identified as the eleventh Panchen Lama—one identified by the Dalai Lama of Tibet and the other identified by the Chinese government—were also raised with the commission. Human Rights Watch findings on police violence and arbitrary detention of children in Guatemala and Kenya were submitted to the U.N. special rapporteur on torture and the U.N. Working Group on Arbitrary Detention.

United States

At the time of writing, the U.N. Convention on the Rights of the Child has been ratified or acceded to by 191 countries. Only two countries had not ratified the treaty: Somalia, which has no internationally-recognized government, and the United States, which had signed but not ratified the convention. The administration had not forwarded the convention to the Senate Foreign Relations Committee, the body charged with reviewing the treaty. Jesse Helms, the chair of that committee, has described the convention as a "pernicious document" and continued in 1997 to advise the administration that submitting the treaty for ratification would be fruitless.

In January 1997 the United States continued its obstructionist tactics with the working group charged with drafting an optional protocol to the Convention on the Rights of the Child on the minimum age for combat. Almost all the nations that have taken part in the drafting sessions have agreed to raise the age from fifteen to eighteen. The United States stood virtually alone in refusing to accept the age of eighteen; U.S. armed forces permit the enlistment of seventeen-year-olds with their parents' permission.

On a more positive note, the administration in August 1996 called together representatives of the footwear and apparel industries, labor, NGOs and consumer groups to examine the issue of sweatshops. In April 1997, President Clinton announced a partnership agreement among those groups that established a workplace code of conduct that would ensure that clothes and shoes bought in the United States would be made under decent and humane conditions. The code would, among other things, prohibit child labor, forced labor, worker abuse and discrimination, and require a safe and healthy work environment. The code has not yet been implemented.

In September 1997, Labor Secretary Alexis Herman announced that the administration would press the Organization for Economic Cooperation and Development to combat child labor and eradicate sweatshops in the garment industry.

The Work of Human Rights Watch

During 1997 Human Rights Watch worked to gather detailed information on violations of children's human rights and carried out advocacy programs to work toward ending the abuses we found. We researched and campaigned to bring to attention the plight of bonded child laborers in India; street children violently attacked by police in India, Guatemala and Kenya; the ill-treatment of children in correctional institutions in those countries, as well as in Colorado in the United States; abuse of unaccompanied minors by the U.S. Immigration and Naturalization Service; and the abduction and killing of children by a rebel group, the Lord's Resistance Army, in Uganda. Human Rights Watch worked closely with local, national, and international nongovernmental organizations in its research and advocacy, and made regular submissions to the human rights mechanism of the United Nations, in particular the Committee on the Rights of the Child.

Bonded Child Labor

In a two-month investigation in India in late 1995 and early 1996, Human Rights Watch researchers talked with more than one hundred bonded child laborers, as well as lawyers, social workers, human rights activists, and government representatives. The fact-finding plan was to look at four industries: three producing for export and one for the domestic market, with a view to using the trade sanction potential as the main advocacy tool. During the investigation, however, our researchers found that the vast majority of children worked in domestic industries; export industries were a small part of the problem. As a result, research and action were redirected toward six industries—five domestic and one export—with findings reported. Meetings with children, NGOs, lawyers, social workers and others, led us to the conclusion that advocating only the firing of child workers—or trade sanctions—could make matters worse. A broader approach was necessary—chiefly to recommend that the Indian government comply with its own constitution and laws that outlaw bonded labor; and that it provide education for those released from servitude, in compensation for, and as a measure of rehabilitation for the wrong done to them and to prevent their return to bondage.

Indian NGOs differed sharply on solutions to the child labor dilemma, but made common cause in contributing to, and supporting the conclusions and recommendations of the report. Moreover, the government of India responded constructively to the findings, and vowed to take steps to end bonded child labor.

Child Soldiers

Human Rights Watch began its work on child soldiers in 1994 in Liberia and has since then met with scores of children, some as young as nine or ten, who were used as soldiers in armed conflicts around the world. Research in southern Sudan documented the plight of boys abducted by rebel groups and government troops and militia and identified means to end their use as child soldiers in 1995, in a practice that continues. In 1996, we documented the use of child soldiers in eight countries; and, in a separate report in 1997 we reported research findings and recommendations on the use of child soldiers in Burma.

In 1997, a team of Human Rights Watch researchers traveled to northern Uganda to investigate the abduction of children for military purposes by a brutal armed opposition group calling itself the Lord's Resistance Army (LRA). The abduction, torture, rape and killing of abducted children was documented in a September 1997 report: this report was launched jointly with an Amnesty International report on abuses by the Lord's Resistance Army.

Human Rights Watch worked to encourage the Ugandan government to take greater steps to protect children from abductions, to secure the release of abducted children, and to actively provide for the support, rehabilitation, and reintegration into society of children upon their return. The international community, in turn, was pressed to provide assistance to all children affected by the armed conflict. There was little progress in mobilizing pressure on the LRA itself to halt its abuse of children.

Documenting children's experiences as military "recruits" around the world has been a means towards ending the horrific practice of using children to fight adult wars. Towards that end, the Children's Rights Project also continued work in support of the drafting of an optional protocol to the Convention on the Rights of the Child that would raise the minimum age for soldiering from fifteen to eighteen. Research was also undertaken to consider the impact that proposed draft legislation to establish an international criminal court could have on furthering the protection of children affected by armed conflicts, including child soldiers. This included work to try to influence the drafting of that legislation to take into account the interests and needs of children affected by armed conflict.

Human Rights Watch informed the U.N. Committee on the Rights of the Child in September 1997 of our findings concerning the Lord's Resistance Army in Uganda and its pattern of abduction and killing of children, as well as the Ugandan government's failure effectively to protect and rehabilitate children who have escaped from the LRA.

Street children
In 1997, Human Rights Watch documented police violence against street children in India, Kenya and Guatemala, and pressed for greater accountability for police who perpetrated abuses against the children. This research, the findings of which were set out in three reports, highlighted the severity of the abuses in these countries, at times rising to deadly levels, and the lack of accountability by police for their actions.

Human Rights Watch findings on police violence and arbitrary detention of children in Guatemala and Kenya were submitted to the U.N. Commission on Human Rights, and to its special rapporteur on torture and Working Group on Arbitrary Detention.

Conditions in Children's Institutions
The correctional institutions in which children are confined, sometimes with adults, present a range of human rights abuses requiring intensive research and programmatic remedies. Conditions in these institutions in the United States and in other regions have been the object of research by Human Rights Watch since the inception of its Children's Rights Project. In 1994 we reported on the inhumane conditions in which children were illegally confined in adult lockups (jails) in Jamaica; the report contributed to the

government's releasing some of the children and ordering the development of alternative facilities.

Fact-finding in eight Colorado juvenile correctional institutions was completed in 1996. Officials in Colorado were extremely open, permitting access to all institutions and children and providing Human Rights Watch with damning internal audits. The findings of the inquiry, published in 1997, were widely covered by the press in Colorado, while contributing to the founding of a local group of lawyers, social workers and others committed to follow up on the investigation's findings and recommendations and to work toward improving the lot of Colorado children in conflict with the law.

In January 1997, the U.N. Committee on the Rights of the Child met with Bulgarian government representatives and cited the Human Rights Watch's submission on shortcomings in the juvenile justice system in its discussions. The committee asked the government to take steps previously sought by Human Rights Watch, including measures to train police, and to provide safeguards to prevent discrimination against minority children, to protect children in "boarding institutions" and "Labor Education Schools" (both are correctional institutions), and to reform the juvenile justice system.

Relevant Human Rights Watch reports:

The Scars of Death: Children Abducted by the Lord's Resistance Army in Uganda, 9/97
High Country Lockup: Children in Confinement in Colorado, 8/97
Guatemala's Forgotten Children: Police Violence and Arbitrary Detention, 7/97
Juvenile Injustice: Police Abuse and Detention of Street Children in Kenya, 6/97
Slipping Through the Cracks: Unaccompanied Children Detained by the U.S. Immigration and Naturalization Service, 4/97
Burma: Children's Rights and the Rule of Law, 1/97

THE WOMEN'S RIGHTS PROJECT

Women's Human Rights

In 1997 voices as disparate as United Nations Secretary-General Kofi Annan, World Bank President James D. Wolfensohn, and U.S. Secretary of State Madeleine K. Albright called for the full integration of women's human rights into the policies and practices of national governments and international agencies. Secretary-General Annan stated that he remained "dedicated to mainstreaming a gender perspective into the work of the entire United Nations system and to ensuring that women's rights and women's programs remain integral parts of the Organization's global mission." Secretary Albright called on all states to act on their responsibility to end violations of women's human rights.

This surge in high-level pronouncements on women's human rights represented a watershed in the decade-long effort by women's rights activists from around the world to highlight human rights issues. Years of often frustrating lobbying by women's rights activists in national, regional, and international fora finally bore significant fruit, with the statements of international leaders reflecting the growing strength and influence of the global women's human rights movement. Whether at the World Trade Organization or during the negotiations for a permanent International Criminal Court, the growing presence of women and increased attention to women's rights concerns were keenly felt.

Unfortunately, as is the case with international human rights practices generally, the political rhetoric surrounding women's human rights was rarely accompanied by any significant action, whether at the international or national level. At the United Nations, the Commission on Human Rights, the two ad hoc war crimes tribunals, and the various specialized agencies continued to give only inconsistent attention to women's human rights and in general acted only when prompted by outside pressure or media coverage. The gap between principle and practice was no less evident at the national level, where governments continued not only to tolerate widespread violence and discrimination against women but to commit such abuses themselves. In fact, as research by the World Bank and others revealed, the world's governments continued more often than not to abuse women's human rights rather than observe them.

One of the most pressing human rights concerns of 1997 was the continued prevalence of violence against women by both state and non-state actors. Conflict-related violence and its effects on women were evident everywhere from Colombia to the Democratic Republic of Congo, and prison abuse of women emerged in several countries as a growing concern. Both wartime and custodial violence continued in large measure to occur with widespread impunity and persistent international inaction. This was no less true of abuse by private actors which, while affecting women everywhere, was adequately addressed by governments virtually nowhere. Police, prosecutors, and judges commonly exhibited indifference to or outright bias against women victims of such abuse who themselves experienced little meaningful relief.

Some bright spots in this otherwise bleak record included important legal reforms in the domestic violence laws of several countries, including South Africa and Peru, lawsuits brought by the U.S. Department of Justice against Arizona and Michigan for the sexual abuse of women in custody, and the decision by the U.N. Human Rights Commission to renew the mandate of the special rapporteur on violence against women.

While violence against women continued to be universally condemned, if infrequently combatted, discrimination against women was still publicly and vigorously defended in many countries. Defending draft legislation that would deny women equal inheritance rights in Nepal, opponents to such equality argued that it would "create a state of social disorder." The U.N. Convention on the Elimination of All Forms of Discrimination Against Women (CEDAW) continued to be the U.N. treaty with the most reservations and did not include an optional protocol—a formal mechanism that establishes the right of individuals as well as governments to petition. Some countries, including the United States, failed to ratify CEDAW altogether.

The worldwide prevalence of violence and discrimination against women was particularly worrisome in the age of economic and labor globalization. In 1997 more women entered the formal and informal economic sectors than ever before, yet too often they were forced to choose between their jobs and their rights. This was particularly evident in the growing problem of the trafficking of women, which is reported in virtually every region of the world. Moreover, while the U.S. National Administrative Office (U.S. NAO), which oversees compliance with the labor rights side agreement to the North American Free Trade Agreement (NAFTA), did take initial steps to investigate violations of anti-discrimination provisions of the labor rights side agreement to NAFTA, such concern for the ways in which workforce discrimination hinders or harms women's participation in the workforce was notably absent from debate about trade regulations—whether bilateral, regional, or transnational—elsewhere.

The inattention to women's human rights in the policies and programs of both national governments and international bodies was mirrored in their failure to commit adequate resources in this area. Thus, the U.N.'s repeated pledge to uphold the rights of women and integrate attention to these issues throughout its programs was not meaningfully reflected in the distribution of its resources. This assessment applied equally to national governments, including the U.S., the 1997 budget of which reflected only a minimal contribution to the protection and promotion of the human rights of women.

The following section is designed to provide an overview of the state of women's human rights in 1997. It focuses in particular on the problems of violence and discrimination against women as committed and tolerated by states and is drawn from the work of Human Rights Watch in these areas over the past year.

Violence Against Women

Violence against women by both state and non-state actors was among the most serious and pervasive human rights abuses that the international community confronted in 1997, yet most countries were at best ineffectual and at worst negligent in taking action to end such abuse. Private actors often committed acts of violence against women, including rape and physical abuse, with impunity because states failed to prosecute and punish them. Moreover, in some countries, state agents themselves, such as military, police, and prison personnel, inflicted rape and other forms of violence on women without sanction.

While no reliable statistics exist regarding the scope of wartime or custodial violence against women, such abuse was clearly common. For example, reports from the Democratic Republic of Congo indicated that violence against women was prevalent during fighting between rebels and government forces. In both Rwanda and Bosnia women continued to face the consequences of wartime violence with little assistance from national governments or international entities. They continued to experience inadequate criminal justice, widespread displacement, and discrimination in access to property and financial resources.

The problem of custodial sexual abuse fared little better in 1997. Because of the routine failure of states to uphold the Standard Minimum Rules for the Treatment of Prisoners, particularly with respect to cross-gender guarding, women were particularly vulnerable to custodial abuse, often by male officers. For a variety of reasons, including the relatively small population of female prisoners in most countries, this abuse was routinely overlooked. In one important exception to this inattention, the European Court of Human Rights, in a September 1997 judgment, found that Sukran Aydin, a young Kurdish woman from southeastern Turkey, was subjected to torture when she was raped by guards who detained her in June 1993. In addition, the Inter-American Court on Human Rights issued an important decision related to custodial violence against women. In a September 17 judgment, the court ordered the immediate release of María Elena Loayza Tamayo, a Peruvian professor who was tortured and raped by police in February 1993 and then convicted of terrorism in Peru's "faceless court" system and given a twenty-year prison sentence. While the Inter-American Court found that there was insufficient evidence to prove rape, Peru was ordered to release her immediately and to pay her reparations for the "grave material and moral injury suffered."

Domestic violence has been one of the principal causes of female injury in almost every country in the world. Because most countries do not collect yearly data on the incidence of domestic violence, there is a dearth of current global statistics tracking the prevalence of this abuse. Nevertheless, the data that are available indicate that domestic violence is widespread. The World Health Organization reported in 1996 that in twenty-four countries across four continents, 20 to 50 percent of adult women had been victims of domestic violence at some point in their lives, and that in 50 to 60 percent of those cases, the violence included rape. In some countries, estimates were higher. For example, in Lima, Peru, over 6,000 cases of domestic violence were reported in 1996. According to the Peruvian Ministry of Justice, only one out of every five domestic violence cases actually gets reported. While the U.S. Department of Justice reported that approximately one million women suffered intimate violence in 1994, the American Medical Association estimated that the true incidence neared four million. In Russia, officials estimated that in 1993 15,000 women were killed and over 50,000 hospitalized because of domestic violence; however, there are no official statistics on its actual incidence, and the statistics department of the general prosecutor's office does not compile statistics on domestic violence. A 1994 study in India found that 91 percent of female murder victims had been killed by their husbands.

In addition to domestic violence, sexual assault was a persistent threat to women globally. Because so little official attention was devoted to the subject, the true dimensions of this problem must be inferred from partial studies. One 1994 study found that 23.3 percent of Canadian college students surveyed had been victims of rape or attempted rape. In the U.S., the Department of Justice reported that in 1994 there was one reported rape for every 270 females twelve years old and older, and a 1996 American Medical Association report estimated that one in five women is sexually assaulted by the time she reaches twenty-one years of age. In Russia, according to the Ministry of Internal Affairs, 10,888 rapes were reported to officials in 1996—a figure believed to be significantly lower than the actual incidence. In Peru, women's rights activists estimated that 25,000 women are raped every year.

In 1997 we investigated the effects of wartime violence in Rwanda, Bosnia, Liberia, Burundi, and the Democratic Republic of Congo; custodial abuse in Peru, the United States, and Venezuela; and private actor violence against women in Pakistan, Peru, Russia, and South Africa.

Wartime Violence and Post-Conflict Abuse

During the 1994 Rwandan genocide, women from both the Tutsi and Hutu ethnic groups were subjected to sexual violence—individual rapes, gang rapes, rapes with objects such as sharpened sticks or gun barrels, sexual slavery, and sexual mutilation—on a massive scale. These crimes were perpetrated, directed, or sanctioned by military and political leaders, as well as heads of militia, with a view toward furthering their political goals. Extremist propaganda denouncing the sexuality of Tutsi women, for example, served as one means to incite the widespread use of rape as an instrument to degrade and destroy the Tutsi community.

Throughout the war from 1991 to 1995 in the former Yugoslavia, countless women were victims of rape and other crimes of sexual violence—forced pregnancy, forced maternity, and sexual slavery. While these crimes were committed by all parties to the conflict, they were undertaken most notably by Bosnian Serb soldiers as a military strategy to seize territorial control in the former Yugoslavia. Whether committed against women in front of their families or in the village square, in the home or in a rape camp, once or repeatedly, the deliberate use of rape advanced a political objective: to humiliate, intimidate, and terrorize women and others affected by their suffering as well as to seize territory through the ethnically motivated expulsion of civilians.

In large part, however, the International Criminal Tribunals for Rwanda (ICTR) and the former Yugoslavia (ICTY) failed to deliver substantive justice to the thousands of women who endured brutal acts of sexual violence. After three years of operation, only in June 1997 did the ICTR levy charges of rape against two alleged war criminals. Moreover, shortcomings plagued the few initiatives undertaken by the ICTR to strengthen its investigative and prosecutorial strategies concerning sexual violence. The nascent sexual assault team, for instance, remained severely understaffed and ineffective. Moreover, the appointment of a gender advisor to address the needs of female witnesses, although a step in the right direction, failed to compensate for the overall absence of sufficient protection for witnesses at all stages of the trial. The ICTY, too, experienced limited success in securing women's access to international justice. Its failure to apprehend persons indicted for war crimes in the former Yugoslavia exacerbated women's fear of reprisals against them and their relatives. Wholly inadequate protection measures before and after trial reinforced these fears and further deterred women's participation with the tribunal.

In the wake of warfare, Rwandan and Bosnian women assumed critical roles in rebuilding the social and economic infrastructures of their transformed societies. At the same time, however, they continued to face discrimination in their access to property or financial resources, social stigmatization resulting from rape, deteriorating physical health, and intensifying poverty. Beyond suffering from psychosocial trauma as a consequence of the sexual violence committed against them during the genocide, Rwandan women faced dire economic difficulties as a result of their second-class citizenship status. Because Rwandan women, pursuant to customary law, are unable to inherit property absent explicit designation as beneficiaries, thousands of widows or orphaned daughters had no legal claim to their late husbands' or fathers' property or finances. Many women were thus rendered destitute, living in abandoned houses or with relatives or friends, struggling to make ends meet, to reclaim their property, and to raise children. Hutu women whose husbands were killed, in exile, or imprisoned on charges of genocide dealt with similar issues of poverty, as well as with the recrimination directed at them on the basis of their ethnicity or their ties to alleged war criminals.

Women in the former Yugoslavia fared no better. "Ethnic cleansing" campaigns during the war there resulted in staggering numbers of refugee and internally displaced women. Many were unable to return home, in part because of the failure to apprehend war criminals, who enjoyed not only freedom but the power to obstruct the return of refugees and displaced persons. In significant numbers, displaced women lived in collective centers, abandoned houses, or other temporary accommodations, dependent on minimal humanitarian aid for basic survival. Moreover, rampant unemployment continued to threaten the future of Bosnian women as they coped with heightened economic responsibilities, particularly after the loss of their husbands, brothers, fathers, and sons to the war.

Despite their obvious needs and vital roles in rebuilding the social and economic infrastructures in their post-war societies, Rwandan and Bosnian women were not viewed as a priority, either by their respective governments or by international donors, humanitarian organizations, and reconstruction and development agencies. Shortchanged in the reconstruction process, Rwandan and

Bosnian women continued to suffer personal, social, and economic hardships, in part because of a dearth of services and programs designed to assist these women in rebuilding their lives. The only monetary aid specifically targeted to assist Bosnian women in the transition—the U.S.$5 million Bosnian Women's Initiative from the United States—was scheduled to end in 1997. Although U.N. High Commissioner for Refugees (UNHCR) pledged to sustain the initiative, the only member of the international community that responded to appeals for support was Denmark with only $150,000. A similar United States Agency for International Development (USAID) initiative in Rwanda commanded almost $1.6 million, but despite praise for the program, it was planned to run only through 1998.

Custodial Violence

Unredressed custodial violence against women affected both political prisoners and those accused or convicted of common crimes. In Nepal, for example, border police allegedly gang-raped a female Tibetan refugee in December 1996. At the time of this writing, more than ten months later, this case has still not been seriously investigated. Similarly, in Peru, against the backdrop of the lingering effects of the armed conflict between the Peruvian military and the Shining Path (Sendero Luminoso), members of the Peruvian police and army continued to enjoy nearly complete impunity while committing sexually violent torture against women. As far as Human Rights Watch could determine, there has been only one successful prosecution of sexually violent torture against a detained civilian. Juana Ibarra Aguirre was gang raped and tortured by members of the Peruvian army at the Monzón base on August 29, 1996. On February 17, 1997, a military court convicted Lt. Cpl. Luis Daniel Figueroa Fernández Dávila of abuse of authority against Ms. Ibarra Aguirre and Jorge Chávez Espinoza (who was beaten to death). Fernández Dávila was permanently separated from the army and sentenced to twenty-five months of prison for both crimes and a reparations payment equivalent to $118 to Ibarra Aguirre.

In the common-crimes context, women were the victims of widespread, unchecked violence. In the United States, for example, where the female prison population increased by nearly 400 percent between 1980 and 1995, a Human Rights Watch investigation revealed that women warehoused in overcrowded prisons were regularly subjected to verbal degradation and harassment, unwarranted visual surveillance, abusive pat frisks, rape, and sexual assault. This situation resulted, in part, from the fact that women prisoners in the United States were guarded predominantly by male officers, most of whom were not properly trained to refrain from custodial abuse. Some guards threatened to deny women visitation by their children unless the women submitted to sexual advances—a glaring instance of the abuse of power by those charged with overseeing and protecting the women prisoners.

This abuse of women prisoners in the United States was compounded by the failure of both the state and federal governments to establish effective grievance and investigatory procedures to sanction abusive officers appropriately. Women who resisted sexual overtures from guards or who filed grievances alleging unprofessional and abusive conduct on the part of the guards were typically subjected to retaliatory actions such as threats by the accused corrections officer or his peers, physical abuse, or disciplinary sanctions, including solitary confinement or transfer to another facility. The U.S. Department of Justice, in charge of investigating civil rights violations of prisoners, does not have a mechanism in place to track complaints of sexual abuse. As a result, despite the filing of numerous complaints, it may be years before official action actually occurs.

Women in prisons in Venezuela also suffered from civil and political rights violations, including regulations that discriminated on the basis of gender. Human Rights Watch investigations found that, like their male counterparts, two-thirds of the women being detained have not been sentenced. For example, one woman with nine children ranging in age from four to nineteen had waited more than four years for her case to be resolved. Incarcerated women were stigmatized by society and many women were rejected by their families and communities. Although Venezuelan law prohibits cross-gender guarding, male National Guard personnel had access to the women, and the cases of brutality Human Rights Watch documented were at the hands of the guardsmen. An example of discriminatory regulations was the contrast between a liberal conjugal visit policy for men and a very stringent conjugal visit policy for women that effectively precluded most women from qualifying for the visits, further alienating them from their families.

Violence by Private Actors

In Pakistan, Peru, Russia, and South Africa, where Human Rights Watch investigated sexual and other violence against women, there were gross deficiencies in the states' response to such abuse by private actors. Access to justice was blocked or extremely difficult at every step of the legal process, from the police to the forensic doctors, prosecutors, and judges. In many cases, survivors who lodged complaints of domestic violence were further victimized by hostile and unsympathetic authorities who refused to accept the gravity of their assaults, routinely acted as if these assaults were provoked or deserved, and ultimately denied complainants protection or redress. These practices reflected both deficiencies in the laws of each country with respect to private actor violence as well as discriminatory and prejudiced practices on the part of state authorities.

Police routinely failed to exercise minimum diligence in the recording and investigation of rape and domestic violence complaints. It was common practice for police to refuse to accept domestic or sexual violence complaints outright, and in many cases victims were told that they deserved to be beaten, or had provoked their rapists, or were simply lying. In Russia, police blamed women for making themselves vulnerable to rape because of the clothing they wore, because they went out late at night, or because they

consumed alcohol. In Peru, women reported that they were told by police, prosecutors, and justices of the peace that they deserved to be beaten for being disobedient, stubborn, or refusing sex with their partners.

Given such official bias against women, medical evidence can be crucial to the effective prosecution of such abuse, despite the fact that the victim's own testimony should be sufficient. Some countries even went so far as to require medical exams for victims while at the same time failing to ensure that those exams were properly or expeditiously conducted. Access to such exams was often geographically or financially impossible to obtain, and the exams themselves were ordinarily inadequate, incomplete, and conducted by poorly trained personnel with distinct biases against corroborating victims' claims. Doctors frequently failed to examine thoroughly sexual assault victims for any evidence other than obvious signs of forced vaginal penetration and usually centered on prejudicial and, in most cases, irrelevant information regarding the victims' imputed sexual history. In Russia and Peru, doctors tended to focus on the condition of the victim's hymen and how recently she was "deflowered," regardless of her age, marital status, or prior sexual experience, in some cases claiming that there was "nothing to find" in women who were not virgins. In Pakistan, it was standard procedure for doctors to insert several fingers into the victim's vagina to determine whether she was "habituated to sex."

The actual prosecution of private actor violence against women was recurrently hampered by the official tendency in both law and practice to treat such abuse as a lesser offence. In Peru and Pakistan, cases of domestic violence and of rape of adult women were seldom prosecuted by the state. (Children's cases were treated more seriously.) Many Peruvian survivors of rape could pursue their cases only through private suits that they or their families initiated. In Pakistan, domestic violence victims could seek redress only through private suits. In Russia, the state rarely prosecuted domestic violence, and the law does not provide for protective orders to prevent the continued abuse of the victim. In the countries we investigated, only a very small percentage of domestic and sexual violence complaints ever reached adjudication. It was considered normal for judges to examine victims' behavior and reputation more exhaustively than the defendants' acts of violence. For example, one Pakistani judge dismissed a divorce case in which domestic violence was alleged, saying that the Koran allows men to admonish their wives. Criminal judges in Peru routinely suspended the sentences of convicted rapists, letting them free.

Another form of violence by private actors practiced in over thirty African countries, in parts of Asia, and among immigrant communities in the U.S. and elsewhere was female genital mutilation (FGM), also called female circumcision. FGM was performed on infants, children, teens, and adult women and was defended by practitioners as an appropriate way of controlling women's sexuality, an important initiation rite, or a prerequisite for marriage. In Egypt, where a 1995 government-supported study indicated that over 90 percent of the female population underwent FGM, a July court decision undermined initial government efforts to combat the practice by overturning the health minister's ban on FGM on the grounds that it exceeded his authority. Egyptian human rights activists lobbied hard for the government to stand by its opposition to FGM, and the government pledged to appeal the court decision.

Discrimination

In addition to violence against women, which itself reflects and perpetuates discrimination, systematic discrimination against women persisted in 1997 in myriad forms throughout the world. Numerous states, including those that have ratified CEDAW, continued to maintain and enforce statutory laws that require differential and discriminatory treatment against women. In many states without such de jure discrimination, de facto discrimination flourished. The belief that discrimination on the basis of sex is acceptable in some forms or on certain occasions frustrated efforts both to eliminate sex discrimination—as called for by CEDAW—and to secure justice for women suffering its consequences.

In a major setback in the struggle to secure equal rights, women in Afghanistan saw their status plunge in 1997 as the Taliban took control over much of their country. Taliban edicts severely restricted women's freedom of movement and denied women and girls' access to education. Women whose dress did not comport with Taliban standards—which outlawed makeup, jewelry, and shoes that make noise—reportedly were beaten in the street. Variations of these extreme forms of sex discrimination exist in countries around the world. In 1997, we investigated state-committed or -tolerated discrimination in Morocco, Russia, Nepal, Egypt, Guatemala, Mexico, Malaysia, and Lebanon.

State-Sponsored Discrimination

As governments adopted the language of women's human rights in the wake of the 1995 Fourth World Conference on Women in Beijing, many pointed to their constitutional guarantees of equal rights to all citizens, equal opportunity regardless of sex, or equal protection of the law. Yet these guarantees were often nullified by specific statutes that, among other things, limited women's access to divorce or their ability to inherit property or denied them equal citizenship rights. Morocco's constitution, for example, provides limited equality: women are guaranteed equality in politics, education, and the workplace but are not guaranteed equality as a civil right that would apply in other areas, such as the family law. The government of Morocco submitted its record on complying with the Convention on the Elimination of All Forms of Discrimination Against Women for the first time in January 1997. Although Morocco could claim that certain forms of discrimination had been eliminated through legal reform—women no longer needed their husbands' express permission to work outside the home—it defended as consistent with religion and tradition the sex discrimination that pervades its Family Code and makes women minors under the law regardless of their age. Morocco succeeded in exporting this discrimination to France. Despite a French constitutional guarantee of equality, the French and Moroccan governments have operated since 1981 under an agreement to apply Moroccan family law to Moroccan nationals living in France.

Egypt's constitution provides a much stronger guarantee of equality, stating, "Citizens are equal before the law. They have equal rights and duties without distinction because of sex, origin, language, religion, or belief." Nonetheless, Egyptian President Hosni Mubarak continued to refuse women equal citizenship by denying their right to pass on their nationality to their children. Instead, in 1997 his government offered to eliminate some of the consequences—high education fees, barriers to residency, visas—faced by families with Egyptian mothers and non-Egyptian fathers but failed to remove the discriminatory provisions from the law.

Women's rights in the workplace were also curtailed by law. In Russia, for example, labor legislation adopted in 1996 denied women the right to work in 400 professions considered inconsistent with their femininity and maternal responsibilities. Morocco also denied women access to certain jobs, specifically prohibiting them from working at night (with some exceptions), from holding jobs that are "immoral," and from serving in particular posts in the ministries of interior and defense, in national security, and in the government post and telecommunications office. In addition, in April 1997, the Taliban, who controlled nearly two-thirds of Afghanistan, announced an outright ban on women working outside the home, except in the health sector.

Unfortunately, tenacious efforts to eliminate sex discrimination continued to be undercut by official and broad-based opposition to women's equality. Nepali women's rights activists lobbied their parliament to grant women equal inheritance rights. As of September 1997, the bill under discussion allowed only unmarried daughters the right to inherit parental property. Opponents of giving women equal inheritance rights argued that, in the words of Supreme Court lawyer Madhab Koirala, it would "create a state of social disorder."

In another example of the state's participating directly in the subordination of women, Guatemala's civil code allows husbands to refuse their wives permission to work outside the home and appoints the husband as the representative of all family concerns. In 1994 María Eugenia Morales de Sierra, represented by the Center for Justice and International Law, challenged these provisions as discriminatory on the basis of sex. Morales de Sierra brought her case to the Inter-American Commission in Human Rights, which inexplicably and uncharacteristically declined to consider the case for eighteen months. At the September 1996 hearing, Guatemala agreed to promote legal reform but did not act on this promise. Despite continued government failure to reform the challenged laws, as of October 1997, the Inter-American Commission has not issued a ruling on the case.

State-Tolerated Discrimination

The state's direct role in perpetuating discrimination and violence against women was evident not only through the promulgation of biased laws but through its complicity with private actors in failing to enforce protective law. By failing to take measures to prohibit discrimination and protect the right of women to nondiscrimination, governments throughout the world contributed to the creation of an environment in which non-state entities could openly discriminate against women without fear of condemnation or prosecution. In 1997 Human Rights Watch focused on the particular abuses suffered as a result of state-tolerated sex discrimination by women in the paid workforce and trafficked women.

Although many countries of the world have outlawed some of the most pernicious forms of workplace discrimination, many de facto discriminatory practices persist. This is a particularly troubling fact given that women participated in the workforce (informal and formal sectors) in increasing numbers in the developing world as well as in industrialized nations. The United Nations estimated that in 1994 approximately 41 percent of the world's women age fifteen and over were economically active but that most of the job growth for women had occurred in low-wage positions. Unfortunately, women's participation was often defined by conditions that kept them chronically poor or subsising. Women worked in segregated, primarily low-wage industries that offered them the least amount of benefits, pay, potential for advance, skills development, or job security. According to a 1995 International Labour Organisation (ILO) report, women were paid less than men for comparable work, including in developed nations. Moreover, the ILO found that when women began to enter in significant numbers any category of work previously dominated by men, there was a simultaneous downgrading of that occupation, in both pay and status; examples included teaching and senior civil service positions.

Regardless of the sector in which women worked or how much they were paid, they continued to face de facto discrimination in the labor force. One glaring example of such discrimination was hiring practices. Associating women primarily with their reproductive capacities, many employers assumed that women would leave the workforce once they bore children and thus saw female workers as bad investments and tried to avoid hiring them. Such biased notions against female job applicants resulted in discriminatory hiring practices in many countries, often despite clear labor laws and international obligations to the contrary.

In Mexico's export processing (maquiladora) sector, for example, Human Rights Watch research in 1996 and 1997 found that women applying for work as line assemblers were required to undergo mandatory, hiring-related pregnancy testing before they were offered work. Those found to be pregnant were denied jobs. Those who became pregnant shortly after being hired risked being forced to resign. Some companies required new female employees to certify that they remained non-pregnant, typically by forcing them, at regular intervals, to undergo mandatory checks of their used sanitary napkins. When confronted with evidence of these discriminatory practices, few of the responsible parties made any effort to address it. General Motors Corp., the largest employer in the maquiladoras, and ITT Corp. were two notable exceptions: after receiving our findings, these corporations pledged to discontinue pregnancy-based sex discrimination. The government of Mexico, however, characterized such discriminatory hiring practices as legal and failed to sanction offending companies, among them Zenith and Johnson Controls, which continued to argue that such discriminatory practices were legally permissible.

Few international remedial bodies exist to explore and make judgments on workforce discrimination against women and to require reforms. The Mexico maquiladora sector, however, is subject to such a mechanism. In July 1997, the United States National Administrative Office (U.S. NAO, the body charged with hearing cases of alleged violations by Canada or Mexico of the North American Agreement on Labor Cooperation, commonly referred to as the labor rights side agreement of the North American Free Trade Agreement, NAFTA) accepted for review a petition filed by Human Rights Watch, the International Labor Rights Fund, and the National Association of Democratic Lawyers (Asociación Nacional de Abogados Democráticos), which charged the Mexican government with failure to enforce its domestic labor code or set up effective mechanisms to adjudicate labor disputes. The U.S. NAO was expected to issue its findings by November 1997. (For more information on the U.S. NAO process, *see* the Mexico chapter.)

The experiences of migrant women workers provided another striking example of de facto discrimination against women. All over the world, women migrated from their home countries to wealthier receiver countries to work in factories or to provide in-home domestic or other services. A variety of government action or inaction, including the implementation of legislation with a negative disparate impact on migrant women workers, the condoning of discriminatory contractual agreements, and the failure to enforce contractual protections for migrant workers, resulted in violations of women workers' rights. Migrant women workers faced not only loss of promised wages but exploitative hours, physical abuse, and confinement by their employers, and arbitrary detentions and summary deportations by the state.

Governments' failure to provide remedies to violations of women workers' rights, at times combined with overtly prejudicial laws and regulations, resulted in discrimination and physical abuse; some governments or their agents tolerated or collaborated in discriminatory, arbitrary detentions and deportations. In Malaysia, for example, the government, by promulgating a law that excludes domestic workers from labor protections, indirectly but nonetheless effectively sanctioned discrimination against migrant women workers. Malaysia's Employment Act, the primary law governing worker rights in that country, extends to both foreign and Malaysian workers but specifically exempts domestic workers from key provisions. These provisions include those guaranteeing maternity leave, those which place limits on advances, and those governing permissible working hours. Although many of the exemptions are couched in gender-neutral language, because the vast majority of domestic workers are women, it is clear that these provisions have had a particularly significant impact on decreasing protections afforded to women workers.

The Malaysian government's complicity with private discrimination against migrant women workers was also evident in its inaction with regard to the discriminatory contracts issued by Malaysian employers. A Human Rights Watch investigation in 1997 found that thousands of Indonesian women migrated to Malaysia to work as either factory workers or domestic servants. Contracts for the domestic servants generally included a standard prohibition on association, barring them from "forming or participating in any social club in Malaysia" during their employment. Contracts for the migrant factory workers often included bans on trade union activity and on pregnancy. With regard to the latter, factory employers were able to enforce the pregnancy provisions because of Malaysian immigration regulations, which require migrant women to have full medical examinations that screen for pregnancy prior to their entry into Malaysia, a follow-up examination one month after entry, and then subsequent yearly examinations. Those found to be pregnant are barred from working in Malaysia and are subject to immediate dismissal and deportation.

Even when women were able to negotiate labor contracts that satisfactorily protected their rights, they were still not safe from abuse by their employers. These situations arose because of some governments' failure to provide adequate mechanisms for the women workers to enforce their contracts or seek remedies for their violation. In Lebanon, for example, women from as far away as Ethiopia migrated with the help of Lebanese employment agencies to work as household servants. In one widely publicized case, an Ethiopian woman, Zenebech Girma, alleged that she had been working in Lebanon as a domestic servant, yet her wages were underpaid (or not paid at all), she was confined to her employers' home and denied freedom of movement, physically and mentally abused, and refused permission to end her contractual relationship with her employer and return to her home country. At this writing, the Lebanese government had initiated an investigation but had yet to take any action on their findings.

The lack of adequate legal protection was particularly stark not only for household domestics, migrant workers, and workers in assembly plants but also for victims of trafficking. In virtually every region of the globe, women were coerced or tricked into migrating to work in prostitution, the garment trade, or other sectors, in addition, frequently, to suffering abuses in the workplace. Human Rights Watch has investigated trafficking in women in the United States, Thailand, Nepal, India,

Brazil, and Pakistan.

Once transported to an unfamiliar and often hostile milieu, women were inevitably left at the mercy of traffickers who then more easily exploited their labor and operated outside of applicable frameworks of labor, criminal, and contractual laws. Trafficking victims were hence particularly susceptible to a range of abuses in the workplace, including debt bondage, forced labor, illegal confinement, enforced isolation, wage withholding, deprivation of identity documents, and sexual and other physical abuse. Women who had not been trafficked into these sectors frequently found themselves suffering such abuse as well.

Trafficking victims were commonly denied access to legal remedies and redress for severe human rights violations both during recruitment and in the workplace. Most trafficked women were socially, linguistically, culturally, and legally isolated in their host countries. Frequently they were under the physical control of their employers, lacking any identity papers and uncertain of their status and rights in the receiving country. Most were illegal migrants, subject to the constant threat of detention and deportation. Women trafficked into prostitution feared, in addition, harsh criminal sanctions. All these factors contributed to an atmosphere that inhibited trafficked persons from speaking out to officials or seeking redress from state agencies.

Human Rights Watch investigations revealed that even when trafficked women did come in contact with law enforcement officials, they were frequently treated as illegal migrants or as criminals or both, routinely detained, and summarily deported. With few exceptions, officials failed to investigate or record the testimony of victims in state custody as to the abuses they suffered during recruitment and in the workplace or to allow them an opportunity to file charges or bring civil suits against their employers and traffickers. Rarely were systematic efforts made to track down and prosecute the employers or traffickers. On the contrary, in many countries law enforcement and immigration officials profited from the traffic in women. For a price they aided and abetted the coercive passage of women and ignored abuses in their jurisdictions.

In the United States, as in many other countries, upon their detection in brothels or sweatshops, trafficked women were generally detained and deported unless their testimony was required for criminal cases against their traffickers or employers. Where criminal suits were instituted against the latter, in many cases, the charges did not reflect the full range of civil and human rights violations committed against the women. Rather, the traffickers and brothel owners were typically prosecuted for harboring illegal aliens and conspiring to commit prostitution. This pattern was due, in part, to domestic criminal laws that failed fully to protect the rights of trafficked women and others held in debt bondage and involuntary servitude and to practices which often reflected an official bias against both immigrants and prostitutes.

Notably Belgium and the Netherlands have domestic laws that afford a measure of due process protection and allow for the provision of basic support services to women believed to be victims of trafficking. The laws allow trafficked women who want to bring charges against their traffickers and employers to obtain temporary residence permits for the duration of the judicial process. Furthermore, victims of trafficking are entitled to social security benefits, safe shelters, legal aid, medical care, and psychological counseling while they consider whether to press charges, and, in some cases, beyond that as well. The Dutch and Belgian governments also support nongovernmental organizations working with trafficked women and cooperate with them in implementing government initiatives for trafficking victims. Neither the Dutch nor Belgian governments criminalize prostitution, although Belgium does outlaw procurement and brothel keeping.

The Role of the International Community

In recent years, the international community has made important advances in the recognition of violence against women as a human rights concern, recognizing the need for states to respond appropriately. In 1992, the U.N.'s Committee on the Elimination of Discrimination Against Women (the CEDAW Committee), which monitors state compliance with the Convention for the Elimination of All Forms of Discrimination Against Women (CEDAW), issued General Recommendation No. 19, finding that gender-based violence is a form of discrimination that states must take measures to eradicate. The U.N. General Assembly subsequently adopted the Declaration on the Elimination of Violence Against Women in 1993. Later that year, at the World Conference on Human Rights in Vienna, states reaffirmed that governments have a duty to eliminate violence against women in order to ensure women's enjoyment of their human rights and fundamental freedoms. In 1994 the Commission on Human Rights appointed a special rapporteur on violence against women. That year the Organization of American States adopted the Inter-American Convention on the Prevention, Punishment and Eradication of Violence against Women (the Belem do Pará Convention). These efforts reached an apex in 1995, at the Fourth World Conference on Women in Beijing, China, where states adopted a Platform of Action and individual states made commitments to take specific actions to promote gender equality, including the eradication of all forms of violence against women.

The international community's commitment to achieving the goal of gender equality did not, however, lead to sustained efforts to eliminate other forms of sex discrimination, including laws and practices that deny women equal rights in the workplace and in the family. For example, in June 1993, governments at the World Conference on Human Rights asked the Commission on the Status of Women (CSW) and the CEDAW Committee to create a stronger enforcement mechanism for victims of sex discrimination. Four years and much discussion later, the CSW had managed only to draft and circulate a proposal for an optional protocol that would give victims of sex discrimination the right to petition the CEDAW Committee. Moreover, in negotiations over the draft proposal, most governments refused to integrate specific means to make the petition mechanism available and functional for actual victims of sex discrimination.

United Nations

While it is widely acknowledged within the United Nations that attention to women's human rights must be integrated into the U.N.'s programs and mission, the international body's actual practice fell far short of its rhetoric during 1997. A press release issued by the Economic and Social Council (ECOSOC) in July 1997, for example, quoted a Russian delegate as stating that the U.N.'s approach to mainstreaming women's issues was over-theoretical and "risked being nothing but arcane paper-churning." This observation followed the release of a June 1997 ECOSOC draft outlining concepts, principles, and specific recommendations for integrating women's concerns and issues into the overall work of the United Nations. In this draft, ECOSOC recognized that "a gender perspective has not been fully integrated." A July 1997 report by Secretary-General Kofi Annan on humanitarian assistance acknowledged that the U.N. had yet to implement specific measures to address the protection of women's human rights in times of conflict.

The U.N.'s failure fully to address women's human rights concerns was perhaps best reflected in its allocation of resources. Although a wide variety of U.N. officials have publicly committed to promoting women's human rights, these commitments have mostly failed to lead to concrete programs or, because of the U.N. accounting system, actual work to promote women's rights cannot be measured. Secretary-General Annan acknowledged in a report issued in June 1997 that the U.N. method of budgeting made it impossible to assess allocation of resources disaggregated by sex or by beneficiary. However, even absent such information for 1997, it was clear that women's human rights got short shrift. In December 1996, United Nations Development Program (UNDP) issued a directive committing 20 percent of its 1997 budget for programs to promote gender equality and the advancement of women, but this purported increase in support could not be assessed because UNDP failed to modify its reporting system so as to clarify whether the goal would be reached. On an even more disturbing note, the United Nations Development Fund for Women (UNIFEM), an autonomous body in association with UNDP and the only U.N. agency that provides direct support to promoting women's human rights and development projects, received less than 2 percent of the UNDP's 1997 budget of $1 billion.

In addition to concerns about budgeting, the U.N. reform process, spearheaded by Secretary-General Annan, prompted concerns both within and outside the United Nations that women's human rights would become increasingly marginalized. Not only was Angela King, the special adviser to the secretary-general on gender issues, excluded from the initial reform process, but the final ninety-page document guiding the process makes only three references to women's human rights. Furthermore, despite repeated pledges to achieve gender parity at all levels within the U.N., in his first round of high-level appointments in January 1997 Secretary-General Annan named two women and seventeen men. On a positive note, he later appointed Mary Robinson to be High Commissioner for Human Rights.

While overall, the U.N.'s actions failed to match its rhetoric, the organization did make some progress in addressing specific women's rights, particularly with respect to human rights bodies. The reports of Special Rapporteur on Violence Against Women Radhika Coomaraswamy continued to make a significant contribution to exposing the issue and securing government action to address it. The rapporteur's February 1997 report on sexual violence in South Africa, for example, highlighted the relationship between the high rate of violence against women and the legacy of apartheid and recommended a complete "overhauling of the criminal justice apparatus to respond to violence in general

and violence against women in particular." The Commission on Human Rights, in recognition of the importance of the rapporteur's work, renewed her mandate for three additional years.

In addition, the Human Rights Committee, responsible for reviewing country reports under the International Covenant on Civil and Political Rights, increased its focus on violence against women. For example, in considering Peru's latest report, the committee focused on violations which were gender specific, including de jure discrimination. Specifically, the committee recommended the repeal of the provision in the Peru's Penal Code that exempted a rapist from punishment if he married the victim. The committee criticized the fact that rape in Peru can only be prosecuted privately as well as provisions in the Civil Code that discriminate against women, including a difference in the minimum age of matrimony.

Though such specific improvements were welcome, the U.N.'s human rights system continued in general to accord too little attention to women. Thus, a UNIFEM review of reports to the U.N. Commission on Human Rights by special rapporteurs and by countries characterized them as providing "inconsistent attention to, and analysis of, gender-specific violations." UNIFEM also noted that few reports included analysis of the relationship between the abuse suffered by women and their subordinate status in public and private life. In a March 1997 letter circulated at the fifty-third session of the Commission on Human Rights, UNIFEM presented specific suggestions on how to analyze human rights violations from a gender-sensitive perspective. The letter called for differentiating gender-specific forms of violence and discrimination, for analyzing the circumstances and consequences of violations which may be gender-specific, and for identifying gender-specific barriers in access to remedies.

The United Nations' uneven treatment of women's human rights was equally evident in its approach to trafficking. The 1997 report of the U.N. special rapporteur on violence against women noted that existing international instruments are clearly inadequate to address the problem. She emphasized that the 1949 Convention on the Suppression of the Traffic in Persons is flawed, lacks widespread support, and has a weak enforcement mechanism. Yet when the Subcommission on Prevention of Discrimination and Protection of Minorities' Working Group on Contemporary Forms of Slavery issued a report five months later, it failed to take into consideration the special rapporteur's analysis and called for widespread ratification of the 1949 Convention.

Attempts to address the human rights of women more fully were increasingly evident in U.N. programs, which until recently have not viewed this work as within their mandate. Both United Nations Po6pulation Fund (UNFPA) and the United Nations Children's Fund (UNICEF) have taken welcome steps in this direction and in 1995 and 1996, respectively, adopted mandates based on promoting human rights and in particular the rights of women and girls. UNFPA adopted a rights approach to family planning which incorporated the objectives set forth at the 1994 International Conference on Population and Development (Cairo Conference), including gender equity and equality; education, especially for girls; infant, child, and maternal mortality reduction; and universal access to reproductive health services. UNICEF officially changed its mandate to make its mission the universal ratification and implementation of Convention on the Rights of the Child (CRC), with an explicit reference to the fact that the well-being of children is directly correlated to that of their mothers. In the *Progress of Nations - 1997*, an annual UNICEF publication, the commentary on women focused on violence against women and girls. Whether these changes will translate into full-fledged programmatic attention to women's rights by these agencies remains to be seen.

The potential gap between policy and practice with respect to the treatment of women's human rights by U.N. agencies was also evident during 1997 at the Office of the United Nations High Commissioner for Refugees (UNHCR). When UNHCR staff did implement procedures to protect women refugees and train workers, we were able to document significant improvements in the situation for women refugees. However, the failure to translate these policies into practice continued, as evidenced by a 1997 International Rescue Committee (IRC) survey of approximately 3,800 women refugees from Burundi who have spent the last three years as refugees in Tanzania that revealed that 26 percent had been victims of sexual violence in the camps. UNHCR had no protection officers assigned to the camp and only conducted trainings on preventing sexual violence after learning of the IRC report.

An important U.N. initiative in the area of accountability and access to justice was the move to create an International Criminal Court, negotiations for which continued through 1997. However, here again women's issues fared poorly and were nearly always at risk of being overlooked entirely without the watchful eyes and targeted efforts of women's rights activists. The proposed establishment of an ICC has great significance for women because they are commonly the targets and victims of egregious international crimes and, at the same time, have frequently been denied access to justice at both national and international levels. The conflicts in Rwanda and the former Yugoslavia are only the most recent examples of horrifying levels of violence against women, including acts of rape, enforced prostitution, and other forms of sexual assault. Although it is well established that these abuses can constitute genocide, serious violations of the laws and customs of war, or crimes against humanity, the prosecution of sexual and gender violence presents unique challenges in terms of developing appropriate investigative methods and legal theories, as well as particular difficulties in ensuring the participation and protection of victims and witnesses. This fact might account, in part, for the initial reluctance of the tribunals for the former Yugoslavia and Rwanda to investigate and prosecute these crimes with the seriousness they deserve. Drawing on lessons learned from the experiences of the ad hoc tribunals, the permanent International Criminal Court must be fully empowered to prosecute sexual and gender violence if it is to fulfill its mandate to end impunity for the most serious violations of international law.

Nevertheless, the Preparatory Committee on the Establishment of an International Criminal Court, convened by the U.N. General Assembly in December 1995, did not deal in any detail with the specific concerns of women victims of violence until February 1997, when, owing to the pioneering efforts of a few committed delegations and a caucus of women's rights activists, these concerns entered the debate on the definitions and scope of crimes within the court's jurisdiction. At the conclusion of the meeting, the draft consolidated text expressly categorized crimes of sexual and gender violence as war crimes and crimes against humanity. Although this move does not represent a progressive development of international law, such express reference is necessary for the prosecution of these crimes to be treated as an integral part of the court's mandate.

Although the momentum created in February was sustained during the August meeting of the preparatory committee, it was again the result of the labors of a small number of dedicated and outspoken delegations and women's rights advocates. Based on their efforts, the draft consolidated text on principles of criminal procedure included an explicit direction to the prosecutor to ensure that the investigation of crimes of sexual violence be carried out in a manner conducive to eliciting relevant testimony from victims and witnesses. It also contained an instruction to the court to take necessary measures to ensure the safety, physical and psychological well-being, dignity, and privacy of victims and witnesses and explicitly referenced victims of sexual and gender violence in this regard. Beyond this hard-won success, the August meeting was marked by setbacks on critical foundational issues (see the discussion of the ICC in the Special Issues section).

World Bank

The World Bank, which is charged with promoting social and economic development through loans, investment, and technical assistance, has publicly recognized the impact of violations of women's rights on women's participation in the social and economic development of their countries. In his address at the 1995 Fourth World Conference on Women in Beijing, World Bank President James D. Wolfensohn stressed the critical role that governments and development institutions have to play "to support the investments which can help women to achieve equality and escape poverty." He called for an end to "empty words" in place of real action to improve the lives of women worldwide.

Unfortunately, the World Bank did not successfully respond to this call for action by its own president. A 1994 study by the bank did acknowledge violence against women as a human rights concern and a health issue that greatly affects women's participation in socioeconomic development, but the bank did not undertake projects to follow up on the report—its first and only comprehensive work on violence against women. This lack of institutional support meant that in 1997 violations of women's human rights committed by recipients of World Bank assistance were not explicitly addressed by bank project work on gender inequity. In a potentially important step, the bank in 1996 and 1997 developed "gender action plans" for every region. However, the extent to which these plans, and particularly their attention to women's rights, were being implemented was difficult to assess given the lack of monitoring of this undertaking.

United States

U.S. leadership shared with that of the U.N. a flair for strong statements in defense of women's rights. Much less obvious were the effects of this rhetoric on the implementation of U.S. policy in countries around the world. With the December 1996 appointment of Madeleine K. Albright as secretary of state, the Clinton administration gained a forceful advocate for making women's human rights a foreign policy priority. President Clinton emphasized his administration's intent to make women's human rights a U.S. foreign policy priority at a Human Rights Day ceremony on December 10, 1996 that honored women's rights activists from around the world. In early March 1997, Secretary Albright underscored that improving the status of women is the "mission" of U.S. foreign policy, saying, "Women will only be able to contribute to their full potential if they have equal access, equal rights, equal protection, and a fair chance at the levers of economic and political power." First Lady Hillary Rodham Clinton also supported women's rights activists in her trips to Asia in late 1996 and to Africa in March 1997 and raised women's human rights in her speeches, including on International Women's Day and in a meeting with human rights activists in Costa Rica in May.

The rhetoric was accompanied by some modest signs of progress within the State Department. The senior advisor on international women's issues, Theresa Loar, appointed in late 1996, increased the scope and reach of her staff's activities in 1997 and created interagency working groups to coordinate U.S. policy on violations of women's human rights such as trafficking and female genital mutilation. Loar's office began work to ensure that a G8 initiative involving the governments of the United States, Russia, Japan, France, Great Britain, Germany, Italy, and Canada to promote democracy building, announced in Denver in early 1997, would translate into aid and trade policies to advance women's human rights, especially their political participation. The State Department's Bureau of Democracy, Human Rights, and Labor also stepped up efforts to integrate women's rights more consistently and prominently into U.S. foreign policy by raising women's human rights concerns in bilateral talks with governments such as Russia and Mexico, requesting more reporting on women's rights from embassies around the world, and supporting small grants for women's rights organizations and programs in different countries. At the U.S. Agency for International Development (USAID), a legal rights initiative supported legal rights education for women in the newer independent states of the former Soviet Union, Bangladesh, Cambodia, Nepal, and Sri Lanka. Breaking new ground in 1997, the Department of Justice brought lawsuits against the states of Arizona and Michigan for violating women's constitutional rights by allowing prison staff to sexually abuse female prisoners with impunity.

Overall though, U.S. government claims to international leadership in promoting women's rights were undermined by its inconsistent pursuit of this mission. In some cases, the U.S. government made no effort to translate verbal pledges into concrete programs. Despite the Clinton administration's repeated commitment to combat domestic and sexual violence against women throughout the world, the State Department's country reports did not denounce the failure of states to prohibit and remedy such abuse. Not surprisingly, U.S.-supported programs also did little to combat such state inaction. Only after pressure from Congress did the administration dedicate $1 million of the $12 million allotted to the State Department Bureau of International Narcotics and Law Enforcement Matters, Office of International Criminal Justice, for work in Russia to train Russian law enforcement to investigate violence against women. Moreover, the department's initial undertaking with these funds—a Washington, D.C. conference on trafficking of women and children for senior Russian and U.S. officials—focused more on child pornography and the Internet than on improving Russian law enforcement's response to violence against women. In the cases of Peru and Pakistan, none of the available U.S. assistance funds for democracy, rule of law, or civil society programs squarely confronted government failure to provide justice to women victims of violence.

Nor did the U.S. actively seek to secure justice for women victims of violence in international negotiations to establish a permanent International Criminal Court (ICC).

Since the beginning of the U.N. process to create this critical body for trying serious human rights abuses, the United States has been conspicuously silent on the need to ensure that the court emerges as a mechanism for justice for women victims of egregious international crimes. In fact, at the August 1997 meeting of the Preparatory Committee for the Establishment of an International Criminal Court, the U.S. questioned the rationale for including in the draft statute an explicit reference to the witness protection needs of victims of sexual and gender violence, hence obstructing efforts toward this end. Furthermore, by aggressively taking restrictive stances on critical issues that bear on the independence and effectiveness of the ICC in general, such as the preconditions for triggering the court's jurisdiction and the independence of the prosecutor to initiate investigations, the U.S. has worked to restrict access to justice at the ICC for all victims of genocide, crimes against humanity, and war crimes.

Even where the U.S. government did initiate specific policies and programs to promote women's rights, they received only small-scale resources. Since its 1995 inception, the USAID women's legal rights initiative, for example, was allocated a total of just over $6 million. By contrast, in 1997 alone, USAID committed over $400 million to democracy programs. And, although Secretary of State Albright stated in March that "we will take part in a global effort to crack down on illegal trafficking in women and girls," the only resources devoted to this problem funded the above-mentioned conference. In late 1996, President Clinton did announce a $5 million initiative to promote women's participation in the economic and social reconstruction of Bosnia, but the initiative was not renewed for fiscal year 1998. On a more positive note, for a similar program in Rwanda to assist women to participate in the rebuilding of their country, USAID increased its funding from $1 million in 1996 to almost $1.6 million in 1997 and extended the program's mandate, but only until the end of 1998.

The U.S. commitment to women's rights as a cornerstone of U.S. policy took backseat in 1997 when other policy concerns conflicted with this goal. In one significant example, the U.S. pursued trade relations with Mexico despite widespread, blatant pregnancy-based sex discrimination in Mexico's maquiladora (export processing) sector. In its *Country Reports on Human Rights Practices* for 1996, 1995, and 1994, the State Department reported this practice but stopped short of condemning the discrimination and the Mexican government's tolerance of it. The U.S. also passed up a key opportunity to press for better labor rights: at an April 1997 meeting on women and work hosted by the Mexican government for all signatories to NAFTA, the U.S. failed to speak out against or even to mention pervasive pregnancy-based sex discrimination in Mexico's private sector. Later in the year, however, the U.S. did express its concern over discrimination in the maquiladoras in human rights meetings with Mexican officials. At the same time, systematic discrimination in other countries with claims to U.S. interests never appeared on the U.S. agenda. Although Secretary Albright invited her counterparts to join her in a discussion on women's status in the region during a September 1997 visit to the Persian Gulf, the administration produced no evidence that it had pressed for women's rights in countries such as Saudi Arabia, where women's mobility, education, job opportunities, and rights are restricted on the basis of sex.

While some U.S. officials called for improved respect for women's rights abroad, U.S. women could not benefit from international standards at home. Despite entreaties from President Clinton and Secretary Albright, chair of the Senate Foreign Relations Committee Jesse Helms refused to move toward ratification of the Convention on the Elimination of All Forms of Discrimination Against Women (CEDAW). That women in the U.S. need the protection of international human rights standards was made pointedly clear by revelations in late 1996 and through 1997 of widespread sexual abuse of women in U.S. state prisons. Although presented with extensive evidence of sexual abuse and harassment by prison staff against female prisoners, state and federal authorities did precious little in 1997 to put an end to the abuse. Thirty-three states and the federal government expressly criminalize custodial sexual misconduct, yet efforts to enforce these prohibitions were wholly inadequate. For example, the U.S. failed to ensure that prison guards were trained to refrain from abusing their authority by having sexual contact with female prisoners, to respect women's privacy, and to avoid subjecting prisoners to cruel, inhuman and degrading treatment. Congress did indicate its interest in ending this custodial abuse by introducing legislation in October 1997 that sought to compel all states to criminalize custodial misconduct. The bill also would establish a hotline for women to report custodial sexual misconduct to the Department of Justice (DOJ) and would prohibit the rehiring of guards found liable for such misconduct.

Work of
Human Rights Watch

In 1997, Human Rights Watch capitalized on high-level pronouncements of support for women's human rights—coming from governments, U.N. officials, and other international actors—to press for programs and policies that would move states toward meeting their international obligations to protect women's rights. We conducted field investigations in Mexico, Peru, Pakistan, Bosnia, the Hague and Arusha, Tanzania that documented violations of women's rights and the international response to such crimes and used this fact base to demonstrate the serious shortcomings in policies promoting women's rights.

Key among our efforts was securing accountability for acts of violence against women, whether committed by soldiers during conflicts, by jailers guarding female prisoners, or by husbands behind apartment doors. In January 1997, Human Rights Watch other women's rights activists, including the International Human Rights Law Group, the Center for Women's Global Leadership, and the International Women's Human Rights Law Clinic, initiated efforts to press governments negotiating the creation of an Interna-

tional Criminal Court at the U.N. to ensure that women's rights concerns were fully integrated into the treaty. We drafted and helped distribute action alerts to concerned organizations around the world on the status of negotiations and prepared position papers in February, August, and November for government delegates to strengthen support for taking up women's rights. We also joined coalitions of nongovernmental organizations (NGOs) to emphasize the need for an effective, independent ICC in meetings with delegates to the negotiations and policy makers in the U.S. government.

The acute need for creating international mechanisms to secure justice for women victims of human rights abuse is underscored by Human Rights Watch's work monitoring the tribunals established to prosecute violations of human rights and humanitarian law in Bosnia-Hercegovina and Rwanda. In 1997, we investigated the progress of the two tribunals in improving efforts to investigate crimes of sexual violence. We pressed governments at the 1997 session of the U.N. Commission on Human Rights to ensure that the resolution on Rwanda expressed concern about ongoing violations of women's rights and stressed the need for justice for victims of sex-specific crimes. In October 1997, Human Rights Watch participated in a workshop convened by Justice Louise Arbour, chief prosecutor for both tribunals, to reinforce her staff's commitment to and develop their skills in investigating and prosecuting sexual violence in both Bosnia and Rwanda.

Human Rights Watch raised the issue of securing justice for women who suffer violence in conflict situations at the first meeting of the Organization for Security and Cooperation in Europe (OSCE) to take up the issue of women's status in the region. At the October meeting in Warsaw, governments agreed on the importance of improving OSCE attention and response to problems of violence against women and several expressed support for creating a high-level advisor on gender integration into OSCE activities.

We also fought to increase access to justice for women abused while in custody.

Following the December 1996 release of our report on sexual abuse of women in U.S. state prisons, we began working with congressional staff to draft and introduce legislation requiring states to make it a crime for prison staff to have any kind of sexual contact with female prisoners and creating a secure hotline for prisoners to report instances of sexual abuse. In June 1997, we wrote to Illinois Gov. James Edgar, urging him to sign into law a bill criminalizing custodial sexual misconduct in Illinois state prisons, a step he did take.

Based on detailed investigations into state responses to violence against women by private actors, we pressed governments to acknowledge their role in denying women access to justice. In August 1997, we released a report on violence against women and the medico-legal system in South Africa detailing the government's failure to respond adequately to violence against women, particularly the obstacles created by the state's forensic medical system which women must navigate in order to prosecute successfully the abuses committed against them. In July 1997, we joined experts and activists at a World Health Organization meeting in Copenhagen to discuss ways of improving the forensic medical treatment of victims of violence.

In the case of the U.S. government, we urged officials to commit foreign assistance to improving law enforcement handling of violent crimes against women. Although the U.S. government devotes millions of dollars each year to training police and judicial authorities around the world, almost none of those monies target law enforcement failures to respond to violence against women. Human Rights Watch thus urged that Congress renew its request—and it did so in October 1997—that the State Department devote a portion of its law enforcement budget in Russia to improving the response to violence against women. We also urged that U.S. assistance support a pilot program in Moscow to serve as a model of an effective, coordinated response to women who report violence, a project now being developed by the State Department.

In November 1997, Human Rights Watch honored Marina Pisklakova and her work fighting official indifference to violence against women in Russia. Ms. Pisklakova is the founder and executive director of the Moscow Crisis Center for Women and started one of the first domestic violence hotlines in Russia. Since its 1993 founding, the center has helped more than 8,500 women, providing them with counseling and social and legal support services.

Although international attention is more and more directed toward violence against women, discrimination on the basis of sex often goes unchallenged. In 1997, Human Rights Watch confronted official indifference to sex discrimination in a variety of fora. In collaboration with the International Labor Rights Fund and Mexico's National Association of Democratic Lawyers, Human Rights Watch filed a petition with the U.S. NAO challenging the Mexican government's failure to enforce its laws protecting labor rights and prohibiting sex discrimination by allowing pregnancy-based discrimination to flourish in its maquiladora sector. The U.S. NAO accepted the petition and scheduled a hearing for November 1997. We raised concern over these practices in a March letter to Secretary of State Madeleine Albright, and in meetings with U.S. human rights officials and representatives of companies perpetuating such discrimination. Our work on sex discrimination in the maquiladoras inspired Working Assets, a long-distance telephone company that promotes social responsibility, to design a call-in and writing campaign to General Motors, one of the chief offenders. Working Assets enclosed in its phone bills information urging its subscribers to send protests to General Motors to urge it to stop discriminating against women workers in its factories in Mexico. The highly successful campaign generated 22,228 letters and 4,425 phone calls from subscribers of Working Assets.

Earlier in the year, we focused on discrimination against women under Morocco's family law and submitted to the members of the CEDAW committee a memorandum presenting our findings on the effects of laws that render women legal minors regardless of their age. Committee members drew upon the memo in critiquing Morocco's failure to comply with CEDAW. In meetings with Senate staff and Clinton administration officials, we joined other groups in urging immediate U.S. ratification of CEDAW.

Human Rights Watch also worked in 1997 to document trafficking of girls and women into forced prostitution, marriage, domestic service, and other forms of labor. Our advocacy strived to turn the international response from cracking down on trafficked women as undocumented migrants to protecting women's rights in the recruitment process and in the abusive situations in which they worked and lived. In April 1997, we submitted a statement to the U.N. Human Rights Commission detailing our findings and recommending action to combat trafficking and abuses against women workers. We also participated in meetings in Uganda and Canada to discuss the international dimensions of trafficking. In July, we worked with Rep. Louise Slaughter's office to prepare a resolution condemning trafficking and calling for improved response by the U.S. and the international community. In November, we joined U.S. officials, congressional staff, and other NGOs to assess the problems associated with trafficking in the U.S. and the needed response.

Much of Human Rights Watch's work on women's human rights in 1997 was directed toward the overarching goal of ensuring that women's human rights were treated as a priority concern by governments and international actors. Thus, in meetings with officials such as U.S. Assistant Secretary of State John Shattuck and his Russian counterpart, Teymuraz Ramashvilli, we urged specific actions to improve their governments' records on ameliorating women's status. At the U.N., we pursued this goal by supporting the renewal of the mandate of the special rapporteur on violence against women and by meeting with the Human Rights Centre staff about integrating women's rights into all aspects of their work.

On another level, we continued our work with women's rights activists to discuss with and train them in using international human rights methods, standards, and mechanisms to increase the power and visibility of their work. To this end, in June 1997 Human Rights Watch released a women's human rights advocacy manual, produced jointly with Women, Law and Development International. This manual is designed to train women rights activists in using women's human rights fact-finding, documentation, and advocacy. The manual is designed to demystify human rights documentation and advocacy to make it accessible to activists the world over in their efforts to promote the human rights of women. We plan to conduct training sessions, to be sponsored by regional women's human rights organizations around the world, aimed at increasing women's awareness of and expertise in human rights law and practice.

Relevant Human Rights Watch reports:
Violence Against Women and the Medico-Legal System in South Africa, 8/97
All Too Familiar: Sexual Abuse of Women in U.S. State Prisons, 12/96

INTERNATIONAL FILM FESTIVAL

The Human Rights Watch Film Festival was created to advance public education by illuminating human rights issues and concerns using the unique medium of film. Each year, the festival exhibits the finest human rights films and videos in theaters, at universities and on cable television throughout the United States and a growing number of cities abroad—a reflection of both the scope of the festival and the increasingly global appeal that the project has generated.

The Human Rights Watch Film Festival was established in 1988, in part to mark the tenth anniversary of the founding of what has become Human Rights Watch. After a hiatus of three years, it was resumed in 1991 and has since been presented annually. The 1997 festival featured twenty new films from fifteen countries over a two-week period first in New York, as a collaborative venture with the Film Society of Lincoln Center, and then in Los Angeles with the Museum of Tolerance, and in London in partnership with the Institute of Contemporary Art. A majority of the screenings were followed by discussions with the filmmakers and Human Rights Watch staff on the issues represented in each work. The festival included feature-length fiction and documentary films as well as works-in-progress and experimental films.

In selecting films for the festival, Human Rights Watch concentrates equally on artistic merit and human rights content. The festival encourages filmmakers around the world to address human rights subject matter in their work and presents films and videos from both new and established international filmmakers. Each year, the festival's programming committee screens over 600 films and videos to create a diverse and challenging program that represents a broad array of countries and issues. Once a film is nominated for a place in the festival, staff of the relevant division of Human Rights Watch also view the work to confirm its accuracy in the portrayal of human rights concerns.

Each year the festival is launched in New York with an opening night that features a film's U.S. premiere. In 1997 the festival's opening night centerpiece was "The Truce", by Italian director, Francesco Rosi. The award-winning film is based on Primo Levi's autobiographical novel which traces his return to Italy at the end of the Second World War.

In conjunction with the opening night, the festival annually awards a prize in the name of cinematographer and director Nestor Almendros, who was a cherished friend of the festival. The award, which includes a cash prize of $5,000, goes to a deserving new filmmaker in recognition of his or her contributions to human rights through film. The 1997 recipient of the Nestor Almendros Award was Zimbabwean filmmaker Ingrid Sinclair,

for her outstanding film "Flame," a fictional account of two young women's fight against white minority rules in what was then Rhodesia. Because of a short scene in the film in which its heroine is raped by her commander, "Flame" was almost banned before its completion and for more than one year provoked widespread debate within Zimbabwe. "Flame" also became the centerpiece of the festival's Women's Day Program—a day and evening exclusively devoted to films and videos that address women's rights around the world.

In 1995, in honor of Irene Diamond, a longtime board member and supporter of Human Rights Watch, the festival launched a new award, the Irene Diamond Lifetime Achievement Award, which is presented annually to a director whose life's work illuminates an outstanding commitment to human rights and film. The 1997 award went to American director Alan J. Pakula, for his role in encouraging American independent filmmakers to produce provocative, challenging human rights films for wider audiences.

Highlights of the 1997 festival featured thematic screenings including films dealing with ethnic conflict, land rights, international conspiracies and the right to education. The 1997 festival also included a retrospective of the work of African-American director Charles Burnett, whose latest film, "Nightjohn," had its commercial theater premiere. Unlike Burnett's other films, "Nightjohn" is a period piece set in the antebellum South, a compelling story of a slave who gives up freedom in order to teach fellow slaves how to read and write. The retrospective of Burnett's work highlighted his thirty-year career of making films chronicling everyday lives in black families and communities and celebrated him as one of America's greatest social realist filmmakers.

In 1997 the festival continued its collaborative screenings with the New York African Film Festival, highlighting human rights themes in new African-American cinema.

During the festival's two-week run in New York, its high school project offered daytime screenings for students followed by interactive discussions among the students, their teachers, visiting filmmakers, and Human Rights Watch staff. Special high school screenings were also held in Los Angeles.

In an effort to reach a wider audience and satisfy the growing demand for these films, the festival continued, for the third year, its "Global Showcase," a touring program of films and videos, which appeared in seven U.S. cities. A tailored version of the global showcase also traveled to Bogotá, Colombia and to Gent, Belgium.

In December, in collaboration with the International American Institute for Human Rights, the festival appeared in San José, Costa Rica exhibiting new films from the Americas dealing with human rights themes. The festival also assisted with the programming for the first human rights festival organized by university students in the Philippines, at the end of December.

The second annual full-scale Human Rights Watch Film Festival in Europe, opened in London on September 30. The collaborative venture between the festival and the Institute of Contemporary Art (ICA) presented an opening-night British premiere of the dramatic feature "Prisoner of the Mountains," about Russian-Chechan conflict. The film was directed by Sergei Bodrov and adapted from a Tolstoy novella. A one-week festival of film and video screenings followed, along with panel discussions with filmmakers from around the world and Human Rights Watch staff. The 1997 London series showcased a weekend of films and discussions with filmmakers from the former Yugoslavia as well as films from Northern Ireland, Japan, Taiwan and the U.S.

SPECIAL ISSUES

The complexity that human rights work has acquired, and the diversity of opportunities for advocacy and action, have increasingly demanded that Human Rights Watch undertake cross-regional or thematic initiatives involving a specialized focus or expertise. At times, those initiatives consist of a single opportunity to make our voice heard on a crucial issue, but often they take the form of campaigns that have become a sensational part of our program. Some of the issues in which we undertook or maintained special initiatives in 1997 included the following:

PRISONS

Prison massacres, dramatic protests, and violent guard abuse earned occasional news headlines in 1997, but the deplorable daily living conditions that were the plight of the great majority of the world's prisoners passed largely unnoticed. With scant public attention to the topic in most countries, correspondingly little progress was made in rectifying the abuses routinely inflicted in prisons and other places of detention. Many countries, moreover, fostered public ignorance of prison inadequacies by denying human rights groups, journalists, and other outside observers nearly all access to their penal facilities. A smaller group of countries, including China, Cuba, and Peru, even barred the International Committee of the Red Cross (ICRC) from providing basic humanitarian relief to people in their prisons.

Unchecked outbursts of prison violence continued to violate prisoners' right to life. The August 28 killings of at least twenty-nine prisoners in a remote jungle facility in Venezuela led the country's Justice Ministry, charged with prison administration, to promise reforms, and its Public Ministry to conduct an extensive investigation of the incident's causes. The Tajikistan government, earlier in the year, chose to cover up an even bloodier prison massacre. Although information about the events was scarce, reports indicated that in mid-April the Tajik security forces stormed a prison in the northern city of Khujand, killing over a hundred prisoners. Earlier that week, inmates had rioted and taken several guards hostage to protest life-threatening detention conditions. Ignoring Human Rights Watch's request for information and its calls for a thorough and impartial investigation of the incident, the Tajik government apparently took no action to punish those responsible for the deaths.

In Morocco's Oukacha prison, twenty-t prisoners were burned alive in early September; they had been crammed together in a cell reportedly built to hold eight. The cause of the fire was not announced, but the country's Justice Ministry did acknowledge that overcrowding might have played a role in the deaths.

The most common cause of death in prison was disease, often the predictable result of severe overcrowding, malnutrition, unhygienic conditions, and lack of medical care. A special commission of inquiry, appointed after the 1995 death of a prominent businessman in India's high-security Tihar Central Jail, reported in September that the 10,000 inmates held in that institution endured serious health hazards, including overcrowding, "appalling" sanitary facilities, and a shortage of medical staff. Similar conditions prevailed in the prisons of the former Soviet Union, where tuberculosis continued its comeback. Russia's prosecutor general announced in March that about 2,000 inmates had died of tuberculosis in the previous year. In Kazakhstan, the disease, including drug resistant strains, reached epidemic proportions. AIDS also plagued many prison populations.

Inadequate supervision by guards, easy access to weapons, lack of separation of different categories of prisoners, and fierce competition for basic necessities encouraged inmate-on-inmate abuse in many penal facilities. In extreme cases—as in certain Venezuelan prisons with one guard for every 150 prisoners, and an underground trade in knives, guns, even grenades—prisoners killed other prisoners with impunity. Rape, extortion, and involuntary servitude were other frequent abuses suffered by inmates at the bottom of the prison hierarchy.

In contrast, powerful inmates in some facilities in Colombia, India, and Mexico, among others, enjoyed cellular phones, rich diets, and comfortable lodgings. With guard corruption rampant in so many prisons around the world, the adage "you get what you pay for" was only too appropriate. Indeed, in Indonesia, two prisoners reportedly escaped in September after bribing guards to bring them to a brothel.

Besides corruption, physical abuse by guards remained a chronic problem. Some countries continued to permit corporal punishment and the routine use of leg irons, fetters, shackles, and chains. The heavy bar fetters used in Pakistani prisons, for example, turned simple movements such as walking into painful ordeals. In many prison systems, unwarranted beatings were so common as to be an integral part of prison life. Women prisoners were particularly vulnerable to custodial sexual abuse. In the aftermath of prison riots or escapes, physical abuse was even more predictable, and typically much more severe.

Overcrowding—prevalent in almost every country for which information was available—was at the root of many of the worst abuses. The problem was often most severe in smaller pretrial detention facilities, where, in many countries, inmates were packed together with no space to stretch or move around. In some of Rwanda's *cachots* (local lockups), where a large proportion of the country's approximately 120,000 detainees were held, overcrowding was so acute as to be life-threatening. In Rwanda and elsewhere, even large prisons were crowded far beyond their capacity. Panama's Modelo prison, for example, held over ten times the number of prisoners it was built to hold. So notorious were its conditions that, in a symbolic choice of dates, the government finally demolished it on International Human Rights Day in December 1996.

The Modelo prison was built in 1917, exemplifying another common problem: that of old, antiquated, and physically decaying prison facilities. Nineteenth-century prisons needing constant upkeep remained in use in some countries, including the United States, Mexico, Russia, and the United Kingdom, although even many modern facilities were in severe disrepair due to lack of maintenance. Notably, many prisons lacked a functional system of plumbing. In Hong Kong, one of the most prosperous and technologically advanced places in the world, prisoners in some older facilities had to "slop out," that is, to defecate in plastic buckets that they were periodically allowed to empty. In Venezuela, inmates in parts of some facilities did not even get buckets; they resorted to defecating in newspapers that they threw out the window.

Conditions in many prisons were, in short, so deficient as to constitute cruel, inhuman or degrading treatment, violating article 7 of the International Covenant on Civil and Political Rights. Their specific failings could also be enumerated under the more detailed provisions of the U.N. Standard Minimum Rules for the Treatment of Prisoners. A widely known set of prison standards, the Standard Minimum Rules describe "the minimum conditions which are accepted as suitable by the United Nations." Although the Standard Minimum Rules have been integrated into the prison laws and regulations of many countries, few if any prison systems observed all of their prescriptions in practice.

The poor prison conditions existing in many countries arose from a complex of causes. Fiscal constraints and competing budget priorities were surely a factor in most countries, although these pressures were never a valid excuse for violating minimum standards of decency. In other countries, an element of deliberate cruelty seemed evident. For example, describing some prisoners as "animals that must never see sunlight again," South Africa's corrections commissioner released a March statement in favor of converting disused mine shafts into super-maximum security penal institutions.

Even those unsympathetic to convicted criminals and entirely skeptical of the idea of rehabilitation should nonetheless be concerned about the inhumane treatment of prisoners. Although comprehensive figures were impossible to obtain, the available statistics showed that an impressive proportion of the world's prisoners had not been convicted of any crime, but were instead being preventively detained at some stage of the trial process. Some of these detainees—who under basic human rights standards are presumed innocent and should be treated as such—had been confined for years before being acquitted of the charges against them. The Nigerian government's national human rights commission reported in September, for example, that at least 60 percent of the country's prisoners were pretrial detainees, and at least half of them had been awaiting trial for more than five years.

Shielded from public view, and populated largely by the poor, uneducated, and politically powerless, prisons tended to remain hidden sites of human rights abuse. By struggling against this natural tendency toward secrecy and silence, the efforts of numerous local human rights groups around the world—who fought to obtain access to prisons, monitored prison conditions, and publicized the abuses they found—were critical in 1997, as in the past. In some countries, moreover, government human rights ombudspersons, parliamentary commissions, and other monitors helped call attention to abuses. In South Africa, notably, the national human rights commission conducted numerous investigations into prison conditions, resulting in substantial public criticism of prison authorities.

At the regional level as well, prison monitoring mechanisms were active. The European Committee for the Prevention of Torture (CPT) continued its important work, inspecting the penal institutions of approximately a dozen countries in 1997, including those of Turkey, Spain, and Estonia. In December 1996, the CPT released a public statement on Turkey, declaring that "the practice of torture and other forms of severe ill-treatment of persons in police custody . . . remained widespread."

In Africa, the recently-appointed special rapporteur on prisons and conditions of detention, an adjunct to the African Commission on Human and Peoples' Rights, began work in January 1997 and made an initial fact-finding mission to Zimbabwe in early March. Human rights organizations with observer status at the commission reported, however, that the special rapporteur's oral report on his mission presented an insufficiently detailed or critical view of the country's prison situation. (As of October, no written report had yet been released.) In August, the special rapporteur inspected prisons in Mali.

Protests, Riots, and Killings in Latin American Prisons

Like 1996, 1997 was an eventful year in the prisons of Latin America, which held approximately half a million inmates. Conditions continued to stagnate—and even to worsen in some countries—inspiring dramatic forms of prisoner protest. Massacres, riots, and other violent incidents struck prisons across the region, further evidencing the failure of Latin America's penal systems.

Prison unrest erupted over the course of the year in Bolivia, Brazil, Colombia, Ecuador, Guyana, Honduras, Jamaica, Mexico, Panama, Peru, and Venezuela. In Brazil alone, there were over sixty prison riots in the first six months of the year. Fifty-two hostages were taken in one such mutiny at a São Paulo prison in August. In Bolivia, thousands of prisoners went on a hunger strike in March to protest the slow pace of the judicial system and the uneven application of the parole law; several of them sewed their mouths shut to dramatize their plight.

As exemplified by the Bolivian protest, prisoners in Latin America were subject not only to horrendous conditions of confinement but to entire criminal justice systems in need of reform. Prisons around the region were filled with *procesados*: inmates whose cases languished at some stage of the criminal process. Indeed, some 90 percent of Honduran, Paraguayan, and Uruguayan inmates were unsentenced, while in the Dominican Republic, Panama, Haiti, El Salvador, Peru and Venezuela, the proportion of unsentenced inmates ranged from 65 to 85 percent. The slow pace of criminal proceedings, combined with the routine denial of pretrial release, was at the origin of these unhappy statistics.

Human rights ombudspersons from all over Latin America discussed the state of the region's prisons at a February conference on prison overcrowding that was organized by ILANUD, the U.N. criminal justice institute

for Latin America; their reports paint a depressing picture of prisons in crisis. The ombudsperson for El Salvador, for example, spoke of the "systematic violation of the human rights of the prison population" and the unfortunate reality of "cruel, inhuman, and degrading treatment." The Guatemalan representative compared his country's prison conditions against the U.N. Standard Minimum Rules for the Treatment of Prisoners and the Guatemalan Constitution, concluding that neither set of standards was obeyed. With regard to Mexico, the capital's human rights commission confirmed that the majority of the country's prisons "lack basic services," and that inmates "enjoy privileges or suffer wants depending on their economic resources." Other countries' delegates made similar reports.

An encouraging contrast to this generally bleak picture were the vigorous efforts of numerous Latin American countries in working to establish a U.N. mechanism to monitor the treatment of persons deprived of their liberty (described below). Latin American delegates, particularly the representatives of Argentina, Chile, Costa Rica, and Uruguay, were key players in the U.N. debates on the proposed monitoring body, presenting compelling arguments in support of a strong and effective mechanism.

U.N. Prison Monitoring Effort

The vast scale and chronic nature of the human rights violations in the world's prisons have long been of concern to the United Nations, as demonstrated by the 1955 promulgation of the U.N. Standard Minimum Rules for the Treatment of Prisoners. Indeed, the international community's failure to adopt these standards in practice, even while it has embraced them in theory, has inspired the United Nations' most recent prisons effort.

For the past several years, a U.N. working group has been hammering out a draft treaty that would establish a U.N. subcommittee authorized to make periodic and *ad hoc* visits to places of detention in states party to the treaty, including prisons, jails, and police lockups. As described in the draft treaty—conceived as an optional protocol to the Convention Against Torture—the basic goal of the subcommittee would be to prevent torture and other ill-treatment. Accordingly, based on the information obtained during its periodic and ad hoc visits, the subcommittee would make detailed recommendations to state authorities regarding necessary improvements to their detention facilities, and the authorities would be expected to implement these recommendations.

Although the proposed monitoring mechanism had great promise, it also had serious potential flaws. Notable among them was the possibility that the subcommittee could be entirely barred from reporting publicly on abuses it discovers, pursuant to a strict rule of confidentiality that some countries have advocated. Although the draft treaty favored cooperation between governments and the subcommittee as a means of instituting remedial measures, it must, if it is to create an effective mechanism, leave open the possibility of public reporting, at least in situations where governments stubbornly refuse to cooperate with the subcommittee or to implement its recommendations.

The working group met for its sixth session in October 1997, reaching negotiated agreement as to the content of several draft provisions. Although most countries active in the deliberations—including South Africa, the Netherlands, Denmark, Sweden, Australia, and several Latin American countries—clearly favored establishing a strong and workable mechanism, a few recalcitrant states were able to hinder the working group's progress toward this goal. Because the proceedings were conducted on a consensus basis, rather than by simple majority vote, a small minority of countries could have an exaggerated impact on the draft text. As of this writing, the working group has not yet taken a definitive position on public reporting and other fundamental issues, but there is fear that given this consensus approach the lowest common denominator could prevail.

Relevant Human Rights Watch reports:
Cold Storage: Super-Maximum Security Confinement in Indiana, 10/97
Hong Kong: Prison Conditions in 1997, 6/97
Punishment Before Trial: Prison Conditions in Venezuela, 3/97
All Too Familiar: Sexual Abuse of Women in U.S. State Prisons, 12/96

CORPORATIONS AND HUMAN RIGHTS

The debate on corporate responsibility for human rights captured broad public interest worldwide in 1997. Local activists at the point of production, supported by advocacy groups in the United States, Canada, the European Union, and Asia, spurred a steady stream of reports, counter-reports, articles, and press releases. These documented and/or refuted allegations of physical abuse and suppression of freedom of association and expression against women workers. In total, this discourse underscored how far the debate had moved from earlier discussions of whether corporations even had a responsibility for human rights. The focus of the intensifying debate increasingly centered on the steps companies needed to take to make their codes of conduct meaningful. Responding to mounting public concern, several U.S. apparel and footwear corporations attempted to grapple with new implementation methods for their codes. At the same time, allegations of human rights abuses at plants contracted by Nike Incorporated in Asia provided a concentrated focus of attention throughout the year.

The debate, while still centered in the apparel, footwear, food and rug industries, expanded beyond these sectors to touch the multinational oil companies. Feeling the sting of allegations of complicity in rights violations and their effect on corporate image, a few of the oil giants made general commitments to human rights without the programmatic steps to implement them. In 1997, the Canadian, British, German and U.S. governments, as well as intergovernmental bodies and agencies like the European Parliament and the International Labour Organisation, were drawn into the debate. There was some progress, stemming in part from Human Rights Watch's work. In March, General Motors, in response to the 1996 Human Rights Watch Women's Rights Project report on forced pregnancy testing in the maquiladoras (export-oriented assembly plants) of northern Mexico, announced that it was ending its practice of pre-hire pregnancy screening; the new policy was implemented on April 1. In August, seventeen U.S. manufacturers of anti-personnel mine components agreed to cease their involvement in landmine production following an April report issued by the Human Rights Watch Arms Project. As a result of campaigning on Burma by an international coalition of human rights groups, including Human Rights Watch, a few companies ceased production there.

The Apparel Industry

Across the globe corporations and their critics debated monitoring. In May, the director-general of the International Labour Organisation floated a proposal for a " global social label" to tag goods produced according to core labor standards. He suggested that specific country labeling would be a more effective check on labor rights violations than voluntary codes of conduct. In May, following reports of worker abuse and child labor in the textile industry in South Asia, members of the European Parliament adopted a resolution calling on the European Commission to adopt E.U. legislation to ensure that clothes, shoes, and carpets imported from developing countries would be labeled to indicate that worker rights had been respected. A high-profile, tripartite attempt occurred in the United States with the work of the White House-convened Apparel Industry Partnership. The partnership, a group of U.S.-based apparel and footwear manufacturers, labor unions, and nongovernmental organizations, was launched by President Clinton in 1996 to formulate a global code of conduct to eradicate sweatshop practices in the companies' operations, both in the U.S. and abroad. The companies included L.L. Bean, Liz Claiborne,

Nike, and Phillips-Van Heusen, among others. After eight months, on April 18, the partnership issued an interim report. Its "Workplace Code of Conduct" consolidated and advanced the best of the existing U.S. voluntary company codes of conduct on freedom of association and expression. It prohibited forced labor, child labor, harassment of employees in the workplace, and discrimination, as well as recognizing the rights to freedom of association and collective bargaining. It also attempted to address minimum standards on health and safety, wages and benefits, and overtime. The provisions on wages, benefits and overtime were criticized by some analysts who saw them as insufficient to meet workers' basic needs and sanctioned excessively long working hours. The report's "Principles of Monitoring" defined company responsibilities in internal monitoring. These required companies to publicize their codes actively in the workplace, articulate employee notification of workers' rights and responsibilities, and conduct periodic audits to ensure compliance with the code.

The most important, and divisive, element of the Apparel Industry Partnership's report was the section on independent external monitoring. In 1996, apparel and footwear companies had resisted independent monitoring of their codes. By 1997, however, several companies had accepted the fact that their voluntary efforts would not be credible unless compliance could be independently verified. Others, however, opposed independent monitoring. Two of the corporate members, Warnaco Incorporated and Karen Kane Incorporated, claimed that independent monitoring would jeopardize essential trade secrets and that internal monitoring procedures afforded adequate safeguards. These corporations withdrew from the partnership in opposition to any plans for independent monitoring involving local religious, labor, or human rights organizations in the countries where operations are based. The April report's section on this issue left the essential elements of independent monitoring unresolved. The report required only that local human rights, labor rights, religious or other similar institutions be "consulted." Furthermore, creating no role for public accountability, the report omitted a disclosure requirement that monitors' evaluation reports be made public. As of November, the partnership was continuing its attempt to resolve the outstanding differences over independent monitoring and establish an association empowered to supervise adherence with the code in a meaningful way. Human Rights Watch, believing that it could better contribute by remaining outside this group, was not a participant in the Apparel Industry Partnership.

The appeal of voluntary codes of conduct and the debate over their implementation spread in 1997. The export manufacturers association in Guatemala, VESTEX, announced the promulgation of its own voluntary code of conduct, and the Guatemalan subsidiary of the U.S. accounting firm, Ernst & Young, conducted several audits of its implementation. In contrast to this auditing, during 1997 a coalition of Guatemalan religious, human rights and labor groups had formed a committee to monitor corporate codes of conduct. Parallel efforts were also underway in El Salvador, where working conditions and hiring practices of multinational corporations and their subcontractors had received bad publicity. In May 1997, the Salvadoran clothing manufacturers association, ASIC, announced that it had formulated its own code of conduct. ASIC likened the code to the Apparel Industry Partnership's effort and stated that it would use international auditing companies "to certify that international norms are not violated." According to one Salvadoran newspaper headline, the widespread adoption of the code would "eliminate the effects of international campaigns." The manufacturers' undertaking stood in contrast to work already in place, specifically that of the Independent Monitoring Commission which is composed of members of Salvadoran nongovernmental organizations and which monitors the Mandarin plant in the San Marco free trade zone.

Responding to the calls for transparency in monitoring, the world's largest accounting firms, such as Ernst & Young and Coopers & Lybrand, presented themselves as independent monitors able to perform social audits. While Ernst & Young did a commendable job in documenting egregious health and safety violations at a Nike contractor in Vietnam, the competence of accounting firms to conduct sensitive human rights investigations, combining testimonial evidence with statistical analysis, was doubtful. Despite the importance of active guidance and participation of local human rights defenders, the large firms' social "auditing" would involve these knowledgeable, activist groups in minimal consultation, at best. In addition, the firms would simply convey their findings to their employers, the contracting companies, with no provision for the public disclosure or accountability necessary to establish and maintain effectiveness and credibility. The effect of this lack of transparency was highlighted in early November with media reports on an Ernst & Young audit of a Nike contractor in Vietnam. The document, issued on January 13, 1997, detailed numerous violations of health and safety and wage and hour standards in Nike's facilities but had remained an internal and confidential report until it was leaked to the press by an inside source.

While several U.S. footwear and apparel companies were actively exploring the possibility of independent monitoring as of November, the only functioning—and quite effective—locally-based independent monitoring program in existence was the program implemented at the Mandarin factory, a supplier to Gap Incorporated, in El Salvador.

Nike

The sharpest and most persistent controversy over corporate responsibility for human rights and independent monitoring of company codes of conduct swirled around the practices of Nike contractors in Vietnam, China, and Indonesia. Vietnam Labor Watch (not affiliated with Human Rights Watch) issued a report in March citing physical abuse of workers at a Nike contractor in Vietnam. In Indonesia, workers at Nike subcontractors went on strike to demand payment of the country's newly promised minimum wage. In the face of repeated allegations by international and regional investigators of abusive labor practices at subcontractor facilities in those three countries, Nike hired former U.S. Ambassador to the United Nations Andrew Young and his consultancy firm, GoodWorks, to conduct an audit of Nike facilities in all three countries. The methodology employed by Ambassador Young was disturbingly flawed: he spent very limited time at each facility; interviewed workers at random on company premises; and conducted the interviews with the assistance of company-supplied translators. Such methods reinforce the strain on those workers selected for interviews and make it difficult, if not impossible, to unearth patterns of subtle but invidious harassment. Ambassador Young's report, released in June, found that Nike facilities were generally respectful of human rights and that there was "no evidence or pattern of widespread or systematic abuse or mistreatment of workers" in the factories he had visited.

Ambassador Young recommended that the company should more actively publicize its code of conduct in supplier factories, implement an independent monitoring system, and organize a committee of "distinguished individuals" to perform spot-checks at their factories abroad. Following the report, Nike took out full-page advertisements in several newspapers, including the *New York Times, USA Today,* and the *Washington Post,* publicizing the findings as a vindication of its corporate image and standards. The subsequent public disclosure of the January Ernst & Young internal report on Nike facilities in Vietnam cast doubt on whether the company would implement these recommendations in good faith.

In contrast to Ambassador Young's findings, the Hong Kong-based Asia Monitor Resource Center and the Hong Kong Christian Industrial Committee released a report drawn from their investigations of Nike (and Reebok) contractors in south China. Highlighting the different findings that emerge from widely varying orientations and methodologies, this investigation documented very different conditions than those reported by Ambassador Young. The two groups found consistent patterns of labor rights violations in Nike contractor facilities in China. They found that freedom of association was "harshly repressed" and that there were no independent trade unions or nongovernmental organizations available to represent workers. The report also documented pregnancy-related discrimination and illegal firings because workers over the age of twenty-five were considered "too old" by factory management.

That report concluded that conditions in the Chinese facilities were in gross violation of the Nike (and Reebok) codes of conduct, the Apparel Industry Partnership's "Workplace Code of Conduct," and Chinese labor law. Based on their findings, the organizations argued that until real independent monitoring could be implemented in Chinese factories, labor rights violations would continue unabated. The report was released just prior to the Nike annual shareholder meeting in September. At that meeting, Nike claimed that it had investigated the report's allegations and had found them to be erroneous. Unfortunately, Nike management responded to the allegations by sharply attacking the bona fides of the Hong Kong-based monitors. A company press release stated, "Enough is enough. It's time for the public magnifying glass to be focused back on these fringe groups, which are again using the Internet and fax modems to promote mis-truths and distortions for their own purposes."

Also at the shareholder meeting, Nike management announced that it had severed relations with four Indonesian contractors on the grounds that they did not meet the company's code of conduct requirements. Specifically, there was a disagreement over payment of wages to workers at these facilities. Nike also announced at the meeting that it would distribute wallet-sized cards, with its code of conduct printed in eleven languages to all its employees. These actions resulted in the withdrawal of a shareholder resolution, filed by the General Board of Pensions and

Social Responsibility of the United Methodist Church, seeking reforms in Nike's overseas labor practices. No further commitments to establish independent monitoring as called for by Ambassador Young were made known by the company.

In October, a coalition of U.S.-based women's groups, including the National Organization for Women, the Ms. Foundation for Women, and the Feminist Majority, launched a campaign against Nike in order to highlight the problems female workers faced at Nike's Asian contractor facilities. The coalition noted that, "While the women who wear Nike shoes in the United States are encouraged to perform their best, the Indonesian, Vietnamese and Chinese women making the shoes often suffer from inadequate wages, corporal punishment, forced overtime and/or sexual harassment." The campaign called on Nike to allow independent monitors into their facilities abroad and to address issues related to the treatment of women and wage issues in Nike contractor operations.

Phillips-Van Heusen

Another example of the critical importance of independent monitoring, this one involving Human Rights Watch, was demonstrated in the controversy at the Phillips-Van Heusen (PVH) factories in Guatemala. Starting in September 1996, Van Heusen was confronted by allegations from union organizers and international labor rights activists that its workers' rights to free association, specifically their right to engage in collective bargaining, at PVH's Camisas Modernas factories was being suppressed. Local labor activists also alleged that union members were being pressured to resign from the union and the company with offers of large severance packages. Because a member of the Human Rights Watch board of directors served as the chief executive officer (CEO) of the company, Human Rights Watch staff members agreed to go to Guatemala to investigate the allegations on-site. In January, Human Rights Watch sent a team to determine whether the union had gathered the 25 percent support necessary under Guatemalan labor law to compel

the company to engage in collective bargaining and whether company management had harassed or discriminated against union activists. Based on the investigation, during which the organization received cooperation from both the company and the union, Human Rights Watch released a report which found that the union had met the critical 25 percent support threshold and that the Guatemalan Labor Ministry had failed in its duty to resolve the conflict between the union and the company over union strength. Furthermore, our investigation found that union members had faced subtle but pernicious forms of discrimination, including deprivation of earnings and large severance packages in exchange for their resignations.

On receiving an advance copy of the report, the CEO of Phillips-Van Heusen announced that the company accepted the findings on union support and would immediately begin collective bargaining negotiations. In August, negotiations between the company and union resulted in the first-ever collective bargaining agreement in the Guatemalan maquiladora sector. At this writing, the agreement awaits approval by the Guatemalan Ministry of Labor.

The Oil Industry

Increasingly, multinational oil companies, expanding exploration and drilling operations to states ruled by governments that are serious human rights violators, were criticized for the human rights consequences of partnering with those governments. Operations in such human rights trouble spots as Colombia, Nigeria, and Burma repeatedly received press attention.

Colombia

In 1997, faced with an increase in guerrilla attacks and paramilitary activity, multinational oil companies operating in the Casanare and Arauca regions of Colombia found themselves deep in controversy over the human rights implications of their security arrangements with the Colombian Defense Ministry. In November 1995, the companies had signed agreements with the armed forces, committing to pay U.S.$2 million annually to a military institution known for abusing human rights with impunity, for protection of their pipelines and installations from guerrilla attack.

In Casanare, the consortium operating the massive Cusiana-Cupiagua oil fields comprised British Petroleum (BP), TOTAL Exploratie en Produktie Maatschippij B.V. (TOTAL), Triton Energy, and the state-owned ECOPETROL. Arauca province was the site of the Occidental Petroleum, Royal Dutch/Shell, and ECOPETROL consortium's Cano Limón-Covenas oil fields and pipeline. By putting the companies in a new relationship to the military, the contracts had raised serious questions. The direct contracts signed with the Ministry of Defense inappropriately tightened the companies' relations with an abusive military and compounded the fundamental problem: that the companies relied on that abusive military institution for security and thereby assumed a responsibility to take concrete, programmatic measures to prevent violations and to confront those that may arise. Yet, the companies took little action regarding human rights. For instance the agreements with the Defense Ministry failed to mention human rights compliance as a condition of contract. In addition, abuses that have been attributed to the military units defending the companies have not received a strong response from the companies. Some have been completely ignored.

Controversy over the companies' relations with Colombian military and police was particularly active in Britain. A *World in Action* documentary on the BBC reported, among other things, that the U.K.-based private security firm that BP had contracted to protest the Casanare installations had been involved in training Colombian police not only in security, but also, in counterinsurgency techniques. Responding to various media reports, British-based rights groups sharply criticized the new Labour government for appointing Sir David Simon, the CEO of British Petroleum, as minister of trade and competitiveness in Europe.

Human Rights Watch called on the partners in the Arauca consortium to disclose publicly the contents of their contract with the Colombian military. As of this writing, neither Occidental nor Shell has made any public statement as to how human rights may be respected in the course of their Colombian operations, but by November some of the companies were saying that they would no longer continue the contract with Colombia's armed forces. Nonetheless, they will continue to rely on the military and police to protect their companies under a payment scheme that, at this writing, is still being negotiated.

Nigeria

In the case of Shell, human rights concerns were not limited to company operations in Colombia. In March, following two years of criticism for its partnership with the Nigerian government and the role the company had played in events leading to killings in Ogoniland, Shell announced that it would explicitly acknowledge respect for human rights and the environment in its revamped internal code of conduct. As part of its general business principles, the company expressed "support for fundamental human rights in line with the legitimate role of business." The announcement was hailed as a breakthrough in that Shell had acknowledged that its operations had a significant impact on human rights. However, beyond the inclusion of this very vague language, it was unclear what specific steps the Royal Dutch/Shell group of companies would take to put those words into practice.

On May 14, at the annual general meeting of the Shell Transport and Trading Company in London, management soundly defeated a resolution brought by the socially responsible investment organization, Pensions and Investment Research Consultancy (PIRC), to conduct an independent audit of its human rights and environmental policies. The resolution was brought on behalf of various nongovernmental organizations including Friends of the Earth, the World Development Movement, and the Movement for the Survival of the Ogoni People (MOSOP). While defeating the resolution, Shell did announce that it agreed in principle to independent auditing, but that a shareholder resolution was not the appropriate mechanism to initiate such an action.

Burma/Thailand

The Burma operations of California-based UNOCAL and French-based TOTAL continued to draw fierce criticism and became the focus of an important lawsuit in U.S. federal court. The suit was brought on behalf of a number of unidentified citizens of Burma and a California resident. The complaint argues that the State Law and Order Restoration Council (SLORC) regime in Burma has been responsible for human rights violations in the course of constructing a pipeline to carry natural gas from the offshore Yadana gas fields to Bangkok. The plaintiffs contend that the companies were liable because residents in the area of the project were "subjected to the death of family members, assault, rape or other torture, and other human rights violations in furtherance of the Yadana gas pipeline project in which defendants are joint venturers."

On March 25, Judge Richard Paez declined to dismiss the lawsuit against UNOCAL and TOTAL and ruled that they could be sued in U.S. federal court, under the Alien Tort Claims Act, for abuses committed by SLORC. Compounding the problems for UNOCAL and other United States-based multinationals invested in Burma was the April 22 executive order by which President Clinton banned new investment in Burma on grounds of SLORC's dismal human rights record. While the order did not affect existing investments in Burma, such as UNOCAL's, it sent a message that, at least in the case of Burma, human rights considerations would be a factor. Roger Beach, the CEO of UNOCAL, defiantly announced that the only way UNOCAL would leave Burma was "if we are forced to by the enactment of law."

Meanwhile, UNOCAL established a second headquarters in Malaysia on April 21, to manage its non-U.S. operations. Oil industry analysts believed this was the beginning of an attempt by the company to withdraw from the United States and to minimize any liability brought by the lawsuit or because of sanctions against U.S. corporations doing business in Burma.

Nongovernmental Organizations' Initiatives

Advocacy and grassroots campaigning spread to more countries in 1997, and it was clear that pressure mounted by grassroots organizations, the press, and the public at large was playing an important role in holding corporations accountable for complicity in governmental human rights and labor rights violations. In the United States, several campaigns centered around sweatshop-like practices of U.S. apparel manufacturers. The National Labor Committee, a nongovernmental lobbying group associated with the U.S. labor movement, launched efforts against the Ralph Lauren apparel company for its sourcing of products from Burma and against Walt Disney Corporation for sourcing from sweatshops in Haiti and Thailand. In July, Ralph Lauren announced that it was ceasing business in Burma "until conditions have changed." Warnaco, a company that had left the Apparel Industry Partnership, made a similar announcement. The U.S.-based organizations Press for Change and Global Exchange continued their campaigns against Nike, and the Union of Needle Trades, Industrial and Textile Employees (UNITE) continued to campaign against the apparel manufacturer GUESS Incorporated because of its labor practices in the United States and abroad. In an effort to hold public actions to maintain pressure on companies, in early October a coalition of labor unions, religious groups and solidarity organizations sponsored a National Day of Conscience in various U.S. cities to focus on child labor and "to affirm the dignity of life and human rights."

Throughout the member states of the European Union, a coalition, based on the Dutch Clean Clothes Campaign, was joined by Labor Behind the Label in the United Kingdom, Les Magasins du Monde in Belgium, Artisans du Monde in France, and the Dutch industry organization, FENECON, in a concerted effort to highlight the problems of manufacturing abroad and to implement an independent monitoring system for European apparel manufacturers.

In Australia, a coalition comprising trade unions and community-based activist groups began the Fairwear campaign—an effort to implement a sourcing code of conduct among Australian retailers and manufacturers. As a result of campaigning by nongovernmental organizations in Germany, members of the Green Party introduced a bill into parliament calling for codes for conduct for German companies operating in China.

Campaigns were not limited to countries in the North. In India the South Asian Coalition on Child Servitude (SACCS) sponsored the Fair Play campaign in June in an attempt to eliminate child labor from the Indian sporting goods industry. In Hong Kong, the Asia Monitor Resource Center (AMRC) continued its campaigns to highlight abuses faced by workers in the Chinese footwear and toy industries. A coalition of groups from Honduras, Thailand, Ecuador, Indonesia, India, and Bangladesh continued their campaign to publicize and curtail activities of the worldwide shrimp industry that have created human rights and environmental problems.

In a surprising success, a four-year boycott of Holiday Inn and its parent company, Bass Private Limited, on the grounds that it was the only multinational hotel chain with operations in Tibet, resulted in Holiday Inn announcing that it would not continue its partnership with the Chinese government and would not extend its contract past the expiration date of October 1997. The campaign was organized by the Free Tibet Campaign, based in the U.K., and included activist groups in the United Kingdom and United States.

Relevant Human Rights Watch reports:

Exposing the Source: U.S. Companies and the Production of Antipersonnel Mines, 4/97
Corporations and Human Rights: Freedom of Association in a Maquila in Guatemala, 3/97

DRUGS AND HUMAN RIGHTS

Efforts to curtail the trafficking, sale and consumption of illegal drugs continued to acerbate prison overcrowding, stress criminal justice systems, and weaken legal protection for civil liberties. In countries with vastly different political, social and economic systems and traditions, anti-narcotics strategies included tactics inconsistent with human rights principles. Drug offenders faced the death penalty in a number of countries, including China, Indonesia, Iran, Iraq, Malaysia, Pakistan, Turkey and Saudi Arabia. Statistics were not available for the number of people executed for drug offenses in 1997. In August, Amnesty International reported that 534 people in China were executed for drug trafficking in 1996; available information suggested the execution rate did not change in 1997. The quantities of drugs that trigger death sentences can be small: one man was executed in China in September for peddling ten ounces of heroin. In Kuala Lumpur, two Indonesians were sentenced to death for trafficking three kilograms of marijuana. In Vietnam, where selling as little as one hundred grams of drugs can be punished with death, at least eighteen people were executed for drug offenses in 1997, including a twenty-eight-year-old sentenced to die by firing squad for trafficking 5.7 kilograms (12.5 pounds) of heroin.

Prisons in countless countries face burgeoning populations because of drug offenses. For example, in Ecuador and Venezuela, thousands accused of drug possession or trafficking languish in prolonged pre-trial detention, some of them for longer than the maximum sentence that would be applicable if convicted. According to the Organization of American States, in 1996 over sixty-three thousand people were detained in the Americas (excluding the United States and Canada) for drug offenses. Thailand's prisons are crowded with individuals serving life sentences for relatively minor roles in drug trafficking enterprises, including working as drug couriers.

Evidence of growing recognition of the problems caused by prevailing anti-drug law enforcement strategies was the concern evidenced in the most recent annual report of the International Narcotics Control Board:

[W]hile many members in the higher echelons of drug trafficking groups go unpunished, the growing number of small-time pushers and drug users being arrested is putting pressure on criminal justice systems by increasing prison populations and prison expenditure, as well as the cost of running law enforcement operations and the judicial system. This may lead to a feeling of injustice in the community and undermine public confidence in the criminal justice system.

The International Narcotics Control Board recommended that states consider giving priority to targeting large-scale drug traffickers and the organizers of drug trafficking operations, and pointed out, "Both the absolute number of drug-related convictions and the often increasing length of prison sentences can have adverse effects upon prison conditions."

The adverse human rights effects of excessively aggressive criminal drug law enforcement were perhaps most starkly displayed in the United States, the world's capital of drug consumption. The arrest and conviction of U.S. drug offenders continued to swell the prison population. According to official statistics released in 1997, 22 percent of state prisoners and fully 60 percent of federal prisoners in the United States were incarcerated for drug offenses. The vast majority were low-level offenders, including persons convicted of drug possession. FBI statistics indicated that approximately one-half million people were arrested in 1996 for marijuana possession. The implementation of anti-drug laws continued to affect black Americans disproportionately: for example, blacks account for 38 percent of arrests for drug offenses, 59 percent of persons convicted of drug felonies in state courts. Such statistics supported the widespread percep-

tion that the "war on drugs" in the United States has unfairly targeted blacks and has been as devastating to black families and communities as drugs themselves.

Prison sentences for U.S. drug offenders are uniquely severe among constitutional democracies. For example, a person convicted of a single sale of two ounces of cocaine in the state of New York faces the same mandatory prison term as a murderer—fifteen years to life. In Michigan, a person with a spotless prior record convicted of a minor role in a drug transaction involving one-and-one-half pounds of cocaine must be sentenced to life without parole. Under U.S. federal law, simple possession of a mere five grams of cocaine base requires a sentence of five years in prison. In 1997 in Oklahoma, a jury imposed a sentence of ninety-three years on a man convicted of growing marijuana plants for sale in the basement of his house. More than three dozen U.S. congressmen supported legislation in 1997 that would have imposed the death penalty for anyone who imported two ounces of marijuana into the U.S. Draconian sentences also arise under legislation that imposes severe mandatory sentences on repeat offenders. For example, in California, conviction of a third felony is punished with mandatory life imprisonment. At least thirteen people in California were serving life sentences for conviction of a third felony consisting of the possession of marijuana for sale.

Prison sentences for drug offenses in many cases are so disproportionate that they constitute cruel punishment in violation of fundamental rights. Human Rights Watch released a report in March which criticized the human rights impact of drug sentences in New York for low-level or marginal drug offenders. While the report did not challenge the state's decision to use criminal sanctions in its effort to curtail drug trafficking and drug abuse, we insisted that such sanctions must be proportional to the gravity of the offense. All too often, however, drug sentences constituted arbitrarily severe punishment, shaped by public concerns and political pressures that have run rough-shod over human rights considerations.

Partisan politics doomed reform of New York's drug laws in the 1997 legislative session. In other states, efforts at drug law reform had mixed results. For example, the Michigan legislature developed proposals for reforms that would have ameliorated some of the harshest aspects of its drug sentencing laws; at this writing, they are pending. Despite the hesitations of politicians, public debate about drug policies and their impact on individual well-being continued to grow. In late 1996, two states, Arizona and California, passed public initiatives endorsing the legal use of marijuana for medical purposes and numerous medical organizations, journals and groups endorsed both access to marijuana for medical purposes and access to clean needles through syringe exchange programs to halt the spread of AIDS. During 1997, however, the federal government strongly opposed efforts to remove criminal sanctions for the medical use of marijuana and continued to refuse to fund needle exchange programs.

Federal drugs laws in the United States require judges to impose dramatically higher penalties for crack than powder cocaine offenses, even though the two drugs are chemically identical. Although the cocaine sentencing laws are racially neutral on their face, their application has created stark racial disparities as far more blacks are convicted of crack offenses than whites and consequently receive the much stiffer penalties. The sentencing laws have been widely criticized as a symbol of the racial injustice many Americans feel characterizes the "war on drugs" in the United States. In July 1997, President Clinton proposed narrowing, although not entirely eliminating, the differential between crack and powder cocaine sentences.

The U.S. Supreme Court has almost uniformly rebuffed constitutional challenges to law enforcement tactics adopted to pursue drug trafficking, thus reducing protections of individual privacy against state intrusion in the form of searches and seizures. In an important departure from this tradition, the Supreme Court in April struck down as unconstitutional a Georgia law that required candidates for public office to submit to a drug test. The court held that the law was not tailored to serve purposes other than that of demonstrating a commitment against drugs, and that such a symbolic purpose was not important enough to override individual privacy interests. The decision had a direct impact on a small group of people, but it may signal a new approach by the Supreme Court to anti-drug measures, one that would weigh individual privacy or liberty interests more heavily against state efforts to "send a message about drugs." In another important decision also announced in April, the court ruled that the constitutional rule requiring police to knock and announce their presence before executing a search warrant does not contain a blanket exception for drug searches.

U.S. supported counternarcotics programs overseas, particularly in Latin America, continued to raise human rights concerns. Bolivia, where Human Rights Watch continued research on anti-drug policies and violence, was a case in point. In 1996, the U.S. and Bolivian government signed agreements for U.S. counter narcotics assistance that included strong human rights provisions. Those provisions appeared to go largely unimplemented in 1997. For example, there was no sign of improved riot and crowd control measures by the police; arbitrary search and seizures continued; impunity for police abuse remained rampant. The government's human rights office in the Chapare region—the center of Bolivia's coca cultivation—continued to be underequipped, understaffed and ignored by the police.

Renewed violence between Chapare coca growers and anti-drug police included deaths from the police's apparently indiscriminate use of lethal force. There were also reports of torture and ill treatment in custody. The worst violence occurred on April 17, 1997 when the Mobile Rural Patrol Unit (Unidad Móvil de Patrullaje Rural, UMOPAR) and other police forces killed six civilians during clashes between local residents and police eradicating new coca seedbeds in Eterezama, in the Chapare. Violence erupted after fifty-three-year-old Alberta Orellana García was shot by police. According to her children, she was unarmed, kneeling and imploring the police not to destroy her crop. Angered by her death, residents armed mainly with sticks and stones went on a rampage, setting fire to a building belonging to the government crop substitution office. Police launched tear gas canisters from helicopters, and reportedly fired indiscriminately at protesters' feet.

According to eyewitnesses, an UMOPAR agent fired six times at Elio Escobar, aged sixteen, while he was entering his house and not presenting a threat. Four bullets struck him in the legs, one in the neck, and another perforated his hand. After he was hit and on the ground, an UMOPAR agent struck him in the head with the butt of his rifle and beat his younger brother, who tried to help him. The police later severely beat people detained after the incident, including unionists and local government officials.

There were also disturbing reports of Chapare peasants being abused after their detention. Seventeen-year-old Cyprian Santos was beaten by UMOPAR agents who, because of his muddy feet, suspected him of working in pits where coca leaves are trampled. Nine peasants detained after the death of a policeman in early July 1997 were beaten and forced to pose for photographs holding dynamite, Mauser rifles and ammunition. One of them, sixteen-year-old Abelardo Iraíso Zelada, told the press that UMOPAR agents beat him all day: "I don't know how many times I passed out, they almost killed me. One of the moments I came to I found bullets and dynamite in my pockets." Seven of the detainees, including Iraíso, were released without charge for lack of evidence.

As the government stepped up its coca eradication efforts in the Chapare, local prisons became stretched to bursting point, and detainees were being held in deplorable, overcrowded conditions in police lockups. Women detainees in the Cochabamba detention center of the Special Force for the Battle Against Drug-trafficking (FELCN) went on hunger strike to protest conditions. They were forced to sleep sitting up, and one alleged that she had to deliver her child chained to a hospital bed.

She told reporters the baby nearly died because police beat her when she was pregnant to force her to sign a statement.

The Clinton administation continued to encourage military involvement in antinarcotics efforts in Latin America and continued to press for significant counternarcotics assistance to military and police forces. In August, for example, the Office of National Drug Control Policy stated that the U.S. would provide more than $100 million worth of equipment and training to the Colombian armed forces and police to assist drug eradication and interdiction efforts.

Following the severe criticism of Colombia's record in the 1996 U.S. State Department Report on Human Rights, the Clinton administration sought to distance itself from the dirty-war tactics of the Colombian military by extending the human rights restrictions contained in foreign assistance appropriations legislation for Fiscal Year 1997 to all counternarcotics assistance. Despite strong pressure from members of Congress who insisted that fighting the war on drugs take precedence over human rights, the Clinton administration withheld military assistance until the Colombian military high command signed a formal agreement containing human rights conditionality and end-use monitoring provisions. U.S. counternarcotics assistance in Colombia was limited to military units that do not have records of unsanctioned human rights violations. Difficulties promptly surfaced with trying to target aid to clean units within a military that, as an institution, has a notorious human rights record. In October, for example, in an area of the country the U.S. had designated as being free of military abuses, the Colombian security forces reportedly supported a paramilitary massacre that left six civilians dead. The commander of the Colombian armed forces in the same month stated that U.S. aid could be used against rebels whether or not they are involved in cocaine operations. Similar problems regarding the use of U.S. anti-drug aid have arisen in other countries.

Relevant Human Rights Watch report:
Cruel and Usual: Disproportionate Sentences for New York Drug Offenders, 3/97

REFUGEES, DISPLACED PERSONS AND ASYLUM SEEKERS

Refugees, displaced persons and asylum seekers are among the most vulnerable victims of human rights abuse. Forced to leave their homes, possessions, friends, and, often, family, traumatized by killings or other crimes that caused them to flee, they find themselves adrift, sometimes alone, dependent on strangers in a foreign region or land. At special risk are women and children who are often subjected to violence and sexual abuse in their place of refuge.

Unfortunately, as ethnic and communal violence continue to create new waves of refugees and displaced persons throughout the world, many countries that have traditionally welcomed refugees are now turning them away or passing legislation restricting their ability to apply for asylum. Moreover, the protection of refugees and asylum seekers has significantly deteriorated over the past few decades. Refugees and displaced persons are subjected to abuse in their places of exile and are in danger of being returned to countries or regions from which they fled, thereby endangering their safety.

Europe

Increased restrictions on the right to asylum were imposed in European Union member states in 1997, reflecting, among other things, a general disinclination to take in refugees from the Bosnian crisis. Asylum seekers were given only limited access to asylum procedures once their asylum claims were deemed either "manifestly unfounded" or the responsibility of a "safe third country," defined as any country where the asylum seeker would be admitted and protected against persecution or *refoulement*. These policies gave immigration officials considerable discretion to deny asylum after little or no substantive review of the asylum claim. The right to appeal was rendered meaningless because the asylum seeker had no right to remain in the country while the appeal was pending. "Safe third country" rules subjected asylum seekers to the risk of chain of deportations from one country to another, and expanded in 1997 as E.U. member states negotiated an ever-widening number of readmission agreements with their eastern and southern neighbors.

Despite the Dayton peace agreement, which brought a fragile peace to Bosnia, local authorities obstructed the return of displaced persons to their prewar homes in 1997, and ethnically motivated expulsions and evictions continued. Of the more than two million Bosnians who were displaced by the war, only some 250,000 had returned to the country by November, and of these very few to their pre-war homes. Since the Dayton accord was signed in 1995, another 80,000 individuals were displaced due to transfers of territory. In Croatia in 1997, the government continued to hamper attempts to return by some of the 200,000 to 350,000 non-Croat refugees who were forced into exile by the war. In May, some one hundred Serbian refugees were expelled after an attempt to return to homes near Sisak. The Federal Republic of Yugoslavia (FRY) maintained an inconsistent and discriminatory policy toward the estimated 600,000 refugees from the former Yugoslavia living in the FRY. Large numbers were denied refugee status, thereby limiting the amount of humanitarian aid they could receive and threatening them with possible repatriation. Discrimination against minorities encouraged emigration from the country, and the influx of Serbian refugees from Bosnia and Croatia to Vojvodina in recent years led to state-sponsored seizures of minorities' homes for Serbian refugees and coerced land swaps.

In September 1997 it was revealed that the prime minister of Slovakia, in August meetings with the Hungarian prime minister, had proposed a "population exchange" of ethnic Hungarians living in Slovakia for ethnic Slovaks living in Hungary.

United States

In the United States, the implementation of the Illegal Immigration Reform and Immigrant Responsibility Act of 1996 hindered the ability of asylum seekers to exercise their right to seek asylum by allowing immigration inspectors at the port of entry to make a determination about the legitimacy of their cases without allowing the applicant to have legal counsel or permitting independent monitoring of this process. Those allowed to make a case had a very limited time in which to do so. The bill provided for the detention of individuals arriving without proper documentation, many of whom were held in substandard conditions. Hundreds of children were detained, including many with no responsible adult present, who were not informed of their rights and were often detained in prison-like conditions.

Confederation
of Independent States

In Russia the situation of asylum seekers from countries of the former Soviet Union remained grave in 1997: they were detained by police, threatened with deportation, and at least thirty were deported without the opportunity to apply for asylum. Amendments to the 1993 Law on Refugees brought some improvements but did not change the refugee determination procedure. Most refugees arriving at Moscow's international airport were sent back to their country of origin without being given a chance to apply for asylum.

In Tajikistan large numbers of refugees and all but a few internally displaced persons were able to return safely to their homes. But hostilities in northern Afghanistan, which led the authorities in Uzbekistan to close the Afghan-Uzbek border, limited repatriation through Uzbekistan for 7,000 refugees in Sakhi camp in northern Afghanistan. Following intense international pressure, Uzbekistan in late October agreed to open its border with Afghanistan to allow for the passage of the Sakhi refugees through Termez to Tajikistan.

Africa

In late 1996, soldiers of the rebel Alliance of Democratic Forces for the Liberation of the Congo (ADFL) and their Rwandan allies attacked camps in the Democratic Republic of Congo (DRC) that sheltered more than one million Rwandans. Most of the Rwandans were refugees, but others were soldiers, militia, or civilian authorities responsible for the 1994 genocide in Rwanda. Some 600,000 Rwandans returned home, many willingly but some against their will. Other refugees fled west, some of them forced to accompany soldiers and militia, and were chased down by the ADFL and its allies. Armed elements among the refugees sometimes used the noncombatants as human shields or even killed them directly if they refused to follow orders. In mid-1997, more than 200,000 persons were still missing, many of them dead from attacks or deprivation of food, water, and medicine. The disaster resulted in part from the refusal of the international community to heed pleas from the UNHCR and others to separate out the armed elements, who were making incursions into Rwanda, from the real refugees. Soon after the massive return from the DRC, more than 470,000 other refugees returned to Rwanda from Tanzania, many of them forcibly repatriated by Tanzanian authorities. Rwandan authorities generally maintained calm, but in subsequent months more than 200 returnees were killed and hundreds more were reported missing from their communities. Up to 15,000 Rwandan refugees fled from the DRC into Angola, where humanitarian organizations had difficulty reaching them; they were reportedly mistreated, and some were conscripted into UNITA forces.

In Burundi, nearly one tenth of the population had fled their homes by mid-1997 in a continuing civil war. Of the 570,000 living in camps, some 223,000 were Hutu forced into the camps by soldiers of the Tutsi-dominated army who used murder, rape, pillage, and destruction of homes to create zones of scorched earth in regions contested by the primarily Hutu rebel movements. Others were Tutsi who had gathered spontaneously in camps to seek protection from rebel attacks. Many died from diseases associated with overcrowded conditions in the camps, particularly in the Hutu camps where relief services were limited by the government.

Close to one million Liberians remained displaced within and outside of the country in 1997, mainly women and children of rural background. In July, elections were held that swept former faction leader Charles Taylor and his party into power, but one of the preconditions for the elections—the return of refugees—was not achieved. In 1997 in South Africa, there allegations of police brutality against foreigners, including the death of at least one asylum seeker shortly after he was released from police custody. A government-appointed committee published a Green Paper on migration policy, proposing a more rights-based approach.

Asia

The government of Thailand failed to protect some 117,000 refugees from Burma in camps along the Thai-Burmese border in 1997. Refugee camps in Thailand were attacked from across the border on several occasions, and refugees were killed and injured. In a reversal of its previous policy, the Thai army and Border Patrol Police either denied entry to or pushed back some 8,500 refugees, violating international strictures against *refoulement*. In several instances, the United Nations High Commissioner for Refugees (UNHCR) was criticized for lending legitimacy to the process by observing some apparently involuntary returns. Refugees from Cambodia faced similar problems in Thailand, where conditions in the refugee camps and immigration detention centers remained poor. Thailand also blocked the establishment of new camps for refugees.

In Burma the number of internally displaced was estimated to be more than 300,000. Forced relocations were accompanied by rapes and killings, and scores are believed to have died from malnutrition and other diseases related to poor conditions at the government-controlled sites.

Before the transfer of sovereignty to Hong Kong, Chinese dissidents who had fled there as political refugees were successfully resettled in third countries. Many Vietnamese asylum seekers, however, were pushed out by the Hong Kong government and the UNHCR, which had made conditions in the camps intolerable in response to Chinese pressure to send all the boat people home before the July 1 transfer of sovereignty. More than 2,000 Vietnamese whom the Vietnamese government refused to take back on the grounds that they were not Vietnamese citizens remained in Hong Kong.

Latin America

In Colombia, between 1985 and 1996, some 920,000 civilians had been forcibly displaced by political violence. The number of displaced continued to grow in 1997 and included an unprecedented exodus of 13,000 peasants from northwest Colombia, most of whom languished in crowded camps without adequate food, health care or physical protection. In April, some 300 Colombians were forcibly repatriated from Panama, only to be evacuated from their place of return in September after one returnee was killed and paramilitaries threatened to kill a list of others. The government responded to the national problem by appointing a presidential counselor on displacement and passing legislation dealing with assistance, prevention, and protection issues, but the law and national policy were criticized for lack of funding and for not guaranteeing the safety of returnees. In June, the UNHCR opened an office at the invitation of the government, but at the time of this writing has not undertaken any formal activities.

The Reponse of the International Community

The protection of refugees ultimately rests with the individual nations involved and with the international community as a whole. Their safety is guaranteed by international human rights and humanitarian law, and by the 1951 Convention on the Status of Refugees and the 1967 Protocol. UNHCR is the preeminent agency for the protection of refugees and has the expertise and experience to ensure refugees' rights. However, many states are hampering the activities of the UNHCR by blocking its access to refugee camps and returnees and otherwise obstructing its work.

United Nations High Commissioner for Refugees

UNHCR, in turn, has shifted its focus from exile-oriented strategies to an emphasis on voluntary repatriation and on the prevention of refugee flows. This has resulted in an erosion of protection standards. Human Rights Watch has documented cases in recent years in which the UNHCR has resorted to the reduction of rations in order to "encourage" refugees to repatriate, or failed to provide a neutral and accurate account of the situation in the region from which the refugees have fled, in an effort to encourage them to repatriate "voluntarily." UNHCR has also assisted in the repatriation of refugees in situations where it did not have adequate control to determine whether the decision to return was truly voluntary and whether their safety would be ensured. UNHCR policies to protect and assist victims of sexual violence were still not being adequately integrated into UNHCR programs and services in the field. Receiving governments should cooperate with UNHCR to institute protection programs to prevent sexual assault of women, which is common during some stage of their flight of refuge, and in some situations rampant.

Human Rights Watch has urged the UNHCR to play a stronger and more active role, including the use of various U.N. channels, in situations where governments are abusing refugees and hindering humanitarian and protection work. We also have urged the UNHCR to work more closely with nongovernmental groups that are experienced in refugee needs and human rights. Governments should cooperate with UNHCR in providing access to refugees and displaced persons and in ensuring their safety both in exile and when they return home. We have called on the international community to use its leverage to encourage governments to cooperate with UNHCR and to cease practices that are abusive to refugees.

Some of our concerns about the UNHCR role were as follows:

* In the case of Rohingya refugees crossing from Burma to Bangladesh in 1991 and 1992 and again in 1996, UNHCR, starting in 1994, encouraged their repatriation, despite the fact that the conditions in Burma that caused them to flee had not been ameliorated. UNHCR failed to supply the refugees with adequate information about conditions that they might face in Burma upon their return. In addition it circulated information indicating that refugees might be arrested in Bangladesh. While such information may have constituted an accurate reflection of the Bangladeshi government's treatment of the new arrivals, UNHCR would have better directed its efforts to seeking protection for newly arrived Rohingya who sought to exercise their fundamental right to seek asylum. In 1997 Rohingya Muslims returning to Burma from Bangladesh reported continued persecution by the Burmese military because of their race and religion; some 20,000 fled once again to Bangladesh after returning home.

* In Tajikistan, where UNHCR's presence had significantly improved the situation for returning refugees, the agency considerably decreased its staff in, despite continuing tensions in the civil war, and also relinquished certain monitoring functions to the Organization for Security and Cooperation in Europe (OSCE).

* With regard to refugees from Bosnia, the UNHCR used the concept of "temporary protected" status, which allowed large numbers of people to get out of harm's way in a short period of time. However, the UNHCR stressed the "return-oriented" nature of the protection, with emphasis on the safety of the return, rather than its voluntary nature, in order to convince governments to receive the asylum seekers. Human Rights Watch has been concerned that "temporary protected" persons may not be afforded a full opportunity to raise claims for traditional refugee status under the 1951 refugee convention.

* UNHCR has traditionally neglected the issue of sexual violence against women in refuge, as in the widespread rape in 1993 of Somali refugee women in camps in Kenya close to the Somali border. Following publicity on this issue, extensive and quite successful efforts were made by the UNHCR and the Kenyan government to improve the situation. Significant steps were taken by the agency, including guidelines for the protection of refugee women in general, but in 1997 implementation remained a problem.

* While UNHCR has issued guidelines on the protection of children in refuge, they have not been adequately implemented. In Ethiopia in 1996, UNHCR failed to protect unaccompanied Sudanese boys from forced military recruitment. Many of the boys, sent to fight on the Sudan-Ethiopia border, reportedly died in battle.

United Nations Development Program (UNDP)

UNDP, the United Nations' development arm, is increasingly administering reintegration programs for the internally displaced. Although human rights functions have not been an established feature of its traditional work, UNDP has formally acknowledged that its mandate and its programs for the internally displaced must incorporate human rights and other issues. UNDP made human rights a central component of its successful reintegration program in Central America between 1989 and 1995. However, the lessons of the Central American program were not translated into UNDP's Kenya program, carried out between 1993 and 1995 to reintegrate an estimated 300,000 displaced persons. In 1997 Human Rights Watch undertook a detailed evaluation of UNDP's Kenya program and made a series of recommendations that we believe, if implemented, would lead to greater success in the implementation of all future UNDP programs for the internally displaced.

Relevant Human Rights Watch reports:

Emerging from the Destruction: Human Rights Challenges Facing the New Liberian Government, 11/97
What Kabila is Hiding: Civilian Killings and Impunity in Congo, 10/97
France—Toward a Just and Humane Asylum Policy, 10/97
Rohingya Refugees in Bangladesh: The Search for a Lasting Solution, 8/97
No Safety in Burma, No Sanctuary in Thailand, 7/97
Failing the Internally Displaced: The UNDP Displaced Persons Program in Kenya, 6/97
Uncertain Refuge: International Failures to Protect Refugees, 4/97
Zaire—Transition, War and Human Rights, 4/97
Slipping Through the Cracks: Unaccompanied Children Detained by the U.S. Immigration and Naturalization Service, 4/97
Zaire— "Attacked by All Sides": Civilians and the War in Eastern Zaire, 3/97
Hong Kong: Abuses against Vietnamese Asylum Seekers, 3/97

ACADEMIC FREEDOM

Educators, researchers and students are frequent targets of state-sponsored violence and repression. In the most notorious cases, such as China during the Cultural Revolution and Kampuchea under Pol Pot, governments bent on imposing a monolithic state ideology have disproportionately targeted teachers and educated individuals for imprisonment, torture and murder. More commonly, governments use intimidation, physical abuse and imprisonment to silence critical scholars and students, deny access to educational institutions to girls, women and members of disfavored minority groups, and censor teaching, research and publication on important historical and social subjects.

The preamble to the Universal Declaration of Human Rights declares that "every individual and every organ of society, keeping this Declaration constantly in mind, shall strive by teaching and education to promote respect for [human rights]." To this end, the declaration specifically provides for the right to education, mandates that access to educational institutions and to the cultural and scientific resources of society shall be available to all, and provides that "education shall be directed to the full development of the human personality and to the strengthening of respect for human rights and fundamental freedoms." Human Rights Watch believes that educational institutions cannot fulfill their mission of strengthening respect for human rights when the basic rights of educators and students themselves are not respected.

In 1997, Human Rights Watch gave particular attention to government attacks on the civil and political rights of university faculty and students, and to the devastating impact such attacks often have on the academic community and on freedom of inquiry, expression and association in society at large. The evidence was not encouraging. As described below, although governments increasingly recognize the importance of higher education in promoting technological and economic progress, many sought to assert rigid control over the speech and activities of members of the university community and greeted perceived noncompliance with force.

Ideological Pressure and Censorship

Prior to 1989, communist governments from the Soviet Union to Czechoslovakia notoriously made affirmation of party loyalty an explicit precondition of scholarship and routinely punished perceived deviations from state ideology with imprisonment and exile. In the 1950s in the United States, requirements in states such as California and New York that faculty take oaths of national loyalty and Congressional investigations of alleged communist "sympathizers" on campus cast a similar pall of orthodoxy over the university.

Ideological litmus tests did not end with the Cold War. In 1997, Indonesia and China were prominent examples of their continued currency. In Indonesia, all applicants for teaching positions were required to pass a background screening to determine whether or not they had what the government called a "clean environment." Those who previously had been imprisoned for political crimes, including hundreds of thousands of people imprisoned without charge following an attempted coup over thirty years ago, were forbidden from teaching. All relatives of such people, including siblings, children, grandchildren, aunts, uncles and in-laws, were considered suspect and were allowed to teach only if the government was satisfied that their records were clear of any evidence of opposition to the government or *Pancasila*, the official state ideology. In addition, all new students and teachers were required to undergo a government-sponsored training program in Pancasila as a condition of entry to the university, and all organizations in society, including student groups and faculty associations, were required to expressly adopt Pancasila as their "sole basis."

Although Pancasila itself literally means "five principles," and consists of vague invocations of monotheism, humanitarianism, national unity, democracy and social justice, the Indonesian government in 1997 continued to use alleged deviations from Pancasila to justify wide-ranging censorship and attacks on critical faculty and student activists. As one researcher told Human Rights Watch, "Critical thinking alone makes you suspect."

During the run-up to elections held in May, numerous student rallies calling for political reforms or advocating a boycott of the elections were dispersed by the military and police, and students routinely were held overnight for questioning. In April, the government sentenced a group of twelve students activists to jail terms ranging from eighteen months to thirteen years in prison. The students initially were accused of having masterminded political riots in Jakarta in July 1996. When the government could come up with no evidence to substantiate such charges, they instead were charged with and convicted of subversion. The first ground for conviction specified in the Indonesian subversion law, punishable with the death penalty, is "distorting, stirring up trouble or deviating from Pancasila." At trial, the prosecution repeatedly accused the activists of endorsing ideas contrary to Pancasila (*see* Indonesia section).

In 1997, four prominent professors, Sri Bintang Pamungkas, Mulyana W. Kusumah, Arief Budiman and George Aditjondro, were among the targets of an ideological smear campaign initiated by a high-ranking military officer. In interviews with the Jakarta press in 1995, Lieutenant General Soeyono, who at the time was chief of staff of the Indonesian armed forces, named the academics as among fifteen individuals who use "communist methods" to spread their ideas, echoing accusations made by President Soeharto that certain "formless organizations" were using democracy and human rights as a ruse to propagate ideas contrary to Pancasila. After riots in Jakarta in July 1996, Lieutenant General Soeyono asserted that the unrest had proven his point, and his list of ideologically suspect individuals gained renewed currency, appearing in press accounts into the early months of 1997. Two of the professors previously had been brought up on charges of insulting the government. Dr. Aditjondro, formerly a professor at Satyawacana Christian University in Java, was charged based on a political joke he had told while serving as a discussant at a university symposium in 1994. He now lives and teaches in exile at Newcastle University in Australia, and faces arrest should he return to Indonesia. Dr. Pamungkas, an economist at the University of Indonesia, an opposition member of Indonesia's parliament and an outspoken critic of President Soeharto, was sentenced to thirty-four months in prison in 1996 for critical remarks about the president made during a presentation at the Berlin Technological University in Germany. The conviction of Dr. Pamungkas demonstrated the government's willingness to apply its repressive laws even to academic speech by Indonesians overseas. Dr. Pamungkas subsequently lost his seat in parliament, and in May 1997, he learned that he had been dismissed from the teaching position at the University of Indonesia he had held for twenty-seven years.

In its attacks on alleged ideological deviation, the Indonesian government also targeted books and academic publications, depriving social science and humanities faculty of important resource materials for classroom study and impoverishing intellectual life throughout Indonesian society. According to one study, over 2,000 books have been banned by the Soeharto government, including a wide range of prominent works by both foreign and domestic scholars, dissertations prepared by Indonesian scholars abroad, and works of fiction regarded as among Indonesia's finest. The Attorney General's office is given wide discretion to ban books, and has been especially aggressive in targeting works of history that challenge the accounts given in books sponsored by the government or army. Titles added to the list in recent years include works by Japanese, American, Australian and Dutch scholars on Indonesia's independence struggle and on the development of a capitalist economy in the Southeast Asia region. Other works that have been banned recently include a political memoir by Oei Tjoe Tat, Indonesia's first minister of state of Chinese ancestry and assistant to former President Sukarno, and a collection of essays aimed at stimulating further academic inquiry into the events in Indonesia in 1965-66 that led to the assumption of power by President Soeharto.

In China, all universities have been under close ideological surveillance since the student uprising at Tienanmen Square was brutally suppressed by government authorities in 1989. In 1997, the government introduced a host of new regulations and restrictions expressly aimed at strengthening ideological training and Communist Party control over universities throughout China.

In January, the government announced new censorship regulations, effective February 1, banning all publications that questioned the legitimacy of communist rule or failed to go along with "socialist morality." In April, the government announced new government restrictions on public opinion research, household surveys and studies of demographics, important tools for understanding citizens' attitudes toward economic reform and other social and political issues. A memo from the Propaganda Ministry, the Office of the Secretary of the Politburo, and the Office of the State Council, also made public in April, announced that all social science projects involving foreign funding henceforth would require approval from the Public Security Bureau and National Security and Foreign ministries. The new restrictions coincided with a campaign at the Chinese Academy of Social Sciences against "theories and opinions that are against Marxism, the leadership of the Party and the people's democratic dictatorship." In June, the well-publicized Sixth National Conference on Party Building in Institutions of Higher Education called on all members of the academic community to firmly pursue the party's line, principles and policies, echoing a government decree issued in October 1996 ordering university administrators to consult campus-based Communist Party representatives on all major decisions.

In recent years, numerous Chinese academics and students have been imprisoned for alleged "counterrevolutionary" crimes. Although the China National People's Congress in 1997 removed the counterrevolutionary acts provision from the criminal code and replaced it with "endangering state security," a number of leading proponents of democratic reforms, including former student leader Wang Dan and marine biology student Chen Lantao, remained behind bars. In December 1996, U.S.-based Tibetan ethnomusicologist Ngawang Choephel and former Beijing University philosophy student Li Hai, accused of political crimes, were sentenced to jail terms of eighteen and nine years, respectively (*see* China section).

Although Human Rights Watch is unaware of evidence directly linking the announcements of renewed restrictions on scholarship to the growing contacts between scholars at mainland and Hong Kong universities, the timing of the announcements made clear that the resumption of Chinese sovereignty in Hong Kong would be accompanied by tightening rather than relaxation of ideological controls on mainland campuses. In Hong Kong itself, new threats to academic freedom emerged both before and after the handover. Early in the year, government-sponsored revisions to school textbooks to reflect Hong Kong's new status went beyond deleting references to Hong Kong as a colony and included censorship of accounts of the Tienanmen massacre and its aftermath. In August, Hong Kong textbook publishers revised modern history texts for primary and secondary schools, removing references to the Cultural Revolution, the "anti-rightist campaign," 1976 dissident protests, and the Tibet conflict, and in some cases reducing texts to one-quarter their pre-handover length.

A number of prominent Hong Kong faculty members also were denied reappointment, and local and Hong Kong-based foreign scholars reported growing ideological tensions on campus. Among the Hong Kong academics ousted from their positions was Prof. Nihal Jayawickarama, an internationally respected legal scholar at Hong Kong University who also served as chairman of the Hong Kong section of the International Commission of Jurists. Dr. Jayawickarama had criticized China's human rights policies and questioned the legal status of the provisional legislature. Although a university spokesperson defended the decision saying that Dr. Jayawickarama reached the retirement age of sixty in 1996, university procedures provided for an additional five-year contract for valued faculty members, and Dr. Jayawickarama had been expressly invited to apply for an extension of his appointment by officers of the university. As Dr. Jayawickarama explained in an interview with the Hong Kong press, "I think the university feels it might be better off without me because I'm not likely to become politically correct after July 1." In a separate incident in August, Hong Kong provisional legislator David Chu Yu-lin sent letters to two universities in an effort to have academic critics fired. The targeted individuals were Prof. Richard Baum, a visiting scholar at Chinese University who had criticized Mr. Chu's proposals for a program of patriotic education, and Tim

Hamlett, a lecturer at Baptist University's Department of Journalism, who had disputed Mr. Chu's account of the Hong Kong public's enthusiastic embrace of the handover. In a positive development, administrators at both Chinese University and Baptist University defended the scholars in interviews with the Hong Kong press. Such public defense of academic freedom was particularly important given the perception by many Hong Kong scholars that political and ideological considerations were increasingly displacing academic standards.

Reprisals against Dissenting Professors

As centers of learning and research, universities play a critical role in shaping and informing debate on a wide range of social, scientific and moral issues. In many countries, however, professors who peacefully express ideas or views that government does not want to hear are subject to intimidation, arrest and loss of livelihood. Professors singled out for such strong-arm tactics typically are highly regarded academics who openly spoke their minds on controversial subjects. Reprisals against such individuals are significant not only for their impact on individual lives and careers, but also, given the high profile of universities in most countries, for their effectiveness in chilling political criticism and stifling intellectual debate more generally. Prominent examples in 1997 included attacks on professors in Egypt, Gaza and Cuba.

In Egypt, Dr. Ahmed al-Ahwany, assistant professor of engineering at Cairo University, was arrested by state security forces in April and subsequently imprisoned for nearly a month merely for possessing and seeking to make copies of a paper critical of a controversial new agrarian law due to take effect in September. The government's arrest of Dr. Ahwany proved to be the first shot in what was to become a concerted government barrage against discussion and criticism of the new law.

Palestinian Authority security forces arrested Dr. Ahmed Subuh, a professor of education at al-Azhar University in Gaza, at his home in July. The arrest came shortly after Dr. Subuh had administered an examination to students in which, among nine short essay questions asking students to analyze the interplay between social and educational problems, he included a question asking students to address the impact of corruption in either the university administration or the Palestinian Authority. Security forces subsequently raided Dr. Subuh's home and seized the exam papers of the students. Dr. Subuh, who has been critical of the leadership of al-Azhar University installed by the government, was also director of the Touffah Educational Development Center, an autonomous non-profit organization widely respected for its innovative community education programs. At the time of this writing, Dr. Subuh remains in custody.

In Cuba, two academics, Dr. Felix A. Bonne Carcasses and Dr. Marta B. Roque Cabello, were among four leaders of a pro-democracy group arrested during a government crackdown in July. Prior to the arrests, the group, called the Internal Dissidents' Working Group for the Analysis of the Cuban Socioeconomic Situation, had publicly urged Cubans to abstain from voting in the upcoming elections and had issued a paper titled "The Homeland Belongs to Everyone," in which they criticized an official Communist Party discussion paper on the Cuban economy and asserted their own view that greater democratization is a prerequisite to effective economic liberalization. Dr. Cabello, economist and director of the Cuban Institute of Independent Economists, was also reported to have angered government officials by criticizing government economic forecasts. The four activists, who remain in prison at the time of this writing, were charged with plotting to disturb the upcoming national election, misrepresenting the condition of Cuba's economy, and threatening foreign investors.

Suppression of Student Protest

Political turmoil in society inevitably finds an important outlet on college campuses, particularly among student groups. Although the university typically is home to advocates of ideas and views across the political spectrum, the most active student groups in times of political upheaval tend to be vocal critics of the political status quo and proponents of reform. Important characteristics of the university facilitate such student activism, including an intellectual climate relatively open to debate and expression of controversial ideas, the ease of organizing group activity in the typically close-knit campus environment and the availability of public spaces suited for assemblies. Unfortunately, those same characteristics make it easy for intolerant government authorities to identify student critics and to intervene to silence dissent. Although campus unrest at times is instigated by student groups who engage in unilateral acts of violence that cannot be condoned, the evidence in 1997 again demonstrated that a far more common source of campus violence is government use of armed force and coercion to suppress student dissent.

Numerous governments mobilized armed security forces to quell student protests in 1997. Prominent examples included Burma, Indonesia, Israel, Kenya, Nigeria, South Korea and Zambia. In most cases, tens if not hundreds of students were seriously injured in the crackdowns, and, in Burma, Kenya and Nigeria, students were killed. The situation in Kenya, in which repeated campus crackdowns claimed the lives of at least six students and led to the closure of leading Kenyan public universities for extended periods of time, illustrated the often tragic consequences of government failure to respect basic civil and political rights on campus.

The recent outbreak of violence on Kenya's campuses began at the end of 1996. On December 17, 1996, Festus okong'o Etaba, an unarmed first-year student at Egerton University, was shot and killed by police during a student demonstration demanding a partial refund of fees allegedly owed students by the university. The following day, police shot and killed Kenneth Makokha Mutabi and Eric Kamundi, both unarmed, who were among a group of students at Kenyatta University who had gathered peacefully to mourn the death of Mr. Etaba and to protest the use of lethal force by police against student protesters.

On February 23, 1997, Solomon Muruli, a student leader at Nairobi University, was killed after a suspicious early morning explosion and fire in his dormitory room. Muruli, who had helped organize a series of campus demonstrations protesting government neglect of the universities and favoritism in the award of student loans, previously reported having been abducted and tortured by police in November 1996 and had identified a senior police officer as one of his abductors. Less than two weeks before his death, Muruli reported having received death threats. Nairobi University was closed for over a month following students protests over the failure of the authorities to protect him.

On July 7, 1997, at least two students were among nine or more individuals killed in a violent government crackdown on opposition groups seeking constitutional reform. On the morning of July 7 police raided the campuses of Kenyatta and Nairobi universities, tracking down dozens of students who supported the reform movement and attacking them in dormitory rooms and classrooms where year-end exams were being held. Numerous students, several bystanders, and at least one professor were hospitalized, some with gunshot wounds. Campus rallies to protest the violence the subsequent day were again violently disrupted by the police, leading to a series of running battles between police and students and to closure of Kenyatta University and all four campuses of Nairobi University on July 9.

The events in Kenya reflected a vicious cycle of student protest, violent government crackdown and angry student counter-response. At the root of the problem has been pervasive government interference in campus affairs, repeated attacks on the right of students and faculty to express their views and grievances, and failure of government security forces to comply with international standards regarding the use of force. The Kenyan government, moreover, repeatedly closed universities in the face of political turmoil, depriving students of their right to further their education, forcing all teaching and research to come to a halt and seriously compromising the ability of the academic community to provide the training and knowledge that the Kenyan government elsewhere said was essential to Kenya's future.

Restrictions on Travel and Exchange

Student and information flows across borders have been essential to the academic enterprise since its inception. Today, such international contacts are more common and more central than ever before, a reflection of the increasing internationalization of scholarship that has accompanied the end of the Cold War, the development of new technologies, most notably the Internet, that facilitate international communication, and the rapid growth in collaboration between academics from different countries who share a range of social and scientific commitments, including the environment, women's issues and human rights. Governments suspicious of ideas that circulate beyond the reach of the state, or fearful that critical domestic scholars will find support for their views among their counterparts in other countries, often deny such scholars travel permits and Internet access. Other governments use travel restrictions on scholars to punish foreign governments, denying their scientists and scholars entry to attend international conferences or to engage in collaborative research. Both forms of abuse continued in 1997.

In the United States, the government in March denied visas to five Cuban scientists who had been invited to present their work at a conference on quantum chemistry in Florida and to working visits to Cornell University and Clark Atlanta University. Although a contingent of prominent United States scientists organized by the New York Academy of Sciences volunteered to attest to the credentials of the Cuban scientists, the visas were not issued. The U.S. government based its denials on the claim that "entry [was] detrimental to the interests of the U.S." The refusal of the U.S. government to issue the visas was particularly troubling in view of long-term U.S. support for the right of scientists to travel freely, including its willingness during the Cold War to issue visas to scientists from the Soviet Union and the nations of eastern Europe.

In Iran, the Ministry of Information seized the passport of prominent scholar Dr. Abdol Karim Soroush, preventing him from attending academic seminars to which he was invited in Germany, Malaysia and England, where the British Society for Middle Eastern Studies had invited him to give a plenary address at a conference held July 6-9, 1997. Dr. Soroush, a philosopher and leading proponent of religious and governmental reform in Iran, was also effectively banned from teaching and warned by a government official that he faced possible imprisonment if he continued to speak his mind.

In Tunisia, two academics were among a group of government critics denied passports. Dr. Moncef Ben Salem, founder of the mathematics department at the University of Sfax and a former visiting scholar at universities in the United States, had been denied permission to travel abroad since 1990 and was banned from teaching in retaliation for his steadfast criticism of the secular orientation of the current government. Dr. Moncef Marzouki, a physician and professor of neurology and preventive medicine at the University of Sousse and an advocate of democratic reform and human rights in Tunisia, was denied a passport and prevented from accepting an invitation to travel to Strasbourg in June to attend European Parliament hearings on human rights in Tunisia.

As the preceding discussion demonstrates, attacks on the civil and political rights of faculty and students were commonplace in 1997. In many cases, the attacks were significant not only for their impact on academic communities but also for their serious and far-reaching impact on citizens' basic rights to freedom of inquiry, expression and association. Because the great majority of universities around the world are public institutions or are dependent on government funding, and because such institutions typically are viewed by governments as "prime instruments of national purpose," governments have considerable power to influence what takes place on campus and an incentive to wield that power. A wide range of governments abused their power in 1997, engaging in arbitrary arrests of critical scholars, censorship of research and publication on matters of public concern, and violent crackdowns on campus protests. Due to the high public profile of universities and, in many cases, of the academics who were targeted, such attacks often played an exemplary role, serving as a warning to individuals throughout society that dissent and political opposition would not be tolerated.

LESBIAN AND GAY RIGHTS

Lesbians and gay men in countries throughout the world continued to face discrimination, harassment, arbitrary arrests and torture in 1997, due to their sexual orientation. They were subjected to discriminatory legislation as well as violent treatment and persecution by police. The year also saw some positive developments in lesbian and gay rights. A decision by the European Court of Justice supported more equitable employment rights for homosexuals, encouraging gay rights groups in their campaign for non-discriminatory treatment in European Union member states. In some other countries, laws criminalizing sodomy—traditionally enforced only against homosexuals—were repealed.

Discrimination and Violence

The following were some instances of discrimination and violence reported and protested by nongovernmental organizations and the press.

Europe

Article 200 of Romania's penal code, which had previously outlawed all homosexual acts, was amended slightly in September 1996 to punish only homosexual acts "committed in public, or which cause public scandal." The improvement was largely illusory, however. In a number of cases reported to Human Rights Watch during 1997, private conduct was made "public" by an informant—an individual who witnessed or participated in a private homosexual act— who gave this information to the state. Critics of the law noted that the key article's wording might also be employed to limit free expression, assembly, and association. Meanwhile, gays and lesbians in Romania continued to be frequent victims of police brutality. Three men from Constanta were arrested in June on charges of having sex in a deserted storage cabin; all three reported of being beaten by civil guards and by a major in the municipal police, one was not been allowed to see his family after his arrest. Another told Human Rights Watch that, under threat of further beatings, he was coerced into signing three statements, the contents of which were unknown to him. Gay men also reported that police often waited in known "cruising areas" in order to extort money in return for not arresting them.

In Bulgaria, gay men were targets of police harassment, even for associating with one another. On March 5, police raided the Flamingo gay bar in Sofia, beating up and harassing several people, some of whom were taken to the police station and handcuffed for as long as twenty hours. According to the Bulgarian Helsinki Committee, on August 29, police raided another gay bar in Sofia and assaulted its patrons, On July 12, Demet Demir, a Turkish transvestite, was reportedly severely beaten and illegally detained by police when she intervened against their assault on a young Kurdish girl selling handkerchiefs in Istanbul. The incident, reported to the U.S.-based International Gay and Lesbian Human Rights Commission (IGLHRC), occurred as Demir emerged from a workshop organized to promote employment skills of members of the transvestite and transsexual community. Demir had previously been imprisoned by the police in the Beyoglu district of Istanbul for her political activities on behalf of transvestites and transsexuals in Turkey.

Africa

In Zimbabwe, virulent anti-homosexual statements made in recent years by President Robert Mugabe, church leaders and various political figures had created a hostile environment for gay men and lesbians. Similarly, in March, while speaking to the Irish press President Mugabe denounced homosexuality and said, "Gays can never be something we can accept in Zimbabwe." Some church leaders have called for the lynching of homosexuals. Although homosexuality is not illegal in Zimbabwe, sodomy remained a criminal offense during 1997. A bill introduced in 1996, and at this writing being debated in Parliament, would make HIV exposure through sodomy an aggravated offense—whether the act was consensual or forced—punishable by up to fifteen years in prison, and would allow for the involuntary HIV testing of alleged sexual offenders

The Zimbabwean government also employed censorship laws to suppress gay-oriented literature, including homosexual-produced material on HIV/AIDS prevention. Gays and Lesbians of Zimbabwe (GALZ), which in 1995 and 1996 was banned from participating in the Zimbabwe International Book Fair, returned to the event in 1997, as the ban had been overturned in court. However, GALZ did not hold an official exhibition for fear of government reprisal, opting instead to distribute materials on the association and its counseling services. The government continued to cut funding for Centre—the only organization in Zimbabwe offering HIV/AIDS counseling— on the basis that the director of the organization was affiliated with GALZ.

At a ruling-party women's congress in December 1996, President Samuel Najoma of Namibia encouraged discrimination and hostility against gays and lesbians, stating, "Homosexuals must be condemned and rejected in our society."

Asia and the Pacific

In December 1996, the Rajabhat Institute Council—the collective governing body of all of Thailand's teachers colleges—declared that it would bar homosexuals from enrolling in any of its colleges nationwide. The announcement brought strong criticism from human rights and lesbian and gay rights groups in Thailand. The organizations urged that the ban be dropped and that an anti-discrimination clause be added to the charter of the colleges. The Rajabhat Institute later lifted the ban but proposed a new rule to keep out what it described as "sexually abnormal" people: applicants would be required to take a test, which would be prepared by the World Health Organization. If approved by the Rajabhat Council, the new rule would take effect in the 1998 academic year.

In Singapore, the government refused to register the grassroots gay and lesbian organization People Like Us (PLU). The PLU was required to cease activity or face heavy penalties on organizers and members, and its leadership was forbidden to meet the press or give interviews regarding the decision.

In China, lesbians and gays were, as previously, harassed by police and jailed or fined. They continued to be unable to organize, meet, or obtain information about HIV/AIDS prevention in order to protect themselves.

South Korean censorship laws prohibit the screening of any films about homosexuality. Therefore, local government officials declared the first Seoul International Queer Film and Video Festival illegal. The festival was due to open on September 19. Authorities threatened to seize screening equipment and materials and warned the organizers of a possible twenty-million Korean won (U.S.$22,000) fine and a three-year jail sentence if they proceeded with the event.

The Australian Human Rights and Equal Opportunity Commission continued to criticize Western Australia as the worst-performing state in the nation on gay issues. Western Australia has the highest age of consent for male homosexuals at twenty-one years, compared with sixteen to eighteen years in the rest of Australia. Same-sex couples in Western Australia also continued to be denied legal entitlement available to heterosexual couples, such as bereavement, career leave, compensation rights, tax concessions, and property rights.

Latin America

On June 14 police arrested fourteen gay men during a raid on a gay bar in Cuenca, Ecuador. According to local gay and lesbian organizations, and IGLHRC, one of the men was raped twice by other inmates while in police custody, and another suffered epileptic seizure but was offered no medical assistance. The men were reportedly released after being charged with intention to commit crimes against morality. Article 516 of the Ecuadorian penal code criminalizes consensual sex between adult men, with sentences of four to eight years in prison. The article violates article 2 (equal protection) and article 17 (right to privacy) of the International Covenant on Civil and Political Rights (ICCPR) as affirmed by the United Nations Human Rights Committee in its 1995 decision *Toonen v. Australia*, which condemned anti-sodomy legislation. The ICCPR has been ratified by Ecuador.

The rights group Collectivo Arco Iris on September 24 released a report that criticized the Morality Brigade of the Police and the 2nd Commissary in Rosario, Sante Fe province, for discriminatory treatment of gay, lesbian, bisexual and transgendered persons. According to the report, despite the anti-discrimination clause adopted by the Rosario town council in December 1996, which covered discrimination based on sexual orientation, transvestites were routinely arrested on charges of prostitution and for cross-dressing, and were forced to undergo HIV testing under threat of accusation of the crime of homicidal intent. The arrests were made on the basis of article 78 (offenses against decency), article 81 (prostitution) and article 87 (cross-dressing) of the penal code of the province of Santa Fe.

In Brazil, a relatively tolerant society, there was growing violence against homosexuals. According to the Gay Group of Bahia (GGB), a monitoring organization, 118 homosexuals and transvestites were murdered in Brazil during 1996 and sixty in the first five months of 1997. There have been a total of 1,528 violent deaths of homosexuals and transvestites since 1980, according to GGB.

On December 16, 1996, following months of threatening phone calls, pranks and minor acts of vandalism, the office of Triangulo Rosa, a gay and lesbian organization in Costa Rica, was forced to close down. IGLHRC received reports that the local police refused to accept Triangulo Rosa's complaints, claiming that the case was not within their jurisdiction.

Middle East

In December 1996, according to Amnesty International, twenty-three Filipino workers in Saudi Arabia were flogged in installments of fifty lashes over a period of four weeks following their arrest for homosexual behavior. Following the punishment, the Filipinos were to be deported.

Twenty Filipinos in Doha, Qatar suspected of engaging in homosexual acts were deported in October 1997, according to press reports. At this writing, sixteen more Filipinos are awaiting deportation on the same charges. The police arrested all the defendants on October 1 in a raid on clothing and barber shops that had been under surveillance. Foreigners convicted of homosexual acts in Qatar are usually sentenced to five years in prison, followed by deportation.

Anti-homosexual remarks were made at a high school on December 20, 1996 by Israeli President Ezer Weizmen, who said gays and lesbians "disgusted" him and called for legal steps to determine the status of homosexuals. Gay and lesbian organizations in Israel and members of the Knesset condemned the president's remarks. The president later apologized.

United States

At this writing, thirty-nine states in the U.S. lack anti-discrimination laws that would protect gays and lesbians for being dismissed from their jobs because of their sexual orientation. In response to this lack of protection, the Employment Non-Discrimination Act (ENDA) was reintroduced in the U.S. Congress in June. The bill would have extended federal employment anti-discrimination protections—currently provided based on race, religion, gender, national origin, age and disability—to sexual orientation. In various parts of the U.S., discrimination against gay and lesbian employees has been justified, in some cases, by noting "anti-sodomy" laws that criminalize many sexual practices. In May 1997, an appellate court upheld the Georgia attorney general on his decision to rescind a job offer made to Robin Shahar, a lesbian; the attorney general's argument had been that a lesbian would confront an inherent conflict of interest in enforcing the laws of Georgia, which include a felony sodomy law.

ENDA did not require an employer to provide benefits for same-sex partners of employees and did not apply to members of the armed forces, thereby having no impact on the "don't ask, don't tell, don't pursue" policy, under which gay service members are not asked about or required to admit their sexual orientation. The policy is designed to keep sexual orientation a "personal and private" matter and prohibits commanders from inquiring about the sexual orientation of their troops. At this writing, no court of appeals actions challenging the constitutionality of the policy have been upheld, although a New York district court judge in June ruled that the policy denied equal treatment under guarantees of due process because only gays and lesbians were subject to separate, discriminatory regulations. Two years earlier, the same judge had ruled that the policy violated the free-speech rights of gay and lesbian troops. The 1997 decision was appealed. According to the Servicemembers Legal Defense Network (SLDN), a legal advocacy group for gay rights, in 1996 there were 443 specific violations of the policy where suspected gay servicemembers were asked, pursued, and harassed; figures for 1997 are not yet available at this writing.

In the state of Hawaii, the state Supreme Court was due to make a decision in early 1998 on the constitutionality of a state law allowing same-sex marriages. Under the Defense of Marriage Act (DOMA), which became national law in 1996, marriage in the United States was defined as a union between a man and woman, and same-sex marriages

legal in one state could not be recognized in other states. At this writing, twenty-six states have passed laws prohibiting same-sex marriages.

In recent years there has been growing trend toward more frequent, more violent hate crimes against gay, lesbian, bisexual and transgendered persons in the U.S. At this writing, final figures for 1997 are not yet available. However, 1995 figure compiled by the Federal Bureau of Investigation (FBI) revealed an increase of 12 percent in reported hate crimes against gays and lesbians. In 1996, according to the National Coalition of Anti-Violence Program (NCAVP), there was a 6 percent increase in reported hate crimes, with an overwhelming majority directed not at property but at individuals. The NCAVP also noted that the intensity and viciousness of attacks against gays and lesbians intensified in 1996. Of those injured, 35 percent suffered physical injury or death. Assaults resulted in injury or death to 867 victims. NCAVP further reported that when victims of violence sought police assistance, 37 percent were met with police indifference and 12 percent were physically abused.

In research on U.S. prison conditions, Human Rights Watch noted that prison guards and officials continued to be indifferent to the sexual abuse of gay prisoners. One gay inmate in Texas told Human Rights Watch that, when he tried to report his abuse to a guard, he met with open hostility and reluctance to intervene. Another prisoner, describing a similar experience, told us that guards' hostility towards gays gave the abusive inmates a sense of "approval to beat, rape and extort gay men in prison."

Positive Developments

In a victory for gay rights in Britain, the European Court of Justice in August ruled that it was a breach of European Union (E.U.) law for an employer to deny the same employment rights to lesbian couples that are extended to unmarried couples. The court ruled that it was wrong for South West Trains to deny a lesbian employee's live-in lover travel concessions that were available for workers' husbands, wives, and common-law spouses of the opposite sex. Gay rights groups described the ruling as a vital change for the estimated thirty-five million gay and lesbian people in the E.U. as opening the way for measures to outlaw discrimination against homosexuals at work. At this writing, following a ruling by the European Commission of Human Rights, the British parliament is also considering at "the earliest opportunity" lowering the age of consent for homosexuals from eighteen years to the age of sixteen that applies to heterosexuals.

After nine years of community organizing to repeal anti-homosexual laws in Tasmania, Australia, which carried jail terms of twenty-one years, the Tasmanian legislature finalized a vote to repeal the statute on May 1, according to IGLHRC.

In another landmark judgment, the Cape High Court of South Africa on August 4 declared the criminalization of same-sex sodomy unconstitutional under the new South African constitution. In *State v. Kampher*, the court overturned the conviction and suspended sentence of a Knysna Correctional Services prisoner for having consensual sex with another prisoner while awaiting trial. This decision, however, does not apply to the other eight provinces, where prisoners are still charged each year.

Access to political asylum for people fleeing persecution based on their sexual orientation became more common in North America and Western Europe. Canada continued to accept more gay and lesbian refugees than any other country. In June, the U.S. Ninth Circuit Court of Appeals reversed a 1995 Board of Immigration Appeals ruling against a Russian lesbian activist seeking asylum on grounds of persecution because of her sexual orientation. The ruling sent *Pitcherskaia v. INS* back to the Board of Immigration Appeals for a new hearing on whether Alla Pitcherskaia had a credible fear of persecution if forced back to Russia. According to Pitcherskaia, she had been arrested and beaten by police several times because of her sexual orientation, was forced to undergo state medical "treatment" as a lesbian, and was threatened with long-term institutionalization, medication, and electric shock therapy.

INTERNATIONAL CRIMINAL COURT

The growing case load at the two ad hoc U.N. tribunals, the fervent but dashed hopes for a genuine trial of Pol Pot, and serious violations of humanitarian law occurring in the Republic of the Congo set the context for the movement towards a permanent International Criminal Court (ICC) in 1997. Most importantly, the 1998 date for a diplomatic conference of plenipotentiaries to finalize the court's statute propelled increased state participation in the negotiations and pushed the process to a new critical stage. During the year civil society groups from around the world became engaged as more and more attended and influenced the Preparatory Committee sessions debating the power of the court to try cases of genocide, crimes against humanity and serious war crimes.

By the end of 1997, the question was no longer whether there would be a permanent court but whether the court that emerged from the negotiations would have the independence and credibility to carry out its crucial tasks. At the August Preparatory Committee session it was clear that there was no advantage to sacrificing principle to conciliate members of the five permanent members of the Security Council (P5), who would not ratify the ICC statute at an early date, and that insistence on points of principle for an effective court was essential. The expected confrontation between the P5 and the "like-minded" states, which would test the latter's commitment and determination, will decide whether the ICC becomes an international criminal court in name only or a great step forward for the rule of law and protection of human rights that deserves the support of civil society worldwide.

The Work of the
Preparatory Committee in 1997

In December 1996, the U.N. General Assembly adopted a resolution setting April 1998 as the completion date for the work of the Preparatory Committee and calling for a diplomatic conference in mid-1998 to finalize the ICC's draft statute. This was a milestone in the negotiations. With an end in sight, a larger number of states, including governments from Africa, Asia and Latin America that had made the transition from dictatorship and had attempted to account for abuses committed under previous regimes, brought their perspective to the debate. By the August 1997 session, approximately one hundred states were sending delegations to the Preparatory Committee session.

The Preparatory Committee moved to fulfill its mandate during 1997. At its February session, delegates made considerable headway in shaping a consolidated text on the definitions of crimes within the court's jurisdiction as well as the accompanying general principles of criminal law. The great majority of delegations agreed that the definition of genocide codified in the 1948 Genocide Convention should be reproduced in the ICC's Statute. While there was overwhelming agreement that crimes against humanity did not require a nexus with armed conflict, the U.S. and U.K. delegations insisted on a limited definition of the acts which would be deemed to constitute these crimes.

The definition of the war crimes committed in internal armed conflict coming within the jurisdiction of the ICC generated intense controversy. The U.S., U.K. and France, insisting that the PrepCom had no mandate to codify new law, argued that the court's jurisdiction must be restricted to a narrow list of crimes under customary international law. Other states, refusing to accept customary international law as the parameter of offenses, proposed a broader list of crimes for the purposes of the court's jurisdiction. In advance of the December Preparatory Committee session several governments met to strike a compromise that would broaden the court's jurisdiction in internal armed conflicts. An important product of discussions at the February meeting conferences was the explicit inclusion in these proposals of rape and other sexual violence as crimes, addressing women's human rights concerns as an issue for the first time.

At intercessional meetings, further progress was made. In June, delegates from forty countries, appearing in their individual capacity, attended a conference at the International Institute of Higher Studies in Criminal Sciences in Siracusa, Sicily. They prepared a consolidated compilation of proposals on the technically complex issue of criminal procedure, including provisions on the rights of suspects, the accused, victims and witnesses. This text became an essential document for the working group at the August Preparatory Committee that was charged with drafting the procedural aspects of the court's statute. Another session at Siracusa was scheduled for mid-November to prepare an abbreviated document on the issues of state cooperation and mutual assistance.

The August PrepCom dealt with the key political issues that would ultimately determine the court's ability to function effectively, independent of political interference. Unfortunately, the permanent members of the Security Council championed proposals that, if adopted, would seriously weaken the court. On complementarity, or the relationship between national courts and the ICC, a consolidated text without brackets emerged, promoted by the U.S., the U.K. and France. The text limited ICC jurisdiction to cases where the national authorities are "unable" or "unwilling" to investigate or prosecute. This draft, if codified, would raise the threshold for the exercise of jurisdiction by the ICC. It put the burden on the court to demonstrate not only the factual situation--that there has been no effective prosecution at the national level--but also the underlying motivation for the state's failure to prosecute or its inability in that respect.

The role of the Security Council remained a point of contention. The permanent members supported its power to prevent the exercise of ICC jurisdiction by veto in cases relating to a matter that the Security Council is considering under its powers to maintain international peace and security. Other delegations vehemently opposed such a potential politicization of the court's docket. Certain delegates, in a compromise effort, expressed a willingness to acknowledge the prerogatives of the Security Council by proposing a provision that would empower it to prevent the ICC from exercising jurisdiction, but only after a majority decision by the Security Council to do so. The U.S. delegation's refusal to consider anything but a right of the Security Council to veto cases represented a major obstruction.

Delegates also debated the power of the prosecutor to initiate an investigation *ex officio,* as opposed to having to wait on a referral from the Security Council or a state party complaint. The majority supported such broad powers as well as ICC authority to determine jurisdiction itself without first obtaining the consent of several state parties. The U.S. and U.K., however, reserved their position on these key questions pending resolution of the complementarity question.

In addition to these more political questions, considerable progress was made in the area of criminal procedure. The willingness of states with common law traditions, such as the U.S. and U.K., to compromise and accept the incorporation of certain procedural features typical of civil law systems, such as a pre-trial chamber and continued proceedings following an admission of guilt, was commendable. Furthermore, significant developments occurred during the course of the August PrepCom with respect to victim and witness protection, and the investigation of gender-related crimes. A witness protection unit was included with the draft text to ensure the adoption of measures necessary for the protection of victims and witnesses. The text that emerged from this session also contained language explicitly calling for the effective and sensitive investigation of crimes of gender and sexual violence.

The Role of Various States

The intransigence of the French delegation—on procedural and other issues and notwith—standing compromises on the part of others—was disturbing. In 1997, France played an especially obstructionist role, and there was no difference in the French position after the change in government in Paris. While the U.K.'s position changed measurably after Labour's electoral victory, and the British delegates were genuinely more accessible and open, substantive changes lagged behind the Labour Party's professions of support for the ICC. The U.S., while supportive of the establishment of a court, pressed for an ICC that it, as a global military power, would be able to call on at its will, or not, more like a permanent ad hoc tribunal than a genuine international criminal court.

The like-minded states, an increasingly diverse group from Africa, the Americas, Europe, and Asia committed to an effective ICC, continued to push the process ahead during and between the 1997 Preparatory Committee sessions. The forty-member group had succeeded in gaining General Assembly approval for the 1998 conference date. As the negotiations moved into drafting, the like-minded states faced new challenges in managing their differences over substantive issues, but they worked to identify a core of common positions for a principled basis of unity.

In 1997, the hardball negotiating strategies of the five permanent Security Council members underscored the need for a cohesive like-minded strategy. The ICC, like so many human rights treaties before it, seemed likely to be established without the P5, whose ratification would be expected to come in time and with the court's growing prestige.

Nongovernmental Organizations and Civil Society

During 1997 the numbers of nongovernmental organizations (NGOs) and individuals playing an active part in the movement for a strong and effective ICC grew dramatically. The Coalition for an International Criminal Court (CICC), with many international human rights groups on its steering committee, continued to facilitate this participation and disseminate information internationally. In 1997, the coalition took significant steps to bring NGOs into the campaign. First, more representatives from around the world attended and lobbied delegates at the 1997 Preparatory Committee sessions. In February, there were representatives from Africa, the Americas, Asia and the Middle East. In August, there was even a larger turnout from Africa, the Americas, the Middle East and Europe. The presence of these international representatives had a pronounced effect on delegates, who understood that their governments' role in the negotiations was being monitored by interested domestic constituencies.

At the same time, there were several important organizational meetings around the world. The Coalition for the International Criminal Court, working with domestic groups, helped to set up national coalitions in France, Italy and the United Kingdom. In Brussels a coalition focusing on the European Union's institutions was launched. Working with national and international human rights groups as well as civil society organizations, these coalitions planned to publicize the need for an effective ICC and the status of the debate, as well as to lobby their respective governments. In February, a nascent women's caucus emerged as a member of the coalition and a dynamic force in its own right. By the August session, the caucus had expanded, with its lobbying efforts reflected in the texts that emerged from both sessions. Meetings were held simultaneously with the August session among advocates of children's' rights to review issues of importance to them and discuss the possibility of working together to press children's issues.

No Peace Without Justice, a group launched by the Europe-based Transnational Radical Party, sponsored meetings for the political leaders in Paris, Montevideo and Atlanta. NPWJ planned similar meeting in Africa and possibly Asia.

The Work of Human Rights Watch

In the face of numerous proposals to weaken the court, in 1997 Human Rights Watch pursued a two-fold strategy. First, Human Rights Watch concentrated on forging a principled partnership with states committed to the establishment of an effective ICC, assisting the like-minded group while working to make it more diverse geographically and politically. In building support leading up to the Diplomatic Conference, Human Rights Watch emphasized the importance of regional events of governments and nongovernmental organizations. We also helped to facilitate a September meeting of member states of the Southern African Development Community (SADC), where representatives of the justice ministries of ten SADC states met in South Africa to discuss the key issues arising from the ICC draft statute. After three days of discussion these representatives agreed to ten basic principles of consensus critical to an effective ICC. In October, during the General Assembly's Sixth Committee debate of the ICC resolution, South Africa's ambassador, speaking on behalf of SADC, cited these same ten principles as "essential to the effective establishment and functioning of such an international criminal court."

Simultaneously, Human Rights Watch approached intergovernmental organizations like the European Union and the African Commission of Human and People's Rights. Our office in Brussels helped launch the Brussels coalition and worked to form a Friends of the ICC group in the European Parliament. The parliament was scheduled to hold a hearing on ICC in late November.

Secondly, Human Rights Watch began reaching out to other concerned organizations to build a constituency in civil society that would both support like-minded states and pressure more obstructive governments, including permanent members of the Security Council. In April, Human Rights Watch prepared a four-page action alert, translated into six languages, in advance of the August Preparatory Committee session for distribution to NGOs throughout the world. Human

Rights Watch staff members made the ICC an important item in their various missions, pursuing support for the ICC at conferences in the Middle East, Latin America, and Africa. In advance of the formation of a French national coalition we engaged in discussions with major human rights organizations in France, and staff raised the ICC among non-governmental organizations attending the meeting of Commonwealth states in Edinburgh.

Human Rights Watch also raised the issues in bilateral meetings with government officials—Diet members and Foreign Ministry officials in Japan, the foreign ministers of Brazil, the president of Venezuela, and senior officials in Bonn and Paris, among others. By actively taking the substantive issues raised by the ICC out to counterpart groups and officials internationally, Human Rights Watch added its support to promote a worldwide discussion of the search for justice and the need for accountability.

FREEDOM OF EXPRESSION ON THE INTERNET

On June 26, 1997, the United States Supreme Court struck down the Communications Decency Act (CDA), which had become national law in February 1996. The CDA was an attempt by Congress to criminalize online communications that were legal in other media, specifically communications that might be deemed "indecent" or "patently offensive" to minors. Because the U.S. remained overwhelmingly the world's largest national market for Internet use and communications, the outcome on the CDA had been closely watched by both governments elsewhere and cyberliberties groups worldwide.

The decision established a fundamental position as articulated by the court that on the Internet, citizens are not mere consumers of content but also creators of content. The court also recognized that content on the Internet is as diverse as human thought. Human Rights Watch had opposed the Communications Decency Act since its inception

and, together with nineteen other organizations led by the American Civil Liberties Union, was a plaintiff in the suit that led to Supreme Court decision.

Despite growing acknowledgment during 1997 among regulators around the world that the Internet undermines their control of the free flow of information, governments continued their rush to restrict expression on the Internet. For example:

* Internet access in Singapore remained curtailed, although the National Internet Advisory Committee, which counsels the Singapore Broadcasting Authority on the regulation and development of its computer network, recommended abolition of the ban on "anti-government propaganda" on the Internet.

* In January, the United Arab Emirates' monopoly Internet provider, the state telecommunications company Etisalat, launched a program to censor web sites.

* In March, a decree was issued by government of Vietnam which established strict controls over Internet use; the decree restricted domestic use of the Internet, supervised all Internet content, and controlled international links between Vietnamese users and the global World Wide Web.

* In July, Australia and Ireland announced proposals for Internet regulation that would threaten free expression and make service providers liable for the content on their sites.

* Also in July, the German Parliament approved similar legislation which made Internet service providers liable for offering a venue for "illegal content" if they do so knowingly and it is "technically possible and reasonable" to prevent it.

* Declaring the Internet as "the end of civilizations, cultures, interests and ethics", the Iraqi government announced a total ban on Internet access.

In the United States, meanwhile, legislative proposals contemplated establishing controls on the access to and use of cryptography, or data-scrambling technology, which is used to protect the privacy of communications online. Encryption software and anonymous way-stations for messages—called "remailers" because, after erasing the identity of the originator, they pass messages on to the destination—came under scrutiny. The U.S. government argued for official access to encryption keys to avert terrorism and other crime that might be planned on the Internet; civil libertarians and human rights organizations argued that privacy rights took precedence and that speech, even when encoded using encryption software and expressed through the use of a medium such as the Internet, is no less speech and deserves the full protection of both international and constitutional law. Of particular concern to Human Rights Watch and others was the need to maintain secure communication on the Internet for human rights activists in countries where authorities routinely monitor and control all forms of communication and take reprisals against unauthorized speech.

Recognizing that the Internet can be a democratizing force and a useful tool for the advocacy of human rights, Human Rights Watch undertook research on how the use of the Internet had already had a positive impact in several campaigns for protection of human rights. While continuing to document and protest attempts to silence the Internet, we began working in coalition with civil liberties, labor, journalists' and other groups internationally in an effort to develop coordinated approaches to defending individuals' access to the Internet and to making their online communications private and secure.

As part of this effort, Human Rights Watch and other organizations filed an amicus brief in the case of *Bernstein v. U.S. Department of Commerce*. The case emerged from the U.S. government's refusal to accept the findings of a court that favored protection of speech over the administration's economic and political agenda. Professor Daniel Bernstein had challenged government export controls that restricted his ability to publish on the Internet an encryption program he called "Snuffle." A federal district court in California had upheld Bernstein's claim that the controls were an impermissible prior restraint on protected speech, but following the judgment, the Clinton administration had transferred authority for such controls from the State Department to the Commerce Department and had reinstituted virtually the same set of controls the court had struck down. This litigation is to enjoin enforcement of the latest set of controls.

POSTSCRIPT

CONGRESSIONAL CASEWORK

Human Rights Watch continued to work closely with three casework groups composed of members of the United States Congress: the Congressional Friends of Human Rights Monitors, the Congressional Committee to Support Writers and Journalists, and the Congressional Working Group on International Women's Human Rights. All three groups are nonpartisan and bicameral.

Human Rights Watch initiated the formation of these groups to enable concerned members of Congress to write letters to governments that commit or condone violations against human rights monitors, writers and journalists, or gender-based abuses of women's human rights. Human Rights Watch supplies the groups with information about appropriate cases of concern; the groups, in turn, determine which cases they would like to pursue.

The goals of the congressional casework groups are threefold. First, their letters help to pressure governments to end their persecution of human rights monitors, writers and journalists, and women — abuses which are either committed or routinely tolerated by governments. Second, members of the congressional groups are informed about important incidents of violence and intimidation. Third, copies of the letters are sent to U.S. ambassadors in the relevant countries to inform them about cases of concern and to local press from the countries in question so that they can consequently bring additional attention to human rights violations.

The Congressional Friends of Human Rights Monitors

Human Rights Watch helped to form the Congressional Friends of Human Rights Monitors in 1983 to support and protect our persecuted colleagues. Letters on their behalf have condemned killings, "disappearances," assaults, harassment, and threats, calling for arrest and prosecution of those responsible.

During 1997, the group consisted of twenty-five senators and one hundred members of the House of Representatives. Steering committee members were Sen. James Jeffords, Sen. Daniel Patrick Moynihan, Rep. Tony Hall, and Rep. Constance A. Morella. In the four letters sent in 1997, the group voiced concern over events in Colombia, Mexico, Nigeria, and Turkey. In Mexico, visits by foreign human rights workers were cut short when the monitors were expelled after government officials claimed that the visitors had the wrong type of visa. In Colombia, there was an attack on the home of two rights activists, Drs. Mario Calderón Villegas and Elsa Constanza Alvarado Chacón of the Center for Investigation and Popular Education (CINEP) in May; both monitors were killed, as was Dr. Alvarado's mother. The Congressional Friends expressed their outrage and deep concern over the attack and the consistent persecution of human rights advocates in Colombia.

The Congressional Committee to Support Writers and Journalists

In 1997, the Congressional Committee to Support Writers and Journalists was made up of sixty-seven representatives and fifteen senators, and was headed by Sen. Bob Graham, Rep. Jim Leach, and Rep. John Lewis. The committee wrote to the heads of state in Argentina, Iran, Kyrgyzstan, Nigeria, and Turkey, focusing on cases in which freedom of expression was threatened, restricted, or otherwise impaired. In Argentina and Iran, journalists and writers were murdered, while in Nigeria, the state ordered the execution of authors who were accused of being "conspirators against the state." In Turkey, Ertu rul Kürkçü and Ay enur Zarakolu—respectively an editor and a publisher of a Turkish translation of a Human Rights Watch report—were tried for "defaming and belittling" the state security service. In Kyrgyzstan, a defamation case was brought against a newspaper editor, Ryspek Omurzakov.

In October, Argentine Minister of Foreign Relations Santos Goñi responded to a letter sent by the Committee regarding the brutal murder of photojournalist José Luis Cabezas. He noted that because of the investigation, "many police officers have been expelled from the police force of the province of Buenos Aires (where the homicide took place) and are being investigated for alleged direct or indirect involvement in criminal activities that could have led to this crime." Minister Goñi further stated his government's commitment to assure press freedom.

Early this year, Taoiseach (Prime Minister) John Bruton of Ireland responded to a letter sent by the committee regarding the July 1996 murder of Irish journalist Veronica Guerin, who had reported on Dublin's criminal underworld. Mr. Bruton echoed the committee's condemnation of the crime and pledged to do everything possible to bring Ms. Guerin's murderer to justice and protect press freedom in Ireland.

Congressional Working Group on International Women's Human Rights

The Congressional Working Group on International Women's Human Rights, which was formed in April 1994 to promote accountability for violations of women's rights worldwide, is a bipartisan group composed of twenty senators and thirty-two members of the House of Representatives. The four members of the working group's steering committee are Sen. Patty Murray, Sen. Olympia J. Snowe, Rep. Joe Moakley, and Rep. Constance A. Morella. In 1997 the group wrote letters of protest to King Birendra Bir Bikram Shah Dev of Nepal on the case of a Tibetan woman refugee who was gang-raped after crossing into Nepal from Tibet and to Minister of Labor Assad Hardan of Lebanon on the abuse of an Ethiopian domestic worker.

MONITORS 1997

Every year Human Rights Watch honors human rights monitors from around the world for their commitment to the defense of human rights. In challenging the worlds powerful human rights abusers, they are often at grave risk. We work closely with them to conduct investigations and devise strategies to end abuses. For 1997, the people we honored were:

ALBANIA

Fatos Lubonja

Fatos T. Lubonha was born in Tirana in 1951. He graduated from Tirana University in theoretical physics in 1974 and was arrested in the same year and sentenced to seven years imprisonment for "agitation and propaganda against the state" because of his political writings. In 1979, while serving his first sentence, he was charged again and sentenced to another ten years in prison and labor camps. He was released in 1991 with most of Albania's political prisoners and co-founded Albania's first ever human rights group (Forum for the Defense of Human Rights, which later became the Albanian Helsinki Committee).

Since then, he has been one of Albania's most outspoken human rights activist, Unlike most former political prisoners, and many of Albania's intellectuals, Lubonja openly criticized the authoritarian government of Sali berisha. Since 1994 he has been both editor and publisher of *Pepjekja* ("Endeavor"), Albania's leading critical social/political journal. He is the author of three books, including a novel he wrote while in prison. In 1997 Fatos served as spokesman of the Forum for Democracy, a coalition of organizations and political parties united in opposition to the government of Sali Berisha.

CAMBODIA

Dr. Lao Mong Hay

Dr. Lao Mong Hay is the Executive Director of the Khmer Institute for Democracy, one of the first non-governmental organizations created to stimulate debate on democracy and human rights in Cambodia after the Khmer Rouge era. Founded in November 1991 shortly after the Paris Accords, the Institute has taken on such diverse and high-profile projects as producing a weekly television round-table on controversial public issues of the day, training provincial police leaders and the diplomatic corps in human rights and international law, and conducting grassroots education in electoral democracy.

Dr. Lao and the Institute have come under government pressure, particularly with regard to their educational television programming, a novelty in a country with little tradition of independent journalism and where the broadcast media have been dominated by political factions. In October the Information Ministry cancelled Dr. Lao's panal discussion show on state-run TVK. The move came in retaliation for Lao Mong Hay's criticism of Cambodia's record on democracy following the July 5-6 coup. Many outspoken democracy activists and politicians left the country after the coup, but Dr. Lao Mong Hay decided to remain, in Phnom Penh and outspoken.

Prior to assuming the leadership of the Institute, Dr. Lao was director of the Cambodian Mine Action Center, a unique government-supported agency dedicated to mine clearance and mine education that grew out of the United Nations peace-keeping mission. In that capacity, Dr. Lao urged the Cambodian government to take a leading role in the campaign to immediately ban the production, stockpiling and use of landmines worldwide, a cause recently awarded the Nobel Prize. Human Rights Watch is honored to have him as a member of the advisory board of the Arms Project since 1996.

CHINA
Wei Jingsheng

Except for a six-month period between September 1993 and March 1994, Wei Jingsheng, China's most prominent dissident, has spent most of his adult life in prison. Now forty-eight, he was first jailed in 1979 for his participation in the Democracy Wall movement. His famous essay, "The Fifth Modernization," argued that in addition to four kinds of modernization advocated by Deng Xiaoping, China also needed democracy. That essay was followed by another calling Deng an autocrat. For these words, Wei Jingsheng was sentenced on October 16, 1979 to fifteen years in prison.

His recently-published collection of prison letters, *The Courage to Stand Alone*, makes it clear that his treatment in prison was always harsh. He spent long periods in solitary confinement, and his health deteriorated sharply. In late 1993, he was released in what was widely interpreted as an attempt by China to deflect human rights criticism in pursuit of its ultimately unsuccessful bid to host the 2000 Olympic Games. Wei immediately went back to advocating political reform, meeting with activists, journalists, and others, and writing for foreign and domestic publications.

On April 1, 1994, he was again taken into custody, and after a delay of eighteen months was convicted of "counterrevolution." In November, the Chinese government released Wei on medical parole.

LEBANON
Dr. Muhamad Mugraby

Dr. Muhamad Mugraby, a Lebanese attorney with a busy corporate and commercial law practice in Beirut, is also a well-known defender of human rights in his country. He has long championed the independence of the judiciary, not only in Lebanon but regionwide. In 1967, he introduced civil rights and civil liberties as courses at the Lebanese University School of Law, where he taught for many years. He is also an outspoken critic of Syria's increasingly tight grip on Lebanon, and believes that human rights in Lebanon cannot be restored without addressing the harmful impact of the ubiquitous Syrian role in the country's affairs.

As a human rights lawyer and activist, Dr. Mugraby has focused on some of the most serious human rights problems in Lebanon, such as incommunicado detention, torture, and the expanding use of military courts to try civilians. He is not afraid to take on politically sensitive cases. He has represented property owners and tenants in the old city of Beirut who have challenged unlawful practices of Prime Minister Hariri's Solidere—the multi-billion-dollar real estate company—carrying out the controversial physical reorganization of downtown Beirut. In March 1997, he made formal written complaints to Lebanon's public prosecutor about the unlawful detention of two Lebanese who "disappeared" in January and in March, were transferred into Syrian custody, and held incommunicado in Damascus. Both demarches called on Lebanese authorities to investigate these cases, and prosecute the perpetrators and their accomplices.

Dr. Mugraby holds degrees from the Lebanese University School of Law, and Columbia University Law School, where he was an International Law Fellow from 1963-65 and where he earned two masters degrees and a doctorate. He is a member of the International Bar Asociation and the International Association of Lawyers.

COLOMBIA
Carlos Rodriguez

Carlos Rodriguez is a distinguished lawyer, teacher, and writer who has dedicated his talents to the defense of human rights in Colombia. Educated at the prestigious Javeriana University in Bogota and the Complutense University of Madrid, he began his professional career in 1974. He is a founding member of one of Colombia's most effective human rights groups, the Colombian Commission of Jurists. There, he has pioneered the international dimension of human rights work in Colombia, heading up the team that finally made Colombia a priority at the regular meetings of the Human Rights Commission in Geneva and at the offices of the United Nations High Commissioner for Human Rights. Largely through his efforts, the high commissioner set up for the first time an office in Bogota to pressure the Colombian government to protect human rights.

Rodriguez has also played a key role in landmark cases in the defense of human rights in Colombia. As a member of the group looking into the 1990 Trujillo massacre, he helped persuade the government to accept responsibility for the killings of 109 people by an army major and his paramilitary allies. Rodriguez continues to work on other important cases, including the Villatina massacre, the Caloto massacre, and the Los Uvos massacre, all of which involved the direct participation of state agents with paramilitary groups.

DEMOCRATIC REPUBLIC OF CONGO
Dieudonne Been Masudi Kingombe

As Director of the Center for Human Rights and Humanitarian Law (CDH) in Lubumbashi, the second largest city in the Democratic Republic of Congo, Dieudonne Been Masudi Kingombe oversees and coordinates the work of a team of three full time investigators, and half a dozen volunteers. During the infamous Mobutu era, the CDH, which was founded by a group of lawyers in 1992, assumed a pivotal role in exposing abuses, in pressing for accountability, and in mediating between victims and the authorities. The Center's reports also exposed the corruption and ineptitude of the judiciary, and denounced national and regional politicians for relying on ethnic manipulation to consolidate their hold on power.

With the advent of the government of the Alliance of Democratic Forces for the Liberation of Congo, the Center, as before, spearheaded the local human rights community's efforts to denounce the far-too-familiar abuses perpetrated by the agents of the new government. On July 31, 1997 Center staff visited detainees held at the headquarters of the new political police. In a scathing, two page open letter to the minister of interior after that visit, CDH denounced the arbitrary detention of 89 individuals, and the torture and beatings some of them had suffered. In the days that followed, most of them, including high-profile political detainees, were released.

Been Masudi is also the inspiration behind the "Concertation," the umbrella forum of all human rights organizations in Lubumbashi that act together to raise human rights cases with government and military officials.

RUSSIA
Marina Pisklakova

Marina Pisklakova founded the Moscow Crisis Center for Women in July 1993, to focus on domestic violence and set up one of the first domestic violence hotlines in Russia. It takes up to 250 calls a month. Marina has emerged as a leader in the fight against violence against women in Russia. She has also done work on sexual violence more generally and on trafficking of Russian women into domestic work and prostitution throughout Europe. She was also one of the cofounders of the Russian Association of Crisis Centers for Women.

Marina is currently involved in two major efforts: To open the first shelter for battered women in Russia, and to develop pilot programs to coordinate the law enforcement, medical and nongovernmental response to violence against women.

UGANDA
Angelina Acheng Atyam

Angelina Acheng Atyam, a nurse-midwife and mother of six, is the vice chair of the Concerned Parents Association, a group of Ugandan parents who came together to demand action when their daughters, 139 girls from the St. Mary's School, were abducted by the Lord's Resistance Army in October 1996. For years in the northern part of Uganda the Lord's Resistance Army has been stealing children for use in their rebel army in their attempt to overthrow the Ugandan government. Children as young as eight-years old have been kidnapped, tortured, raped, virtually enslaved, and sometimes killed by the rebel army. Angelina's daughter was fourteen when she was abducted and remains in rebel captivity today.

The Concerned Parents have worked tirelessly to secure the release of their daughters, and all children in rebel captivity, encouraging other families to speak out about the abductions of their children. Families have been reluctant to come forward for fear of reprisals. Angelina and the Concerned Parents have made it clear, by their own example, that families do not have to watch silently as their children are stolen from them. They have shown that they do not have to tolerate the intolerable. The Concerned Parents have succeeded in bringing national and international attention to their cause, and have raised their concerns with Ugandan President Yoweri Museveni and at high-level meetings between representatives of the governments of Uganda and Sudan. Although they were drawn into the turmoil surrounding the conflict in the north only when their own children were stolen from them, the Concerned Parents have become a powerful voice for all children in rebel captivity.

Hellman/Hammett Grants

Human Rights Watch administers the Hellman/Hammett grant program for writers who have been victims of political persecution and are in financial need. Every year, between $150,000 and $200,000 from the estates of Lillian Heilman and Dashiell Hammett is given to writers all over the world. In addition to providing much needed financial assistance, the Hellman/Harnmett grants focus attention on repression of free speech and censorship by publicizing the persecution that the grant recipients endured. In some cases the publicity is a protection against further abuse. In other cases, the writers request anonymity because of the dangerous circumstances in which they and their families are living.

The recipients are a tiny portion of the many writers of the world whose books have been banned or who have been exiled, imprisoned, tortured, and harassed because of their work. For the third consecutive year, eight or more Chinese writers have received Hellman/Hammett grants as the government targets all who dare to express ideas that conflict with the ruling party line. Relying on the lure of its enormous economic potential to mute international protest, China continues to repress criticism in flagrant disregard for international free expression standards. This year twelve Turkish writers received grants, representing the wide range of thought (Islamist, Kurdish, leftist, and mainstream) that is often subject to harsh repression in Turkey. Their persecution for writing about a number of issues, including the Kurdish question, the role of Islam in society, and the nature of the Turkish state, co-exists with high degrees of free expression on almost all other topics, creating a national dichotomy that permeates public debate.

In 1997, forty-five writers from sixteen countries received Hellman/Hammett grants. In addition to the recipients from Turkey and China, there were six from Vietnam and two each from Indonesia, Iran, Liberia, and Nigeria.

The recipients whose names can be safely released are:

Ahmet Altan, Turkish journalist, was prosecuted for "insulting the government" based on two articles he wrote about the war in southeast Turkey.

Nnimmo Bassey, Nigerian poet and environmental activist, was arrested and held without charge for six weeks.

Bui Minh Quoc, Vietnamese poet and former Communist patriot, was forced from his job and banned from publishing for criticizing the government.

Chan Tin, dissident Vietnamese Catholic priest, was sentenced to five years at hard labor for giving sermons and writing articles demanding the release of political prisoners.

Ragip Duran, journalist for Turkish and international papers, was sentenced to ten months in prison and fined $4,000 for making "separatist propaganda."

Ah Erol, Turkish journalist, is the subject of thirty-seven law suits stemming from his tenure as editor of *Evrensel,* the leftist daily paper that was forced to close in October 1996.

Gertrude Fester, South African prison poet and short story writer, spent two years in prison for African National Congress activities and is writing a history of the women's movement within the African National Congess.

Houshang Goishiri, Iranian novelist, was jailed by the Shah, fired from his job by the Islamic Republic, and continues to speak out in defense of basic human freedoms.

Atilla Halis, journalist, was convicted under Turkey's antiterror law for writing articles about new books on the cultural page of the now closed, pro-Kurdish *Ozgur Gundem.*

Mustafa Islamoglu, poet and newspaper columnist, was convicted for giving a speech that "insulted the republic" and convicted again for writing an article that was found to violate a law that protects Ataturk, the founder of modern Turkey.

Sefa Kaplan, reporter for a mainstream weekly magazine in Turkey, was convicted of "insulting Ataturk. Rather than go to prison, he fled to England.

Siaka Konneh, Liberian journalist, was arrested and tortured for exposing the Doe regime's secret killings and arbitrary arrests in 1988. In 1996, when he tried to report on the renewed fighting, his life was threatened, forcing him to flee to Guinea and Ghana and finally to seek asylum in the United States.

Ertugul Kurkcu, Turkish journalist, was charged several times, most notably for writing about an interview with Abdulah Ocal an, the leader of the PKK, a militant Kurdish rebel group.

Abdellatif Laabi, Moroccan poet and novelist, was tortured and sentenced to ten years in prison for "crimes of opinion" and then forced into exile.

Liu Hongbin, Chinese poet, whose poems were posted in Tiananmen Square during the 1989 demonstrations, fled to London. While on a return visit to his mother in 1997, he was arrested and expelled.

Liu Xiaobo, literary critic, has been repeatedly harassed and arrested for dissenting from the Chinese government party line. In October 1996, he was sentenced to three years of re-education through labor.

Ababas Maroufi, Iranian novelist and journalist, whose books are banned, has been legally barred from working in Iran.

Emad El-Meky, journalist, questioned and tortured for reporting on the political situation in Sudan, fled to Egypt. Still at risk from Sudanese agents, he has applied for asylum in the United States.

Nguyen Dinh Huy, Vietnamese journalist, is serving a fifteen-year prison term for planning to hold an international conference to promote peaceful support for democracy.

Nguyen Ngoc Lan, philosophy professor, is under strict surveillance for writing articles calling for freedom of expression and political pluralism in Vietnam.

Nguyen Van Tran, Vietnamese political commentator and communist party elder statesman, gradually became alienated and published a humorous collection of articles disparaging the Vietnamese Communist Party. Though under an order of suppression, he continues to publish.

Mehmet Oguz, Turkish journalist, faces a ten-month prison term for an editorial he wrote for a pro-Kurdish weekly. Several cases are pending against him for articles published in other pro-Kurdish publications.

Phan Thanh Hoai, Vietnamese physician turned author, was barred from publishing but kept writing. As the political issues that forced his "retirement" faded, he published his first book at age 67.

Fahmida Riaz, Pakistani poet, novelist, and journalist, was charged with treason by the Zia government because of her views on co-existence with India and Bangladesh.

Ahmet Sik, Turkish journalist and photographer, fled to England when he started receiving death threats after he photographed and testified about the arrest of a journalist who died in police custody.

Su Xiao Kang, author of a widely acclaimed book about the historical reasons for persistent authoritarianism in China, was put on China's "most wanted" list after the massacre at Tianamen Square.

Wang Dan, columnist and editor, sentenced to four years in prison for his role in the June 1989 Beijing demonstrations, was released as part of China's effort to win Most Favored Nation trade status. Wang refused to be silenced and was rearrested in May 1995, held incommunicado for seventeen months, convicted in a closed trial of "conspiring to subvert the government," and is serving an eleven-year prison sentence.

Wang Xizhe was sentenced to fourteen years in prison for the major role his essays played in Democracy Wall movement in China. Released on parole (under close police surveillance) two years early, he continued talking to foreign journalists and publishing articles in Hong Kong. As his parole was about to expire, he was told it had been extended for two years.

Isik Yurtcu, editor responsible for the pro-Kurdish daily *Ozgur Gundem* when it was closed by the Turkish government, was the target of numerous law suits resulting in sentences totaling five years, ten months in prison and more than U.S.$10,000 in fines. Cases pending in the Appeals Court would add time and dollars to his sentences.

Aysenur Zarakolu has served multiple prison terms for publishing books on the Kurds and other minorities in Turkey. Most recently she was convicted for publishing a translation of the Human Rights Watch report, *Weapons Thansfers and Violations of the Laws of War in Turkey.*

Zhang Xian Liang, author of numerous articles and poems attacking corruption and autocracy in the Chinese government, was most recently imprisoned for arranging a commemoration of the Tiananmen Square massacre. His treatment in labor camps permanently damaged his health.

Three *La Voje* **journalists,** Abou Drahamane Sangare, Freedom Neruda, and Emmanuel Kore, were sentenced to two years in prison for publishing a satirical article that offended the president of Ivory Coast. Offered a pardon if they would withdraw the appeal of their conviction, they refused.

The Hellman/Hammett grants were awarded after nominations were reviewed by a five-person selection committee composed of writers and editors. In the course of the year, the selection committee approved nine additional grants to writers who needed emergency funds to help in situations where their lives were in immediate danger.

MISSIONS

Human Rights Watch/Africa

December 1996-January 1997/Democratic Republic of Congo: Respect for rights under new government.

February/Mozambique: Advocacy on landmines.

February/Zambia: Research on human rights since 1996 elections.

March/U.N. Commission on Human Rights: Submission on Internally displaced persons in Kenya, Somali refugees, women and refugees in South Africa.

April/Zambia: Human rights since the 1996 elections.

April/ICTR: Monitor efficacy of the International Criminal Tribunal on Rwanda; investigate gender-based crimes; workshop on prosecution of sexual violence.

May/ICTR: Testimony at the International Criminal Tribunal on Rwanda.

May/Belgium: Testimony at the Belgian Senate Commission investigating role of Belgium in the genocide in Rwanda.

June-July/Burundi: Human rights abuses against civilians during the civil war.

July/Liberia: Prospects for respect for human rights under the new Liberian government.

July/Nigeria: Corporate responsibility in the Niger delta.

July-August/Ethiopia: Current civil and political rights situation.

July-August/Democratic Republic of Congo: Civilian killings and government impunity.

August/Democratic Republic of Congo: Rights under the new government.

August-September/Nigeria: Investigated transition to civilian rule.

October/Southern Sudan: Updated the state of human rights in the 14 year-old civil war (monitored and engaged parties to the conflict in dialogue on rules of war)..

November 1996/South Africa: Researched violence against women and the medico-legal system.

Human Rights Watch/Americas

March/Venezuela: Released the "Punishment Before Trial: Prison Conditions in Venezuela" report. Met with high-level government officials, including the Venezuelan President, members of the Cabinet, Congress and non-governmental organizations (NGOs).

March/Colombia: Advocacy mission. Met with President Samper, members of the Cabinet, NGOs and the media.

April/Mexico: Released "Implausible Deniability: State Responsibility for Rural Violence in Mexico" report. Met with government authorities including the Attorney General, as well as NGOs.

April/Miami: Researched human rights violations in Cuba.

April/Peru: Investigated reports of torture for a forthcoming report.

May/Colombia: International humanitarian law impact of drug eradication in Colombia.

June/Brazil: Released the Portuguese version of the report "Police Brutality in Urban Brazil." Met with state and federal officials in Rio de Janeiro, Sao Paulo and Brasilia, as well as the media.

June-July/Honduras and Guatemala: Researched violations for the 1998 World Report, as well as the specific issue of impunity in Guatemala.

July/Venezuela: Researched police brutality and violence in the country.

July-August/Colombia: Researched forced displacement of Colombians.

July-August/Haiti and the Dominican Republic: Researched violations for the 1998 World Report.

July-August/ Spain: Met with governmental officials, NGOs, the press and members of the political opposition.

August/Guatemala: Released "Guatemala's Forgotten Children" report. Met with high-level government officials and the press.

September/Brazil: Met with President Cardoso and the Brazilian Minister of Justice.

September/Colombia: Advocacy Mission. Met with the President and other high-level officials, members of Parliament, and

NGOs.

Human Rights Watch/Asia

January/ Indonesia: Investigated outbreaks of ethnic violence.

March-April/Hong Kong: Investigated prison conditions in Hong Kong.

March/Malaysia: Observer mission to the trial of labor rights activist Irene Fernandez and investigation of abuses against migrant workers.

March-April/Thailand: Lead sessions on using international law and on forging linkages among NGOs as part of a two-week Asian regional study session on human rights

April/ Geneva: Monitored debates on the China resolution at the meeting of the United Nations Human Rights Commission.

May-June/Thailand: Examined the situation of Burmese refugees in Thailand in light of an influx of 20,000 Karen refugees since February 1997.

May-June/Hong Kong: Investigated China's control of religious practice.

May/Japan: Advocacy mission. Discussed Japanese foreign policy with government officials and NGOs and attended the Asian Development Bank meetings in Fukuoka.

July/Thailand and Indonesia: Investigated causes of ethnic violence in West Kalimantan and collected information on East Timor.

August/Geneva: Advocacy mission for the protection of the rights of Burmese refugees in Thailand.

October/Vietnam: Investigated human rights violations occurring in the course of rural unrest.

October/North Korea: Investigated links between the North Korean famine and human rights violations.

November/Indonesia: Investigated alleged labor rights abuses.

November/APEC - Vancouver: Advocacy Mission. Attended the People's Summit on APEC (Asia Pacific Economic Cooperation), the parallel NGO meeting to the APEC summit, to participate in meetings on worker rights, media freedom, women's rights

and cooperative NGO strategies on human rights.

Human Rights Watch/Helsinki

January-July/Uzbekistan: Maintained presence in Toshkent office, investigated abuses of media freedom, police brutality.

January-March/Northern Ireland: Investigated police brutality and encouraged emergency legislation.

February/Serbia: Researched post-election crackdown, police brutality.

February/ Eastern Slavonia, Croatia: Preparations for the transfer of authority in the region to Croatian control.

February/Bosnia and Hercegovina: Maintained presence in Sarajevo office. Researched Bihac.

March/Bosnia and Hercegovina: Researched ethnic tension and influence of war criminals in Mostar.

March/Tajikistan: Maintained presence in Dushanbe office, general monitoring, prison conditions, etc.

May/Armenia: Investigated freedom of association and the press.

June/Bosnia and Hercegovina: Investigated central Bosnia

June/Northern Ireland: Researched summer marching season and report follow-up.

June/Khojent, Tajikistan: Investigated problems of Uzbek minority.

July/Romania: Researched anti-homosexual legislation.

August/Bosnia and Hercegovina: Investigated post-conflict problems for women.

August/Turkey and Greece: Investigated free expression (Turkey) and problems of Turkish minority (Greece).

September/Bosnia and Hercegovina: Researched municipal elections.

September-October/Bosnia and Hercegovina: Researched efficacy of International Police Task Force.

September - November/Russia: Investigated prison conditions throughout Russia.

September - October/Eastern Slavonia and Krajina, Croatia: Reassessed situation in Eastern Slavonia.

November/Azerbaijan and Armenia: Investigated repression of civil and political rights in increasingly authoritarian atmosphere.

November/Bosnia and Hercegovina: Investigated ethnic tension in Sarajevo suburbs

Human Rights Watch/Middle East

December 1996 & February1997/Europe: Advocacy on Euro-Mediterranean Association-Agreement with Israel, Tunisia and Morocco.

January-February/Europe: Interviewed minorities in Iran.

March-April/Algeria: Looked at human rights conditions on the eve of legislative elections. Interviewed journalists, lawyers, political party leaders, government officials, victims of human rights violations or their relatives.

May/Tunisia: Attended meeting of the Arab Lawyers Union

June/France: Testified at European Parliament hearing on Tunisia.

June/Egypt: Consulted with Egyptian human rights organizations on possible collaboration.

July/Egypt: Researched deaths in custody and the state's investigation of these deaths.

July/UK: Interviewed an Iraqi military defector and do advocacy on Bahrain.

The Arms Project

January/Turkey: Attended trial of publisher and translator of Human Rights Watch report.

February/Japan: Advocacy at mine clearance conference

February/Vienna: Advocacy mission to landmine ban treaty conference

February/Mozambique: Advocacy mission at NGO conference on landmines

February-July/ Eritrea, Ethiopia, Sudan: Researched arms flows.

March/Turkey: Attended trial of publisher and translator of Human Rights Watch report.

March/Former Yugoslavia: Researched on chemical weapons use.

April/Bonn: Advocacy mission to landmine ban treaty conference.

May/South Africa: Advocacy mission for mine-free zone in Southern Africa at landmine ban treaty conference.

September/Oslo: Advocacy mission to landmine ban treaty conference.

The Children's Rights Project

May/Uganda: Investigated of abductions of children by the Lord's Resistance Army in northern Uganda.

June/In-country release of "Juvenile Injustice: Police Abuse and Detention of Street Children in Kenya." Advocacy trip to Nairobi, Kenya.

The Women's Rights Project

April/Tanzania: Advocacy mission to International Criminal Tribunal for Rwanda

May/ Pakistan: Investigated state response to violence against women.

May/Mexico: Follow-up mission on sex discrimination in the maquiladoras in Mexico.

June/The Hague: Advocacy mission to International Criminal Tribunal for former Yugoslavia.

September-August/Bosnia and Hercegovina: Investigated post-conflict problems for women.

October/Mexico: Follow-up mission on sex discrimination in the maquiladora in Mexico

Prisons

March/Hong Kong: Investigated prison conditions.

July/Indiana: Examined conditions at two super-maximum security prisons in Indiana.

October/Geneva: Advocacy mission to session of the Working Group on the draft Optional Protocol to the Convention Against Torture.

November-December/Brazil: Investigated prison conditions in Brazil.

Drugs

1996-1997/US: Researched on the human rights impact of drug sentencing in New York for nonviolent, and low-level drug offenders.

May/Colombia: International humanitarian law impact of drug eradication in Colombia.

Academic Freedom

September/Indonesia: Explored academic freedom issues in Indonesia.

1997 PUBLICATIONS

To order any of the following titles, please call our Publications Department at (212) 986-1980 and ask for our publications catalog. Order reports online via secure credit card at our site on the World Wide Web at http://www.hrw.org.

Algeria
Algeria—Elections in the Shadow of Violence and Repression, 6/97, 35 pp.

Bahrain
Routine Abuse, Routine Denial: Civil Rights and the Political Crisis in Bahrain, 6/97, 120 pp.

Bangladesh
Bangladesh/Burma—Rohingya Refugees in Bangladesh: The Search for a Lasting Solution, 8/97, 15 pp.

Belarus
Republic of Belarus: Crushing Civil Society, 8/97, 52 pp.

Bosnia-Hercegovina
Bosnia-Hercegovina: The Continuing Influence of Bosnia's Warlords, 12/96, 47 pp.
Bosnia and Hercegovina—The Unindicted: Reaping the Rewards of "Ethnic Cleansing," 1/97, 76 pp.
Bosnia and Hercegovina—Politics of Revenge: The Misuse of Authority in Bihac, Cazin, and Velika Kladusa, 8/97, 44 pp.

Brazil
Police Brutality in Urban Brazil, 4/97, 128 pp.

Burma
Bangladesh/Burma—Rohingya Refugees in Bangladesh: The Search for a Lasting Solution, 8/97, 15 pp.
Burma: Children's Rights and the Rule of Law, 1/97, 27 pp. 1/97
Burma/Thailand: No Safety in Burma, No Sanctuary in Thailand, 7/97, 27 pp.

Cambodia
Deterioration of Human Rights in Cambodia, 12/96, 25 pp.
Cambodia: Aftermath of the Coup, 8/97, 14 pp.

China
China: Chinese Diplomacy, Western Hypocrisy and the U.N. Human Rights Commission, 3/97, 14 pp.
China—Whose Security?: State Security in China's New Criminal Code, 4/97, 56 pp.
China: State Control of Religion, 10/97, 152 pp.

Croatia
Croatia: Human Rights in Eastern Slavonia During and After the Transition of Authority, 4/97, 21 pp.

Democratic Republic of Congo
Democratic Republic of Congo—What Kabila is Hiding: Civilian Killings and Impunity in Congo, 10/97, 42 pp.

France
France—Toward a Just and Humane Asylum Policy, 10/97, 31pp.

General
Human Rights Watch World Report 1997, 12/96, 416 pp.
Uncertain Refuge: International Failures to Protect Refugees, 4/97, 26 pp.

Exposing the Source: U.S. Companies and the Production of Antipersonnel Mines, 4/97, 47 pp.

Still Killing: Landmines in Southern Africa, 5/97, 224 pp.

In its Own Words: The U.S. Army and Antipersonnel Mines in the Korean and Vietnam Wars, 7/97, 14 pp.

Killers in the Commonwealth: Antiperson nel Landmine Policies of the Com monwealth Nations, 10/97, 21 pp.

Guatemala
Guatemala: Freedom of Association in a Maquila in Guatemala, 3/97, 62 pp.

Haiti
Haiti: The Human Rights Record of the Haitian National Police, 1/97, 40 pp.

Hong Kong
Hong Kong: Abuses against Vietnamese Asylum Seekers, 3/97, 22 pp.

Hong Kong: Prison Conditions in 1997, 6/97, 51 pp.

Indonesia & East Timor
Indonesia/East Timor—Deteriorating Human Rights in East Timor, 9/97, 22 pp.,

Iran
Iran—Leaving Human Rights Behind: The Context of the Presidential Elections, 5/97, 10 pp.

Iran—Religious and Ethnic Minorities: Discrimination in Law and Practice, 9/97, 36 pp.

Israel & Israeli-Occupied Territories
Israel—Legislating Impunity: The Draft Law to Halt Palestinian Tort Claims, 7/97, 9 pp.

Israel/Lebanon: "Operation Grapes of Wrath", 9/97, 49pp.

Palestinian Self-Rule Areas: Human Rights under the Palestinian Authority, 10/97, 80pp.

Israel—Without Status or Protection: Lebanese Detainnes in Israel, 10/97, 47 pp.

Jordan
Jordan—A Death Knell for Free Expres sion?: The New Amendments to the Press and Publications Law, 6/97, 15 pp.

Jordan: Clamping Down on Critics--H.R. Violations in Advance of the Parliamentary Elections, 10/97, 34 pp.

Kenya
Failing the Internally Displaced: The UNDP Displaced Persons Program in Kenya, 6/97, 164 pp

Juvenile Injustice: Police Abuse and Detention of Street Children in Kenya, 6/97, 168 pp.

Lebanon
Lebanon—Restrictions on Broadcasting: In Whose Interest?, 4/97, 29 pp

Syria/Lebanon—An Alliance Beyond the Law: Enforced Disappearances in Lebanon, 5/97

Israel/Lebanon: "Operation Grapes of Wrath", 9/97, 49pp.

Mexico
Implausible Deniability: State Responsibil ity for Rural Violence in Mexico, 4/97, 112 pp.

Nigeria
Nigeria— Transition or Travesty: Nigeria's Endless Process of Return to Civilian Rule, 10/97, 52 pp.

Northern Ireland
To Serve Without Favor: Policing, Human Rights, and Accountablity in Northern Ireland, 5/97, 192 pp.

Russia
Russia/Chechnya: A Legacy of Abuse, 1/97, 26 pp.

Russian Federation: A Review of the
Compliance of the Russian
Federation with Council of
Europe Commitments and Other
Human Rights Obligations on the
First Anniversary of its
Accession to the Council of
Europe, 2/97, 34 pp.

Russia—Moscow: Open Season, Closed
City, 9/97, 40pp.

Saudi Arabia

Saudi Arabia —Flawed Justice: The
Execution of 'Abd al-Karim Mara'i al-
Nashquabandi, 10/97, 31pp.

Serbia and Montenegro

Serbia and Montenegro— Persecution
Persists: Human Rights Violations in
Kosovo, 12/96, 44 pp.

Serbia and Montenegro—Discouraging
Democracy:Elections & H.R.,
09/97, 31pp.

South Africa

South Africa—Violence Against Women
and the Medico-Legal System, 8/97,
54 pp.

Syria

Syria/Lebanon—An Alliance Beyond the
Law: Enforced Disappearances in
Lebanon, 5/97, 42 pp.

Turkey

Turkey: Torture and Mistreatment in Pre-
Trial Detention by Anti-Terror
Police, 3/97, 49 pp

United Kingdom

Racist Violence in the United Kingdom,
5/97, 112 pp.

United States

U.S.—Cruel and Usual Punishment:
Disproportionate Sentences for New
York Drug Offenders, 3/97, 39 pp.

Slipping through the Cracks: Unaccompa
nied Children Detained by the United
States Immigration and Naturalization
Service, 4/97, 128 pp.

High Country Lockup: Children in
Confinement in Colorado, 8/97,
120pp.

Cold Storage: Supermaximum Security
Confinement in Indiana, 11/97, 92 pp.

Uganda

Uganda —Scars of Death: Children
Abducted By The Lord's Resistance
Army, 9/97, 152pp.

Uzbekistan

Uzbekistan—Violations of Media
Freedom: Journalism and Censorship
in Uzbekistan, 7/97, 18 pp.

Venezuela

Punishment Before Trial: Prison Condi
tions in Venezuela, 3/97, 128 pp.,

Former Yugoslavia

Former Yugoslavia—Clouds of War:
Chemical Weapons in the Former
Yugoslavia, 3/97, 16 pp

Zaire

Zaire— "Attacked by All Sides": Civilians
and the War in Eastern Zaire, 3/97,
14 pp.

Zaire—Transition, War and Human Rights,
4/97, 63 pp.

Zambia

Zambia: Elections and Human Rights in the
Third Republic, 12/96, 53 pp.

Zambia—The Reality Amidst Contradic
tions: Human Rights since the 1996
Elections, 7/97, 71 pp.

STAFF AND COMMITTEES

Human Rights Watch Staff

Executive: Kenneth Roth, Executive Director; Associate Director, Susan Osnos; Anne Hughes-Hinnen Executive Assistant.
Advocacy: Allyson Collins, Washington Associate Director; Lotte Leicht, Brussels Office Director; Joanna Weschler, United Nations Representative; Robby Peckerar, Associate, Mayke Huijbregts, Associate, Brussels Office.
Communications: Susan Osno, Communications Director; Jean-Paul Marthoz, European Press Director, Brussels Office; Liz Reynoso, Communications Associate; Patrick Minges, Publications Director; Sobeira Genao, Publications Manager; Doris Joe, Publications Associate; Lenny Thomas, Production Manager; Fitzroy Hepkins, Mail Manager.
Development: Michele Alexander, Director of Development; Rachel Weintraub, Director of Special Events; Michele Demers, Major Gifts Officer; Pamela Bruns, California Director; Sue Jares, LA Associate Director; Heather Cooper, Associate; Marianne Law, Special Events Coordinator; Amy Poueymirou, Associate; Veronica Matushaj, Associate.
Finance and Administration: Barbara Guglielmo, Director of Finance & Administration; Maria Pignataro Nielsen, Director of Administration and Human Resources; Iris Yang, Accountant; Walid Ayoub, Systems Manager; Bessie Skoures, Bookkeeper/Departmental Associate; Mia Roman, Receptionist/Office Assistant/Internship Coordinator; Christian Peña, Receptionist/Office Assistant; Lolita Woodward, Network Aide; Ernest Ulrich, Consultant; Anderson Allen, Office Manager, DC Office; Andrea Rodriguez, Receptionist/Office Assistant, DC Office; Urmi Shah, Office Manager, UK Office; Isabelle Tin-Aung, Office Manager, Brussels Office.

General Counsel: Wilder Tayler, General Counsel; Dinah PoKempner, Deputy General Counsel.
Program: Cynthia Brown, Program Director; Michael McClintock, Deputy Program Director; Jeri Laber, Senior Advisor; Allyson Collins, Associate Director, Sr. Researcher; Sahr Muhammed Ally, Associate; Richard Dicker, Associate Counsel; Arvind Ganesan, Research Associate; Helen Duffy, Counsel; Matt McGowan, Associate; Jamie Fellner, Associate Counsel; Christina Portillo, Associate; Joanne Mariner, Associate Counsel; Awali Samara, Associate; Jagdish Parikh, On-Line Research Associate; Joe Saunders, Associate Counsel; Marcia Allina, Associate.
International Film Festival: Bruni Burres, Director; Heather Harding, Associate Director.
1997 Fellowship Recipients: Peter Bouckaert, Orville Schell Fellow; Sinsi Hernàndez Cancio, Sophie Silberberg Fellow; Smita Narula, Sophie Silberberg Fellow; Jennifer Scheuese, Leonard H. Sandler Fellow

Board of Directors
Robert L. Bernstein, Chair; Adrian W. DeWind, Vice Chair; Roland Algrant, Lisa Anderson, William Carmichael, Dorothy Cullman, Gina Despres, Irene Diamond, Fiona Druckenmiller, Edith Everett, Jonathan Fanton, Jack Greenberg, Vartan Gregorian, Alice H. Henkin, Stephen L. Kass, Marina Pinto Kaufman, Bruce Klatsky, Harold Hongju Koh, Joshua Mailman, Samuel K. Murumba, Andrew Nathan, Jane Olson, Peter Osnos, Kathleen Peratis, Bruce Rabb, Sigrid Rausing, Anita Roddick, Orville Schell, Sid Sheinberg, Gary G. Sick, Malcolm Smith, Domna Stanton, Maureen White, Maya Wiley.

Human Rights Watch/Africa

Staff
Peter Takirambudde, Executive Director; Janet Fleischman, Washington Director; Jemera Rone, Counsel; Suliman Ali Baldo, Senior Researcher; Binaifer Nowrojee; Coun-

sel, Alex Vines, Research Associate; Bronwen Manby, Research Associate; Alison L. DesForges, Consultant; Ariana Pearlroth, Associate; Juliet Wilson, Associate; Peter Bouckaert, Orville Schell Fellow; Scott Campbell, Consultant.

Advisory Committee

William Carmichael, Chair; Roland Algrant; Robert L. Bernstein, Julius L. Chambers, Michael Clough, Roberta Cohen, Carol Corillon, Alison L. DesForges, Adrian W. DeWind, R. Harcourt Dodds, Stephen Ellman, Aaron Etra, Thomas M. Franck, Gail M. Gerhart, Jack Greenberg, Arthur C. Helton, Alice H. Henkin, Robert Joffe, Jeh Johnson, Richard A. Joseph, Thomas Karis, Stephen L. Kass, Vincent Mai, John A. Marcum, Gay McDougall, Toni Morrison, Samuel K. Murumba, Muna Ndulo, James C. N. Paul, Robert Preiskel, Norman Redlich, Randall Robinson, Sidney S. Rosdeitcher, Dirk van Zyl Smit, Howard P. Venable, Claude E. Welch, Jr., Maureen White, Aristide R. Zolberg.

Human Rights Watch/Americas

Staff

José Miguel Vivanco, Executive Director; Anne Manuel, Deputy Director; Joel Solomon, Research Director; James Cavallaro, Brazil Office Director; Sarah DeCosse, Research Associate; Jennifer Bailey, Research Associate; Sebastian Brett, Research Associate; Robin Kirk, Research Associate; Steven Hernandez, Associate; Megan Himan, Associate.

Advisory Committee

Stephen L. Kass, Chair; Marina Pinto Kaufman, David E. Nachman, Vice Chairs; Roland Algrant, Michael Barnes, Peter D. Bell, Robert L. Bernstein, Albert Bildner, Reed Brody, Paul Chevigny, Roberto Cuéllar, Dorothy Cullman, Patricia Derian, Adrian W. DeWind, Tom J. Farer, Tricia Feeney, Alejandro Garro, Wendy Gimbel, John S. Gitlitz, James Goldston, Peter Hakim, Ronald G. Hellman, Wade J. Henderson, Alice H.

Henkin, Bianca Jagger, Margaret A. Lang, Robert S. Lawrence, MD, Jocelyn McCalla, Theodor Meron, John B. Oakes, Victor Penchaszadeh, Clara A. "Zazi" Pope, Bruce Rabb, Jean-Marie Simon, Malcolm Smith, George Soros, Eric Stover, Rose Styron, Jorge Valls, Horacio Verbitsky, José Zalaquett.

Human Rights Watch/Asia

Staff

Sidney Jones, Executive Director; Mike Jendrzejczyk, Washington Director; Robin Munro, Hong Kong Office Director; Patricia Gossman, Senior Researcher; Zunetta Liddell, Research Associate; Jeannine Guthrie, NGO Liaison; Mickey Spiegel, Consultant; Tom Kellogg, Associate; Olga Nousias, Associate; Smita Narula, Silberberg Fellow.

Advisory Committee

Andrew Nathan, Chair; Orville Schell, Vice Chair; Maureen Aung-Thwin, Edward J. Baker, Harry Barnes, Robert L. Bernstein, Jagdish Bhagwati, Julie Brill, Jerome Cohen, Clarence Dias, Dolores A. Donovan, Adrienne Germain, Merle Goldman, James C. Goodale, Deborah M. Greenberg, Jack Greenberg, Paul Hoffman, Sharon Hom, Rounaq Jahan, Virginia Leary, Daniel Lev, Perry Link, Rt. Rev. Paul Moore, Jr., Yuri Orlov, Victoria Riskin, Sheila Rothman, Barnett Rubin, James Scott, Stephen Shapiro, Eric Stover, Ko-Yung Tung, Maya Wiley.

Human Rights Watch/Helsinki

Staff

Holly Cartner, Executive Director; Rachel Denber, Deputy Director; Elizabeth Andersen, Advocacy Director; Fred Abrahams, Research Associate; Erika Dailey, Research Associate; Julia A. Hall, Research Associate Chris Panico, Research Associate; Diane Paul, Research Associate; Marie Struthers, Research Associate; Max Marcus, Research Associate; Andreas Lommen, Research Associate; Emily Shaw, Associate; Juliet Wilson, Associate; Pamela Gomez, Caucasus Office Director; Acacia Shields, Central Asia/

Caucasus Coordinator; Diederik Lohman, Moscow Office Director; Sasha (Alexander) Petrov, Deputy Director, Moscow Office; Malcolm Hawkes, Research Associate, Moscow Office; Liuda Belova, Associate, Moscow Office.

Steering Committee

Jonathan Fanton, Chair; Alice H. Henkin, Peter Osnos, Co-Vice Chairs; Morton Abramowitz, Barbara Finberg, Felice Gaer, Michael Gellert, Paul Goble, Bill Green, Stanley Hoffmann, Robert James, Jack Matlock, Herbert Okun, Jane Olson, Barnett Rubin, Leon Sigal, Malcolm Smith, George Soros, Donald J. Sutherland, Ruti Teitel, William D. Zabel, Warren Zimmermann.

Human Rights Watch/Middle East

Staff

Hanny Megally, Executive Director; Ricky Goldstein, Research Director; Virginia Sherry, Associate Director; Joe Stork, Advocacy Director; Clarisa Bencomo, Research Associate; Elahé Sharifpour-Hicks, Research Associate; Nejla Sammakia, Research Associate; Pamela Pensock, Consultant; Awali Samara, Associate; Georgina Copty, Associate; Avner Gidron, Consultant.

Advisory Committee

Gary G. Sick, Chair; Lisa Anderson, Bruce Rabb, Vice Chairs; Shaul Bakhash, M. Cherif Bassiouni, Martin Blumenthal, Paul Chevigny, Helena Cobban, Patricia Derian, Stanley Engelstein, Edith Everett, Mansour Farhang, Christopher George, Rita E. Hauser, Ulrich Haynes, Rev. J. Bryan Hehir, Edy Kaufman, Marina Pinto Kaufman, Samir Khalaf, Judith Kipper, Pnina Lahav, Ann M. Lesch, Stephen P. Marks, Rolando Matalon, Philip Mattar, David K. Shipler, Sanford Solender, Mary Ann Stein, Shibley Telhami, Andrew Whitley, Napoleon B. Williams, Jr., James J Zogby.

Human Rights Watch Arms Project

Staff

Joost R. Hiltermann, Director; Stephen D. Goose, Program Director; Loretta Bondì, Advocacy Coordinator; Ernst Jan Hogendoorn, Research Assistant; Alex Vines, Research Associate; Andrew Cooper, Research Assistant; Kathi Austin, Consultant; Monica Schurtman, Consultant; Dan Connell, Consultant; Frank Smyth, Consultant, Rebecca Bell, Associate.

Advisory Committee

Torsten N. Wiesel, Chair; Nicole Ball, Vincent McGee, Co-Vice Chairs; Ken Anderson, Frank Blackaby, Ahmed H. Esa, Bill Green, Alastair Hay, Lao Mong Hay, Frederick J. Knecht, Edward J. Laurance, Janne E. Nolan, Andrew J. Pierre, David Rieff, Julian Perry Robinson, Kumar Rupesinghe, John Ryle, Gary G. Sick, Thomas Winship.

Human Rights Watch Children's Rights Project

Staff

Lois Whitman, Director; Yodon Thonden, Counsel; Jo Becker, Advocacy Coordinator; Vikram Parekh, Research Associate; Linda Shipley, Associate.

Advisory Committee

Jane Green Schaller, Chair; Roland Algrant, Vice-Chair; Goldie Alfasi-Siffert, Michelle India Baird, Phyllis W. Beck, James Bell, Albina du Boisrouvray, Rachel Brett, Nicole Burrowes, Bernadine Dohrn, Fr. Robert Drinan, Rosa Ehrenreich, Barbara Finberg, Sanford J. Fox, Gail Furman, Lisa Hedley, Anita Howe-Waxman, Eugene Isenberg, Sheila Kamerman, Kela Leon, Alan Levine, Hadassah Brooks Morgan, Prexy Nesbitt, Elena Nightingale, Martha J. Olson, Marta Santos Pais, Susan Rappaport, Jack Rendler, Robert G. Schwartz, Mark I. Soler, Lisa Sullivan, William Taggart, William L. Taylor, Geraldine Van Bueren, Peter Volmink, James D. Weill, Derrick Wong.

Human Rights Watch Women's Rights Project

Staff
Dorothy Q. Thomas, Director; Regan Ralph, Washington Director; LaShawn Jefferson, Research Associate; Samya Burney, Research Associate; Widney Brown, Research Associate; Rumbi Mabuwa, Research Associate; Sinsi Hernandez-Cancio, Silberberg Fellow; Kerry McArthur, Associate, Evelyn Miah, Associate; Jane Kim, Women's Law and Public Policy Fellow.

Advisory Committee
Kathleen Peratis, Chair; Nahid Toubia, Vice Chair; Mahnaz Afkhami, Roland Algrant, Abdullahi An-Na'im, Helen Bernstein, Charlotte Bunch, Holly Burkhalter, Rhonda Copelon, Lisa Crooms, Patricia Derian, Gina Despres, Joan Dunlop, Mallika Dutt, Martha Fineman, Claire Flom, Adrienne Germain, Leslie Glass, Lisa Hedley, Zhu Hong, Stephen Isaacs, Marina Pinto Kaufman, Gara LaMarche, Joyce Mends-Cole, Marysa Navarro-Aranguren, Donna Nevel, Susan Petersen, Catherine Powell, Celina Romany, Margaret Schuler, Domna Stanton.

Human Rights Watch California

Advisory Committee
Stanley K. Sheinbaum, Honorary, Chair; Mike Farrell, Jane Olson, Vicki Riskin. Co-Chairs; Clara A. "Zazi" Pope, Vice Chair; Elaine Attias, Joan Willens Beerman, Rabbi Leonard Beerman, Justin Connolly, Chiara Di Geronimo, Alan Gleitsman, Danny Glover, Paul Hoffman, Barry Kemp, Maggie Kemp, Li Lu, Lynda Palevsky, Tom Parker, Alison Dundes Renteln, Tracy Rice, Cheri Rosche, Lawrence Rose, Pippa Scott, Bill Temko, Andrea Van de Kamp, Dianne Wittenberg, Stanley Wolpert.